Handbook of Eclectic Psychotherapy

Edited by

John C. Norcross, Ph.D.

Department of Psychology
University of Scranton/University of Rhode Island
and
Department of Psychiatry and Human Behavior
Brown University School of Medicine

BRUNNER/MAZEL, *Publishers* • New York

Library of Congress Cataloging-in-Publication Data
Main entry under title:

Handbook of eclectic psychotherapy.

   Includes bibliographies and index.
   1. Psychotherapy. I. Norcross, John C.,
1957-   . [DNLM: 1. Psychotherapy. WM 420 H236]
RC480.H284 1986   616.89′14   85-30848
ISBN 0-87630-422-6

Published by
BRUNNER/MAZEL, INC.
19 Union Square West
New York, New York 10003

MANUFACTURED IN THE UNITED STATES OF AMERICA

To Nancy

Handbook of
Eclectic
Psychotherapy

Contents

PART III: *Concepts, Research, and Directions*

Preface

Eclectic psychotherapies have proliferated in recent years as a response to the perceived fragmentation and conflict within the field. Whether seeking whole-hearted integration of diverse systems or cautious exploration of other technical procedures from the refuge of their own paradigms, clinicians are increasingly enamored with eclecticism. The psychotherapy *Zeitgeist* of the 1980s is rapprochement, convergence, and integration.

Indeed, the field has grown to the point where a comprehensive source and critique of systematic eclectic psychotherapy is sorely needed. However, no such compendium currently exists.

The *Handbook of Eclectic Psychotherapy* was designed to fill this void. This volume represents a unique compilation of the historical, conceptual, clinical, and research issues related to psychotherapy integration and eclecticism. The *Handbook* is intended as a state-of-the-art description of the major systems and principles of eclectic psychotherapy. These pages will hopefully serve as a guide for practicing clinicians interested in therapeutic eclecticism, as a textbook for students in the mental health professions, and as a resource for theoreticians and researchers. The nature of the subject presumes some knowledge of the various systems of psychotherapy.

As editor, I was particularly concerned that the book would be balanced, scholarly, and integrative. Toward these ends, only original contributions were accepted and these were subjected to two independent critiques. Contributors were instructed to consider both the advantages and disadvantages of their systematic eclectic approaches, and an entire chapter (13) was devoted to the underlying limitations and trade-offs of eclecticism. In addition, the authors of chapters 12 through 17 received advance copies of Part II chapters for review in their respective chapters.

More importantly, to facilitate comparative analyses and to ensure comprehensiveness, chapters in Part II followed standard guidelines provided by the editor. Similar guidelines were employed in the critically acclaimed *Handbook of Family Therapy* edited by Alan Gurman and David Kniskern. The guidelines include what I considered to be the central dimensions of any eclectic approach to psychotherapy. It was not expected that contributors would address every point under each of the main headings. Rather, these focal points were illustrative of the types of issues pertinent to each section.

These guidelines would have surely tested the wisdom of Solomon and the patience of Job. The contributors deserve special praise for confronting and acknowledging the unknowns in their approaches. The Guidelines for Contributors (for chapters in Part II) are reproduced here as a guide to the reader.

I. BACKGROUND OF THE APPROACH

Aim: To describe the development of the approach and to place it in historical perspective.

(1) What were the primary influences that contributed to the development of the approach (e.g., people, experiences, research, books, conferences)?
(2) What were the direct antecedents of the approach?
(3) How was the approach originally conceptualized and constructed?
(4) What were some of the early theoretical speculations and/or therapy interventions?

II. THE APPROACH

Aim: To describe the advantages, guiding principles, and current status of the approach.

(1) What is the promise of eclecticism?
(2) What are the advantages of eclectic psychotherapy, in particular your approach?
(3) What are the guiding principles and central tenets of the approach?
(4) What form of eclecticism (e.g., syn-

thetic, technical, atheoretical) did you adopt for your approach?
(5) Which, if any, therapy systems are excluded from your approach (e.g., bioenergetics, orthodox psychoanalysis)?
(6) Are some orientations more prominent contributors to your approach than others?
(7) What is the basis for selecting therapy interventions (e.g., proven efficacy, theoretical considerations, intuition)?

III. PATIENT ASSESSMENT

Aim: To describe the conceptualization and methods used to gain an understanding of patient functioning and treatment goals.

(1) What are the formal and informal systems for diagnosing or typing patients?
(2) Do you employ tests, devices, or questionnaires in your assessment?
(3) What major client and/or environmental variables are assessed?
(4) At which *unit* levels (e.g., individual, dyadic, system) are the assessments made?
(5) At which *psychological* levels (e.g., intrapsychic, behavioral) are the assessments made?
(6) How do you integrate assessment and treatment?
(7) How do you select and prioritize treatment goals?

IV. TREATMENT APPLICABILITY

Aim: To describe those situations and patients for which the approach are particularly relevant.

(1) For which types of patients (e.g., diagnostic types, client characteristics) is the approach relevant?

(2) For which types of patients is the approach not appropriate or of uncertain relevance?

(3) For what situations (e.g., clinical settings, time limitations) is/is not the approach relevant?

(4) What are the therapy modalities (e.g., individual, family, group) for which the approach is/is not relevant?

(5) Under what circumstances would a referral be made to another type of psychotherapy (e.g., psychoanalysis, behavioral) or to another type of treatment (e.g., chemotherapy, milieu therapy)?

V. TREATMENT STRUCTURE

Aim: To describe the typical setting, frequency, duration, and structure of the approach.

(1) What are the clinical settings for the approach? Are there any specific contraindicated settings?

(2) What is the spatial arrangement within the therapy room? Is it a sigificant structural aspect of therapy?

(3) What is the typical frequency and length of sessions?

(4) Is the therapy typically time-limited or unlimited? What is the typical duration of therapy (mean number and range of sessions)?

(5) How do you negotiate treatment decisions (e.g., location, fees)?

(6) Are combined therapy modalities used (e.g., individual therapy plus family therapy)?

VI. TREATMENT SPECIFICITY AND MATCHING

Aim: To describe the methods and rationale for matching patient and therapist as well as patient and interventions.

(1) How do you select specific treatments for specific disorders?

(2) How is the decision made to use a particular intervention at a particular time?

(3) What is the basis for patient-therapist matching?

(4) What is the basis for patient-intervention matching?

(5) Is it possible or desirable to match all patients/disorders with specific treatments?

VII. TREATMENT INTERVENTIONS AND STRATEGIES

Aim: To describe the therapeutic interventions and strategies frequently employed in the approach.

(1) How much structure do you provide in therapy sessions?

(2) What are some of the interventions used to engage patients?

(3) What is the therapist's work in treatment?

(4) What is the client's work in treatment?

(5) How do you deal with resistances and blocks in treatment?

(6) What are the most common *and* most serious technical errors a therapist can make when operating within your approach?

(7) On what basis is termination decided and how is termination effected?

VIII. THERAPIST BEHAVIORS

Aim: To describe the stances the therapist takes with patients in the approach.

(1) How active and directive is the therapist in the approach?

(2) How much and on what basis does the therapist self-disclose?

(3) How do you view and use the therapeutic relationship (e.g., as a precondition of change, as a mechanism of change, as content to be changed)?

(4) How do you determine the appropriate level of involvement/intimacy with patients?
(5) Does the therapist's role change as therapy progresses? Does it change as termination approaches?

IX. MECHANISMS OF CHANGE

Aim: To describe the mechanisms or processes that produce change in therapy, and to assess their relative impact.

(1) What is the role of insight and understanding in change, distinguishing between historical-genetic insight and interactional insight?
(2) What is the relative importance of (a) interpretations, (b) skill acquisition, (c) transference analysis, and (d) the therapeutic relationship in the approach?
(3) What are the relative contributions of "specific" versus "nonspecific" factors to outcome?
(4) Does the therapist's personality and psychological health play an important part?
(5) What other therapist factors influence the course and outcome of treatment?
(6) Which patient variables enhance or limit the probability of successful treatment?
(7) What characterizes "successful" versus "unsuccessful" termination of therapy?

X. CASE EXAMPLE

Aim: To describe the initiation, process, and outcome of therapy using the approach.

To maintain comparability among the examples, the case should ideally deal with the treatment of a client with general anxiety and unipolar depression (psychological distress).

The case example should illustrate and discuss the initiation of treatment, patient assessment, formulation, matching patient to treatment, interventions and strategies, therapeutic relationship, termination, and outcome.

XI. RESEARCH ON THE APPROACH

Aim: To summarize the clinical and empirical research on the approach.

(1) What research has been conducted on the conceptual framework of the approach?
(2) What evidence exists for the efficacy and efficiency of the approach?
(3) What are the percentages of drop-outs and negative outcomes?
(4) Are there important unresolved theoretical or practical questions about the approach?
(5) What are the most pressing future research directions for the approach?

XII. CLINICAL TRAINING

Aim: To describe the proper training and qualifications of an eclectic therapist.

(1) Should a therapist learn specific therapy systems (e.g., behavioral, psychoanalytic) before or after an eclectic approach?
(2) Is prior competence in some/many/all therapy systems required before becoming a true eclectic therapist?
(3) What amount of clinical experience is required?
(4) Is previous personal therapy important?
(5) Is any research experience necessary?
(6) What is an ideal program and sequence of training for the approach?

XIII. FUTURE DIRECTIONS AND NEEDS

Aim: To explicate the future directions and needs of eclectic psychotherapy.

(1) What are the most important issues that eclectic psychotherapies need to address?
(2) What further work (clinical, research, theoretical) is required to improve eclecticism?
(3) In what directions are eclecticism, and your approach in particular, heading in the next decade?

A work of such interest will inevitably generate its share of criticism. The errors of commission will have to speak for themselves, but a few words on the errors of omission are in order. The selection of eclectic approaches was necessarily restricted by the length of the book; however, they do represent a fair sampling of the published literature and, in my judgment, are among the most promising of the lot. The pioneering work of Frederick Thorne is not represented here due to his untimely death. Intentionally excluded were the numerous systems designed to integrate psychoanalytic and behavioral therapies. These approaches accommodate *two* "schools of thoughts" and represent an early stage of mature eclecticism, which seeks to integrate *many* schools of thought.

I experienced a recurring irony in putting this book together. The eclectic approaches in this book are orderly, public, and systematic. And yet, most eclectic therapists are guided by some idiosyncratic, unsystematic, almost ineffable creations of their own. Although I am not encouraging the promulgation of 250 eclectic systems to complement the extant 250 theoretical orientations, it will be increasingly necessary to tap the clinical acumen of these unsung eclectic psychotherapists.

In fact, I am firmly convinced that it is premature to advance any *one* eclectic approach or to pit them against each other like rival orientations. Such strategies have proved historically unproductive. Instead, as several contributors in Part II have noted, these are preliminary attempts at integrating diverse psychotherapy systems which require maturation and concomitant change. I would urge you—in the integrationist spirit—to take the "best" from each approach and to discern converging themes for yourself.

It has been a genuine pleasure to organize and edit a volume dedicated to eclectic psychotherapy. This publication represents a much-needed departure from traditional texts which detail competing orientations, i.e., 40 pages to School A, 40 pages to School B, *ad infinitum,* without attempts to synthesize them. I hope the change of scenery is refreshing and enduring.

My efforts in this enterprise have been aided immeasurably by my family and colleagues. There are not words to express my appreciation for the love and honesty of my wife, Nancy, to whom this book is dedicated. My stepdaughter Rebecca, parents, and brothers have a special place in my life and in this book. I am also grateful to Jim Prochaska, Tom Paolino, and Ann Alhadeff for their assistance in selecting contributors and organizing the book. I thank Michael Wogan and Andy Bondy for their early and sustained encouragement of my work. The clerical skills of Terri Javarey and Elaine Taylor of the University of Rhode Island and Becky Diaz and Ann Goulet of Brown University are also gratefully acknowledged. Lastly, I am indebted to the contributors, each an eminent clinician in his or her own right.

J.C.N.

About the Editor

John C. Norcross, Ph.D., completed his undergraduate work at Rutgers University, his graduate work in clinical psychology at the University of Rhode Island, and his internship at the Brown University School of Medicine. He is currently a Research Fellow in the Self-Change Lab at the University of Rhode Island and an Associate Professor of Psychology at the University of Scranton. He also maintains a part-time independent practice in psychotherapy. Dr. Norcross is author of over 50 scholarly publications and editor of the forthcoming *Casebook of Eclectic Psychotherapy* (Brunner/Mazel, in press).

About the Contributors

Michael J. Apter, Ph.D., is Reader in Psychology at University College-Cardiff in the University of Wales. He has lectured or carried out research at a number of universities including Bristol University (U.K.), Princeton University (U.S.A.), University of California at Berkeley (U.S.A.), University of British Columbia (Canada), and the University of Bergen (Norway). He is the author of five books, including *The Experience of Motivation, Cybernetics and Developments,* and *The Computer Simulation of Behaviour,* and is co-editor of two further books.

Larry E. Beutler, Ph.D., is Professor of Psychiatry and Psychology at the University of Arizona, College of Medicine. Formerly, he has been employed by Duke University Medical Center, Stephen F. Austin State University, Baylor College of Medicine, and the University of Arizona. He is a diplomate of the American Board of Professional Psychology, and is Associate Editor of the *Journal of Consulting and Clinical Psychology.* He is author of *Eclectic Psychotherapy: A Systematic Approach* and co-author of *Cognitive Group Therapy for the Treatment of Older Adults.*

Gary M. Burlingame, Ph.D., is on the core faculty of the Comprehensive Clinic and is affiliated with the Clinical Psychology program at Brigham Young University. He maintains an active program of research and writing in short-term individual and group psychotherapy, and has conducted numerous training workshops in short-term therapy techniques.

Carlo C. DiClemente, Ph.D., is Chief of the Addictive Behavior and Psychosocial Research Section at the Texas Research Institute of Mental Sciences and an adjunct faculty member at the University of Houston. He is active in both psychology and psychiatry training programs, administers an outpatient Alcoholism Treatment Program, and conducts psychotherapy and behavioral medicine research. He is co-author of *The Transtheoretical Approach: Crossing the Traditional Boundaries of Therapy.*

Windy Dryden, Ph.D., is Lecturer in Psychology, Goldsmiths' College, University of London, and Director of the U.K. Branch of the International Academy of Eclectic Psychotherapists. He maintains a part-time independent practice in psychotherapy. He is author of *Rational-Emotive Therapy: Fundamentals and Innovations* and editor of *Individual Therapy in Brit-*

ain. His most recent book is entitled *Therapists' Dilemmas.*

Joel Fischer, D.S.W., is Professor of Social Work, Assistant for Curriculum Development, and Chair of the Ph.D. program at the University of Hawaii School of Social Work. He has published 11 books and well over 100 articles, chapters, and reviews. He has presented lectures and workshops all over the United States and in 10 foreign countries.

Addie Fuhriman, Ph.D., is Chair and Professor of Educational Psychology at the University of Utah. She is actively involved with training and research in individual and group therapy in the specialty of counseling psychology.

Sol L. Garfield, Ph.D., is Professor of Psychology at Washington University, St. Louis, Missouri. He is author of *Psychotherapy: An Eclectic Approach; Clinical Psychology: The Study of Personality and Behavior;* and co-editor with Allen E. Bergin of the *Handbook of Psychotherapy and Behavior Change.* A former president of the APA's Division of Clinical Psychology as well as the Society for Psychotherapy Research, he was editor of the *Journal of Consulting and Clinical Psychology,* 1979-1984.

Marvin R. Goldfried, Ph.D., is Professor of Psychology and Psychiatry at the State University of New York at Stony Brook. In addition to his teaching, supervision, and research, he maintains a limited private practice in New York City. He is co-author of *Clinical Behavior Therapy,* and editor of *Converging Themes in Psychotherapy.*

Lawrence C. Grebstein, Ph.D., is Professor of Psychology and Director of the Clinical Psychology Training Program at the University of Rhode Island. He has served as a consultant to a variety of agencies, and maintains a part-time independent practice. He is a diplomate in Clinical Psychology of the American Board of Professional Psychology, author of *Toward Self-Understanding: Studies in Personality and Adjustment,* and has been a Fellow in Family Therapy and Research at the Center for Family Research, George Washington University Medical Center.

Joseph T. Hart, Ph.D., is Director of Counseling and Testing Services at California Polytechnic University in Pomona, California. He is also a consultant, specializing in occupational psychology, stress management, and wellness programs, with Hart and Associates and The University Consulting Group in Los Angeles. He is the author of *Modern Eclectic Therapy: A Functional Approach to Counseling and Psychotherapy,* co-author of *Psychological Fitness,* and co-editor of *New Directions in Client-Centered Therapy.*

Michael J. Lambert, Ph.D., is Professor of Psychology and a member of the Clinical Training Committee at Brigham Young University. He serves as an editoral consultant to numerous professional journals and maintains a part-time practice in psychotherapy. He is co-editor of *Psychotherapy and Patient Relationships* and co-editor of *The Assessment of Psychotherapy Outcome.*

Arnold A. Lazarus, Ph.D., is a Professor II in the Graduate School of Applied and Professional Psychology, Rutgers University. He has founded several Multimodal Therapy Institutes, serves as a consultant to a number of state and private agencies, and has a part-time private practice in Princeton, New Jersey. He has published over 120 scientific articles and 10 books, of which *Casebook of Multimodal Therapy* is his most recent volume.

Stanley B. Messer, Ph.D., is Professor of Psychology in the Graduate School of Applied and Professional Psychology at Rutgers University, where he directs the psychodynamic track in Clinical Psychology. He is co-editor (with Hal Arkowitz) of *Psychoanalytic Therapy and Behavior Therapy: Is Integration Possible?,* and is a consulting editor of the *Journal of Consulting and Clinical Psychology.* Dr. Messer is a consultant to the Office of the Public Defender in several New Jersey counties, and maintains a part-time independent practice in psychotherapy and psychological assessment.

Stephen Murgatroyd, M.Phil., is Professor of Applied Psychology and Dean of Administrative Studies at Athabasca University, Alberta, Canada. He has worked as a counseling psychologist in a variety of settings, and has specialized in adult counseling, crisis counseling, and psychotherapy. Stephen is editor of the *British Journal of Guidance and Counseling* and author of *Helping the Troubled Child—Interprofessional Case Studies, Coping with Crisis* (with Ray Woolfe), and *Helping Families in Distress.*

Edward J. Murray, Ph.D., is Professor of Psychology at the University of Miami and maintains a private practice in psychotherapy. He has published about 100 articles, chapters, and books on personality, motivation, emotion, and various forms of therapy, including psychoanalysis, transcendental meditation, encounter groups, systematic desensitization, and cognitive-behavior therapy. He has served on the editorial boards of *Contemporary Psychology, Journal of Personality Research, Psychotherapy,* and *Cognitive Therapy and Research.* He has also served as a research consultant for the National Institute of Mental Health.

Cory Newman, M.A., received his B.A. at the University of Pennsylvania, and is currently a doctoral candidate at the State University of New York at Stony Brook. His dissertation research represents the first stage in a project aimed at generating an empirically-based, cross-theoretical set of principles of successful therapeutic feedback. On the side, he is a classical pianist-composer, and a Senior League baseball coach in the Stony Brook area.

Stephen C. Paul, Ph.D., is Assistant Professor of Educational Psychology and Associate Director of the University Counseling Center at the University of Utah. He is also President of Consult West, a firm specializing in organizational consultation and individual, couple, and family counseling.

James O. Prochaska, Ph.D., is Professor of Psychology and Director of the Self-Change Laboratory at the University of Rhode Island. He also serves as a consultant to numerous institutions and maintains a part-time independent practice in psychotherapy. He is author of *Systems of Psychotherapy: A Transtheoretical Analysis,* and co-author of *The Transtheoretical Approach: Crossing the Traditional Boundaries of Therapy.*

Malcolm H. Robertson, Ph.D., is Professor of Psychology and Director of Clinical Psychology Training at Western Michigan University. He is an ABPP Diplomate in Clinical Psychology. He also serves as a consultant to several community agencies and maintains a part-time independent practice in psychotherapy. He is the author of several articles on eclectic psychotherapy and clinical training.

Jeremy D. Safran, Ph.D., is Associate Director of the Cognitive Therapy Unit at the Clarke Institute of Psychiatry in Toronto, Canada. His interests include psychotherapy change process research, clarifying the role of client affective experience, integration of cognitive and interpersonal approaches, and the development of integrative psychotherapy paradigms in general. He is author of "Some Implications of Sullivan's Interpersonal Theory for Cognitive Therapy," in *Cognitive Psychotherapies,* and co-author (with Leslie S. Greenberg) of *Affect, Cognition, and the Process of Change.*

PART I

History and Overview

CHAPTER 1

Eclectic Psychotherapy: An Introduction and Overview

John C. Norcross

Psychotherapeutic innovations appear and vanish with bewildering rapidity on the diffuse, heterodox American scene. In 1959, Harper identified 36 distinct systems of psychotherapy, and in 1976, Parloff discovered over 130 therapies on the marketplace, or more appropriately, the "jungle place." By 1980, several estimates put the number well over 250 (Corsini, 1981; Herink, 1980). The proliferation of therapies has been accompanied by a deafening cacophony of rival claims. The result has been variously characterized as confusion, fragmentation, and discontent.

Sibling rivalry among theoretical orientations has a long and undistinguished history in psychotherapy, dating back to Freud. In the infancy of the field, therapy systems, like battling siblings, competed for attention and affection in a "dogma eat dogma" environment (Larson, 1980). Clinicians traditionally operated from within their own particular theoretical frameworks, often to the point of being blind to alternative conceptualizations and interventions (Goldfried, 1980). Mutual antipathy and exchange of puerile insults

between adherents of rival orientations were very much the order of the day.

Perhaps these conflicts were a necessary developmental stage to sophisticated, mature eclecticism. Kuhn (1970) has described this period as a pre-paradigmatic crisis. Feyerabend (1970), another philosopher of science, has concluded that "the interplay between tenacity and proliferation is an essential feature in the actual development of science. It seems that it is not the puzzle-solving activity that is responsible for the growth of our knowledge, but the active interplay of various tenaciously held views" (p. 209).

Amid this strife and bewilderment, a therapeutic "underground" slowly emerged (Wachtel, 1977). Though not associated with any particular school and not detailed in the literature, the underground reflected an unofficial consensus of what experienced clinicians believed to be true. Adventuresome clinicians gradually employed strategies that they found successful without regard for theoretical origin.

The notion of integrating various therapeutic approaches has intrigued mental health professionals for some time (see, e.g., Goldfried, 1982; Chapter 2); however, it has been only within the past 15 years that eclecticism has developed into a clearly delineated area of interest. And this has occurred less as an orderly scientific advance than as a developing climate of opinion (Murray, 1983).

The last decade in particular has witnessed both a general decline in ideological struggle and the stirrings of rapprochement. The debates across theoretical systems appear to be less polemical, or at least more issue-specific. The theoretical substrate of each system is undergoing intensive reappraisal, as psychotherapists acknowledge the inadequacies of any one system and the potential value of others.

Clinicians of all persuasions are increasingly seeking a rapprochement of various systems and an integration of therapeutic interventions. Eclecticism has become the modal orientation of psychologists, with between one third and one half ascribing to it (Garfield & Kurtz, 1976; Norcross & Prochaska, 1982). Psychologists generally believe that eclecticism offers the best hope for a truly comprehensive approach to treatment (Smith, 1982). A recent panel of psychotherapy experts predicted that eclecticism would increase in popularity more than any individual system in the forthcoming decade (Prochaska & Norcross, 1982).

The concomitant openness to contributions from diverse persuasions has given rise to numerous publications, organizations, and conferences. Specific systems of eclectic practice (e.g., Beutler, 1983; Garfield, 1980; Hart, 1983; Lazarus, 1981; Palmer, 1980; Prochaska & DiClemente, 1984; Thorne, 1973), influential anthologies (e.g., Goldfried, 1982; Marmor & Woods, 1980; Wachtel, 1977), and compilations of prescriptive treatments (e.g., Frances, Clarkin, & Perry, 1984; Goldstein & Stein, 1976) have flourished. Several eclectic journals (e.g., *International Journal of Eclectic Psychotherapy, Comprehensive Psychotherapy*) and special series of articles (e.g., Brady et al, 1980; Garfield, 1982; Goldfried, 1982; Kendall, 1982; Wachtel, 1982) have appeared. Three interdisciplinary and nonideological organizations—the Society for Psychotherapy Research (SPR), the Society for the Exploration of Psychotherapy Integration (SEPI), and the International Academy of Eclectic Psychotherapists (IAEP)—also exemplify the spirit of open inquiry and growing collaboration. Regular conferences and symposia on eclecticism (see, e.g., Bergin, 1981; Goldfried, 1982; Goldfried & Strupp, 1980; Norcross, 1984a) are another manifestation of this trend.

Clearly, we have not yet arrived at a consensus or convergence. Most clinicians express considerable satisfaction with their respective "schools" of therapy (Norcross & Prochaska, 1983; Norcross & Wogan, 1983). Like any movement on the rise, eclecticism has met with adverse reactions and pleas for caution (see, e.g., Abroms, 1983; Arkowitz & Messer, 1984; Messer & Winokur, 1984; Norcross, 1981; Yates, 1983; Wilson, 1982). Even here though, most antagonists believe the movement "deserves a fair hearing and a substantial trial" (Messer, 1983, p. 132). Moreover, if Kuhn (1970) is correct in his analysis and an eclectic paradigm is created, then most dissidents "can be reached in one way or another." Although the older and more experienced scientist may resist indefinitely, "conversions will occur a few at a time until, after the last holdouts have died, the whole profession will again be practicing under a single, but now different paradigm" (Kuhn, 1970, p. 152). Until that day, we will have to settle for less than unanimity.

In the meantime, there are numerous psychotherapists working toward integration and on the development of systematic eclecticism. There is also a promising and growing number of clinicians who, while maintaining their own theoretical identities, are nonetheless willing to explore potential sources of enrichment and convergence. This is the important first step: to view rival systems not as an adversity, but as a healthy diversity (Landsman, 1974); not as contradictory, but as complementary. It is to this spirit of open inquiry that this book is directed.

ORGANIZATION OF THE BOOK

The *Handbook* is divided into three sections. Part I features an overview and the history of therapeutic eclecticism. Part II presents, in general chronological order of their development, nine leading exemplars of systematic eclectic psychotherapy, followed by a critique of these systems. Part III considers the limitations and possibilities of eclecticism, the training of eclectic clinicians, research on eclectic psychotherapy, and the future directions of the field.

The present chapter is designed to explicate the broad context of eclectic psychotherapy. The paramount task, as the title indicates, is to provide a brief overview rather than an exhaustive treatment of the issues. To begin, I consider the various definitions and manifestations of eclecticism. Relevant data on eclectic practitioners are reviewed, and several reasons for the dramatic increase in eclecticism are offered. The chapter concludes with a discussion of the conceptual, practical, and training challenges faced by systematic eclectic psychotherapies.

DEFINING ECLECTICISM

The term *eclectic* has been employed indiscriminately and inconsistently. A vague and nebulous term, its connotations range from "a worn-out synonym for theoretical laziness" to the "only means to a comprehensive psychotherapy" (Smith, 1982). The following sections review several definitions and manifestations of

eclecticism in an effort to clarify our thinking and to bring about some consistency in our vocabulary.

Apart from its definition, the utility of eclecticism and the motivation of eclectic practitioners have been seriously questioned. In some corners, eclecticism is prized as complex, relativistic thinking by people united in their respect for the evidence and in their willingness to learn about what may be clinically effective. In other corners, eclecticism connotes undisciplined subjectivity, "muddle-headedness," even minimal brain damage. Robertson (1979) quotes colleagues who refer to eclecticism as the "last refuge for mediocrity, the seal of incompetency" and "a classic case of professional anomie." As Garfield (1982) observes, it is surprising that so many clinicians admit to being eclectic in their work, given the negative valence the term has acquired.

There is some debate whether eclecticism constitutes another theoretical orientation or simply the absence of one. Thorne (1973), among others, insists that eclecticism is the active acceptance of an orientation, in its own right, albeit broader and more integrative. Garfield (1980), in contrast, uses *eclectic* to indicate that one is not an adherent of a particular school of psychotherapy. Beyond this, the term does not have any precise meaning. What binds most eclectics together is a stated dislike for a single orientation, selection from two or more theories, and the belief that no present theory is adequate to explain or predict all of the behavior a clinician observes (Garfield & Kurtz, 1977).

Probably the most accurate definition of eclecticism comes from the dictionary. *Webster's Collegiate Dictionary* defines eclecticism as the "method or practice of selecting what seems best from various systems." Similarly, Brammer and Shostrom (1982) define therapeutic eclecticism as the "process of selecting concepts, methods, and strategies from a variety of current theories which work" (p. 35).

Though somewhat vague, these are suitable working definitions. If eclectics do indeed choose what appears to work best, few will oppose the movement or criticize them (Garfield, 1982).

Other descriptive terms have been proposed to replace *eclecticism*. These include creative synthesis, metamodeling, ecological therapy, comprehensive therapy, prescriptive counseling, and differential therapeutics. Each term has a slightly altered emphasis and connotation, but all generally denote a trend toward a comprehensive approach to clinical work predicated on demonstrated efficacy.

The terms "rapprochement," "convergence," and "integration" are widely employed with reference to eclecticism. Rapprochement refers to a "coming together, the establishment of a state of cordial relations" (*Webster's Collegiate Dictionary*). This concept denotes an earlier developmental stage than mature eclecticism as cordial relations typically precede incorporation. Convergence is the tendency to grow alike, to develop similarities in form. Integration refers to incorporating parts into a whole. Integrationists, many of whom abhor the label "eclectic," are persons who work toward or from an integrative perspective.

Integrationism should *not* be equated with eclecticism since integrationism is only one form of eclecticism. All integrationists are probably eclectics, but not all eclectics are integrationists. Judging from the literature and the content of this book, integrationism is currently the most prevalent form of eclecticism.

Clinical practice can be viewed on a continuum ranging from a single orientation at one pole to an integration of all orientations at the other. The practice of orthodox psychoanalysis or radical behaviorism would represent one end. A hyphenated approach—say, the cognitive-behavioral approach—would be one step further along the continuum. And just how many hyphens constitute eclecti-

cism? Does interpersonal-cognitive-behavioral therapy qualify as an eclectic therapy? There is no arbitrary cutoff on a continuum, of course, and this seems to be a matter of labeling and taste. The ideal of integrating *all* available psychotherapy systems is not likely to be met either. Somewhere between the hyphenated two-orientation approach and the unattained integration of all theories lie the obscure boundaries of eclecticism.

Not all clinicians sympathetic to eclecticism label themselves eclectics. Conversely, many self-proclaimed eclectics do not adhere to similar principles. At best, eclectics are a loosely formed, self-designated group who are united in their interest in pursuing effective procedures without restricting themselves to a single theory.

The Society for the Exploration of Psychotherapy Integration, much akin to eclecticism, consists of diverse clinicians with different goals in mind (see, e.g., Goldfried & Wachtel, 1983). Some subscribe to a particular paradigm but recognize that other schools have something to offer. Some are searching for commonalities across therapies. Others are concerned with the feasibility of integrating rationales and techniques. Still others are hoping to construct a new, comprehensive approach to psychotherapy.

Four Stances

Weiner (1983) has developed a typology of four "stances" to accommodating lines of convergence. Those who adopt the *stonewalling* stance ignore or deny the existence of convergence or the possibility of integration. These clinicians generally adhere strictly to a single point of view, delining to consider that other frames of reference might add something useful to the understanding and treatment of psychological disorders. In the *reformulation* stance, therapists translate the concepts of other theoretical formulations into a language of some preferred paradigm. Psychotherapists embracing either of these first two stances would probably not qualify as eclectics according to our working definition.

A third stance, which Weiner (1983) calls *amalgamation*, posits that the distinctive theoretical formulations associated with different schools of thought are little more than "window dressing." From this perspective, talented and experienced clinicians end up working with their clients in pretty much the same ways, regardless of the theories they espouse. In other words, all roads lead to Rome. This stance is conceptually akin to the therapeutic underground described by Wachtel (1977) and reminiscent of Fiedler's (1950a, 1950b) seminal finding that experienced therapists of different orientations are more similar to each other than they are to less experienced therapists of their own orientations. This perspective is also frequently associated with the identification of common principles of behavior change and the "nonspecific" factors that transcend orientation.

From the point of view of *complementarity,* the fourth stance, various orientations complement each other and enrich the ability of clinicians to understand and work effectively with their clients. The complete clinician in this view will appreciate the lessons taught by various theories and will draw on methods of many different approaches. This stance is clearly indicative of the committed, systematic eclectic psychotherapist.

Four Stages

Given the pluralistic nature of knowledge, educated people tend to structure knowledge according to their particular level of cognitive development. Prochaska (1984), applying Perry's (1970) model of intellectual and ethical development to personal views of diverse theories of psychotherapy, posits the following four primary stages of intellectual and ethical development:

DUALISTIC → MULTIPLISTIC → RELATIVISTIC → COMMITTED

Dualistic psychotherapists believe that the truth has been revealed to them. They are the true believers among us who think that one therapy system is correct and all others are erroneous. These dualistic therapists, found in all orientations, are the result not of the structure of the systems in which they believe, but rather the structure of their own intellects.

To *multiplistic* psychotherapists, the current state of diversity and uncertainty in the field is only a temporary stage in our knowledge. The multiplistic therapist is a bettor who is convinced that betting his or her energies on a particular theory will pay off in the future when that particular system is shown to be more effective, efficient, or applicable.

In contrast, *relativistic* psychotherapists see diversity and uncertainty as givens, knowledge as contextual and relative. For them the truth about psychotherapy is that it is pluralistic with a variety of valid alternatives. According to Prochaska (1984), the relativistic therapist is likely to be an eclectic for whom the usefulness of any particular system is relative to some particular issue, e.g., relative to the patient's problem, the patient's personality, the therapist's personality. Given the relativistic nature of knowledge, the eclectic thinks that no one theory will ever be found to be the "best."

Committed psychotherapists accept undeniable relativism and maintain a humility that comes with knowing that other systems of therapy may be equally valid for other professionals. These eclectic psychotherapists form a community of committed professionals who realize that at this point in our development the questions we share are more important than the answers we give. A committed therapist "is centrally concerned with questions of what is the best way to be in therapy; what is the most valuable model we can provide for our clients, our colleagues, and our students, and how we can help our clients attain a better life" (Prochaska, 1984, p. 367).

Three Stages

Werner's (1948; Werner & Kaplan, 1963) organismic–developmental theory is also instructive for conceptualizing psychotherapists' development of an eclectic stance (also see Kaplan et al., 1983; Rebecca, Hefner, & Oleshansky, 1976). In the first of three developmental stages in learning new information, one perceives or experiences a global whole, with no clear distinctions among component parts. Unsophisticated laypersons and undergraduates probably fall into this category.

In the second stage, one perceives or experiences differentiation of the whole into parts, with a more precise and distinct perspective of components within the whole. However, one no longer has a perspective on the whole, and subsequently loses the "big picture." Most psychotherapy courses, textbooks, and formally educated practitioners fall into this category.

In the third stage, the differentiated parts are organized and integrated into the whole at a higher level. Here, the unity *and* complexity of psychotherapy are appreciated. Few psychotherapists have successfully reached this summit, but many more are scaling the slope.

VARIETIES OF ECLECTIC EXPERIENCE

Eclecticism comes in many guises and manifestations. It is clearly not a monolithic entity or a single operationalized system; to refer to *the* eclectic approach to therapy falls prey to the "uniformity myth"

(Dryden, 1984; Kiesler, 1966). It is more accurate to speak of "the eclectic therapies." The goals of this section are to explicate the immense variability among these therapies and to identify several available forms of eclecticism. As our research and practice evolve, it is expected that much of this information will be revised or replaced.

Survey Results

Definitions of eclecticism do not tell us what individual psychotherapists actually do or what it means to be an eclectic therapist. In their survey of eclectic psychologists, Garfield and Kurtz (1977) discerned 32 different theoretical combinations used by 145 eclectic clinicians. The most popular two-orientation combinations, in order of frequency, were as follows:

- Psychoanalytic and learning theory
- Neo-Freudian and learning theory
- Neo-Freudian and Rogerian theory
- Learning theory and humanistic theory
- Rogerian and learning theory

Sixty-five percent of Larson's (1980) respondents indicated allegiances to two or more schools. For example, of the behaviorally oriented respondents who chose another school, approximately 17% selected phenomenological, 15% gestalt, and 13% client-centered.

In both studies, most combinations were blended and employed in an idiosyncratic fashion. It could not be determined whether the most efficacious procedures were indeed selected from the combined perspectives. The investigators concluded that the designation of eclectic covers a wide range of views, some of which are apparently quite the opposite of others.

Garfield and Kurtz (1977) asked their sample of eclectic clinicians to define or explain their eclectic perspective, resulting in a diverse set of rationales. Almost half responded that they employed "whatever theory seemed best for the client." These clinicians reportedly select procedures according to the requirements of individual clients. They consider themselves "pragmatic" insofar as they use "what works best." A second group of respondents, accounting for 12% of the sample, replied that they basically combine two or three theories in their clinical work. These therapists consider themselves eclectic because they do not adhere to just one perspective. A third group, 14% of the sample, reported an amalgamation of theories or aspects of theories. Five percent of these eclectics, representing a fourth vantage point, responded rather vaguely that "no theory is adequate and some are better for some purposes than others" (Garfield & Kurtz, 1977, p. 82). Whether they favor pragmatism, combination, amalgamation, or vague relativism as their explanation, all are self-described eclectics.

Systematic Versus Unsystematic Eclecticism

Systematic eclecticism, as opposed to the unsystematic brand, is the product of years of painstaking clinical, research, and theoretical work. It is truly eclecticism "by design"; that is, clinicians competent in several therapeutic systems who selectively choose interventions based on clinical experience and/or research findings. By contrast, haphazard or unsystematic eclecticism is primarily an outgrowth of pet techniques and inadequate training. It is eclecticism "by default," lacking sufficient competence for an eclectic approach, and selecting interventions on the basis of subjective appeal. Eysenck (1970) has characterized this form of eclecticism as a "mish-mash of theories, a huggermugger of procedures, a gallimaufry of therapies" (p. 145) having no proper rationale or empirical evaluation.

It has been traditional to criticize un-

systematic eclectics for their haphazard practice. However, one should not blame clinicians for not adopting what is not available. Systematic eclectic therapies have just recently been developed, and training has not been widely available to date.

By necessity, idiosyncratic eclecticism appears to have been the rule rather than the exception (Garfield & Kurtz, 1977). In the extreme, such eclectics attend numerous weekend workshops and then experiment with new procedures whether or not their clients warrant such methods. According to Dryden (1984), many of these psychotherapists wander around in a daze of professional nihilism experimenting with new "fad" methods indiscriminately.

Several intrepid clinicians have tried to decipher the psychotherapeutic maze and to operationalize their rationales, resulting in systematic eclectic approaches. Part II of this book contains many of the leading exemplars of sophisticated systematic eclecticism. The strengths of systematic eclectic psychotherapies lie in their ability to be taught, replicated, and evaluated. Anything less spells disaster for those interested in pursuing an eclectic approach grounded in clinical experience and research.

Atheoretical, Synthetic, and Technical Eclecticism

Eclectic practice and theory can, for heuristic purposes, be further divided into three subtypes. Atheoretical eclecticism is an integrative perspective governed by no preferred theoretical approach (e.g., London, 1964, 1972). Synthetic eclecticism strives toward an integration of diverse contemporary theories (e.g., Goldfried, 1980; Prochaska & DiClemente, 1984). Technical eclecticism endorses the use of a variety of techniques within a preferred theory (e.g., Lazarus, 1967). These three subtypes are all evident in contemporary systematic eclectic psychotherapies and parallel the spontaneously generated divisions within Garfield and Kurtz's (1977) sample.

Norcross and Prochaska (1982) asked their subsample of eclectic clinicians to select the one type of eclecticism that best approximated their own views. Over half (61%) of these eclectics indicated they integrated a diversity of contemporary approaches, 29% responded that they use a variety of techniques within a preferred theory, and 10% claimed that they had no preferred theoretical orientation. Results from a second sample (Prochaska & Norcross, 1983) replicated the order of preference, namely, synthetic, technical, and atheoretical.

A related but not identical distinction can be made between the integration of diverse theories and the integration of diverse techniques (traditionally associated with certain theories). Much controversy and misunderstanding can be attributed to the failure to maintain this distinction. Except where specifically noted, as with Lazarus's technical eclecticism below, this chapter deals primarily with integration of theories.

Lazarus (1967, 1977, 1984), the most eloquent proponent of technical eclecticism, emphasizes the distinction between the theoretical eclectic and the technical eclectic. The theoretical eclectic draws from diverse systems that may be epistemologically incompatible, whereas the technical eclectic uses procedures drawn from different sources without necessarily subscribing to the theories that spawned them. For Lazarus and other technical eclectics, no necessary connection exists between metabeliefs and techniques. It is not necessary to build a composite from divergent theories, on the one hand, nor to accept divergent conceptions, on the other, in order to utilize their technical procedures. "To attempt a theoretical rapprochement is as futile as trying to picture the edge of the universe. But to read through the vast amount of literature on psychotherapy, *in search of techniques,* can be clinically enriching and therapeutically rewarding" (Lazarus, 1967, p. 416).

Synthetic eclecticism has the greatest support among eclectic therapists to date. However, persistent difficulties in integrating epistemologically and ontologically incompatible orientations may spawn additional technical eclectic systems in the near future.

Psychodynamic, Phenomenological, and Behavioral Eclecticism

In their research on American Psychological Association members who were eclectic psychotherapists, Prochaska and Norcross (1983a) asked respondents to select one of four theoretical perspectives underlying their eclecticism. Among this group, 45% chose psychodynamic, 25% humanistic–existential (phenomenological), 17% behavioral, and 13% "other." Similarly, the most used theoretical orientations among eclectic social workers were psychoanalytic (47%), reality therapy (29%), humanistic (26%), neo-Freudian (24%), and behavioral (17%) (Jayaratne, 1982).

It would appear that the practice of eclecticism is influenced by all orientations, and that eclectic practitioners bring definite theoretical biases to their integrative work. Psychodynamic orientations, in particular, comprise a significant and sustained element in eclectic approaches. Quite naturally, the pervasive influence of a therapist's philosophical biases and visions of reality enter into his/her eclectic approach. Although eclectics may indeed integrate interventions from diverse sources, their selection is guided by their clinical training, professional history, and personal values.

Quilt-Making

The distinctions made earlier —systematic vs. unsystematic, synthetic vs. technical—enable us to delineate more accurately the heterogeneity of eclecticism. These distinctions are well-illustrated by quilt-making, which is offered as an analogy for eclecticism. Metaphorically, the quilting experience demonstrates the construction of an eclectic approach and the process of integrating diverse methods. Metaphoric thinking also results in a more "primary process" exposition than a prevalent "secondary process" explanation.

The selection of materials and the construction of a quilt are reciprocally determined by the craftsperson's training, experiences, and preferences. Quilt-makers do not mechanically select their swatches from the entire universe of possible materials. Instead, the possible materials are restricted to those in their possession, to remnants of old projects, and to those that can be readily acquired. The final selection of material is guided by the quilter's previous experience and personal preferences (psychoanalytic vs. behavioral vs. phenomenological). And it is certainly the case that one cannot include materials that one does not possess. Consequently, the patchwork is somewhat arbitrary and personalized.

Furthermore, one can construct a quilt out of incomplete materials and scraps (by default) or, alternatively, from an abundance of rich and diverse materials (by design). Some quilters are therefore forced to sew a quilt because they lack requisite resources for even a single cloth covering, whereas others, although capable of making a conventional blanket, prefer a more varied and colorful creation. In the latter case, there are still no definitive rules as to the most beautiful, as beauty lies in the eyes of the beholder.

Because quilt-makers must peddle their wares in the public marketplace, they create products to match consumers' desires. Increasingly, quilts are tailored to the recipient, not the artisan. However, each recipient's needs differ, resulting in greater demands on the quilt-maker. Some quilt-makers refuse to sacrifice their own preferences to cater to others' needs. These craftspeople continue in their own tradition, although to a smaller and narrower range of clientele. The new line of quilt-makers scurry about trying to acquire the necessary resources to meet more varied demands and agonize over the conflict between their personal tastes and the consumers' desires.

Lest this analogy sound too far-fetched, it is actually the fate of quilt-makers in the Great Smokey Mountains of Tennessee. Like eclecticism, it does not have a fairy-tale ending. True to life, many eclectics have sacrificed personal preferences and one-theory security to better meet the needs of clients. However, "how to better meet the needs of clients" has yet to be consensually or conclusively established.

THE PROMISE OF ECLECTICISM

The promise of eclecticism is the development of a comprehensive psychotherapy based on a unified and empirical body of work. It is the opportunity to construct a new integrative paradigm and, at the same time, to transcend more narrow "schools" of therapy.

The price of theoretical purity is the exclusion of variables that the theory overlooks or ignores (Garfield, 1982). People who adhere closely to one school tend to have restricted vision and selective perception—theoretical "blinders"—that limit their perception of relevant phenomena. Eclecticism can potentially transcend the constraints of factionalism "where cloistered adherents of rival schools, movements, and systems each cling to their separate illusions" (Lazarus, 1977, p. 11). Eclectic psychotherapies attempt to avoid this "polarized thinking of the older veterans of the ideological cold war" (Murray, 1983, p. 127).

An eclectic paradigm promises sense out of multiple etiologies, formulations, and treatments. It facilitates greater choice and flexibility in clinical work and access to a wider range of skills, both technical and interpersonal. Eventually, the varied needs of clients, the therapeutic demands of psychological disorders, and the challenges of different stages in the helping process will be better met by drawing on what is most effective and efficient across therapy systems. Eclecticism addresses a central concern of mental health professionals: the prescription of specific interventions to meet specific needs of patients.

In short, eclectic psychotherapy promises increased efficacy, applicability, and efficiency. Systematic eclecticism can direct the clinician to an appropriate intervention and can provide indications of the level at which to begin and of when to switch levels. It can generate alternatives if a particular strategy or method fails. With increasing refinement of the categorization of patients and more precise delineation of central change strategies, further advantages of specific therapies for specific conditions may be found. At that point, effective therapy will be "defined not by its brand name, but by how well it meets the need of the patient" (Weiner, 1975, p. 44).

ECLECTIC THERAPISTS

Between 30% and 40% of contemporary American psychologists embrace eclecticism as their primary theoretical orientation. And according to recent national surveys, eclecticism is invariably the most popular approach to psychotherapy. This holds true for 30% of active clinical psychologists (Norcross & Prochaska, 1982), 33% of academic clinical psychologists (Shemberg & Leventhal, 1978), 40% of counseling psychologists (Smith, 1982), 30 to 32% of psychologists conducting psy-

chotherapy (Prochaska & Norcross, 1983a; Smith & Kraft, 1983), 35% of independent practitioners (Nash, Norcross, & Prochaska, 1984), 37% of Psy.D. recipients (Peterson, Eaton, Levine, & Snepp, 1982), 36% of master-level psychologists (Perlman, 1985), 37% of master-level counselors (Norcross, in press), and 54% of clinical social workers (Jayaratne, 1982). Interestingly, surveys of psychologists belonging to behavioral (Association for Advancement of Behavior Therapy) and humanistic (APA Division of Humanistic Psychology) organizations also reveal sizable percentages of respondents who indicate an eclectic orientation; 42% in the former case (Swan, 1979; Swan & MacDonald, 1979) and 31% in the latter (Norcross & Wogan, 1983). In other words, one-third to one-half of present-day clinicians disavow any affiliation with a particular therapeutic school, preferring instead the label of "eclectic."

With such large proportions of contemporary therapists embracing eclecticism, it would be informative to identify distinguishing characteristics or attitudes of eclectics as compared to noneclectics. There do not appear to be, however, any consistent differences in personal characteristics between the two groups, with the exception of clinical experience (Norcross & Prochaska, 1982; Norcross & Wogan, 1983; Walton, 1978). Clinicians ascribing to eclecticism tend to be older and, concomitantly, more experienced. Inexperienced therapists are more likely to endorse exclusive theoretical orientations (Norcross & Prochaska, 1982; Smith, 1982). Several empirical studies have suggested that reliance on one theory and a few techniques may be the product of inexperience or, conversely, that with experience comes diversity and resourcefulness (cf. Auerbach & Johnson, 1977; Fey, 1958; Parloff, Waskow, & Wolfe, 1978; Strupp, 1955; Wogan & Norcross, 1985).

Attitudinally, eclectic clinicians also differ from their noneclectic colleagues in several respects. First, eclectics report relatively greater dissatisfaction with their current conceptual frameworks and technical procedures (Norcross & Prochaska, 1983; Norcross & Wogan, 1983). This increased dissatisfaction may serve as an impetus to create an integrative approach or it may result from the elevated expectations that eclecticism can engender. Second, consistent with the prescriptive ideology, eclectics rate themselves as less influenced than noneclectics by particular theories but more influenced by their clientele and by pragmatic considerations (e.g., setting and length of treatment) in their clinical practice. A central goal of systematic eclecticism is the optimal match among the intervention, the patient, the problem, and the setting.

From a personal–historical perspective, Robertson (1979) identified six factors that may facilitate the choice of eclecticism. The first is the lack of pressures in training and professional environments to bend to a doctrinaire position. Also included here would be the absence of a charismatic figure to emulate. A second factor, which we have already discussed, is length of clinical experience. As therapists experience heterogeneous clients and problems over time, they may be more likely to reject a single theory. A third factor is the extent to which doing psychotherapy is making a living or making a philosophy of life; Robertson asserts that eclecticism is more likely to follow the former. The remaining three factors are personality variables: an obsessive– compulsive drive to pull together all the interventions of the therapeutic universe; a maverick temperament to move beyond some theoretical camp; and a skeptical attitude toward the *status quo*. Although these factors require further confirmation, they are supported by our common training experiences and the personal histories of prominent eclectics. These factors are repeatedly cited as influential variables in the development of the eclectic approaches presented in this compendium (see Chapters 3 through 11). In the future, we can hope that psychotherapists will not have to travel such circuitous and rocky roads in opting for eclecticism. Intensive training in extant systematic eclectic psychotherapies will provide smooth and direct paths.

Several empirical studies (Prochaska & Norcross, 1983b; Swan & MacDonald, 1979; Wogan & Norcross, 1985) have indicated that eclectics, as a whole, do indeed use a broader range of interventions than do other groups bound closely to a specific orientation. These findings tend to support the observation that eclectics, in theory, favor a wide range of clinical procedures and suggest that eclectic philosophy translates into eclectic clinical practice.

However, it must be emphasized that these conclusions are based on self-report data. It remains to be demonstrated that systematic eclectics do in fact employ more varied interventions and conceptualizations. More important—and this is the proof of the pudding—it has yet to be shown that eclectics are differentially effective, for their integrative efforts.

WHY ECLECTICISM NOW?

The recent and rapid increase in eclectic psychotherapies leads one to inquire "Why now?" What is there about the present environment or the discipline's development that intensifies the spirit of open inquiry? It has been persuasively argued that the stirrings of rapprochement have always been with us but recently given specific attention and credence.

At least six interacting, mutually reinforcing factors have fostered the development of eclecticism in the past decade:

1. Proliferation of therapies
2. Inadequacies of any one specific therapy

3. Absence of differential effectiveness among therapies
4. Growing recognition that patient characteristics and the helping relationship are the most efficacious components of successful treatment
5. Resultant search for common components of effective treatment
6. External sociopolitical contingencies

The sheer proliferation of diverse schools has been one important reason for the surge of eclecticism. The field of psychotherapy has been staggered by over-choice and fragmented by future shock. Which of 250 therapies should be studied, taught, or bought? Conflicting and untested theories are advanced almost daily, and no single theory has been able to corner the market on validity or utility. The task of the eclectic has become to determine which approach works best with each type of problem.

A related and second factor is the growing awareness that no one approach is clinically adequate. Beutler (1983) suggests that the proliferation of theories is both a cause and symptom of the problem —that neither the theories nor the techniques are adequate to deal with the complexity of psychological problems. Clinical realities demand an eclectic perspective.

The field has entered a period of intense self-examination in which the failures and limitations of our pet theories are reappraised. It is becoming increasingly clear that not all the answers may be found within any given school of therapy. Eclecticism reflects, to some degree, this dissatisfaction with current approaches. Garfield and Kurtz (1972) noted that most of their respondents embraced eclecticism out of disillusionment with a single therapy system.

This dissatisfaction generates movement and experimentation. For example, behaviorism has undergone a "cognitive revolution" (e.g., Mahoney, 1976; Mei-

chenbaum, 1974), and the psychodynamic approaches have succumbed to pressures for short-term treatment (e.g., Malan, 1976; Mann, 1973; Sifneos, 1979; Strupp & Binder, 1982). Eclecticism is a natural extension of combined two-theory approaches to systematic multiple-theory approaches.

Despite a noticeable increase in the quantity and quality of research on psychotherapy, a third reason for the surge of eclecticism is that it has not been possible to show that one therapeutic approach is clearly superior to another (see, e.g., Bergin & Lambert, 1978; Frank, 1979; Landman & Dawes, 1982; Luborsky, Singer, & Luborsky, 1975; Meltzoff & Kornreich, 1970; Sloane, Staples, Cristol, Yorkston, & Whipple, 1975; Smith, Glass, & Miller, 1980). There are few conditions in which the therapy system leads to differential success in outcome, and with a couple of exceptions, there is little evidence to recommend the use of one type over another in the treatment of specific problems. Luborsky et al. (1975), borrowing a phrase from the Dodo bird in *Alice in Wonderland,* wryly observe that "everybody has won and all must have prizes."

As empirical studies and comprehensive reviews are unable to show differential outcomes attributable to therapy systems, the field has slowly departed on a new direction to determine factors common to successful treatments (see, e.g., Gomes-Schwartz, Hadley, & Strupp, 1978). These common ingredients appear to exert tremendous impact on therapeutic relationships and hence outcome.

A fourth contributor to the rise of eclecticism is the recognition that the powerful determinants of therapeutic success lie in the personal qualities of patient and therapist and in the interaction between them. The particular therapeutic method appears to have little discernible influence. That is, success in therapy can best be predicted by the properties of the patient, therapist, and their particular therapeutic relationship.

The client, the psychotherapist, and the nature of their therapeutic relationship are still considered more crucial for outcome than technique (Frank, 1979; Hynan, 1981). Experts estimate that about one-third of treatment outcome is due to the therapist and two-thirds to the client (Prochaska & Norcross, 1982). Less than 10% of outcome variance is generally accounted for by technique variables (Lambert, 1979, 1983; Smith, Glass, & Miller, 1980).

Echoing the consensus on the issue, Bergin and Lambert (1978) conclude: "We believe . . . that the largest variation in therapy outcome is accounted for by preexisting client factors, such as motivation for change, and the like. Therapist personal factors account for the second largest proportion of change, with technique variables coming in a distant third" (p. 180).

Consequently, it would appear that singular attempts to improve techniques within one orientation would have negligible effect on therapeutic outcome. Instead, eclecticism strives to tailor the method to the patient's personality, problem, motivation, and so on in order to maximize treatment success. To the degree that therapists are able to modify and broaden their practices to fit the patient's needs and characteristics, the benefits are potentiated. This is truly the promise of eclecticism: integrated, prescriptive psychosocial treatment based on patients' needs rather than therapists' preferences.

A fifth and more general factor contributing to the eclectic spirit has been the search for commonalities across therapies. The identification of common change processes or therapeutic factors has been called the most important trend in the 1980s (Bergin, 1982).

In his classic *Persuasion and Healing,* Frank (1973) posited that all psychotherapeutic methods are elaborations and variations of age-old procedures of psychological healing. The features that distinguish psychotherapies from each other, however, receive special emphasis in the pluralistic, competitive American society. Since the prestige and financial security of psychotherapists hinge on their being able to show that their particular approach is more successful than that of their rivals, little glory has been traditionally accorded the identification of shared or common components.

Frank (1973, 1979, 1982) further argued that therapeutic change is predominantly a function of factors common to all therapeutic approaches. These include an emotionally charged, confiding relationship; a healing setting; a rationale or conceptual scheme; and a therapeutic ritual. He and others conclude that features shared by all therapies account for an appreciable amount of observed improvement in clients.

Strupp (1973, 1982) noted that the significant advances in psychotherapy research have resulted from better conceptual analyses of basic processes operating in all forms of therapy rather than from premature comparisons of techniques. This observation is based on the emerging view that the commonalities in all forms of therapy are far more impressive than their apparent differences, which may be no more than relative emphases. Limited progress may be expected until therapists and researchers manage to gain some distance from their deeply held emotional commitments.

A truly eclectic psychotherapy may begin with and be based on an operationalization of common variables that play an important role in most therapies (Garfield, 1973, 1980; Goldfried, 1980, 1982; Prochaska & DiClemente, 1984). A transtheoretical analysis of extant systems of psychotherapy demonstrated how much therapeutic systems agree on the processes producing change while disagreeing on the content to be changed (Prochaska, 1984). To the extent that clinicians of varying orientations are able to arrive at a common set of change principles, what is likely to emerge will be robust and efficacious strategies in that they have managed to survive the distortions imposed by varying theories (Goldfried, 1980). Common features may in fact be the most efficacious features of psychotherapy.

In "selecting what works best" from disparate orientations, eclectics may also be choosing what is common across orientations. Systematic eclecticism is not simply selecting from the different, but also conceptualizing the contradictory as complementary on a different level (Goldfried, 1980). Convergence refers both to our methods becoming more alike and to our thinking about psychotherapy becoming increasingly similar.

Finally, eclecticism is also an adaptive response to external contingencies. Attacks from outside the mental health professions have started to propel them together. Psychotherapy is experiencing mounting pressures from such not easily disregarded sources as the courts, insurance companies, and national health insurance planners. Third-parties and the public are demanding crisp and informative answers regarding the quality, durability, and efficiency of psychosocial treatments (Parloff, 1979). The confrontation between psychotherapy and third-parties has been dramatically characterized as Bambi meeting Godzilla (Parloff, 1981).

Until recently the field has had the luxury of "doing its own thing," functioning within a culture of individual professional freedom. Clinical services had been in steady demand in the marketplace, generally oblivious to economic forces, sociopolitical realities, and the noisy yammerings of the secular world. However, the shrinking job market, increased competition, and diminishing public support portend a future discontinuous with our expansive past (Fishman & Neigher, 1982).

The assault from without is already well underway. Government support for mental health services (Kiesler, 1980) and research (Brown, 1977) has decreased steadily over the past ten years. In addition to these economic realities, the general distrust of public psychosocial treatments has led to an increasing number of malpractice suits, demands for accountability, and calls for reform of professional self-regulation (Fishman & Neigher, 1982; Keppler-Seid, Windle, & Way, 1980; VandenBos, 1980). Standard professional review of treatment and tightening insurance reimbursement have just begun to startle clinical practitioners out of their complacency. By choice or force, psychotherapy in the United States is becoming decidedly brief and pragmatic (Koss, 1980; Phillips & Bierman, 1981; Budman & Gurman, 1983).

Within the profession, these and related developments have us increasingly pulling together rather than apart. Mental health professionals report that the impact of political and economic changes have led them to work harder, to be more creative, and to adjust their treatments to meet the needs of their clients (Brown, 1983). Interprofessional collaboration and intertheoretical cooperation are products of these sociopolitical forces. As the external demands escalate, so too will the spirit of open inquiry and eclecticism.

CURRENT CHALLENGES

The task of constructing and disseminating a systematic eclectic approach is a formidable one. The intent of this closing section is to outline several practical, training, and conceptual challenges likely to be encountered by eclectic psychotherapies. These challenges are presented as eradicable barriers, not as unsolvable puzzles, in the hope that we can address them forthrightly.

Practical

Possible practical barriers to the integration of psychotherapies include language and network problems (Goldfried, 1982). The language problem is manifested in our difficulty in understanding various concepts and in actively tuning out buzz words associated with another orientation. Many a behaviorist's mind has wandered when case discussions turn to "transference issues" and "warded-off conflicts." Similarly, psychodynamic therapists are typically unwilling or unable to engage in serious discussion of "conditioning procedures" and "discriminative stimuli." In the short run, use of the vernacular or purely descriptive language will suffice. In the long run, a new common language may need to be developed.

Another barrier to eclecticism is the existence of numerous professional networks, which reflect a particular theoretical outlook. "Without a specific therapeutic orientation, how would we know what journals to subscribe to or which conventions to attend?" (Goldfried, 1980, p. 996). Our current networks may not be able to advance the field very much beyond its current development. Sorely needed are networks of dedicated professionals who are interested in taking steps toward the achievement of some kind of rapprochement and eclecticism.

A third pressing practical concern is bringing more clinicians into the eclectic fold. On the one hand, the pull of eclecticism is strong. Most therapists do not believe a one-school approach is particularly effective, and most already profess at least a dual allegiance (Garfield & Kurtz, 1977; Larson, 1980; Norcross & Prochaska, 1983; Sundland, 1977). On the other hand, schools are not without their advantages. Clinicians need structured

theories, readily use them, and report considerable satisfaction with them (Frank, 1971; Norcross & Prochaska, 1983; Sundland, 1977). Furthermore, to be an eclectic is to have a marginal professional identity. By contrast, identification with a particular school of therapy has powerful economic, political, and social support. Theoretical purity provides one with an organized system, a rationale, and circumscribed practices.

The principal allure and ultimate challenge of systematic eclecticism are identical: the development of clinical models that have *clinical utility* and *empirical validity*. The criteria of meaningfulness (experienced worth) and effectiveness (demonstrated worth) need to be satisfied to attract clinicians—practitioners and academicians alike—to eclecticism (Kisch & Kroll, 1980). We need to discover, in *functional* terms, which therapist behaviors and treatment strategies are more effective with which types of patients (Cross & Sheehan, 1981; Paul, 1967). Beyond conceptual relativity and personal appeal, eclecticism to date has made little progress in matching type of treatment to type of patient or problem.

The adequacy of the various systems promising a synthesis remains to be further investigated; that is one goal of the present volume. Yates (1983) points out that the evidence is anecdotal or grossly flawed. As yet, there is little unambiguous evidence of the clinical superiority of an eclectic approach over existing systems. It is important to note, though, that the reverse is true as well (Wachtel, 1983).

A fourth and broader challenge concerns the resolution of theoretical controversies. Adams (1984, p. 92) pointedly inquires how clinicians settle their differences: "by negotiation, 'kissing and making up,' taking a vote, or gathering data?" The question is less problematic for technical eclectics who integrate techniques separate from their "theoretical baggage," but it remains a thorny issue for synthetic eclectics who integrate theories. Most authors have opted to circumvent rather than try to resolve these theoretical conflicts. Predominant avoidance responses in the early literature include: deemphasizing or dismissing the disparities as unimportant; building an open bridge between the two sides; and creating a new level of conceptualization somewhere between theory and technique.

The success of these ventures is debatable, but the process of cross-orientation dialogue is encouraging. The questions still persist: Will we ever be able to resolve our differences? Is it even possible? If possible, would it be profitable? Can scientific research, interpersonal persuasion, or sociopolitical pressures help us reach a common ground, or are these inherently unsolvable theoretical quandaries? Tracing the history of psychotherapy does not leave one optimistic, but the recent spirit of open inquiry offers us an opportunity to chart a new course.

Training

There are now literally hundreds of therapies, thousands of tests, and endless myths jumbled together with solid facts. Those trainees who gamely try to pick their way through the morass without firm knowledge and training are handicapped to say the least. Those who do not even recognize that there is a morass are in even deeper trouble (Meltzoff, 1984).

The critical training question is how to facilitate adequate knowledge of and competence in the various psychotherapeutic systems. On the one hand, while intense concentration on a single theoretical system can be myopic and misleading, it is often complete and secure. On the other, cursory exposure to dominant therapeutic systems leaves students with a few clichés and disunited techniques, but it does encourage integration. The challenge is to steer a course between the superficiality

of easy eclecticism on one hand and isolationist entrenchment on the other.

Given the knowledge explosion in the psychotherapy domain, can any clinician be expected to master all theories and techniques? It may not be realistic to aspire to work comfortably with several different therapeutic orientations and modalities. Thorne (1973) maintains that the true eclectic will be competent in all available forms of clinical intervention; only such a highly skilled and experienced therapist can possibly have the flexibility to be therapeutic for all clients. By contrast, Lazarus (1967) asks "Who, even in a life-time of endeavor, can hope to encompass such a diverse and multifarious range of thought and theory? Indeed, an attempt to imbibe and digest this overwhelming mass of information (and misinformation) may be no more rewarding than gluttony at any other level" (p. 415).

Even were a psychotherapist to master all current methods, could he or she be expected to maintain the high level of competence over the years while keeping abreast of the newest fads? Articles double in quantity every 12 to 15 years, and by the end of the century, informed specialists will need to read four times as much as they now do (Barlow, 1981; Boice & Jones, 1984; Hartley, 1982). Beutler (1983, p. 225) conceded that even eclectics are "not so naive as to believe that most therapists will expand the energy, effort, and money required to develop the broad range of therapeutic procedures." If not all the procedures, then which ones? Clinical research provides few directions, and when on rare occassions it does, few respond to it (Barlow, 1981; Luborsky, 1969). We may then again be guided by selective perception and personal preference, a situation eclecticism seeks to avoid.

Clinical trainers need to think carefully how to expand and liberate our theories of psychotherapy. Extremist articles, irrational accusations, and proximity to open-minded parties tend to broaden our awareness (Mischel, 1973, 1979). Demanding work lies before those wishing to translate eclectic theory into eclectic training, and finally, into eclectic practice.

Conceptual

A pressing conceptual challenge is that of *balance*—balance between competing theories, balance between superficiality and complexity, balance between rigidity and flexibility. As for the first, given professionals' penchants for pet theories and biases, few clinicians will agree on the appropriate mix of theories constituting an eclectic approach. Although eclectic at heart, I find many contemporary eclectic approaches overemphasizing behavioral methods for my tastes, while seriously underemphasizing psychodynamic contributions. Each psychotherapist's clinical experiences and visions of reality guide his/her integration, and thus we may arrive at hundreds of eclectic systems of psychotherapy.

Eclectic theories also struggle with a second delicate balance between bare superficiality and overwhelming complexity. Glossing over critical distinctions, simplifying complex phenomena, and relabeling incompatible phenomena under broader terms do not begin to satisfy the needs of sophisticated eclecticism. To be sure, many clinicians already believe that eclectic systems are likely to exhibit superficiality (Smith, 1982). There is a real danger that, in our rush to identify common change principles and to create integrative paradigms, we may neglect the diversity, complexity, and uniqueness of the philosophies and people involved in psychotherapy. Nor is it the case that only theoretical orientations guide clinical practice; eclecticism needs to address the disparate beliefs and behaviors associated with the psychotherapist's values, mental health, personality, gender, experience, and the like.

Many observers (e.g., Norcross, 1981, 1985; Messer & Winokur, 1980, 1984; Wilson, 1982; Yates, 1983) have remarked that much of what passes for integration seems to be denial or ignorance of these fundamental differences among clinicians. However, genuine integration does not try to show there are no real differences, that one is equivalent to the other. Integrationism is concerned with the chasm, not by denying there is a distance between the two sides, but by building a bridge that unites them. Systematic eclecticism recombines elements of several approaches into a *new* structure that shows some similarities to each but possesses its own logic and coherence (Wachtel, 1983, 1984).

An equally perilous path is that of excessive complexity. Clinicians currently suffer from information overload and do not need weighty theoretical contributions. A deluge of contingency tables and flow diagrams will deservedly be ignored. However, a complex but integrative theory could provide more clarity and, ultimately, more simplicity than a diversity of unintegrated information.

A third precarious balance is weighted by rigidity on one end and flexibility on the other. Psychotherapists' beliefs, training, and values will inevitably influence their clinical work, be it eclectic or not. Needed are eclectic schemes with sufficient rigor and direction to be valued, but with room for personal style and improvisation.

Aside from balance, *specification* and *evaluation* of systematic eclectic approaches are paramount challenges. Describing oneself as an eclectic does not adequately communicate what one actually practices in therapy. Survey research does not reveal what self-professed eclectics do with patients, on what basis they make decisions, and which factors influence their actions. It is not sufficient to simply know that some type of "eclectic psychotherapy" has been successful, if our ultimate goal is to determine the best possible form of treatment for each patient (Waskow, 1984).

The resultant challenge is to operationalize fully treatment procedures and to concretize, as much as possible, therapists' decision-making processes. One reason for the difficulty in drawing conclusions and generalizing from psychotherapy research is the vagueness and poor specification of treatment variables. In reading the literature one is frequently hard presed to know what transpired during the treatment and what the therapist actually did during the sessions. Garfield (1982) has eloquently argued for corrective research in this area if we are to unravel the mysteries of eclecticism.

The literature on eclecticism is growing by leaps and bounds, and there is no dearth of theoretical writings on the subject. There is, however, a striking dearth of case histories, particularly of verbatim accounts. We need to see what eclectic therapists actually do rather than what they say they do or recommend to others. Transcripts, videotapes, treatment manuals, and detailed case accounts would be steps in the right direction. At a minimum, eclectic therapists can more fully specify their operations and decision-making processes, and eclectic theorists can address meaningful clinical phenomena, such as treatability, patient selection, and focal issues.

Once the eclectic treatment has been specified, it will need to be rigorously evaluated. Several studies of "eclectic therapy" have been conducted (e.g., Koss et al, 1983; Thorne, 1957) but the treatment is described in a sentence or two as "eclectic in nature." Since eclectic therapies are so diverse and idiosyncratic, evaluators will need to pay particular attention to actual operations and interactions. It is precisely this complex interaction of patient qualities, clinician skills, and therapeutic interventions that needs to be explicated.

A final challenge concerns the connotation of the label "eclecticism" and the reputation of "eclectic" therapists. Eclecticism should not be embraced as an intuitive "whatever feels right" approach to clinical work. There is a persistent danger that being eclectic will justify a superficial, chaotic approach in which practitioners fly by the seats of their pants.

Clearly, eclecticism needs to stand for more than a nondescript brand name for clinicians dissatisfied with orthodox schoolism. For too long eclecticism has been defined negatively, against something. It is my hope that, in the not too distant future, eclecticism will be defined positively, namely, systematic prescriptive psychotherapy.

REFERENCES

Abroms, E. M. (1983). Beyond eclecticism. *American Journal of Psychiatry, 140,* 740–744.

Adams, H. E. (1984). The pernicious effects of theoretical orientations in clinical psychology. *The Clinical Psychologists, 37,* 90–93.

Arkowitz, H., & Messer, S. B. (Eds.). (1984). *Psychoanalytic and behavior therapy: Is integration possible?* New York: Plenum.

Auerbach, A. H., & Johnson, M. (1977). Research on the therapist's level of experience. In A. S. Gurman & A. M. Razin (Eds.), *Effective psychotherapy: A handbook of research.* New York: Pergamon.

Barlow, D. H. (1981). On the relation of clinical research to clinical practice: Current issues, new directions. *Journal of Consulting and Clinical Psychology, 49,* 147–155.

Bergin, A. E. (1981, August). *Toward a systematic eclecticism.* Symposium chaired at the annual meeting of the American Psychological Association, Los Angeles, CA.

Bergin, A. (1982). Comment on *Converging themes in psychotherapy.* New York: Springer.

Bergin, A. E., & Lambert, M. J. (1978). The evaluation of therapeutic outcomes. In S. L. Garfield & A. E. Bergin (Eds.), *Handbook of psychotherapy and behavior change* (2nd ed.). New York: Wiley.

Beutler, L. E. (1983). *Eclectic psychotherapy: A systematic approach.* New York: Pergamon.

Boice, R., & Jones, F. (1984). Why academicians don't write. *Journal of Higher Education.*

Brady, J. P., Davison, G. C., Dewald, P. A., Egan, G., Fadiman, J., Frank, J. D., Gill, M. M., Hoffman, I., Kempler, W., Lazarus, A. A., Raimy, V., Rotter, J. B., & Strupp, H. H. (1980). Some views on effective principles of psychotherapy. *Cognitive Therapy and Research, 4,* 271–306.

Brammer, L. M., & Shostrom, E. L. (1982). *Therapeutic psychology: Fundamentals of counseling and psychotherapy* (4th ed.). Englewood Cliffs, NJ: Prentice-Hall.

Brown, B. S. (1977). The crisis in mental health research. *American Journal of Psychiatry, 134,* 213–232.

Brown, B. S. (1983). The impact of political and economic changes upon mental health. *American Journal of Orthopsychiatry, 53,* 583–592.

Budman, S. H., & Gurman, A. S. (1983). The practice of brief therapy. *Professional Psychology: Research and Practice, 14,* 277–292.

Carkhuff, R. R., & Berenson, B. G. (1977). *Beyond counseling and therapy.* New York: Holt, Rinehart & Winston.

Corsini, R. J. (Ed.). (1981). *Handbook of innovative psychotherapies.* New York: Wiley.

Cross, D. G., & Sheehan, P. W. (1981). Classification of variables in psychotherapy research: Therapeutic change and the concept of artifact. *Psychotherapy: Theory, Research, and Practice, 18,* 345–355.

Dryden, W. (1984). Issues in the eclectic practice of individual therapy. In W. Dryden (Ed.), *Individual therapy in Britain.* London: Harper & Row.

Eysenck, H. J. (1970). A mish-mash of theories. *International Journal of Psychiatry, 9,* 140–146.

Fey, W. F. (1958). Doctrine and experience: Their influence upon the psychotherapist. *Journal of Consulting Psychology, 22,* 103–112.

Feyerabend, P. (1970). Consolations for the specialist. In I. Lakatos & A. E. Musgrave (Eds.), *Criticism and the growth of knowledge.* Cambridge: Cambridge University Press.

Fiedler, F. E. (1950a). The concept of the ideal therapeutic relationship. *Journal of Consulting Psychology, 14,* 239–245.

Fiedler, F. E. (1950b). Comparison of therapeutic relationships in psychoanalytic, nondirective, and Alderian therapy. *Journal of Consulting Psychology, 14,* 436–445.

Fishman, D. B., & Neigher, W. D. (1982). American psychology in the eighties: Who will buy? *American Psychologist, 37,* 533–546.

Frances A., Clarkin, J., & Perry, S. (1984). *Differential therapeutics in psychiatry.* New York: Brunner/Mazel.

Frank, J. D. (1971). Psychotherapists need theories. *International Journal of Psychiatry, 9,* 146–149.

Frank, J. D. (1973). *Persuasion and healing* (2nd ed.). Baltimore: Johns Hopkins University Press.

Frank, J. D. (1979). The present status of outcome studies. *Journal of Consulting and Clinical Psychology, 47,* 310–316.

Frank, J. D. (1982). Therapeutic components shared by all psychotherapies. In J. H. Harvey & M. M. Parks (Eds.), *The Master Lecture Series.* Vol. 1. Washington, DC: American Psychological Association.

Garfield, S. L. (1973). Basic ingredients or common factors in psychotherapy? *Journal of Consulting and Clinical Psychology, 41,* 9–12.

Garfield, S. L. (1980). *Psychotherapy: An eclectic approach.* New York: Wiley.

Garfield, S. L. (1982). Eclecticism and integration in psychotherapy. *Behavior Therapy, 13,* 610–623.

Garfield, S. L., & Kurtz, R. (1976). Clinical psychologists in the 1970's. *American Psychologist, 31,* 1–9.

Garfield, S. L., & Kurtz, R. (1977). A study of eclectic views. *Journal of Consulting and Clinical Psychology, 45,* 78–83.

Goldfried, M. R. (1980). Toward the delineation of therapeutic change principles. *American Psychologist, 35,* 991–999.

Goldfried, M. R. (1982, August). *Multiple therapies with one client.* Symposium chaired at the annual meeting of the American Psychological Association, Washington, DC.

Goldfried, M. R. (Ed.). (1982). *Converging themes in psychotherapy.* New York: Springer.

Goldfried, M. R. (1982). On the history of therapeutic integration. *Behavior Therapy, 13,* 572–593.

Goldfried, M. R., & Strupp, H. H. (1980, November). *Empirical clinical practice: A dialogue on rapprochement.* Presented at the convention of the Association for Advancement of Behavior Therapy, New York, NY.

Goldfried, M. R., & Wachtel, P. L. (Eds.). (1983). *Newsletter of the Society for the Exploration of Psychotherapy Integration.* Volume 1 (1).

Goldstein, A. P., & Stein, N. (1976). *Prescriptive psychotherapies.* New York: Pergamon.

Gomes-Schwartz, B., Hadley, S. W., & Strupp, H. H. (1978). Individual psychotherapy and behavior therapy. *Annual Review of Psychology, 29,* 435–471.

Harper, R. A. (1959). *Psychoanalysis and psychotherapy: 36 systems.* Englewood Cliffs, NJ: Prentice-Hall.

Hart, J. (1983). *Modern eclectic therapy: A functional orientation to counseling and psychotherapy.* New York: Plenum.

Hartley, J. (1982). Scientific communication: So where do we go from here? *Behavioral and Brain Science, 5,* 215–216.

Herink, R. (Ed.). (1980). *The psychotherapy handbook.* New York: Meridian.

Hynan, M. T. (1981). On the advantages of assuming that the techniques of psychotherapy are ineffective. *Psychotherapy: Theory, Research and Practice, 18,* 11–13.

Jayaratne, S. (1982). Characteristics and theoretical orientations of clinical social workers: A national survey. *Journal of Social Service Research, 4,* (2), 17–30.

Kaplan, A. G., et al. (1983). The process of sex-role integration in psychotherapy. *Psychotherapy: Theory, Research and Practice, 20,* 476–485.

Kelly, E. L. (1961). Clinical psychology—1960. Report of survey findings. *Newsletter: Division of Clinical Psychology of the American Psychological Association, 14* (1), 1–11.

Kendell, P. C. (1982). Integration: Behavior therapy and other schools of thought. *Behavior Therapy, 13,* 559–571.

Keppler-Seid, H., Windle, C., & Way, J. R. (1980). Performance measures for mental health programs. *Community Mental Health Journal, 16,* 217–234.

Kiesler, C. (1980). Mental health policy as a field of inquiry for psychology. *American Psychologist, 55,* 1066–1080.

Kiesler, D. J. (1966). Some myths of psychotherapy research and the search for a paradigm. *Psychological Bulletin, 65,* 110–136.

Kisch, J., & Kroll, J. (1980). Meaningfulness versus effectiveness: Paradoxical implications in the evaluation of psychotherapy. *Psychotherapy: Theory, Research and Practice, 17,* 401–413.

Koss, M. P. (1980). Descriptive characteristics and length of psychotherapy of child and adult clients seen in private psychological practice. *Psychotherapy: Theory, Research and Practice, 17,* 268–271.

Koss, M. P., Graham, J. R., Kirkhart, K., Post, G., Kirkhart, R. O., & Silverberg, R. S. (1983). Outcome of eclectic psychotherapy in private psychological practice. *American Journal of Psychotherapy, 38,* 400–410.

Kuhn, T. S. (1970). *The structure of scientific revolutions* (2nd ed.). Chicago: University of Chicago Press.

Lambert, M. J. (1979). *The effects of psychotherapy.* St. Albans, VT: Eden Press.

Lambert, M. (1983). *Psychotherapy and patient relationships.* Homewood, IL: Dow-Jones-Irwin.

Landman, J. T., & Dawes, R. M. (1982). Smith and Glass' conclusions stand up under scrutiny. *American Psychologist, 37,* 504–516.

Landsman, T. (1974, August). *Not an adversity but a welcome diversity.* Paper presented at the annual meeting of the American Psychological Association, New Orleans, LA.

Larson, D. (1980). Therapeutic schools, styles, and schoolism: A national survey. *Journal of Humanistic Psychology, 20,* 3–20.

Lazarus, A. A. (1967). In support of technical eclecticism. *Psychological Reports, 21* 415–416.

Lazarus, A. A. (1977). Has behavior therapy outlived its usefulness? *American Psychologist, 32,* 550–554.

Lazarus, A. A. (1981). *The practice of multimodal therapy.* Hightstown, NJ: McGraw-Hill.

Lazarus, A. A. (1984). Multimodal therapy. In R. J. Corsini (Ed.), *Current psychotherapies* (3rd ed.). Itasca, IL: F. E. Peacock.

London, P. (1964). *The modes and morals of psychotherapy.* New York: Holt, Rinehart & Winston.

London, P. (1972). The end of ideology in behavior modification. *American Psychologist, 27,* 913–920.

Luborsky, L. (1969). Research cannot yet influence clinical practice. *International Journal of Psychiatry, 7,* 135–140.

Luborsky, L., Singer, B., & Luborsky, L. (1975). Comparative studies of psychotherapies: Is it true that "Everbody has won and all must have prizes?" *Archives of General Psychiatry, 32,* 995–1008.

Mahoney, M. J. (1976). *Cognition and behavior modification.* Cambridge, MA: Ballinger.

Malan, D. M. (1976). *The frontier of brief psychotherapy.* New York: Plenum.

Mann, J. (1973). *Time-limited psychotherapy.* Cambridge, MA: Harvard University Press.

Marmor J., & Woods, S. M. (Eds.). (1980). *The interface between the psychodynamic and behavioral therapies.* New York: Plenum.

Meichenbaum, D. H. (1974). *Cognitive behavior modification.* Morristown, NJ: General Learning Press.

Meltzoff, J. (1984). Research training for clinical psychologists: Point-counterpoint. *Professional Psychology: Research and Practice, 15,* 203–209.

Meltzoff, J., & Kornreich, M. (1970). *Research in psychotherapy.* New York: Atherton.

Messer, S. B. (1983). Integrating psychoanalytic and behavior therapy: Limitations, possibilities and trade-offs. *British Journal of Clinical Psychology, 22,* 341–132.

Messer, S. B., & Winokur, M. (1980). Some limits to the integration of psychoanalytic and behavior therapy. *American Psychologist, 35,* 818–827.

Messer, S. B., & Winokur, M. (1984). Ways of knowing and visions of reality in psychoanalytic therapy and behavior therapy. In H. Arkowitz & S. B. Messer (Eds.), *Psychoanalytic therapy and behavior therapy: Is integration possible?* New York: Plenum Press.

Mischel, W. (1973). Toward a cognitive social-learning reconceptualization of personality. *Psychological Review, 80,* 252–283.

Mischel, W. (1979). On the interface of cognition and personality: Beyond the person–situation debate. *American Psychologist, 34,* 740–754.

Murray, E. J. (1983). Beyond behavioral and dynamic therapy. *British Journal of Clinical Psychology, 22,* 127–128.

Nash, J., Norcross, J. C., & Prochaska, J. O. (1984). Satisfactions and stresses of independent practice. *Psychotherapy in Private Practice, 2* (4), 39–48.

Norcross, J. C. (1981). All in the family?: On therapeutic commonalities. *American Psychologist, 36,* 1544–1545.

Norcross, J. C. (1984, August). *Systematic eclectic psychotherapy.* Symposium chaired at the annual meeting of the American Psychological Association, Toronto, Canada.

Norcross, J. C. (1985). In defense of theoretical orientations for clinicians. *The Clinical Psychologist, 38* (1), 13–17.

Norcross, J. C. (in press). Psychotherapist heal thyself: The self-change and therapy-change experiences of psychologists, counselors, and laypersons. *Psychotherapy.*

Norcross, J. C., & Prochaska, J. O. (1982). A national survey of clinical psychologists: Affiliations and orientations. *The Clinical Psychologist, 35* (3), 1, 4–6.

Norcross, J. C., & Prochaska, J. O. (1983). Clinicians' theoretical orientations: Selection, utilization, and efficacy. *Professional Psychology: Research and Practice, 14,* 197–208.

Norcross, J. C., & Wogan, M. (1983). American psychotherapists of diverse persuasions: Characteristics, theories, practices, and clients. *Professional Psychology, 4,* 529–539.

Palmer, J. E. (1980). *A primer of eclectic psychotherapy.* Monterey, CA: Brooks/Cole.

Parloff, M. B. (1976). Shopping for the right therapy. *Saturday Review,* February 21, 135–142.

Parloff, M. B. (1979). Can psychotherapy research guide the policymaker? A little knowledge may be a dangerous thing. *American Psychologist, 34,* 296–306.

Parloff, M. B. (1981, June). *Psychotherapy and reimbursement decisions: Bambi meets Godzilla.* Paper presented at the 12th annual meeting of the Society for Psychotherapy Research, Aspen, CO.

Parloff, M. B., Waskow, I. E., & Wolfe, B. E. (1978). Research on therapist variables in relation to process and outcome. In S. L. Garfield & A. E. Bergin (Eds.), *Handbook of psychotherapy and behavior change: An empirical analysis* (2nd ed.). New York: Wiley.

Paul, G. L. (1967). Strategy of outcome research in psychotherapy. *Journal of Consulting Psychology, 31,* 109–119.

Perlman, B. (1985). A national survey of APA affiliated master-level clinicians: Description and comparison. *Professional Psychology: Research and Practice, 16,* 553–564.

Perry, W. (1970). *Forms of intellectual and ethical development in the college years: A scheme.* New York: Holt, Rinehart & Winston.

Peterson, D. R., Eaton, M. M., Levine, A. R., & Snepp, F. P. (1982). Career experience of doctors of psychology. *Professional Psychology, 13,* 268–277.

Phillips, J. S., & Bierman, K. L. (1981). Clinical psychology: Individual methods. *Annual Review of Psychology, 32,* 415–438.

Prochaska, J. O. (1984). *Systems of psychotherapy: A transtheoretical analysis* (2nd ed.). Homewood, IL: Dorsey Press.

Prochaska, J. O., & DiClemente, C. C. (1984). *The transtheoretical approach: Crossing the traditional boundaries of therapy.* Homewood, IL: Dow Jones-Irvin.

Prochaska, J. O., & Norcross, J. C. (1982). The future of psychotherapy: A Delphi poll. *Professional Psychology, 13,* 620–627.

Prochaska, J. O., & Norcross, J. C. (1983a). Contemporary psychotherapists: A national survey of characteristics, practices, orientations, and attitudes. *Psychotherapy: Theory, Research and Practice, 20,* 161–173.

Prochaska, J. O., & Norcross, J. C. (1983b). Psychotherapists' perspectives on treating themselves and their clients for psychic distress. *Professional Psychology: Research and Practice, 14,* 642–655.

Rebecca, M., Hefner, R., & Oleshansky, B. (1976). A model of sex role transcendence. *Journal of Social Issues, 32,* 197–206.

Robertson, M. (1979). Some observations from an eclectic therapist. *Psychotherapy: Theory, Research and Practice, 16,* 18–21.

Shemberg, K. M., & Leventhal, D. B. (1978). A survey of activities of academic clinicians. *Professional Psychology, 9,* 580–586.

Sifneos, P. E. (1979). *Short-term dynamic psychotherapy: Evaluation and technique.* New York: Plenum.

Sloane, R. B., Staples, F. R., Cristol, A. H., Yorkston, N. J., & Whipple, K. (1975). *Short-term analytically oriented psychotherapy versus behavior therapy.* Cambridge, MA: Harvard University Press.

Smith, D. S. (1982). Trends in counseling and psychotherapy. *American Psychologist, 37,* 802–809.

Smith, D., & Kraft, W. A. (1983). DSM-III: Do psychologists really want an alternative? *American Psychologist, 38,* 777–785.

Smith, M. L., Glass, G. V., & Miller, T. I. (1980). *The benefits of psychotherapy.* Baltimore, MD: Johns Hopkins University Press.

Strupp, H. H. (1955). An objective comparison of Rogerian and psychoanalytic techniques. *Journal of Consulting Psychology, 19,* 1–7.

Strupp, H. H. (1973). On the basic ingredients of psychotherapy. *Journal of Consulting and Clinical Psychology, 41,* 1–8.

Strupp, H. H. (1982). The outcome problem in psychotherapy: Contemporary perspectives. In J. H. Harvey & M. M. Parks (Eds.), *Master Lecture Series.* Vol. I. Washington, DC: American Psychologial Association.

Strupp, H. H., & Binder, J. L. (1982). *Time-Limited Dynamic Psychotherapy (TLDP): A treatment manual.* Nashville, TN: Vanderbilt University Center for Psychotherapy Research.

Sundland, D. M. (1977). Theoretical orientations of psychotherapists. In A. S. Gurman & A. M. Razin (Eds.), *Effective psychotherapy: A handbook of research.* New York: Pergamon.

Swan, G. E. (1979). On the structure of eclecticism: Cluster analysis of eclectic behavior therapists. *Professional Psychology, 10,* 732–739.

Swan, G. E., & MacDonald, M. L. (1979). Behavior therapy in practice: A national survey of behavior therapists. *Behavior Therapy, 9,* 799–807.

Thorne, F. C. (1957). An evaluation of eclectically oriented psychotherapy. *Journal of Consulting Psychology, 21,* 459–464.

Thorne, F. C. (1973). Eclectic psychotherapy. In R. Corsini (Ed.), *Current psychotherapies.* Itasca, IL: F. E. Peacock.

VandenBos, G. R. (1980). Introduction. In G. R. VandenBos (Ed.), *Psychotherapy: Practice, research, policy.* Beverly Hills, CA: Sage.

Wachtel, P. L. (1977). *Psychoanalysis and behavior therapy: Toward an integration.* New York: Basic Books.

Wachtel, P. L. (1982). What can dynamic therapies contribute to behavior therapy? *Behavior Therapy, 13,* 594–609.

Wachtel, P. L. (1983). Integration misunderstood. *British Journal of Clinical Psychology, 22,* 129–130.

Wachtel, P. L. (1984). On theory, practice, and the nature of integration. In H. Arkowitz & S. Messer (Eds.), *Psychoanalytic and behavior therapy:*

Is integration possible? New York: Plenum.

Walton, D. E. (1978). An exploratory study: Personality factors and theoretical orientations of therapists. *Psychotherapy: Theory, Research and Practice, 15,* 390–395.

Waskow, I. E. (1984). Specification of the technique variable. In J. B. W. Spitzer & R. L. Spitzer (Eds.), *Psychotherapy research: Where are we and where should we go?* New York: Guilford Press.

Weiner, I. B. (1975). *Principles of psychotherapy.* New York: Wiley.

Weiner, I. B. (1983). Theoretical foundations of clinical psychology. In M. Hersen, A. E. Kazdin, & A. S. Bellack (Eds.), *The clinical psychology handbook.* New York: Pergamon.

Werner, H. (1948). *Comparative psychology of mental development.* Chicago: Follett.

Werner, H., & Kaplan, B. (1963). *Symbol formation: An organismic–developmental approach to language and the expression of thought.* New York: Wiley.

Wilson, G. T. (1982). Psychotherapy process and procedure: The behavioral mandate. *Behavior Therapy, 13,* 291–312.

Wogan, N., & Norcross, J. C. (1985). Dimensions of therapeutic skills and techniques: Empirical identification, therapist correlates, and predictive utility. *Psychotherapy, 22,* 63–64.

Yates, A. J. (1983). Behavior therapy and psychodynamic therapy: Basic conflict or reconciliation and integration? *British Journal of Clinical Psychology, 22,* 107–125.

CHAPTER 2

Psychotherapy Integration: An Historical Perspective

Marvin R. Goldfried and Cory Newman

The progress of science is the work of creative minds. Every creative mind that contributes to scientific advances works, however, within two limitations. It is limited, first, by ignorance, for one discovery waits upon that other which opens the way to it. Discovery and its acceptance are, however, limited also by the habits of thought that pertain to the culture of any region and period, that is to say, by the *Zeitgeist*: an idea too strange or preposterous to be thought in one period of western civilization may be readily accepted as true only a century or two later.

—E.G. Boring

The idea of being able to integrate varying approaches to psychotherapy has intrigued mental health professionals for more than 50 years. It is only within the

last decade or so, however, that the issue of psychotherapy integration has begun to develop into a clearly delineated area of interest. Prior to that time, it was more of a latent theme that ran through the literature.

As is the case with any attempt to trace the historical origins of contemporary thought, one never knows for certain the specific influence that earlier contributions have made to later thinking. More often than not, innovative ideas and findings are initially ignored, only to become assimilated into the mainstream at a later point in time (Barber, 1961). It is possible that the ultimate contribution of an idea lies in its consciousness-raising function. Quite apart from their specific merits, new ideas sensitize us to otherwise neglected areas of thought. With regard to psychotherapy, some notions have continued to live on over the years, whereas others have failed to pass the test of time. Still others disappear after their introduction only to reappear at a later time when the *Zeitgeist* has become more hospitable. The recent dramatic interest in

Portions of this chapter have been adapted from Goldfried, M. R. (1982). On the history of therapeutic integration. *Behavior Therapy, 13,* 572–593. Preparation of the chapter was facilitated by Grants MH 24327 and 40196 from the National Institute of Mental Health. The authors would like to thank John C. Norcross, Jeremy D. Safran, and Paul L. Wachtel for their helpful comments on an earlier version of this paper.

developing a rapprochement across the psychotherapies fits into this last category.

In the present chapter, we begin with a historical review of past efforts at psychotherapy integration, touching on the directions that were taken in the early 1980s. We then highlight some of the recurrent themes that have appeared over the years and continue to remain salient, such as the complementary nature of divergent approaches to therapy; the interplay between thought, emotion, and behavior; the need for therapy to be guided by empirical findings; the importance of a common language; and the need to reformulate commonalities into transtheoretical principles of change. The concerns of the anti-integrationists are discussed, along with the various social, economic, and political forces that serve to prevent rapprochement, on the one hand, and encourage it, on the other. Finally, we describe the recent development of a professional reference group that will hopefully support continued work in this area.

EARLY ATTEMPTS AT INTEGRATION

In what perhaps represented one of the earliest attempts at integrating the psychotherapies, French delivered an address—at the 1932 meeting of the American Psychiatric Association—in which he drew certain parallels between psychoanalysis and Pavlovian conditioning. Acknowledging the wide discrepancy between these two approaches, French discussed the similarities between the psychoanalytic concept of repression and Pavlovian concepts of extinction and inhibition. Trying to tie sublimation to learning principles, he invoked the principle of differentiation, suggesting that some sort of discrimination training had probably taken place to differentiate the unacceptable from the more socially accepted manifestations of certain impulses. He also suggested that a pa-

tient's adjustment to reality might be explained in terms of the individual's earlier conditioned experiences.

The following year, the text of French's presentation was published, together with comments by members of the original audience (French, 1933). As one might expect, French's presentation resulted in very mixed audience reaction. As one of the most unabashedly negative responses by a member of the audience, Myerson acknowleged:

I was tempted to call for a bell-boy and ask him to page John B. Watson, Ivan Pavlov, and Sigmund Freud, while Dr. French was reading his paper. I think Pavlov would have exploded; and what would have happened to Watson is scandalous to contemplate, since the whole of his behavioristic school is founded on the conditioned reflex. . . . Freud . . . would be scandalized by such a rapprochement made by one of his pupils, reading a paper of this kind. (In French, 1933, p. 1201)

Meyer was not nearly as unsympathetic. Although he stated that the field should encourage separate lines of inquiry and should not attempt to substitute any one for another too prematurely, Meyer nonetheless suggested that one should "enjoy the convergences which show in such discussions as we have had this morning" (French, 1933, p. 1201). Zilboorg, who was also in the audience at the time, took an even more favorable stand, noting:

I do not believe that these two lines of investigation could be passed over very lightly. . . . There is here an attempt to point out, regardless of structure and gross pathology, that while dealing with extremely complex functional units both in the physiological laboratory and in the clinic, we can yet reduce them to comparatively simple phenomena. (French, 1933, pp. 1198-1199)

In an extension of French's attempts, Kubie (1934) maintained that certain aspects of psychoanalytic technique itself could be explained in terms of the conditioned reflex. Noting that Pavlov hypothesized that certain associations might exist outside of an individual's awareness because they took place under a state of inhibition, Kubie suggested that the encouragement of free association on the part of the patient, together with the relatively passive role of the therapist, might serve to remove the conditions of inhibition and thus allow such unconscious associations to emerge into conscious awareness.

In 1936, Rosenzweig published a brief article in which he described what he believed were common factors among the psychotherapies. In contrast to French's and Kubie's attempts to link two separate theoretical orientations, Rosenzweig argued that the effectiveness of various therapeutic approaches probably had more to do with their common elements than with the theoretical explanations on which they were based. Rosenzweig suggested three common factors: (a) Regardless of any particular orientation a therapist adopts, it is the therapist's personality that has much to do with the effectiveness of the change process; this influence may be related to the therapist's ability to inspire hope in patients or clients. (b) Interpretations that therapists make to patients/clients are helpful because they provide alternative and perhaps more plausible ways of understanding a particular problem. It makes little difference what the interpretation is, argued Rosenzweig, as long as it serves to make a problem more understandable. (c) Even though varying theoretical orientations may focus on different aspects of human functioning, they can all be effective because of the synergistic effects that one area of functioning may have on another.

At the 1940 meeting of the American Orthopsychiatric Association (Watson, 1940), a small group of therapists got together to discuss areas of agreement in psychotherapy. Commenting on the points of commonality (e.g., the importance of the therapeutic interaction), Watson observed that "if we were to apply to our colleagues the distinction, so important with patients, between what they tell us and what they do, we might find that agreement is greater in practice than in theory" (p. 708).

Woodworth's 1948 text, *Contemporary Schools of Psychology,* explored the development and substantive content of the then existing schools of psychological thought. More than simply presenting an overview of different approaches and philosophies, Woodworth sought to address the problem of the lack of reconciliation between such areas of psychology as behaviorism, gestalt psychology, and the psychoanalytic schools. He recognized that although each school had made gains in its own respective chosen direction, "no one [school] is good enough" (p. 255). Observing that psychology was advancing in many different directions, Woodworth wondered "whether synthesis of the different lines of advance [might] not sometime prove to be possible" (p. 10). In this way, he reasoned, psychology would most likely find the path or paths that would yield the greatest discoveries for the field as a whole.

Close on the heels of this thesis was a landmark work in the history of the integration of the psychotherapies, namely Dollard and Miller's classic book *Personality and Psychotherapy,* published in 1950 and dedicated to "Freud and Pavlov and their students." The importance of Dollard and Miller's work in the history of psychotherapy can be attested to by the fact that this book has remained in print for over 30 years. Although behavior therapists have traditionally argued that Dollard and Miller's thinking had little impact on the development of behavior therapy, the fact that the work is continually referred to suggests that it has been widely read. In their work, Dollard and Miller described in detail how such psychoanalytic concepts as regression, anxiety, repression, and displacement may be understood within the framework of learning theory. For the most part, Dollard and Miller merely translated one language system into another. Nonetheless, they did point to certain factors that may very well be common to all therapeutic approaches, such as the need for the therapist to support an individual's attempt at changing by expressing empathy, interest, and approval for such attempts.

Even though Dollard and Miller (1950) stayed fairly close to the intervention procedures associated with psychoanalytic therapy, they made continual reference to principles and procedures on which contemporary behavior therapy is based. Thus, Dollard and Miller suggest the value of modeling procedures (e.g., "watching a demonstration of the correct response may enable the student to perform perfectly on the first trial," pp. 37-38); the use of hierarchically arranged tasks (e.g., "the ideal of the therapist is to set up a series of graded situations where the patient can learn," p. 350); reinforcement of gradual approximations toward a goal (e.g., "if a long and complex habit must be learned, the therapist should reward the subunits of the habit as they occur," p. 350); the principle of reciprocal inhibition (e.g., "like any other response, fear apparently can be inhibited by responses that are incompatible with it," p. 74); the significance of the reinforcing characteristics of the therapist (e.g., "the therapist uses approval to reward good efforts on the part of the patient," p. 395); the importance of teaching the individual self-control or coping skills to be used following therapy (e.g., "it is theoretically possible that special practice in self-study might be given during the latter part of a course of therapeutic interviews. The patient might be asked to practice solving particular problems . . . [under conditions] as similar as possible to those to be used after therapy," p. 438); the treatment of orgasmic dysfunctions via masturbation (e.g., "at one point in a therapeutic sequence, the therapist might have to reward masturbation so that the patients may experience the sexual orgasm for the first time" p. 350);

and the importance of environmental contingencies for maintaining behavior change (e.g., "the conditions of real life must be favorable if new responses are to become strong habits," p. 427).

Dollard and Miller also emphasized yet another behavioral tenet, the importance of between-session assignments (e.g., "behavioral changes must be made in the real world of the patient's current life. If benevolent changes are to occur, the patient must begin doing something new," p. 319). All the more striking is the source that they cite in support of this notion. Freud himself is quoted as writing, "Actually it is quite unimportant for his cure whether or not the patient can overcome this or that anxiety or inhibition in the institution; what is of importance, on the contrary, is whether or not he will be free from them in real life" (Freud, 1924, Vol. II, p. 320).

Unlike Dollard and Miller (1950), whose primary emphasis was on the integration of different theoretical orientations, Thorne (1950) was interested in pursuing therapeutic integration on the basis of what we know empirically about how people function and change. Thorne's book on eclectic psychotherapy (*Principles of Personality Counseling*) was based on some of his work published in the *Journal of Clinical Psychology,* which he had founded five years earlier. From the time that he was a medical student, Thorne was struck by the fact that medicine was not divided up into different schools of thought, but rather that basic principles of bodily functioning were what guided actual practice. One objective throughout his career was to establish a similar set of principles for the field of psychology and psychotherapy. Like Thorne, Garfield has long been interested in an empirically based approach to therapy, and in 1957 he outlined what appeared to be common points among the psychotherapies. In an introductory clinical psychology text, Garfield noted such universal factors as an understanding and supportive therapist, the opportunity for emotional catharsis, and the provision of self-understanding.

Glad's (1959) *Operational Values in Psychotherapy* took issue with the relative inflexibility of psychotherapy when practiced, to the letter, according to any given theoretical persuasion. Glad felt that the value systems instilled by doctrinaire approaches posed major limitations for adequately understanding and treating psychological problems. The selective characteristics of the methods and theory for each orientation, in his view, were likely to "produce biases in the phenomenon produced, the data selected for representation and the conceptual structure imposed as explanation" (Glad, 1959, p. 38). Glad therefore recommended that the practicing therapist be exposed to (if not specifically trained in) systematic operations of psychotherapists from the major theoretical approaches of the time, including client-centered and psychodynamic therapies. It was reasoned that this would provide a wider variety of procedures to use in the treatment of complex cases.

MORE RECENT TRENDS TOWARD RAPPROCHEMENT

The topic of therapeutic rapprochement was seriously addressed by only a handful of writers in the 1950s, due, perhaps, to the fact that no single approach to psychotherapy had yet gained enough momentum to challenge psychoanalytic therapy. Perhaps it was also the conservative social and political climate of the 1950s that served to discourage therapists from questioning their paradigms. The 1960s, by contrast, brought an increase in the number of books and articles dealing with rapprochement.

1960s

The most significant contribution to the integration of psychotherapies made in the early 1960s was Frank's (1961) *Persuasion and Healing*. This book addressed itself to commonalities cutting across varying attempts at personal influence and healing in general. Frank suggested that psychotherapy serves to correct people's misconceptions about themselves and others. It is not the only method for influencing people, however; similar change processes, Frank observed, can be seen in such diverse methods as religious conversion, primitive healing, brainwashing, and the placebo effects that occur in the practice of medicine. When distressed individuals are placed in any of these contexts, the effectiveness of the interaction is due to an expectancy for improvement and an arousal of hope, which in turns results in a concomitant increase in self-esteem and improved functioning. It should be pointed out that although Frank continued, in his later writings, to stress common factors across the psychotherapies, in one of his more recent reviews of the field (Frank, 1979) he acknowledges that certain clinical problems (e.g., fears, phobias, compulsive rituals) may be effectively dealt with by methods that go beyond the general nature of the therapeutic interaction.

In one of the last papers to be published before his death, Alexander (1963), a colleague of French, suggested that psychoanalytic therapy might profitably be understood in terms of learning theory. Based on an analysis of tape recordings of psychoanalytic therapy sessions, Alexander concluded that many of the therapeutic changes that occurred, "can best be understood in terms of learning theory. Particularly the principle of reward and punishment and also the influence of repetitive experiences can be clearly recognized" (p. 446). A therapist who was dedicated throughout his career to the advancement of the field, Alexander suggested that "we are witnessing the beginnings of a most promising integration of psychoanalytic theory with learning theory, which may lead to unpredictable advances in the theory and practice of the psychotherapies" (p. 448). A year later, Marmor, involved in the same program of research on psychotherapy, described in detail the learning principles that he believed to underlie psychoanalytic therapy (Marmor, 1964).

About this time, Carl Rogers (1963), published an article dealing with the current status of psychotherapy. He noted that the field was "in a mess," but that the theoretical orientations within which therapists had typically functioned were starting to break down. He stated that the field was now ready to shed itself of the limitations inherent in specific orientations—including client-centered therapy—and that it was essential to observe more directly exactly what goes on during the course of psychotherapy.

London (1964), in a short but insightful book entitled *The Modes and Morals of Psychotherapy,* pointed to the inherent limitations associated with both the psychodynamic and behavioral orientations, suggesting:

There is a quiet blending of techniques by artful therapists of either school: a blending that takes account of the fact that people are considerably simpler than the Insight schools give them credit for, but that they are also more complicated than the Action therapists would like to believe. (p. 39)

Marks and Gelder (1966) also compared behavioral therapy and psychodynamic procedures, looking at their historical antecedents, theoretical underpinnings, practical procedures, and claims to success. Although acknowledging that there was probably common ground between the two approaches, Marks and Gelder also underscored certain differences. They further suggested that the two approaches should be viewed as potentially contributing to each other, rather than necessarily being antagonistic in nature. Arguing

for the integration of learning theory with psychoanalysis, Wolf (1966) noted:

I submit that their integration is sooner or later inevitable, however passionately some or many of us may choose to resist it. Psychoanalysis cannot remain for much longer outside the behavioural sciences, nor can the science of human behaviour for much longer ignore the body of knowledge amassed by the psychoanalytic schools of thought. (p. 535)

The concept of "technical eclecticism" was introduced in 1967 by Lazarus, who maintained that clinicians can use techniques from various therapeutic systems without necessarily accepting the theoretical underpinnings associated with these methods. Starting from this pragmatic /clinical point of view, Lazarus suggested that the ultimate standard of utility should rest on empirical, not theoretical grounds. Appearing in that same year were an article by Patterson (1967) on divergent and convergent elements across the psychotherapies; a paper by Whitehouse (1967) on the generic principles underlying a wide variety of therapeutic interventions; and a discussion by Weitzman (1967) of how systematic desensitization may profitably be used within a psychoanalytic context.

Brady (1968), responding to the practical demands of doing actual clinical work, argued that behavioral and psychodynamic approaches were not necessarily contradictory in nature but could, in certain cases, be used in combination. He described the treatment of a preorgasmic woman who experienced anxiety associated with sexual activities, systematic desensitization and short-term psychodynamic therapy focusing on the woman's relationship with her husband. In a similar vein, Leventhal (1968) described a case of a woman experiencing anxiety over sexuality who was successfully treated with combined behavioral and traditional therapeutic interventions.

Developing this line of reasoning, Bergin (1968) asserted that systematic desensitization could be made into an even more powerful treatment procedure if accompanied by therapist warmth, empathy, and moderate interpretation. Bergin reasoned that such extra-behavioral activities were important because they elicited cognitive and emotional responses that were intimately tied to the behavioral situations addressed in the desensitization hierarchies. Bergin maintained that a theory of therapy that addressed a more universal set of psychological events would be less likely to lead therapists to conceptual dead-ends in the face of particularly complex cases. Along these same lines, in an article offering a rationale for "psychobehavioral therapy," Woody (1968) observed that the integration of behavior therapy and psychodynamic therapy was particularly relevant for cases that were unresponsive to treatment.

In the following year, Kraft (1969) presented clinical evidence that systematic desensitization could help clients/patients gain insight into a wealth of unconscious material through both imagery and relaxation in the face of previously feared objects or situations. In a theoretical paper examining the similarities among psychoanalytic, behavioral, and client-centered therapy, Sloane (1969) maintained that common factors ran through all three orientations. Sloane suggested that, in the final analysis, the underlying process of therapeutic change probably involves principles of learning. Commenting on Sloane's paper, Marmor (1969) agreed that all therapies involve some application of learning principles, either directly or unwittingly, but argued that the simple S–R model could not explain some of the more complex aspects of human functioning. Moreover, like London (1964), Marks and Gelder (1966), Lazarus (1967), Brady (1968), Bergin (1968), and others, Marmor concluded that behavioral and psychodynamic therapies are probably best viewed as complementary in nature, with neither model being totally applicable to all cases. Cautioning against a haphazard piecing together of techniques from different orientations, Brammer (1969) maintained that what was needed was an eclecticism based on research findings about the effectiveness of various clinical procedures.

1970s

The year 1970 marked the inauguration of a new journal, *Behavior Therapy*. Given the enthusiasm that had been building among those who associated themselves with this orientation, one might have expected the first articles to be part of a gala opening-ceremony of sorts, complete with grandiose statements about the "proven" effectiveness of behavior therapy over all other approaches. Such was not at all the case. Editors and contributors, from the first issue of *Behavior Therapy,* devoted serious attention to aspects of theory and therapy that were not strictly "behavioral." The implicit message seemed to be that the relevant quest was one of advancing the field of psychotherapy, not simply behavior therapy per se. Birk (1970), writing in this new journal, described two clinical cases to illustrate the potential integration of behavior therapy with psychodynamic theory. Bergin (1970a) followed his earlier treatise on nonbehavioral "adjuncts" to systematic desensitization with a paper that went so far as to claim that desensitization proper was, in fact, much more than a simple counterconditioning process. Begin's work suggested that desensitization drew heavily upon cognitive and relationship variables, while also influencing the dream process, i.e., evoking changes in the symbolic domain.

In addition to those articles that dealt with the convergence of behavioral and psychodynamic techniques, space in *Behavior Therapy* was devoted to a discussion of cognitive techniques in therapy (Beck, 1970), a move that was applauded by Bergin (1970b): "Such an attitude is a welcome sign of maturity in a field which needs a good deal more willingness to focus on the broad spectrum of phenomena instead of simply strengthening in-group identifications" (p. 205). Bergin (1970b) went on to say:

For so many neobehaviorists to acknowledge the importance of introspection, cognitive mediation, and symbolic monitoring and control may seem gratuitous to those who have been devoted to these phenomena for many years, but the sociological and historical importance of the movement should not be underestimated for it has three important consequences. It significantly reduces barriers to progress due to narrow school allegiances, it brings the energies of a highly talented and experimentally sophisticated group to bear upon the intricate and often baffling problems of objectifying and managing the subjective, and it underscores the notion that a pure behavior therapy does not exist. (p. 207)

As it turned out, Bergin's observations were very much on the mark; many of the behavior therapists who became involved in the development of cognitive procedures (e.g., Beck, Davison, Goldfried, Lazarus, Mahoney, Meichenbaum) later moved on to an interest in therapeutic integration.

In a consideration of the importance of the therapeutic relationship within a behavioral approach, Truax and Mitchell (1971) noted that the successful techniques and procedures of behavior therapy were not being delivered in an interpersonal vacuum. They cautioned against the reifying techniques and encouraged the exploration of how these useful procedures interact with the human qualities of the therapist to bring about therapeutic change. Although they lamented the evident difficulties involved

in conducting research on the therapy interaction, they suggested—as Rosenzweig (1936) had done some 35 years earlier—that there existed important therapist characteristics that contributed to the change process, regardless of therapeutic orientation.

Commenting on how existing cultural values contribute to the development of different schools of therapy, Frank (1971) outlined features that nonetheless were common to all approaches. Marmor published an article on therapeutic integration in that same year (Marmor, 1971), in which he suggested:

The research on the nature of the psychotherapeutic process in which I participated with Franz Alexander, beginning in 1958, has convinced me that all psychotherapy, regardless of the techniques used, is a learning process. . . . Dynamic psychotherapies and behavior therapies simply represent different teaching techniques, and their differences are based in part on differences in their goals and in part on their assumptions of the nature of psychopathology. (p. 26)

Many contemporary behavior therapists probably would now agree with Marmor's clinical observation that not only simple conditioning but cognitive learning occurs during the course of therapy.

In a comprehensive and scholarly review of the psychotherapy outcome literature, Bergin (1971) recognized the important empirical contributions that behavior therapy had begun to make. Nonetheless, he concluded that the field needed to remain open to the "many fertile leads yet to be extracted from traditional therapy" (p. 254). Responding to Bergin's clinical observations that behavior therapy alone was not always effective clinically, Lazarus (1971) described in *Behavior Therapy and Beyond* a wide array of both behavioral and nonbehavioral techniques that may be employed by broad-spectrum behavior therapists. In the same year, Woody (1971) also published a book integrating behavioral and insight-oriented procedures. Echoing Lazarus's concept of technical eclecticism, Woody suggested that, providing one is able to set aside varying theoretical allegiances, the practicing clinician is capable of selecting and integrating procedures from varying sources based purely on pragmatic grounds. Marks (1971) similarly noted the beginning trends toward rapprochement, observing that therapists "are growing less reluctant to adopt methods with pedigrees outside their own theoretical systems" (p. 69).

Houts and Serber's (1972) edited book *After the Turn On, What?* described the experiences of a group of seven researchers and practitioners who spent a weekend together in a humanistic-group-type experience. Ranging from radical behaviorism to cognitive learning in orientation, the participants described what they saw to be both assets and liabilities of their group experience. As a part of a larger project to try to determine the future course of psychotherapy research, Bergin and Strupp (1972) reported on their contacts with researchers throughout the country. Among those interviewed was Neal Miller, who predicted that as behavior therapy began to become involved with more complicated types of cases, and as psychodynamic therapy focused more on ego mechanisms and the working-through process, the two therapeutic approaches would eventually start to converge in some interesting ways.

In a provocative article on the "end of ideology" in behavior therapy, London (1972) asked his behavioral colleagues to call a truce in their strife with other orientations and to look more realistically and pragmatically at what we are able to do clinically. Very much the clinical pragmatist, London cautioned against becoming overly enamored with theories, noting that "the first issue, scientifically as well as clinically, is the factual one—do they work? On whom? When? The how and why

come later" (p. 919). And if techniques exist that are not necessarily within the behavioral school but are found to be effective, continued London, these cannot afford to be ignored.

Other efforts at therapaeutic integration that appeared in 1972 included a book by Martin that attempted to integrate learning theory with client-centered therapy; a description of universal healing processes, seen among psychotherapists and witchdoctors alike (Torrey, 1972); and a set of papers dealing with the theoretical and clinical aspects of the integration of psychodynamic and behavior therapies (Feather & Rhoads, 1972a, 1972b). Feather and Rhoads (1972a) argued that in psychology, as in medicine, the existence of many treatments for a given disorder probably signalled a poor understanding of the disorder, and that none of the separate individual treatments was likely to be adequate. Hence, they suggested, it was important to search for a more all-encompassing, integrative psychotherapy theory.

Commenting on one of Feather and Rhoads's articles appearing in the previous year, Birk (1973) noted that one area of complementarity between a behavioral and psychodynamic approach was that the former dealt more with external stimuli, whereas the latter tended to focus on stimuli that are more internal in nature. Strupp (1973), stressing the common elements underlying all psychotherapies, underscored the therapeutic relationship as a vehicle for change, providing the client/patient with a corrective learning experience. Strupp likened the therapeutic interaction to a parent–child relationship, a phenomenon that Freud had called "after-education." Thoresen (1973) suggested that many of the philosophical underpinnings of behaviorism and humanism were in agreement, and that it was possible to view a behavioral approach as providing the technology by which certain humanistic goals might be achieved. Appearing in that same year was a report of two cases of sexual deviance (Woody, 1973), in which successful treatment was accomplished by aversion therapy and short-term psychodynamic therapy, administered concurrently by separate therapists.

A fair number of articles appeared in 1974 on the issue of therapeutic rapprochement. In an intriguing discussion of behavioral and psychodynamic approaches as "complementary" rather than mutually exclusive, Ferster (1974)—a well-known Skinnerian—described what he considered to be some of the merits of psychoanalytically oriented therapy. Birk and Brinkley-Birk (1974) provided a conceptual integration of psychoanalysis and behavior therapy, viewing the two approaches as complementing "the weak links in the therapeutic input–outcome chain of the other" (p. 505). They specifically suggested that with an integrated model, insight can set the stage for change, whereas behavior therapy provides some of the actual procedures by which the change process may be brought about. They went on to suggest: "what is really required at this stage, however, is a dialogue between clinicians of both schools whose aim is genuine rapprochement, mutual understanding, and the tentative forging of a new clinical learning theory for psychotherapy" (p. 500). Birk (1974) illustrated how intensive group therapy might be implemented by combining behavioral and psychoanalytic principles, and Rhoads and Feather (1974) described cases treated with desensitization procedures that were modified along psychodynamic lines.

Kaplan (1974), in her book *The New Sex Therapy,* outlined how a psychodynamic approach to therapy may be integrated with performance-based methods, and Sollod's (1975) article expounded on the merits of this structured and synergistic integrative approach to sex therapy. In a report of the Menninger Foundation Psychotherapy Research Project, Horwitz (1974, 1976) noted that inasmuch as supportive treatment procedures were just as effective, in terms of outcomes, as insight-oriented therapy, the psychodynamic approach needed to consider alternative methods of producing therapeutic change that might not readily fit into its usual conceptual model. Similarly, Silverman (1974) similarly made suggestions to his psychoanalytic colleagues that there is much to learn from "other approaches that can make (unmodified) psychoanalytic treatment more effective" (p. 305). In a paper delivered at the 1974 meeting of the American Psychological Association, Landsman (1974) urged his humanistically oriented colleagues to attend to some of the important contributions of behavior therapy, such as "attention to specifics, to details, careful quantification, modesty in claims, demonstrable results" (p. 15).

In his book *Misunderstandings of the Self,* Raimy (1975), like Frank (1961), suggested that various approaches to therapy all seem to be directed toward changing patients'/clients' misconceptions of themselves and of others. All therapies are alike in that they "present evidence" to assist individuals in changing these misconceptions; the type of evidence and the way it is presented, however, vary across different therapeutic orientations. An article by Bastine (1975), amplified upon a few years later (Bastine, 1978), similarly outlined common therapeutic strategies together with the specific techniques by which they may be implemented. In his clinically oriented book on the therapeutic change process, Egan (1975) modified his original humanistic orientation to acknowledge that there comes a time when the therapist must assume a more active role in helping a client to change. Although the contributions of Rogers (1963) and others are essential for establishing the type of therapeutic relationship in which change can take place, Egan suggested, behavior therapy may offer the clinician methods to implement specific action programs.

Also in 1975 Sloane, Staples, Cristol, Yorkston, and Whipple published their findings on psychodynamic and behavior therapists' activities. Although the title of their book, *Psychotherapy Versus Behavior Therapy,* connoted a confrontation, their findings actually underscored a theme of rapprochement. Sloane et al. reported that behavior therapists and psychotherapists demonstrated comparable degrees of warmth and positive regard toward patients/clients; that patients/clients of both types of therapists exhibited the same depth of self-exploration; and that "there were no differences between therapists in the extent to which they used statements interpreting and clarifying the patient's problem" (pp. 158–159).

On a theoretical level, Shectman (1975) suggested that behavioral principles might provide psychoanalysis with a more adequate theory of learning. Wachtel (1975), in the first of his many writings on the topic of therapy integration, cited the contributions made to psychodynamic therapy by Alexander, Horney, and Sullivan as evidence that behavioral approaches, which attempt to deal directly with certain problematic behaviors, could readily be incorporated into a psychodynamic framework. This is a two-way street, argued Wachtel, in that many instances of relapse following behavior therapy might possibly be linked to certain maladaptive patterns on the part of the client-patient. These patterns in turn might more readily be identified when viewed from within a psychodynamic framework.

Wachtel (1977) went on to explore such integration at greater length in his well-known and challenging book, *Psychoanalysis and Behavior Therapy,* in which he maintained that the convergence of clinical procedures from each orientation would be likely to enhance the effectiveness of our intervention attempts. For example, a psychodynamic orientation might help us to better understand the implicit meaning structure and distortions that our patients/clients carry with them in their current life situation, whereas the behavioral approach could provide us with techniques for actively intervening in changing such distortions. Wachtel emphasized the need for patients/clients to act on their therapy-facilitated insights, and argued that enhanced awareness, along with behavioral testing and validation, would facilitate additional introspection and insights. This notion was presented as an "insight → behavior change → insight → behavior change" positive feedback loop.

The year 1976 also witnessed a number of articles and books that touched on the topic of therapeutic integration. Strupp (1976) criticized psychoanalytic therapy for not keeping up with the times, using therapeutic procedures more on the basis of faith than data. Fortunately, observed Strupp, younger therapists seem less constrained by orthodoxy and are more willing to experiment with newer techniques. In a commentary on Strupp's article, Grinker (1976) underscored the need for a therapeutic approach based on research findings and noted that with added clinical experience, even the most orthodox of psychoanalysts learn that other methods are needed to help facilitate change. As a practicing psychoanalyst with personal experience in the human potential movement, Appelbaum (1976) suggested that some gestalt therapy methods may complement more traditional psychoanalytic techniques. Appelbaum's excursions into more humanistically oriented activities are described in fascinating detail in a later book (Appelbaum, 1979).

Wandersman, Poppen, and Ricks' (1976) *Humanism and Behaviorism* offered discussions by members of each orientation, which attempted to acknowledge points of potential integration. In Burton's (1976) edited volume, *What Makes Behavior Change Possible?,* 16 representatives of diverse therapeutic orientations addressed themselves to some of the basic questions about the essential ingredients of therapeutic change. Noting that behavior therapy was a useful framework for dealing with clinical cases but still incomplete in and of itself, Hunt (1976) argued that there currently exists no single orientation that can deal with all clinical material. Just as separate laser beams function together to obtain a three-dimensional holographic image, observed Hunt, so are different therapeutic orientations required in order to provide us with a comprehensive treatment approach.

In their book *Clinical Behavior Therapy,* Goldfried and Davison (1976) maintained that behavior therapy need no longer assume an antagonistic stance vis-à-vis other orientations. Acknowledging that there is much that clinicians of different orientations have to say to each other, they suggested: "It is time for behavior therapists to stop regarding themselves as an outgroup and instead to enter into serious and hopefully mutually fruitful dialogues with their nonbehavioral colleagues" p. 15. That many clinicians were in effect already doing this was reflected in Garfield and Kurtz's (1976) findings that approximately 55% of clinical psychologists in the United States considered themselves eclectic. Most frequently used in combination were the psychodynamic and learning orientations. The single most frequent reason for using more than one framework was found to be based on the pragmatics of doing clinic work (Garfield & Kurtz, 1977). Integration at a clinical level was dealt with in several articles (Lambley, 1976; Levay, Weissberg, & Blaustein, 1976; Murray, 1976; Segraves & Smith, 1976). Also Lazarus's (1976) book, *Multimodal Behavior Therapy,* extended and refined his broad-spectrum approach to behavior therapy so as to systematically take into account the individual's behaviors, affects, sensations, images, cognitions, interpersonal relationships, and physiological states.

In the following year, Lazarus (1977), then having practiced behavior therapy for approximately 20 years, questioned whether behavior therapy, as a delimited school of thought, had "outlived its usefulness." He recognized the need to "transcend the constraints of factionalism, where cloistered adherents of rival schools, movements, and systems each cling to their separate illusions" (p. 11). Also, Lazarus reiterated his earlier statement on technical eclecticism, suggesting that empirically determined effectiveness and not therapeutic school should dictate intervention procedures.

An editorial comment appearing in the *Journal of Humanistic Psychology* (Greening, 1978) applauded Lazarus's 1977 paper and urged readers of the journal to be open to such suggestions for rapprochement. Commenting on the gap that frequently exists between theory and practice, Davison (1978) delivered a talk at the Association for Advancement of Behavior Therapy (AABT) Convention in which he suggested that behavior therapists consider the possibility of using certain humanistic procedures in their clinical work. Krasner (1978) outlined the history of both behaviorism and humanism, noting that the two orientations shared some common view of human functioning (e.g., importance of situational factors, the uniqueness of the individual). He looked forward to the time when representatives in "both camps will decrease mutual battling and recriminations."

Gurman (1978) challenged the usefulness of approaching a psychological problem through the eyes of one of many existing theories. He argued that theories are generally biased toward a single presentation of the human condition, and that human experience is more accurately conceptualized as the result of multiple factors. Gurman went on to suggest that "a theoretical base which can be expanded to include the range of useful interventions ultimately is preferable to an approach excluding such augmentation. . . .

Therapy is not viewed as a reified set of procedures, but as an evolving science" (p. 131). Diamond, Havens, and Jones (1978) independently came to the same conclusion, stressing the need for an eclectic approach to therapy that would be tied to research and theory yet flexible enough to provide highly individualized treatment. In that same year, Baer and Stolz (1978) provided a behavioral analysis of *est,* Fischer (1978) outlined an eclectic approach to social casework, and O'Leary and Turkewitz (1978) described how a communications analysis of marital interaction might be used within the context of behavioral marital therapy. Some of the points of overlap between behavior therapy and Zen Buddhism were outlined by Mikulas (1978) and Shapiro (1978).

A symposium on the compatibility and incompatibility of behavior therapy and psychoanalysis, chaired by Arkowitz (1978), was held at the 1978 AABT Convention. In a subsequently published 1978 convention paper entitled "Are Psychoanalytic Therapists Beginning to Practice Cognitive Behavior Therapy or is Behavior Therapy Turning Psychoanalytic?", Strupp (1983) commented on some of the converging trends that seem to be occurring within each of these orientations. In a reanalysis of agoraphobia, Goldstein and Chambless (1978) described some of the complicating features in dealing with this problem clinically, outlining a comprehensive treatment plan that went beyond the straightforward methods typically associated with a behavioral approach. Also in the same year, Brown (1978) presented case material reflecting the integration of psychodynamic and behavior therapies, and Ryle (1978) suggested that experimental cognitive psychology might provide a common language for the psychotherapies.

Prochaska (1979), in a textbook describing various approaches to psychotherapy, concluded with a chapter that made the case for ultimately developing a transtheoretical orientation that will encom-pass what may have been found to be effective across different approaches to psychotherapy. Presenting some interesting parallels between cognitive therapy and psychodynamic therapy, Sarason (1979) suggested that experimental cognitive psychology may provide us with a conceptual system for understanding both orientations. Goldfried (1979) proposed that cognitive behavior therapy might more usefully be construed as dealing at times with an individual's implicit meaning structures, and that use of association techniques from experimental cognitive psychology to study such phenomena should be equally acceptable to clinicians and theorists of a psychodynamic orientation. It is interesting to note that Sarason and Goldfried drew their conclusions independently and without any apparent knowledge of Ryle's (1978) very similar conclusion the year before.

Robertson (1979) speculated on some of the reasons for the existence of eclecticism, such as lack of pressures, in one's training or professional setting, to take a given viewpoint; the tendency for clinical experience to make a therapist more open to other procedures; a personal tendency to be a nonjoiner; and a therapeutic orientation reaching a point where "the bloom is off the rose." Related to this last point are the results of Mahoney's (1979) survey of leading cognitive and noncognitive behavior therapists. Among the several questions asked of the respondents was: "I feel satisfied with the adequacy of my current understanding of human behavior." Although there were no statistically significant differences between the two groups on this item, the absolute rating was indeed instructive. Using a 7-point scale, Mahoney found that the average rating of satisfaction was *less than 2!*

1980s

Noting past attempts to find commonalities across the psychotherapies, Goldfried (1980) argued that a fruitful level of abstraction at which such a comparative analysis might take place would be somewhere between the specific technique and the theoretical explanation for the potential effectiveness of that technique. He maintained that it is at this intermediate level of abstraction—at the level of clinical strategy—that potential points of overlap may exist. One clinical strategy that may very well cut across orientations entails providing the patient/client with corrective experiences, particularly with regard to fear-related activities. For example, Fenichel (1941), on the topic of fear reduction, noted that

when a person is afraid but experiences a situation in which what was feared occurs without any harm resulting, he will not immediately trust the outcome of his new experience; however, the second time he will have a little less fear, the third time still less. (p. 83)

This very same conclusion was reached by Bandura (1969), who observed:

Extinction of avoidance behavior is achieved by repeated exposure to subjectively threatening stimuli under conditions designed to ensure that neither the avoidance responses nor the anticipated adverse consequences occur. (p. 414)

Relevant to this general theme was Nielsen's (1980) description of how certain psychoanalytic concepts are reflected in the practice of gestalt therapy.

Personality differences were found by Shuger and Bebout (1980) between clients/patients who had just completed a gestalt therapy experience and those who were treated psychoanalytically. However, these differences had been present *before* therapy as well, leading the authors to suggest that self-selective biases of clients/patients in part might be responsible for creating apparent differences between therapies of different orientations.

In a 1980 special issue of *Cognitive*

Therapy and Research, therapists of various orientations answered a set of questions about what they believe to be the most effective ingredients in therapeutic change (Brady, Davison, Dewald, Egan, Fadiman, Frank, Gill, Hoffman, Kempler, Lazarus, Raimy, Rotter, and Strupp, 1980). At the 1980 AABT Convention, Goldfried and Strupp (1980) held a dialogue on the issue of rapprochement in which they agreed that in the final analysis, any attempt at finding points of commonality must be based on what clinicians do, rather than what they say they do. Bastine (1980) observed that a problem-oriented approach to intervention is likely to facilitate psychotherapy integration, and Linsenhoff, Bastine, and Kommer (1980) emphasized that the field of psychotherapy could benefit most from an integration that would be both theoretical and practical.

Marmor and Woods' (1980) edited book *The Interface Between the Psychodynamic and Behavioral Therapies* illustrated the theme that no single approach to therapy can deal with all of human functioning. This general theme was reflected in a case report by Cohen and Pope (1980), in which a single patient/client was significantly helped by two cooperating therapists, one behavioral and the other analytic. A survey by Larson (1980) found that although therapists typically used a single orientation as their primary reference point, 65% acknowledged that their clinical work included contributions from a number of other therapeutic approaches. Garfield (1980), drawing on different therapeutic orientations in his *Psychotherapy: An Eclectic Approach,* described an empirically oriented view of psychotherapy. He viewed the introduction of cognitive variables into behavior therapy as a particularly important advance, noting:

Whether or not it really portends a beginning realization of the limitations of a single approach and the possible rapprochement of some of the different emphases in psychotherapy remains to be seen. However, it is a step in this direction, and, therefore, a very welcome development. (p. 290)

Relevant to this point was a convention presentation by Meichenbaum, in which he acknowledged the importance of considering unconscious as well as conscious processes in the development of assessment procedures. In an unpublished manuscript, Ryle (1980) outlined how cognitive psychology might provide opposing theoretical orientations with a unifying model of various clinical disorders. Along these same lines, Dowd and Kelly (1980) noted that cognitive concepts such as "self-efficacy" represent points of rapprochement, in that client's/patient's subjective strivings are considered on an equal footing with actual environmental consequences.

In 1981 a number of writers furthered the argument that different orientations present different strengths that can be combined into a more broad-based and useful approach. For example, Schwartz (1981) reported that therapists who led *groups* in psychotherapy were moving toward "technical and theoretical eclecticism" in increasing numbers. He likened such a development to patients'/clients' healthy attempts to broaden their perceptual horizon as part of the process of treatment. Addressing the issue of integrative conceptual models, Landau and Goldfried (1981) described in detail how certain concepts from experimental cognitive psychology (e.g., schema, scripts) can offer the field a consistent framework within which cognitive, behavioral, and psychodynamic assessment may fit. Also addressing himself to the need for a framework, Staats (1981) remarked that the field of psychology had the means for creating empirical knowledge in abundance, but that the lack of conceptual unification in the field was creating greater confusion, not clarity. Staats (1981) added this powerful statement: "The growth of unrelated

knowledge is such that without the benefit of organizing principles, we are being inundated and drowned by our own scientific products" (p. 259).

Also appearing in 1981 was a book by Lazarus that detailed clinical procedures for the practice of multimodal therapy, an article by Rhoads (1981) outlining and illustrating the clinical integration of behavior therapy and psychoanalytic therapy, a chapter by Gurman (1981) that described how different therapeutic orientations may be fitted into a multifaceted empirical approach to marital intervention, and a convention presentation by Sears (1981) describing his own personal observations of the early attempts to link behavior theory with psychoanalytic therapy.

As the discussion of therapeutic integration was becoming increasingly widespread, it became desirable for concerned professionals to arrange meetings, so as to facilitate a more efficient and meaningful exchange of views. Bergin (1981), for example, chaired a symposium at the 1981 meetings of the American Psychological Association on "Systematic Eclectic Therapy," in which participants discussed the growing trends toward convergence among the psychotherapies. In the same year, a small group of clinicians and clinical researchers (Garfield, Goldfried, Horwitz, Imber, Kendall, Strupp, Wachtel, and Wolf) held an informal, two-day conference to determine whether clinicians of different orientations could communicate with each other about actual clinical material. This group did not attempt to derive any particular product as their goal; their primary objective was to have the opportunity to initiate a dialogue with each other.

Elaborating on the theme that different therapeutic orientations are needed for a multidimensional intervention approach, Bergin (1982) pointed out that nobody attempting to understand the workings of the human body would ever try to invoke a single set of principles. Depending upon which aspect of bodily functioning is of interest, different principles may be required. Thus, principles of fluid mechanics are needed to understand how the heart operates, whereas electrochemical principles are needed for an understanding of neural transmission. A true rapprochement across the psychotherapies is needed, suggested Bergin, if we are to deal effectively with those complex human problems requiring psychotherapeutic intervention. As a way of illustrating how such rapprochement might be implemented, Mahoney and Wachtel (1982) presented a day-long dialogue and discussion of actual clinical material.

In 1982 the issue of theoretical integration acquired still greater visibility through the publication of a number of relevant books on the topic, authored by clinicians and researchers from divergent training backgrounds. In *Converging Themes in Psychotherapy*, Goldfried (1982a) provided a compendium of articles dealing with the issue of rapprochement, together with an overview of the current status and future direction in psychotherapy as it relates to the development of a more comprehensive paradigm for intervention. In *Resistance*, Wachtel (1982) elicited the views of experienced and well-known therapists in an attempt to explore the possibility that a synthesis of the psychodynamic and behavioral approaches might shed light on resistance to therapeutic change. In addition to the obvious benefits of this volume for therapists, it served the much desired function of bringing psychodynamic and behavior therapists together in dialogue.

Using concepts from cognitive psychology, Ryle's (1982) volume *Psychotherapy: A Cognitive Integration of Theory and Practice* offered an account of psychological problems and psychotherapy in an endeavor to assimilate theories and methods of a diverse set of orientations into a common language system. In *Marital Therapy*, Segraves (1982), like Ryle, at-

tempted to integrate elements of seemingly disparate theoretical systems by translating them into the language of cognitive social psychology. Segraves borrowed from psychoanalytic theory to address the influence of individual past experiences on the genesis of marital discord, and from behavior marital therapy and general systems theory to explain the role of current interpersonal forces maintaining individual psychopathology. The utility of his cognitive–social psychology terminology is exemplified by the persuasive presentation of the concept of "interpersonal schemas," analogous to the analytic concept of "transference," to explain the influence of early-life significant relationships on a person's perceptions of his/her spouse.

In 1983, the frequently asked question of "what therapy activities are most appropriate for what type of problem, by which therapist, for what kind of client?" was addressed by Beutler in his book, *Eclectic Psychotherapy*. The latter volume represented an attempt to define the fundamental ingredients of successful psychotherapy across orientations, suggesting ways of maximizing their effective use by reviewing what is known about the optimal *matching* of patients/clients to therapists and techniques. Fensterheim and Glazer (1983), in *Behavioral Psychotherapy*, highlighted the complementarity of psychoanalytic and behavioral approaches to therapy. Consistent with the thesis outlined by Wachtel (1977), the contributors to this volume suggested that a psychoanalytic style be used to formulate assessment hypotheses and to select target behaviors, and that a behavioral style be employed to change these problematic behaviors in a systematic, empirically verifiable manner.

Another framework for organizing and integrating various approaches to psychotherapy is presented by Driscoll (1984) in *Pragmatic Psychotherapy*. Substituting the vernacular for theoretical jargon, Driscoll presents a method (the pragmatic "survey") by which any given psychological problem can be described and conceptualized legitimately in a diversity of ways, so as to generate numerous hypotheses that *together* may present a better portrayal of the whole picture. Again, this suggests complementarity, rather than competition, between differing viewpoints regarding the etiology, maintenance, and treatment of psychological problems.

The issue of rapprochement is certainly a controversial topic. In the early years, one was more likely to witness ruthless, antagonistic debates between proponents of differing schools of thought than cautious but thoughtful dialogue. One was also likely to find that members of one camp were in the dark about the complete picture presented by the other theoretical persuasions. Today, knowledge and communication seem to be replacing voluntary ignorance and intolerance. Such a trend is epitomized by Arkowitz and Messer's (1984) edited volume, *Psychoanalytic Therapy and Behavior Therapy: Is Integration Possible?* The editors, along with ten contributing authors, explore the clinical, theoretical, and empirical issues and implications of a serious attempt at rapprochement. Although there is still no clear consensus on such matters, it is apparent that Arkowitz and Messer have provided an invaluable opportunity for the generation and exchange of fruitful philosophical and practical ideas toward the advancement of the field as a whole.

In addition to the aforementioned books, numerous others on therapeutic integration have begun to appear (e.g., Guidano & Liotti, 1983; Hart, 1983; Meyer, 1982; Prochaska & DiClemente, 1984; Wittman, 1981). Moreover, journals have started to feature discussions on this topic. A special 1982 issue of *Behavior Therapy* contained a series of articles examining the potential benefits and drawbacks of complementing a behavioral approach with those of other orientations (Garfield, 1982; Goldfried, 1982b; Kendall, 1982; Wachtel, 1982), and a 1983 issue of the *British*

Journal of Clinical Psychology presented spirited "point–counterpoint" commentary between Yates (1983a, 1983b) and Davis (1983), Messer (1983), Murray (1983), and Wachtel (1983) on the topic of the plausibility of rapprochement.

There is another important trend that we should underscore, namely the work that has recently begun on integrating psychodynamic, behavioral, and systems approaches to marital and family therapy. This trend is more recent, but nonetheless growing very rapidly, and it is typified by the work of Duhl and Duhl (1980), Feldman (1979), Feldman and Pinsof (1982), Friedman (1980a, 1980b, 1981), Gurman (1981), Hatcher (1978), Lebow (1984), Pinsof (1983), Rosenberg (1978), Segraves (1982), and Steinfeld (1980). As testimony to the momentum this work has gathered, a special interest group within the American Family Therapy Association has been organized to support these efforts.

Another significant event in the history of rapprochement has been the formation of an international organization devoted specifically to therapy integration. Formed in 1983, the Society for the Exploration of Psychotherapy Integration (SEPI) was established as a way of bringing together the growing number of professionals interested in this area. We shall have more to say about SEPI later in this chapter.

It is strikingly evident that in the 1980s we have witnessed a geometric increase in the numbers of publications and presentations on therapeutic integration. Indeed, it has reached the point where it is unwieldy and impractical in a review such as this to offer an adequate description of each and every article and book that has begun to appear on the topic. Besides, we may already have overstepped our bounds by extending our "historical" account to the 1980s. It would nevertheless be reasonable and instructive to deal with some of these more recent works collectively, according to the general issues that they raise. In this next section, we examine such issues, including thematic arguments that support or cast doubt on the usefulness of therapeutic integration.

RECURRENT THEMES

When examining the rapidly growing body of literature that has appeared in recent years, one is tempted to conclude that the field is only now beginning to sort out the issues that need to be addressed on the topic of rapprochement. However, one need only glance at the work cited earlier in this review to see that many of these issues have been dealt with repeatedly throughout the past half century. Such recurrent themes include:

• The potential for divergent modes of therapy to complement each other
• The advantages of focusing on the interactions of cognitions, behavior, and affect in clients/patients
• The desire for therapeutic procedures to be guided by empirical findings
• The importance of a common theoretical language
• The need to organize commonalities into a universal "meta-theoretical" set of principles of therapeutic change.

What is significant about the recent attention that is being given to these issues, however, is that they are being discussed by a larger and more diversified body of clinicians and researchers, and are being read by a more widespread and enthusiastic audience than ever before. The following sections summarize the most recent views regarding these historical yet timely areas of concern.

Complementarity of Divergent Approaches

Different approaches to therapy claim to have their areas of expertise, whereby certain well-described therapist and client/patient activities are seen as resulting in significant gains. However, no therapy or therapist is immune from the more than occasional therapeutic failure, whereby a client/patient either voluntarily terminates before changes can be made or, stays in therapy for what is deemed an excessive period of time, with major goals continuing to remain unfulfilled. It is at such times that experienced clinicians often wonder if the approaches from orientations other than their own might more appropriately have been included in the treatment program—if another orientation's strength in dealing with the particular therapeutic problem might complement the therapist's own orientational weakness in this area. This idea is the basis of Pinsof's (1983) "Integrative Problem-Centered Therapy," which "rests upon the twin assumptions that each modality and orientation has its particular 'domain of expertise,' and that these domains can be interrelated to maximize their assets and minimize their deficits" (p. 20).

Messer and Winokur (1980), in an article examining the potential benefits and pitfalls of an integrative approach, acknowledge that client/patient variables play a large role in determining what kind of treatment will be most successful. For example, a person who has below-average verbal skills and/or is not accustomed to deep introspection may flounder in a psychodynamic treatment that might have greater therapeutic impact on another individual who is more adept at self-exploration. In the case of the former client/patient, a more concrete action-oriented (behavioral) therapy may be a boon to progress. Messer and Winokur go on to suggest that action-oriented and introspective therapeutic approaches may also be used together to help a single client/patient. In this regard, they express a willingness to test Wachtel's (1977) contention that people are helped most if they are guided towards translating their insights into action—which can reinforce and stimulate further introspection in a positive-feedback loop.

Yates (1983a), even as he addresses problematic aspects in any attempt to integrate therapies of divergent viewpoints, reviews some powerful arguments in support of the need for a more eclectic stance (e.g., Birk, 1973; Birk & Brinkley-Birk, 1974). Among these is the argument that analytic techniques do not necessarily lead to *objective* behavioral changes in a client/patient, nor do behavior therapy techniques always lead to a *subjective* sense of improvement. Yates summarizes this position by stating that "If *both* kinds of change are regarded as desirable for change to be 'truly' significant, then it seems clear, on this analysis, that behaviour therapy and psychodynamic psychotherapy are genuinely complementary". (p. 114)

Fensterheim (1983) presents another way to look at the potential for inter-orientation complementarity. Consistent with Wachtel's (1977) thesis, Fensterheim suggests that the therapist can make use of the psychoanalytic style to formulate hypotheses concerning the way a client/patient organizes his perceptions of the world and to select behavior patterns that pertain to the individual's particular problem. Following this, a behavior therapy style may be applied to change these behaviors in a systematic and verifiable manner.

Beck (1984) describes depression as consisting of a universal, transtheoretical theme of loss, including loss of reinforcement and of object, as deprivation and defeat, and/or as depletion of important catecholamines. In his view, the varying treatment orientations are complementary in that they facilitate more positive experiencing through restoration of each of the lost components. Therefore, therapy becomes more powerful by doing *all* of the following: (a) It reestablishes positive reinforcements; (b) forms a less negative cognitive set, and (c) increases the availability of noradrenaline and serotonin.

Driscoll's *Pragmatic Psychotherapy* (1984) advocates a clinical method whereby an extensive list of plausible etiological and maintaining factors is generated for a particular client/patient problem. These hypotheses extend over theoretical boundaries, but are expressed in ordinary language. The result is a pragmatic/eclectic "survey" that thoroughly describes the nature and causes of the problem. The components of this survey do not compete but complement each other by presenting connecting pieces of the whole therapeutic puzzle. Similarly, in *Marital Therapy: A Combined Psychodynamic–Behavioral Approach,* Segraves (1982) presents a marital case, and taking a cognitive–social integrative approach, proceeds to list and explicate hypotheses as to why the husband is deficient in processing information about his wife (i.e., why he consistently misperceives his wife's motivations and character). Segraves then generates more hypotheses as to why the husband's views of his wife persist in spite of objective disconfirming evidence, and later limits further hypotheses regarding mechanisms of change. None of these hypotheses are mutually exclusive; together, they help the therapist to obtain a more holistic view of the couple's problems.

Finally, Messer (1984) has identified a theme of complementarity also expressed by Rhoads (1984) and Salzman (1984). Here, a behavioral slant to therapy is viewed as being an excellent way of focusing on a presenting complaint, intervening promptly to provide some measure of relief at the very start of therapy, thereby gaining the client's/patient's trust and cooperation to discuss broader lifestyle problems in a more introspective fashion. As insight is gained, learning theory can once again be utilized to teach the client/patient more adaptive behaviors, so as to test out the everyday-life effects of this heightened self-awareness.

Interaction of Cognition, Behavior, and Affect

Depending on the theoretical perspective being taken, the cognitions, behaviors, and emotions of the client/patient have been given varying degrees of relative emphasis. Generally speaking, cognitive therapy has focused on the more consciously accessible side of the cognitive continuum, psychoanalytic therapy has delved into the unconscious aspects of cognitive processing, experiential orientations have tended to focus more on emotionality, and behavior therapy has been well known for its emphasis on action.

Lazarus' (1967, 1976) work on a "multimodal" therapy may have paved the way for some of the questions that the integrative psychotherapist seems to be asking today, such as, "Why not be prepared to give strong emphasis to the *interaction* of cognitions, behavior, and affect?" (e.g., Schwartz, 1982), and "Shouldn't the choice to concentrate on one component more than the others be a function of client/patient characteristics instead of the therapist's training background?" (e.g., Driscoll, 1984). Ward (1983) has observed that the field of psychotherapy has been inundated with various models of pathology and treatment. It is therefore important, he notes, to employ a three-dimensional affective–cognitive–behavioral schema in therapy, as a more parsimonious guide in the selection of specific theories for conceptualization and intervention. Steinfeld (1980) and Staats (1981) have similarly supported the adoption of a unified-interactive approach that includes cognition, behavior, and affect, adding that there must be an accompanying theoretical model as well as a systematic program of research.

Safran (1984) has dealt with the interaction of cognition, behavior, and affect in an intriguing article on the incorporation of Sullivanian principles into a cognitive–behavioral approach. He argues that the integration of these models can provide

a systematic framework which will allow cognitive–behavior therapists to broaden their conceptualization of the role of emotions in psychotherapy from one which views emotions only as undesirable experiences which should be controlled to one which recognizes the adaptive role of emotions in human functioning. (p. 335)

Safran suggests that Sullivanian concepts (of self-perception and perception of others), if translated into a language consistent with experimental cognitive and social psychology, can supplement a cognitive–behavioral assessment by providing the conceptual framework within which to examine "hot" information processing, occurring within an emotional and/or interpersonal context. Greenberg and Safran (1984) go on to make a serious attempt at conceptualizing the integration of affective and cognitive processes, based on experimental data and models of information processing. Although this is a rigorous undertaking, they are quick to acknowledge that "it is essential to recognize the complex interdependence of the thinking, feeling, and action systems" (p. 561).

An Empirically Based Therapy

An important ideal that has long been shared by researchers and clinicians of differing orientations is that of the need for a theory of therapy based on empirical foundations. Maslow (1966) expounded on the advantages of an approach to therapy based on empirical knowledge. He saw such a therapy as being in constant touch with clinical realities and therefore in a continual self-correcting flux, modifying itself as new information became available. Strupp (1968) emphasizes that any given therapy must be a *testable* therapy, such that impartial observers can specify the clinical phenomena, communicate about them, and reach a consensus on the presence or absence of change. Lazarus (1967, 1971) has viewed therapy as being most potent when clinicians could make use of (and further experiment with) a set of empirically useful methods, instead of using static theory as the a priori predictor of what would and would not succeed therapeutically.

Not surprisingly, similar opinions are continuing to be voiced. For example, Segraves (1982) writes that "empirical foundations for clinical activities are both necessary and possible (p. viii). Beutler's (1983), Dryden's (1984), Fensterheim and Glazer's (1983), and Garfield's (1980) respective volumes also aspire to an empirical approach, toward a more comprehensive, flexible, and effective therapy.

Although many authors have enumerated what appear to be common therapeutic strategies cutting across different orientations, the generation of these strategies has been based primarily on what therapists *say* they do, not on direct observations of what they *actually* do. In previous years, writers such as Bergin (1970b), Diamond et al. (1978), Grinker (1976), Gurman (1978), Lazarus and Davison (1971), London (1964, 1972), and Thorne (1950) stressed that clinical skills and concomitant efficacy of therapy could be enhanced by the identification, understanding, and use of data-based principles of psychotherapeutic change. More recently, it has been suggested that the identification of general mechanisms of change can be facilitated by the investigation of those similarities that exist across different orientations (Goldfried & Padawer, 1982). Unfortunately, a commonly expressed concern amongst contemporary authors is that such research is sorely lacking (e.g., Arkowitz, 1984; Beutler, 1983; Gurman, 1978; Yates, 1983a). A direct result of this concern is the emergence of a new theme in the lit-

erature, that of the push for the development of a workable methodology for the study of psychotherapy integration (e.g., Goldfried & Padawer, 1982; Goldfried & Safran, Chapter 17, this volume).

The need to develop an empirically based integration of the psychotherapies is perhaps best summarized by Appelbaum (1979):

If any of us are to benefit from the ideas and experiences of others, then the whole has to be defined . . . as knowledge. Only knowledge can unite disparate schools, techniques, and views of man and change. Only knowledge is boundaryless and infinite. (p. 501)

Need for a Common Language

Each approach to psychotherapy has its own jargon, which presents obstacles to bridging the gap across schools. The problem is manifested not only by difficulty in understanding various concepts, but also by an active tuning out when one hears certain buzz words associated with another orientation (e.g., "transference", "warded-off conflict", "extinction", "negative reinforcement", or "self-actualization"). Gurman (1978) has warned us that jargon impedes communication and that without a common language the field resembles a Tower of Babel.

Although the use of the vernacular may be helpful in facilitating communication, as it was in the special issue of *Cognitive Therapy and Research* (Brady et al., 1980), the field of psychotherapy ultimately needs a language system that is tied to a data base. A number of contemporary writers have independently suggested the possibility that a common language may ultimately come from the field of experimental cognitive psychology and social cognition (Goldfried, 1979; Kazdin, 1984; Landau & Goldfried, 1981; Messer & Winokur, 1980; Ryle, 1978, 1982; Safran, 1984; Sarason, 1979; Segraves, 1982; Shevrin & Dickman, 1980). Concepts such as "schema," "scripts," and "meta-cognition" have the potential for covering therapeutic phenomena observed by clinicians of varying orientations. Summarizing the position of Messer and Winokur (1980), Kazdin (1984) writes that the concepts of cognitive psychology

deal with meaning of events, underlying processes, and ways of structuring and interpreting experience. They can encompass affect, perception, and behavior. Consequently, cognitive processes and their referents probably provide the place where the gap between psychodynamic and behavioral views is the least wide. (p. 163)

An illustration of this language system was given earlier, when we noted Segraves' (1982) reference to a married couple's "interpersonal schemas," roughly equivalent to the analytic notion of transference. The term refers to the tendency for each partner to distort the perception of the other by unwittingly perpetuating old cognitive–emotional ties with significant others of the opposite sex.

Ryle's (1982) support for integration via a cognitively based common language is particularly strong. He argues that a therapist is faced with the task of understanding clients'/patients' worlds as a function of their mental representations of themselves and their environment. It then follows that an important aspect of therapy is to help clients/patients change their understanding of themselves and their relation to the world by examining the way they think, feel, act, and learn. Ryle contends that such an approach demands a cognitive psychology model

because cognitive psychology offers the best available, and least reductive, account of mental processes. Cognitive psychology is concerned with knowledge, that is to say with how information is received, stored, coded, evaluated, and revised; and with how action is learned, selected, organized, carried through, evaluated and modified: in brief, with how we know [the] world and know ourselves. (pp. 11-12)

Common Therapeutic Principles: In Search of a Meta-Theory

There is a great deal of clinical evidence, and a small but corroborating amount of experimental data, to the effect that the activities of experienced therapists of differing orientations are highly similar, even though their conceptualizations of cases may be articulated quite differently (e.g., Friedling, Goldfried, & Stricker, 1984; Goldfried & Padawer, 1982; Kazdin, 1984; Sloane et al., 1975). In other words, therapists of varying orientations are making use of therapeutic activities that are successful, but not necessarily congruent with their theoretical persuasions and mandates (Davis, 1983; Murray, 1983; Yates, 1983b). Wachtel (1977) has observed that there exists a therapeutic "underground," reflecting an unofficial consensus of what experienced clinicians know to be true. Many of these factors are not associated with any particular school, and one rarely sees them described in the literature. Moreover, a number of writers (e.g., Alexander, 1963; London, 1964; Rosenzweig, 1936) have suggested that therapeutic techniques may in fact prove effective for reasons unrelated to the theoretical ideas that spawned them. If this is so, our understanding of the effects of psychotherapy may not be significantly enhanced until a more encompassing, unified metatheory is developed and revised with continual empirical evaluation (Staats, 1981).

Beutler (1983) has suggested that the frequently observed lack of congruence between theoretical orientation and technique is a result of the fact that therapists have found current paradigms inadequate to deal with the complexity of the problems they are confronted with clinically. "While each theory operationally functions on the myth of therapy uniformity" (Kiesler, 1966), "reality demands an eclectic perspective" (Beutler, 1983, p. 2). In a similar vein, Lazarus (1976, 1981) has contended that successful therapy does not require a theory from which to work. Taking a purely empirical–pragmatic stance, he argues that the most objective and helpful therapy is devoid of the "bias" of theory. In his multimodal approach, Lazarus assesses clinical problems with regard to several areas of client/patient functioning (e.g., behavior, affect, cognition, interpersonal relationships), generates potential points of intervention, applies them, and systematically evaluates their impact.

Lazarus reports success with his approach, but other writers express doubt that a clinician and/or researcher can truly formulate hypotheses without some sort of implicit theoretical framework. Murray (1983) suggests that the field needs to develop a new, higher order theory that will help us to better understand the connections between cognitive, affective, and behavioral systems. With such an evolving theory, argues Murray, therapists would be better able to make predictions about how to achieve objective and subjective therapeutic change in any given case. Murray (1983) notes:

If we could get beyond . . . polarized philosophical questions we could address the real issues. For example, how do the cognitive, affective, and behavioral systems affect one another (Murray & Jacobson, 1978)? Under what circumstances can you produce change in one system by changing another? (p. 128)

Murray, along with others (e.g., Beck, 1984; Beutler, 1983; Mahoney, 1984), maintains that attempts to answer such questions will move the field toward the development of a more adequate, unified paradigm.

POINTS OF CONTENTION: IS INTEGRATION INACHIEVABLE?

Ever since Myerson's horrified response to French's (1933) presentation on the commonalities between behaviorism and psychoanalysis, staunch supporters of cir-cumscribed orientations have argued that rapprochement is neither possible nor desirable. For the most part, these viewpoints have not been expressed in publications specifically designated to attack the concept of integration (perhaps it was deemed not even necessary to address such a "preposterous" notion). Instead, this sentiment has been communicated implicitly, by authors writing on the exclusive merits of their own theoretical persuasions. As the field has become more intrigued with the possibility of therapy integration, we have been witnessing the emergence of publications that are making explicit those long-standing implicit reservations toward rapprochement (e.g., Franks, 1984; Schacht, 1984; Yates, 1983a). Moreover, there now appears to be a willingness among enthusiasts and skeptics to have open dialogues concerning the plausibility of rapprochement (e.g., *British Journal of Psychiatry*, 1983; Arkowitz & Messer, 1984; Wachtel, 1982). Such communication can only be helpful. It encourages an exchange of ideas between dedicated professionals of all persuasions, it helps to clarify the important issues as viewed from varying perspectives, and it raises important questions that must be addressed by supporters of theoretical integration.

The following is an overview of current arguments concerning those aspects of psychotherapy that traditionally have been considered to represent fundamental points of contention between behavioral and psychoanalytic approaches to therapy.

Differing Perspectives on Reality

Although the list of publications discussing similarities across differing theoretical orientations is impressive, some authors express great concern that the search for commonalities is a trivial pursuit. For example, in referring to the work of Sloane et al. (1975), Farkas (1981) writes that they

... have taken a microscopic look at the commonalities of behavior therapy and psychotherapy. Their list included taking a history, showing interest, correcting misperceptions, answering questions, and elucidating objectives. However, they neglected to mention talking, sitting, walking, and hearing, and one wonders when an analysis of commonalities has reached infinite regress. As Garfield (1973) has questioned, are we considering mere common factors as opposed to fundamental ingredients? (p. 14)

Authors such as Messer and Winokur (1980), Yates (1983a) and Schacht (1984) maintain that the fundamental ingredients represent points of considerable divergence. One of these is the "world view" that is taken respectively by members of a behavioral and a psychodynamic orientation. Yates (1983a) finds little hope for rapprochement between orientations that stereotypically have such different perspectives on reality. Whereas behavior therapy may be characterized as emphasizing *realism* (the world existing independently of its observers), *objectivity* (the existence of a common frame of reference for all), and *extraspection* (seeking the external motivators of behavior), psychoanalytic therapy reflects *idealism* (the world is of one's own making), *subjectivity* (each person's frame of reference is unique), and *introspection* (searching for the internal motivators of behavior). Additionally, Messer and Winokur (1980) and Messer (Chapter 13) view a behavioral approach as being consonant with a "comic" view, whereby happiness can be obtained if environmental barriers and complications are identified and removed. A psychoanalytic approach, by contrast, follows a "tragic" view, whereby internal conflicts rage, and all one can ever hope for is an enlightened acceptance of the human psychological condition.

According to Yates (1983b), such marked differences in basic philosophic viewpoints result in contrasting notions as to what constitute appropriate therapeutic goals. For example, the behavior therapist would stress changes in readily observable client/patient behaviors, and would view sorrow as a negative affect to be extinguished rapidly. The psychoanalytic therapist, on the other hand, would focus on the feeling of sorrow, view it as a natural concomitant of the person's life history and current circumstances, and would strive to help the client/patient more fully experience, accept, and work through this emotionality with an understanding of associated real and perceived losses.

Wachtel's (1983) reply to the above issue is straightforward. He notes that these differences in philosophy are real and that, indeed, an integrative effort would be pointless were there an absence of such differences. Wachtel goes on to suggest: "What makes an integration interesting is its bringing the strengths, the different strengths, of each together in a new combination that is more comprehensive" (p. 129). Echoing this very sentiment is Beck (1984), who writes,

Despite the obvious philosophical, theoretical, and technical differences among cognitive therapy, psychoanalysis, behavior therapy, and pharmacotherapy, there are enough subtle but important similarities to justify attempts to construct a maxi-model to encompass those systems of therapy.... The various perspectives have varying degrees of explanatory power. By relating them to each other we can attempt to construct an integrated model that will have greater explanatory power than the individual perspectives. (p. 115)

Mahoney (1984) has also commented on the differences in world view between behavior therapy and psychoanalytic therapy, and concludes that incompatibility does not diminish the value of an exchange of ideas, nor does it eliminate the possibility that "both behaviorism and psychoanalysis are contributing to the evolution of a more adequate paradigm." (p. 320)

It is important to bear in mind that philosophical differences represent a barrier to integration only at a *theoretical* level of abstraction, not at lower levels of abstraction, such as the *clinical strategy* (Goldfried, 1980). Goldfried has maintained that, at a level of abstraction somewhere between theory and technique, these strategies may be thought of as clinical heuristics that implicitly guide the efforts of most experienced therapists.

> To the extent that clinicians of varying orientations are able to arrive at a common set of strategies, it is likely that what emerges will consist of robust phenomena, as they have managed to survive the distortions imposed by the therapists' varying theoretical biases. (Goldfried, 1980, p. 996)

A review of the available literature dealing with points of commonality across different therapeutic approaches reveals a number of similarities that have been described at this intermediate level of abstraction (Goldfried & Padawer, 1982). Among these are the initially induced expectations that therapy can be helpful; the client's/patient's participation in a therapeutic relationship; the possibility of obtaining an external perspective on one's problems; the encouragement of corrective experiences; and the opportunity to repeatedly test reality. Although the specific techniques that are used to implement each of these strategies may vary from orientation to orientation, the strategies themselves nonetheless represent common threads.

The Role of the Unconscious in Therapy

It has been argued that a discussion of "the unconscious mind" clearly separates a psychodynamic approach from a behavioral approach. Psychodynamic theory and practice has given considerable attention to the complex network of intrapsychic motivators that lie out of the client's/patient's awareness, whereas behavior therapy traditionally has cast doubt on the very existence of such unconscious processes. Supporters of a psychodynamic orientation have insisted that an adequate understanding of a client's/patient's problems necessitates a search for repressed conflicts and needs that have grown out of arrested psychosexual development. Champions of a behavioral viewpoint eschew such an approach as being unparsimonious and unverifiable, and instead focus on the client's/patient's current life situation.

Thus, at first glance, the concept of the unconscious would appear to represent an irreconcilable point of divergence between psychodynamic and behavior therapy. But this is only so if we adhere to the traditional tenets of classical psychoanalysis and radical behaviorism. Authors such as Arkowitz and Messer (1984), Goldfried (1979), Mahoney (1980), Meichenbaum and Gilmore (1982), Safran (1984), and Wachtel (1977) point out that dynamic psychotherapists have grown to recognize the importance of conscious thoughts and environmental factors, whereas behaviorists have adopted a position that accepts a person's explicit (and even implicit) thoughts as useful data.

As cognitive processes have come to be introduced into the behavioral camp, the consideration of "unconscious" events has become inevitable (Mahoney, 1980). Meichenbaum and Gilmore (1982) explain how conscious thoughts and actions, once practiced and learned, become more integrated and automatic. Such "automatic thinking" (Beck, 1976) is latent and/or unobserved. Beck (1984) states that a cognitive approach involves more than consciousness, with cognitive organization existing at several levels, only the highest of which are characterized by rationality, objectivity, and free decisionmaking. Beck's view is reminiscent of Kelly's (1955) conceptualization of a "complicated unverbalized meaning" and Polanyi's (1958) notion of "tacit knowledge," whereby persons know a great deal more than they can articulate and act on this knowleldge as a trusted and important clue to reality. Like Beck, Polanyi and Kelly do not dichotomize the conscious and unconscious processes, but instead speak of different levels of cognitive awareness.

Meichenbaum and Gilmore (1984) believe that, to some extent, all psychotherapy deals with the client's/patient's hypothesized cognitive structures. One such structure (in experimental cognitive psychology) is the "schema," which is construed as an unconscious entity that *can* be accessible to awareness. The authors point out that the psychodynamic therapist's attempt to bring the unconscious to awareness is analogous to the cognitive-behavior therapist's attempt to have the client look for negative automatic assumptions, and that each of these represents an endeavor to make sense out of client's/patient's verbalizations and behaviors that on the surface seem bewildering.

Mahoney (1984) presents a thought-provoking conceptualization of the unconscious:

More recent advances in clinical science and some of its associated psychobiology have suggested that the more central and core features of our nervous system tend to precede and potentiate our conscious experience in such a way that they would be more aptly termed "metaconscious" rather than "unconscious." [Metaconsciousness refers to] interdependent preconscious processes that limit the range and nature of potential experiences. (p. 313)

Although there *are* differences between the cognitive–behavioral and the psychodynamic view of the unconscious (e.g., the psychodynamic premise that the unconscious is maintained by the energies of repression, as contrasted with a cognitive–behavioral view of unconscious processes in terms of information-processing mechanisms), we seem to be witnessing a convergence between traditionally opposing orientations regarding the clinical phenomena that are given emphasis and attention.

The Importance of Transference

A strict psychoanalytic edict prohibits therapists from intervening on the client's/patient's behalf in a direct behavioral fashion, lest they hamper or contaminate the development of the client's/patient's idiosyncratic attitudes towards the analyst. The ambiguous and restrained analytic stance is designed to enable the client's/patient's a priori expectations about the therapeutic relationship to show themselves more clearly (Gill, 1984). With more direct intervention, the transference phenomena are altered, as clients/patients can attribute their feelings for the therapist to actual, as opposed to perceived, therapist demands. In light of these transference considerations, Gill (1984) expresses doubts that classical psychoanalysis can be combined with interventions that are more directive. Acknowledging that analysis is quite different from psychoanalytic psychotherapy, however, Gill admits that the possibility of advantageously implementing behavioral techniques within a psychodynamic framework is still an open issue.

Writing from within a Sullivanian conception of the therapeutic interaction, Wachtel (1977) suggests that the therapist can never really be a totally "blank screen" onto which patients/clients project aspects of their past. The therapist's role as participant–observer needs to be acknowledged as creating the actual context within which therapy takes place. Consequently, the therapist "is as much a part of the context if he is silent and invisible as if he is face to face with the patient and overtly discernibly responding to him" (Wachtel, 1977, p. 69). It is within this context, argues Wachtel, that direct interventions—sometimes in the form of procedures suggested by behavior therapy—can reasonably be made.

Segraves (1982) has discussed transference-like issues within the context of marital therapy. As we noted earlier, he broadens the analytic definition of transference to include any systematic misperception of a significant other, such that those in current reality are erroneously perceived as being similar to important others in the client's/patient's past. Such problems can be conceptualized within a cognitive–social psychology framework, whereby individuals learn a tacit set of "rules" or "interpersonal schemas" earlier in life about what to expect in interpersonal relationships with persons of varying characteristics. This conceptualization is closer to Sullivan's (1954) notion of "parataxic distortion," in that such prototypic expectations do not necessarily require the existence of unresolved conflicts in order to be present.

Arnkoff (1983) examines Strupp's (1977) definition of transference, and concludes that similarities do exist between psychodynamic therapy and cognitive behavior therapy in the use of the therapeutic relationship. She notes that cognitive behavior therapy focuses on relationship issues and agrees with Beck et al. (1979) that there are times when such an area of exploration provides in vivo information that can be used therapeutically. The same argument has been made by Goldfried and Davison (1976) and Goldfried (in press), who have conceptualized the therapeutic relationship as frequently offering a sample of the client's/patient's relevant thoughts, emotions, and behavior. The essential difference between the psychodynamic and behavioral use of the relationship as a sample for in vivo intervention is the extent to which it is viewed as central or peripheral to the change process. Clearly, numerous questions surrounding the relative importance of the therapeutic relationships across the various therapies have yet to be answered.

Goals of Therapy

Beutler (1983) has maintained that the different theories of psychotherapy probably do not direct the application of specific treatment techniques as much as they determine the therapeutic goals. If this is indeed the case, one may say that it is fruitless to strive for therapeutic integration, as each therapy has its own set of objectives about what needs to be changed.

Wachtel (1977) points out that behavior therapists are more likely than dynamic psychotherapists to conceptualize the client's/patient's problems as involving difficulties in attaining conventional and socially acceptable aims in life. In contrast, dynamic therapists are apt to see their clients/patients as having conflicting wants and needs, some socially censured. As a result, the goals of treatment are likely to differ. A behavior therapist may assess the situations, behaviors, cognitions, and consequences that are problematic, and then attempt to make the necessary alterations in these domains so that clients/patients may be free to seek their conventional desires. In psychodynamic therapies, the therapist works with clients/patients in a joint effort to understand the development of their personalities and concomitant problems in living. In an analytic approach, the assessment —in the sense of increased self-understanding—and the goals of therapy are one and the same. Wachtel (1977) goes on to add, however, that there is nothing to prevent a behavior therapist from intervening with regard to presenting problems, and *then* assisting the client/patient in further self-exploration. A concurring viewpoint is held by Llewelyn (1980), who states that the therapist can agree to pay serious attention to the presenting complaint, deal with it behaviorally, and additionally raise the question of whether the now trusting client/patient wants to go "deeper." In this way, both extraspective and introspective changes can be achieved, which is a value to any therapeutic endeavor (Murray, 1983). At the same time, it has been the client/patient who has determined the course of treatment, rather than any particular theoretical model.

Other authors have found similarities in therapeutic goals across orientations. Bastine (1975) observes that psychoanalytic and behavior therapies converge at the level of therapeutic subgoals. Farkas (1981) understands that a dynamic approach attempts the modification of personality, but sees this as inextricably tied to a modification of the person's overt behaviors. Prochaska and Di Clemente (1982) view all approaches to therapy as involving a consciousness-raising experience, where therapists increase the information available to individuals so that they can make effective responses and decisions in the face of internal and external demands. Perhaps most fundamental of all, Strupp (1978b) and Anchin (1982) view all therapy as sharing a meta-goal: to boost an individual's morale and to help him or her achieve a more gratifying and pleasurable existence.

SOCIAL, POLITICAL, AND ECONOMIC INFLUENCES ON INTEGRATION

Thus far we have examined the history of the movement toward therapeutic integration as a body of knowledge that has accumulated over the years. At this point, it is important for us to address ourselves to two important questions: (a) If the concept of therapeutic integration has been around for over half a century, why has so little progress been made toward developing a comprehensive paradigm? (b) Given the above, what present conditions have encouraged the field to develop an increased interest in pursuing this elusive

goal? An overview of the social, economic, and political influences on the field of psychotherapy will help to answer these questions.

What Are the Barriers to Integration?

Although the issue of rapprochement across therapeutic orientations has been discussed by many professionals in the past and seems to make good sense, there exist a number of barriers to therapeutic integration. One of these barriers has been documented within the sociology of science, which has described the competitive set of rules by which the scientific community operates (Hagstrom, 1965; Merton, 1969; Rappaport, 1977; Reif, 1961). The system fosters competition rather than cooperation; scientists are encouraged to outdo each other. This has led to the proliferation of different schools of therapy, compounded by the financial benefits that are often associated with following a given orientation (Goldfried & Padawer, 1982). As noted by Farkas (1981), "Individuals find lucrative contracts writing books and editing journals that would not exist but for an identified and homogeneous market" (p. 24). Additionally, professionals often attain greater recognition and prestige within a delimited reference group, and "notoriety is much easier to attain amongst members of a small collective with shared values than in a larger, more diversified organization" (Farkas, 1981, p. 24). Although the scientist's initial motivation may have involved an honest attempt to advance the field, there is always the danger that the extrinsic rewards of fame and position can subvert such original motives (Merton, 1969).

The field of psychotherapy is comprised of numerous professional networks, most of which reflect a particular theoretical outlook. As noted elsewhere, "Without a specific therapeutic orientation, how would we know what journals to subscribe to or which conventions to attend?" (Goldfried, 1980, p. 996). This is not to say that professional networks are not needed, but rather that the particular kind we now have may not provide us with enough scope to advance the field very much beyond its current point. In a vehement statement on this position, Basch (1982) has maintained: "We have much to learn from each other, but, given the parochial and doctrinaire atmospheres of our training programs and professional societies, little incentives or opportunity to do so" (p. 196).

Still another barrier to rapprochement lies in the costs of committing oneself to the kind of painstaking, long-term process and outcome research that is needed in order to generate common principles of successful psychotherapy. Much of the impetus for integration comes from anecdotal reports regarding the similarities of therapist activities across orientations. Consequently, if the concept of integration is to be properly evaluated and systematically advanced, there will be a need for empirical research on what therapists *do* in actual practice, instead of simply what they *say* they do. Groundbreaking research, by its very nature, involves a good deal of work, along with the possibility of abandoning work in which one has invested a great amount of time, money, and personal dedication. Going "back to the drawing board" seems unrewarding. Successful publication is much easier when one writes papers that fit into existing paradigms (Rappaport, 1977). Consequently, there exists the tendency for research activities and organizational policies to remain static (Farkas, 1981).

Another significant barrier, noted earlier in this chapter, involves the different language systems associated with the various therapeutic orientations. It is difficult enough to keep up with developments in one's own school of therapy, let alone try to understand advances that are couched in another orientation's jargon.

Even with all of the aforementioned barriers, the field is nevertheless striving more than ever before to generate successful methodologies to advance the field as a unified whole. The question is: Why is this happening?

Why the Move Toward Integration?

Kuhn (1970), in describing how scientific revolutions occur, has indicated that the abandonment of any given paradigm is usually preceeded by a period of "crisis," characterized by the proliferation of different orientations and the open expression of discontent about the current state of affairs. It appears that the field of psychotherapy is currently undergoing such a crisis (Goldfried & Padawer, 1982).

London (1983) suggests that this crisis was precipitated by the economic and social pressures in the 1960s created by such occurrences as the advent of legal accreditation of psychologists, with a resultant surge in professional practice and growth of psychological trade schools; the destigmatization of psychological services, spurred by the encounter movement and the establishment of "growth centers"; and the onset of federal financial support for clinical training, as well as insurance companies' financing of psychotherapeutic treatment. The result of these pressures, according to London, was a proliferation of brand-named therapies— Herink's (1980) count exceeds 250. According to London, socioeconomic pressures brought forth a Kuhnian crisis, which has been followed by a new wave of political and socioeconomic pressures to *resolve* the crisis. There are at present increasing pressures for accountability coming from insurance companies, government policymakers, and consumer groups. The field must pool its resources in order to demonstrate the viability, efficacy, and cost effectiveness of psychotherapy. Without some drastic changes (not the least of which is the movement for therapeutic integration), psychotherapists stand to lose prestige, customers, and money. As Mahoney (1984) put it, there is something to be said for having the different therapies "hang together," rather than "hang separately."

In addressing himself to third party reimbursement, Parloff (1979) noted that, as health care costs continue to soar, "private and public health insurance planners will seek to impose clean and restrictive rules of eligibility on both patient and psychotherapist" (p. 299). The danger here is that questions of health insurance eligibility are heavily influenced by political pressures, which leads Parloff to worry about "the potential soundness or unsoundness of the inferences that the policymaker may draw from research evidence in making decisions that may materially affect the field of psychotherapy" (p. 292). These decisions may take the form of the kind of arbitrary restrictions alluded to above, or may lead to the establishment of national health insurance for psychological services. The political pendulum may swing in either direction, with enormous implications for the field as a whole.

Consumers of psychological treatment are also a force to be reckoned with. In the past two decades, we have come to see an ever-increasing psychological sophistication on the part of the general population. Lichtenstein (1980) explains that, paradoxically, the recent surge of "self-help" books available to the public has sensitized readers to psychological issues, thereby actually producing a *greater* demand for therapy. These clients/patients approach treatment with some understanding of what to expect from a competent therapist and an efficacious therapy program. Adding to this consumer knowledge is The Public Citizen Health Research Group, a Ralph Nader organization, that compiles and publishes consumer guides to instruct potential clients/patients on what issues they should consider before choosing from the overwhelming array of available therapies (Lichtenstein, 1980). As the populace becomes more psychologically sophisticated, the need for notable advances in the field becomes more salient. The search for a unified psychotherapy paradigm represents an attempt to respond to this need.

THE DEVELOPMENT OF A PROFESSIONAL NETWORK

Recognizing the need to provide the field with a reference group that was oriented toward rapprochement among the therapies, Goldfried and Strupp, in 1979, compiled a list of professionals who were likely to be interested in efforts toward therapeutic integration and wrote all of these individuals, inviting them to add their names to an informal professional network. Little was done with this list until 1982, when Wachtel and Goldfried decided to poll those included in the network about potential future directions. Taking the list that we already had, and expanding it on the basis of the correspondence we each had with other professionals over the years on the topic of therapy integration, we mailed out a questionnaire. A total of 162 individuals completed the survey. They expressed their continued interest in rapprochement and offered their views on what should be done next—namely, the establishment of a newsletter and the formation of an organization.

In the summer of 1983, an organizing committee, consisting of Lee Birk, Marvin Goldfried, Jeanne Phillips, George Stricker, Paul Wachtel, and Barry Wolfe, met to discuss the results of the questionnaire. It was immediately apparent to all six that the time was ripe to do something with this rapidly growing network, and it was agreed that a newsletter was in order. The group discussed the advisability of creating an organization, especially in light of some of the comments on the questionnaire expressing reservations about formalizing something that might best be dealt with informally. It finally was decided that *without* the existence of some sort of organization, it would be difficult to maintain any sense of continuity. As later noted by Goldfried and Wachtel (1983), "It was concluded that we needed to achieve a delicate balance: a formal organization that would facilitate informal contacts among the members" (p. 3). Hence, the Society for the Exploration of Psychotherapy Integration (SEPI) was formed.

SEPI members represent diverse orientations and interests. Some are professionals who clearly identify themselves with a particular theoretical framework but openly acknowledge that other schools have something to offer; some are people who are interested in finding commonalities among the therapies; some would like to find a way to integrate existing approaches; some would like eventually to develop a totally new approach based on research findings; and some are professionals who have gradually drifted away from their original orientation and are interested in developing clearer guidelines that are more consistent with their clinical experience. A common thread that runs through this diversity is a respect for research evidence and an openness to anything that can be demonstrated to be clinically effective. Goldfried and Wachtel have described SEPI as an umbrella organization that is designed to serve the following objectives:

To begin with, it will function as a reference group for those professionals interested in working toward the development of an approach to psychotherapy that is not necessarily associated with a single theoretical orientation. There are many in the field who find it difficult to align themselves with any particular persuasion, and consequently would probably welcome such a group with which they can identify. A second function of the society is educational, directed toward those practitioners who may be looking for clearer clinical guidelines, not tied to a specific orientation, within which they might operate. To fulfill this need, conferences, workshops, and reading materials will be made available to the membership. A third function of the society will be to serve those members who might be interested in becoming involved in ongoing collaborative research on the process of psychotherapy. (Goldfried & Wachtel, 1983, p. 4)

The hope is that SEPI will serve to further raise our consciousness about the field's need for a more comprehensive model of therapeutic intervention, and will encourage the clinical and research efforts of an increasing number of professionals interested in pursuing this goal. The *Zeitgeist* is more receptive to integrative efforts than it has ever been before, and it is our hope within this context, significant advances will be made.*

REFERENCES

Alexander, F. (1963). The dynamics of psychotherapy in light of learning theory. *American Journal of Psychiatry, 120,* 440–448.

Anchin, J. C. (1982). Sequence, pattern, and style: Integration and treatment implications of some interpersonal concepts. In J. C. Anchin & D. J. Kiesler (Eds.), *Handbook of interpersonal psychotherapy.* Elmsford, N.Y.: Pergamon.

Appelbaum, S. A. (1976). A psychoanalyst looks at gestalt therapy. In C. Hatcher & P. Himmelstein (Eds.), *The handbook of gestalt therapy.* New York: Jason Aronson.

Appelbaum, S. A. (1979). *Out in inner space: A psychoanalyst explores the therapies.* Garden City, NY: Anchor.

Arkowitz, H. (Chair). (1978, November). *Behavior therapy and psychoanalysis: Compatible or incompatible. Symposium presented at the Convention of the Association for Advancement of Behavior Therapy. Chicago.*

Arkowitz, H. (1984). *Historical perspective on the integration of psychoanalytic and behavior therapies.* In H. Arkowitz & S. B. Messer (Eds.), *Psychoanalytic and behavior therapy: Is integration possible?* (pp. 1–30). New York: Plenum.

Arkowitz, H., & Messer, S. B. (Eds.). (1984). *Psychoanalytic and behavior therapy: Is integration possible?* New York: Plenum.

---

* For further information about SEPI, write to Dr. Lee Birk, 398 Walnut Street, Newton, MA 02160.

Arnkoff, D. B. (1983). Common and specific factors in cognitive therapy. In M. J. Lambert (Ed.), *Psychotherapy and patient relationships*. Homewood, IL: Dorsey.

Baer, D. M., & Stolz, S. B. (1978). A description of the Erhard Seminars Training (est) in the terms of behavior analysis. *Behaviorism, 6,* 45–70.

Bandura, A. (1969). *Principles of behavior modification*. New York: Holt, Rinehart, & Winston.

Barber, B. (1961). Resistance by scientists to scientific discovery. *Science, 134,* 596–602.

Basch, M. F. (1982). Behavioral and psychodynamic psychotherapies: Mutually exclusive or reinforcing? In P. L. Wachtel (Ed.), *Resistance: Psychodynamic and behavioral approaches*. New York: Plenum.

Bastine, R. (1975). Auf dem Wege zu einer integrierten Psychotherapie. *Psychologie Heute,* 53–58.

Bastine, R. (1978). Strategien psychotherapeutischen Handelns. In F. Reimer (Ed.), *Moglichkeiten und Grenzen der Psychotherapie im psychiatrischen Krankenhaus* (pp. 59–66). Stuttgart: Thieme.

Bastine, R. (1980). Ausbildung in psychotherapeutischen methoden und strategien. In V. Birtsch & D. Tscheulin (Eds.), *Ausbildung in klinischer psychologie und psychotherapie* (pp. 71–85). Weinheim: Beltz.

Beck, A. T. (1970). Cognitive therapy: Nature and relation to behavior therapy. *Behavior Therapy, 1,* 184–200.

Beck, A. T. (1976). *Cognitive therapy and the emotional disorders*. New York: Plenum.

Beck, A. T. (1984). Cognitive therapy, behavior therapy, psychoanalysis, and pharmacotherapy: The cognitive continuum. In J. B. W. Williams & R. L. Spitzer (Eds.), *Psychotherapy research: Where are we and where should we go?* New York: Guilford Press.

Beck, A. T., Rush, A., Shaw, B., & Emery, G. (1979). *Cognitive therapy of depression*. New York: Guilford Press.

Bergin, A. E. (1968). Technique for improving desensitization via warmth, empathy, and emotional re-experiencing of hierarchy events. In R. Rubin & C. M. Franks (Eds.), *Advances in Behavior Therapy*. New York: Academic Press.

Bergin, A. E. (1970a). A note on dream changes following desensitization. *Behavior Therapy, 1,* 546–549.

Bergin, A. E. (1970b). Cognitive therapy and behavior therapy: Foci for a multidimensional approach to treatment. *Behavior Therapy, 1,* 205–212.

Bergin, A. E. (1971). The evaluation of therapeutic outcomes. In A. E. Bergin & S. L. Garfield (Eds.), *Handbook of psychotherapy and behavior change*. New York: Wiley.

Bergin, A. E. (Chair). (1981, August). *Toward a systematic eclectic therapy*. Symposium presented at the meeting of the American Psychological Association, Los Angeles.

Bergin, A. E. (1982). The search for a psychotherapy of value. *Tigdschrift voor Psychotherapie (Journal of Psychotherapy)*. Amsterdam, 8.

Bergin, A. E., & Strupp, H. H. (1972). *Changing frontiers in the science of psychotherapy*. Chicago: Aldine-Atherton.

Beutler, L. E. (1983). *Eclectic psychotherapy: A systematic approach*. New York: Pergamon.

Birk, L. (1970). Behavior therapy: Integration with dynamic psychiatry. *Behavior Therapy, 1,* 522–526.

Birk, L. (1973). Psychoanalysis and behavioral analysis: Natural resonance and complementarity. *International Journal of Psychiatry, 11,* 160–166.

Birk, L. (1974). Intensive group therapy: An effective behavioral–psychoanalytic method. *American Journal of Psychiatry, 131,* 11–16.

Birk, L., & Brinkley-Birk, A. (1974). Psychoanalysis and behavior therapy. *American Journal of Psychiatry, 131,* 499–510.

Boring, E. G. (1950). *A history of experimental psychology* (Rev. ed.). New York: Appleton-Century-Crofts.

Brady, J. P. (1968). Psychotherapy by combined behavioral and dynamic approaches. *Comprehensive Psychiatry, 9,* 536–543.

Brady, J. P., Davison, G. C., Dewald, P. A., Egan, G., Fadiman, J., Frank, J. D., Gill, M. M., Hoffman, I., Kempler, W., Lazarus, A. A., Raimy, V., Rotter, J. B., & Strupp, H. H. (1980). Some views on effective principles of psychotherapy. *Cognitive Therapy and Research, 4,* 271–306.

Brammer, L. M. (1969). Eclecticism revisited. *Personnel and Guidance Journal, 48,* 192–197.

Brown, M. A. (1978). Psychodynamics and behavior therapy. *Psychiatric Clinics of North America, 1,* 435–448.

Burton, A. (Ed.). (1976). *What makes behavior change possible?* New York: Brunner/Mazel.

Cohen, L. H., & Pope, B. (1980). Concurrent use of insight and desensitization therapy. *Psychiatry, 43,* 146–154.

Davis, J. D. (1983). Slaying the psychoanalytic dragon: An integrationist's commentary on Yates. *British Journal of Clinical Psychology, 22,* 133–134.

Davison, G. C. (1978). *Theory and practice in behavior therapy: An unconsummated marriage*. (Audiocassette). New York: BMA Audio Cassettes.

Diamond, R. E., Havens, R. A., & Jones, A. C. (1978). A conceptual framework for the practice of prescriptive eclecticism in psychotherapy. *American Psychologist, 33,* 239–248.

Dollard, J., & Miller, N. E. (1950). *Personality and psychotherapy*. New York: McGraw-Hill

Dowd, E. T., & Kelly, F. D. (1980). Adlerian psychology and cognitive behavior therapy: Convergences. *Journal of Individual Psychology, 36,* 119–135.

Driscoll, R. (1984). *Pragmatic psychotherapy*. New York: Van Nostrand Reinhold Co.

Dryden, W. (Ed.). (1984). *Individual therapy in Britain*. London: Harper & Row.

Duhl, B., & Duhl, F. (1980). Integrative family therapy. In A. Gurman & D. Kniskern (Eds.), *The handbook of family therapy*. New York: Brunner/Mazel.

Egan, G. (1975). *The skilled helper.* Monterey, CA: Brooks/Cole.

Farkas, G. M. (1981). Toward a pluralistic psychology of behavior change. In M. Hersen, R. M. Eisler, & P. M. Miller (Eds.), *Progress in behavior modification* (Vol. 11). New York: Academic Press.

Feather, B. W., & Rhoads, J. M. (1972a). Psychodynamic behavior therapy: I. Theory and rationale. *Archives of General Psychiatry, 26,* 496–502.

Feather, B. W., & Rhoads, J. M. (1972b). Psychodynamic behavior therapy: II. Clinical aspects. *Archives of General Psychiatry, 26,* 503–511.

Feldman, L. B. (1979). Marital conflict and marital intimacy: An integrative psychodynamic-behavioral-systemic model. *Family Process, 18,* 69–78.

Feldman, L. B., & Pinsof, W. M. (1982). Problem maintenance in family systems: An integrative model. *Journal of Marriage and Family Therapy, 8,* 295–308.

Fenichel, O. (1941). *Problems of psychoanalytic technique.* Albany, NY: Psychoanalytic Quarterly.

Fensterheim, H. (1983). Introduction to behavioral psychotherapy. In H. Fensterheim & H. I. Glazer (Eds.), *Behavioral psychotherapy: Basic principles and case studies in an integrative clinical model.* New York: Brunner/Mazel.

Fensterheim, H., & Glazer, H. I. (Eds.). (1983). *Behavioral psychotherapy: Basic principles and case studies in an integrative clinical model.* New York: Brunner/Mazel.

Ferster, C. B. (1974). The difference between behavioral and conventional psychology. *Journal of Nervous and Mental Disease, 159,* 153–157.

Fischer, J. (1978). *Effective casework practice: An eclectic approach.* New York: McGraw-Hill.

Frank, J. D. (1961). *Persuasion and healing.* Baltimore: Johns Hopkins.

Frank, J. D. (1971). Therapeutic factors in psychotherapy. *American Journal of Psychotherapy, 25,* 350–361.

Frank, J. D. (1979). The present status of outcome research. *Journal of Consulting and Clinical Psychology, 47,* 310–316.

Franks, C. M. (1984). On conceptual and technical integrity in psychoanalysis and behavior therapy: Two fundamentally incompatible systems. In H. Arkowitz & S. B. Messer (Eds.), *Psychoanalytic therapy and behavior therapy: Is integration possible?* (pp. 223–247). New York: Plenum.

French, T. M. (1933). Interrelations between psychoanalysis and the experimental work of Pavlov. *American Journal of Psychiatry, 89,* 1165–1203.

Freud, S. (1924). *Collected papers: Vols. I–II.* (2nd ed.). London: Hogarth.

Friedling, C., Goldfried, M. R. & Stricker, G. (1984). *Convergences in psychodynamic and behavior therapy.* Paper presented at the meetings of the Eastern Psychological Association, Baltimore.

Friedman, P. (1980a). An integrative approach to the creation and alleviation of disease within the family. *Family Therapy, 3,* 179–195.

Friedman, P. (1980b). Integrative psychotherapy. In R. Herink (Ed.), *Psychotherapy handbook* (pp. 308–313). New York: New American Library.

Friedman, P. (1981). Integrative family therapy. *Family Therapy, 8,* 171–178.

Garfield, S. L. (1957). *Introductory clinical psychology.* New York: Macmillan.

Garfield, S. L. (1973). Basic ingredients or common factors in psychotherapy? *Journal of Consulting and Clinical Psychology, 41,* 9-12.

Garfield, S. L. (1980). *Psychotherapy: An eclectic approach.* New York: Wiley.

Garfield, S. L. (1982). Eclecticism and integration in psychotherapy. *Behavior Therapy, 13,* 610–623.

Garfield, S. L., & Kurtz, R. (1976). Clinical psychologists in the 1970s. *American Psychologist, 31,* 1–9.

Garfield, S. L., & Kurtz, R. (1977). A study of eclectic views. *Journal of Consulting and Clinical Psychology, 45,* 78–83.

Gill, M. M. (1984). Psychoanalytic, psychodynamic, cognitive behavior, and behavior therapies compared. In H. Arkowitz & S. B. Messer (Eds.), *Psychoanalytic therapy and behavior therapy: Is integration possible?* (pp. 179–187). New York: Plenum.

Glad, D. D. (1959). *Operational values in psychotherapy.* New York: Oxford University Press.

Goldfried, M. R. (1979). Anxiety reduction through cognitive–behavioral intervention. In P. C. Kendall & S. D. Hollon (Eds.), *Cognitive-behavioral-interventions: Theory, research, and procedures.* New York: Academic Press.

Goldfried, M. R. (1980). Toward the delineation of therapeutic change principles. *American Psychologist, 35,* 991–999.

Goldfried, M. R. (Ed.), (1982a). *Converging themes in psychotherapy: Trends in psychodynamic, humanistic, and behavioral practice.* New York: Springer.

Goldfried, M. R. (1982b). On the history of therapeutic integration. *Behavior Therapy, 13,* 572–593.

Goldfried, M. R. (in press). In vivo intervention or transference? In W. Dryden (Ed.), *Therapists' dilemmas.* London: Harper & Row.

Goldfried, M. R., & Davison, G. C. (1976). *Clinical behavior therapy.* New York: Holt, Rinehart, & Winston.

Goldfried, M. R., & Padawer, W. (1982). Current status and future directions in psychotherapy. In M. R. Goldfried (Ed.), *Converging themes in psychotherapy* (pp. 3–49). New York: Springer.

Goldfried, M. R., & Strupp, H. H. (1980, November). *Empirical clinical practice: A dialogue on rapprochement.* Presented at the Convention of the Association for Advancement of Behavior Therapy, New York.

Goldfried, M. R., & Wachtel, P. L. (Eds.). (1983). *Newsletter of the Society for the Exploration of Psychotherapy Integration.* Vol. 1, No. 1.

Goldstein, A. J., & Chambless, D. L. (1978). A reanalysis of agoraphobia. *Behavior Therapy, 9,* 47–59.

Greenberg, L. S., & Safran, J. D. (1984). Integrating

affect and cognitions: A perspective on the process of therapeutic change. *Cognitive Therapy and Research, 8,* 559–578.

Greening, T. C. (1978). Commentary. *Journal of Humanistic Psychology, 18,* 1–4.

Grinker, R. R. (1976). Discussion of Strupp's, "Some critical comments on the future of psychoanalytic therapy." *Bulletin of the Menninger Clinic, 40,* 247–254.

Guidano, V. S., & Liotti, G. (1983). *Cognitive processes and emotional disorders: A structural approach to psychotherapy.* New York: Guilford.

Gurman, A. S. (1978). Contemporary marital therapies. In T. Paolino & B. McCrady (Eds.), *Marriage and marital therapy.* New York: Brunner/Mazel.

Gurman, A. S. (1981). Integrative marital therapy: Toward the development of an interpersonal approach. In S. Budman (Ed.), *Forms of brief therapy.* New York: Guilford.

Hagstrom, W. O. (1965). *The scientific community.* Carbondale, IL: Southern Illinois University Press.

Hart, J. (1983). *Modern eclectic therapy: A functional orientation to counselling and psychotherapy.* New York: Plenum.

Hatcher, C. (1978). Intrapersonal and interpersonal models: Blending gestalt and family therapies. *Journal of Marriage and Family Counseling, 4,* 63–68.

Herink, R. (1980). *The psychotherapy handbook: The A to Z guide to more than 250 different therapies in use today.* New York: New American Library.

Horwitz, L. (1974). *Clinical prediction in psychotherapy.* New York: Jason Aronson.

Horwitz, L. (1976). New perspectives for psychoanalytic psychotherapy. *Bulletin of the Menninger Clinic, 40,* 263–271.

Houts, P. S., & Serber, M. (1972). *After the turn on, what? Learning perspectives on humanistic groups.* Champaign, IL: Research Press.

Hunt, H. F. (1976). Recurrent dilemmas in behavior therapy. In G. Serban (Ed.), *Psychopathology of human adaptation.* New York: Plenum.

Kaplan, H. S. (1974). *The new sex therapy.* New York: Brunner/Mazel.

Kazdin, A. E. (1984). Integration of psychodynamic and behavioral psychotherapies: Conceptual versus empirical synthesis. In H. Arkowitz & S. B. Messer (Eds.), *Psychoanalytic therapy and behavior therapy? Is integration possible?* (pp. 139–70). New York: Plenum.

Kelly, G. A. (1955). *The psychology of personal constructs.* New York: Norton.

Kendall, P. C. (1982). Integration: Behavior therapy and other schools of thought. *Behavior Therapy, 13,* 559–571.

Kiesler, D. J. (1966). Some myths of psychotherapy research and the search for a paradigm. *Psychological Bulletin, 65,* 110–136.

Kraft, T. (1969). Psychoanalysis and behaviorism: A false antithesis. *American Journal of Psychotherapy, 23,* 482–487.

Krasner, L. (1978). The future and the past in the behaviorism–humanism dialogue. *American Psychologist, 33,* 799–804.

Kubie, L. S. (1934). Relation of the conditioned reflex to psychoanalytic technic. *Archives of Neurology and Psychiatry, 32,* 1137–1142.

Kuhn, T. S. (1970). *The structure of scientific revolutions* (2nd ed.). Chicago: University of Chicago Press.

Lambley, P. (1976). The use of assertive training and psychodynamic insight in the treatment of migraine headaches: A case study. *Journal of Nervous and Mental Disease, 163,* 61–64.

Landau, R. J., & Goldfried, M. R. (1981). The assessment of schemata: A unifying framework for cognitive, behavioral, and traditional assessment. In P. C. Kendall & S. D. Hollon (Eds.), *Assessment strategies for cognitive–behavioral interventions* (pp. 363–399). New York: Academic Press.

Landsman, T. (1974, August). *Not an adversity but a welcome diversity.* Paper presented at the meeting of the American Psychological Association, New Orleans.

Larson, D. (1980). Therapeutic schools, styles, and schoolism: A national survey. *Journal of Humanistic Psychology, 20,* 3–20.

Lazarus, A. A. (1967). In support of technical eclecticism. *Psychological Reports, 21,* 415–416.

Lazarus, A. A. (1971). *Behavior therapy and beyond.* New York: McGraw-Hill.

Lazarus, A. A. (1976). *Multimodal behavior therapy.* New York: Springer.

Lazarus, A. A. (1977). Has behavior therapy outlived its usefulness? *American Psychologist, 32,* 550–554.

Lazarus, A. A. (1981). *The practice of multimodal therapy.* New York: McGraw-Hill.

Lazarus, A. A., & Davison, G. C. (1971). Clinical innovation in research and practice. In A. E. Bergin & S. L. Garfield (Eds.), *Handbook of psychotherapy and behavior change.* New York: John Wiley and Sons.

Lebow, J. L. (1984). On the value of integrating approaches to family therapy. *Journal of Marital and Family Therapy, 10,* 127–138.

Levay, A. N., Weissberg, J. H., & Blaustein, A. B. (1976). Concurrent sex therapy and psychoanalytic psychotherapy by separate therapists: Effectiveness and implications. *Psychiatry, 39,* 355–363.

Leventhal, A. M. (1968). Use of a behavioral approach within a traditional psychotherapeutic context: A case study. *Journal of Abnormal Psychology, 73,* 178–182.

Lichtenstein, E. (1980). *Psychotherapy: Approaches and applications.* Monterey, CA: Brooks/Cole.

Linsenhoff, A., Bastine, R., & Kommer, D. (1980). Schulenubergergreifende Perspektiven in der Psychotherapie. *Integrative Psychotherapie, 4,* 302–322.

Llewelyn, S. P. (1980). The uses of an eclectic approach: A case study. *British Journal of Medical Psychology, 53,* 145–149.

London, P. (1964). *The modes and morals of psy-*

chotherapy. New York: Holt, Rinehart, & Winston.

London, P. (1972). The end of ideology in behavior modification. *American Psychologist, 27,* 913–920.

London, P. (1983). Ecumenism in psychotherapy. *Contemporary psychology, 28,* 507–508.

Mahoney, M. J. (1979). Cognitive and non-cognitive views in behavior modification. In P. O. Sjoden & S. Bates (Eds.), *Trends in behavior therapy.* New York: Plenum.

Mahoney, M. J. (1980). Psychotherapy and the structure of personal revolutions. In M. J. Mahoney (Ed.), *Psychotherapy process.* New York: Plenum

Mahoney, M. J. (1984). Psychoanalysis and behaviorism: The yin and yang of determinism. In H. Arkowitz & S. B. Messer (Eds.), *Psychoanalytic therapy and behavior therapy: Is integration possible?* (pp. 303–325). New York: Plenum.

Mahoney, M. J., & Wachtel, P. L. (1982, May). *Convergence of psychoanalytic and behavioral therapy.* Presentation at the Institute for Psychosocial Study, New York.

Marks, I. M. (1971). The future of the psychotherapies. *British Journal of Psychiatry, 118,* 69–73.

Marks, I. M., & Gelder, M. G. (1966). Common ground between behavior therapy and psychodynamic methods. *British Journal of Medical Psychology, 39,* 11–23.

Marmor, J. (1964). Psychoanalytic therapy and theories of learning. In J. Masserman (Ed.), *Science and psychoanalysis* (Vol. 7). New York: Grune & Stratton.

Marmor, J. (1969). Neurosis and the psychotherapeutic process: Similarities and differences in the behavioral and psychodynamic conceptions. *International Journal of Psychiatry, 7,* 514–519.

Marmor, J. (1971). Dynamic psychotherapy and behavior therapy: Are they irreconcilable? *Archives of General Psychiatry, 24,* 22–28.

Marmor, J., & Woods, S. M. (Eds.). (1980). *The interface between psychodynamic and behavioral therapies.* New York: Plenum.

Martin, C. G. (1972). *Learning-based client-centered therapy.* Monterey, CA: Brooks/Cole.

Maslow, A. H. (1966). Abstracting and theorizing. In A. H. Maslow (Ed.), *The psychology of science: A reconnaissance.* New York: Harper & Row.

Meichenbaum, D. (1980, April). *Nature of conscious and unconscious processes: Issues in cognitive assessment.* Invited address presented at the meeting of the Eastern Psychological Association, Hartford, CT.

Meichenbaum, D. & Gilmore, J. B. (1984). The nature of unconscious processes: A cognitive-behavioral perspective. In K. Bowers & D. Meichenbaum (Eds.), *The unconscious reconsidered* (pp. 273–298). New York: Wiley-Interscience.

Merton, R. K. (1969). Behavior patterns of scientists. *American Scholar, 38,* 197–225.

Messer, S. B. (1983). Integrating psychoanalytic and behaviour therapy: Limitations, possibilities, and trade-offs. *British Journal of Clinical Psychology, 22,* 131–132.

Messer, S. B. (1984). The integration of psychoan-

alytic therapy and behavior therapy: Summing up. In H. Arkowitz & S. B. Messer (Eds.), *Psychoanalytic therapy and behavior therapy: Is integration possible?* (pp. 359–369). New York: Plenum.

Messer, S. B., & Winokur, M. (1980). Some limits to the integration of psychoanalytic and behavior therapy. *American Psychologist, 35,* 818–827.

Meyer, R. (1982). *Le corps assui: De la psychoanalyse à la somatanalyse.* Paris: Maloine S. A., Editeur.

Mikulas, W. L. (1978). Four noble truths of Buddhism related to behavior therapy. *Psychological Record, 28,* 59–67.

Murray, E. J. (1983). Beyond behavioural and dynamic therapy. *British Journal of Clinical Psychology, 23,* 127–128.

Murray, E. J., & Jacobson, L. I. (1978). Cognition and learning in traditional and behavioral psychology. In S. L. Garfield & A. E. Bergin (Eds.), *Handbook of psychotherapy and behavior change: An empirical analysis.* New York: Wiley.

Murray, N. E. (1976). A dynamic synthesis of analytic and behavioral approaches to symptoms. *American Journal of Psychotherapy, 30,* 561–569.

Nielsen, A. C. (1980). Gestalt and psychoanalytic therapies: Structural analysis and rapprochement. *American Journal of Psychotherapy, 34,* 534–544.

O'Leary, K. D., & Turkewitz, H. (1978). Marital therapy from a behavioral perspective. In T. J. Paolino & B. S. McCrady (Eds.), *Marriage and marital therapy: Psychoanalytic, behavioral, and systems theory perspectives.* New York: Brunner/Mazel.

Parloff, M. B. (1979). Can psychotherapy research guide the policy maker? A little knowledge may be a dangerous thing. *American Psychologist, 34,* 296–306.

Patterson, C. H. (1967). Divergence and convergence in psychotherapy. *American Journal of Psychotherapy, 21,* 4–17.

Pinsof, W. M. (1980). The family therapist coding system (coding manual). Unpublished manuscript. The Family Institute of Chicago.

Pinsof, W. M. (1983). Integrative problem-centered therapy: Toward the synthesis of family and individual psychotherapies. *Journal of Marital and Family Therapy, 9,* 19–35.

Polanyi, M. (1958). *Personal knowledge: Towards a post-critical philosophy.* Chicago: University of Chicago Press.

Prochaska, J. O. (1979). *Systems of psychotherapy: A transtheoretical analysis.* Homewood, IL: Dorsey.

Prochaska, J. O., & DiClemente, C. C. (1982). Transtheoretical therapy: Toward a more integrative model of change. *Psychotherapy: Theory, Research, and Practice, 19,* 276–288.

Prochaska, J. O., & DiClemente, C. C. (1984). *The transtheoretical approach: Crossing the traditional boundaries of therapy.* Homewood, IL: Dow Jones-Irwin.

Raimy, V. (1975). *Misunderstandings of the self.* San Francisco: Jossey-Bass.

Rappaport, J. (1977). *Community psychology: Values, research, and action.* New York: Holt, Rinehart, and Winston.

Reif, F. (1961). The competitive world of the pure scientist. *Science, 134,* 1958–1962.

Rhoads, J. M. (1981). The integration of behavior therapy and psychoanalytic theory. *Journal of Psychiatric Treatment and Evaluation, 3,* 1–6.

Rhoads, J. M. (1984). Relationships between psychodynamic and behavior therapies. In H. Arkowitz & S. B. Messer (Eds.), *Psychoanalytic therapy and behavior therapy: Is integration possible?* (pp. 195–211). New York: Plenum.

Rhoads, J. M., & Feather, B. W. (1974). The application of psychodynamic to behavior therapy. *American Journal of Psychiatry, 131,* 17–20.

Robertson, M. (1979). Some observations from an eclectic therapist. *Psychotherapy: Theory, Research, and Practice, 16,* 18–21.

Rogers, C. R. (1963). Psychotherapy today or where do we go from here? *American Journal of Psychotherapy, 17,* 5–15.

Rosenberg, J. (1978). Two is better than one: Use of behavioral techniques within a structural family therapy model. *Journal of Marriage and Family Counseling, 4,* 31–40.

Rosenzweig, S. (1936). Some implicit common factors in diverse methods in psychotherapy. *American Journal of Orthopsychiatry, 6,* 412–415.

Ryle, A. (1978). A common language for the psychotherapies? *British Journal of Psychiatry, 132,* 585–594.

Ryle, A. (1980). *Integrating opposing theories in a cognitive model of neurotic problems.* Unpublished manuscript. University of Sussex.

Ryle, A. (1982). *Psychotherapy: A cognitive integration of theory and practice.* London: Academic Press.

Safran, J. (1984). Assessing the cognitive–interpersonal cycle. *Cognitive Therapy and Research, 8,* 333–347.

Salzman, L. (1984). Psychoanalysis and behavior therapy. In H. Arkowitz & S. B. Messer (Eds.), *Psychoanalytic therapy and behavior therapy: Is integration possible?* (pp. 335–349). New York: Plenum.

Sarason, J. G. (1979). Three lacunae of cognitive therapy. *Cognitive Therapy and Research, 3,* 223–235.

Schacht, T. E. (1984). The varieties of integrative experience. In H. Arkowitz & S. B. Messer (Eds.), *Psychoanalytic therapy and behavior therapy: Is integration possible?* (pp. 107–131). New York: Plenum.

Schwartz, B. D. (1981). An eclectic group therapy course for graduate students in professional psychology. *Psychotherapy: Theory, Research, and Practice, 18,* 417–423.

Schwartz, R. M. (1982). Cognitive-behavior modification: A conceptual review. *Clinical Psychology Review, 2,* 267–293.

Sears, R. R. (1981, August). *Psychoanalysis and behavior therapy: 1907–1965.* Paper presented at the meeting of the American Psychological Association, Los Angeles.

Segraves, R. T. (1982). *Marital therapy: A combined psychodynamic–behavioral approach.* New York: Plenum.

Segraves, R. T., & Smith, R. C. (1976). Concurrent psychotherapy and behavior therapy: Treatment of psychoneurotic outpatients. *Archives of General Psychiatry, 33,* 756–763.

Shapiro, D. H., Jr. (1978). *Precision nirvana.* Englewood Cliffs, NJ: Prentice-Hall.

Shectman, F. A. (1975). Operant conditioning and psychoanalysis: Contrasts, similarities, and some thoughts about integration. *American Journal of Psychotherapy, 29,* 72–78.

Shevrin, H., & Dickman, S. (1980). The psychological unconscious: A necessary assumption for all psychological theory? *American Psychologist, 35,* 421–434.

Shuger, D., & Bebout, J. (1980). Contrasts in Gestalt and analytic therapy. *Journal of Humanistic Psychology, 20,* 21–39.

Silverman, L. H. (1974). Some psychoanalytic considerations of non-psychoanalytic therapies: On the possibility of integrating treatment approaches and related issues. *Psychotherapy: Theory, Research, and Practice, 11,* 298–305.

Sloane, R. B. (1969). The converging paths of behavior therapy and psychotherapy. *American Journal of Psychiatry, 125,* 877–885.

Sloane, R. B., Staples, F. R., Cristol, A. H., Yorkston, N.J., & Whipple, K. (1975). *Psychotherapy versus behavior therapy.* Cambridge, MA: Harvard University Press.

Sollod, R. (1975). Behavioral and psychodynamic dimensions of the new sex therapy. *Journal of Sex and Marital Therapy, 1,* 335–340.

Staats, A. W. (1981). Paradigmatic behaviorism, unified theory construction methods, and the zeitgeist of separatism. *American Psychologist, 36,* 239–256.

Steinfeld, G. J. (1980). *Target systems: An integrative approach to individual and family therapy.* Jonesboro, TN: Pilgrimage.

Strupp, H. H. (1968). Psychotherapists and (or versus?) researchers. *Voices: The Art and Science of Psychotherapy, 4,* 28–37.

Strupp, H. H. (1973). On the basic ingredients of psychotherapy. *Journal of Consulting and Clinical Psychology, 41,* 1–8.

Strupp, H. H. (1976). Some critical comments on the future of psychoanalytic therapy. *Bulletin of the Menninger Clinic, 40,* 238–254.

Strupp, H. H. (1978a, August). *Are psychoanalytic therapists beginning to practice cognitive behavior therapy or is behavior therapy turning psychoanalytic?* Presented at symposium, Clinical–cognitive theories of psychotherapy, American Psychological Association, Toronto.

Strupp, H. H. (1978b). Psychotherapy research and practice: An overview. In S. L. Garfield & A. E. Bergin (Eds.), *Handbook of psychotherapy and behavior change: An empirical analysis.* New York: Wiley.

Strupp, H. H. (1983). Are psychoanalytic therapists beginning to practice cognitive behavior therapy or is behavior therapy turning psychoanalytic? *British Journal of Cognitive Therapy, 1,* 17–27.

Sullivan, H. S. (1954). *The psychiatric interview.* New York: Norton.

Thoresen, C. E. (1973). Behavioral humanism. In C. E. Thoresen (Ed.), *Behavior modification in education.* Chicago: University of Chicago Press.

Thorne, F. C. (1950). *Principles of personality counseling.* Brandon, VT: Journal of Clinical Psychology.

Torrey, E. F. (1972). What Western psychotherapists can learn from witchdoctors. *American Journal of Orthopsychiatry, 42,* 69–72.

Truax, C. B., & Mitchell, K. M. (1971). Research on certain therapist interpersonal skills in relation to process and outcome. In A. E. Bergin & S. L. Garfield (Eds.), *Handbook of psychotherapy and behavior change: An empirical analysis.* New York: Wiley.

Wachtel, P. L. (1975). Behavior therapy and the facilitation of psychoanalytic exploration. *Psychotherapy: Theory, Research, and Practice, 12,* 68–72.

Wachtel, P. L. (1977). *Psychoanalysis and behavior therapy: Toward an integration.* New York: Basic Books.

Wachtel, P. L. (Ed.). (1982). *Resistance: Psychodynamic and behavioral approaches.* New York: Plenum.

Wachtel, P. L. (1983). Integration misunderstood. *British Journal of Clinical Psychology, 22,* 129–130.

Wandersman, A., Poppen, P. J., & Ricks, D. F. (Eds.). (1976). *Humanism and behaviorism: Dialogue and growth.* Elmsford, NY: Pergamon.

Ward, D. E. (1983). The trend toward eclecticism and the development of comprehensive models to guide counseling and psychotherapy. *Personnel and Guidance Journal, 67,* 154–157.

Watson, G. (1940). Areas of agreement in psychotherapy. *American Journal of Orthopsychiatry, 10,* 698–709.

Weitzman, B. (1967). Behavior therapy and psychotherapy. *Psychological Review, 74,* 300–317.

Whitehouse, F. A. (1967). The concept of therapy: A review of some essentials. *Rehabilitation Literature, 28,* 238–347.

Wittman, L. (1981). *Verhaltenstherapie und psychodynamik. Therapeutisches Handeln jenseits der Schulengrensen.* Weinheim: Beltz.

Wolf, E. (1966). Learning theory and psychoanalysis. *British Journal of Medical Psychology, 39,* 1–10.

Woodworth, R. S. (1948). *Contemporary schools of psychology.* New York: Ronald Press.

Woody, R. H. (1968). Toward a rationale for psychobehavioral therapy. *Archives of General Psychiatry, 19,* 197–204.

Woody, R. H. (1971). *Psychobehavioral counseling and therapy: Integrating behavioral and insight techniques.* New York: Appleton-Century-Crofts.

Woody, R. H. (1973). Integrated aversion therapy and psychotherapy: Two sexual deviation case studies. *Journal of Sex Research, 9,* 313–324.

Yates, A. J. (1983a). Behaviour therapy and psychodynamic psychotherapy: Basic conflict or reconciliation and integration? *British Journal of Clinical Psychology, 22,* 107–125.

Yates, A. J. (1983b). Reply. *British Journal of Clinical Psychology, 22,* 135–136.

PART II

Eclectic Approaches

CHAPTER 3

Multimodal Therapy

Arnold A. Lazarus

BACKGROUND OF THE APPROACH

After having embraced a "pure" behavior therapy approach (Wolpe & Lazarus, 1966), this author (Lazarus, 1967, 1971) briefly propounded the virtues of *technical eclecticism* (as opposed to theoretical eclecticism) and strongly emphasized the specific advantages of adding "cognitive" procedures to the behavioral armamentarium. These developments arose out of treatment results and follow-up studies that showed that whereas behavioral interventions frequently enabled disturbed individuals to make impressive headway, these gains were often not maintained. The search for additional systematic interventions that could yield more stable outcomes led to an appreciation of the synergy of behavioral and cognitive methods. Clients who had maintained their therapeutic improvements tended to achieve "a different outlook and philosophy of life and increased self-esteem in addition to an increased range of interpersonal and behavioral skills, presumably as a result of therapy" (Lazarus, 1971, p. 18).

A broad-based outlook was apparent even in my earliest writings. In 1956, re- ferring to the treatment of alcoholism, I stressed that "the problem is generally tackled within a unitary, or at best a 'bimodal,' frame of reference," and called for "a *synthesis,* which would embrace active measures combined with educative procedures and psychotherapeutic and socioeconomic procedures, as well as innumerable adjunctive measures such as drug therapy, vitamin therapy, and the like" (Lazarus, 1956, pp. 709–710). It seems axiomatic to postulate that the more coping responses a person learns in therapy, the less likely he or she is to relapse; that lasting change is at the very least a function of combined *techniques, strategies,* and *modalities.* Because a point of diminishing returns obviously exists, it is important to avoid a random mélange of techniques based on subjective preferences and impressions. Instead, the aim is to formulate a consistent framework that permits (a) specification of goals and problems; (b) specification of treatment techniques to achieve these goals and remedy these problems; and (c) systematic measurement of the relative success of these techniques.

With the foregoing in mind, when gathering outcome and follow-up data, several questions arose repeatedly. When do behavior therapy techniques suffice? What sorts of people, with which particular problems, require more than behavior therapy? When stepping outside the confines of behavior therapy, which effective "nonbehavioral" methods are best incorporated? The upshot was that comprehensive treatment at the very least called for the correction of maladaptive and deviant behaviors, unpleasant feelings, negative sensations, intrusive images, dysfunctional beliefs, stressful relationships, and possible biochemical imbalance. "To the extent that problem identification (diagnosis) systematically explores each of these modalities, whereupon therapeutic intervention remedies whatever deficits and maladaptive patterns emerge, treatment outcomes will be positive and long-lasting" (Lazarus, 1973, p. 408).

The need to go beyond the "trimodal" methods advocated by most cognitive-behavior therapists—Affect, Behavior, Cognition (ABC)—became evident when several clients showed little or no affective improvements despite clear-cut evidence of rational and positive "self-talk." Closer scrutiny revealed that it is possible to "think positively" and yet be able to maintain "negative imagery" that tends to override the final affective process. This discovery led to the formulation of a specificity hypothesis: The presence of negative images calls for changes in the actual images themselves; sensory complaints (e.g., tension headaches, muscle spasms, bruxism) require specific sensory techniques in addition to behavioral change, cognitive shifts, affective expression, and attention to other aspects of functioning. It seemed important to separate "affect" from "sensation" as well as "imagery" from "cognition." A comprehensive appraisal of human interactions called for an examination of behavior, affect, sensation, imagery, cognition, and interpersonal relationships. (The first letters of these terms form the acronym BASIC I.). In addition, it would be nearsighted and foolish to ignore the neurophysiological–biochemical elements that contribute to human conduct, personality, and temperament. Hence if we add "D" which stands for "drugs/biology" to the BASIC I., we have the complete multimodal spectrum BASIC I.D. (It must be remembered that the "D" modality stands for more than recreational drugs or prescribed medications, but addresses all issues of physical well-being—diet, sleep habits, exercise—and all significant physical problems, such as CNS pathology, endocrinopathy, and metabolic disorders.)

Wilson (1982) inquired: "If we began with overt behavior in the 1950's and 1960's, then added cognition in the 1970's, can affect be far behind? In looking for a new emphasis in behavior therapy, it might be 'affect in the eighties' " (p. 298). This conception of human functioning appears to be an incomplete statement of multimodal therapy. By covering the entire BASIC I.D., it would seem that multimodal therapy transcends the usual cognitive-behavior therapy framework. It offers an assessment template that is intended to "Leave no stone unturned."

THE APPROACH

What is the alternative to eclecticism? The most obvious answer is: close adherence to one or two particular schools of thought. The limitations of orthodoxy have become widely recognized, and the value of empiricism—basing one's knowledge on evidence from experimentation, observation, and measurement and not on theoretical speculation—has been incorporated into the realm of several psychotherapeutic approaches. Many no longer question the wisdom of employing terms that are verifiable, experimental, and scientific in place of metaphysical concepts and theories. It is encouraging to note that more and more therapists are inclined to place the practical exigencies of their patients' problems before the theoretical constraints of their own ideologies (Frances, Clarkin & Perry, 1984). Nevertheless, several dangers loom large.

What Is Eclecticism?

Webster's Ninth New Collegiate Dictionary (1984) provides two definitions of *eclectic*: "1. Selecting what appears to be best in various doctrines, methods, or styles. 2. Composed of elements drawn from various sources." The first definition seems to fit what is sometimes termed "synthetic eclecticism" or "theoretical eclecticism," wherein an attempt is made to integrate diverse theories. In so doing, to quote the recondite Eysenck (1970), many have embraced "a mish-mash of theories, a hugger-mugger of procedures, a gallimaufry of therapies, and a charivaria of activities having no proper rationale, and incapable of being tested or evaluated" (p. 145). Indeed, for an eclectic therapist to choose his or her theories and techniques largely on the basis of subjective appeal can only breed confusion worse confounded. If we look very closely at the theories, metatheories, and assumptions that underlie the different psychotherapeutic systems, contradictory notions and divergent points of reference are readily discerned. These differences are not merely terminological or semantic—they often go to the core of fundamental differences in ideology and rest on entirely different epistemological foundations (cf. Franks, 1984). When examining various theoretical assumptions, many superficial similarities may exist and, from a slight distance, they may seem to be virtually identical. It is difficult to appreciate the difference between water and vodka until you taste them! Similarly, those seemingly identical theories and systems, upon closer inspection, reveal basic paradigmatic and other irreconcilable differences, so that rapprochement or integration is quite impossible. It cannot be overemphasized that phenotypical similarities need not reflect genotypical commonalities.

Unlike theoretical or synthetic eclecticism, *technical eclecticism,* or *systematic eclecticism* (using a variety of techniques within a theoretical structure that is open to verification and disproof), fits the second dictionary meaning "composed of elements drawn from various sources." Although they employ techniques from many sources, multimodal therapists do not necessarily subscribe to any of their underlying theories. Methods and techniques may be effective for reasons other than those their originators propound. Thus, technical eclecticism sidesteps the syncretistic muddles that arise when attempting to blend divergent models into a super-organizing theory. Eventually, our field might generate a theoretical superstructure under whose umbrella present-day differences and clash-points can be subsumed and reconciled, but the pre-paradigmatic phase in which we function at present, calls for extreme caution in the face of any of our existing theories. Besides, as London (1964) pointed out: "However interesting, plausible, and appealing a theory may be, it is techniques, not theories, that are actually used on people. Study of the effects of psychotherapy, therefore, is always the study of the effectiveness of techniques" (p. 33).

The foregoing should not be misconstrued as an argument in favor of *atheoretical eclecticism.* Every practitioner has, at the very least, an implicit theory that determines how he or she conceptualizes problems and that influences his or her choice of techniques. Multimodal therapy rests primarily on the theoretical base of *social learning theory* (Bandura, 1969, 1977) but draws also from *general system theory* (von Bertalanffy, 1974; Buckley, 1967) and *group and communications the-*

ory (Watzlawick, Weakland, & Fisch, 1974). These theoretical systems blend harmoniously into a congruent framework.

Whereas a therapist who wishes to achieve constructive outcomes with a wide range of problems has to be flexible, versatile, and technically eclectic, a rigorous scientist cannot afford to be eclectic. In laboratories it is essential to test one or two variables at a time to separate the inert and incidental ingredients from those that are active and specific. Scientific research often requires the withholding of potentially helpful methods so as to determine *what* actually works and to discover *why* it works. Such procedures in clinical practice—withholding potentially helpful interventions—are unprofessional and inhumane. An effective therapist will not withhold seemingly helpful techniques, regardless of their point of origin.

What Is Affect?

The bulk of psychotherapy is concerned with the treatment of "emotional disorders." Thus, the way in which a practitioner understands, perceives, and conceptualizes strong feelings and emotions—*affective processes*—will speak to the essence of his or her ministrations. The multimodal position is that *affect is the product of the reciprocal interaction of behavior, sensation, imagery, cognitive factors, and biological inputs, usually within an interpersonal context.* Clearly, there can be no emotion without a neurophysiological–biochemical substrate. The reciprocal and interactive properties of the specific modalities can be clearly depicted in a simple figure (cf. Lazarus, Kreitzberg, & Sasserath, 1981) (see Fig. 1).

The basis of all human functioning is ultimately biological; hence, biology is placed at the base of the hierarchy. Sensation is most closely related to biology since it is physically experienced. The sensory system triggers affective reactions or

is a concomitant thereof; this activity occurs in concert with mediation and stimulation from cognition and imagery (i.e., behaviors on a covert level). The overt behaviors that precede and accompany the affective reaction will influence its intensity and duration. Few responses occur in a social vacuum; thus, the interpersonal modality is placed at the top of the hierarchy. There is a close-knit interaction among the various modalities; hence, the arrows go in both directions.

How can one deal *directly* with affects or emotions? One cannot! Affect or emotion can be worked with only indirectly. "I arouse emotions directly by getting people to scream while pounding foam rubber cushions," one therapist informed me. "No," I replied, "you are arousing emotions via behaviors (screaming and pounding are not emotions) and by generating sensations and images." If asked to deal specifically with behavior, we can readily show someone how to act and react, what to do, what not to do, what to say, and so on. The sensory modality can be directly stimulated at all levels—see this, hear that, smell this, feel that, taste this. In the interpersonal modality, specific interventions such as role-playing, imitation, and modeling are among the most common. In the biological modality, of course, direct interventions come in the form of drugs, surgery, and a myriad of substances that can be introduced into one's body. Even images and cognitions, although inferred constructs, are amenable to direct intervention. "You have just reached a false conclusion. Think about it this way and you will spot your mistake." "Imagine a pink elephant standing under a big green tree." But affect is derived from and can only be reached through behavior, sensation, imagery, cognition, interpersonal relationships, and biological processes. This conception is at the core of the multimodal position. Regardless of the affective disorder under scrutiny, it holds that thoroughness in assess-

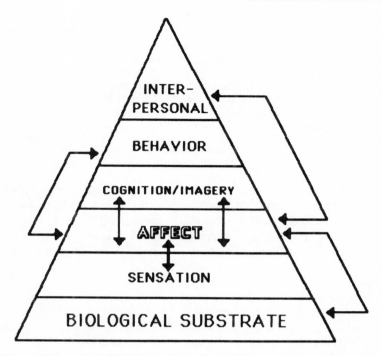

Figure 1. Affect as the reciprocal product of the other six modalities.*

ment requires an inquiry into behavioral, sensory, imagery, cognitive, interpersonal and biological factors. Thus, the Modality Profile of a client who complains of "anxiety" might contain the interactive items as shown in Table 1.

A multimodal therapist would address each specific problem. The client would be encouraged to make approach responses (and would be rehearsed and trained via role-playing if necessary, with additional modeling and *in vivo* excursions if called for). Relaxation training would go hand-in-hand with positive imagery exercises and cognitive restructuring (e.g., focusing on constructive rather than destructive outcomes). Social skills training and assertive responses would be implemented, and at the biological level, the client would be urged to cut down on, if not eliminate, cigarettes and coffee. Thus, specific

changes in behavior, sensation, imagery, cognition, interpersonal relationships and biological elements would be expected to reduce, if not extinguish, the affective disorder (anxiety) for which therapy was sought. Of course, the order in which specific modalities were addressed, the way in which the specific techniques were introduced, the number of dimensions dealt with at any particular time, would all depend on the client's receptivity and the practitioner's clinical skills (Lazarus, 1981).

PATIENT ASSESSMENT

Space limitations permit me to address only the treatment of adult outpatients in this chapter. For multimodal therapy with inpatients see Brunell and Young (1982); Keat (1979) has described multimodal therapy with children. Other publications (e.g., Lazarus, 1976, 1981, 1985) have covered specific applications of multimodal

---

* I thank Clifford N. Lazarus for his cogent criticisms and for designing and executing Figure 1.

TABLE 1

Behavior:	Avoidance responses. Fidgets.
Affect:	Anxiety. [The presenting complaint.]
Sensation:	Tremors. Palpitations. Sweaty palms. Muscular tension.
Imagery:	Dwells on agitating pictures out of the past.
Cognition:	Thinks about innumerable things that could go wrong and have dire consequences.
Interpersonal:	Timid. Inhibited. Unassertive.
Drugs/Biology:	Smokes 2 packs of cigarettes a day. Drinks ±5 cups of coffee a day.

methods to particular problems or populations (e.g., mental retardation, obesity, anorexia nervosa, and "ghetto clients") and in various contexts (e.g., marriage therapy, group therapy, family therapy).

With adult outpatients, the backbone of multimodal assessment is the *Multimodal Life History Questionnaire.* This 12-page printed booklet first obtains routine background information, and then turns to a "Modality Analysis of Current Problems" via behavior, affect, sensation, imagery, cognition, interpersonal relationships, and biological factors. This instrument started out as a general anamnestic survey (Lazarus, 1971), and with the aid of colleagues, it was refined and amplified (Lazarus, 1976) and further developed to its present form (Lazarus, 1981).*

It is a simple matter, after the client has completed and returned the *Life History Questionnaire,* to determine a central range of problems in each area of the BASIC I.D and to appreciate their interactive effects. (Items that are omitted by the client or cursorily answered also supply grist for the therapeutic mill). In addition to factual information about the client and his/her significant others, the questionnaire addresses items that reveal specific excesses and deficits in behavior, affective reactions, sensations, images, cognitions, interpersonal relationships, and biological functioning. There are also

various sentence completion items, checklists, and a section that underscores common cognitive errors (Lazarus & Fay, 1977). Another important section on "Expectations Regarding Therapy" asks the following questions:

• In a few words, what do you think therapy is all about?
• How long do you think your therapy should last?
• How do you think a therapist should interact with his or her clients?
• What personal qualities do you think the ideal therapist should possess?

These questions establish the interactive cadence that is most likely to yield compliance and respect from the client. Someone who thinks that therapy is all about the past and its current implications is likely to be displeased with exclusively here-and-now points of inquiry. A person who anticipates a three-to-six month course of treatment may be nonplussed in the hands of a long-term psychotherapist. A client who considers a good therapist "someone who is an active listener, who says very little but takes in a whole lot," will probably take unkindly to an active–directive, task-oriented clinician.

It would be naive to assume that the client necessarily knows what is best for her or him or that the therapist must comply with each of the client's expectations. Nevertheless, in my experience it is wise, initially, to follow the client's script fairly closely so that adequate rapport is estab-

---

* *The Multimodal Life History Questionnaire* is published by Research Press, Box 31779, Champaign, Illinois 61821.

lished. Thereafter, it is more acceptable and less threatening when the therapist rewrites parts of the scenario and develops a modus operandi that seems better suited to overcome the client's fundamental problems.

Initial Interviews

In multimodal assessment, there is no slavish attention to order. A person in a crisis needs a good listener and someone who can offer immediate support, reassurance, and perhaps guidance. There are those who enter therapy with so many misgivings, such as low levels of basic trust, that it would be foolhardy to trot out questionnaires, to administer formal tests, or to recommend homework assignments. Clients who are deeply depressed, or agitated, or otherwise unduly upset are unlikely to comply if asked to fill out forms, chart their specific behaviors, or read prescribed self-help books. In the majority of cases, the initial interview focuses on the establishment of rapport, on assessing and evaluating presenting complaints, and in determining the best course of treatment. Any good clinician will be on the alert for signs of psychosis, homicidal or suicidal tendencies, and other indications of serious psychopathology.

Presenting complaints are placed in a meaningful context by answering two main questions: (a) What has led to the current situation? and (b) Who or what is maintaining it? Thorough assessment requires the therapist to take careful note of *what* the clients says and *how* the client says it. The verbal content of a person's remarks is often less revealing than the manner and delivery of the statement. People have distinctive ways of *saying* things and of *concealing* them. It is most important to notice what clients gloss over; to observe any hesitations, blocks, or evidence of confusion; to note whether the pitch and timbre of the client's voice

tends to change when different topics are introduced. Body position, facial expression, posture, gestures and movement are significant, as are changes in pallor, or evidence of flushing, moist palms, frequent swallowing, dry mouth, and rapid breathing rates. The minutiae are important.

Multimodal therapists emphasize flexibility and versatility above all else. One begins the initial interview in an accepting, neutral, and open manner. It is then necessary to gauge how best to augment the level of rapport. Some clients, for instance, require clarification of their affective reactions, and in these instances, a reflective atmosphere is made to order. Others require direct confrontation, and cognitive disputation. When response deficits are the focus of therapeutic attention, methods such as active coaching, modeling, and social skills training are indicated. A primary purpose of the initial interview is to determine how to fit the treatment to the patient (and not vice versa). It is necessary to tailor one's general clinical knowledge to fit the given individual.

Whenever there is a definite discrepancy between the client's apparent pre-symptomatic stress and the severity of the ongoing disorder, particular attention should be paid to biological factors. When in doubt, a typical mental-status examination is performed. If this examination suggests neurological impairment, a thorough testing of the client's comprehension, attention, grasp, reasoning, judgment and other neuropsychological factors is called for.

Constructing the Modality Profile (BASIC I.D. Chart)

The BASIC I.D. Chart, or Modality Profile, is a distinctive feature of multimodal therapy. By writing down the salient features of the client's BASIC I.D. problems, a clear nexus develops between diagnosis and treatment. Usually, the initial interview, and details from the *Life History Questionnaire,* enable the therapist to draw up a fairly comprehensive Modality Profile (which ordinarily takes 15–20 minutes). The items on the Profile are viewed as specific problem areas that call for direct therapeutic attention. They serve as "working hypotheses" that may be modified or revised by ensuing discussions.

Clients are frequently asked to draw up their own Modality Profiles; it is sometimes particularly valuable for therapist and client to perform this exercise independently and then compare notes. Clients are provided with a brief explanation of each term in the BASIC I.D. A typewritten instruction sheet with the following information usually suffices:

Behavior: This refers mainly to overt behaviors: to acts, habits, gestures, responses, and reactions that are observable and measurable. Make a list of those acts, habits, etc., that you want to increase and those that you would like to decrease. What would you like to start doing? What would you like to stop doing?

Affect: This refers to emotions, moods, and strong feelings. What emotions do you experience most often? Write down your unwanted emotions (e.g., anxiety, guilt, anger, depression, etc.). Note under "behavior" what you tend to *do* when you feel a certain way.

Sensation: Touching, tasting, smelling, seeing, and hearing are our five basic senses. Make a list of any negative sensations (e.g., tension, dizziness, pain, blushing, butterflies in stomach, etc.) that apply to you. If any of these sensations cause you to act or feel in certain ways, make sure you note them under "behavior" or "affect."

Imagery: Write down any bothersome recurring dreams and vivid memories. Include any negative features about the way you see yourself—your "self-image." Make a list of any "mental pictures"—past, present, or future—that may be troubling you. If any "auditory images"—tunes or sounds that you keep hearing—constitute a problem, jot them down. If your images arouse any significant actions, feelings, or sensations, make sure these items are added to "behavior," "affect," and "sensation."

Cognition: What types of attitudes, values, opinions, and ideas get in the way of your happiness? Make a list of negative things you often say to yourself (e.g., "I am a failure," or "I am stupid," or "Others dislike me," or "I'm no good"). Write down some of your most irrational ideas. Be sure to note down how these ideas and thoughts influence your behaviors, feelings, sensations, and images.

Interpersonal Relationships: Write down any bothersome interactions with other people (relatives, friends, lovers, employers, acquaintances, etc.). Any concerns you have about the way other people treat you should appear here. Check through the items under "behavior," "affect," "sensation," "imagery," and "cognition," and try to determine how they influence and are influenced by your interpersonal relationships. (Note that there is some overlap between the modalities, but don't hesitate to list the same problem more than once, e.g., under "behavior" and "interpersonal relationships.")

Drugs/Biology: Make a list of all drugs you are taking, whether prescribed by a doctor or not. Include any health problems, medical concerns, and illnesses that you have or have had.

A 32-year-old housewife and mother who had been diagnosed as suffering from Alcohol Dependence (DSM-III category, Axis I 303.9x) drew up the Modality Profile as shown in Table 2.

It should be clear from the Modality Profile, that Alcohol Dependence fits into an interactive context that calls for specific attention to several interrelated problem areas. Every item needs to be discussed with the client in an effort to

TABLE 2

Behavior:	I tend to avoid many things, withdraw from others, and I also procrastinate.
Affect:	I am afraid of taking a job. I have a lot of anxiety in general. I also have guilty feelings tied into religion. I also know that anger is in there somewhere.
Sensation:	I suffer from pains and tensions in my jaws, neck, and stomach. I often get to feeling nausea. I think I hyperventilate.
Imagery:	I have a poor self-image. I have lots of painful memories (images?) especially about my father.
Cognition:	I am inferior. I am stupid. I can't do most things I am expected to do.
Interpersonal relationships:	I am always apologetic. I have no confidence about raising my 4-year-old son. I have no friends. I don't get along with my family (parents and sister).
Drugs/Biology:	I abuse alcohol, coffee, cigarettes. I eat junk and I get little exercise.

eliminate ambiguity, and each problem is best assessed in terms of its antecedents and consequences so that one can better appreciate its functional significance. Nevertheless, even a preliminary list of problems across the BASIC I.D. will provide the therapist with immediate ideas about potentially useful therapeutic interventions.

Given a Modality Profile, how does one proceed to select and prioritize treatment goals? A basic rule is to start with items that are likely to respond to one's ministrations, thereby augmenting one's credibility. In many instances, certain problems call for immediate attention (e.g., someone who is unduly tense may require some form of relaxation training before other measures can be introduced; a client with a clearly dysfunctional belief that appears to undermine several areas of discourse may require "cognitive disputation" as an initial intervention). Generally, the choice of problem areas to be addressed, and the techniques to be administered are discussed with the client, and decisions are made in concert with his or her input. Thus, in the foregoing case of Alcohol Dependence, the client agreed that three initial changes would have far-reaching effects:

1. She would join Alcoholics Anonymous, which would provide several essential functions: dealing with her abuse of alcohol in particular, providing a support group, augmenting the chances of making friends, and providing a milieu in which she could start to practice interpersonal skills that would be rehearsed during our sessions.

2. She would undertake relaxation training which, combined with certain meditation and positive imagery procedures (Lazarus, 1984), would address several interrelated problems—anxiety, sensory discomforts, and generalized tension.

3. Cognitive disputation concerning her self-derogation could be added to the foregoing without overloading the system.

The Use of Structural Profiles

In addition to Modality Profiles (i.e., specific problems and proposed treatments across a client's BASIC I.D.) the use of Structural Profiles often yields important information, especially in couples therapy. The format for a Structural Profile is presented in Table 3.

The therapist can administer the test, or have the client(s) do it alone. These subjective ratings are easily depicted on a graph. Despite their arbitrary nature, these ratings often enable one to derive useful clinical information. Important insights are gained when the therapist ex-

TABLE 3

Here are seven rating scales that pertain to various tendencies that people have. Using a scale of 0 to 6 (0 means that it does not describe you, or you rarely rely on it; 6 means that the description characterizes you, or you rely on it greatly) please rate yourself in the following areas:

1. *Behavior*: How active are you? How much of a "doer" are you? Do you like to keep busy?
   Rating: 6 5 4 3 2 1 0

2. *Affect*: How emotional are you? How deeply do you feel things? Are you inclined to impassioned, or soul-stirring inner reactions?
   Rating: 6 5 4 3 2 1 0

3. *Sensation*: How much do you focus on the pleasures and pains derived from your senses? How "tuned in" are you to your bodily sensations—to sex, food, music, art?
   Rating: 6 5 4 3 2 1 0

4. *Imagery*: Do you have a vivid imagination? Do you engage in fantasy and daydreaming? Do you "think in pictures"?
   Rating: 6 5 4 3 2 1 0

5. *Cognition*: How much of a "thinker" are you? Do you like to analyze things, make plans, reason things through?
   Rating: 6 5 4 3 2 1 0

6. *Interpersonal*: How much of a "social being" are you? How important are other people to you? Do you gravitate to people? Do you desire intimacy with others?
   Rating: 6 5 4 3 2 1 0

7. *Drugs/Biology*: Are you healthy and health conscious? Do you take good care of your body and physical health? Do you avoid overeating, ingestion of unnecessary drugs, excessive amounts of alcohol, and exposure to other substances that may be harmful?
   Rating: 6 5 4 3 2 1 0

plores the meaning and relevance of each rating. In couples therapy, when husband and wife each fill out a Structural Profile, various differences and areas of potential incompatibility are readily discerned. With couples, it is also useful to have them rate how they think their spouse would depict them. This metacommunication usually provides additional inputs that can be put to good effect. Furthermore, it is also useful to compare the way a person rates himself or herself with the way he or she rates his or her spouse.

When necessary, the multimodal therapist may call for standardized tests and additional diagnostic and assessment procedures (in the same technically eclectic spirit as a therapeutic method may be employed), but the mainstay of multimodal assessment centers on Modality Profiles and Structural Profiles.

TREATMENT APPLICABILITY

The entire content of DSM-III can be shown to intersect to some extent with the multimodal armamentarium. The range and flexibility of this orientation renders it applicable to almost every problem that people bring to psychotherapeutic practitioners. When primary biological interventions are indicated, the adjunctive use of psychological techniques across the other six modalities tends to enhance treatment outcomes and follow-ups (Lazarus, 1981, 1985). The point about multimodal assessment is that it encompasses a broad range of symptoms, dysfunctions, deficits, and relationship problems.

The range of problems addressed by multimodal therapy (with varying degrees of success) includes anxiety states, phobias, depression, obsessive–compulsive disorders, alcohol abuse, obesity, sexual dysfunctions, marital discord, pain, anorexia nervosa, somatization disorders, schizophrenia, several children's disorders, post-traumatic stress disorder, insomnia, shyness, and various habit disorders. In addition, the principles and techniques of multimodal therapy cut across distinctions of schools and settings, so that multimodal methods are relevant to sex therapy, couples therapy, family therapy, and group therapy. Multimodal assessment and therapy have been applied to hospitalized psychiatric patients (Brunell & Young, 1982), and to an entire clinical service delivery unit (Roberts, Jackson, & Phelps, 1980). The multimodal orientation was selected as the best framework to meet the challenges of assisting the nondisclosing black client (Ridley, 1984), and the multimodal format was even shown to be relevant to the aftermath of community disasters (Sank, 1979).

The foregoing list would appear to suggest that apart from such recalcitrant populations as hard-core drug addicts, encrusted character disorders, grossly inadequate personality disorders, and one or two other malignant psychiatric dysfunctions, the multimodal practitioner will handle virtually every aspect of psychopathology with ease and alacrity. In fact, a puzzling problem has been that certain "easy problems" remain unresponsive to our best efforts despite the absence of serious psychological or biological dysfunctions. For example, certain people with simple phobias did not respond to treatment; others with mild anxiety or depression (who appeared to be eminently treatable) were minimally helped. Yet it is difficult to state exactly what specific types of clients are not helped by multimodal therapy. Clearly, when a definite mismatch is evident between client and therapist (e.g., in terms of clients' expectations, their respective "personalities," or similar relationship variables) unfavorable outcomes or premature termination are likely.

When a multimodal practitioner's assessment of a client reveals major biological disturbances that are amenable to somatic interventions, referral to a biologically sophisticated psychiatrist for neuroleptic medication and other drug treatments is a matter of course. Similarly, if the multimodal assessment points to the need for extensive biofeedback therapy, referral to an expert in this area would be a probable recommendation. Failures are minimized by a strong willingness to use teamwork and cross-referrals, and by explicitly seeking second and third opinions when doubts arise. Nevertheless, failures do occur.

In examining the reasons for failures, we have not been able to single out specific problems, nosological categories, or particular patient populations that consistently prove refractory (other than those listed in the previous paragraph with which therapists of all persuasions are equally ineffective). At times, one can offer no more than the lame and obvious comment that some people simply seem to be unreachable and remain intractable. In other cases, one can pinpoint more definite reasons; for example, someone in the client's network is undermining or sabotaging the therapy, or there may be evidence that the client is receiving far too many secondary gains to relinquish his or her maladaptive behavior. One might also mention that there are some highly accomplished "passive-resisters" who derive an enormous sense of power or gratification from the therapist's frustration.

Earnest attempts to match the client to the type of therapist and therapy that he or she seems most likely to profit from, also tend to promote success rather than failure. This raises a significant question. If a client's problems and expectancies call for a supportive, essentially nondirective treatment style—the provision of a caring relationship and little else—is this "multimodal therapy?" If biofeedback and hypnosis appear to be the major treatments of choice in a given case, is this "multimodal therapy?" The multimodal orientation is an approach rather than a system. The BASIC I.D. assessment permits the clinician to pinpoint the types of interventions that are most likely to be of genuine help in each instance. Whether or not the practitioner who carries out the multimodal assessment will perform the necessary treatments depends on his or her technical armamentarium. Ideally, a multimodal therapist is as broadly trained as possible—able to work with individuals, couples, families, and groups and well-versed in specific behavioral, affective, sensory, imagery, cognitive, interpersonal, and somatic techniques—although most somatic interventions require medical training (see Lazarus, 1981, for a glossary of 39 most frequently used techniques). Nevertheless, although one may be competent in a particular area or with a specific technique, some clients require a level of expertise that calls for referral to a specialist.

For example, I was consulted by a young man with a myriad of problems whose overriding symptoms were extreme tension. "I'm tight as a drum," he would say. Despite my best efforts at deep muscle relaxation training augmented by imagery, meditation, and EMG biofeedback procedures, his degree of tension remained unchanged. Referral to a "bioenergetic analyst" who applied much more heroic sensory exercises to "pierce his armor" proved effective, while I simultaneously worked on his dysfunctional beliefs and interpersonal deficits. Again, technical eclecticism encouraged me to draw on a discipline whose theoretical underpinnings I totally reject, but whose sensory techniques can prove effective in specific instances.

TREATMENT STRUCTURE

The various Multimodal Therapy Institutes (situated in New York, Illinois, Pennsylvania, Ohio, and Virginia at present) have tastefully and comfortably furnished waiting rooms and offices to maximize the "placebo effect." Soft background music from FM radio stations or cassette tapes in the waiting and reception areas are common. Receptionists are informed that they play a crucial role in setting the interpersonal ambience and emotional tone for putting each client at ease. They are told to offer tea or other beverages if clients are early or if the therapist is running overtime. They are schooled to be sure that their telephone manner is tolerant, polite, and patient. A friendly, unharried atmosphere is essential to offset the tensions and anxieties that many clients experience while waiting for their sessions.

An attempt is made to create a homelike atmosphere—the consulting rooms are carpeted and many have indirect adjustable lighting. They are relatively soundproof and have books, artwork, and plants. Comfortable chairs are carefully selected; usually a couch or a recliner (especially for relaxation and hypnosis purposes) is part of the office furniture. Most of the therapists prefer no desk between themselves and the client. Many clients are encouraged to tape-record each session and to study the recordings as a homework assignment between meetings. Consequently, I encourage my colleagues to make sure that there are accessible electrical outlets and a supply of blank cassettes on hand.

Although most of the meetings take place in the therapist's office, the flexibility of the multimodal approach leaves open a variety of other settings. On occasion, it may be helpful to shift the locus of therapy outside of the office, such as outdoor walking sessions or a session in a park, or, under certain circumstances, a home visit by the therapist. The use of ancillary personnel is also often useful. Thus, parents, teachers, nurses, psychiatric aides, and other paraprofessional volunteers may expedite several *in vivo* excursions, provide reinforcement for adaptive responses, and offer useful modeling experiences.

The typical frequency and length of sessions is once a week for approximately an hour. Generally, 50–60 minutes is sufficient time for client and therapist to review the week's events, to focus on specific problems, to implement new techniques, and to develop relevant homework assignments. Flexibility is essential in these matters. Some clients have an attention span that seldom exceeds 30 minutes, and they may fare far better being seen twice a week for half-hour sessions. Others do best with 90-minute sessions. Initially, some clients who are in various crisis situations may benefit from two or three hour-long sessions a week until the more critical events die down. I have seen many clients for whom one 60-minute session every two weeks proved ideal. Some have preferred what physicians call PRN ("as needed") appointments and have tended to call for a session once a month or even less often.

While some clients have received time-limited therapy, this has usually been due to external circumstances; for example, the client was leaving the area after a specified period. In my view, time-limited therapy across the board seems arbitrary. It is very difficult to predict how much time a particular individual is likely to require before deriving significant benefits. Temperamentally and ethically I favor short-term therapy, but on many occasions, clients have indicated that they were in no great hurry to conclude therapy. The average number of sessions is about 25 (n = 210) but the range extends from one to over 200 in a few cases.

Fees are on a sliding scale and depend entirely on the client's socioeconomic position and insurance coverage. I think that most of my associates follow my example of treating at least a couple of clients without any fee or for a nominal $1 or $5 a session. It is not my policy to charge for sessions that are missed or cancelled, unless this behavior is a clear-cut pattern. I feel strongly opposed to charging for services not rendered!

We have found it unwise to see the same client in group therapy and individually. Here, the inclination is to save those embarrassing and affectively laden issues for the easier one-on-one situation. Nevertheless, there appear to be no untoward effects when treating couples conjointly and individually, and when combining other therapy modalities such as individual therapy plus family therapy. Multimodal therapy places particular emphasis on the identification of appropriate treatment goals, and calls for a broad repertoire of techniques and an especially high level of flexibility.

TREATMENT SPECIFICITY AND MATCHING

Technique selection commences with the most obvious and logical procedures. By ascertaining what clients have found to be unsuccessful in the past, one may avoid problem-engendering pseudosolutions. Although it is necessary to avoid push-button panaceas, it is also necessary to overcome any penchant for making straightforward problems needlessly complicated. The selection of techniques is probably the least difficult aspect of multimodal therapy. The BASIC I.D. analysis takes vague, general, and diffuse problems (unhappiness, depression, anxiety, family conflicts, etc.) and reduces them to specific, discrete, and interactive difficulties. Thereafter, the selection of techniques is usually straightforward. In the final analysis, successful therapy depends on what techniques are selected, how they are implemented, and by whom they are delivered.

If a client is timid and unassertive, "assertiveness training" will be implemented; if she or he is tense, "relaxation therapy" will be applied; if faulty cognitions and dysfunctional beliefs abound, the "correction of misconceptions" will be a priority. If obsessive–compulsive disorders are part of the clinical picture, "response prevention and flooding techniques" will be introduced (Steketee, Foa, & Grayson, 1982). When phobias undermine the client's adaptive functioning, some form of "exposure"—imaginal and/or in vivo—will be called for. Even among psychodynamically oriented authorities, there is some consensus that behavioral procedures are the preferred treatments for sexual problems such as impotence, premature ejaculation, and orgasmic dysfunction (LoPiccolo & LoPiccolo, 1978; Leiblum & Pervin, 1980). Marital dysfunction will usually call for training procedures aimed at teaching more positive and productive interpersonal behaviors (e.g., Jacobson & Margolin, 1979). A person in the manic phase of a bipolar depressive disorder will often require lithium under the direction of a biologically sophisticated psychiatrist.

The major emphasis in the foregoing paragraph is that there are specific therapies for specific problems. From a multimodal perspective, although certain techniques (such as some form of exposure in the treatment of agoraphobia) are a *sine qua non* for effective outcomes, it is still necessary to cover the BASIC I.D. to ensure stable results. Moreover, the way the necessary techniques are explained to the client, their manner of application and their style of presentation (i.e., the artistic components) will determine their overall effectiveness.

Multimodal therapists attempt to reach a wide range of clients via their therapeutic flexibility and versatility. They eschew any unitary mode of approach. Thus, the therapist who exudes warmth and empathy with everyone will offend, or at least prove less effective with, clients who prefer a business-like, distant, or formal interaction. One remains constantly on the alert for individual and personalistic differences. Despite these caveats, impasses sometimes arise. Clearly, if the therapist's personality and approach do not jibe with the client's fundamental expectancies, treatment is unlikely to prove especially beneficial. Treatment outcomes often depend on a reasonable degree of similarity between the client's BASIC I.D. and the therapist's BASIC I.D. For example, a therapist whose Structural Profile reveals especially high self-ratings in cognitive and behavioral modes (thinkers and doers) may have problems understanding clients who are predominantly affective and imagery reactors (emotional dreamers). Still more significant are the tensions and misunderstandings that may arise when client and therapist come from divergent cultural backgrounds and/or have opposing political, religious, and other ideologies. When inappropriate matching results in the absence of rapport, it often makes sense to refer the client to a more compatible resource, rather than try to "work through" the difficulties.

On occasion, educated guesses based purely on "gut reactions" may be used to determine to whom a client should be referred. In most instances, the reasons for referring clients to one's colleagues are not based on intuitive or subjective inferences. It may be evident that a female therapist will do better than a male; a Spanish-speaking therapist is needed; someone younger or someone older may be required; someone highly skilled in handling drug-related problems is made to order; and so forth.

In addition to the foregoing, the multimodal therapist has two specific procedures available to him or her for determining technique selection—the use of *Second-Order BASIC I.D. Assessments*, and a method called *tracking*.

Second-Order BASIC I.D. Assessments

When treatment impasses arise, it is often helpful to subject a problematic item on the initial Modality Profile to a more

TABLE 4

Behavior:	I would report directly to the Vice President.
	I would move to a different office (larger).
	I would spend more time in meetings.
Affect:	I would feel more conspicuous (the chief executives would be watching me).
	I would feel proud of myself.
Sensation:	At times, very tense, very guarded, often skipping lunch break, but also excited in a positive sense.
Imagery:	I picture myself impressing the Board Members.
	I picture my father dying and my brothers blaming me.

detailed inquiry in terms of behavior, affect, sensation, imagery, cognition, interpersonal factors, and drugs or biological considerations. This recursive application of the BASIC I.D. to itself adds depth and detail to problematic items on the overall Modality Profile. Thus, one of several specific fears listed by a generally anxious client was that he felt strong trepidation at the prospect of being promoted at work. Friends in whom he had confided uttered cliches about his "fear of success," but he remained puzzled since he viewed himself as "ambitious" and a "go getter." By analyzing his reaction through a Second-Order BASIC I.D., the items emerged as shown in Table 4.

There was no need to proceed any further with the second-order assessment. The last item under "Imagery" called for closer scrutiny and fit into a convoluted pattern of reasoning that proceeded more or less as follows:

The youngest son, with three older brothers, the client had already exceeded his own expectations regarding his station in life. He was the only college graduate in a blue-collar family, and he sensed real or imaged envy from his siblings, especially his oldest brother. A rebellious child, he had a turbulent relationship with his father, who disapproved of his academic aspirations and often accused him of wanting to look down on the entire family. Nevertheless, he had "written his own script" and had obtained a liberal arts education instead of following the family tradition of becoming a tradesman. In part, he missed the comradery that his brothers had with each other and with their father, but he also felt superior to them—a feeling that was tainted with guilt.

All of this information had been obtained from the *Life History Questionnaire,* but only while focusing on the Second-Order BASIC I.D. did he realize to what extent additional achievements on his job symbolized the demise of his father and signaled total alienation from his siblings. This opened up a productive discussion of his entitlements and his family attachments and obligations and eventuated in a decision to "go full steam ahead." Thus, the systematic second-order assessment yielded a specific focus instead of the pat "fear of success" diagnosis. Later he said: "I knew I wasn't afraid of the added responsibility and new demands that would be placed on me, but I couldn't figure out what was holding me back." I also indicated that he may have adopted a standoffish attitude toward his family and recommended that he make deliberate overtures to participate with them in mutually enjoyable activities—bowling, family dinners, picnics, and other sporting events. The net result was decidedly positive. In this case a Second-Order BASIC I.D. rapidly brought to the fore some important issues that eluded other avenues of inquiry.

Tracking

A careful examination of the "firing order" of the different modalities is referred to as *tracking*. For example, some clients tend to generate negative emotions by dwelling first on aversive images (I) (e.g., pictures of dire consequences befalling them), followed by unpleasant sensations (S) (e.g., muscle tension and heart palpitations) to which they attach negative cognitions (C) (e.g., ideas about imminent cardiac arrest), culminating in maladaptive behavior (B) (e.g., unnecessary avoidance). A person who usually adheres to such an ISCB pattern (Imagery–Sensory–Cognitive–Behavioral) tends to require a different treatment sequence than say a CISB reactor (Cognitive–Imagery–Sensory–Behavior) or someone with yet a different firing order.

By tracking the precise sequence that results in an affective disturbance, one gains insight into the antecedent events that tend to generate various disturbed feelings. The client is also thereby shown how to intercede appropriately. Thus, someone with a SICA sequence (Sensation–Image–Cognition–Affect) might first be taught slow abdominal breathing and differential relaxation, followed by positive and coping images, whereas a CISA (Cognition–Image–Sensation–Affect) reactor would start with positive self-statements, rational disputation, and other cognitive restructuring techniques, followed by imagery. Only then would sensory techniques be introduced (biofeedback, relaxation, etc.). Clinical observations suggest that when one selects techniques that follow the client's habitual sequence, the therapeutic impact is greater.

TREATMENT INTERVENTIONS AND STRATEGIES

The emphasis on flexibility and specificity calls for the multimodal therapist to adopt a variety of treatment styles and structures. Unlike some clinicians (e.g., psychoanalysts, or Rogerian person-centered practitioners) who treat all their clients with essentially interpretive or nondirective methods, and unlike other systems that are basically directive (e.g., behavior therapy, or rational–emotive therapy), multimodal therapy calls for a much more precise tailoring of the therapeutic climate to fit each client's idiosyncratic needs and expectancies. With some clients it is counterproductive to offer more than a sympathetic ear; with others, unless therapy is highly structured, active, and directive, significant progress will not be made. As mentioned in the section on "Patient Assessment," the decision to adopt a particular style and the way to determine the type of liaison that will facilitate meaningful gains stem from certain answers on the *Multimodal Life History Questionnaire,* and from clues derived during the initial interview.

Quite frequently, clients are rather explicit. A 32-year-old sixth-grade teacher stated:

As a teacher, I approach psychotherapy as a form of education—I don't want to be spoonfed, but do want to be taught, shown how to achieve certain things. . . . My previous therapist never showed me how to do some of the things I know I should do. Every question was fed back to me as a question—I got no answers.

She responded most gratifyingly to techniques such as behavior rehearsal and assertiveness and relaxation training; she kept quantitative records of specific behaviors, read prescribed books, and made significant gains in twelve sessions over three months of "behavior therapy." During this time, I was seeing another woman with very similar complaints, but in her case, she took unkindly to the very structure that proved so effective with the school teacher. The reasons were soon apparent. Whereas the teacher had certain response *deficits,* the other woman had all the instrumental skills in her repertoire, but she demonstrated several basic *conflicts,* and she required the opportunity to develop greater clarity concerning her entitlements. Thus, the treatment trajectory in the latter case was entirely "insight oriented."

There are clients for whom, as Schofield (1964) pointed out many years ago, psychotherapy is essentially the purchase of friendship. Indeed, for some, the opportunity to have good conversations, or merely to chit-chat with a person who listens and responds intelligently, goes far toward alleviating anomie. The client–therapist relationship is the soil that enables specific techniques to take root, but in some instances "relationship therapy" is both necessary and sufficient. In my experience, however, such cases are in the minority. If measurable gains are to be derived, client and therapist have to *work*—not merely *relate*. It is generally more edifying and stimulating to discuss love, politics, sex, religion, and existential realities than to carry out relaxation training, desensitization, contingency management, and so forth. It may be fascinating to plumb the depths of a client's imagination, or to examine the subtle nuances of his or her "object relations." But what is fascinating is not necessarily helpful. Moreover, the use of "homework" and in vivo excursions are often essential for promoting generalization and maintenance of treatment gains (Lazarus & Fay, 1984).

The most successful clients are those who do not deliberately lie, distort, or withhold information; who attend sessions regularly; are willing to practice relaxation when appropriate; role play; study prescribed reading materials; keep activity charts; and carry out other assignments between sessions. Nevertheless, many people are inclined to resist efforts by others to modify their behavior. *Telling* a client to relax, imagine scenes, or to act more assertively is likely to foster some degree of opposition; *asking* for these performance-based responses is more likely to meet with cooperation.

Perhaps one of the most pernicious assumptions that many therapists embrace is that clients often do not want to get better. In some cases, the client may be receiving far too many secondary gains to relinquish certain maladaptive behaviors, but in most instances, when clients appear "resistant" it is likely that the therapist has failed to deal effectively with various special therapeutic problems (see Lazarus & Fay, 1982 for an extended discussion of this viewpoint). When resistances and blocks arise, seven questions should be addressed:

1. Is there inappropriate matching or absence of rapport?
2. Has the therapist failed to identify relevant antecedents and/or maintaining consequences?
3. Did the therapist overlook saboteurs in the client's social network by dwelling too heavily on intra-individual factors?
4. Has the therapist made too many blunders and perhaps used incorrect techniques?
5. Were the appropriate techniques incorrectly administered?
6. Does the client suffer from irreversible dysfunctions?
7. Is the desired outcome not valued highly enough by the client, so that he or she finds that the amount of effort needed to effect change is too costly?

These seven factors seem to cover the range of explanations for most treatment impasses. Note that while I consider it mainly the therapist's responsibility to inspire and to assist the client to take the necessary steps to effect change, I do not place the entire onus on the clinician.

Among the most common and most serious technical errors that a practitioner of any persuasion can commit is that of labeling a client and interacting with him or her in a pejorative manner. Quite often, a label (e.g., "hysterical," "schizophrenic," "borderline") becomes either an excuse and/or a reason for repeated failures and bizarre conduct. But even more damaging are those clinicians who overtly or covertly ridicule, blame, or exploit their clients. Indeed, one of the cardinal arts of effective therapy is the ability to express criticism in a supportive, constructive, and almost complimentary manner. Among my trainees, perhaps the most frequent shortcoming is their excessive need to make people change, and their haste to see results.

The foregoing points tie into the issue of termination. It is quite frequent for a client to terminate therapy when he or she is feeling and doing considerably better—despite more than residual dysfunctions in several areas of his or her life. It is not my practice to discourage clients from discontinuing therapy unless I have good reason to suspect that by so doing, serious consequences may result. It is fairly common for clients to undergo several different courses of therapy, preferring to deal with different problems at different times (and perhaps with different therapists). Typically, when most of the problems on the client's BASIC I.D. have been successfully attenuated, if not eliminated, termination is an obvious next step. Weekly sessions may then be scheduled every two weeks, then once in every three or four weeks. In some cases, booster or check-up sessions are made at three-month intervals. In my experience, it is rare to find a client wishing to cling dependently and unnecessarily while prolonging treatment beyond a point of diminishing returns.

THERAPIST BEHAVIORS

The principle of individuality speaks to the fact that there is no unitary way to approach peoples' problems. If a number of clinicians, unfamiliar with me or my therapeutic orientation, were to observe me with different clients, their views and conclusions about my methods and school identification would differ considerably. One might say: "I think he's a gestalt therapist because he relied so heavily on sensory and imagery techniques." With a different client, another might venture: "He seems pretty behavioral to me, having used desensitization, behavior rehearsal, and assertiveness training." Yet another observer who had seen me with yet a different client might say: "He's a Rogerian through and through. All he did for the entire session was reflect back the client's affective reactions." Someone else might say: "He reminded me of Albert Ellis as he actively disputed the client's dysfunctional beliefs." It is even possible that someone might conclude: "He's a psychoanalytic therapist because most of the hour was spent listening to and making occasional comments about childhood events."

Again, it must be emphasized that, when drawing upon Freud, Rogers, Ellis, Perls, or any other personage, one need not accept any of their theories. Technical eclecticism draws on all and any effective techniques without necessarily subscribing to the theories or systems that gave rise to them. The therapist who prefers to learn how to apply one or two procedures extremely well (rather than using ten or twenty reasonably well) will probably not be attracted to multimodal therapy. Clinically, there is support for the contention that it is usually better to cover seven areas fairly thoroughly than to deal with only one or two modalities in extreme detail (Lazarus, 1981, 1985).

Unlike psychoanalysts, who eschew self-disclosure because their theory demands detachment and distance for the facilitation of transference, multimodal therapists have no such proscriptions. It is clear that self-disclosure often tends to enhance the therapeutic relationship and proves especially valuable when using modeling and behavior rehearsal techniques (see

Rimm & Masters, 1979, pp. 119–120). Nevertheless, as with all procedures, some clients respond positively, others neutrally, and a few react negatively to therapist self-disclosure. There appears to be no way to avoid a certain degree of trial and error when making these determinations. I have at times regretted sharing a personal frailty with a client after having it used against me, but one can capitalize on such events by pointing out their interpersonal significance to the client. "Perhaps you have problems keeping friends because you batter them with their own shortcomings."

I was treating a financially successful accountant who reacted negatively to my statement: "Let me tell you about a time when that happened to me." He pointed at me and said: "I haven't come here to learn about you. I'm paying good money to learn about myself." Of course, this served as an important stimulus to examine his basic ideas of give-and-take. At the opposite end of the continuum are those individuals who appear to need therapist self-disclosure as a sign of trust, confidence, and caring. Similarly, there are clients who prefer a formal, if not somewhat distant, and decidedly business-like relationship. Only surnames and titles are used. And then there are those who respond to an egalitarian friendship-type of interaction where first names or nicknames go hand-in-hand with humor, informality, and even socializing in some instances.

The principal clues for determining the appropriate level of involvement/intimacy with clients are derived from "countertransference" factors (there are some people with whom there is instant rapport, a common sense of identity and compatibility) and from the general ambience that develops as therapy progresses. In 25 years, having seen about 2,000 clients, I have made six close friendships, and have enjoyed frequent social contacts with no more than 20 former clients. I adhere to only a couple of absolute taboos—any form of exploitation and any type of sexual involvement.

MECHANISMS OF CHANGE

I would characterize most of my clients' suffering as due to one or more of the following:

1. Conflicting or ambivalent feelings and reactions
2. Misinformation
3. Missing information (includes skill deficits, ignorance, and naiveté)
4. Maladaptive habits (includes conditioned emotional reactions)
5. Interpersonal disturbances (e.g., undue dependency, misplaced affection, excessive antipathy)
6. Issues pertaining to low self-esteem
7. Biological dysfunctions.

The mechanisms or processes that produce change in therapy will depend on the specific factors responsible for clients' distress. When problems seem due to lacunae in the person's understanding of how historical events are influencing his or her current feelings and reactions, traditional "insight" is likely to be an important ingredient. A different form of "insight" prevails when a client recognizes the "firing order" that typically engenders anxiety or other negative emotional reactions. Yet a third form of "insight" follows the disputation of dysfunctional beliefs, the correction of misconceptions, and the educational impact of new information. Specific skill acquisition invariably opens new channels of communication, information, and self-understanding. Ultimately, most forms of therapy try to provide clients with a new way of seeing life, a different view of self and others, and with methods for combatting emotional

TABLE 5
Techniques and Ingredients of Multimodal Therapeutic Change

Technique/Ingredient	Example
BEHAVIOR	
Positive reinforcement, negative reinforcement, punishment	Contingent praise, time out, aversion therapy
Counterconditioning	Graded exposure, desensitization
Extinction	Flooding, massed practice responsive prevention
AFFECT	
Owning and accepting feelings	Bringing affect-laden material into awareness
Abreaction	Reliving painful emotions in the presence of a trusted ally
SENSATION	
Tension release	Relaxation, physical exercise, biofeedback
Sensory pleasuring	Sensate focus methods for sexual retraining
IMAGERY	
Coping images	Picturing self-achievement and self-control
Changes in self-image	More positive reactions to one's body and to other areas of functioning
COGNITION	
Greater awareness	Less ignorance and naivete, awareness of past-present linkages, awareness of how specific "firing orders" culminate in affective reactions
Cognitive restructuring	Less self-derogation, overgeneralization, dichotomous reasoning, categorical imperatives, non sequiturs
INTERPERSONAL	
Nonjudgmental acceptance	When clients are offered desiderata not usually available in social situations
Modeling	Therapist serving as a role model through selective self-disclosure and using deliberate modeling during role reversal exercises
Dispersing unhealthy collusions	Treating a family and changing counterproductive alliances
DRUGS/BIOLOGICAL	
Exercise and nutrition	
Substance use cessation	
Use of psychotropic medication when indicated	
Complete physical check-ups when warranted	

distress. Some of the main techniques and ingredients of psychotherapeutic change from a multimodal perspective are summarized in Table 5.

The mechanisms of change cannot be divorced from the person administering the particular procedures. The therapist's style and personality are integral to the treatment processes and outcomes. Highly successful therapists whom I have been privileged to know seem to share certain common characteristics. They all seem to possess a high and genuine respect for people, and tend to be essentially flexible and responsible individuals. They are nonjudgmental and firmly comitted to the view that infringement on the rights of others is to be strongly discouraged. They are generally warm, witty, funloving, articulate, and possess a good sense of humor. They practice what they preach and are authentic, congruent, and willing to reveal their shortcomings. As surgeons are apt to point out, it is the person wielding the scalpel who can use it as an instrument of destruction or healing. In psychotherapy, it is even more difficult to separate specific mechanisms and techniques from the person who administers them.

CASE EXAMPLE

Ted, a 32-year-old systems engineer complained of general anxiety and inter-mittent bouts of depression. He was particularly concerned about possibly losing his job and obsessed about it almost constantly. After graduation from college, he had obtained a good position with the firm for which he was still working; he had received substantial salary increases and three significant promotions in the ten years he had been with the company. Nevertheless, he felt that his job was always in jeopardy. Whereas he had found these problems manageable without seeking professional help, they had tended to escalate over the past two years following his marriage. His wife's pregnancy (although planned) finally "sent me through the roof!"

He had consulted two therapists. First, he saw a psychiatrist who prescribed a tricyclic antidepressant which Ted took for about a month. "It just gave me a dry mouth and blurred vision." Next, he saw a psychologist who employed "thought stopping" and "imaginal flooding" ("He had me imagining myself fired from work and ending up on welfare. . . . I couldn't see the point of it!"). After our initial interview, Ted filled out the *Multimodal Life History Questionnaire* and mailed it to me before his second session. The Modality Profile, as shown in Table 6, was drawn up.

The questionnaire also indicated that the client expected therapy to last no more than 3–6 months, and that he favored a

TABLE 6

Behavior:	Disorganized; leaves things to the last minute; "can't get out of bed in the mornings."
Affect:	Anxiety; intermittent depression.
Sensation:	Feels fatigued much of the time; experiences tension in his shoulders and jaws; bouts of dizziness; frequent headaches.
Imagery:	Images of failure; being laughed at; not coping.
Cognition:	Ruminates over negatives; catastrophic thinking; excessively achievement-oriented.
Interpersonal:	Feels too dependent on his wife; tends to be obsequious with his employers; basically reticent.
Drugs/Biology:	Frequent use of aspirin; smokes a pack of cigarettes a day; overeats; gets far too little exercise.

didactic and structured format. Consequently, during the second session, I emphasized that a change in his smoking, eating habits, and lack of physical exercise would have a significant impact on some of his emotional difficulties. He accepted the basic rationale that by improving his physical health, his emotional responses were likely to benefit in tandem. At my instigation, he joined a health club, attended a weekend "smoke-enders" workshop in the community, and read Fay's (1980) book on permanent weight control. Next, I focused on various relaxation techniques and abdominal breathing methods, and urged him to practice these procedures several times a day for 2–3 minute intervals. At my suggestion, he also underwent a thorough physical check-up.

Ted was particularly taken with my distinction between "parasitic" and "healthy" dependency, and concluded that his attachment to his wife fell into the latter category. We also discussed better time-management techniques, used cognitive disputation à la Ellis (1975) to point out that what he perceived as catastrophic was, at most, merely inconvenient. We engaged in dialogues on the importance of fun and the deemphasis of over-achievement. Through behavior rehearsal, we focused on assertiveness and other interpersonal skills. By the twelfth session, some three months into the therapy, Ted had made some significant gains. He certainly looked better, had lost weight, had quit smoking, and felt less fatigued. The one area in which he displayed zero progress was with his anticipatory anxieties about losing his job.

Following the use of "cognitive disputation," Ted acknowledged that he firmly believed that being fired or laid off from work was "very inconvenient" but hardly "terrible and dreadful." Nevertheless, his obsessive thoughts and undue fears remained as intrusive as ever. A Second-Order BASIC I.D. revealed a "right-brain"

pattern of imagery that seemed to account for his "resistance."

It transpired that Ted's maternal grandfather had lived with the family until his death when Ted was 10 years old. Ted described his grandfather as "a parasite" and indicated that he had been a burden on the family and was treated as an object of derision. He had been a successful mason and had worked for a construction company. However, during a time of economic depression, he lost his job and could find no other gainful employment. "I think that's when he fell apart and ended up being a nonperson." As Ted and I discussed the significance of his grandfather's unhappy plight, it became clear that Ted had somehow associated job loss with inevitable emotional dissipation leading to subhuman functioning. Despite his "left brain" or cognitive awareness of the utter irrationality of these perceptions, his nonverbal, indeed preverbal, "right brain" seemed to possess images of doom. Consequently, the focus of our meeting turned into "imagery therapy" (Lazarus, 1984).

In essence, while Ted was relaxed, with his eyes closed, sitting comfortably on a recliner, I had him picture a series of vivid images. He was to see himself losing his present job, seeking employment elsewhere, looking in the newspapers for possible jobs, contacting an employment agency. He was to see himself—unlike his grandfather—obtaining new employment, after receiving unemployment compensation if necessary. He would then lose his next job and have to go through the inconvenience of job hunting all over again. Nevertheless, in imagery, he was to practice seeing himself coping, picturing himself being distinctly different from his unfortunate grandfather, vividly seeing himself not falling apart.

During these imagery exercises, Ted recalled his grandfather's demise and remembered that for reasons unknown, it was extremely upsetting to him. "It wasn't as if I was fond of that old codger," he said. I had him picture the following scenario:

"Imagine yourself going into a Time Machine and traveling back in time to the day of your grandfather's funeral. Out of the future comes 32-year-old Ted to comfort and educate little 10-year-old Ted. Please nod your head when you can picture 32-year-old Ted walking up to 10-year-old Ted. . . . Now little Ted senses something very special about this 32-year-old man who comes up to him. Obviously, he can't verbalize that this man is none other than himself 22 years into the future, but he has a close affinity for this man. Nod your head if you can visualize that scene. . . . Now you explain to little Ted that he is not like his grandfather, that he is a completely different person, that he will never follow in his grandfather's footsteps." As a homework assignment, Ted was asked to practice the foregoing images several times daily.

The full course of multimodal therapy lasted over four months and extended over 18 sessions. Ted was not a difficult client. He was cooperative, intelligent, competent, and willing to change. Nevertheless, let it be recalled that two previous therapists had failed to make significant inroads. Interestingly, about 10 months post-therapy, Ted called to report that he had in fact lost his job. The company was relocating out of state and Ted decided to seek other employment "which took longer than I had imagined, but I didn't fall apart." He had obtained a good position with managerial and engineering duties that he found more stimulating than the purely technical position he had held in the past. His treatment gains seemed to be well maintained.

RESEARCH ON THE APPROACH

Multimodal therapy is an approach that endeavors to incorporate "state of the art" research and findings into its framework.

It is not intended as yet another "system" to be added to the hundreds in existence. Rather, it is an approach that attempts to be at the cutting edge of clinical effectiveness by continually scanning the field for better assessment and treatment methods. The majority of techniques currently employed within this discipline come from the field of cognitive behavior therapy because the evidence (e.g., Rachman & Wilson, 1980) points to the efficacy of behavioral and cognitive–behavioral procedures over most (but not all) other interventions. In time, if other schools of thought spawn superior techniques for particular problems, our technically eclectic stance will permit their immediate adoption into the multimodal armamentarium.

The multimodal orientation has several unique assessment operations:

1. The construction of Modality Profiles
2. The use of Structural Profiles
3. Recourse to Second-Order BASIC I.D. analyses
4. Tracking the "firing order" of sequential modalities

Whether or not these methods augment the clinician's overall effectiveness is an empirical question. Attempts to obtain funding for the necessary controlled research have not been fruitful. Nevertheless, a "stock-taking mentality" (stemming, no doubt, from observing my father, uncles, and older brother reviewing and taking stock of the merchandise in their small retail businesses) has led me to keep careful inventories. Over the years, I have used several outcome and follow-up measures (Lazarus, 1971, 1981). A three-year follow-up of 20 "complex cases" who had completed a course of multimodal therapy (e.g., people suffering from extreme agoraphobia, pervasive anxiety and panic, obsessive–compulsive rituals, or enmeshed marital or family problems) showed that fourteen maintained their gains or had made additional progress without further therapy.

A recent survey of 100 clients who had not responded to at least three previous therapists before seeking multimodal therapy (thus excluding the "placebo reactors" and those common-or-garden variety "neurotics" who require little more than a good listener, or a touch of empathy) revealed that 61 achieved objective and unequivocal benefits (i.e., quantifiable *decreases* in compulsive behaviors, depressive reactions, panic attacks, marital and family disputes, sexual inadequacy, avoidance behaviors; and corresponding *increases* in assertive responses, work-related achievements, and prosocial behaviors). Many of these clients were considered "intractable" by their former therapists.

In terms of overall statistics, during the past seven or eight years, more than 75% of the people who have consulted me have achieved their major treatment goals. Data from other practitioners who consider themselves "multimodal therapists" are in keeping with my own results.

The most ambitious research undertaking involving multimodal therapy is a study conducted in Holland (Kwee, 1984). The subjects were 44 obsessive–compulsive clients and 40 severely phobic clients who were treated in a general psychiatric hospital. Approximately 70% had been suffering from their disorders for more than four years and 90% had previously undergone some form of psychiatric treatment. Kwee administered various process measures at intake, admission, after 12 weeks, at discharge, and at follow-up nine months later. Follow-up findings for the obsessive–compulsive clients ($n=31$) revealed that 64% were significantly improved, 26% were unchanged, and 10% had deteriorated. Among the phobic clients ($n=31$), 55% showed significant improvement, 39% were unchanged, and 6% had deteriorated. In all instances where deterioration was evident, Kwee was able to demonstrate unbroken levels of primary and/or secondary gain.

Rosenblad (1985) administered Structural Profiles to distressed and nondistressed couples. Her most significant finding was that among the dysfunctional couples, the spouses tended to be incorrect in the way they estimated that the other person would rate them (i.e., their metacommunications were faulty). This was particularly true in the Sensory and Interpersonal modalities. In their Sensory estimates, the discrepancies were such that $P<.02$ for wives, $P<.03$ for husbands, and for husbands + wives, $P<.003$. With regard to their Interpersonal estimates, $P<.05$ for wives, $P<.02$ for husbands, and $P<.003$ for husbands + wives.

At the time of writing, a study is being designed to test inter-rater reliability in drawing up a Modality Profile after observing an intake interview on video tape.

CLINICAL TRAINING

It is a historical fact that most of our present-day eclectic therapists were trained fairly thoroughly in one or two specific disciplines. Thereafter, for various reasons, they branched out into other directions. Is it necessary to achieve a degree of expertise at one or two systems before venturing into other domains? Is prior competence in some/many/all therapy systems required to become an effective multimodal practitioner?

Since I know of no formal research or systematic studies that have been conducted to answer these questions, I shall confine my remarks to the actual training that has been delivered to the personnel who work at the various Multimodal Therapy Institutes, and to those who function as independent practitioners. My base of teaching and research since 1972 has been at Rutgers University where, since the founding of the Graduate School of Applied and Professional Psychology in 1974, I have offered formal courses and supervision in multimodal therapy. Most of my trainees have been enrolled in the Doctor of Psychology (Psy.D.) program, which has an eclectic curriculum. Students select "tracks" (e.g., behavioral, psychodynamic, or family-systems) but are required to take introductory courses in all three disciplines. Thus, all Rutgers University graduates who now function as multimodal therapists have been exposed to several disciplines and different areas of inquiry.

In training multimodal clinicians, I place heavy emphasis on a data-oriented base, one that stresses research-awareness. This is not meant to imply that any given individual can be equally at home in the laboratory and the clinic, nor does it mean that one should be both a contributing scientist and a practicing therapist. What I consider of paramount importance is that those who practice multimodal therapy be trained to understand the workings of science, to appreciate the meaning and value of the scientific method, and thus to become critical consumers of research—not necessarily researchers per se (see Peterson, 1976).

The ideal training program, in my opinion, would be one in which, in addition to a sound grounding in psychology as a science and a profession, the trainee is exposed to additional social and biological sciences. I look with favor on graduate students who bring to our program a background in biology and psychology as majors, with courses in sociology, anthropology, and the history and philosophy of science. Their graduate training, which consists of formal courses in developmental psychology, psychopathology, tests and measurements, interviewing techniques, research design, and a wide range of electives, should have a built-in *apprenticeship model*. In other words, the opportunity to work closely with expert therapists—to observe them in action, to sit in on cases, to assist as cotherapists—to receive formal supervision—must be carefully written into the training program.

Training in ethics is also important. Allied to ethics is the need to impart genuine respect for the dignity of the client. Although many therapists pay lip service to the fact that human rights and dignity should not be compromised, the very theories to which they subscribe may demand a pejorative outlook (Wile, 1981). Therapists who believe that they are superior to their clients will obviously deliver very different messages than those who view all human beings as different, indeed unique, but equal. Some clients are prone to elevate the therapist to godlike eminence; the therapist who perpetuates this, or much worse, believes it, is likely to prove noxious rather than helpful.

In addition to the published material on multimodal assessment and therapy per se, I presently require advanced trainees to read two books most thoroughly: Corsini's *Handbook of Innovative Psychotherapies* (1981) and Corsini's *Current Psychotherapies,* Third Edition (1984). These two books present over 75 different therapeutic approaches in considerable detail. Of course, the capacity to be able to read critically is a sine qua non for the effective application of technical eclecticism!

Corsini (1981) lists over 240 different forms of psychotherapy; Herink (1980) described over 250 different therapies in use today. Given this knowledge explosion, how can any clinician master all the theories and techniques? It is not necessary to peruse volumes and tomes to determine whether or not a given theoretical system is viable. Ask only for the fundamental premises on which the system rests. Some years ago, at a social gathering, I was conversing with a clinician who waxed eloquently about the problems of adulthood being derived not from childhood encounters but from the agonies of puberty and adolescence. This fundamental premise seemed to warrant further discussion until it became clear that the gentleman was referring to pubertal crises in a previous life! Inasmuch as I regard reincarnation as outside the confines of scientific discourse, it was not necessary for me to listen any further to his theoretical propositions nor to read the tomes he might have written on the subject.

Useful techniques may be garnered from any source and, if necessary, totally divorced from their origins. Nevertheless, even here, despite the plethora of methods that have been devised to mitigate psychological suffering, there is no need for panic. As a "technique collector," I employ fewer than four dozen—despite my familiarity with perhaps several hundred. First, many different techniques are not really different—they are essentially variations on a theme. Second, a scientifically minded technical eclectic typically requires "proof of effectiveness" before incorporating a specific procedure into his or her repertoire. This cuts down a sizeable number of esoteric and way-out modes of treatment! (At the very least, one would generally not use a technique of unproven effectiveness that could not readily be understood by one's theoretical framework. Thus, when I experimented with techniques such as The Deserted Island Fantasy (Lazarus, 1971, 1981) and when I tried out Time Projection for the treatment of certain types of depression (Lazarus, 1968), I did so, not because these procedures had been shown to be effective, but because they did not conflict with the learning theory base to which I subscribe).

The multimodal position is that by enabling clients to make changes across their BASIC I.D. dysfunctions, a salubrious outcome is more likely than it would be if only one, two, or three dimensions were treated. Nevertheless, one does not have to be a B.F. Skinner in the behavioral modality, an Albert Ellis in the cognitive modality, a Harry Stack Sullivan in the interpersonal modality, to practice effective multimodal therapy. The training calls for as much breadth as the individual clinician can muster. Regardless of one's level of expertise, it is not possible for any clinician to be therapeutic for and with all clients. The goal is adequacy—never perfection!

How important is personal therapy? Obviously, if personal problems are such that they may interfere with the successful implementation of multimodal assessment and therapy, it is necessary to remedy the situation. During one of my internship programs, it was obligatory for all trainees to be in therapy. I consulted a therapist who regarded himself as eclectic, with a view to gaining better self-understanding. In retrospect, this was largely a waste of time! The hours (and the money) spent in therapy would have been put to far better use had I taken tennis lessons, joined a health club, or learned how to ski! Several of my colleagues who practice multimodal therapy have never received personal therapy. Unlike the psychoanalysts, I do not regard personal therapy as mandatory for all trainees. Nevertheless, while supervising certain students, I have recognized areas of "psychopathology" in them that would benefit from treatment, and in these instances, I have not only strongly recommended that they seek therapy, but have helped them find the "right" therapist.

FUTURE DIRECTIONS AND NEEDS

Norcross (Chapter 1, this volume) has eloquently emphasized the need for greater rigor, for broader integrative theoretical bases, for clearly operationalized and concretized therapist-decision-making processes, and for a systematic prescriptive eclecticism. He has also stressed the need for an objective body of actual operations and client–therapist interactions across many conditions. The multimodal viewpoints are entirely in accord with these worthy objectives.

To my mind, one of the greatest gaps in our knowledge is the question of etiology, of our need to identify basic causative factors that lead to psychological dysfunction. In a broad sense, we are products of the interplay among our genetic endowment, our physical environment, and our social learning history. To state that *learning* plays a central role in the development and resolution of our emotional problems is to communicate very little. Exactly how, when, where, and why are certain movements, habits, responses, expectancies, values, outlooks, insights, fantasies, and interpersonal patterns acquired? We all recognize that conflicts, traumata, and other adverse environmental factors play a role in psychological disturbances, but this is far too global. Psychodynamic theorists have endeavored to pinpoint the developmental processes that enter into our "object relations" and fuel our emotional fires, but they have couched their findings in terms that are untestable and often unprovable by any accepted scientific criterion. While in many therapeutic areas, effective remedies have existed, and diseases have been cured without any understanding of etiological factors, ultimately, a truly effective theory of treatment will have to rest on a proper theory of the origins of psychological disturbance.

Again, let me underscore that the aim of eclecticism is not to produce such tremendous openness to every new development that one falls prey to each new fad. This type of hodgepodge is no better than those who adhere with dogma, narrowness, and rigidity to a particular orthodoxy. Greater specificity is required—we need tests and measurements that predict responses to specific treatments, and instruments with highly focused predictive validity and high reliability for clinical decision making. Instead of having rela-

tively inexperienced therapists and trainees serving as research models, we need to study in detail what outstanding experts really do (not what they say they do). This ties into the need to comprehend the true nature of iatrogenic harm and negative outcome in psychotherapy (Mays & Franks, 1985). A most provocative statement is that only 20% of therapists are truly competent (Zilbergeld, 1983).

There are already several factions in existence that are addressing each of the foregoing points. Within the next decade, some much-needed answers are likely to result. I think that one major advance will be in the development of complete treatment plans that factor in each client's idiosyncrasies and carefully weigh items such as choice of treatment setting, orientation, format, frequency and duration of sessions, choice of somatic treatments, and ways of combining treatments (cf. Frances, Clarkin, & Perry, 1984). When specific treatment selection becomes more of a science and less of an art, our field will truly take a quantum leap. And in my view, without systematic eclecticism, this goal will never be reached. Those who adhere to particular theories and specific schools of treatment cannot possibly address the need for *differential therapeutics*.

Halleck (1978) pointed out: "We will achieve the goal of multi-dimensional treatment more quickly to the extent that we approach our patients with open minds and a relentless commitment to study and confront the complexities of human behavior" (p. 501). The multimodal framework is eclectic without being fragmented; it provides integration without a futile rapprochement of conflicting theories; and it calls for broad-based clinical training without sacrificing "depth."

REFERENCES

Bandura, A. (1969). *Principles of behavior modification.* New York: Holt, Rinehart, & Winston.

Bandura, A. (1977). *Social learning theory*. Englewood Cliffs, N.J.: Prentice-Hall.

Brunell, L. F., & Young, W. T. (Eds.). (1982). *A multimodal handbook for a mental hospital: Designing specific treatments for specific problems.* New York: Springer.

Buckley, W. (1967). *Modern systems research for the behavioral scientist.* Chicago: Aldine.

Corsini, R. J. (Ed.). (1981). *Handbook of innovative psychotherapies.* New York: Wiley.

Corsini, R. J. (Ed.). (1984). *Current psychotherapies* (3rd ed.). Itasca, IL.: Peacock.

Ellis, A. (1975). *How to live with a neurotic, at home and at work.* New York: Crown.

Eysenck, H. J. (1970). A mish-mash of theories. *International Journal of Psychiatry, 9,* 140–146.

Fay, A. (1980). *The invisible diet.* New York: Manor.

Frances, A., Clarkin, J., & Perry, S. (1984). *Differential therapeutics in psychiatry: The art and science of treatment selection.* New York: Brunner/Mazel.

Franks, C. M. (Ed.). (1984). *New developments in behavior therapy: From research to clinical application.* New York: Haworth.

Halleck, S. L. (1978). *The treatment of emotional disorders.* New York: Aronson.

Herink, R. (Ed.), (1980). *The psychotherapy handbook.* New York: New American Library.

Jacobson, N. S., & Margolin, G. (1979). *Marital therapy: Strategies based on social learning and behavior exchange principles.* New York: Brunner/Mazel.

Keat, D. B. (1979). *Multimodal therapy with children.* New York: Pergamon.

Kwee, M. G. T. (1984). *Klinische multimodale gedragstherapie.* Lisse, Holland: Swets & Zeitlinger.

Lazarus, A. A. (1956). A psychological approach to alcoholism. *South African Medical Journal, 30,* 707–710.

Lazarus, A. A. (1967). In support of technical eclecticism. *Psychological Reports, 21,* 415–416.

Lazarus, A. A. (1968). Learning theory and the treatment of depression. *Behaviour Research and Therapy, 6,* 83–89.

Lazarus, A. A. (1971). *Behavior therapy and beyond.* New York: McGraw-Hill.

Lazarus, A. A. (1973). Multimodal behavior therapy: Treating the BASIC ID. *Journal of Nervous and Mental Disease, 156,* 404–411.

Lazarus, A. A. (1976). *Multimodal behavior therapy.* New York: Springer.

Lazarus, A. A. (1981). *The practice of multimodal therapy.* New York: McGraw-Hill.

Lazarus, A. A. (1984). *In the mind's eye.* New York: Guilford.

Lazarus, A. A. (Ed.). (1985). *Casebook of multimodal therapy.* New York: Guilford.

Lazarus, A. A., & Fay, A. (1977). *I can if I want to.* New York: Warner.

Lazarus, A. A., & Fay, A. (1982). Resistance or rationalization? A cognitive–behavioral perspective. In P.L. Watchel (Ed.), *Resistance: Psychodynamic and behavioral approaches.* New York: Plenum.

Lazarus, A. A., & Fay, A. (1984). Some strategies for promoting generalization and maintenance. *The Cognitive Behaviorist, 6,* 7–9.

Lazarus, A. A., Kreitzberg, C. B., & Sasserath, V. J. (1981). Multimodal therapy. In R. J. Corsini (ed.), *Handbook of innovative psychotherapies.* New York: Wiley.

Leiblum, S. R., & Pervin, L. A. (Eds.). (1980). *Principles and practice of sex therapy.* New York: Guilford.

London, P. (1964). *The modes and morals of psychotherapy.* New York: Holt, Rinehart, & Winston.

LoPiccolo, J., & LoPiccolo, L. (Eds.). (1978). *Handbook of sex therapy.* New York: Plenum.

Mays, D. T., & Franks, C. M. (Eds.). (1985). *Negative outcome in psychotherapy and what to do about it.* New York: Springer.

Peterson, D. R. (1976). Is psychology a profession? *American Psychologist, 31,* 572–581.

Rachman, S. J., & Wilson, G. T. (1980). *The effects of psychological therapy* (2nd ed.). New York: Pergamon.

Ridley, C. R. (1984). Clinical treatment of the nondisclosing black client: A therapeutic paradox. *American Psychologist, 39,* 1234–1244.

Rimm, D. C., & Masters, J. C. (1979). *Behavior therapy: Techniques and empirical findings* (2nd ed.). New York: Academic Press.

Roberts, T. K., Jackson, L. J., & Phelps, R. (1980). Lazarus' multimodal therapy model applied in an institutional setting. *Professional Psychology,* February 150–156.

Rosenblad, L. V. (1985). *A multimodal assessment of perception and communication in distressed and nondistressed married couples.* Unpublished master's thesis, Department of Psychology, Rutgers University, New Brunswick, New Jersey.

Sank, L. I. (1979). Community disasters: Primary prevention and treatment in a health maintenance organization. *American Psychologist, 34,* 334–338.

Schofield, W. (1964). *Psychotherapy: The purchase of friendship.* Englewood Cliffs, N.J.: Prentice-Hall.

Steketee, G., Foa, E. B., & Grayson, J. B. (1982). Recent advances in the behavioral treatment of obsessive–compulsives. *Archives of General Psychiatry, 39,* 1365–1371.

von Bertalanffy, L. (1974). General system theory and psychiatry. In S. Arieti (Ed.), *American handbook of psychiatry* (Vol. 1). New York: Basic Books.

Watzlawick, P., Weakland, J., & Fisch, R. (1974). *Change: Principles of problem formation and problem resolution.* New York: Norton.

Wile, D. (1981). *Couples therapy: A nontraditional approach.* New York: Wiley.

Wilson, G. T. (1982). Clinical issues and strategies in the practice of behavior therapy. In C. M. Franks, G. T. Wilson, P. C. Kendall, & K. D. Brownell, *Annual review of behavior therapy: Theory and practice.* (Vol. 8.). New York: Guilford.

Wolpe, J., & Lazarus, A. (1966). *Behavior therapy techniques*. New York: Pergamon.

Zilbergeld, B. (1983). *The shrinking of America: Myths of psychological change*. Boston: Little Brown.

CHAPTER 4

Systematic Eclectic Psychotherapy

Larry E. Beutler

In writing this chapter I have found myself in an interesting quandary. In order to understand this quandary I must explain three observations which have underwritten my effort to define an eclectic psychotherapy (Beutler, 1983). First, the past two decades have seen an exponential growth in the number of psychotherapies being offered and the variety of theories underlying them. Each theory has taken the position that it and it alone offers fundamental and consistent answers to the problems of human behavior and emotions. This observation has suggested to me that all of these theories have failed to respond adequately to the very broad spectrum of human behavior. This failure, in turn, suggests the need for truly integrative approaches, wherein specific interventions can be designed to specific populations.

Second, it has always intrigued me that although over 80% of the literature on psychotherapy theory is devoted to specific technologies and procedures, most of the effectiveness of psychotherapy can be attributed to factors that are common across approaches and that characterize most effective therapists and treatable conditions. Indeed, Lambert and DeJulio

(1978) as well as Shapiro and Shapiro (1982) have suggested that only 10-15% of the variation in outcome can be attributed to specific approaches. Hence, over 80% of the literature is devoted to focusing on 10% of change.

Third, there has been a chronic lack of communication between practitioners and psychotherapy researchers (Barlow, 1981; Strupp, 1981a). Most psychotherapy theories have little or no foundation in research; as a result they generate relatively little *new* research. With over 240 different psychotherapy theories (Corsini, 1981) devoted to the task of explaining 10-15% of change clearly we need a superordinate language system to facilitate communication both between clinicians and researchers and among theoreticians.

Having said the foregoing, I am now drawn to ponder the significance of a volume that, in pursuing its objectives, undertakes to describe many different eclectic psychotherapies. In providing such a description we, like the theoreticians before us, may become so concerned with our pet viewpoints that we will fail to provide a truly eclectic approach. At this point in the development of integrative approaches, we are still talking in different language systems and proposing different theories, albeit now under the heading of "eclecticism." The potential for both positive and negative outcomes of this endeavor leads me to approach this task with some degree of trepidation. Yet integration and advancement can come only with continued discussion. And I would caution the reader that in science, it is often as important to be wrong as to be right, as long as theories are established in such a way as to allow one to tell the difference. We find ourselves, in fact, in a situation not unlike that confronting the paleontologist: One theory which purports to explain the extinction of dinosaurs has held that the earth's temperatures rose suddenly enough to produce sterilization. Unfortunately, there is no satisfactory way to disprove this theory. First, we do not know at what temperature gonadal destruction would occur among species that no longer exist. Second, we have no way of assessing whether that temperature was achieved. Third, the mechanism by which temperatures might rise poses a further problem for explanation. However, because this theory is logical, many have accepted it as true.

BACKGROUND

My interest in developing an integrative psychotherapy dates my professional existence. The early observations of Cole and Magnussen (1966) persuaded me that diagnostic labels carried little weight in determining what treatments were offered to patients. My early research, moreover, persuaded me that compatible patient–therapist matches were more important sources of therapeutic influence than particular strategies. Summarizing this work a few years ago (Beutler, 1981), I argued that attitudinal convergence between patients and therapists may be an important ingredient in successful psychotherapy and that it can be predicted on

the basis of complex interactions of initial similarity and dissimilarity between patients' and therapists' attitudinal systems.

I have also been influenced by numerous authors who have argued that there is relatively little to distinguish the outcomes of one type of psychotherapy from those of another (Luborsky et al., 1975; Sloane et al., 1975; Smith, Glass & Miller, 1980). If, as Luborsky et al. (1975) suggest, "all [theories] have won and all must have prizes," one must either become committed to the role of nonspecific effects in psychotherapy influence or explore interrelationships between therapists' techniques and patients' characteristics. Ultimately, like the legendary mugwamp, I turned in both directions. I first became committed to defining the dimensions of compatibility that would facilitate the therapy relationship, regardless of theoretical approach. Later I investigated what characteristics of patients might predispose a favorable response to certain strategies.

In pursuit of the first objective, I investigated the A–B psychotherapy matching dimension; methods of enhancing Rogerian conditions; and the convergence of patients' and therapists' attitudes. These explorations into nontechnical change variables have held my attention over most of my professional career, partially bolstered by the work of Frank (1973), Goldstein (Goldstein & Simonson, 1971; Goldstein, Heller & Sechrest, 1966), and to a lesser extent, that of Strong (1968). Studying these authors, I became impressed with the power of interpersonal persuasion and with the potential ability of interpersonal influence theory to describe and predict the parameters of psychotherapy change.

On the other hand, the writings of Goldstein (e.g., Goldstein & Stein, 1976) and Kiesler (1976) also influenced my decision to explore the role both of specific therapy techniques and of patient characteristics in affecting outcome. My initial effort to describe eclecticism (Beutler, 1979a) entailed a close inspection of over 50 comparative psychotherapy studies, utilizing the criteria of adequacy suggested by Luborsky et al. (1975). While Luborsky and others had concluded that different psychotherapies produced little differential outcome, none of these authors had committed themselves—at least sufficiently for my taste—to a consideration of how various patient variables may have affected these conclusions. An inspection of the patient characteristics represented among those studies in which one psychotherapy did demonstrate itself to be more effective than another led me to extract certain patient variables that seemed relevant to the derivation of a successful, prescriptive psychotherapy program. Though admittedly post hoc, the advantage of having extracted such a set of patient-related variables on the basis of differential response rates lies in the potential for integrating empirical and theoretical literature.

These dimensions and their implications for treatment came together in my 1983 book on systematic eclectic psychotherapy. It was not then nor is it my intent now to establish a new psychotherapy theory. Neither is it my intent to reify the importance of the dimensions described. It is my intent, however, to provoke thought and research and in this process also to provide a systematic framework in which the technologies derived from numerous psychotherapy theories can be applied in a rational and consistent fashion to diverse client populations.

CONCEPTS OF SYSTEMATIC ECLECTIC PSYCHOTHERAPY

To be practical, an eclectic psychotherapy must emphasize three working principles. First, it must consider all or most psychotherapy approaches as potentially beneficial to some individuals. Second, it must act on the assumption that therapeutic procedures are capable of being implemented independently of their originating theories. Third, eclectic psychotherapy must provide a superordinate, functional theory that encourages and dictates the utilization of the preponderance of these approaches without sacrificing the integrity or the value derived from any. This is a tall order and may seem impossible to those who maintain that certain procedures are, per force, incorrect and inappropriate. However, most psychotherapists identify themselves as eclectic (Garfield & Kurtz, 1977; Norcross & Prochaska, 1983). That is, psychotherapists claim to utilize whatever procedure seems to fit the client best, regardless of its theoretical origins and regardless of their own theoretical preferences. Yet, it is unlikely that all professed eclectic psychotherapists would perform the same procedure at any given moment with a given client. Moreover, psychotherapists may change less to accommodate their patients than they believe they do (Strupp, 1981b). If they have a guiding theory, however, the process of accommodating to client needs may be facilitated.

If eclectic psychotherapy is to be effective, it must provide a sound theory to direct the modification of procedures in accordance with defined patient characteristics. To this end, three questions face a systematic eclectic psychotherapy: (a) On what dimensions should patients and therapists be matched to be maximally effective? (b) Within compatible patient–therapist matches, what is the best combination of patient and procedure? (c) What considerations can best dictate the alteration of therapeutic procedures in treatment across time? The promise of eclectic psychotherapy rests in the faith that one can extract, from research and theory, a superordinate theory of the dimensions, characteristics, and patterns that will provide suitable and researchable answers to these questions.

In view of the foregoing, some attention must be given to what constitutes a suitable superordinate theory. If eclectic psychotherapy is to attract the attention of practitioners who represent diverse theoretical approaches, communication must be possible. Moreover, practitioners must be able to apply an eclectic approach without sacrificing the things they value from their own theories. A superordinate theory, in other words, must be capable of several things. First, it must facilitate communication. Second, it must be able to describe and encompass therapeutic change agents from diverse points of view. Third, it must provide a focus of treatment. The significance of this latter factor deserves some special clarification.

Ample research literature suggests that while psychotherapists do not necessarily do what they say they do, the degree to which they follow some theoretical and integrative system facilitates treatment process (Strupp, 1981). For example, in comparing various psychotherapy approaches, both Luborsky et al. (1983) and Shaw (1983) have observed that treatment effectiveness is more a function of whether therapists consistently follow their particular theories of intervention than of what techniques or philosophies they employ. Theoretically, at least, one's view of human behavior and psychopathology provides such a focus and allows the therapeutic interventions to impact upon "relevant" patterns of behavior. In developing a short-term, psychodynamically oriented psychotherapy, therefore, Strupp (1981b) has emphasized the role of theory in directing the therapist's attention to cardinal conflicts that form the core of the patient's difficulty. Strupp's focus is designed to maximize the impact of psychotherapeutic interventions by concentrating attention on salient issues. Theoretical systems dictate the values that therapists assign to certain kinds of behaviors, and define the meaning of "relevant." Theories also determine, at least

to some degree, the patterns that are perceived in the patient's behavior and provide the backdrop against which all change agents are applied.

There are several potential candidates for a superordinate theory by which to direct focus and prescribe interventions. To be useful, such a theory must be capable of describing a broad range of human behaviors and emotional disturbances while encompassing or translating, in a logical way, the principles derived from an array of specific theories of psychopathology and sources of therapeutic influence. General learning theory represents one such candidate. The concepts of reinforcement theory are broad and flexible. A wide variety of specific therapeutic approaches can be understood by invoking the terms utilized by behavior theorists. However, reinforcement theory has typically been applied very narrowly and cast in an antagonistic role other psychotherapy theories. For this reason, its ability to facilitate communication may have been compromised.

Systems theory is another general theory that might possibly serve as a vehicle for communication and as an umbrella under which all therapeutic approaches could be described. The application of such a theory to marital and group functioning has been well defined and holds much promise. Its utility for individual psychotherapy is somewhat less clearly specified at present, however, and thus its usefulness may be limited.

Cognitive theory provides yet another viewpoint and it is probable that most theoretical systems can be translated into terms of information processing and cognition. Advantages of selecting this point of view include its increasing acceptance within psychotherapy generally and its utilization of relatively conventional terminology. The disadvantage of this approach, however, may be in its ties to specific therapeutic frameworks and orientations (e.g., cognitive therapy). The theory may also place an unwarranted constraint on the number and type of therapeutic procedures considered appropriate.

My own choice of a general theory is derived from interpersonal influence models of social persuasion. Persuasion theory is really not *a* theory but a descriptive framework that embodies empirical observations. The most salient of these observations, insofar as psychotherapy is concerned, are the following:

1. Cognitive, behavioral, and emotional experience represent separate but interactive dimensions of human functioning that are collectively called *attitudes*. A treatment that impacts one of these dimensions does not necessarily impact another. Hence, attitude persuasion must be focused on the realm of experience that is most problematic to the patient. Disturbances of cognitive control or distortion can be most directly impacted by interventions designed to bring about change specifically in the cognitive realm. Similarly, behavioral disturbances might best be impacted by treatments that focus on behaviors, while emotional distress or constraint might best be addressed by treatments that focus on enhancing or controlling emotional experiences.

2. Other things being equal, discrepancies between the point of view taken by a valued persuader (e.g., the therapist) and the point of view held by a willing recipient (e.g., the patient) of a persuasive message will be predictive of the amount of attitude change or persuasion initiated. The strength of this relationship, however, will be affected by factors that determine the patient's view of the therapist as a credible, empathic, helpful, and expert source of new knowledge. To the degree that the therapist is perceived as a safe, knowledgeable, trustworthy, and receptive individual, the relationship between patient–therapist attitudinal discrepancy and subsequent persuasion will become stronger.

3. Recipients of persuasive communications vary in their receptivity to direct persuasive efforts. Hence, patient variables determine the potential usefulness of various persuasive strategies, and these strategies can be selected to "fit" with patient expectancies and response sets to enhance or retard persuasive efforts.

Because persuasion theory is comprised of a collection of empirical observations, its constructs are sufficiently broad and flexible to encompass psychodynamic formulations, behavioral interventions, and general systems orientations. Moreover, this framework has some specific strengths in its ability to encompass many of the concepts that are often considered "nonspecific" to psychotherapy influence. Characteristics of patient, therapist, and intervention are easily included within a general persuasion model. Certainly, there is great need to reintroduce the variables that are often labeled as "nonspecific" influences back into a general formulation of psychotherapy which makes them equally legitimate as targets of investigation as are "specific" sources of therapeutic influence. Persuasion theory accomplishes this by focusing on those characteristics of the listener or patient that make them susceptible to specific types of external influence, including the personal and technical characteristics of the influence force (i.e., both the therapy and the therapist).

There are other advantages of persuasion theory as a general model of therapeutic intervention. For example, it is intuitively logical to see psychotherapy as an interpersonal influence situation in which an authoritative other attempts to encourage a receptive individual to change feelings, thoughts, behavior, and/or interpersonal relationships. Additionally, much of psychotherapy seems to be directed at teaching the patient a view of life from which to construct adaptive behaviors. The fact that successful psychotherapy results in patients' and therapists' beliefs and philosophies converging is well documented (Beutler, 1981). Moreover, those characteristics that enhance therapists' and persuaders' power seem to be clearly in operation in the psychotherapy relationship (Beutler, 1979c; Corrigan, Dell, Lewis & Schmidt, 1980; Frank, 1973; Goldstein, 1971). That is, therapeutic power seems to rest, in part, with the ability of the therapist to convince (i.e., persuade) the patient that the therapist is credible, trustworthy, supportive, and knowledgeable. Hence, persuasion theory is compatible with the need to match patient and therapist, technique and patient/problem and to adjust interventions as patients change.

PATIENT–THERAPIST COMPATIBILITY

Patient–therapist compatibility is the most powerful of all therapeutic ingredients. If this relationship is solid and safe, progress can be consistent. If it is not, change will be retarded, inconsistent, or absent. Yet, there are currently no empirically defined and consensually valid dimensions on which patients and therapists can be matched before treatment starts, so as to facilitate both treatment process and outcome. However, the literature does reveal several potentially important dimensions. Among notable attempts at patient–therapist matching, investigations of the A–B therapist typology have drawn the most attention. Based on the early effort of Whitehorn and Betz (1960) to define a set of therapist characteristics that predispose the effective treatment of schizophrenic patients, an interactive hypothesis emerged. A-Type

therapists, described as person-oriented and independent, were found to produce better results with schizophrenic inpatients than were their problem-centered and more mechanically oriented B-Type counterparts. B-Type therapists, however, were subsequently found to be more effective than A-Types in working with neurotic outpatients (McNair, Callahan & Lorr, 1962). Over the course of the last 25 years, much research has been devoted to the A–B typology but with sufficiently mixed results that few firm conclusions can be established. Indeed, Cox (1978) proposes that the concept was initially developed from a statistical artifact and has outlived its usefulness. Although research on the A–B dimension continues to be done with mixed results (e.g., Kaplan, 1979; Patterson & Heilbron, 1978), it seems clear at this point that the early promise of this approach cannot be realized. Interestingly, however, recent research (e.g., Kennedy & Chartier, 1976) has attempted to investigate patient and therapist responses to the same assessment situation, rather than deriving two separate dimensions for patient (a diagnostic dimension) and therapist (an interest or A–B dimension). This research suggests that dissimilar dyads seem to be most highly disposed to positive outcomes.

The observation that dissimilarity between patients and therapists may be an important factor in psychotherapy process and outcome has been suggested by others as well. Among the best studies available, Berzins (1977) undertook a large-scale matching study with cross validation, utilizing standard personality assessment devices. This is the best single matching study yet conducted, largely because of its concise and clear cross-validation effort. The results suggest that therapists who are unlike their patients on dimensions that reflect dependency and autonomy needs are most likely to produce positive therapeutic change.

Somewhat similar findings have been

obtained in research studies of patient and therapist attitude similarity. Beutler (1981) reviewed 21 studies, fifteen of which found that patients who acquired their therapists' belief systems over the course of treatment tended to have a higher likelihood of improvement than those who did not change or who diverged from the belief systems of their therapists. Concomitantly, a number of clinically relevant studies (e.g. Mendelsohn & Geller, 1963; Beutler et al., 1975) have suggested that this convergence process is facilitated by the presence of initial dissimilarity between a patient and a therapist. However, "dissimilarity" must be specified more precisely. Research also suggests that similarity in some attitudes may be coupled with dissimilarity in others to produce the most effective gains. After summarizing this literature, Beutler (1983) concluded that aspects of background and demographic similarity along with disparity in those belief systems related to the value of interpersonal attachment, friendship, and dependency may comprise a facilitative match between patient and therapist. Interestingly, this latter disparity appears to facilitate improvement regardless of whether the patient or the therapist places the highest value on these dimensions.

Although intentional assignment of patients and therapists on dimensions of belief similarity–dissimilarity is unlikely to occur in most clinical settings, the implications of patient–therapist matching has additional significance. For example, demographic and background similarities between patients and therapists may be most advantageous early in treatment and may serve to facilitate the patients' adherence to treatment regimens and maintenance in the treatment process (Beutler, Crago, & Arizmendi, in press). Hence, by emphasizing demographic and background similarities during the early stages, the therapist may establish the initial relationship on sound footing. It is likely, however, that the attitudinal and conceptual changes that we frequently call "improvement" in psychotherapy are based on the patients' perceiving and struggling to assimilate the therapist's attitudinal differences. For this reason, one observes that patients and therapists from widely different ethnic, cultural, and social backgrounds are not distinguishable on the basis of outcome, although similarities in these dimensions do seem to result in longer treatment relationships and fewer dropouts (Beutler et al., in press). From a persuasion perspective, one may suggest that as patients come to perceive therapists' discrepant beliefs and attitudes they are forced to confront dissonances in their own cognitive systems. Perceived dissonance between one's own beliefs and those of a valued therapist may motivate acquisition of that therapist's beliefs, attitudes, and perspectives. This motivation to change, in itself, may well determine treatment gain. Indeed, from this persuasion perspective, psychotherapy is a cognitive-dissonance-inducing process that is designed to confront the patient with discrepancies both within his or her own belief systems and between the patient's behavior and beliefs, on the one hand, and those of a valued therapist, on the other.

From the standpoint of therapeutic process, the foregoing suggests that the therapist does well to introduce elements of relevant dissonance for the patient's consideration throughout treatment. This must be accomplished, however, within the context of procedures that maintain the therapist's persuasive potential and perceived credibility. These procedures include the selective use of voice, posture, interpersonal distance, and self-disclosure. At the same time, the methods used to develop compatibility, like the implementation of therapy techniques themselves, must vary as a function of the patient. We will be considering their importance throughout the chapter.

MATCHING THERAPY TECHNIQUE TO PATIENT CHARACTERISTICS

Matching treatment strategies to certain patient qualities or characteristics is a common objective of all integrative and eclectic psychotherapies. How to accomplish this task is among the most interesting and intriguing of questions. To begin with, one must assume that effective interventions from numerous approaches can be separated from their originating theories and applied within a framework designed to make these interventions specific to certain patient characteristics and qualities. Beyond this, it must be emphasized that effective treatment planning requires that procedures be defined in ways that are not usually captured by brand-name labels. To say this is to recognize, for example, that "psychoanalytic therapy" is composed of many elements that distinguish it from "Gestalt therapy" and "behavior therapy" as well as many ingredients that resemble these other therapies. To apply a systematic eclectic intervention strategy, one must speak in terms of specific interventions rather than in terms of global theories.

By the same token, clinical diagnoses are too broad and nonspecific to dictate the application of specific psychological treatments. While formal diagnoses have a role in the derivation of medical treatments (Frances, Clarkin, & Perry, 1984), psychological interventions must be tailored to more refined or specific qualities of patients' personalities, styles of coping, and knowledge repertoires than clinical diagnoses allow.

Patient Variables

There are numerous patient dimensions to which one may attend in attempting to define characteristics that will be suitable to the predictive efficacy of psychotherapy. My initial effort (Beutler, 1979a) extracted from comparative psychotherapy studies those dimensions that were present when the application of one theory emerged as more effective and powerful than the application of another, but the dimensions extracted do not represent all potentially useful ones. However, research has accumulated on each and they do appear to represent reliably established entities. This being the case, the dimensions extracted in the earlier review compose a reasonable place to begin our search for effective patterns of interplay between therapists' interventions and patients' characteristics.

Symptom complexity. The first patient dimension that I proposed as significant for differentiating among psychotherapy effectiveness rates is that of patient problem and symptom *complexity*. Simplistically, this dimension ranges from "habit" to neurotiform "adjustment" patterns and may be similar to the process–reactive distinction. Symptom complexity is defined on the basis of several interwoven clinical concerns, collectively representing both problem *intensity* and coping *adequacy*. For example, the less intense the distress around the problem and the less disruptive it is to one's life, the more likely it is that it constitutes a transitory pattern or positively reinforced "habit." More specifically, the number of areas affected by the problem (e.g., home, work, interpersonal relationships, marriage), the number of concomitant symptoms associated with the conditions and the degree to which the problem represents a direct, generalized expression of the reinforcing conditions that initiated it, all index its position on this first dimension. If one's current symptoms and precipitating environments bear a direct, linear relationship and similarity to the situations and symptoms as they originally occurred or developed, the problem usually can be considered to be a "habit disorder." If, on the other hand, the current symptom only indirectly or symbolically represents the events that initiated it and evokes interruptive distress, one must consider it to express a "neurotiform adjustment disorder."

We will return to the issue of assessing this dimension, but it is worth noting that one must weigh several factors in determining whether or not a given problem represents a direct expression of positive reinforcement (e.g., "habit") or represents a symbolic and idiosyncratically generalized or distorted avoidance pattern in which overt behavior misrepresents the driving motives (e.g. "adjustment"). Yet, the designation of a problem along the dimension of "adjustment" to "habit" is necessary in order to select the focus of treatment. Neurotiform adjustment disturbances merit a *broad-band* treatment that is aimed at conflict resolution. Such a determination, therefore, directs the therapist to define the nature of the focal conflict or interpersonal theme that seems to represent, promote, and maintain the problem. In contrast, if the problem is determined to be a "habit disorder," one may expect that treatment can proceed with a symptom-oriented or *narrow-band* focus.

In the event that one determines that an adjustment pattern is being presented, the next major task is to define the focal theme. The exact framework by which one formulates a dynamic focus, however, though not irrelevant, is not specifically dictated by a systematic eclectic psychotherapy. The eclectic approach simply emphasizes the importance of defining an interpersonal theme or conflict in whatever terminology one finds compatible, and then to orient therapeutic strategies around this focus. Strupp (1981b) has proposed that a reliable theme is defined by the interplay of the patient's underlying motive, the patient's expectation of what could happen if the motive were enacted, and one's subsequent introject that inhibits or encourages action. In my own approach, I first make a global judgment of the principal need or desire which appears to guide the individual's interpersonal behavior. In the interests of simplicity and consistency, I assess this motive by categorizing patients into classes of need enactment: Attachment Oriented, Individuated Oriented, Ambivalently Oriented, or Detachment Oriented. This categorical scale is selected both because of its rational appeal (Millon, 1969) and because of the evidence cited earlier that patient–therapist differences in the dimension of autonomy (individuation) to dependency (attachment) have a bearing on patient–therapist compatibility. Specifically, I ask myself, "Do the patient's relationships seem cemented by efforts to achieve attachment and closeness or distance and individuation? Neither? Both?" Among those who are neither pure *attachment* nor *individuating* types, the *ambivalent* individual may vacillate between both, equally dominant strivings and the *detached* individual may invest in neither. This determination is based on patient descriptions of how important relationships actually begin and end, rather than simply on the basis of verbalized wants or needs. Once defined, however, this global motive or behaviorally expressed "want" is then considered along with two other patient dimensions to complete a thematic focus which will be used to direct treatment.

Coping style. The second major patient dimension represents the patients' *coping style* or method of avoiding anxiety and/or achieving interpersonal goals. If the disturbance has been defined as a "habit pattern," the patient's standing on this dimension simply represents an indication of the degree to which the behavior is one of behavioral excess (e.g., acting out) or behavioral insufficiency (e.g., lack of skill or social withdrawal). If it is the former, treatment procedures are selected that are designed to limit, reduce, or bring the excessive behaviors under control. If there is judged to be a problem of insufficiency of behavior, the treatment is oriented toward enhancing cognitive knowledge or behavioral repertoires. Skill building and directive instruction may be appropriate interventions in this latter case.

Among individuals representing disorders of neurotiform adjustment, this second dimension represents a description of the patient's dominant style of defending against anxiety. Originally (Beutler, 1979a, 1983) conceptualized as a dichotomy, it is clear that the dimension of internal to external coping style represents a continuum. However, three broad subcategories can be defined, clinically. The most primitive defenses are those that attempt to avoid anxiety through displacement, acting out, conversion symptoms, and projection. Individuals characterized by these defenses are *anxiety avoiders*. At a higher level of functioning, individuals may employ internalized and intellectualized defense mechanisms that often seem to heighten and magnify the experience of anxiety. These individuals can be seen as *anxiety magnifiers*. Individuals who are acutely sensitized to their own physiological functioning and to internal experiences that are assumed to cue them to danger represent this level of defensive development. People whose internalizing defenses are more extreme may become overcontrolled and so rigidly compartmentalized that they do not express even limited emotions from any defined source. They may be overwhelmed with anxiety but quite unable to identify it as such. These individuals are *anxiety containers*. The dimension of coping style, in other words, represents the degree to which one's intellectual resources dominate affective experience. In the very externalized—and to a lesser extent in the

very internalized—patient, subjective distress may be low. In the middle group, subjective distress is relatively high.

External (avoidant) coping styles emphasize projection, acting out, attention seeking, development of conversion symptoms, and phobias. These undercontrolled patterns merit a therapeutic strategy that focuses initially on limiting or controlling these external behaviors. At this level there are likely to be similarities in treatments of monosymptomatic (habit) and multisymptomatic (adjustment) patterns. Complex phobias, for example, may be treated through an initial program that is symptom centered and emphasizes gradual exposure and extinction. Similarly, individuals who act out aggressively must first be controlled, utilizing behavioral contingencies and environmental structure. The feature that distinguishes broad-band approaches to adjustment patterns from the narrow-band approaches applied to individuals with habit patterns, however, is the therapist's continual awareness of and emphasis on the underlying conflict or theme when treating patients of the former type. If through these behaviors, the individual is attempting to establish relationships (e.g., attachment themes) or break relationships (e.g., individuation themes), the interventions must be so constructed as to magnify and then to explore, through either behavioral or intellectual experiments, the underpinnings of this method of adjustment and the way in which it expresses both overt and covert ends. This level of concentrated, conflict focus is not required for an individual who presents a habit disorder.

Both anxiety magnifiers and anxiety containers are characterized by constraint of impulses to act out and by prominent self-critical evaluations. However, those whom we have called *magnifiers* undercontrol emotions while overcontrolling behavior. This pattern is manifest in exaggerated subjective anxiety or rumination, without behavioral impulsivity. Anxiety containment patterns, on the other hand, are manifest in low subjective arousal, emotional and behavioral overcontrol, and little emotional sensitivity or insight.

Anxiety magnification defenses emphasize hypervigilance and sensitization to internal states. When relying on such defenses, a patient is likely to present as behaviorally inhibited but also as worrisome, emotionally labile, and distraught. In this case, the treatment strategy is to strengthen the patient's cognitive resources for controlling or reducing emotions. Efforts to increase or produce awareness of emotional states may be unproductive.

If the patient in question presents with a coping style that emphasizes anxiety containment, patterns that include internalization, intellectualization, emotional compartmentalization, undoing, and introjection will be observed. For such patients, the therapeutic strategy must focus primarily on the emotions and cognitions giving rise to this constricted affect rather than on the behavior itself. Because these individuals present a picture of emotional as well as behavioral overcontrol and inhibition, the treatment strategy proposed is to enhance emotional awareness through procedures that arouse and increase emotional conflict.

In other words, with impulsive and undercontrolled emotionality (e.g., avoiders –externalizers), externally focused treatments and strategies are called for. For the ruminative and sensitized middle group (anxiety magnifiers), treatments that emphasize cognitive control and reinforcements of internal cognitive structure are advantageous. Finally, for those with little emotional awareness and overcontrolling intellectual resources (anxiety containers), enhancing and increasing emotional arousal and awareness is the treatment of choice.

Reactive level. The third patient dimensions reflects interpersonal sensitivity; more specifically, vulnerability to the threatened loss of interpersonal freedom. This dimension, described as "reactance level" (Brehm, 1976; Brehm & Brehm, 1981) is drawn directly from persuasion theory and models of interpersonal influence and is reflected in attributional processes. Those who desire *and* seek personal control are more highly reactant than those who perceive and seek external control. Though this dimension may not be empirically orthogonal to the other variables discussed, it is logically distinguished and empirically related to the amount of direction and confrontation that will be tolerable to the patient. That is, those who have both a strong need for external control and a strong perception of external influence are most susceptible to therapeutic strategies that are relatively directive and confrontive and are therapist controlled. On the other hand, those who have strong needs both to perceive themselves as personally controlled and to resist external limitations of freedom may do best with a therapist who is relatively nondirective and takes a stance that deemphasizes the therapist's control in favor of the patient's self-direction. Indeed, these latter individuals may deteriorate if the therapeutic intervention robs them of their sense of personal control (e.g., Forsyth & Forsyth, 1982).

Together, symptom complexity, coping style and reactance level describe neurotiform patients' dynamic conflict. Among neurotiform patients, defining a dominant motive directs the focus of treatment; defining coping style identifies the method by which patients attempt to achieve their wants and determines the level (behavioral, cognitive, or affective) at which treatment strategies will be aimed; and defining reactance level pinpoints the level of patients' probable resistance to interpersonal influence and indicates the degree of directive control the therapist needs to assume.

Interventions

Before we can be more specific in prescribing applications, we must explore the technologies and objectives that characterize different therapeutic schools. This process is necessary in order to support the viewpoint that therapeutic procedures can be divorced from their originating philosophies. To this end, it will be helpful to summarize psychotherapy literature in which the processes of various treatments are compared and contrasted. The task of differentiating among various theories was undertaken in my original volume on eclectic psychotherapy (Beutler, 1983). This review was accomplished by systematically summarizing the various studies that have empirically compared and contrasted the treatment process of two or more treatment approaches. There are many more therapeutic models of treatment than there are systematic comparative studies of them. However, both the obvious similarities among the theories and the research conducted on them suggested that most well known psychotherapies could be represented by five basic groupings: psychoanalytic therapies, interpersonal psychotherapies, experiential–humanistic therapies, cognitive therapies, and behavioral therapies.

Among these five groups, psychoanalytic therapy was found to rely on evocative procedures such as interpreting and analyzing and on such directed procedures as free association and dream analysis. Interpersonal psychotherapies, on the other hand, were found to be characterized by an emphasis on teaching and informing on the part of the therapist, who also directed the patient to engage in free association and structured problem-solving activities. Experiential therapists were found to contrast with the foregoing psychotherapy models by being highly reliant on reframing and reflection. Experiential therapists also directed patients in activities that included physical release or expression, role playing, and the construction of structured images or dreams.

Cognitive therapy was distinguished from other therapies by the high verbal activity level of the therapist, the therapist's reliance on questioning as an evocative strategy, and the use of therapist directives, which included teaching and informing the client. The directed activities used by cognitive therapists emphasized instruction in systematic problem-solving strategies and role playing, both of which were often accompanied by the use of specific reinforcements.

Finally, behavior therapists, like cognitive therapists, were found to be more verbal than other therapist types. Behavior therapists utilized more reframing and reflection than did most of their colleagues, and they emphasized teaching and informing. Even more than cognitive therapists, behavior therapists relied on reinforcement procedures to teach systematic problem-solving skills and behavioral activities. They also were found to be relatively more reliant on encouraging environmental exposure than other therapists.

In sum, most treatment models are distinguishable from one another on the basis of the degree to which the therapist directs the patient's attention or activity (e.g., behavior modification vs. client-centered therapy) and in the nature and focus (internal or external) of the topics selected for discussion. At one reach of the directive dimension, for example, the therapist determines and explicitly requests a patient's response or action. At the other extreme, the therapist serves the function of stimulating patients' creative processes through evocative, verbal behaviors that invite but do not directly require patient action. Similarly, different schools emphasize, to a greater or lesser extent, the role of a personal, informal relationship and vary in their emphasis on extra-therapy experience or activity.

Matching

Notwithstanding the foregoing distinctions in therapeutic styles, it is important to classify and distinguish among the objectives of the interventions used in each approach. These objectives reflect areas of intended influence and can be summarized by six general categories (see Table 1). Each objective reflects the intent to modify various combinations of affective, cognitive, and behavioral experience. Selection from among these objectives, therefore, may be made by an assessment of patient defensive styles.

Although similar procedures can be modified to fit different objectives, some

TABLE 1
Representative Interventions and Indicators

Objective/Interventions	Indicators
I—*Insight Enhancement*	*Anxiety Magnification*
Free association	High reactant, conflict focused
Interpretation	Low reactant, conflict focused
Questioning (event-specific)	High reactant, symptom focused
Role playing	Low reactant, symptom focused
II—*Emotional Awareness*	*Anxiety Containment*
Reflection	High reactant, conflict focused
Reframing	Low reactant, conflict focused
Enactment	High reactant, symptom focused
Playing opposites	Low reactant, symptom focused
III—*Emotional Escalation*	*Both Anxiety Magnification and Containment*
Interpretation/confronting	High reactant, conflict focused
Focusing	Low reactant, conflict focused
Paradoxical instruction	High reactant, symptom focused
Questioning (event-specific)	Low reactant, symptom focused
IV—*Emotion Reducing*	*Both Anxiety Magnification and Avoidance*
Reassurance	High reactant, conflict focused
Teaching/instructing	Low reactant, conflict focused
Relaxation/desensitization	High reactant, symptom focused
In vivo desensitization	Low reactant, symptom focused
V—*Behavioral Control*	*Both Anxiety Avoidance and Insufficient/Excessive Behavior*
Contingency contracting	High reactant, conflict focused
Advising/interpersonal homework	Low reactant, conflict focused
Self monitoring	High reactant, symptom focused
Token economy	Low reactant, symptom focused
VI—*Perceptual Change*	*Both Anxiety Avoidance and Containment*
Questioning (schematic thoughts)	High reactant, conflict focused
Cognitive substitution/practice	Low reactant, conflict focused
Evidence gathering/collaborative	High reactant, symptom focused
Role playing opposites	Low reactant, symptom focused

procedures are relatively unique in terms of the aspects of experience impacted. Space limitations prevent a detailed exploration of these permutations in this chapter, but Table 1 provides a sampling of interventions, drawn from a variety of therapeutic theories, that may be useful in meeting each objective. The usefulness of a given procedure can be estimated from a knowledge of the demand characteristics inherent in the procedure and from an assessment of the patient's needs for (a) symptom or conflict resolution; (b) changing cognitive, affective, or behavioral experience; and (c) more or less therapist control.

A schematic representation of the proposed relationship between general classes of interventions and patient types is presented in Figure 1. The figure illustrates the way treatment objectives and relevant interventions may be determined for specific patients.

Whether or not the speculations presented in Table 1 and Figure 1 are ultimately found useful will depend partially on the ability and willingness of psychotherapy research to address complex interactions of patient behavior and therapeutic intervention and to give up concerns with either broadly defined schools or global and unidimensional patient characteristics. For example, one must study specific therapeutic procedures rather than global interventions and apply them to individuals who selectively represent complex permutations of several patient dimensions at once in order to make an adequate assessment of this approach. Past literature has relied too heavily on global interventions under brand-name theories and has investigated relatively few patient characteristics as these interact with the interventions. The hope of systematic eclectic psychotherapy is to define interventions on the basis of such efficacy studies and to derive a conceptual plan for prescribing patterns of interventions, utilizing both good clinical sense and empirical findings.

MODIFYING TREATMENT STRATEGY AS PATIENTS CHANGE

Two separate factors underlie the need to modify the therapeutic procedures that are used at different points in therapy. First, many patients do not maintain a consistent level of either reactance or coping style and may vary on these dimensions when stressed. Hence, one must modify the therapeutic procedure from moment to moment as the patient vacillates on these dimensions. Second, with effective treatment, patients may be expected to move on all three major character dimensions. That is, if therapy is effective, it can be anticipated that patients with severe adjustment problems will come to present fewer and less severe problems as emotional conflicts become resolved. Similarly, patients who present a dominance of external defenses may become more internalized and introspective; the reverse is often true for those with strong internalizing defenses. In my experience, many patients tend to become more reliant on internal sources of control and reinforcement than on external ones, as treatment progresses, and as a result, they become less reactant. Among other overly compliant patients, treatment may actually be designed to induce increased levels of reactance.

The process of tailoring and modifying therapeutic interventions over time is directed by the same general guidelines as those used for initially implementing treatment. By evaluating patients on the three dimensions specified, one makes decisions about treatment processes and procedures that can be revisited as the process of patient change unfolds. In this way, treatment includes an ongoing process of diagnosis by which treatments are inter-

Habit/Monosymptomatic Problems

Expressive Level	Interpersonal Level		General Rule
	High Reactance	Low Reactance	
Behavioral Excess	1. Contracting 2. Relaxation training/SDT 3. Self-charting behavior 4. Covert sensitization	1. Direct reinforcement 2. Contingency management 3. SDT-therapist controlled	Behavioral control/extinction
Behavioral Insufficiency	1. Problem solving 2. Information 3. Questioning 4. Contracting 5. Self-monitoring/cognitions 6. Graded practice	1. Skill training 2. Advising 3. Instructing 4. Overt reinforcement 5. Alternative giving 6. Role playing	Behavioral training/cognitive emphasis
General Rule	Patient controlled	Therapist controlled	

Neurotiform/Multisymptomatic

Intrapsychic Level	Interpersonal Level		General Rule
	High Reactance	Low Reactance	
Externalizers/Anxiety Avoiders	1. Exercise 2. Problem solving 3. Contingency 4. Self-charting/monitoring	1. Role analysis 2. Exposure 3. Hypnosis 4. SDT-therapist 5. Modeling	Behavioral control/reduction perceptual change
Sensitized Internalizers/Anxiety Magnifiers	1. Alternative thinking 2. Self-instruction 3. Relaxation 4. Questioning 5. Reflecting 6. Paradoxical/injunction	1. Interpreting 2. Restating 3. Association 4. Role play 5. Dream interpretation 6. Sculpturing roles	Cognitive/perceptual change/emotion reducing
Overcontrolled Internalizers/Anxiety Containers	1. Prescribing symptom 2. Two-chair work 3. Free fantasy 4. Audio/video feedback 5. Questioning/reflecting	1. Enactment 2. Dream work/gestalt 3. Group feedback 4. Exaggeration 5. Playing opposites 6. Directed fantasy	Affective awareness/escalation
General Rule	Patient controlled/paradoxical interventions	Therapist controlled interventions	

Figure 1. Schematic: Intervention model.

woven over time. At least among individuals with adjustment disorders, the therapy processes are ultimately interwoven in order to systematically address the expression of conflictual themes in all three realms of experience that constitute interpersonal relationships: cognitions, affects, and behaviors.

In my experience, there are two common scenarios that occur across time for the patient with adjustment problems. In the first scenario, the patient initially has a very high level of affectivity and experiences a great deal of subjective discomfort. For the avoidant and anxiety-magnifying patient, the initial process of therapy is aimed either at controlling destructive behavioral patterns or reducing affective intensity. Hence, therapeutic strategies that impact upon behavior and emotion may be selected at first. As the patient's anxiety and stress diminish, however, one may increasingly rely on more internally oriented therapeutic procedures designed to create insight or cognitive control.

A second scenario often unfolds for individuals who rely on anxiety containment (and who are overcontrolled and avoid the experience of affect). For these individuals, the initial stages of therapy are designed to increase affectivity and affective awareness. Only later in therapy does one move to procedures that emphasize behavioral control and skill training.

PATIENT ASSESSMENT

Assessment of the patient dimensions specified in the earlier pages of this chapter relies on a combination of both formal and informal procedures. In many cases, the evaluation process is not clearly distinct from the therapeutic one. Indeed, for most patients who are referred from other professional sources, the interweaving of assessment and treatment can be almost complete. However, if not determined in advance by the referral process, one must become satisfied that the patient does not represent a current risk and is suitable for psychotherapy, and that the patient–therapist match is appropriate to initiate treatment. Beyond this point, the evaluation of the patients' characteristics can be undertaken as a process activity, using initial speculations as a basis for defining the start of treatment and then revisiting these assessment decisions as therapy unfolds.

Three fundamental questions are to be answered when a patient enters the consultation relationship with a prospective therapist: "*Why* are you here?" "Why are you *here*?" and "Why are you here *now*?" In the context of answering questions about safety and suitability for psychotherapy, one must explore relevant history. The latter can also be used to determine if the patient's difficulty represents a habit pattern or a more long-standing and debilitating neurotiform pattern of adjustment. One must also determine each patient's expectations in approaching therapy. This information is used during the early sessions of treatment in order to provide the patient with corrective information that will bring these expectations into line with likely therapy activities.

In making an initial assessment of the patient's ability to respond to psychotherapy, one must address history, previous treatment, and the nature of the disturbance. In certain disorders, psychotherapy should be considered only as an adjunctive treatment. In other kinds of conditions, psychotherapy, while the primary intervention, must be supported through other forms of intervention (e.g., group therapy, psychoactive medication). There may be still other conditions in which psychotherapy is directly contraindicated. It is at this stage of the decisional process that formal diagnoses may have a place. Assessment of the patient's mental status, family history, medication history, and health status, as well as of the nature of the problem and the events that have brought the patient to treatment are all critical. Once suicide risk, bipolar disorder, psychoses, organicity, and major medical problems have been ruled out as primary problems, one can make a better decision about the patient's potential for effecting a helpful psychotherapy relationship.

In my own assessment, I prefer to have patients send, or bring with them to the first appointment, pertinent medical records, including recent physical exam findings which may be of relevance to their specific complaints. If patients initially present with suicidal ideation, the first decisional alternative must address the control of this behavior and the protection of the patient, rather than the resolution of the distressing conflict. If a patient is sufficiently intact and the intensity of the problem is such that he or she is willing to make a nonsuicide contract, the potential for a helpful therapeutic relationship is more certain.

In a similar way, patients presenting with psychotic ideation, dementia, or major physical complaints must be considered for alternative forms of treatment first. Frances, Clarkin and Perry (1984) have described some of the indicators and contraindicators for such protective interventions and externally controlled treatments. If patients present with either treatable habit or neurotiform disorders, based on this initial assessment, the process of establishing their suitability for psychotherapy can then continue.

Initial assessment is facilitated by the use of formal psychological devices that can be integrated with background material and clinical impressions. The differentiation among organic, psychotic, neurotic, or habitform disturbances may entail either relatively little or a great deal of intensive psychological investiga-

tion for ultimate clarification. One must remain open too all of these possibilities. In most patients, however, the initial decisions about working diagnosis and the appropriateness of treatment can be made within the first one or two treatment sessions, especially if the therapist has pertinent medical history at hand and the patient is supplied with self-administered psychological assessment devices in advance of or at the end of the first appointment. Paper and pencil tests of intellectual level and efficiency, personality functioning, and level of psychotherapy are all readily available and adaptable to this purpose (see Beutler, 1983).

I find instruments such as the Shipley Institute of Living Scale (Paulson & Lin, 1970), the SCL-90R (Derogatis, Rickels & Rock, 1976), the Locus of Control Scale (Rotter, 1966), and the MMPI (Dahlstrom, Welsh & Dahlstrom, 1972) particularly useful in defining the three primary treatment-related patient variables, while history, the Millon Clinical Multiaxial Inventory (MCMI; Millon, 1982) and direct observations both supplement these decisions and define primary conflictual themes. The SCL-90R is particularly useful for assessing symptom complexity, because it presents estimates of both intensity of distress and symptom generality or spread. Monosymptomatic symptoms and habit patterns are easily separated from multisymptomatic and neurotiform ones by this means. Moreover, the various dimensions on which significant symptomatology is found can also be considered in juxtaposition with general personality measures and historical data in order to define the patient's coping style.

The MMPI is especially helpful in obtaining an estimate of the patient's defensive style. Although this instrument is most useful in assessing coping style among individuals with adjustment disorders, when it is combined with clinical history a final determination of symptom expression in habit disorders is usually quite easy to accomplish. Welsh (1952) proposed that elevations on such MMPI scales as hysteria, psychopathic deviance, paranoia, and hypomania indexed externalized styles of coping with anxiety. To me, such elevations suggest the potential value of behaviorally and environmentally oriented treatment interventions. By the same token, Welsh suggested that individuals who score very high on hypochondriasis, psychasthenia, and social introversion scales rely on internalizing, overcontrolled patterns of defense against anxiety. Such patterns may suggest the need of treatment inteventions whose focus is either cognitive or affective.

We have found (Beutler & Mitchell, 1981) that many of these latter individuals maintain both internalizing and externalizing defenses. This group of people are characterized as "sensitizing," because they are both emotionally expressive and behaviorally restricted. Because of their heightened levels of arousal and their excessive impulse control, the therapeutic strategy is to focus on cognitive procedures that will assist them to control affective experiences while loosening their behavioral restrictions. Differentiations between the potential value of cognitive and affective interventions among these defensive styles are made on the basis of overcontrol versus sensitizing patterns, particularly of angry emotions. Clinical history is helpful in making these determinations but may be supplemented by such specialized MMPI scales as the Overcontrol–Hostility Scale, the Hysteria Scale, or subscales from the Buss–Durkey Hostility Inventory.

Of the three major dimensions on which patients are assessed for matching to treatment procedure, interpersonal reactance is the one wherein the least methodology exists for making formal assessments. Because reactance corresponds somewhat with attributions of internal or external control, various locus of control formulations may be helpful (e.g., Rotter,

1966). It should be understood that reactance is not isomorphic with attribution of control, however, for reactance expresses the patient's investment in both predicting and controlling experience. Therefore, one must ultimately look for the patient's reactance level in prior history and in situations in which authoritative control has been established by others.

Although some effort has been devoted to defining expectations and demands for control within the specific context of psychotherapy (e.g., Osborn, 1981), these efforts are too primitive at present to provide a sound methodology for clearly defining the reactance dimension. Nonetheless, such efforts suggest that therapy-specific scales can be developed by which reactance level can be defined. Until more work is completed on these tasks, however, one must obtain, through the patient's history and by means of therapeutic "tests," the information that is relevant to establishing the patient's reactance level. Patients who present an orientation of compliance to authorities must be considered to be relatively low-reactant individuals. Those who maintain a steady, resistant state in the face of external threats to their control have moderate levels of reactance; those who frequently perform in a way that is opposite to the external demand are seen as possessing high reactance levels.

It is important to emphasize that reactance combines with one's coping style to reflect variations to the degree of passivity or activity with which reactance levels are expressed. Individuals who are externalized and highly reactant may be overtly rebellious and hostile. On the other hand, those who have strong internalizing defenses but who are highly reactant may utilize very indirect and passive–aggressive procedures to be oppositional. One must not attend simply to what the patient describes as a pattern, therefore, but must also observe and experiment with the implementation of therapist control in order to see reactance levels in action. Frequently, the use of homework assignments can experimentally determine if patients are compliant, resistant or reactant. Do they comply? avoid? or incorrectly execute?

Once it is determined that the patient presents an adjustment disorder, concern must be given to definition of the dynamic conflict or interpersonal theme that characterizes the patient's life patterns. Malan (1976) has been most specific in describing the procedures by which such a dynamic theme may be formulated. Luborsky, McLellan, et al. (1983) have also described a procedure for defining core themes and have been able to obtain relatively high levels of reliability in measuring these themes by asking patients to describe several past relationships: how each began; how each was maintained; and how each subsequently ended. External raters then infer the underlying motive or need represented in each relationship, the patient's expectancy in expressing that need, what the actual consequences have been, and the usual introject and behavior exhibited by the patient as a result of these consequences. Variations of a similar process are used by others (e.g., Malan, 1976; Strupp & Binder, 1984).

In the present framework, the process of defining an underlying motive or need may be complemented by the use of the personality scales of the MCMI (Millon, 1982). This patient motive, coupled with estimates of reactance and coping style, defines an interpersonal style. Reactance level defines the interpersonal consequences the patient expects in response to expressing needs. On the other hand, knowledge of the patient's coping style tells us both what s/he does as a result of that need and how s/he attempts to avoid the confronting conflict. Consider, for example, a patient who has a characteristic pattern of moving towards others, seeking attachments, and who engages in this pattern both in an active, attention-seeking way and with a morbid anticipation that

any expression of this need will result in loss of power and influence. We have described an individual with unmet dependency wants, externalized coping styles, and high levels of reactance. Contrast this person with the patient whose life course seems destined to draw boundaries between self and others and to maintain personal autonomy. We observe that the latter patient accomplishes this objective by emotional retreat, refusal to share or express feelings, and constraint of impulses, and only superficially complies with external controls, structures, and authorities. This characterizes the autonomy strivings of an internalizing and moderately reactant person. Various other permutations could also be proposed.

To facilitate focus on the dynamic theme, one must assess patients' attitudes quite directly, relative to issues of dependency and autonomy. Because ideally therapists should place themselves in contrast to patients on these dimensions as treatment proceeds, a fairly precise knowledge of the strength of patients' attachment drives and struggles for autonomy is important. Formal assessment scales can assist in this process; elsewhere we have presented some preliminary devices for matching patient and therapist along these personal compatibility dimensions (Beutler, 1983). Patterns of patient–therapist similarity and dissimilarity, as assessed on attitude scales appear to predict treatment outcome. Knowledge of these patterns may help therapists to emphasize similarities in demographic attitudes and intellectual strivings in the beginning of treatment, and to emphasize dissimilarities on dimensions of attachment and autonomy as treatment progresses.

TREATMENT APPLICABILITY

The avowed purpose of eclectic psychotherapy is to impact a broad range of patients by differentially altering the therapeutic procedure applied. However, the value of psychotherapy itself is subject to some question for some populations. Psychotherapy seems least relevant for individuals with active thinking disorders, those with bipolar affective disorders, and those whose psychiatric and psychological symptoms are the result of some medical or biological impairment. Eclectic psychotherapy's effectiveness, at least theoretically, is limited only by the broader limits of psychotherapy's effectiveness, combined with the creative genius of the psychotherapist. The creative therapist who is highly skilled in a variety of procedures will be likely to succeed with the patients for whom the creatively developed treatment repertoire or menu is applicable. If the creative therapist can also adjust the treatment menu to comply with the changes experienced by these patients during intervention, treatment efficacy is further enhanced.

Although the concepts of eclectic psychotherapy have been applied primarily to individual treatment there is no reason why they cannot be applied to group or family treatment. To do so, however, one must incorporate concepts of systems theory into the general persuasion framework. That is, the collection of individuals being treated must be considered to be a unit and at least to some degree, differentiation of the relevant patient dimensions must be applied to this expanded definition of the "patient." The ease with which this can be accomplished has not yet been assessed. If applied, however, the concepts of eclectic psychotherapy would probably be best suited to those group and family exchanges in which the therapist functions individual-to-individual.

There is also nothing inherent in the concepts described here to insist on either short-term or long-term treatment. Since this form of eclectic therapy is a practical approach, however, one must consider psychotherapy as short term in most cases, being limited either by external require-

ments or by the patient's decision to terminate. More important than the specific length of therapy is the therapist's effort to make the treatment relevant to the patient. If treatment is relevant and focused, patients probably tend to seek their own level of treatment exposure, and within a collaborative environment, contracts that are suitable to both parties can usually be negotiated. It is a central tenet of this form of eclectic psychotherapy, however, that patient and therapist should test their compatibility in a trial period. It is remarkable and interesting that the outcome of psychotherapy seems to be capable of prediction within the first few treatment sessions, based upon these compatibilities (Luborsky et al., 1983; Luborsky, Mintz, Auerbach, et al., 1980).

A guiding rule of thumb for most conditions is to establish an initial treatment period during which time both patient and therapist can explore responses to treatment and make a decision about whether treatment is likely to have long-term effects. I generally like to establish an initial contract for 20 sessions, with an understanding that a new contract can be negotiated at the end of that time. A few patients do not accept a contract of this length, and adjustments to as few as five sessions are occasionally made. Since the initial sessions of psychotherapy, compared to later sessions, tend to result in relatively rapid rates of improvement, about one-third of the patients in my own practice do not continue treatment beyond the 20-session contract. In any case, by the end of 10 sessions the therapist should have an idea of how rapidly the patient is moving through the phases of therapy, initially resolving symptoms and progressing onto explorations of interpersonal, behavioral, cognitive, and affective environments. This awareness can help in the assessment of treatment goals and, eventually, in the establishment of another contract, if the patient is willing.

By the end of the initial contract period,

patients should have a reasonably clear idea of whether or not they are able to estabish a collaborative sense of working with the therapist and should be sufficiently excited by the experiences of treatment to continue. The early sessions of therapy are devoted primarily to compatibility issues, and most early treatment outcomes reflect such compatibility. Thus, if treatment is stalled within the first five to 10 sessions, it may indicate the lack of a suitable patient–therapist match, and appropriate referrals should be forthcoming. It is relevant that clinical literature suggests that there is a natural transition point between long-term and short-term treatment in most individual psychotherapy. In the midst of this natural transition period, which usually occurs between 15 and 20 sessions, termination may be especially problematic for a patient and result in less improvement than if termination takes place at an earlier or later but more stable time (Smith, Glass, & Miller, 1980). Hence, initial contractual negotiations are important to define the limits and boundaries of these transition periods.

The transition from short-term to long-term therapy is most notable and relevant among patients with adjustment difficulties. Individuals with habit problems or situational disturbances may resolve them within 10–20 sessions and have no need to continue into a longer term phase of conflict exploration. The post-transition phase of therapy promises fewer dramatic changes in symptoms and affective state but progresses systematically by confronting avoided experiences and developing concepts that are significant for resolving the patient's conflicts and interpersonal problems. Typically, somewhere around the tenth therapy session, I find patients moving through the symptom-reduction process, wherein there is some resolution of the initial problem. At this point, one must decide whether or not to extend to another, farsighted phase of treatment that includes inoculation against further problems, skill development, insight, and even personality reconstruction. For many patients, short-term treatment is entirely adequate, and it is appropriate to terminate treatment at the end of the initial, contract period. One exception to this rule is those individuals who are forced into treatment by some external agency. For these patients, external motivation may provide the only resource that maintains them in treatment, and subjective distress is a much poorer index of progress, treatment commitment or improvement.

A central assumption for the application of most psychotherapies rests upon the motivation of the patient. Psychotherapies are best applied if the patient is motivated to undertake them. However, this motivation can come from either internal or external sources. The more internal the motivation, the more the likelihood of positive gain. It is the general assumption of eclectic approaches, however, that if the therapist responds appropriately to the patient, the patient's investment and motivation for treatment will increase over the course of time. There is some research support for this proposition, largely based upon the observed effects of inducing common expectancies and enhancing therapist flexibility (e.g., Beutler et al., in press; Parloff et al., 1978).

Psychotherapy should not be considered as a process with a given beginning and a final end. Patients are best prepared to face the world when they understand their difficulties within the context of an ongoing life struggle. This is true as much of symptomatic behaviors as it is of adjustment patterns. The door to therapy is advisably left open, even though planned vacations and terminations may occur. Termination may best be seen as a *phase of treatment,* rather than the *end of treatment,* therefore.

TREATMENT STRUCTURE

The limitations placed on the duration, setting, frequency, or structure of eclectic psychotherapy are those which are also placed on psychotherapy generally. The duration and structure of the intervention as well as the setting depend largely on the contract of mutual expectation that is entered into which the patient. The critical features, rather than setting, frequency, or duration, are the patient's compliance, the therapist's flexibility, and indications of common expectations and of a compatible patient–therapist match. Beyond this, the therapist's ability to adequately assess the patient's needs and to apply a suitable treatment menu that maintains the patient's investment in the treatment process are limiting factors.

The concepts of my particular form of eclectic psychotherapy were extracted from research and theory of individual, formalized psychotherapy intervention. Within this environment it is important to draw from research on the interpersonal influence power of different learning environments. This literature has been reviewed by numerous authors (e.g., Corrigan et al., 1980) and suggests that one does well to vary interpersonal distance, posture, emotional expressions, self-disclosure, and even office decor as a function of various patient characteristics. For example, highly reactive, externalizing patients respond poorly to therapists' self-disclosures of emotional experience and even therapists' expressions of liking (Tennen et al., 1981; Kolb et al., in press). As a result, the empathic therapist does relatively poorly with this type of patient. Adjustment to a patient who presents with high levels of external defense and reactance may require a formal and non-disclosing verbal pattern. With this type of patient, one may not be disposed to penetrate interpersonal boundaries or to directly express the degree of caring that one might with less reactant patients. Highly reactant patients tend to respond best if their therapist is seen as distant, occasionally unsure, and without a great deal of emotional or charismatic appeal. Interestingly, such patients may also do better if their therapist is found to have faults. If a therapist discloses problems with the therapy process and admits occasional confusion, these patients seem to experience a sense of competence and power in the relationship that appears to be helpful. Unlike most patients with lower levels of reactance, patients with high reactance also do best if they are able to avoid adopting the therapist's attitudes and beliefs (Kolb et al., in press).

In contrast, patients with relatively low levels of reactance are tolerant of a broad range of therapist behaviors and therapeutic interventions. They tend to respond best to individuals who emphasize personal contact, who disclose positive feelings, and who may even engage in supportive physical contact. A forward-balanced posture and relatively informal attire and environment might respond to their need for relationships with benign, egalitarian, and friendly authorities.

With the foregoing as a backdrop, one can see that to maximize therapeutic impact, the therapist should be comfortable with a wide range of interpersonal relationship styles. A formal office environment that allows some sense of comfort and the discrete use of informality, self-disclosure, posture, and interpersonal distance can serve to alter the patient's perceptions of the therapist in a manner that both facilitiates treatment process and maintains the treatment relationship (Beutler et al., in press). All of this is simply to say that the therapist must deal with the patient within the framework of the patient's experience, expectations, and hopes. One should initially meet enough expectations of patients to avoid driving them out of treatment, and one should not threaten their sense of integrity or interpersonal stability. The therapist's assigned power, which is derived from the title, the office, and the expectancy inherent in the term "psychotherapist," carries a great deal of weight and may sustain treatment contact for a considerable amount of time if it is not severely discordant with the patient's desires and expectancies (e.g., Corrigan et al., 1980). As treatment proceeds, however, the therapist's individual style emerges and begins exerting increasing influence on the treatment process and outcome. In this process, superficial stylistic variables become less relevant, and patients begin to separate their expectations of the assigned role of the therapist from the roles adopted by their particular therapists (Martin et al., 1977).

As the process of psychotherapy unfolds, it is the task of the therapist to interpose effective, technical interventions on the more powerful, persuasion influences of the facilitative treatment relationship. Persuasion theory argues that patients will more easily be persuaded to adopt a new viewpoint or set of behaviors if the technical procedures used in the persuasion effort are consistent both with preexisting expectations and needs for control, ascendance, and power. This match between patient styles and technical interventions must be accomplished with great care so that the strategies that are used enable the patient to attain greater attitudinal consonance without impeding their ability to adapt to a changing environment. This is to say that certain kinds of techniques and procedures, if inappropriately applied, may retard the benefit that would otherwise accrue simply from relating to a therapist who is perceived as credible, trustworthy, and interpersonally attractive. By matching therapist directiveness with patient needs for external control, while at the same time focusing therapy on that realm of experience most in need of persuasive alteration, suitable matches of technique and patient can be accomplished. It is hypothesized that by matching the patient who utilizes ineffective externalizing coping strategies with a persuasion method that is designed to limit the use of these strategies, the patient can be persuaded to acquire a view of the world that emphasizes positive self-control. It is also hypothesized that individuals whose defensive style both limits the expression of feelings and overcontrols otherwise appropriate behavior can be persuaded to express feelings and explore behavior when confronted with procedures that exaggerate feeling states, reinforce freer expression, and model social roles that have built-in reinforcements.

The effectiveness of persuasion efforts, however, is not to be found solely in the specific match between techniques and patient types. Indeed, these techniques simply serve the mechanism of persuasion. The primary element of change is considered to be the strength of the interpersonal tie that exists between the patient and the therapist. Patients perceptions of the therapist as an individual who is different from themselves but who is, nonetheless, good and kind and healthy, is cardinal to the process of persuasion. The persuasion process is facilitated both by attitudinal and viewpoint discordance between the patient and therapist and by the strength of the therapeutic alliance, which determines how strongly this discordance can be conveyed and confronted.

MECHANISMS OF CHANGE

Systematic eclectic psychotherapy is an integration of therapy procedures, not of personality theories. Although one needs a superordinate theory of human functioning to direct and guide one's interventions, the nature of this theory is directed by one's personal preferences, not by any specific aspects of eclecticism. My own integrating theory of change is extracted from theories of interpersonal influence and persuasion, but there is no inherent need for this particular theory to be seen as any closer to "reality" than is behavior theory, systems theory, or cognitive theory. Theories are conveniences that allow communication, facilitate exploration and prediction, and provide a focus by which to direct therapist interventions. Within my own framework of interpersonal persuasion, the primary concept involved to understand change is *cognitive dissonance*. Therapeutically facilitative dissonance induction relies heavily on the therapist's ability to establish a credible role, to convey safety and care, and to be an object of sufficient attraction that confrontation of dissonance will not result in patient withdrawal.

In order to understand the therapeutic role of dissonance induction, one must be familiar with the concept of *attitudes*. Persuasion theory assumes that the central goal of any persuasion is to modify attitudes. Attitudes, however, are defined in terms of the behaviors, cognitive sets, and affective experiences that are attached to attitudinal objects. Attitudes can also be arranged along evaluative dimensions, and if they are so constructed, they are referred to as "values."

Dissonance induction can occur in three modes. First, a patient may become aware that two different attitudinal objects are in contradiction. For example, the patient may become aware that his or her belief in human rights is at odds with his or her prejudicial view of some minority group. When placed in this situation, the patient must either accept a new superordinate construct to explain both attitudes, change one attitude in order to become consistent with the other, or erect defenses around each in order to limit their contact.

A second type of dissonance may occur when a patient becomes aware that his or her attitudinal system is discrepant from that of a valued other, perhaps that of the therapist. When confronted with this situation, a patient has a choice of either changing his or her own attitudinal construct in order to become similar to that of the valued other, devaluing the significant other, or exiting the system. The therapist's task in this process is to maintain sufficient power and value in the eyes of the patient so that the patient will seriously question his or her own attitudinal systems when such dissonances arise and will not prematurely either exit the system or disregard the therapist's viewpoint. The role of managing transference phenomena can readily be seen in this process.

A third type of conflict exists when the three fundamental components of one's attitude (cognitions, feelings, and behaviors) about a given object are in conflict with one another. If patients become aware that their actions differ from their feelings, for example, they may be induced to change either their behavior or their beliefs. This process is analogous to "working through" a problem and relies on the therapist's ability to keep the patient in cognitive contact with the conflict. The therapist's task is to keep the patient in direct confrontation with relevant dissonant elements and to reinduce the cognitive dissonance whenever it slips from the patient's awareness or becomes distorted. The therapist draws into question the patient's own beliefs when those beliefs reflect issues of significance to the patient's problem. The patient, in turn, struggles to reduce dissonance with minimal effort, thus resulting in perceptual distortions and transference attachments that signal that conflict is being engaged. The therapist is not required to direct the method in which the patient will resolve dissonance at these times but relies selectively on the patient's own resources to bring discrepant elements into line eventually. It is noteworthy that patients tend to utilize their therapists as attitudinal models, not only for defining the internal constructs that will supplant old, unworkable ones, but for modeling the methods of resolution as well. That is, both instrumental and terminal values tend to change over the course of psychotherapy and to become increasingly similar to those of the therapist (Arizmendi et al., 1985; Beutler et al., 1983). A relationship that balances the ability to maintain interpersonal attachment with the ability to confront and model attitudes provides the basis for the corrective emotional experience described by Frank (1973).

Given that the central mechanism of change and maintenance in this system is cognitive dissonance, one sees that therapeutic procedures are mechanisms by which to induce such dissonance; therapeutic theory is only a working construct that the therapist utilizes to define the relevant dimensions on which dissonance should be invoked. It is possible to employ a superordinate theory in developing an initial view of the patient and then to elaborate this theory in accordance with a more specific theory of psychopathology. One of the advantages of persuasion theory, for example, is that psychoanalytic, behavioral, and interpersonal concepts are all incorporated within it and allow one both to develop foci for therapeutic interventions and to maintain specific language concepts that help describe therapeutic change. The superordinate framework of persuasion theory, in the meantime, can still draw one's attention to the context in which therapy takes place, the nonverbal and verbal therapy styles of the therapist and the environment in which the patient lives, putting these various elements into a perspective that emphasizes the specific interventions that may be useful.

In reviewing the foregoing points, it is helpful to distinguish between "inferential" theories of psychopathology, which characterize most psychotherapeutic approaches, and "descriptive" theories of behavior, which provide a framework or backdrop by which change is described and human motivation is discussed. The superordinate, descriptive theory helps us maintain a perspective on the broad context of behavior, while the specific, inferential theory may help us understand moment-to-moment process transactions and the impact of specific interventions. Within this context, termination occurs when the patient derives a workable amount of cognitive consonance in the context of a set of behaviors that do not produce undue alienation from interpersonal support systems. For most volunteer patients, termination is at the patient's initiation, and my own preference is to gradually experiment with reducing the frequency of sessions rather than engage in abrupt termination. This tends to facilitate generalization and allows the patient to reenter treatment without a sense of failure, if behavioral experiments result in disastrous consequences.

Occasionally, one works with a patient who has a strong need to continue interpersonal attachments, and this type of patient may find it difficult to terminate even when this is indicated. Patients with strong attachment needs frequently find themselves afraid to give up their "problems" because to do so means, per force, losing a significant attachment object. Hence, psychotherapy must be seen as something more than simply a process of dealing with "problems." Termination can be simply another "experiment" with breaking attachments that are outgrown and initiating new and more healthy ones. Gradually disengaging the treatment act from the problem itself is also important with many patients. Certain dependent patients should be reassured that they can have the therapist's time even if they don't have a problem and can return to treatment even in moments of happiness. Planned treatment vacations and reducing the frequency of sessions may, thereby, encourage patients to establish more independent lifestyles.

CASE EXAMPLE

The patient was 31-years-old, white, male, and a recently graduated attorney. He initially presented with complaints of acute anxiety and depression in the two months since he and his wife had undergone a temporary, career-development separation. He reported a five-pound weight loss, a disturbed sleeping pattern, and crying spells over a two-week period. He also reported loss of interest in external events and an exacerbation of a long-standing preoccupation about his eyes crossing and of losing urinary control.

The patient's medical condition was largely unremarkable. He had no history of urinary incontinence nor was there evidence of any oculomotor disturbance. Several years before the first therapy contact, he had been diagnosed with myocarditis, which had resolved after six months of treatment. Additionally, the patient reported a history of excessive alcohol usage while an undergraduate in college, but he had experienced no difficulty of this nature for several years.

My initial contact with the patient was in response to a consultation request from the psychiatric resident who saw the patient in the hospital emergency room subsequent to an anxiety attack. In response to the consultation request, psychological evaluation revealed that the patient was functioning within the superior range of intelligence but had increasingly impaired work and marital functioning over a two-year period, with no known precipitating event. His preoccupations with urinary incontinence and with oculomotor difficulties had been evidenced over a period of nine years, also with no evidence of a specific precipitating event. Accord-

ing to the patient, the preoccupations occurred spontaneously when he was touring Europe. He "suddenly" found himself becoming afraid both about being unable to find satisfactory bathroom facilities and about appearing unusual. This preoccupation persisted upon his return home and, with time, increased in severity to the point of impairing, but not severely threatening, his marital relationship and scholastic endeavors. At the time of admission the patient indicated that he had not been able to be seated long enough to pass the bar exam and could not seek work as an attorney. He was certain that he would be unable to make courtroom appearances or meet with clients because of his fear of urinating on himself. He had sought no prior mental health treatment in spite of the fact that his preoccupations had interfered with his school and marriage for years. These fears required him to maintain residence close to people with whom he was familiar. He and his wife had moved to a neighboring state, for example, but his anxiety had increased sufficiently that he was forced to leave both his employment and his wife in order to return to his hometown. His wife planned to join him after he was settled, even though she preferred the other geographic locale.

Formal diagnosis rendered at the time of the initial consultation was Major Depression with an Obsessive–Compulsive Disorder. The anxiety and depression were considered to be acute exacerbations of a long-standing and recurrent obsessive pattern. The psychological consultation also assisted in the delineation of the patient's status on the following dimensions of functioning:

Symptom severity/complexity. The patient was judged to have a neurotiform adjustment disorder both on the basis of his previous history and on the basis of the amount of impairment rendered to current functioning. Several factors contributed to this determination. These considerations included moderate symptom severity, impairment to multiple life activities, manifestation of a wide variety of symptoms, and the lack of a symptom-relevant precipitating condition. That is, the patient's preoccupations occurred without a prior experience with, or exposure to, individuals who had urinary incontinence or nystagmus.

Based on the conclusion that the patient presented a neurotiform adjustment disorder, therapy became focused on resolution of underlying conflicts rather than on symptomatic relief. Following the rationale and reasoning of Strupp and Binder (1984), the patient's relationship behaviors were explored and efforts were made to define underlying motives. Exploration of the patient's interpersonal desires and fears led to his desire to establish interpersonal dependencies and attachments. Evidence for this assumption came from several sources. First, his anxiety and depression became most acute with the anticipation of and following a separation, both from his wife and from his school, even though both were planned and designed to further his growth. Second, his obsessive fears required that he return to his hometown, closer to his parents and other sources of familiar nurturing support, even though this also meant a temporary separation from his wife. The thematic pattern of using obsessive symptoms to break down interpersonal boundaries, to maintain dependencies, and to extend his areas of self-identity to include other objects in his environment, was observed in numerous relationships. The definition of this need comprised a first step in reconstructing a general pattern of behavior that represented the fundamental focus around which treatment would be directed.

Defensive style. This patient was judged to represent a level of internalization that consisted primarily of anxiety magnification. His defenses included psychophysiological sensitization, compartmentalization, and intropunitiveness. When confronted with separation, he became depressed, self-critical, and guilty and remained hypervigilant to internal bodily states, which he construed as sources of danger. Throughout, however, he was quite expressive and animated in the display of intense feelings. The patient could not be characterized as being emotionally overcontrolled in spite of his best obsessive efforts, although he did inhibit behavioral impulses severely. Consistent with the anxiety magnification pattern, his obsessive symptoms were not presented in a bland or unaffected manner, but through expressive and tearful emotion.

The patient's initial depression passed, once treatment arrangements were made, and he then produced MMPI scale scores that were all below the 70 T score line. The most prominent scales were those suggesting impulsivity, passivity, and dependency. The pattern represented a vacillation between internal and external defensive styles, with some emotional display and impulsiveness coupled with emotional and social withdrawal. This pattern confirmed our placement of the patient within the range of individuals who represented an intropunitive, internalized but sensitizing style of coping.

Reactance level. Neither the patient's history nor psychological assessment performance revealed evidence of intense reactance. Reactance is defined as the tendency to do the opposite of that demanded by an authoritative source. Reflected in this pattern is an individual's need for personal and internalized control. This patient presented both a history of overcompliance with authorities and evidence of reliance on external reinforcement and control. However, reactance is also a dimension for which no entirely satisfactory measurement procedure is available. Hence, it sometimes is helpful to apply a critical test to assess the patient's ability to respond to therapeutic injunctions. Homework assignments, for example, can frequently be used as experiments for determining the patient's reactance level. The patient who complies with several types of highly structured and directive homework assignments can be considered to be low on the reactance dimension. Those who do not complete assignments on any regular basis tend to fall into the middle range of reactance, while individuals who repeatedly do the assignment incorrectly or do the opposite of what is suggested present high levels of reactance. By this standard, an initial homework assignment was given to the patient to monitor obsessive thoughts. He responded to the homework assignment willingly and compliantly. This confirmed the hypothesis that the patient represented relatively low levels of reactance. Thus, it was decided that relatively directive therapeutic strategies could be employed safely.

Therapist–patient compatibility. Interpersonal compatibility was assessed by soliciting feedback and by making direct tests of the relationship power during treatment. No formal assessment of therapist–patient differences on the dimensions of attachment was undertaken initially. However, from previous research explorations on this issue in which I had been a therapist–subject, it is relatively clear that my own interpersonal values emphasize autonomy and the development of interpersonal boundaries. Hence, when the patient began treatment, I concluded that his valuing of attachment relationships represented a suitable and potentially productive value contrast to my own. Likewise, demographic similarity was appropriately present, with the patient having come from a middle class background and from a family which emphasized intellectual and academic achievements. Because of this, I felt quite capable of providing an empathic and credible response.

Formulation and Treatment Plan

Collectively, the patient was found to represent a neurotiform adjustment pattern requiring resolution of his intense needs for attachment and dependence. Additionally, the presence of a sensitized, internalizing, and behaviorally overcontrolled (anxiety magnification) defensive style suggested the potential advantage of perceptual change procedures, which included those designed to enhance insight and reduce arousal. Finally, the patient's low reactance level indicated his probable susceptibility to directive therapeutic procedures. A list of potentially evocative and directive procedures was extracted from the list reproduced in Figure 1. Behavioral change procedures were rejected because the patient's defenses emphasized overcontrol of behavioral impulses rather than externalized avoidance of anxiety. Emotional awareness and escalation procedures were also ruled out in the current procedure, both because of the already intense level of the patient's emotional experience and because of his emotionally expressive style. This left us to select primarily procedures designed to produce insight, reduce arousal, and evoke perceptual change. From among the procedures in these categories, we selected those that, at least initially, would include a relatively high level of therapist direction and would be conducive to conflict resolution. This resulted in the menu of procedures listed in Table 2. Among the evocative procedures, transference interpretation, questioning, and teaching were the ones that seemed most useful in the service of our objectives.

Among directive procedures, two-chair dialogues, direct feedback and confrontation procedures, free fantasy, alternative

TABLE 2
Representative Treatment Menu

PATIENT DESCRIPTION
  Conflict: attachment seeking
  Internalizing defenses: emotionally expressive vacillating with overcontrol
  Reactance: low

MENU: **Tolerance of procedures for both high and low reactance**
       Interpretation of parental relations
       Reframing feelings/cognitions
       Periodic affective focusing as patient overcontrols
       Teaching/instructing
       Homework: interpersonal assertion
       Cognitive substitution/practice
       Confrontation
       Questioning schematic cognitions
       Evidence gathering/analysis

---

thinking, evidence gathering, and cognitive rehearsal strategies seemed most amenable to a conflict-oriented focus. These procedures formed the basis of a cognitively oriented therapy that was designed both to initiate change and to explore the evolution of current fears and fantasies in early attachments to parental objects. Initially, the focus was on the patient's depressive symptoms, not directly on uncovering dynamic conflicts. Indeed, I used this attachment dynamic to facilitate the relationship by directly conveying my genuine liking and support for the patient. This approach encouraged his needs for nurturance and attachment within therapy as a means of establishing a base which could then be explored and confronted.

As the relationship continued, verbal and directive responses increasingly emphasized the values of autonomy and of freedom from mandatory reliance on approval and love. Concomitantly, the amount of directive support was reduced. While my effort was not to directly convey my own autonomy-oriented belief system, it seemed clear that I could not avoid doing so, covertly. In the process of frustrating the patient's intense attachment needs, a failure to place value on autonomy seeking would not be in the patient's interests. I do not accept the position that it is possible for the therapist to remain neutral and undisclosing. The very fact that I perceived his concern with dependency as a "problem" conveys the value placed on autonomy and underwrites my determination to provide a treatment oriented toward resolving that conflict. Rather than being a neutral object, however, I perceived myself as an active change agent who presented a point of view that contrasted with the patient's dynamic conflicts. I did not attempt to overwhelm the patient with my own viewpoint, but it is clear that it was both conveyed and adopted during treatment.

The patient responded eagerly to the treatment employed, and he was subsequently seen for ten initially contracted sessions followed by five additional weekly sessions, a prescheduled session two months later and another session four months after that. The latter two appointments were designed in order to taper off treatment and to provide an opportunity to reenter active treatment should the need arise. This procedure is particularly useful for individuals who become terrified of treatment endings, as is often true of those with dependency-based themes.

For a patient with a problem as severe as that presented by this man, I would ordinarily anticipate more than 15 treatment sessions. The early sessions were devoted primarily to helping the patient establish increasing control over his cognitive patterns, anxiety, and depressive symptoms by means of a variety of procedures, including thought monitoring and rational evidence gathering. He was asked to systematically monitor bladder sensations and, during times of anxiety, to reconstruct his interpretation of anxiety-provoking thought patterns, challenging them and providing rational alternatives.

As the patient continued to present his symptoms of obsessive preoccupation, efforts were made to translate these, metaphorically, into terms that reflected his angry feelings when his efforts to please others were frustrated. His urinary urges, for example, were explored as symbolized expressions of the patient's anger and his metaphorical desire to "piss" on those who frustrated his dependencies. These explorations led into two-chair dialogues with the patient's internalized courtroom "judge" and then to discussions of the patient's family attachments and, particularly, his frustrated dependency on his authoritative father. During session number nine, the patient's intense need for other people's approval and love, as well as his effort to remain attached to parental figures by assuming a childlike role, came into full view. The patient began expressing the awareness that his urinary continence might be an effort to return to a more childlike state and in that process to avoid responsibility while being nurtured. His explorations into his marriage confirmed this pattern, and he expressed fear of having children who would compete with him for the attention of his wife.

By the time we reached session number 12, the patient's depression and anxiety had lifted. He had experienced momentary anxiety at the anticipation of a job interview but had pursued this interview as a homework assignment. During the course of the job interview he experienced a momentary urinary urge but reinterpreted this as both an effort to avoid an autonomous, professional role and an expression of his anger at his potential rejection. He was able to stop the thought and replace it with a more realistic one. The urinary urge dissipated.

By session 13 the patient had received a job offer and was anticipating his new employment. As we explored the option of terminating therapy, the patient ambivalently expressed the desire to continue but was concerned about his lack of funds. Given his plan to reunite with his wife, and the anticipated cost of her lost employment, a decision evolved to terminate active treatment but to maintain follow-up at periodic intervals. The patient expressed continuing fear of his symptoms returning, but by session fifteen he experienced virtually no preoccupation with lack of ocular control and had only rare experiences of anxiety about urinary control. He indicated that relationships with his parents had improved and that he was even looking forward to the possibility of starting a family. At the time of his two-month follow-up, the patient was doing well in his practice and now no longer felt the need for continuing treatment. He had exprienced no preoccupation either with urinary incontinence or nystagmus for the prior month and reported that his wife was both employed and pregnant.

Four months later the patient continued to report satisfactory results and expressed great pleasure at how far he had progressed. His wife was beginning to experience some job-related stress in her new employment, particularly as she also anticipated the forthcoming child. I subsequently saw his wife for seven treatment sessions prior to the birth of their baby. A follow-up contact approximately three months later indicated that the couple continued to do very well and revealed that there had been no symptom recurrence.

It is my conviction that longer term treatment would have been helpful to this individual. We did not have sufficient time to explore his nuclear conflicts at great length. However, focused conflict-resolution strategies, combining both symptomatic and dynamic conflict-oriented procedures had a significant and positive effect. The patient's new employment, the return of his wife and other environmental factors supported the changes that he made in psychotherapy. It would probably be inaccurate to attribute either the maintenance of his change or the amount of his change to the therapeutic interventions alone. However, the patient was convinced that the procedures were helpful, expressed great joy at the structured nature of them, and indicated that he had both learned a great many coping strategies and achieved a good deal of insight into the nature of his problem. No formal psychological assessment was undertaken at termination, although this is often done in order to document improvement.

RESEARCH

Research in systematic eclectic psychotherapy has been in two fundamental areas. The first area has addressed the matching of patients and therapists; the second area has emphasized matching of patients to therapeutic procedures. The first area of research is much more clearly developed and specific than the second.

My own research on patient–therapist matching has emphasized the roles of similarities and dissimilarities in belief and value systems. Two related programs of investigation have been undertaken in this regard. The first applies to *similarities and dissimilarities* between the belief systems of patients and therapists. The second applies to the *acceptability* of belief

systems, a concept which is only indirectly associated with similarity. Both of these lines of research rely in part on the demonstration that effective psychotherapy is accompanied by attitudinal convergence between the two participants. This latter point of view is supported by a large number of research studies that have used a wide variety of personality, attitudinal, and value concepts. In a recent view of this literature (Beutler, 1981), it was determined that 15 of 21 studies confirmed the observation that successful psychotherapy outcome was accompanied by attitudinal personality convergence between the patient and therapist.

In our own investigations, five separate studies, utilizing a variety of assessment procedures and populations, have confirmed the observation that initial (pretreatment) patient–therapist dissimilarity on global attitudinal value dimensions is positively associated with the development of facilitative and productive therapeutic processes (Beutler, 1971a; Beutler, 1971b; Beutler et al., 1974; Beutler et al., 1975; Beutler et al., 1983). The strength of this relationship is consistent. For example, in a recent investigation (Beutler et al., 1983), which corrected for statistical artifacts that may affect the relationships between dissimilarity and convergence, we obtained a linear correlation of .59 between patient and therapist dissimilarity in terminal values or life goals (e.g., Rokeach, 1973) and subsequent convergence and a correlation of .44 between patients' and therapists' dissimilarity of instrumental values and subsequent attitudinal convergence.

While global attitudinal dissimilarity seems to facilitate the process of attitudinal convergence, its relationship to therapy outcome is more difficult to assess. Attitudinal *acceptability* must be considered along with the dimension of attitude *similarity* in order to understand therapeutic improvement. The relationship between initial patient–therapist value and attitude similarity and subsequent improvement must also consider the often contradictory influences of specific attitudes. The value of this specificity is seen in a recent investigation (Arizmendi et al., 1985) in which it was determined that improvement could be statistically described as a complex function of initial similarities of academic, intellectual, and social values combined with dissimilarities of interpersonal attachment values. More specifically, effective therapist–patient dyads were those in which participants placed similar amounts of value on courage, forgiveness and politeness but placed differing levels of value on such concepts as independence, social recognition, friendship, and love.

While many of these investigations have utilized a strictly correlational analysis, the introduction of *attitudinal acceptability* as an appropriate target of investigation has allowed the matching of patients and therapists before treatment is initiated. We have employed a variant of social judgment theory to determine, in advance of therapy assignment, the patient's and therapist's latitudes (i.e., range) of attitudinal acceptance and rejection. Using the methodology of social judgment theory, it is possible to define both the patient's and therapist's *preferred* beliefs toward any given object and the *range* of acceptable beliefs that characterize both participants. In our initial investigation of this issue, for example, Beutler (1971a) evaluated both the patient's and therapist's preferred attitudes on a series of dimensions reflecting attitudinal dispositions toward sex, aggression, and authority. The degree to which the therapist's preferred attitudes fell within a range of positions agreeable to the patient (i.e., latitude of acceptance) was concomitantly assessed. It was determined that if the therapist's attitudes were acceptable to the patient, the patient subsequently perceived the therapist to be more similar to him- or herself than he or she was in real-

ity and was more likely to adopt the therapist's belief systems about sex, authority, and discipline.

In subsequent investigations we have confirmed that the therapist's attitudes about personal ideology and personal identity are conducive to enhancing therapeutic outcome if they are both initially very distant from the patient's beliefs about these issues and are initially rejected by the patient (Beutler et al., 1974; Beutler, 1979b). Not surprisingly, we have also discovered that if the therapist's latitudes of acceptance are broad enough to encompass the preferred viewpoints of the patient, both therapeutic process and outcome are facilitated even if the patient finds the therapist's preferred viewpoint unacceptable. In such circumstances, a priori assignment of patients to therapists on the basis of the therapist's latitude of acceptance results in the patient feeling more committed to the treatment relationship and showing more positive treatment gains (Beutler et al., 1978).

A fewer number of studies have been devoted to the matching of specific therapeutic technologies with patient dimensions. Although the derivation of the treatment-matching dimensions was based on an intensive reanalysis of psychotherapy outcome studies (Beutler, 1979a), future investigations must be directed at the explorations of patient groups in which several patient variables are either explored or controlled simultaneously.

In an initial effort to develop this latter area of research, for example, Beutler and Mitchell (1981) compared individual treatment procedures which characterized either the analytically oriented therapists or the experientially oriented therapists of patients who represented two different personality styles. We studied homogeneous groups of neurotic patients and compared those who adopted a predominantly externalized defensive style with those who were characterized by internalizing defensive styles.

Retrospective analysis revealed that the "externalizing patients" actually had internalizing patterns as well and were very similar to those whom I now have come to define as anxiety magnifiers. They were emotionally poorly controlled, reactive internalizers, rather than pure externalizers. The other group was composed of emotionally overcontrolled and constricted internalizers. Among both groups, we found that the broad classes of experiential procedures were more effective than analytically oriented ones. However, individual procedures within both broad categories were effective, others within both broad categories were minimally effective. For example, both exploration of early childhood relationships and the use of visual imagery were shown to be negatively related to improvement in both patient groups. Other procedures designed to increase emotional awareness were consistently effective in both groups, especially in the emotionally expressive group. Although reactance level was not assessed in this study, visual inspection suggested that it was higher among those Ss who presented internalizing and expressive defenses than in overcontrolled internalizers. Hence, the effectiveness of experiential procedures for treating this group may have been a function of high reactance levels, consistent with the hypothesis that the low levels of therapist confrontation embodied in experiential therapy may be more helpful to highly reactant patients than the authoritative procedures of the analytically oriented therapist.

In a later investigation, three highly structured forms of psychotherapy were explored among acutely disturbed psychiatric inpatients (Beutler et al., 1984). In this study of individuals who were emotionally undercontrolled, psychotherapeutic procedures designed to increase emotional arousal and awareness were found to provoke deterioration. In contrast, procedures that emphasized interpretation and emotional support facilitated treatment gain, whereas behavioral treatments exerted virtually no substantial treatment effect. This finding partially confirms the negative value of utilizing emotional awareness and arousal methods among patients who are emotionally expressive and functioning at high levels of distress.

At the present time, we are engaged in two investigations designed to specify the relationships among patient dimensions, therapeutic interventions, and treatment outcome. We are utilizing a variety of therapeutic procedures and are also assessing patients along several dimensions simultaneously. Our results are quite promising at this point and suggest that patients' coping styles are particularly important variables in determining the effects of specific treatments on outcome. We are less certain about the dimension of symptom complexity, although literature on this issue continues to be quite consistent in suggesting that constricted problems are more easily handled by symptom-oriented procedures than by dynamically focused ones (Wolpe et al., 1973).

IMPLICATIONS FOR CLINICAL TRAINING

Integrative psychotherapy maintains that therapists should be simultaneously trained to competency levels in a variety of highly specific models. Whether or not therapists can in fact become equally or even minimally proficient in such a broad range of procedures is uncertain. We are currently exploring this issue, but it is too early to provide definitive results. The eclectic model proposes, however, that at least some therapy procedures should be learned from each of the categories of objectives presented in Table 1 and that these procedures should be learned in a way that allows their implementation through both high and low therapist directiveness.

Training programs for eclectic psychotherapy would ideally be based on competency criteria for procedures representing all of the six categories of objectives. The alternative is to consider psychotherapists as specialists and to determine those skill areas in which they are able to achieve competence or with which they are most comfortable. In this model, eclectic approaches would encourage therapists to define and limit their practices to those patient groups for whom their particular strategies and orientations will be most productive. It is rather naive to assume that therapists will thereafter only treat the patients for whom they and their skills are most fitted. It is somewhat reassuring to observe, however, that there may be an automatic selection process that directs patients to therapists by whom they are likely to be most helped. This is demonstrated, for example, in the observation that referrants who are familiar with therapists in the community tend to make referrals to therapists in a way that is consistent with matching interest and personality patterns (King & Blaney, 1977).

If nothing else is certain, literature to date suggests that training programs that emphasize accreditation and credentialing on the basis of time spent and classes taken, rather than competence, are outmoded. Even highly trained and experienced therapists from such programs do not achieve the ability to define appropriate therapeutic foci or to adjust treatment strategies appropriately (Strupp, 1981b). Beck et al. (1979) maintain that it takes two years of competency-based education to teach highly trained psychiatrists and psychologists to perform cognitive therapy. Special training and feedback is required to teach people to do what they say they do and to do it well. The importance of competency-based programs is also seen in recent observations that therapists' ability to comply with the procedures they say they implement are stronger contributors to treatment outcome than the procedures themselves (Shaw, 1983; Luborsky, 1983). Competency-based programs with criteria levels of performance will be necessary in order to implement any integrative eclectic psychotherapeutic treatment.

To be an effective eclectic psychotherapist, one must be familiar with a wide range of therapeutic procedures. One must have demonstrated competence in implementing those procedures, and one must be trained to observe and assess conflictual themes in a way that allows these themes to be the focus of concentrated treatment. Additionally, and even more importantly, the therapist should be able to facilitate and utilize relationship-enhancement procedures that are generally characteristics of effective therapists, independent of any particular theory or therapeutic school. These tasks are probably best accomplished in a training program that first and foremost emphasizes the development of skills for establishing and maintaining therapeutic relationships. Active listening skills, methods of exploring interpersonal relationships, and a solid foundation in relationship-oriented procedures should be established. Only subsequently, should specific technologies be emphasized. A well-rounded eclectic psychotherapist will receive ample supervision in the development of behavioral methodologies, cognitive change interventions, and the many techniques for exaggerating or escalating affective states that are borrowed from Gestalt therapies. The therapist will also receive supervised experience with interventions that highlight interpersonal processes and psychoanalytically oriented procedures for enhancing and interpreting transference relationships. In each of these areas the therapist should be exposed to the foundations of theory as well as to a sampling of the technologies employed. Subsequently, and as a final step in the training process, the therapist should concentrate on exploring integrative models such as the one proposed here.

Although research experience and training may be important to the training endeavor, it is probably not a necessary —and certainly not a sufficient —ingredient for becoming an effective, integrative therapist. Nonetheless, a research orientation assists one to perceive relationships between therapeutic strategies and subsequent changes and to be a thinking therapist. Research training may also give one an appreciation for methods of questioning, measuring, and assessing one's impact. Hence, such a research perspective should be acquired during training. Beck et al. (1979) maintain—and I concur—that the therapist is a personal scientist who assists patients to develop a scientific view of cause and effect in their own behavior. Therapeutic procedures are implemented as experiments with outcomes usually assessed subjectively, but both patients and therapists can be taught to look for external referents for subjective states. From the outcomes of these *experiments,* new interventions may be developed. These interventions are not developed randomly, however. One must be a thinking and planful interventionist. A guiding model such as that proposed here is useful in developing therapeutic menus for directing research and clinical efforts. However, it does not supplant the thoughtful and systematic clinician.

FUTURE DIRECTIONS

The most critical questions currently facing the eclectic psychotherapist are:

1. Can one actually become equally or minimally proficient in employing a wide variety of therapeutic strategies?
2. To what degree does such proficiency enhance therapeutic outcome?

3. How can we develop more refined methods of defining and assessing both relevant patient dimensions and patterns of patient–therapist compatibility?
4. How can we operationally define and teach the application of specific therapeutic procedures in ways that include both common and specific variables?
5. Are there behaviors and methods that will help the therapist to enhance and strengthen the quality of therapeutic contacts in those cases where patients and therapists cannot be suitably matched?

These questions are in need of definition and answer and are expected to direct the field of psychotherapy research over the next several decades. At this point, it is not certain whether all patients or disorders can be matched with specific therapy procedures. Systematic research is needed in order to determine if the procedures currently available are sufficiently broad and flexible to encompass most patient patterns. Moreover, clinical impressions make it clear that some patient groups are not impacted significantly or consistently through psychotherapy. We need to develop more powerful procedures as well as clearer indications of what types of patients are inappropriate for psychotherapeutic processes in existence at this time.

If any of our eclectic approaches to psychotherapy prove to be more beneficial than the theories they attempt to integrate, they must stand the empirical as well as the clinical test. Researchable concepts must be incorporated under a superordinate language system in order to separate real differences among approaches from label differences. Additionally, researchers and clinicians must acknowledge that many different interventions may have positive impact and must direct their efforts to developing a system by which that impact can be predicted and controlled. Finally, we must abandon simple arguments about the superiority of one or another theory in order to determine which individuals will respond best to what particular approaches, therapists, and environments. The concepts derived must, therefore, be useful to the clinician, verifiable to the scientist, and acceptable to a diversity of practitioners and theoreticians.

REFERENCES

Arizmendi, T. G., Beutler, L. E., Shanfield, S., Crago, M., & Hagaman, R. (1985). Client–therapist value similarity and psychotherapy outcome: A microscopic approach. *Psychotherapy: Theory, Research and Practice, 22,* 16–21.

Barlow, D. H. (1981). On the relation of clinical research to clinical practice: Current issues, new directions. *Journal of Consulting and Clinical Psychology, 49,* 147–155.

Beck, A. T., Rush, A. J., Shaw, B. F., & Emery, G. (1979). *Cognitive therapy of depression.* New York: Guilford Press.

Berzins, J. I. (1977). Therapist–patient matching. In A. S. Gurman & A. M. Razin (Eds.), *Effective psychotherapy: A handbook of research* (pp. 222–251). New York: Pergamon Press.

Beutler, L. E. (1971a). Attitude similarity in marital therapy. *Journal of Consulting and Clinical Psychology, 37,* 298–301.

Beutler, L. E. (1971b). Predicting outcomes of psychotherapy: A comparison of predictions from two attitude theories. *Journal of Consulting and Clinical Psychology, 37,* 411–416.

Beutler, L. E. (1979a). Toward specific, psychological therapies for specific conditions. *Journal of Consulting and Clinical Psychology, 47,* 882–897.

Beutler, L. E. (1979b). Individual, group, and family therapy modes: Patient–therapist value compatibility and treatment effectiveness. *Journal of Counseling and Psychotherapy, 47,* 43–59.

Beutler, L. E. (1979c). Values, beliefs, religion and the persuasive influence of psychotherapy. *Psychotherapy: Theory, Research & Practice, 16,* 432–440.

Beutler, L. E., (1981). Convergence in counseling and psychotherapy: A current look. *Clinical Psychology Review, 1,* 79–101.

Beutler, L. E. (1983). *Eclectic psychotherapy: A systematic approach.* New York: Pergamon Press.

Beutler, L. E., Arizmendi, T. G., Crago, M., Shanfield, S., & Hagaman, R. (1983). The effects of value similarity and clients' persuadability on value convergence and psychotherapy improvement. *Journal of Social and Clinical Psychology, 1,* 231–245.

Beutler, L. E., Crago, M., & Arizmendi, T. G. (in press). Therapist variables in psychotherapy process and outcome. In S. L. Garfield & A. E. Bergin (Eds.), *Handbook of psychotherapy and behavior change* (3rd Edition). New York: John Wiley & Sons.

Beutler, L. E., Frank, M., Scheiber, S. C., Calvert, S., & Gaines, J. (1984). Comparative effects of group psychotherapies in a short-term inpatient setting: An experience with deterioration effects. *Psychiatry, 47,* 66–76.

Beutler, L. E., Jobe, A. M., & Elkins, D. (1974). Outcomes in group psychotherapy: Using persuasion theory to increase treatment efficiency. *Journal of Consulting and Clinical Psychology, 42,* 547–553.

Beutler, L. E., Johnson, D. T., Neville, C. W., Jr., Elkins, D., & Jobe, A. M. (1975). Attitude similarity and therapist credibility as predictors of attitude change and improvement in psychotherapy. *Journal of Consulting and Clinical Psychology, 43,* 90–91.

Beutler, L. E., & Mitchell, R. (1981). Differential psychotherapy outcome among depressed and impulsive patients as a function of analytic and experiential treatment procedures. *Psychiatry, 44,* 297–306.

Beutler, L. E., Pollack, S., & Jobe, A. M. (1978). "Acceptance," values and therapeutic change. *Journal of Consulting and Clinical Psychology, 46,* 198–199.

Brehm, S. S. (1976). *The application of social psychology to clinical practice.* Washington, DC: Hemisphere.

Brehm, S. S., & Brehm, J. W. (1981). *Psychological reactance: A theory of freedom and control.* New York: Academic Press.

Cole, J. K., & Magnussen, M. (1966). Where the action is. *Journal of Consulting Psychology, 30,* 539–543.

Corrigan, J. D., Dell, D. M., Lewis, K. N., & Schmidt, L. D. (1980). Counseling as a social influence process: A review. *Journal of Counseling Psychology Monograph, 27,* 395–441.

Corsini, R. J. (Ed.) (1981). *Handbook of innovative psychotherapies.* New York: John Wiley & Sons.

Cox, W. M., (1978). Where are the A and B therapists, 1970–1975? *Psychotherapy: Theory, Research and Practice, 15,* 108–121.

Dahlstrom, W. G., Welsh, G. S., & Dahlstrom, L. E. (1972). *An MMPI handbook: Volume I: Clinical interpretation.* Minneapolis: University of Minnesota Press.

Derogatis, L. R., Rickels, K., & Rock, A. F. (1976). The SCL–90 and the MMPI: A step in the validation of a new self-report scale. *British Journal of Psychiatry, 128,* 280–289.

Forsyth, N. L., & Forsyth, D. R. (1982). Internality, controllability, and the effectiveness of attributional interpretations in counseling. *Journal of Counseling Psychology, 29,* 140–150.

Frances, A., Clarkin, J., & Perry, S. (1984). *Differential therapeutics in psychiatry.* New York: Brunner/Mazel.

Frank, J. D. (1973). *Persuasion and healing: A comparative study of psychotherapy* (Rev. Ed.). Baltimore: Johns Hopkins University Press.

Garfield, S. L., & Kurtz, R. (1977). A study of eclectic views. *Journal of Consulting and Clinical Psychology, 45,* 78–83.

Goldstein, A. P. (1971). *Psychotherapeutic attraction.* New York: Pergamon Press.

Goldstein, A. P., Heller, K., & Sechrest, L. B. (1966). *Psychotherapy and the psychology of behavior change.* New York: Wiley.

Goldstein, A. P., & Simonson, N. R. (1971). Social psychological approaches to psychotherapy research. In A. E. Bergin & S. L. Garfield (Eds.), *Handbook of psychotherapy and behavior change* (pp. 154–195). New York: Wiley.

Goldstein, A. P., & Stein, N. (1976). *Prescriptive psychotherapies.* New York: Pergamon.

Kaplan, A. G. (1979). Toward an analysis of sex-role related issues in the therapeutic relationship. *Psychiatry, 42,* 112–120.

Kennedy, J. L., & Chartier, G. M. (1976). Effects of client and therapist on the process of A–B status on the process of psychotherapy. *Psychotherapy: Theory, Research and Practice, 13,* 412–417.

Kiesler, D. J. (1976). Some myths of psychotherapy research and the search for a paradigm. In A. P. Goldstein and N. Stein (Eds.), *Prescriptive psychotherapies.* New York: Pergamon.

King, D. G., & Blaney, P. H. (1977). Effectiveness of A and B therapists with schizophrenics and neurotics. A referral study. *Journal of Consulting and Clinical Psychology, 45,* 407–411.

Kolb, D. L., Beutler, L. E., Davis, C. S., Crago, M., & Shanfield, S. (in press). Patient personality, locus of control, involvement, therapy relationship, drop-out and change in psychotherapy. *Psychotherapy: Theory, Research and Practice.*

Lambert, M. J., & DeJulio, S. S. (1978, March). *The relative importance of client, therapist, and technique variables as predictors of psychotherapy outcome: The place of therapist "nonspecific" factors.* Paper presented at the meeting of the American Psychological Association, Scottsdale, AZ.

Luborsky, L., Crits-Christoph, P., Alexander, L., Margolis, M., & Cohen, M. (1983). Two helping alliance methods for predicting outcomes of psychotherapy: A counting-signs vs. a global rating method. *Journal of Nervous and Mental Disease, 171,* 480–491.

Luborsky, L., McLellan, A. T., Woody, G. E., & O'Brien, C. P. (1983, July). *Therapists' success rates and their determinants.* Paper presented at the meeting of the Society for Psychotherapy Research, Sheffield, England.

Luborsky, L., Mintz, J., Auerbach, A., Christoph, P., Bachrach, H., Todd, T., Johnson, M., Cohen, M., & O'Brien, C. P. (1980). Predicting the outcome of psychotherapy: Findings of the Penn Psychotherapy Project. *Archives of General Psychiatry, 37,* 471–481.

Luborsky, L., Singer, B., & Luborsky, L. (1975). Comparative studies of psychotherapies: Is it true that "everyone has won and all must have prizes?" *Archives of General Psychiatry, 32,* 995–1008.

Malan, D. H. (1976). *Toward the validation of dynamic psychotherapy.* New York: Plenum Press.

Martin, P. J., Moore, J. E., & Sterne, A. L. (1977). Therapists as prophets: Their expectancies and treatment outcome. *Psychotherapy: Theory, Research and Practice, 14,* 188–195.

McNair, D. M., Callahan, D. M., & Lorr, M. (1962). Therapist "type" and patient response to psychotherapy. *Journal of Consulting Psychology, 26,* 425–429.

Mendelsohn, G. A., & Geller, M. H. (1963). Effects of counselor–client similarity on the outcome of counseling. *Journal of Counseling Psychology, 10,* 71–77.

Millon, T. (1969). *Modern psychopathology.* Philadelphia: W. B. Saunders.

Millon, T. (1982). *Millon clinical multiaxial inventory manual* (2nd Edition). Minneapolis: National Computer Systems, Inc.

Norcross, J. C., & Prochaska, J. O. (1983). Clinicians' theoretical orientations: Selection, utilization, and efficacy. *Professional Psychology: Research and Practice, 14,* 197–208.

Osborn, K. (1981). *Validation of the psychotherapy preference questionnaire.* Unpublished doctoral dissertation, Virginia Polytechnic Institute and State University.

Parloff, M. B., Waskow, I. E., & Wolfe, B. E. (1978). Research on therapist variables in relation to process and outcome. In S. L. Garfield & A. E. Bergin (Eds.), *Handbook of psychotherapy and behavior change* (2nd edition). New York: John Wiley & Sons.

Patterson, V., & Heilbron, D. (1978). Therapist personality and treatment outcome: A test of the interaction hypothesis using the Campbell A–B scale. *Psychiatric Quarterly, 50,* 320–332.

Paulson, J. J., & Lin, T. T. (1970). Predicting WAIS IQ from Shipley–Hartford scores. *Journal of Clinical Psychology, 26,* 453–461.

Rokeach, M. (1973). *The nature of human values.* New York: Free Press.

Rotter, J. B. (1966). Generalized expectancies for internal versus external control of reinforcement. *Psychological Monographs, 80,* 1 (Whole No. 609).

Shapiro, D. A., & Shapiro, D. (1982). Meta-analysis of comparative therapy outcome studies: A replication and refinement. *Psychological Bulletin, 92,* 581–604.

Shaw, B. F. (1983, July). *Training therapists for the treatment of depression: Collaborative study.* Paper presented at the meeting of the Society for Psychotherapy Research, Sheffield, England.

Sloane, R. B., Staples, F. R., Cristol, A. H., Yorkston, N. J., & Whipple, K. (1975). *Psychotherapy versus behavior therapy.* Cambridge, MA: Howard University Press.

Smith, M. L., Glass, G. V., & Miller, T. I. (1980). *The benefits of psychotherapy.* Baltimore: Johns Hopkins University Press.

Strong, S. R. (1968). Counseling: An interpersonal influence process. *Journal of Counseling Psychology, 15,* 215–224.

Strupp, H. H. (1981a). Clinical research, practice and the crisis of confidence. *Journal of Consulting and Clinical Psychology, 49,* 216–219.

Strupp, H. H. (1981b). Toward the refinement of time-limited dynamic psychotherapy. In S. H. Budman (Ed.), *Forms of brief therapy* (pp. 219–242). New York: Guilford Press.

Strupp, H. H., & Binder, J. L. (1984). *Psychotherapy in a new key: A guide to time limited dynamic psychotherapy.* New York: Basic Books.

Tennen, H., Rohrbaugh, M., Press, S., & White, L. (1981). Reactance theory and therapeutic paradox: A compliance–defiance model. *Psychotherapy: Theory, Research and Practice, 18,* 14–22.

Welsh, G. S. (1952). An anxiety index on an internalization ratio for the MMPI. *Journal of Consulting Psychology, 16,* 65–72.

Whitehorn, J. C., & Betz, B. J. (1960). Further studies of the doctor as a crucial variable in the outcome of treatment with schizophrenic patients. *American Journal of Psychiatry, 117,* 215–223.

Wolpe, J., Brady, J. P., Serber, M., Argas, W. S., & Liberman, R. P. (1973). The current status of systematic desensitization. *American Journal of Psychiatry, 130,* 961–965.

CHAPTER 5

An Eclectic Psychotherapy

Sol L. Garfield

BACKGROUND

As I look back over the years to the early part of my career, there were undoubtedly several factors that played a role in the development of my own orientation to psychotherapy. Although I am really unable to say what influences were primary or how they interacted, I believe I can recall with reasonable confidence the factors that did influence my views of psychotherapy.

During the time that I was a graduate student at Northwestern University, 1938–1942, the only truly influential and available therapeutic orientation, apart from a somewhat directive form of counseling, was that of psychoanalysis. It is true that we were introduced to Adlerian, Jungian, and Lewinian theories of personality, but Freud was the significant figure when it came to discussions of psychotherapy—a rather awesome and psychiatrically dominated area of clinical practice in the early 1940s. Like most other beginning psychotherapists, probably, I attempted to use psychoanalytic theory and procedures during my first real experience as a therapist during World

War II. I was not particularly impressed with the results of my attempts at applying analytic procedures, although I eventually came to the conclusion that the military cases probably were not similar to cases in civilian life.

However, there were not too many other models or resources to emulate or follow. Grinker and Spiegel's (1945) treatment procedures for combat casualties appeared to be quite effective and impressive, but did not necessarily seem applicable to cases in a military hospital in the United States. In any event, I was not overly impressed with the efficacy of the attempts by me or my colleagues to apply analytically oriented therapy in the army hospital to which I was assigned. Nevertheless, I was regarded as a good therapist by my psychiatric colleagues, and I was asked to lecture on Freudian theories in psychotherapy.

Another important influence, and one that has persisted, was my expectation that empirical evidence should be provided in support of a given clinical or therapeutic procedure. Although Freudian theories were interesting and provocative, they were also speculative. They provided a great many interesting hypotheses for both clinical practice and research but relatively little in the way of empirical evidence in support of the theories. This was certainly true as far as the efficacy of psychoanalytically oriented therapy was concerned. Although I did find several published reports by well-known psychoanalysts on failures in psychoanalysis and some critical discussions of the need for evaluations of psychotherapy (Obendorf, 1943; Obendorf, Greenacre, & Kubie, 1948), actual research studies were limited.

Still another important influence was the publication of *Counseling and Psychotherapy* by Carl Rogers in 1942. I did not get a copy of this work until two or three years later, but it did have an impact. There were several reasons for this. As far as I know, Rogers was the first psychologist to author a text on psychotherapy. Furthermore, his whole approach, criticizing the "expert" role of the psychotherapist, was almost diametrically opposed to that of the psychoanalysts. Finally, there was a certain quality to Rogers' work that was different from that of the psychoanalysts and was more congruent with the value system I had acquired in my graduate training in psychology. Rogers was more likely to refer to research studies and to formulate statements as hypotheses requiring study and verification. For example, in his 1942 book Rogers made reference to "a research program in which counseling and therapeutic interviews have been phonographically recorded. . . . This procedure holds much promise for the future" (pp. viii–ix).

Frederick Allen's *Psychotherapy with Children,* also published in 1942, was another early influence. The active and responsible role of the therapist with the emphasis on the current behaviors of the child in the therapy situation made a definite impression on my thinking. Gordon Allport, relatively unknown to today's graduate students in clinical psychology,

also influenced my thinking in a different way. Allport was not a psychotherapist or clinician, but an academic psychologist who published one of the first scholarly books on personality (1937). His emphasis on the ideographic view of personality as compared to the nomethetic view made a profound impression. Whether or not it was related to my own view of the limited value of psychiatric diagnosis (Garfield, 1957, 1983), I do not know. However, my own clinical experience seemed to support the ideographic emphasis and to be critical of the generalizations applied to patients with specific diagnoses. Although now, particularly as a result of third-party payments and DSM-III, there has been an increased emphasis on psychiatric diagnosis and more specific treatments for specific disorders, I still perceive too much variability among patients to follow suit blindly.

Without question, my scientific research training has influenced me throughout my life. As a result, I have generally tried to keep an open mind about the process and outcome of psychotherapy and to see what research data were available to support a given view. The lack of such data for psychotherapeutic approaches seemed somewhat surprising since in the area of psychological testing psychologists usually required information on the reliability, standardization, and validity of such instruments. However, it became apparent that at least a number of dynamically oriented psychologists held the view that psychotherapy was an art and therefore could not be subject to empirical research.

Consequently, the fact that even in the 1940s there were a number of different theoretical orientations and approaches to psychotherapy suggested that there were different and opposing explanations of what was effective in psychotherapy. There were also some materials that suggested the possibility of some common factors operating in the various approaches to psychotherapy. Very early, relatively, Rosenzweig (1936) had actually suggested the possibility of a few common factors in psychotherapy. Levine (1948), in his book on psychotherapy in medical practice, discussed a number of so-called supportive therapeutic techniques that to me appeared as potential variables common to most of the different forms of psychotherapy.

Finally, an important supporting influence on my thinking was the doctoral dissertation conducted by Ralph Heine (1953). Heine studied the evaluations provided by patients treated by three different groups of therapists: client-centered, psychoanalytic, and Adlerian. These patients tended to account for comparable changes in very similar ways and led Heine to conclude that a common factor (or factors) was operating in the different forms of therapy investigated.

The net impact of these influences as well as my own clinical experience with patients in a military hospital, in a Veterans Administration hospital, in two V.A. outpatient clinics, and in a university clinic led me to reach certain conclusions. One was that it was not wise to choose and adhere to only one psychotherapeutic system. The second was to consider seriously the possibility that there were common factors operative in most forms of psychotherapy that actually might be among the most important variables in psychotherapy. And the third was that the research available for evaluating psychotherapy was too limited for drawing any really solid conclusions. Only research in the future would allow us to be more definitive in our appraisals of what was of consequence in psychotherapy. These thus constituted the bases for my views of the psychotherapeutic process and led me early to an eclectic orientation. My first published reference to possible common factors, however, did not appear until 1957 when I devoted 10 pages to this topic in my first book, *Introductory Clinical Psychology*.

THE APPROACH

Eclecticism generally refers to the utilization of features or procedures from a number of theoretical orientations or approaches. Depending on one's point of view, eclecticism represents an improvement over a single approach, or it reflects a nonsystematic conglomeration of ill-fitting parts. Clearly, both views contain some elements of the truth. It is my view, however, that eclecticism is a manifestation of dissatisfaction with particular orientations. If an individual who followed a specific orientation were satisfied with that orientation, he or she would not become an eclectic. However, when one finds that a specific approach has limitations, one of the possible outcomes is to become an eclectic. Another, of course, is to simply choose a new orientation.

It is obvious from what has been presented earlier that I chose an eclectic approach as a means of going beyond adherence to one theoretical system. Although this allows me the freedom to use techniques and procedures from practically any orientation and to use them as I see fit in the individual case, there are negative consequences as well. The primary one is that I do not have a truly organized system of therapy. Although I believe that this is not really a problem in teaching psychotherapy, and in fact I believe it is desirable, following my type of eclectic approach limits the kind of research that can be done. One reason for this is that many of the concepts or procedures used are somewhat general and lack specific operational definition.

Before proceeding to a discussion of some of the emphases in my eclectic approach, I would like to make a brief mention of some surveys of clinical psychologists that illustrate some features of eclecticism. An earlier survey by Lowell Kelly (1961) indicated that eclectic views were held by a relatively large number of clinical psychologists. Actually, 40% of Kelly's sample indicated that they were eclectics. A later comparable survey again indicated the popularity of an eclectic orientation among clinical psychologists (Garfield & Kurtz, 1976a). This time, almost 55% of the sample identified themselves as eclectic.

As a result of this, Kurtz and I followed up with a study of a sample of those who had identified themselves previously as eclectics (Garfield & Kurtz, 1977). In this study, 154 individuals completed and returned the study questionnaires. Apart from the fact that there was considerable variability among the sample in the various theoretical orientations they tended to combine, one theme appeared to be most prominent. The eclectic clinicians tended to emphasize that they used the theory or methods they thought were best for the individual client. In essence, procedures were selected for a given patient in terms of that client's problems, instead of trying to make the client adhere to a particular form of therapy. An eclectic therapy thus allows the therapist to use potentially a wide range of therapeutic techniques. The type of view expressed was similar to my own in most respects.

There is a large degree of freedom in an eclectic approach. One does not have to adhere theoretically to one orientation or keep from using procedures that are inconsistent or frowned upon from that particular orientation. This is particularly interesting in the light of certain recent developments in research in psychotherapy, particularly the emphasis on the use of psychotherapy manuals to train psychotherapists to adhere rather strictly to a specific form of therapy. The reason for the emphasis is to specify more clearly the form of psychotherapy being evaluated. In the past, psychotherapies were simply named or labeled without specifying what was involved in the therapy and without monitoring the therapy to guarantee that a particular form of therapy was in fact being conducted. The new emphasis, therefore, is an attempt to operationalize the forms of psychotherapy being studied and appraised. To the extent that this practice will tend to particularize the forms of therapy being investigated, it would appear to be going in a direction opposite to both the spread of eclecticism and the more recent move toward integration in psychotherapy (Garfield, 1982; Goldfried, 1980, 1982; Marmor & Woods, 1980). It will be interesting to see what develops in the future in terms of these different emphases.

Some Guiding Principles

As mentioned earlier, one of the guiding principles for my views of the psychotherapeutic process is that most of the accepted and apparently successful forms of psychotherapy rely on common therapeutic factors for many of the positive outcomes secured. Each of the psychotherapies may have some individual components that have been emphasized by them and are of some potential utility. However, these unique aspects have been overemphasized at the expense of the potentially important common factors. It is understandable that therapists who have been trained in a given form of therapy and have been identified with it are reluctant to acknowledge the importance of common factors—factors they essentially share with other forms of psychotherapy.

Because the different forms of psychotherapy are derived from different theoretical orientations and use different terms and concepts, the various forms of psychotherapy appear more different than they actually are. Some common variables or processes are consequently viewed as different even when they are essentially similar. Even potentially more significant is the fact that some basic and important processes are overlooked because they are not stressed in the formal descriptions of the individual forms of therapy. Investigators usually investigate the processes and procedures hypothesized to be of significance in the particular orientations. Others tend to be disregarded. However, when different forms of psychotherapy are compared, the research findings on outcome are largely comparable (Garfield, 1980, 1984; Smith, Glass, & Miller, 1980). What is one to make of such findings? Although some find fault with this body of research (Rachman & Wilson, 1980), I view the research results as providing evidence for possible common factors.

In most of the presentations on psychotherapy the emphasis has usually been on specific forms of psychotherapy, such as psychoanalysis or client-centered therapy, or on different approaches to psychotherapy (Binder, Binder, & Rimland, 1976; Morse & Watson, 1977). It appears to be a common procedure in teaching a beginning course in psychotherapy to introduce students to a number of therapeutic orientations and to emphasize the differences among them. Although each of the therapies discussed may be characterized as having some unique features that distinguish it from the others, for the most part they are viewed as alternative approaches to psychotherapy. One is expected to select the form of therapy that appears best or most appealing to the individual, and that one form of therapy is supposed to be adequate to handle all or most types of psychological disorders. The possibility of common factors among the psychotherapies or the possibility of combining aspects of several of the therapies generally has received little emphasis.

However, if one shifts one's focus from the differences among the psychotherapies to possible commonalities among

them, some intriguing possibilities become apparent. Certainly, without trying too hard, one can note at least some superficial commonalities. Almost all forms of psychotherapy consist of at least one therapist and one patient who meet together for a stipulated amount of time for one or more scheduled therapy sessions. Furthermore, most use an interview type of format in which talk or verbal interchange takes place. The therapist generally is a socially designated and sanctioned healer with all the powers, status, and privileges accorded to such individuals. The patient, on the other hand, is a person with some type of psychological discomfort or affliction, generally anxiety, depression, or both, who is seeking to be helped and relieved of discomfort by the therapist.

In addition to the above, there are some other potentially common aspects of many therapies that can be suggested. The patient seeks out therapy because of feelings of demoralization and the hope of being helped (Frank, 1971, 1973, 1979). In meeting with a therapist the patient will also have an opportunity to talk about problems, hopes, and fears regardless of the therapist's theoretical orientation. Most therapists will have some ideas or formulations about how to conduct therapy. Although these may differ, they may provide the therapist with a way of proceeding and generally give the patient the feeling that the therapist knows what he or she is doing. This may heighten the patient's confidence and acceptance of the therapy and the therapist. The therapist also can be expected to say something about the patient's disturbance and the treatment to be received. The explanations offered, even though they may differ from one orientation to another, may also be comforting to the patient. In essence, such communication conveys an indication of the therapist's knowledge and skill as well as indicating familiarity with the patient's problems. All of these factors

AN ECLECTIC PSYCHOTHERAPY 137

conceivably may have a positive influence on the patient.

More will be said about possible common factors in psychotherapy shortly. However, what has just been presented suggests several possible commonalities that are not difficult to perceive or to understand. The usual response of therapists has been to ignore such commonalities or to view them as relatively superficial variables as far as psychotherapeutic change is concerned.

Common Therapeutic Variables—The Relationship in Psychotherapy

We have mentioned previously that all forms of therapy require or consist of a therapist and a client-patient, and that some kind of communication takes place between them. This characterization of psychotherapy is at a purely descriptive level and would not by itself distinguish this interaction of two people from other types of social interaction. What distinguishes the therapeutic situation from most other interpersonal situations are the specific roles of the participants, the objectives of their interactions, and the kind of relationship that develops between them. It is these features that characterize psychotherapy and are also common to almost all forms or variants of psychotherapy. Furthermore, some components or aspects of these features of psychotherapy are hypothesized to play a role in the attainment of positive change.

The relationship in psychotherapy has been accorded a place of importance in many of the more traditional approaches to psychotherapy. Although behavioral approaches did not at first place much emphasis on relationship factors, they recently have also recognized the role they play in the psychotherapeutic process (Goldfried & Davison, 1976; Wilson & Evans, 1977). Although the views concerning the therapeutic relationship and the

emphasis placed on it may vary from orientation to orientation, the therapeutic relationship would still be seen as an important aspect of therapy. Some of the more basic aspects can be noted here.

At the most obvious level, a positive relationship is necessary in most cases if therapy is to continue beyond the first interview. If the patient, for whatever reason, develops a negative view of the therapist and the way therapy is being conducted, he or she may abruptly terminate therapy. The patient must perceive the therapy as potentially helpful and must also be willing to do what is required by the therapist. If not, it is doubtful whether any real gains will be made. It is evident also that both participants contribute to the kind of relationship that develops and that may eventually contribute to the type of outcome achieved.

Most therapeutic approaches appear to agree that the patient must have an adequate degree of motivation in order to continue and eventually to profit from psychotherapy. Thus, a "properly" motivated patient is an important component of the therapeutic relationship. Although patients vary on this dimension, it also seems probable that patient motivation may be influenced by the person of the therapist and by the particular procedures the therapist is using. Other features of the patient may also influence the relationship, but these can be discussed later. Let us now say a few words about the therapist.

The therapist's expectations and perceptions of the patient may also influence the therapeutic relationship. If he perceives the patient as difficult, resistant, or psychologically naïve, or as having false expectations about therapy, the relationship may be adversely affected. On the other hand, if the therapist perceives the client as motivated and willing to collaborate in the therapeutic endeavor, there is a higher probability of a desirable therapeutic relationship.

Thus, a good relationship between therapist and patient is necessary for progress in therapy. Furthermore, this is true for any form of psychotherapy. This should not be taken to imply that the relationship is all there is to psychotherapy or that all other aspects are of minor significance. Rather, a good therapeutic relationship appears to be a necessary, but not sufficient, condition for a worthwhile positive outcome in psychotherapy.

It is also of interest that the therapeutic relationship has received increased attention and research in recent years, particularly among dynamically oriented investigators. Attempts have been made to define aspects of a good therapeutic relationship and to develop scales for measuring these components. For example, one of the components of the Vanderbilt Psychotherapy Process Scale, patient involvement, was found to have a relationship to outcome (O'Malley, Suh, & Strupp, 1983). This relationship was not evident during the initial therapy session, but was apparent at the third interview. Thus, the patient's involvement in therapy is a sign that therapy is progressing satisfactorily and that the relationship between therapist and patient is adequate. However, the exact means of securing such involvement has not been spelled out clearly or demonstrated.

Other "helping alliance" measures have been developed at the University of Pennsylvania. One method is a global rating method, whereas the other consists of counting specified patient experiences. In the latter, the patient experiences the therapist as providing the help needed, or therapy is experienced as working together with the therapist toward therapeutic goals (Luborsky, Crits-Christoph, Alexander, Margolis, & Cohen, 1983). Both procedures showed modest-to-moderate correlations with some measures of outcome when extreme groups were compared. In this investigation, the most positive helping alliance signs dealt with items where the patient felt helped or changed. In other words, if the patient is involved in therapy and feels that something positive is underway, there is a greater likelihood of positive outcome. How this is secured is by no means clear. However, it is hypothesized that a good relationship is essential for this to occur, and it is worth exploring this feature of therapy further.

Thus far we have discussed the importance of developing a worthwhile relationship between therapist and patient but have said little about how such a relationship is established. Although the patient obviously contributes importantly to the development of this relationship, we shall focus here on the therapist's contribution to the relationship. As therapists, we could, of course, select only those highly motivated patients with supposedly very good prognoses who would be likely to develop positive therapeutic relationships and good outcomes. This, however, would be a negative policy in which individuals who are in great need of help are bypassed or rejected because they do not guarantee a successful outcome. Another limitation of such a policy is the fact that our ability to predict outcome *prior* to therapy is quite poor (Garfield, 1978). Thus, it seems best to focus on the role and contribution of the therapist to the development of a positive therapeutic relationship.

If the appraisals of therapy offered by patients are viewed as one means of appraising the relationship, certain perceived qualities of the therapist are viewed as being of great importance. In one study, the patients stressed the personal qualities of the therapist and the opportunity to discuss the personal problems that were bothering them as the important factors in their psychotherapy (Feifel & Eels, 1963). In a study of behavior therapy, "The patients felt . . . that the most universally helpful elements of their experience were the therapists' calm, sympathetic listening, support and approval, advice and 'faith'" (Ryan & Gizynski, 1971, p. 8).

The factors emphasized by the successful patients in the well-known study conducted by Sloane and his colleagues are also pertinent in the present context (Sloane, Staples, Cristol, Yorkston, & Whipple, 1975). The five items considered "extremely important" or "very important" by at least 70% of the successful patients who received *either* analytically oriented psychotherapy or behavior therapy were the following:

1. The personality of your doctor.
2. His helping you to understand your problem.
3. Encouraging you gradually to practice facing the things that bother you.
4. Being able to talk to an understanding person.
5. Helping you to understand yourself. (p. 206)

In addition to the above, at least 70% of the patients who received the analytically oriented psychotherapy also referred to such factors as the therapist's confidence that the patient would improve and his "encouraging you to shoulder your own responsibilities by restoring confidence in yourself" (Sloane et al., p. 207). Several reasonable inferences can be drawn from these evaluations that appear to be highly pertinent to the therapeutic relationship. Statements about the personality of the therapist are clearly important but by themselves they do not indicate any specific features or behavior that would be useful in fully understanding the phenomenon in question. However, the other factors mentioned are more specific and potentially more helpful.

Among the factors that appear to be of potential importance in promoting a good therapeutic relationship on the part of the therapist is the ability to be a sympathetic or empathic listener. Although listening is an obvious feature of the therapist's role in psychotherapy, it is an aspect that is not easily mastered by aspiring psychotherapists, at least in my experience. However, it does appear to be of some consequence in establishing a feeling on the part of the patient that the therapist is truly interested in his case.

Some of the other aspects that appear to be part of a good therapeutic relationship are the patient's feeling of being understood and being free to express his or her feelings, the providing of information and advice by the therapist, and the latter's encouraging the patient to accept his or her responsibilities and to try out new behaviors. Since all of these have been perceived by patients as being very important to them, it is plausible to assume that they are factors that facilitate a desirable therapeutic relationship.

The preceding discussion of the therapeutic relationship is meant to illustrate the general approach that has focused on the importance of common factors in psychotherapy. The therapeutic relationship, however, is only one of many possible variables in psychotherapy that are common to different forms of psychotherapy and are hypothesized to play a significant role in the therapeutic process. A discussion of other common therapeutic variables will be presented later in this chapter in the section on mechanisms of change.

Before proceeding to the next section, a few other general comments can be offered about the eclectic approach described here. I really can't tell whether the approach should be described as synthetic, atheoretical, or anything else. There is no truly systematic theory guiding the approach, and thus it could be called atheoretical. For myself, I prefer to view it simply as an empirically oriented eclectic approach emphasizing common therapeutic variables. It has been derived from my attempt to understand what variables influence change and to account for the comparable results among the diverse forms of psychotherapy that have been evaluated empirically.

PATIENT ASSESSMENT AND TREATMENT APPLICABILITY

I have been opposed for some time to routine diagnostic testing and assessment except for research purposes. A number of factors undoubtedly have contributed to my views in this area. Early in my career, patient assessment meant an intensive battery of tests that required at least two visits by the patient. After the testing was completed, several weeks were required for the scoring, interpretation, and writeup of the results. This generally was followed by a staff conference. Whether the emphasis was on psychiatric diagnosis or on intrapsychic dynamics, I saw the assessment process as primarily a ritual that delayed therapy, increased the cost of professional services, and generally contributed little to the efficacy or efficiency of treatment.

This view is based in great part on empirical research in the area of psychological assessment (Garfield, 1957, 1974, 1983), and in the area of psychotherapy (Garfield, 1978). The reliability of clinical diagnosis in the past has left very much to be desired, and the validity of psychological tests for both clinical diagnosis and psychodynamic predictions was distinctly unimpressive. Furthermore, prediction of therapeutic outcome on the basis of pretherapy appraisals is disappointingly low with the average correlation ranging from 0.10 to 0.20.

I should make clear also that the above statements refer to the routine assessment of every patient, not to the intensive assessment required for very difficult diagnostic cases where such problems as possible brain pathology or incipient psychotic disorders need to be clarified. In most instances, the initial interview generally suffices as both the assessment interview and the first therapeutic interview, thus allowing therapy to begin immediately.

In the first interview, however, a number of areas need to be assessed and discussed. These include such items as the patient's reasons for seeking help now, the problems the patient has personally and socially, the duration of the difficulties, previous therapy, and the patient's expectations about psychotherapy. The extent to which each of these areas is pursued and clarified will depend on the particular patient. I, personally, do not attempt to make a formal psychiatric diagnosis since this is not critical in my judgment. However, this is generally required where third-party payments are involved. Of greater concern are variables that are potentially related more closely to psychotherapy process and outcome. One aspect concerns the estimate of positive outcome—in other words, is psychotherapy a viable therapy for the patient and can I be of help?

It is not easy to predict positive outcome. In fact, if approximately two-thirds of the patients improve by means of psychotherapy, then our predictive measures would have to do considerably better if the base rates are to be exceeded. Therefore, one may state his or her opinions or beliefs but should not necessarily be too strongly attached to them.

In most respects, my views are probably not very different from most that have appeared in the research literature. I prefer individuals as patients who have "reasonably" clear problems, are not psychotically impaired, exhibit some degree of anxiety or depression, appear to want to work on their problems, and show no serious occupational or social disorganization. Such individuals are usually referred to in psychotherapeutic lore as "good patients." Of course, predictions of outcome based on evaluations at intake or the first therapy interview do not add much to the base rates. At the same time, it should be recognized that psychotherapy is not a panacea for extremely severe psychological disorders.

During the first interview, I also attempt to clarify the individual's expectations about therapy, including such matters as what may take place, the possible length of therapy, the problem or problems considered most important, and the probabilities for and extent of positive change. I allow the person to ask any questions he or she may have, and I may indicate that we can take stock of how therapy is progressing after a few sessions. There does seem to be some empirical research in both behavioral and psychodynamic psychotherapy that indicates that beginning with the third interview, signs of progress are positively correlated with some criteria of outcome (Bandura, Jeffrey, & Wright, 1974; Mathews, Johnston, Shaw, & Gelder, 1974; Sachs, 1983). Consequently, one can reappraise some of the issues that were not particularly clear at the initial session. It is also possible that at a later session the patient may present what appears to be the "real" problem, the one that appears to be the cause of the person's current discomfort. Some individuals need to have more than one session before they feel free to trust the therapist with their innermost problems.

I do not have any set scheme for prioritizing treatment goals. In general, we should attempt to deal with the problems that the patient presents to us, not some goals set by the therapist. If, in terms of the general criteria mentioned earlier, it appears that the patient's difficulties can be ameliorated by means of psychotherapy, I would be guided by the patient's ranking of his problems and by what problem might be handled most quickly. When the patient mentions several problems, making some tangible progress quickly on one problem may have an overall positive effect. It demonstrates that change is possible, it increases hope and possibly self-efficacy, and it may also increase the patient's active cooperation in working on other problems.

TREATMENT STRUCTURE

An eclectic approach of this type can be used in most typical clinical settings, particularly outpatient settings. I have only used it for individual and couples' therapy, but it could be adapted for work with families. Obviously, in the latter instance the family would be the unit to consider, and particular attention would have to be paid to the family system and its interactions.

The therapy is essentially brief therapy and sometimes time-limited. As indicated earlier, the client should be given some reasonably clear idea of how long therapy will last. After all, the client's time and money are considerations here as well as the client's desire for improvement as quickly as possible. Most of my cases have taken between 14 and 20 sessions, and I usually indicate this amount of time in the first session. In a few cases, sometimes determined by the reality needs of the patient (e.g., having to make a decision quickly, moving away, not sure about therapy) I have set or agreed to a specific time limit.

Fees, though obviously an important concern to those in private practice, have not been a big issue for me. I have used the sliding scale of the university psychological service center as a rough guide but have generally discussed the fee with the client and agreed on a fee that does not appear to be an undue strain to the client.

I usually see my therapy clients on a once-per-week basis for the usual 50-minute period. However, when it appears warranted, or as the termination of therapy approaches, I usually modify this to a once-every-two-weeks schedule. This change in the arrangement hopefully signifies to the client that progress is being made, there is less need for dependence on the therapist, and the end of therapy is close at hand. This would seem to be a desirable practice for most forms of psychotherapy or counseling since it prepares the client for the termination of therapy and makes this process a gradual and natural one.

In most instances I do not see patients on a more frequent basis than once per week. Increasing the frequency of therapy increases the dependency of the client on the therapist and thus is undesirable. Also, spaced learning is more effective than massed learning. Related to this is my clinical belief or bias that significant change in the client occurs or is secured in the client's actual social environment and not in the consulting room. To the extent also that "time heals all wounds," it seems best to space appointments in a moderate or reasonable fashion. A final reason is the matter of the cost of therapy to the client. Meeting with a client two or three times a week generally leads to a greatly increased cost for therapy since there does not appear to be a corresponding decrease in the length of therapy.

No special structural or spatial arrangements have been made for this version of eclectic psychotherapy. I have usually met with my patients in whatever office I happened to have at the particular time. Seating arrangements have varied although I usually have individuals in my office seated at the side of my desk. Again, these practical aspects of psychotherapy do not appear to be of great importance. What takes place between therapist and client, including the attitudes and perceptions of the participants, is what really counts.

TREATMENT SPECIFICITY AND MATCHING

In the psychotherapeutic literature there has been a moderate amount of discussion about the matching of patient and therapist, and more recently, about treatment specificity. The former has been stressed primarily by psychodynamic therapists, has some face validity, but has not been a topic of much systematic research. The existing work on similarity or complementarity of client and therapist has not been impressive. Furthermore, patient-therapist matching is only possible theoretically when there are many therapists and patients who are readily available for matching purposes. In most practical clinical situations this is just not possible. Patients are assigned to the most available therapist, and if therapists have free time, they are very likely to accept the next patient who comes their way. Furthermore, I believe that most of the matching that we try to do with student therapists and patients in practica and internships is no more effective than chance assignments. Most of the reseach on patient-therapist matching has centered on sex and race as the primary variables, and the results thus far are not robust enough upon which to base practice (Garfield, in press).

The independent practitioner obviously is in a poor position to arrange the best matching of patient and therapist since he or she is the only available therapist. Also, patients tend to present themselves singly in spaced intervals rather than all at one time. Thus, rather than a strict matching process, what actually occurs is a selection or acceptance process. Ideally, therapists should select patients for therapy whom they feel they can help. This should be the only criterion. Admittedly, our selection criteria and predictive ability leave a bit to be desired, and one cannot expect a perfect performance. However, therapists should try to be as honest and forthright as possible in their appraisal of the patient and should not let other considerations, such as economic factors, pride, and egotism, influence their judgment.

Once therapy has begun and it appears

that there is some "mismatch" between therapist and client, or if the therapist for any reason believes the therapeutic relationship is a poor one, he or she should seriously consider discussing a possible referral of the client elsewhere. Similarly, if the therapist experiences feelings of anxiety, fear, hostility, or heightened sexual arousal toward the client, a referral elsewhere should be made. Within limits, these different problems can be discussed with the client in a reasonably open manner and a mutual decision reached. In some instances, this may result in a better therapeutic relationship. In the other instances, what seems to be a more expeditious solution of a problem situation is obtained. Otherwise therapy may proceed with little progress and great cost, or the client may drop out of therapy.

The matter of treatment specificity is another complex issue that has been emphasized in the last two decades or so, particularly by the behavior therapists. This orientation, in actuality, is similar to the accepted medical practice of selecting the appropriate treatment for a particular disorder or disease. This is a reasonable view since an inappropriate treatment may be ineffective, and in the worst scenario, the patient may die. Furthermore, specificity in psychotherapy was advanced as an alternative to the more traditional practice of one general form of therapy for more or less all psychological disorders, what I have called "universal therapy" (Garfield, 1980). The concept of specificity, therefore, has a definite and logical appeal for it does appear to promise a more effective and efficient form of psychotherapy.

It should be pointed out, however, that the theoretical conceptions underlying the ideas of matching and treatment specificity are essentially different and in opposition to each other, even though they are included in the same section here. In matching, the focus is on the personalities of the therapist and client and on the particular kind of therapeutic relationship

that is presumed to develop from the interaction of the two participants. When one speaks of treatment specificity, on the other hand, one emphasizes the client's disorder and the specific treatment that is considered to be the most effective for that disorder. In this case, personal and interactional variables receive scant attention—at least in the conceptualization of treatment specificity.

In my eclectic approach, and I would conjecture in most eclectic approaches, both of the above emphases receive attention. Although strict matching procedures would not be followed for the reasons mentioned earlier, close attention would be paid to the client's behavior in therapy, to the feelings of the therapist, and to the relationship in therapy. However, consideration would also be given to procedures or treatments that empirical research have demonstrated to be effective for specific types of problems. Such a decision would be based on the type of problem presented by the client, the importance of the particular problem in the total picture presented by the client, the client's attitude toward the proposed procedures, and the therapist's skill in administering the specific treatment. There would not necessarily be an automatic matching of reported symptom pattern and treatment although such a possibility would be considered as one component of therapy. However, attention also would be paid to the general factors discussed earlier in the chapter. In this sense, the treatment approach is an eclectic one.

TREATMENT INTERVENTION, STRATEGIES, AND THERAPIST BEHAVIOR

The amount of structure to be provided in the therapy sessions depends on the particular patient and the specific circumstances, even though this sounds like an overly general and evasive answer. However, I have to admit that there is no consistent plan that I appear to follow.

The first session is probably the most highly structured in that there are several specific topics or areas that I try to cover. At the beginning I ask the patients to tell me about the problem or problems that have been troubling them and that have led them to seek therapy. I then proceed to discuss some of the other topics mentioned earlier in the section on patient assessment. From that point on, the type and extent of therapeutic intervention are determined by the presenting problem, the individual patient, and not infrequently, by the amount of time available for therapeutic work. However, after the initial interview, which is structured to a large extent by the therapist, the client is given considerable opportunity to discuss his or her problems and to express or ventilate feelings. To a great extent also, I allow the client to determine the content of the sessions in these interviews.

There are several considerations that I view as potentially important during these early sessions. First, I do not want to indicate and reinforce a passive role for the client. Thus, I try to create the expectancy that the client will be participating actively in the therapy. Second, I believe that empathic listening on the part of the therapist helps to convey the therapist's sincere interest in the client and his or her desire to help him. This, in turn, is of some importance in facilitating a positive relationship in therapy and in motivating the client to collaborate in the therapeutic enterprise. Third, at least some patients need to develop trust in the therapist before they really reveal the problem that is most disturbing to them. The pattern of therapy described here thus may facilitate this process and allow a great potentiality for positive change.

In addition to the considerations mentioned above, at least two features or processes may occur when the client is encouraged to discuss his or her problems or feelings in a favorable therapeutic climate. One is the opportunity for emotional release or catharsis. This may occur with only a small percentage of clients, but when it does, it is a most impressive phenomenon. Such a catharsis may be most therapeutic for individuals experiencing acute guilt. Another process that may occur as the client discusses his or her difficulties is desensitization. The client has the opportunity to discuss problems at some length, and as a result, they may not appear to be as troublesome as originally viewed.

Consequently, the emphasis in the early sessions is on encouraging the patient to discuss personal problems and to express feelings openly. Although the therapist should have a flexible stance, it is best if he or she has some general plan in mind as a guide for intervention, which can be modified as new material and observations arise. It is also possible that some patients will not make use of the opportunity to express themselves and to explore possible difficulties, in which case the therapist must make a special effort to engage the patient in therapy if at all possible.

Such behavior on the part of the patient has been called resistance by psychodynamic therapists. Regardless of what it is called, it may have different causes and may be a hindrance to progress in therapy. There is no simple solution to the problem. The therapist can offer an explanation to the patient and encourage him to try to express his thoughts and feelings. However, I personally do not attempt to "wait out" the patient's lack of participation or resistance, which some more traditional dynamic therapists may do. Such a procedure tends to drag out therapy, increasing its length and cost, but not necessarily its efficacy. For example, a graduate student was seeing a 12-year-old boy in a community outpatient clinic. The boy resented being forced into therapy and was sullen and unresponsive in the early therapy sessions. The clinic supervisor advised the student to simply "wait out" the young child. This process went on for about 14 sessions with no discernible progress until termination at this point. It was a very trying experience for the graduate student and, no doubt, for the client as well.

Psychotherapy, like psychological testing, requires the cooperation of the client. Although it is possible to force-feed individuals and to administer medical injections against a person's will, the situation in psychotherapy is quite different. Consequently, the patient's attitudes and behaviors during the early sessions are important indicators of later progress in therapy and of developing problems. If the patient appears unresponsive, this should be discussed with him or her without undue delay. Such discussions may also reveal more clearly the patient's expectations about therapy, feelings toward the therapist, and early dissatisfactions with therapy. Hopefully, these matters can be resolved by this type of open discussion and therapy continued on a more positive basis. On the other hand, if this is not possible, perhaps a mutual decision to terminate therapy can be reached with the understanding that therapy can be reinstituted when the patient feels inclined to do so. My own bias is to try to handle such matters early in therapy, at least by the fifth interview, so that long impasses do not develop and the patient does not drop out of therapy.

Thus far, our discussion has focused on the early sessions. Although the emphasis has been on the patient's discussing his or her problems and expressing his or her thoughts and feelings, with the therapist as an empathic listener, other therapist behaviors can begin to be brought into play as deemed appropriate for the given case. The therapist may ask the client for clarification of certain points, may ask direct questions, may offer suggestions, and may assign specific tasks to be performed by the client in the interval between therapy sessions. Unfortunately, I cannot spell out concretely and in specific detail the precise and orderly behaviors the therapist will use for each specific kind of patient. My approach to therapy is simply not that refined, methodical, or orderly. I have no prepared therapy manual like those used for Beck's cognitive therapy and the interpersonal therapy being evaluated in the collaborative study of depression administered by the National Institute of Mental Health (Elkin, Parloff, Hadley, & Autry, 1985). These have been designed as time-limited therapies for designated cases of unipolar depression, and each of the sessions is spelled out in some detail. I can only offer some general guidelines.

Apart from showing sincere interest in the client and evaluating the client and his or her problems as adequately as possible, the therapist does not, and should not, respond in exactly the same way to each client. Clients vary in a number of ways that may influence the process of therapy and the therapist's behavior. Clients vary in age, sex, family situation, socioeconomic status, education, motivation, personality, and type of psychopathology. What might be indicated as important or useful for one client may not be of much value for a different client. Thus, the therapist usually cannot follow one specific set of procedures for all patients, even if they appear to have similar diagnoses. Rather, the therapist has to continually evaluate and reevaluate the client and the process of therapy, selecting procedures that appear useful and discarding ones that do not appear to be aiding the progress of therapy.

In this process, the therapist should make use of any procedures or techniques that appear applicable to the problem at hand and that have received research support. For example, if a client has a specific phobia as one feature of the reasons for seeking help, systematic desensitization can be used as one part of the therapeutic plan. If this works out satisfactorily, it will have potentially positive effects not only on the phobic behavior, but also on other aspects of the client's total functioning. First, it demonstrates to the client that positive change is possible and thus increases the client's hope and confidence in the therapeutic process and in further progress. Second, it tends to increase the client's self-esteem and self-efficacy. As a result of these changes, the client is both better equipped and more highly motivated to work on the other problems that present difficulties.

In a similar fashion, other cognitive or behavioral techniques that have been shown on the basis of empirical research to produce positive outcomes can also be employed as deemed appropriate. Attempts to modify distorted cognitions, providing information, practicing social skills, modeling, homework assignments, daily logs, and similar techniques may be of use in the individual cases. A primary difference in my use of such techniques and what appears to be their use by more cognitively and behaviorally oriented therapists is the emphasis placed on these procedures and how they are viewed theoretically. In my view, the application of these procedures may produce positive results even though the theoretical explanation advanced by the originators may not explain adequately the actual process of change. For example, Wolpe's theory of reciprocal inhibition has not been widely accepted by his fellow behaviorists, although they accept generally the finding that systematic desensitization produces positive results. Part of the success of the procedure could be due to the expectations brought by the patient, the confidence of the therapist, the rationale given to the patient, and the fact that the patient does confront his or her problem to some extent by means of the procedure.

Such procedures might best be viewed as one part of the therapeutic process, in which the therapeutic relationship and potential common factors provide the essential frame of reference. As a consequence, I would not emphasize them as much as their originators and would not use them in quite as rigid a manner. For example, in one instance where mild obesity was mentioned as one problem, I had the client keep a detailed log of all she ate and the time and place of eating. After several sessions in which she failed to bring the log to the therapy session, I did not force the issue with the client. I pointed out this rather unusual pattern and asked her what she made of it. It became clear that the weight problem was not a major concern, and by not stressing it, I was accepting this fact. These sessions, however, gave her the opportunity to decide to trust me and to finally bring forth the main source of her difficulty. Later, on her own, she told me that she had lost 10 pounds and was seemingly proud of the fact that it was of her own doing.

A final aspect of the therapist's work that should be mentioned here is the importance of observing the patient's behavior in the therapy hour. Although the patient may have one or more specific symptoms or problems, the patient's style of interpersonal behavior is of some importance in his overall adjustment —whether it be a cause or a result of his current difficulties. In either case, an attempt to modify the behavior may be worthwhile. As the therapist observes the client's behavior in the clinical situation, he should be able to note certain characteristic patterns that may account, at least in part, for the client's difficulties. Focusing on these patterns and discussing them with the client become more than a mere verbal interaction since the focus is on actual behavior that can be pointed out by the therapist. Obviously, this has to be done in a sensitive and understanding manner. However, since the intent is to help the client function in a more satisfying manner and also since such discussion can be followed by attempts to modify the behaviors in question, the client can respond positively. In such instances, use can be made of role playing and of exercises and tasks carried out in the client's social environment.

In this approach, therefore, the therapist is considered to play an active role, even when he or she is ostensibly just listening to the verbalizations of the client. The therapist has the responsibility to evaluate the client, to plan the therapy, to guide the process, and to evaluate it and institute changes when possible. I emphasize this point even though the type of client clearly has an important influence on the process of therapy and its outcome. Still, we have too frequently blamed the client when therapy has not progressed in the manner we would have desired. The client may be difficult or recalcitrant, and the possibility of helping him or her by means of psychotherapy may be extremely limited. Nevertheless, the therapist, as the professional, is responsible for what takes place. If the prognosis for positive outcome is very poor, this should be made explicit at the start and an appraisal as to whether it is worth initiating therapy or not made at that point. A responsible therapist should not continue to see a client over a long period of time with no significant change and then place the responsiblity for lack of progress on the client.

The above discussion leads rather naturally into the topic of termination. Most experiences are finite and have both a beginning and an end, and the same is true of psychotherapy even though in some instances the therapy has appeared to go on forever. Viewed in this naturalistic manner, there should be few difficulties, if any, in bringing therapy to a close.

The kind of client, the goals of therapy, and the particular type of therapy all may influence the actual process of termination. In dynamically oriented, long-term

psychotherapy, the dependency of the client on the therapy and the therapist appears to be increased, and termination has been viewed as a problem. In relatively short-term therapy of the type described here, this does not appear to be the case. Furthermore, references to termination are made in a natural manner at various stages of therapy. In the initial session some reference is made to the possible length of treatment, and this gives the client some potential termination dates. As therapy proceeds and as some of the goals of therapy are being reached, mention of the impending termination of therapy can also be made. At this juncture, termination can be discussed with the client and an agreed-upon date set. I generally discuss termination about two or three sessions before the end of therapy. In addition, I usually stagger the final couple of sessions so that we meet every two weeks instead of weekly.

The above description, of course, applies to the "normal" or modal cases of psychotherapy—those cases in which there are no unusual problems. Although the problems of termination in short-term eclectic therapy do not appear to be as frequent or serious as they seemingly have been in therapy that lasts for several years or a decade, a few potential problems may be mentioned briefly here.

Probably the most serious issue is presented when there is an obvious lack of progress in therapy. The reasons may be diverse or obscure, but the fact remains that satisfactory progress has not been obtained. This is clearly a disappointment to most therapists and frequently is difficult to face. Nevertheless, as emphasized earlier, the therapist has a responsibility to evaluate the progress of therapy and to face the facts of therapy, unpleasant though they may be. In some instances, there may be good reasons for shifting to a different therapeutic strategy and trying some other potentially helpful procedures. However, in other instances, this does not seem reasonable, and steps should be taken to terminate the therapy. In this process I would be open and frank with the patient, indicating that our goals have not been reached and that it is probably not worth continuing. Unless the therapist feels confident that someone else has a high probability of helping the patient, it does not seem wise to refer the patient elsewhere. Although this may make the therapist feel somewhat better, in the long run it may not be beneficial for the patient, who may again experience failure and increased financial costs.

Sometimes a problem in terminating therapy may occur with an usually dependent patient. The therapist, of course, should be alerted early to such a problem by the behavior of the patient in therapy. Reference to future termination, therefore, should be made whenever there is an appropriate opportunity to do so and earlier than would otherwise be the case. Furthermore, in such cases, it is particularly important to begin spacing out the last few visits. In most instances, the staggered visits appear to indicate to the patient that he or she is fully capable of getting along without needing to see the therapist. In one instance, I agreed to see a patient an additional time one month after what was to have been the last therapy session. However, before the time of the appointment the patient called to say that he no longer felt the need for the extra session.

In general, termination should be determined by the progress (or lack of progress) of the patient. When the goals of therapy have been reasonably met and the patient's comments in therapy are generally of a positive nature, it is time to think of terminating therapy. Sometimes, this situation may occur in a relatively brief period of time. Although some therapists, particularly therapists in training, are reluctant to face up to this positive trend and to release the patient from ther-

apy, this is clearly counterproductive. When a patient reports consistent progress, has little to discuss pertaining to the initial reasons for seeking therapy, or asks the therapist when therapy will end, it is time to discuss termination! There is no reason to continue a patient in therapy when there are no real problems that are bothering the patient, even when therapy has lasted for only a few sessions.

MECHANISMS OF CHANGE

This topic has already been alluded to in an earlier section of this chapter when reference was made to the possibility of common factors as factors of some importance in facilitating client change. Such factors have been referred to by some as nonspecific because a proper understanding of their role has not been obtained and because factors other than those hypothesized by a particular orientation apparently have had some therapeutic impact. For these reasons, the unknown variables have been referred to as nonspecific. I prefer to refer to such potential factors as common factors since they appear to be present in most forms of psychotherapy.

At this stage it is difficult to spell out what the relative contribution of the various hypothesized therapeutic variables actually are. What exist at present are for the most part opinions or formulations, and not clearly demonstrated empirical facts. Thus, statements in this regard should be viewed as hypotheses. Within this context, I believe some aspects such as a "good" therapeutic relationship, discussed previously, are a prerequisite for potential progress in psychotherapy. However, a good relationship alone does not ensure positive change; it is only a prerequisite.

The skill of the therapist is of potential importance, although we have not clearly defined skill in psychotherapy nor have we conducted much in the way of systematic research. We have compared therapists in terms of theoretical orientation, gender, years of experience, professional discipline, and personal therapy, but not in terms of skill. This is an interesting commentary on psychotherapy.

In a related fashion, I am inclined to hypothesize that the personality and the psychological health of the therapist also play a role in effective therapy, although data to support my hypotheses are hard to come by. The personality of the therapist, however, has to be evaluated in terms of interactions with different clients. It is a commonly accepted belief in the field of psychotherapy that each therapist works more successfully with some clients than with others. Thus, we cannot speak only of the therapist's personality, but must consider it in relation to client variables.

With respect to the mental health or integration of the therapist, it is again a matter of what kind of conclusion to draw. On a clinical level, a disturbed therapist is capable of producing negative results. Some years ago, Allen Bergin and I conducted a small study of student therapists and did find a positive relationship between the adjustment level of the therapists as measured by the MMPI and the outcomes of the clients treated (Garfield & Bergin, 1971). Although this is encouraging, the finding cannot be viewed as truly robust without more systematic replication.

On the other hand, there has been little disagreement that patient variables have been considered to be extremely important as far as outcome in psychotherapy is concerned. Although prediction of outcome on this basis is usually only slightly better than chance, many well-known psychotherapists have stated that the client is the most important variable as far as outcome is concerned (Frank, 1979; Strupp, 1973). Although I have been somewhat critical of this view in the past since it allows us to place the blame for

therapeutic failure too easily on the client (Garfield, 1973), the latter does influence the outcome. The cooperation of the client is a necessary prerequisite for practically all psychological work. However, once such cooperation is secured, other variables or mechanisms of change are necessarily involved.

The therapist who is perceived favorably by the client first of all provides a source of hope for the client. If a positive relationship develops, the initial hope is reinforced and increases the client's confidence in the therapist and in himself. This, in turn, helps to foster the possibility or release of a number of other potentially therapeutic variables. Which ones come into play in a particular instance depend to some extent on the particular client and his or her problems. In some instances, some of these change-inducing variables have appeared to play a critical role in fostering change. In other instances, it has sometimes been difficult to specify clearly the change mechanisms. Although I have sometimes discussed what I thought were the reasons for a client's positive change, I have tried to emphasize that such views were essentially inferential. Unfortunately, I have conducted no research in this area, and the systematic investigation of therapeutic variables and mechanisms in general has received very little research—for understandable reasons. Such research is very difficult and time-consuming. At some point, however, it will have to be done if we are to understand clearly what brings about therapeutic change.

In the meantime, we present our best hypotheses about the possible mechanisms or interactions that facilitate patient change in psychotherapy. In the present context, only a brief presentation of some of the potential therapeutic variables will be made. A more detailed exposition is available elsewhere (Garfield, 1980).

Emotional Release or Catharsis

Besides the central role of the therapeutic relationship, which has been discussed previously, other potential variables appear to be important in psychotherapy. One of these, long recognized in psychotherapy, has been designated as emotional release, catharsis, or abreaction. Some forms of therapy have deliberately sought to induce or foster such strong emotional reactions in patients, whereas such reactions have occurred more or less spontaneously in more conventional forms of psychotherapy. When a patient is in a state of tension or turmoil, the opportunity to fully confide and express one's feelings and emotions to a trusted therapist may lead to a strong emotional discharge with positive consequences. This has only occurred a few times in my own clinical experience, but when it does, it is noticeable and sometimes dramatic. One brief example can be given here.

A young man had called for an appointment to discuss a personal problem that involved his relationship with his girl friend. When he came into the office, he was acutely upset and his palms were very wet. I offered him a seat and asked him to tell me about his difficulties. He described his relationship with his girl friend, and as he got into his story he began to talk quickly and very emotionally. My interactions were limited primarily to listening, nodding, and trying to be empathic. The few times I tried to offer some therapeutic wisdom to the client, he ignored me and continued with his emotional outpouring. As he described his difficulties, the solution to his problem, which he could not fully face earlier, became clear to him. Although he had thought of marrying his girl friend, he now saw clearly that it was not a good decision. Although he had strong feelings of guilt about this, these seemed to be rather fully expressed in the session, and he ended with a great sigh of relief. Before I could offer any more therapeutic wisdom, he said, "Thank you very much, Doctor. You've been a great help," and quickly departed.

Of course, not all clients will respond as the preceding one did. However, I have noted significant improvement in several cases where the emotional release or catharsis was not anywhere near as vivid or evident. Nevertheless, in two cases that come to mind, bringing out and discussing something that was decidedly guilt-producing in the individual gave evidence of some relief and marked the beginning of positive change.

Explanation, Rationale, and Interpretation

Another aspect of psychotherapy that appears to contribute to positive change pertains to the therapist's providing the patient with some type of explanation of the latter's difficulties and how psychotherapy may improve the situation. Again, this is a common factor in almost all forms of psychotherapy, although it has been viewed and labeled differently within the different therapeutic systems. Whether one emphasizes interpretation of unconscious conflicts, distorted perceptions and cognitions, or irrational beliefs, the patient is being given some type of explanation or rationale for his or her behavior. Even behavior therapists, who pay no attention to such dynamic concepts as interpretation and insight, do provide their patients with some explanation of how their behavioral difficulties have arisen as well as a rationale for the procedures they will employ in therapy. The emergence of cognitive behavior therapy is also an indication of how explanatory concepts are being incorporated into behavioral approaches.

One of the fascinating aspects of interpretation and explanation in psychotherapy is the fact that they appear to vary tremendously among the diverse approaches to psychotherapy. This need not be spelled out here in any detail. It is apparent that the explanations offered by Freudians, Adlerians, Jungians, Sullivanians, cognitive therapists, rational therapists, and a host of others differ, but supposedly they all are therapeutic. Frank (1971, 1973) has also described this as a process of providing the patient with a rationale or myth, but a process of some importance in psychotherapy.

It is also interesting that in the large-scale investigation of encounter groups by Lieberman, Yalom, and Miles (1973), the groups that secured better outcomes tended to give some emphasis to explanations and cognitions. It thus appears that some type of explanation offered by the therapist during psychotherapy has a positive impact on the patient. It seems that whether or not the explanation or interpretation given is "true" in the theoretical or scientific sense is really of little significance in the therapeutic situation. This is a rather strong pronouncement on my part, and when I have presented this view to groups of therapists, I have been aware that it tends to be rather coolly received —and understandably so. It challenges the therapist's own professional-scientific belief system and appears also to denigrate his or her professional work. Nevertheless, the implications of comparable outcomes among the major forms of psychotherapy, particularly recently, should make us face this issue in a forthright manner. Even more important, we should try to use this information as best we can to improve the efficacy and efficiency of psychotherapy.

The important point appears to be that providing the patient with some type of rationale or belief system appears to be of some therapeutic value. In an attempt to explain the plausibility of this view previously, I have stated the matter as follows:

The fact that the therapist appears to understand the patient's problems and is able to provide this understanding to the patient appears to reduce the latter's anxiety about his problems and to engender hope for alleviating them. When an individual is experiencing discomfort and does not understand what his symptoms signify, what has caused this unhappy state of affairs, or how serious his condition may be, it is reassuring to contact a professional therapist who seems to know what the problem is, what factors are responsible for it, and who also offers a treatment which supposedly can alleviate the patient's situation. (Garfield, 1980, p. 101)

Thus, the *particular* explanations or interpretations offered by the therapist do not appear to be of primary importance. Rather, the critical factor appears to be whether or not the patient finds them to be creditable and acceptable. If the explanation is not convincing or incomprehensible, it is likely that the patient will not accept it. In such instances, the proffered rationale will have little positive effect. On the other hand, if the patient fully accepts the explanation, several positive effects may take place. Uncertainties and doubts may be lessened, the patient may be reassured, and his hopes and expectations about therapy may be increased. In addition, the patient may be motivated to collaborate more intensively with the therapist and to try out new behaviors. The above includes a lot of "maybe's," but it appears to be a reasonable hypothesis.

Some possible support for the above supposition is apparent in the way at least some prospective clients shop around for specific kinds of therapy. People have become more sophisticated about psychotherapy than they were in the past owing to the increasing popularity of psychotherapy. Paperback editions of a variety of therapeutic orientations are available in bookstores and elsewhere, and I suspect that they outsell our more scholarly tomes on psychotherapy. It is possible that certain clients are more receptive to certain rationales than others, and that therapy would be more effective if the proper matching of rationale and client occurred. However, it also seems reasonable to believe that how good the therapeutic relationship is may also influence the client's receptivity to the therapist's explanations and rationale. Although how the process actually works is not fully understood, I adhere to the view that we should try to give the client some clear explanation of his difficulties as well as providing him with some rationale for the approach to be undertaken in therapy.

Reinforcement in Psychotherapy

Although many nonbehavioral approaches make no specific theoretical reference to reinforcement in psychotherapy, it appears that reinforcement is a commonly used therapeutic technique. All therapists tend to respond positively to verbal reports or behaviors that appear positive to them, and thus they differentially reinforce both in-therapy and out-of-therapy behaviors. Such therapist behaviors as nodding, smiling, frowning, and verbal responses of selected kinds can influence the behavior of the client. Even nondirective or client-oriented therapists such as Carl Rogers tend to reinforce certain client responses (Murray, 1956; Truax, 1966).

To say that the therapist is potentially capable of influencing the behavior of the patient would not be a surprising statement by any means. Certainly, most therapeutic approaches appear to have this as an implicit assumption. However, how the influence process works or how it can be used most effectively gets into more controversial areas. Learning-oriented therapists do make more conscious use of reinforcement principles than do humanistic- or dynamically oriented therapists, and in a sense the comparison is between structured learning and incidental learning. However, theoretically, all therapists are desirous of promoting positive change

in the client, and thus we do want to reinforce certain behaviors and to modify, diminish, or extinguish others.

Consequently, therapists should be aware of their role in influencing patients by means of reinforcement and should also use such knowledge to secure changes in patients. This does not mean being a "social reinforcement machine" or a "manipulator." Actually, the strongest reinforcement effects are secured when the client under the guidance of the therapist attempts behaviors that are personally and socially rewarding for him/her. Thus, the therapist can utilize reinforcement for a variety of therapeutic purposes.

Desensitization

By now, desensitization has become a well-known behavioral technique usually referred to as systematic desensitization. However, even before the latter procedure was described by Wolpe (1958), a more general description of desensitization had been presented by others (Garfield, 1957; Levine, 1948; Rosenzweig, 1936). It was noted that as patients discuss their problems in the understanding and accepting climate of therapy, over time these problems appear less threatening. It is as if the process of bringing out concerns into the open and examining them or sharing them with the therapist lessens their impact. Problems may be perceived differently as the client discusses them. By having to communicate items that are disturbing, the individual has to organize his experience and to be relatively more objective and realistic in appraising his life situation. In terms of a learning orientation, the client's anxieties about his difficulties are gradually extinguished as he discusses them in the security of the therapeutic setting and no negative consequences follow.

Whether or not this process is actually one of gradual extinction or whether other processes are also involved is not clear. However, it does seem as if a process of desensitization occurs with at least some patients. As in the case with the other therapeutic mechanisms hypothesized to operate in successful psychotherapy, it may be just one of the mechanisms operating in therapy in any given case. Nevertheless, its potential importance should not be overlooked by the therapist.

As indicated earlier, the concept of desensitization has become well known in more recent years as a result of Wolpe's formulation and description of systematic desensitization (Wolpe, 1958, 1961). Since this procedure has received considerable clinical and research attention, little description of it need be given here. Essentially, the procedure is based on the view that in order to diminish anxiety, the therapist must use a process that is antagonistic to it. Although several processes can be used, relaxation has been the most common one. By definition, if a person is fully relaxed, he/she cannot be anxious, and Wolpe has tended to use muscle relaxation procedures to attain this objective. What follows is then a systematic pairing of relaxation with a list of anxiety-provoking stimuli, arranged in terms of degree of arousal, with the patient gradually imagining these scenes and proceeding from the weakest to the most frightening.

Wolpe's approach clearly is a more structured and focused one which emphasizes desensitization. Although Wolpe's theoretical formulations have been criticized, the practical results of systematic desensitization have for the most part been positive (Davison & Wilson, 1973). Thus, although, in vivo exposure treatment has been more heavily favored for agoraphobia in recent years (Marks, 1978; Mathews, Gelder, & Johnston, 1981), systematic desensitization can be used with positive effect in the outpatient setting as one aspect or component of the overall treatment.

Facing or Confronting a Problem

This particular aspect of the psychotherapeutic process has something in common with exposure treatment but is not synonymous with it. It does not necessarily have to be limited to the treatment of phobic behaviors, and it can begin on the basis of verbal discussions in therapy. In fact, the term "confrontation" has been used for some time in strictly verbal psychodynamic psychotherapy where the therapists confront the patient with any one of a number of things that the patient has avoided facing or needs to be informed about. These include such matters as interpretation of content, behaviors in therapy, problems of resistance, and the like.

It is certainly true that many people tend to avoid certain situations that make them feel uncomfortable or inadequate, even if the behaviors are not pronounced enough to be labeled as clinical phobias, e.g., some levels of shyness. However, if the avoidance behaviors can be clearly pointed out to the patient in a sympathetic manner as the source of much of his/her discomfort, the patient may gradually acknowledge this. Furthermore, and most important, the patient may then be willing to enter situations that frequently have been avoided. If these experiences are successful, both anticipation of negative consequences and actual discomfort should decrease and more socially adaptable behaviors result.

The last sentence does indicate the similarity of "facing one's problem" and in vivo exposure. However, I would point out that several other therapeutic techniques, such as systematic desensitization, flooding, implosion, and modeling, have also reported positive results when applied to different fears and avoidance behaviors. Thus, there appears to be a possible common factor operating in all these approaches, and it appears to be that the client in some way is confronted with the negative situation and learns that he can face it without any catastrophic consequences.

In my own experience, I have made use of this procedure after at least a few sessions of therapy. By this time I have felt that I did have an understanding of the client and his/her problem and that some confidence and trust in the therapist had developed. As a consequence, suggestions can be made that the client is willing to attempt. I favor beginning with activities that are less threatening and which the client will most likely attempt. One can then go on to activities that are more important for the client's overall adjustment. Nothing succeeds like success, and positive feedback is the strongest form of reinforcement. As the client succeeds in situations that previously were avoided or caused discomfort, increases in self-confidence and self-esteem are likely to occur. Furthermore, "visible evidence of improvement also facilitates an increased expectancy of positive outcome in psychotherapy on the part of the client, which is also of some benefit" (Garfield, 1980, p. 122).

Information and Training in Psychotherapy

At least a certain number of individuals who seek out psychotherapy are poorly informed about topics of importance or are deficient in desired social skills. In such instances, providing information or attempting to improve social skills can be beneficial. In fact, some recent approaches to psychotherapy have emphasized the training of certain personal skills, e.g., social skills training and assertiveness training. The main difference between these approaches and my eclectic approach is that the former tend to focus on a specific type of problem and to emphasize skill training as the form of therapy,

whereas I might use such procedures as one aspect of therapy at a particular time.

Traditional dynamically oriented therapists have been reluctant to provide information or to answer directly certain questions asked by the patient for fear this would foster an overly dependent role in the patient. There is some validity to this view, but I believe that it was too rigidly adhered to in the past. If the patient asks a question about something of real concern, a direct answer may be very therapeutic. This appears to be particularly true if the patient had a false fear as to his condition and prognosis and correct information could dispel this. I can recall two patients with excessive anxiety and guilt about masturbation who seemed to improve noticeably when the correct information was provided in an understanding and empathic manner. Obviously, how important the providing of information is will depend on the patient and the circumstances.

Somewhat similar comments can be made for the training of certain social skills. Again, this would be just one component or aspect of psychotherapy and would be used to help the individual become more adept and self-confident in his social adjustment. If certain social inadequacies or skills are not fully acknowledged by the patient initially, then the process would be one of confronting the patient with this problem. In this instance it would be as described in the earlier section. However, if these inadequacies are clearly seen by the patient as a personal deficiency, no confrontation is necessary and the focus is on improving the patient's skills. Some role playing can be used along with suggestions for activities to be attempted in the social environment.

Time as a Variable in Psychotherapy

A final variable or "mechanism" that I want to mention here is time. Although we all recognize that a certain amount of time is required for therapy to be conducted, experts do not agree as to what the optimum time for different kinds of problems is. However, time per se is not given much emphasis, despite the old folk saying that "time heals." Also, the importance of time is recognized in medicine where the course of an illness is described in part in terms of time; and the concept of spontaneous remission is also related. It is, of course, difficult to appraise its role in psychotherapy because it appears as a "given" and as more or less a background variable for the introduction and interaction of other variables.

Another possible reason why time is accorded little specific emphasis as a therapeutic variable is that it is not viewed as being under the control or direction of the therapist. For example, it requires no special skill to let time go by—anyone can do it. Furthermore, if the mere passing of time is therapeutically important, it would appear to detract from the other activities that are guided more directly by the therapist.

Since a number of different influences may affect the individual over time, it is difficult to isolate the role that time or other variables play in this process. For example, certain maturational or recuperative processes may occur within the individual and may account to a large extent for the positive changes evident. Anyone who has worked with children is aware of the changes that take place as a result of growth and maturation. It is also possible that very positive (or negative) events may occur in the patient's life that affect the process and outcome of psychotherapy. In some cases these may be extremely potent influences. Sometimes, also, patients get support and psychological help from significant others, and the therapist may be unaware of such help.

In addition to possible organismic processes and external events, psychotherapy is also a potential variable for producing change. Thus, it is frequently difficult to clearly specify the actual variables that have produced change in any given case. As therapists, we are inclined to emphasize the 50 minutes per week that we spend with a patient. However, some people have more favorable social support systems and recover more quickly from crises and stress situations. Psychotherapy may be a worthwhile vehicle for facilitating these potential changes and adding another variable to the process. To this extent, time provides the opportunity for the various mechanisms to operate and is also part of the process.

Finally, I would add that time is a variable or factor that is used in common by all forms of psychotherapy. To the extent that most form of psychotherapy have obtained roughly comparable results, time is an additional variable that may contribute to this finding.

CASE EXAMPLE

This section will be a brief one since I have no recorded cases of my own. There are a number of reasons for this, the main one being that it is a tedious and time-consuming task to listen to a number of tapes and to take notes on them. As part of a study I conducted some years ago, I listened to first therapy interviews and along with two colleagues completed a number of rating scales (Garfield, Affleck, & Muffley, 1963). I found it to be a most demanding task, and when our attempts to predict continuation in psychotherapy on this basis were rather disappointing, I developed an even more negative view toward taping. However, I do require taped sessions in supervision of students.

There are, of course, problems in using therapy notes or in relying on memories that over time tend to get more selective and somehow more positive. It is exceedingly difficult to evaluate what might have been the truly important variables accounting for whatever positive change occurred. Nevertheless, that is what I have to draw upon here.

I accepted a woman as a patient whose major complaint centered around marital difficulties. She had been seen twice before at the outpatient clinic by different therapists for periods ranging from 18 to 24 sessions. However, although she apparently had been a cooperative patient, she had made relatively little progress. She had a variety of symptomatic complaints, primarily depression and fears centering around her marital difficulties. Apparently, her husband was abusive at times, and because there were two young children in the family, leaving her husband or attempting to dissolve the marriage were not seen as really adequate solutions. Despite the fact that the marital situation appeared to be central in terms of this woman's difficulties, apparently little or no attempt had been made to involve the husband in therapy.

Consequently, I agreed to see this woman, but only on condition that her husband agree to participate as well. Thus, his presence was requested for our first meeting. It was apparent to me that the wife was highly motivated to try to improve her situation and was, in my view, a reasonably good case for psychotherapy. At the same time, it was apparent that the husband was essentially the opposite. The wife indicated that she had wanted her husband to participate in therapy previously, but that he had balked. Consequently, she had undertaken therapy herself. However, the husband made an appearance at this first session because I had insisted on it as a condition for accepting the wife as a patient and the wife in turn had threatened to leave him if he did not comply.

Both patients were in their early thirties, ran a small business, and had been married for about eight years. The difficulties between them were largely related to the husband's drinking, sometimes stimulated by economic pressures. His drinking bouts were episodic, but his abusive treatment of his wife was related to them. They were both high-school graduates and appeared to be of average intelligence. Both also wanted to avert a marital breakup.

Although the husband rather clearly indicated little interest in participating in therapy and stated that his wife was the one who had this interest, I emphasized that two people were involved in the current difficulties. Therefore, treatment had to be conducted with both of them. We started on a weekly basis, and my first impressions were clearly supported. Nevertheless, although the wife participated actively and the husband only defensively or in response to questions or reflections from the therapist, I felt it was important to have the therapy oriented to the two of them. There were several reasons for this, and I believe they were sound. The husband had avoided therapy previously, and I felt it was important to have him see that he was involved in this problem and had a responsibility in this regard. I also took the view that marital problems are best resolved when both partners participate in therapy. Third, the different perceptions or appraisals of husband and wife can be most directly handled when both are in therapy; and last, the previous therapy of the wife alone had not resulted in real or sustained progress.

The patients were seen on a weekly basis for eight sessions. During this period things were going along satisfactorily, but I felt this was mainly due to the husband's "behaving himself" while he was in therapy. During these sessions the same behavior was noted in therapy as mentioned earlier. The wife seemed to welcome the opportunity to express her concerns and feelings, demonstrated a strong interest in therapy, and was responsive to comments and suggestions from the therapist.

Her husband said relatively little, appeared to be uncomfortable, and showed little interest in the therapy sessions. Consequently, I decided to make a change at this point. I pointed out their different attitudes and behaviors and said that I thought the wife would like to continue in therapy and to talk about her situation and her feelings. On the other hand, it was clear that the husband now realized his role in the marital problems but was somewhat uncomfortable in talking about himself and his feelings. I tried to present this in an understanding and empathic manner, and both agreed with my appraisal. From that point on I said I would see the wife individually for two weekly sessions and then the husband for one weekly session. This was agreed to and became the plan we followed for a couple of months. Using the same rationale, after some progress was made, I saw the wife every two weeks and the husband once a month.

My goals were to clarify the patients' patterns of interactions, to increase the wife's self-esteem, confidence, and assertiveness, to confront the husband with the implications of his behavior and to help him accept his positive features, and hopefully, to make their life a more harmonious one. In line with what has been described earlier in this chapter, I attempted to develop a good relationship with both patients and in this regard succeeded mainly with the wife. I avoided partiality to either patient, communicated interest and sincerity in helping them, allowed each of them an opportunity to express his/her thoughts and feelings, reinforced positive statements and behaviors, provided some explanations about the causes of their difficulties, made suggestions, and, where appropriate, offered encouragement and reassurances. I also had the patients pay particular attention to events that appeared to precipitate conflict and abusive behavior, and to work out behaviors to avoid this type of build-up.

I saw the wife for a total of 30 individual sessions and the husband for 13 sessions. The wife clearly appeared to profit from our sessions. She expressed her concerns, discussed different ways of responding to the husband, and tried to be consistent and confident in her reactions. Therapy seemed to have a very reassuring effect on her. There were fewer abusive incidents, the mood of both parties seemed much more positive, and the marriage appeared more stable. Although I did not see a great deal of change in the husband, he at least appeared less defensive and was somewhat better able to accept his share of responsibility in the problems discussed. Prior to therapy he had tended to call his wife "crazy" because she had sought psychiatric care. This pattern was no longer evident.

The wife had made what I regarded as significant progress—and that is one reason I remember this case. She was much more self-confident, she was no longer depressed, and she stated that she had profited a great deal from therapy. She also stated that she felt she could handle future problems more adequately than she was capable of doing in the past. In our final session, she mentioned that I was the first man that she felt she could trust and that this was an important aspect of therapy for her. I am inclined to agree that trust is a feature of a desirable therapeutic relationship and that it is particularly important with patients whose lives have been deficient in adequate interpersonal relationships. At least in this case, it did appear to be a significant feature.

RESEARCH ON THE APPROACH

Unfortunately, no systematic research has been conducted on this approach, and thus this section will be painfully brief.

The only evidence that exists to support the efficacy of this approach are clinical observations and anecdotes, and this is not really adequate. On the other hand, as mentioned earlier, there is a considerable body of research data that can be viewed as providing indirect support for the approach described here. Meltzoff and Kornreich (1970), in their view of comparative studies of psychotherapy, concluded that "there is no current evidence that one traditional method is more successful than another in modifying psychopathology, alleviating symptoms or improving adjustment" (p. 200). This conclusion has been reaffirmed in most major reviews since that time (Garfield, 1984; Smith, Glass, & Miller, 1980).

The fact that comparative research has revealed few, if any, significant differences between the psychotherapies evaluated suggests the possibility of common factors operating within the various psychotherapies. As already emphasized, it was the idea of common factors that led to the present eclectic formulation of the psychotherapeutic process. Although this eclectic approach lacks detailed specific guidelines or a training manual, it is potentially researchable. However, to conduct a truly worthwhile study would be a large undertaking, and at this time I have neither the resources nor the drive to undertake such research. The fact that differences between the various therapeutic approaches have been small has led to the present formulation, even though I have not viewed it as a distinctly worked-out system of psychotherapy. For very sound reasons, I have not pictured myself as leading a new school of psychotherapy. We have too many as it is. Instead, I viewed my own work as an attempt to foster a greater rapprochement and integration among the diverse schools of psychotherapy, a movement that now appears to be gaining a following among a number of distinguished psychotherapists.

CLINICAL TRAINING

This section on training, of necessity, will be a brief presentation of my own beliefs and biases on this topic. I have made more comprehensive presentations elsewhere (Garfield, 1977, 1980). Unfortunately, the training of psychotherapists is another area of psychotherapy where only limited research of consequence has been conducted. Thus, beliefs predominate and let the reader beware!

I have taught what is essentially an eclectic approach for over 35 years and see no need to learn a specific therapy system if one wants to become an eclectic therapist. I have always believed that it is best to take a direct path toward one's objective. Some learning of the main essentials of major orientations can and should be provided at the beginning of training, and contributions of importance can be emphasized. However, I would also point out the common elements in these therapies. I tend to make reference to some emphases from psychodynamic approaches, client-centered therapy, and cognitive approaches. Several behavioral procedures are also worthwhile learning since they are not overly complex and have a positive degree of utility. However, since we have always had a course in behavior therapy for our doctoral students, I have not actually taught these procedures.

No prior competence in any therapy system is required before one becomes a "true eclectic therapist"—whatever that is. In fact, if one is truly competent in some therapeutic approach, and achieving what appear to be positive results, there would seem to be little motivation for changing one's approach. It is also possible that all good therapists are already eclectic therapists to some degree.

There is no particular amount of clinical experience that would be appropriate for all therapists since aptitudes and learning ability vary. Rather, ideally, I would prefer that the learners reach a certain level of competence before they are terminated from their training and that progress be evaluated in terms of patient change. However, one year of practicum training with about four active cases and one year of internship with about eight cases as an active case load would appear to be a minimum amount of clinical experience during the training period.

I am one of those, apparently in the minority, who does not view personal therapy as important in the training of psychotherapists. However, this is a strongly held belief on the part of a large number of psychotherapists. The reasons for my contrary view are several. I have known a small number of individuals who have undergone analysis or long-term dynamic therapy and have had an opportunity to observe them both professionally and socially. Although some changes occurred, both positive and negative, they did not become really good therapists.

There is also the possibility that some individuals over-identify with their own therapy or therapist and in essence become overly fixated on a specific form of therapy. Thus, they are not as open to research data or new ideas.

Finally, the few and admittedly limited research studies reported on this issue show no advantage for therapists who have had personal therapy (Garfield, 1980; Garfield & Kurtz, 1976b). Thus, except for personal reasons, I would not recommend personal therapy.

I also do not believe that research experience is necessary for training psychotherapists. However, this statement requires some qualification. Research expertise is not necessarily correlated with therapeutic expertise, and I know of no studies that indicate that it is. Thus, if I were to train psychotherapists exclusively, I would concentrate on psychotherapeutic skills and not on research skills. However, in such instances I would provide some instruction in evaluating psychotherapy outcome, and I would want

the therapists to work in a setting where individuals trained in clinical research were available for consultation and in-service training. This is, of course, hypothetical since I have only been involved in the training of clinical psychologists and psychiatrists. However, with proper selection, a program resembling the experimental program of Rioch and her colleagues with middle-aged housewives could be carried out (Rioch, 1967).

I have no ideal training program in mind, nor have I given much thought to it. However, the essentials of a good program can be noted briefly. The proper selection of candidates for training is an obvious first step. Although there are lists of ideal criteria for clinical psychologists (American Psychological Association, 1947) and psychoanalysts and psychotherapists (Holt & Luborsky, 1958), they are not particularly useful. Almost no one would meet the criteria if they were applied strictly, and they have actually never been validated in any systematic way. Thus, I would not obsess particularly about selection criteria but select perhaps six or eight criteria as guides, e.g., maturity, sensitivity, "reasonable" level of adjustment, empathy, common sense, interest in working with people, and perceptiveness. Even though we have not been particularly successful in selecting people in the past, it is still important to weed out the more obvious cases of psychosis or organic brain damage.

The curriculum should center mainly on a few areas. I would include courses in personality, psychopathology, motivation, learning, development, and interviewing but focus on psychotherapy, with the emphasis on controlled practicum work. In the latter instance, in addition to individual supervision, I would want a four-hour session in which the therapy cases, with taped sessions, are discussed in a small group setting. In this way, viewpoints other than just the supervisor's can be discussed and critically evaluated. In addition, all cases would be research cases to the extent that some basic measures would be used before and after therapy to evaluate change and also as a means of evaluating progress in psychotherapy for both therapist-in-training and client. As training progressed, the student could be introduced to the existing research in the field by means of the *Handbook of Psychotherapy and Behavior Change* (Garfield & Bergin, 1978).

It should be emphasized that the above description of training applies to programs designed to train psychotherapists *only*. At present, we have no truly exclusive programs for training psychotherapists. Rather, we have programs for training psychiatrists, clinical psychologists, counseling psychologists, psychiatric social workers, and the like. In all these programs individuals are being educated for specific professions in which psychotherapy may play a greater or lesser role. Selection criteria and training programs for these professions would necessarily differ one from the other, and they would also differ from programs designed to train psychotherapists exclusively. Psychiatrists, by definition, require training in medicine, which is not really a requirement for psychotherapists. Similarly, I would like to see clinical psychologists trained in research procedures, which also is not required for training psychotherapists. Existing programs for training psychotherapists, usually in a specific type of psychotherapy, are essentially postgraduate programs for individuals who have already completed a professional program in one of the mental health fields. They are not programs for training psychotherapists as delineated here.

It is doubtful that specific programs to train psychotherapists exclusively as a distinct profession will succeed, although there have been conferences to discuss such a possibility (Holt, 1971). I have discussed such developments and related matters in more detail elsewhere (Garfield, 1977) and will not repeat them here. However, it does appear that the established professions will continue, and thus psychotherapy training will be provided largely within the existing professional programs. Without doubt, these will vary greatly in quantity and quality. However, there does appear to be some trend for the broadening of such programs so that they are more eclectic than they were in the past. From at least some points of view, this may be regarded as progress.

FUTURE DIRECTIONS

The most important issue that needs to be addressed is "What are the variables in psychotherapy that are really therapeutic?" Thus far, very little systematic research has been conducted in this regard. At present, it is hypothesized that some common factors are important for therapeutic success regardless of the type of problem. A positive therapeutic relationship is one such factor, and in general I have tended to emphasize such common factors in my eclectic approach. However, beyond common factors, it is reasonable to believe that specific techniques or procedures may be required for particular disorders, or that perhaps some of the common factors are more important for particular disorders than for others. Unraveling the relative importance of various potential therapeutic variables for specific types of problems thus appears to be the prime need.

Apart from the above, and relatively easier to do, would be a study comparing eclectic psychotherapy with a cognitive-behavioral therapy and a form of brief psychodynamic therapy. The results could be extremely interesting and also potentially quite significant in our quest to understand the psychotherapeutic process. I would very much like to see such a research project undertaken in the future and would be willing to participate in some way, although I could not now undertake to direct such a project.

It is always difficult to make predictions for the future. However, I do believe that there is a much stronger interest in and desire for some type of rapprochement and integration in psychotherapy now than there was previously. Whether or not this trend will grow and the multiplication of therapeutic schools will diminish is debatable, at least for the near term. However, in the long run, as research data accumulate, it would appear to be inevitable. When one approach to psychotherapy clearly demonstrates superior efficacy or efficiency, the less efficacious approaches will gradually disappear. That is the history of medicine and of science.

REFERENCES

Allen, F. H. (1942). *Psychotherapy with children.* New York: Norton.

Allport, G. W. (1937). *Personality: A psychological interpretation.* New York: Henry Holt.

American Psychological Association, Committee on Training in Clinical Psychology. (1947). Recommended graduate training program in clinical psychology. *American Psychologist, 2,* 539–558.

Bandura, A., Jeffrey, R. W., & Wright, C. L. (1974). Efficacy of participant modeling as a function of response induction aids. *Journal of Abnormal Psychology, 83,* 56–64.

Binder, V., Binder, A., & Rimland, B. (1976). *Modern therapies.* Englewood Cliffs, NJ: Prentice-Hall.

Davison, G. C., & Wilson, G. T. (1973). Processes of fear reduction in systematic desensitization: Cognitive and social reinforcement factors in humans. *Behavior Therapy, 4,* 1–21.

Elkin, I., Parloff, M. B., Hadley, S. W., & Autry, J. H. (1985). NIMH treatment of depression collaborative research program. Background and research plan. *Archives of General Psychiatry, 42,* 305–316.

Feifel, H., & Eels, J. (1963). Patients and therapists assess the same psychotherapy. *Journal of Consulting Psychology, 27,* 310–318.

Frank, J. D. (1971). Therapeutic factors in psychotherapy. *American Journal of Psychotherapy, 25,* 350–361.

Frank, J. D. (1973). *Persuasion and healing* (2nd edition). Baltimore: The Johns Hopkins Press.

Frank, J. D. (1979). The present status of outcome studies. *Journal of Consulting and Clinical Psychology, 47,* 310–316.

Garfield, S. L. (1957). *Introductory clinical psychol-ogy.* New York: Macmillan.

Garfield, S. L. (1973). Basic ingredients or common factors in psychotherapy? *Journal of Consulting and Clinical Psychology, 41,* 9–12.

Garfield, S. L. (1974). *Clinical psychology: The study of personality and behavior.* Chicago: Aldine.

Garfield, S. L. (1977). Research on training the professional psychotherapist. In A. S. Gurman and A. M. Razin (Eds.), *Effective Psychotherapy. A handbook of research.* New York: Pergamon Press.

Garfield, S. L. (1978). Research on client variables in psychotherapy. In S. L. Garfield and A. E. Bergin (Eds.), *Handbook of psychotherapy and behavior change* (2nd ed.). New York: Wiley.

Garfield, S. L. (1980). *Psychotherapy: An eclectic approach.* New York: Wiley.

Garfield, S. L. (1982). Eclecticism and integration in psychotherapy. *Behavior Therapy, 13,* 610–623.

Garfield, S. L. (1983). *Clinical psychology. The study of personality and behavior.* Revised edition. Hawthorne, NY: Aldine.

Garfield, S. L. (1984). Psychotherapy: Efficacy, generality and specificity. In J. B. Williams & R. L. Spitzer (Eds.), *Psychotherapy research; Where are we and where should we go?* (pp. 295–305) New York: Guilford Press.

Garfield, S. L. (in press). Research on client variables in psychotherapy. In S. L. Garfield & A. E. Bergin (Eds.), *Handbook of psychotherapy and behavior change* (3rd ed.). New York: Wiley.

Garfield, S. L., Affleck, D. C., & Muffley, R. A. (1963). A study of psychotherapy interaction and continuation in psychotherapy. *Journal of Clinical Psychology, 19,* 473–478.

Garfield, S. L., & Bergin, A. E. (1971). Personal therapy, outcome and some therapist variables. *Psychotherapy: Theory, Research and Practice, 8,* 251–253.

Garfield, S. L., & Bergin, A. E. (Eds.). (1978). *Handbook of psychotherapy and behavior change* (2nd ed.). New York: Wiley.

Garfield, S. L., & Kurtz, R. (1976a). Clinical psychologists in the 1970s. *American Psychologist, 31,* 1–9.

Garfield, S. L., & Kurtz, R. (1976b). Personal therapy for the psychotherapist: Some findings and issues. *Psychotherapy: Theory, Research and Practice, 13,* 188–192.

Garfield, S. L., & Kurtz, R. (1977). A study of eclectic views. *Journal of Consulting and Clinical Psychology, 45,* 78–83.

Goldfried, M. R. (1980). Toward the delineation of therapeutic change principles. *American Psychologist, 35,* 991–999.

Goldfried, M. R. (Ed.). (1982). *Converging themes in psychotherapy.* New York: Springer.

Goldfried, M. R., & Davison, G. C. (1976). *Clinical behavior therapy.* New York: Holt, Rinehart, & Winston.

Grinker, R. R., & Spiegel, J. P. (1945). *Men under stress.* Philadelphia: Blakiston.

Heine, R. W. (1953). A comparison of patients' reports on psychotherapeutic experience with psychoanalytic, nondirective and Adlerian therapists. *American Journal of Psychotherapy, 7*, 16–23.

Holt, R. R. (Ed.). (1971). *New horizon for psychotherapy.* New York: International Universities Press, Inc.

Holt, R. R., & Luborsky, L. (1958). *Personality patterns of psychiatrists.* New York: Basic Books.

Kelly, E. L. (1961). Clinical psychology—1960. Report of survey findings. *Newsletter, Division of Clinical Psychology, 14* (1), 1–11.

Levine, M. (1948). *Psychotherapy in medical practice.* New York: Macmillan.

Lieberman, M. A., Yalom, I. D., & Miles, M. B. (1973). *Encounter groups: First facts.* New York: Basic Books.

Luborsky, L., Crits-Christoph, P., Alexander, L., Margolis, M., & Cohen, M. (1983). Two helping alliance methods of predicting outcomes of psychotherapy. *Journal of Nervous and Mental Disease, 171*, 480–491.

Marks, I. (1978). Behavioral psychotherapy of adult neurosis. In S. L. Garfield and A. E. Bergin (Eds.), *Handbook of psychotherapy and behavior change* (2nd edition). New York: Wiley.

Marmor, J., & Woods, S. M. (Eds.). (1980). *The interface between the psychodynamic and behavioral therapies.* New York: Plenum.

Mathews, A. M., Gelder, M. G., & Johnston, D. W. (1981). *Agoraphobia, nature and treatment.* London: Tavistock Publications.

Mathews, A. M., Johnston, D. W., Shaw, P. M., & Gelder, M. G. (1974). Process variables and the prediction of outcome in behaviour therapy. *British Journal of Psychiatry, 125*, 256–264.

Meltzoff, J., & Kornreich, M. (1970). *Research in psychotherapy.* New York: Atherton Press.

Morse, S. J., & Watson, R. I., Jr. (1977). *Psychotherapies. A comparative casebook.* New York: Holt, Rinehart, and Winston.

Murray, E. J. (1956). A content-analysis method for studying psychotherapy. *Psychological Monographs, 70*, (13, Whole No. 420).

Obendorf, C. P. (1943). Results of psychoanalytic therapy. *International Journal of psychoanalysis, 24*, 107–114.

Obendorf, C. P., Greenacre, P., & Kubie, L. (1948). Symposium on the evaluation of therapeutic results. *International Journal of Psychoanalysis, 29*, 7–33.

O'Malley, S. S., Suh, C. S., & Strupp, H. H. (1983). The Vanderbilt Psychotherapy Process Scale: A report on the scale development and a process-outcome study. *Journal of Consulting and Clinical Psychology, 51*, 581–586.

Rachman, S. J., & Wilson, G. T. (1980). *The effects of psychological therapy* (2nd edition). New York: Pergamon.

Rioch, M. J. (1967). Pilot projects in training mental health counselors. In E. L. Cowen, E. A. Gardner, and M. Zax (Eds.), *Emergent approaches to mental health problems,* (pp. 110–127). New York: Appleton-Century-Crofts.

Rogers, C. R. (1942). *Counseling and psychotherapy.* Boston: Houghton Mifflin.

Rosenzweig, S. (1936). Some implicit common factors in diverse methods of psychotherapy. *American Journal of Orthopsychiatry, 6*, 412–415.

Ryan, V. L., & Gizynski, M. N. (1971). Behavior therapy in retrospect: Patients' feelings about their behavior therapies. *Journal of Consulting and Clinical Psychology, 37*, 1–9.

Sachs, J. S. (1983). Negative factors in brief psychotherapy: An empirical assessment. *Journal of Consulting and Clinical Psychology,* 557–564.

Sloane, R. B., Staples, F. R., Criston, A. H., Yorkston, N. J., & Whipple, K. (1975). *Psychotherapy versus behavior therapy.* Cambridge: Harvard University Press.

Smith, M. L., Glass, G. V., & Miller, T. I. (1980). *The benefits of psychotherapy.* Baltimore: The Johns Hopkins University Press.

Strupp, H. H. (1973). On the basic ingredients of psychotherapy. *Journal of Consulting and Clinical Psychology, 41*, 1–8.

Truax, C. B. (1966). Reinforcement and nonreinforcement in Rogerian psychotherapy. *Journal of Abnormal Psychology, 71*, 1–9.

Wilson, G. T., & Evans, I. M. (1977). The therapist-client relationship in behavior therapy. In A. S. Gurman and A. M. Razin (Eds.), *Effective psychotherapy. A handbook of research* (pp. 544–565) New York: Pergamon.

Wolpe, J. (1958). *Psychotherapy by reciprocal inhibition.* Stanford, CA: Stanford University Press.

Wolpe, J. (1961). The systematic desensitization treatment of neuroses. *Journal of Nervous and Mental Disease, 132*, 189–203.

CHAPTER 6

The Transtheoretical Approach

James O. Prochaska and Carlo C. DiClemente

Impetus for the transtheoretical approach came from several different sources. First and foremost was a discontent with the state of affairs in psychotherapy theory, research, and practice. Alternate analyses were encouraged by the bewildering number of therapy approaches, the narrowness and frequent dogmatism of the proponents and followers of many therapies, and the consistent research findings of few, if any, differences in outcome between therapy systems. Each therapy system appeared limited and focused more on theories of psychopathology and single mechanisms of change rather than an exploration of the process of change. Unconditional positive regard, authenticity, living in the here and now, confrontation of beliefs, social interest, conditioning, and contingencies seem to be rules for human functioning that are valuable but are not sufficient to explain therapy change. On the other hand, the search for the unique common denominator in all therapy systems seemed overly simplistic and reductionistic.

In 1977, Prochaska, with the help of his students, embarked on a journey through the various systems of therapy seeking the commonalities across the rigid bound-

aries of the most popular theories of psychotherapy. His *Systems of Psychotherapy: A Transtheoretical Analysis* (1979, 1984) represents the culmination of this journey. The map used for the journey indicated that therapy theories can be summarized by five separate processes of change operating at two levels: experiential and environmental. Adding the nonspecific processes of attention and expectation and the important dimension of the therapeutic relationship, he was able to examine the various systems within an integrative framework which illustrated the processes of change utilized by the different therapy systems.

Although the framework used in this analysis appeared to have face validity and good explanatory power, it remained a theoretical construct with no empirical basis. Since that initial work, both Prochaska and DiClemente, with a number of collaborators, applied the model, expanded its scope, and explored its limitations in studies of intentional change, in surveys of practitioners and patients, and in the creation of assessment instruments. This research supported and expanded our theorizing and encouraged us to continue the development of what we have called *The Transtheoretical Approach: Crossing the Traditional Boundaries of Therapy* (1984).

A final impetus for our work was found in the general *Zeitgeist* among practitioners and theorists of psychotherapy. We heard clearly the pleas of the participants of a 1981 APA Symposium on psychotherapy who called for a more integrated and comprehensive approach to psychotherapy. What seemed to be needed was an approach that would take into account the differences in the attributions and experiences of therapists and clients (Sloane et al., 1975). Moreover, in our thinking, a comprehensive eclecticism should be able to account for how individuals change on their own (unaided by psychotherapy) as well as how individuals change as the result of psychotherapy.

THE TRANSTHEORETICAL APPROACH

The proliferation of psychotherapy systems reflects the complex, interactive nature of psychotherapy involving the varied dimensions of client, therapist, relationship, problem, and interventions. The daily dilemma facing the clinician is what to do, when, with whom, in what way, and with which problem. Both in the research literature and in the experience of many clinicians, it has become clear that no one system of therapy addresses adequately all these questions.

From our perspective, eclecticism reflects the search for an integrated paradigm of psychotherapy that would accomplish the following goals:

1. Preserve the valuable insights of major systems of psychotherapy. Trying to reduce all therapy systems to their least common denominator, such as the therapeutic relationship (Lambert, 1983), results in an eclecticism that

fails to reflect the richness of the major therapy systems.
2. Provide some practical answers to the questions faced by clinicians. However theoretically elegant it might be, an impractical, overly simplistic, or irrelevant or incomplete eclecticism would never be adopted.
3. Bring some order to the chaotic diversity and divisions in the field of psychotherapy. However, if we act like children ordered to clean up their rooms, throwing an assorted collection of techniques into the toybox will offer some relief but only hide the chaos.
4. Offer a researchable alternative to single-system and comparative types of research. An eclecticism that cannot be researched will open the field of psychotherapy to more strident and justified criticism. Explanation without experimentation will not silence the critics of both eclecticism and psychotherapy.

Integration, collaboration, and rapprochement represent the promise and hope of eclecticism—at least the systematic type of eclecticism we believe is needed. What is required for a systematic eclecticism is a structure or set of principles and constructs that are comprehensive enough to include the critical dimensions of psychotherapy and, at the same time, are adequately flexible or open to modification in order to promote collaboration, creativity, and choice, which are the lifeblood of eclecticism.

Analysis of the 24 most popular theories of psychotherapy (Prochaska, 1984) yielded the first of the three basic elements of the transtheoretical approach—the processes of change. Transtheoretical therapy began with the assumption that integration across a diversity of therapy systems most likely could occur at an analytical level between theory and technique, the level of processes of change. Interestingly,

Goldfried (1980, 1982), in his well-known call for a rapprochement, independently suggested that the principles or processes of change were the appropriate theoretical starting point at which rapprochement could begin.

The processes of change, then, represent a middle level of abstraction between the basic theoretical assumptions of a system of psychotherapy and the techniques proposed by the theory. Basic coping activities that the individual engages in to modify a particular problem could be categorized as representing defined processes of change. Thus, a process of change represents a type of activity that is initiated or experienced by an individual in modifying thinking, behavior, or affect related to a particular problem. Although there are a large number of coping activities, there are a finite or limited set of processes that represent the basic change principles behind these activities. Similarly, techniques of therapy can be analyzed to see which type of process they would draw on or promote. Thus, confrontation by the therapist would provide new information, challenge current thinking about the problem, and offer feedback. All these therapist activities would enable the individual to engage in more accurate information processing. From a transtheoretical perspective, these activities represent the process of change called consciousness raising.

Subsequent modifications of the original formulation through research on self-change and therapist surveys yielded 10 separate and distinct processes of change (Table 1). Our studies indicate that people in the natural environment generally use these 10 different processes of change to modify problem behaviors. Most major systems of therapy, however, theoretically employ only two or three processes (Prochaska, 1984). One of the assumptions of the transtheoretical approach is that therapists should be at least as cognitively

complex as their clients. They should be able to think in terms of a more comprehensive set of processes and be able to apply techniques to engage each process when appropriate.

A second basic element in the transtheoretical approach is the stages of change. The stages reflect the temporal and motivational aspects of change. Early in our research on the processes of change it became evident that the utilization of the processes varied according to where an individual was in the cycle of change. Therapists have often talked about clients' motivation, defenses, and readiness to change. With certain problems like addictive behaviors, clinicians also discuss maintenance and relapse. However, theories of therapy have not proposed a sophisticated structure or framework to deal with these phenomena. Intentional change is not an all-or-none phenomenon but a gradual movement through specific stages of change. Lack of awareness of this staging phenomenon has led some theories of therapy to assure that all clients presenting for therapy are in the same stage of change and are ready for the same type of change. Studies of various outpatient populations (McConnaughy, Prochaska, & Velicer, 1983; McConnaughy, Prochaska, Velicer, & DiClemente, 1984; DiClemente & Hughes, 1985) have found

TABLE 1

Ten Change Processes of the Transtheoretical Approach

1. Consciousness raising
2. Self-liberation
3. Social liberation
4. Counterconditioning
5. Stimulus control
6. Self-reevaluation
7. Environmental reevaluation
8. Contingency management
9. Dramatic relief
10. Helping relationships

a variety of profiles on the stages-of-change scale. All individuals who come to therapy are not at the same stage of change. We have been able to isolate four basic stages of change: precontemplation, contemplation, action, and maintenance. A decision-making stage between contemplation and action has been difficult to isolate. Decision making may represent simply a mechanism for movement from contemplation to action or may ultimately be considered a separate stage of change.

The concept of stages is extremely important in understanding change. In the dictionary definition, a stage is a "period, level of degree in a process of development, growth, or change." In our conceptualization, a stage of change represents both a period of time as well as a set of tasks needed for movement to the next stage. Although the time an individual spends in each stage may vary, the tasks to be accomplished in order to achieve successful movement to the next stage are assumed to be invariant. In the move from precontemplation to contemplation, an individual must become aware of the problem, make some admission or take ownership of the problem, confront defenses and habit aspects of the problem that make it difficult to control, and begin to see some of the negative aspects of the problem in order to move to the next stage of seriously contemplating change.

Since each stage requires certain tasks to be accomplished, it follows that particular processes of change are more important at certain stages of change. Although it may appear obvious at this point that the processes of counterconditioning or stimulus control are inappropriate for an individual in the precontemplation or contemplation stage of change, some of the field's clinical and research strategies have in effect proposed just that kind of mismatch. Appropriate use of the specific processes at particular stages of change represents a basic integrative framework of the transtheoretical approach.

One of the most helpful findings to emerge from our research with self-changers and therapy changers is that particular processes of change are emphasized during particular stages of change (Prochaska & DiClemente, 1983). The integration of stages and processes of change can serve as an important guide for therapists. Once it is clear what stage of change a client is in, the therapist would know which processes to apply in order to help the client progress to the next stage of change. Rather than apply change processes in a haphazard or trial-and-error approach, eclectic therapists can begin to use change processes in a much more systematic style.

Table 2 presents a diagram showing the integration that was revealed from our research between the stages and processes of change (Prochaska & DiClemente, 1983). During the precontemplation stage, individuals use the change processes significantly less than people in any other stage. Precontemplators process less information about their problems; they spend less time and energy reevaluating themselves; they experience fewer emotional reactions to the negative aspects of their problems; they are less open with significant others about their problems; and they do little to shift their attention or their environment in the direction of overcoming their problems. In therapy these are clients who are resistant to the therapists' efforts to help them change.

Clients in the contemplation stage are most open to consciousness raising interventions, such as observations, confrontations, and interpretations. Contemplators are much more likely to use bibliotherapy and other educational interventions. As clients become increasingly more conscious about themselves and the nature of their problems, they are freer to reevaluate themselves both affectively and cognitively. Self-reevaluation includes an assessment of which values clients will try to actualize, to act upon, and to make real.

Clients also need to assess which values they will let die. The more central their problem behaviors are to the core of themselves, the more will their reevaluation involve changes in their sense of self. Clients ask themselves, "Will I like myself better as a nondrinker or nonsmoker? Will others I care about like me better? What if I am a more anxious or irritable person after I change? If my shared community is primarily with drinkers or smokers, will I risk rejection? If I fail to change, will I feel coerced, guilty, or weak?"

During the action stage it is important that clients act from a sense of self-liberation. They need to believe that they have the autonomy to change their lives in key ways. Yet they also need to accept that coercion is as much a part of life as autonomy. Thus, if they slip during action and attribute it all to a lack of willpower, they can experience considerable guilt or shame that can keep them from trying to take action again. On the other hand, if clients attribute all their success to the therapist or to the helping relationship, they risk becoming unduly dependent on the therapist.

Self-liberation is based in part on a sense of self-efficacy (Bandura, 1977, 1982), the belief that one's own efforts play a critical role in succeeding in the face of difficult situations. Self-liberation, however, cannot have just an affective and cognitive foundation. Clients must also be effective enough with behavioral processes, such as counterconditioning and stimulus control, to modify the conditional stimuli that can coerce them into relapsing. Therapists can assess how adequately clients are able to apply processes such as contingency management and stimulus control. Therapists can provide training, if necessary, in behavioral processes to increase the probability that clients will be successful when they do take action. As action proceeds, therapists can serve as consultants to the clients as self-changers, to help clients identify any errors they may be making in their attempts to modify their behavior and environment in a freer and healthier direction.

Since action is a particularly stressful stage of change that involves considerable opportunities for experiencing coercion, guilt, failure, and the limits of personal freedom, clients are particularly in need of support and understanding from helping relationships. For clients, taking action tends to mean taking risks with rejection. Knowing that there is at least one person who cares and is committed to helping serves to ease some of the distress and dread of taking life-changing actions.

Just as preparation for action is essential for success, so too is preparation for

TABLE 2
The Stages of Change in Which Particular Processes of Change Are Emphasized the Most and the Least

Precontemplation	Contemplation	Action & Maintenance
Eight processes used the least	Consciousness raising	
		Self-reevaluation
		Self-liberation
		Helping relationship
		Reinforcement management
		Counterconditioning
		Stimulus control

maintenance. Successful maintenance builds on each of the processes that has come before. Specific preparation for maintenance, however, involves an open assessment of the conditions under which a person is likely to be coerced into relapsing. Clients need to assess the alternatives they have for coping with such coercive conditions without resorting to self-defeating defenses and pathological patterns of response. Perhaps most important is the sense that one is becoming more of the kind of person one wants to be. Continuing to apply counterconditioning and stimulus control is most effective when it is based on the conviction that maintaining change maintains a sense of self that is highly valued by oneself and at least one significant other.

At this point in our analysis it appears that we are discussing only how to approach a single, well-defined problem. However, as all of us realize from clinical practice and knowledge of psychopathology, reality is not so accommodating, and human behavior change is not so simple a process. Although we can identify and isolate certain symptoms and syndromes, these occur in the context of complex, interrelated levels of human functioning. The third basic element of the transtheoretical approach addresses this issue. The levels of change represents a hierarchical organization of five distinct but interrelated levels of psychological problems that are addressed in psychotherapy. These levels are:

1. Symptom/situational
2. Maladaptive cognitions
3. Current interpersonal conflicts
4. Family/systems conflicts
5. Intrapersonal conflicts.

Historically, systems of psychotherapy have attributed psychological problems primarily to one or two levels and focused their interventions on these levels. Behaviorists have focused on the symptom and situational determinants; cognitive therapists on maladaptive cognitions; family therapists on the family/systems level; and analytic therapists on intrapersonal conflicts. It appears to us to be critical in the process of change that both therapists and clients be in agreement as to which level they attribute the problem and at which level or levels thay are willing to mutually engage in as they work to change the problem behavior. Once again, it is extremely important that the therapist engage the client at an appropriate and at least implicitly agreed-upon level or levels for the work of therapy to progress.

In the transtheoretical approach we prefer to intervene initially at the symptom/situational level because change tends to occur more quickly at this more conscious and contemporary level of problems and because this level often represents the primary reason for which the individual entered therapy. The farther down the hierarchy we focus, the farther removed from awareness are the determinants of the problem likely to be. Moreover, as we progress down the levels, the farther back in history are the determinants of the problem and the more interrelated the problem is with the sense of self. Thus, we predict that the deeper the level that needs to be changed, the longer and more complex therapy is likely to be and the greater the resistance of the client (Prochaska & DiClemente, 1984). In addition, these levels are not completely separated from one another. Change at any one level is likely to produce change at other levels. Symptoms often involve intrapersonal conflicts; maladaptive cognitions often reflect family/system beliefs or rules. In the transtheoretical approach, the complete therapist is prepared to intervene at any of the five levels of change, though the preference is to begin at the highest level that clinical assessment and judgment can justify.

In summary, the transtheoretical approach sees eclectic psychotherapy as the differential application of the processes of change at the four stages of change according to the problem level being addressed. Integrating the levels with the stages and processes of change provides a model for intervening hierarchically and systematically across a broad range of therapeutic content. Table 3 presents an overview of the integration of levels, stages, and processes of change.

Three basic strategies can be employed for intervening across multiple levels of change. The first is a *shifting-levels* strategy. Therapy would typically focus first on the client's symptoms and the situations supporting the symptoms. If the processes could be applied effectively at the first level and the client could progress through each stage of change, therapy could be completed without shifting to a more complex level of analysis. If this approach were not effective, therapy would necessarily shift to other levels in sequence in order to achieve the desired change. The strategy of shifting from a higher to a deeper level is illustrated in Table 3 by the arrows moving first across one level and then down to the next level.

The second is the *key level* strategy. If the available evidence points to one key level of causality of a problem and the client can be effectively engaged at that level, the therapist would work almost exclusively at this key level.

The third alternative is the *maximum-impact* strategy. In many complex clinical cases, it is evident that multiple levels are involved as a cause, an effect, or a maintainer of the client's problems. In this case, interventions can be created that attempt to affect clients at multiple levels

TABLE 3
Levels, Stages, and Processes of Change

Levels	Stages			
	Precontemplation	Contemplation	Action	Maintenance
Symptom/situational		Consciousness raising Self-reevaluation	Self-liberation Contingency management Helping relationship	Counter-conditioning Stimulus control
Maladaptive cognitions				
Interpersonal conflicts				
Family/systems conflicts				
Intrapersonal conflicts				

of change in order to establish a maximum impact for change in a synergistic rather than a sequential manner.

The transtheoretical approach is an intergrative eclecticism that is designed to synthesize processes and levels of change that have been emphasized by the leading systems of psychotherapy (Prochaska, 1984). Table 4 illustrates where leading systems of therapy fit best within the integrative framework of the transtheoretical approach.

The therapy systems included in Table 4 have been the most prominent contributors to the transtheoretical approach. Depending on which level and which stage we are working with, with particular clients, different therapy systems will play a more or less prominent role. Behavior therapy, for example, has developed specific interventions for clients at the symptom/situational level who are ready for action. At the maladaptive cognition level, however, Ellis's rational emotive therapy and Beck's cognitive therapy are most prominent for clients in the contemplation and action stages.

We have not by definition excluded any therapy systems from the transtheoretical approach. The transtheoretical approach is an open framework that allows for integration of new and innovative interventions as well as the inclusion of existing therapy systems that research or clinical experience suggests are most helpful for clients in particular stages at particular levels of change. Depending on their previous training and experiences, for example, some therapists may find bioenergetics to be more useful than Gestalt therapy for clients ready for action at the intrapersonal level of change. The therapy systems that have been emphasized in our transtheoretical approach have been selected on the basis of a variety of criteria. At a theoretical level we analyze the level and stage for which particular therapy systems are designed. Behavior therapy is an excellent example of a system that is theoretically well designed for clients at the symptom and situational level who are ready for action. We would expect behavior therapy not to be particularly appropriate, however, for

TABLE 4

Integration of Major Therapy Systems Within the Transtheoretical Framework

	Stages			
Levels	Precontemplation	Contemplation	Action	Maintenance
Symptom/ situational			Behavior therapy	
Maladaptive cognitions	Adlerian therapy	Rational emotive therapy Cognitive therapy		
Interpersonal conflicts	Sullivanian therapy	Couples communication Transactional analysis		
Family/ system conflicts	Strategic therapy	Bowenian therapy	Structural therapy	
Intrapersonal conflicts	Psychoanalytic therapies	Existential therapy	Gestalt therapy	

clients in the precontemplation stage or for clients suffering primarily from intrapersonal conflicts.

Therapy systems have also been selected that have the most empirical support for their effectiveness. Behavior therapy, cognitive therapy, structural therapy, and psychoanalytic therapy have all received considerable research attention. Though the research on these systems varies in quality and quantity, the outcome research on these systems has been positive for the most part (Prochaska, 1984).

Other systems such as existential therapy and Gestalt therapy have not received as much empirical attention. Existential therapy, however, has had a major impact on our thinking about intentional change and the role of self-liberation in facilitating self-change and therapy change. Gestalt therapy has generated a variety of creative interventions that clinically we have found to be especially useful in helping clients move to action at the intrapersonal level of change.

A major therapy system that is not included in Table 4 is Rogers' (1951, 1959) client-centered therapy. Rogers' system has been most prominent in articulating and demonstrating the importance of the therapeutic relationship as a critical process of change. Our own thinking and research on the helping relationship as a major process of change has been most influenced by client-centered therapy even though we don't rely just on client-centered techniques for developing a helping relationship. Thus, Rogers' influence on the transtheoretical approach cuts across the levels of change.

PATIENT ASSESSMENT

Accurate assessments of the stage of change and the problem level or levels, as well as the processes of change currently being used by clients, are critical to the transtheoretical approach to therapy from our perspective. Therapy would be most effective if patient and therapist were working at the same stage and level of change. The joining of the patient and therapist is centered around the structure and process of intentional change. The therapist's role is one of maximizing self-change efforts by facilitating neglected processes, deemphasizing overused processes, correcting inappropriately applied processes, teaching new or unknown processes, and redirecting change efforts to the appropriate stages and levels of change.

Clinical assessment of the stages, levels, and processes requires some modification of the traditional interview. Knowledge of both the attitude toward a problem behavior, as well as the actions taken with regard to it, is needed for assessment of the stages of change. It is important to know that an individual stopped drinking one week ago when his wife left him. However, equally important is knowing whether this is an attempt to change his wife's behavior or the first step in taking significant action toward intentional change of problem drinking. Another important aspect of assessing the stages of change is to evaluate both time and energy used in accomplishing the tasks of any prior stage of change.

Assessment of the levels of change requires a clinical interview that addresses each of the levels. In the case of vaginismus, we must know the symptomatic expression and situational determinants of the sexual dysfunction but should also explore self-statements, the couple's interpersonal functioning, family/system involvement, and any possible intrapersonal conflicts regarding identity, self-esteem, etc. In this assessment it would be important to establish at which level or levels the patient perceives the problem, as well as the levels that the clinician assesses are integrally involved in the problem.

Evaluating the processes of change being employed by the patient can be a rather extensive task. Therapists should explore what the patient is currently doing with regard to the problem, how often these activities are occurring, and what has been done in the past in attempts to overcome the problem. An obsessive individual may be relying heavily on consciousness raising as the most important process, while neglecting self-liberation and more action-oriented processes.

In our labs, we have begun to develop assessment instruments to aid in the evaluation of the stages, levels, and processes of change. The University of Rhode Island Change Assessment Scale (URICA) is a 32-item questionnaire with four subcomponents representing the four basic stages of change. Patients respond to each item on a five-point Likert scale of agreement (1 = strongly disagree; 5 = strongly agree). This scale has yielded several profiles based on scores on the four subcomponents. Research on these profiles continues, with some of the profiles needing more empirical interpretations. However, these profiles can be used clinically to direct therapy interventions based on patient scores on precontemplation, contemplation, action, and maintenance.

Several forms of a questionnaire to assess the processes of change have also been developed and tested. The questionnaires typically contain four to five questions about activities that would represent each of the processes. Clients are asked to indicate how frequently each activity occurs on a five-point Likert scale (1 = not at all; 5 = very frequently). Since change process activity is somewhat different for diverse problems, we have attempted to adapt the basic format to problems of alcoholism, overeating, psychic distress, and smoking. A more general form for psychotherapy is currently being tested. These questionnaires have shown remarkable consistency across problem areas (Prochaska & DiClemente, in press). Principal component analyses have yielded 10 or more consistent components in their use with both clients and therapists. This type of questionnaire can be used to assess change processes used before entering therapy and during therapy to examine how therapy interventions affect the utilization of the processes. Change process activity has been found to relate to therapist theoretical orientation (Prochaska & Norcross, 1983) and client activity in the various stages of change and to be predictive of successful movement through the stages of change.

TREATMENT APPLICABILITY AND STRUCTURE

What we are attempting to develop in the transtheoretical approach is a framework applicable to all clinical problems of psychological origin. The levels of change represent a means of categorizing patient problems which is compatible with current DSM-III diagnosis but is somewhat more comprehensive, since it includes systems and interpersonal types of problems. Thus, we envision the framework as appropriate for all types of psychopathology, behavioral medicine, and health-related problems. In addition, the framework can be used to categorize treatment delivery systems as to which types of clients and problems they primarily address.

Since we propose to intervene first at the symptom/situational level, the transtheoretical approach can be used in both a short-term and long-term format. Length of therapy, setting, and modality are determined more by the stage of change, level of problem involvement, and type of processes employed rather than a predetermined set on the part of the therapist. Thus, a family intervention that brings family members and other significant persons together to make an effective confrontation of the patient can be used for a precontemplative alcoholic. Individual and couples therapy can be used to work through contemplation issues and achieve effective action when working with sexual dysfunctions.

At the same time, other resources can be used to assist the client to move successfully through the stages of change. In an alcoholism treatment program based on the transtheoretical approach, a referral to Alcoholics Anonymous is used to provide helping relationships and reinforcement for clients in action and maintenance with their alcoholism problem. Bibliotherapy can be used to assist the client with consciousness raising during the contemplation stage at any particular level of the problem.

Duration and timing of the therapy also depend on the problem levels and the stage of change. An individual with a rather circumscribed problem who is in the action stage can achieve successful modification of the problem in a relatively brief period of time. An individual with multiple problems who may be at the precontemplation stage with several problems would necessarily require significantly longer treatment. In this context, several important considerations should be kept in mind. Action and maintenance are separate and important stages of change. Discontinuation of therapy when the client has taken action could do a disservice to the client, especially a client who is at high risk for relapse.

Therapists have the responsibility of helping clients become aware of the possiblity of relapse, while at the same time increasing their efficacy to control the problem and implement alternative coping strategies. This is a delicate task. Although the therapist must avoid demoralizing clients who may be somewhat overconfident in their new-found ability to control problems, the therapist must also be careful not to create a "confident incompetent" headed for relapse.

Since our approach concentrates on intentional change, contraindications to the use of the transtheoretical approach would indicate any setting or problem where intentional change was not the primary goal. In a correctional setting or in managing the self-destructive behavior of a child, control, not intentional change, may be the primary goal. In this context, being aware of the stages and levels of change may be desirable. However, external behavioral control appears to be the treatment of choice using the processes of contingency control and stimulus control. Once the immediate threat to self or others has been managed, therapists can work to bring the problem behaviors under intentional self-control rather than external control. In fact, this should be an important secondary goal if treatment or incarceration goals are to be maintained after the individual is released into the community. This distinction is an important one in order to avoid the confusion between a problem that is brought under control in a highly structured environment and one that is managed through intentional change. In any controlled setting, such as a prison or hospital, treatment personnel should consider this distinction. It is often easy to bring a problem behavior under control in a structured setting which limits access, opportunity, or temptation and provides ever-present social controls. The important dimension of generalization, however, is whether the problem behavior has been brought under intentional control. What has been called recidivism in these settings may not be a relapse in the maintenance of intentional change but may simply reflect the lack of external controls once individuals are released to their communities.

In working with intentional change the transtheoretical approach is quite compatible with the traditional treatment structure of psychotherapy. Weekly, hour-long sessions can be used to implement the treatment process. Since we envision psychotherapy as an adjunct to self-change, what occurs between therapy sessions is as important as what happens within therapy sessions. However, modifications of the traditional treatment structure may be negotiated with a client depending on the stage and level being addressed. A longer, more intense therapy session with the inclusion of significant others may be needed for an individual in precontemplation to overcome defenses. Less frequent sessions can be used for individuals in contemplation and maintenance. For the former, more time between sessions can allow individuals time to use the processes of consciousness raising and self-reevaluation in the service of decision making. For the latter, time between sessions can be used to monitor temptation levels and encounter any obstacles to continued action or maintenance which occur less frequently. Thus, in effect, therapy sessions become booster sessions. For individuals beginning to take action, therapy sessions may need to be more frequent—at times daily or two to three times a week for some problems like alcoholism. The rationale for this approach is that an individual beginning to use the behavioral processes may need more intensive instruction and support during this initiative phase. Both frequency and duration of sessions may need to be individualized for a particular client. However, for most clients in action, weekly sessions are adequate, with the therapist available by phone, if needed.

TREATMENT SPECIFICITY AND MATCHING

The goals of our research on intentional change are to identify the processes and other variables that are most effective in helping clients move through the stages of change with regard to a particular problem or set of problems. In this context, treatment selection is too generic a term. The more specific question is which process would be most effective in helping to move an individual from one particular stage of change to the next with regard to a certain level or levels of change. The

decision to use a particular process is multiply determined. Rather than stating a priori that counterconditioning is the treatment of choice for phobic problems, we prefer to analyze first the stages and levels of change, as well as the processes currently being used, before making any kind of prescription.

We realize that this approach places a sizable burden on the therapist and is not a simple matter. However, in the case of psychotherapy, we believe that simplicity is the mother of mediocrity and confusion. We have found for example, that insufficient use of consciousness raising in the contemplation stage forces individuals to rely excessively on self-liberation or willpower in their efforts to change and opens the way to what Janis and Mann (1977) have called "post-decisional regret." The overuse of self-reevaluation during maintenance, on the other hand, is predictive of relapse (DiClemente & Prochaska, in press). Thus, matching patients with processes requires both a general knowledge of the stages, processes, and levels of change and how they interact, as well as specific knowledge about individual clients and what they have been doing to effect changes in their lives.

While matching is a complex process which has not yet been adequately researched, mismatches from our perspective are more readily apparent. A therapist committed to consciousness raising and exploration of all the levels of change prior to taking action will frustrate a client ready to take action at the symptomatic level. An action-oriented behavior therapist will be constantly disappointed by precontemplative clients who consistently fail to implement the suggested behavioral techniques. The family therapist, who insists that change take place at the family/systems level with the whole family present, may be unable to engage a system that has a critical member who is in precontemplation.

Therapists must become aware of their

preferences for particular stages, processes, and levels of change. Certain therapists by constitution or training do not have the temperament or skills to adequately address certain stages, processes, or levels. Awareness of these limitations is essential in approaching the question of patient-therapist matching. If a therapist does not have the patience to handle what may be experienced as endless contemplation on the part of the client, it is unlikely that a therapeutic relationship would be developed. Respecting a client's position on the stages of change is an important first step in the joining of therapist and client.

Treatment matching should not simply focus on disorders. The concentration on disorders is really a continuation of the medical model approach to psychotherapy. From our perspective, the problem with using this model as the framework for psychotherapy is that the medical model is not applicable to intentional change. Even with physical problems which require some health behavior modification, the medical model has been problematic. Compliance, diet control, and exercise, all require intentional change and are extremely difficult problems for a medical model that relies on processes of change such as surgery which are invasive, externally applied procedures. Disorder is an important concept for developing a taxonomy that enables us to bring together certain symptoms and syndromes for classification. Although this information is important in understanding a problem, knowledge of a disorder by itself has limited value in prescribing therapy interventions.

TREATMENT INTERVENTIONS AND STRATEGIES

As has already been stated, the structure and strategies for the transtheoretical approach to psychotherapy grow from the assessment of the stages, levels, and processes of change. We have found that, after an initial assessment, an effective way to engage a client is to explain the model of change that we are working with. The stages of change have an intuitive appeal which seems to allow clients to see themselves in the process of change regardless of the stage they are currently in. It also allows the therapist to delineate the different responsibilities of therapist and client. In this framework, defenses may be seen not as irrational forces battling the more reasonable part of the client's psyche, but as once useful coping mechanisms that may have outlived their usefulness. The therapist, then, does not get classified as another person who is determined to impose change on the client but as a consultant or coach concerned with helping the individual cope with change. Implementing the processes and making the decision to change are clearly the province of the client. Teaching the client about the problem and the process of change, offering techniques related to the processes, assisting in decisional balance considerations and the development of self-efficacy, and helping the client to focus on the appropriate level or levels of change are all the work of the therapist. In this manner, therapy is conceived of as a collaborative, interpersonal endeavor focused on therapeutic learning and taking into account critical individual differences (Strupp, 1978).

Termination of therapy can occur at any stage of change. Successful termination occurs when clients are better prepared to continue their self-change efforts. Thus, termination can occur after very brief encounters with therapy, if clients have progressed toward the next stage and are better prepared to change on their own. Dropouts can occur when clients decide to exit from the cycle of change prior to successful maintenance. It is extremely important to realize that there are a variety of exits from the cycle of change. Successful maintenance of change for a problem behavior is the most desirable, but clearly not the only, exit. Contemplators, for example, may decide that the costs of intentional change, such as the time, energy, and money involved in therapy, outweigh the anticipated benefits of taking action. While therapists may be disappointed in the client's decision to drop out, therapists do need to respect that clients can intentionally choose not to change or can choose to postpone further change efforts to another time. The most troubling dropouts occur when clients decide that therapy is not helping and may even be hindering their efforts at intentionally changing significant aspects of their lives. The challenge for therapists is to develop more effective ways to help clients at each of the stages and levels of change and to promote movement from one stage of change to the next. It can also be a challenge for therapists to know when to get out of the way. Although psychotherapy has been in existence for almost 100 years, it is still in its infancy as an applied science, and there is much we need to know about the determination and termination of change.

THERAPIST BEHAVIORS

While therapists have not struggled with all the particular problems faced by different clients, all therapists have had some experience with the processes of change. This is the common experiential ground that forms the basis of the relationship between therapist and client. In general, the therapist is seen as the expert on change, not in having all the answers, but in being aware of the critical dimensions of change and being able to offer some assistance in this regard. Clients are individuals—already at some point in the stages of change—needing help to move to the next stage. They have potential resources as self-changers which must be used in order to effect a change. In fact,

clients need to shoulder much of the burden of change and look to the therapist for consultation on how to conceptualize the problem and ways to free themselves to move from one stage to another.

We believe that the transtheoretical model lends itself most often to a consultant-client style of interaction (Prochaska and DiClemente, 1984). As with any interactive endeavor, rapport must be built in order to accomplish the work. However, the type of relationship needed for the work of psychotherapy can vary somewhat with the stage and level of change being addressed. The consultant-client relationship needs to be modulated according to the client's particular issues.

Initiation of therapy with a precontemplation client, for example, takes on a different flavor with the transtheoretical approach. A client's unwillingness to see or admit a problem is not viewed as resisting the therapist and being uncooperative but as resisting change. Therapists must become aware of how frightening and anxiety provoking the prospect of change can be. With this shift in perspective, the therapist can take on the role of a concerned advisor who can help the individual explore the problem. The therapist becomes an ally rather than another person attempting to coerce change.

For an individual contemplating change, the therapist should take care not to be too impatient. Contemplation can be a lengthy, frustrating stage of change. While therapists should not support chronic contemplation, they must also avoid blame, guilt, or a rush to action. In order to make a decision to change a problem behavior, individuals must see that change is possible and in their own best interests. The therapist can challenge clients by making explicit the pros and cons of both the problem behavior and the change. Support, understanding, and a relationship that would enable the therapist to make explicit the fears and concerns of the client are needed during this time.

During the action and maintenance stages, the therapist can assume a more formal teaching relationship. During these stages, the client is likely to idealize the therapist. When initiating action, the client needs the support of a helping relationship and may need to lean on the confidence of the therapist rather than a self-generated sense of efficacy. Initial efforts are likely to be tentative. Seeing the therapist as the expert on change can be comforting to the client. However, as soon as it is feasible, it is important to have the client develop more self-confidence and independence from the therapist. For therapists who need to be needed this can pose a difficult problem. Letting go and allowing the client to take ownership of the change are the final stages of the therapist-client relationship.

MECHANISMS OF CHANGE

A central principle of the transtheoretical approach is that different mechanisms or processes are most important in producing change at different stages of overcoming a problem. The mechanisms that move someone from precontemplation to contemplation are different, for example, from the processes that move someone from contemplaton to action.

What moves people from precontemplation into the contemplation stage of change? What facilitates or forces people to become aware that previously acceptable patterns of behavior are now problematical or pathological? To respond to these important questions we have had to go beyond research data and rely more on clinical experience and clinical theory (Prochaska and DiClemente, 1984).

Progress from precontemplation into the contemplation stage appears to be due to either developmental changes or environmental changes that occur in peoples' lives. Many individuals begin to contemplate changing particular aspects of their lives because of developmental processes that move them into a new stage of life. As Levinson and his colleagues (1978) suggest in *The Seasons of a Man's Life*, many men find themselves quite satisfied with a particular spouse during their 20s. When they enter the transition into the 30s, however, they begin to contemplate radical changes in their marriages. Similarly, many smokers seriously begin to contemplate stopping smoking as they approach age 40 and feel pressured to face the finiteness of their lives. It is not coincidental that the self-changers in our research who have been most successful in quitting smoking took action at a mean age of 39. And 39 is a mean age. Developmentally, facing 40 is a key time for many people to reevaluate their lives to determine where changes are needed.

Other individuals appear ready for change not because of internal developmental changes but because their external environment has changed. Perhaps a spouse or a child has reached a new developmental stage and asks or insists that they stop drinking. Or they begin to realize that their environment no longer reinforces their drinking or smoking as it once did but now responds with subtle and not so subtle punishments to their old habits. A poignant example of such an environmental event occurred with a married couple who participated in our self-change research. Both spouses were heavy smokers for over 20 years. Then their dog died from lung cancer. The husband quit smoking. The wife bought a new dog.

The important theoretical issue here is that intentional change, such as occurs in therapy, is only one type of change that can move people. Developmental and environmental changes are other events that can cause people to alter their lives. The transtheoretical approach focuses primarily on facilitating *intentional change*, but it recognizes and, at times, relies on other types of change when working with clients. It is assumed, however, that unless developmental or environmental changes produce intentional change as well, then clients will feel coerced and will be likely to revert to previous patterns once the coercion is removed.

Therapists can help clients progress more freely into the contemplation stage of change if they can help their clients identify with the developmental or environmental forces that are pressuring them to change. Clients may, for example, have difficulty identifying with the developmental process of aging even though it comes from within their skin. Whether entering a new age becomes a life crisis or an opportunity for growth may be determined by whether we experience aging as imposed on use or as part of us. Most of us, for example, identify with aging when we become 21. Our sense of self includes becoming more independent, mature, and adult. Becoming 40 or 50, on the other hand, is more often experienced as an imposition in a society that identifies with youth.

Self-defeating defenses can occur against environmental pressures to change. A client named Harold was in marital therapy for three months when he said, "You know, I still don't know why I am coming here. I am coping perfectly fine with all the stresses in my life. It's my wife who can't cope, and yet she insists that I come to therapy or she will leave." Of course, it didn't help his wife to repeat for the umpteenth time that Harold was spending money until they were nearly bankrupt; that he was at risk of losing his job for the third time in four years; that the children were afraid to be around him because of his violent temper; and that she was seriously considering separating because all his energy was going into his skiing club and none into their marriage. But Harold could no longer identify with his wife or with her reasons for changing. He experienced her as a manipulating mother trying to take away his freedom and fun.

How can therapists intervene in a manner that allows them to be experienced by defensive clients as freeing influences rather than as coercive forces? Obviously, the more clients can identify with the therapist and the elements of therapy, the more therapy can be experienced as a freeing influence. With precontemplators, in particular, the therapeutic relationship becomes a precondition for further change. Identification with the therapist is more likely to occur if the client feels that the therapist genuinely cares and that the therapist is trying to truly understand the client's unique experience. Identification is also more likely to occur if the client believes that the therapist is committed to helping the client change in ways that are best for the client and not some other agent, such as the courts or the schools.

Ironically, clients first need to feel that the therapist is free to identify with the client before the client is free to identify with the therapist. If the client feels that the therapist cannot identify with the client's predicament in life because the therapist doesn't care, doesn't understand, or isn't committed, then the client is likely to terminate therapy before it begins. If clients believe the therapist cannot identify with them because the therapist is of the wrong gender, ethnic background, social class, or sexual orientation, then clients will not feel free in therapy. Clients are likely to avoid such therapists lest they risk coercion to change according to stereotypes of gender, ethnicity, social class, or sexual orientation.

As clients and therapists begin to develop a shared identity that is the essence of a therapeutic relationship, clients become much more open to influence from therapists. Clients are much freer to respond to feedback and education about the alienated aspects of their lives. Clients are particularly free to process information from therapists or others with whom they have a helping relationship. Therapists also become more open to influence from their clients, such as to have a favored formulation invalidated by further information from the client. But our focus shall remain centered on how clients change in therapy rather than on how therapists change over the course of therapy.

A helping relationship, such as a therapeutic alliance, provides people with the freedom to process developmental or environmental events in a friendly rather than a coercive atmosphere. Easing up on their defenses, they can begin to see themselves more clearly. They can begin to contemplate making intentional changes in their lives without feeling that they are entirely coerced by developmental or environmental events. Movement into the contemplation stage, like many changes in life, is usually experienced as a combination of coercion and personal freedom.

Once clients begin to move into the contemplation stage, their insight and understanding are critical for further progress. Whether the insight is historical-genetic, interactive, cognitive, or situational depends on the level of change that is needed. For clients working at the symptom/situational level, a functional analysis of the immediate antecedents and consequences of troubled behavior may be all the understanding that is needed. Clients attempting to change troubled relationships, however, will need insight into the interactive nature of their problems. Clients who are not free enough from their family of origin or who are plagued by internalized intrapersonal conflicts are more likely to need insight into the historical-genetic causes of their conflicts.

Insight and understanding can become an endless process of consciousness raising, however, if clients wish to have a complete grasp of all that influences them. Some personalities have a propensity to become bogged down in prolonged contemplation of a problem. Obsessive personalities in particular prefer to believe that if they keep thinking enough about an is-sue, eventually the problem will go away or enough understanding will be gained that points to a perfect solution to a complex problem.

Moving from contemplation to action involves both consciousness raising and self-reevaluation processes. Consciousness-raising interventions, such as observations, confrontations, and interpretations, are most important during the contemplation stage. Value clarification techniques are also important in preparing clients for taking effective action. Helping clients to work through a decisional balance, for example, can clarify which course of action is most likely to reflect the type of person the client wants to become. Balancing the pros and cons of a particular course of action also prepares clients to pay the price that comes with any major change in life.

When it comes to action, skill acquisition and/or utilization is most important for therapeutic progress. If a therapist is skilled only in consciousness-raising interventions, such as interpretations, then the contemplation stage can become excessively and obsessively long. Applying such behavioral skills as desensitization, assertion, communication, or negotiation is an important aspect of the action stage. Which skills are employed depends on the client's level of change. Desensitization, for example, is used most often at the symptom/situational level, whereas communication training is much more important for the interpersonal level. Renegotiating dysfunctional family rules can be particularly liberating at the family/systems level. An existentially based assertiveness can be one of the most liberating means for expressing the enhanced sense of self that emerges when intrapersonal conflicts are being resolved.

From a transtheoretical perspective, the therapeutic relationship, interpretations, skill acquisition, and utilization are all fundamentally important to producing change. Their relative importance varies from stage to stage, with therapeutic relationships most important for facilitating movement from precontemplation to comtemplation, interpretations most important during contemplation, and skill acquisition and utilization most important during action and maintenance.

Part of the purpose of the transtheoretical approach is to help specify what to date have been the nonspecific factors involved in change. "Nonspecific" factors have generally referred to the factors that are common to all effective therapies, rather than being specific to any one system of therapy. The transtheoretical approach has attempted to go beyond this search to identify processes of change that are common to all forms of intentional change and not just to psychotherapy.

One of the common change processes is the presence of a helping relationship. Clients, especially resistant clients, need to experience the therapist as caring, understanding, and committed to the clients' well-being. To the extent that caring, understanding, and commitment to the well-being of clients are values that are essential to the identity of a therapist, the therapist would be healthy enough to develop a helping relationship with clients. To the extent that therapists are too narcissistic, egocentric, or psychologically distressed that they cannot actualize these therapeutic values, they are likely to have serious trouble maintaining a helping relationship with clients. Since a helping relationship is both a precondition for change, as well as a process of change, therapists who have trouble caring, understanding, or being committed to the clients' well-being are expected to produce less effective and more troubling outcomes.

If it is true, as experts estimate, that two-thirds of therapy outcome variance is due to the clients' efforts (Prochaska & Norcorss, 1982), then client variables should be more important for outcome than therapist variables. The client variables focused on in the transtheoretical approach are the stages, levels, and processes of change of particular clients. The further along in the stages of change that clients are, the briefer therapy will be. Clients in the precontemplation stage are seen as being at greater risk of dropping out of therapy. If these clients stay in therapy, the resistance that they experience will impede initial progress and lead to a longer course of treatment. Clients in the maintenance stage, on the other hand, may need only a booster session or two, to help them prevent relapse from occurring.

Similar relationships are expected for the clients' level of change: the higher the level of change that can be used in therapy, the briefer therapy is likely to be. Conversely, the deeper the level of change needed, the longer therapy is likely to be. The more problems clients have at the intrapersonal level, the less able they are to shoulder their share of the burden of change. Progress can be inhibited by intrapersonal difficulties that interfere with the clients' abilities to apply each of the fundamental processes of change.

Consciousness raising, for example, can be very difficult for people to apply if they are troubled by very rigid defense mechanisms. People who rigidly rely on projection, for example, may find it nearly impossible to process feedback about their own roles in producing problems. If they enter therapy, they usually feel coerced by others. Their goals in therapy are to learn how to use processes of change to change others, not themselves.

What are realistic goals for multiproblemed clients? What is successful termination of therapy from a transtheoretical perspective? First, we have to be realistic about how much opportunity we actually have to intervene. National household surveys of representative samples indicate that the mean number of office visits for people going to psychologists and psychiatrists is 12.5 and 10.9, respectively (Taube, Burns, & Kessler, 1984). The median was 5 and 4, respectively. Only about one-quarter of patients stay in therapy for more than 15 sessions. Forty-five percent of patients were seen for less than four sessions.

Several conclusions can be drawn from these figures. First, therapy will be terminated before the client's problems are terminated. Many therapists can set themselves and their clients up for disappointment if they expect short-term therapy to lead to successful termination of problems. Successful short-term therapy facilitates movement through one stage of change, such as movement from precontemplation to contemplation, contemplation to action, or action to maintenance. Therapists and clients need to appreciate that successfully progressing from one stage of change to the next in 5 or 10 sessions is a remarkable achievement. Successful therapy also enables individuals to better manage the remaining stages of change on their own.

In longer-term therapy, ranging from 25 to 75 sessions, successful termination would involve clients progressing at least into the maintenance stage. Successful therapy seems able to reduce remarkably the time it takes individuals to move through each of the stages of change. Therapy involves more conscious and planned interventions in which the therapist can help clients apply the most appropriate processes in the most effective manner. Therapy can help clients avoid having to go through a trial-and-error search for the best processes to apply at each stage of overcoming a problem. Successful therapy involves clients becoming more conscious of a systematic and integrative approach to change that they can apply to new problems that will inevitably occur in life. For growth-oriented clients, successful therapy helps clients to develop the personal autonomy and responsibility to be all that they can be and to accept that limits in life never allow us to be all that we want to be.

CASE EXAMPLES

By its very nature, an eclectic approach to therapy cannot be illustrated by a single case. Rather, it would take a long series of cases to reflect the full range of stages, levels, and processes of change used with a diversity of clients. One of the essential values of an eclectic orientation is that it encourages therapists to be rich, diverse, and creative in their choice of interventions with individual clients.

If the reader were looking over the shoulder of a systematic eclectic therapist, the therapist's interventions would be seen to vary tremendously depending on the needs of particular clients. To capture a little of this diversity, Prochaska will present a brief description of part of his current case load from his part-time private practice that is limited to 10 hours per week. He will then present a more detailed description of an individual client suffering from psychological distress.

In the first case, Prochaska is seen doing systematic desensitization with a somewhat obsessive 26-year-old counselor who has progressed from contemplation to action during the six weeks of therapy for a disruptive phobia of speaking in front of any size group. The client is seen relaxing and raising a finger when a scene was clearly imagined. The client is also seen taping the session for use at home during the three weeks between sessions. The therapist also reviews the next steps in in vivo desensitization as the client is ready to take action with another counterconditioning procedure designed to change the effects of conditional stimuli in specific situations.

The observer might conclude that Prochaska is a behavior therapist until the next session begins. With a 55-year-old engineer who had been severely distressed, Prochaska responds like Albert Ellis as he reviews the client's problems with completing any task in the ABC paradigm of rational emotive therapy. One difference is that Prochaska doesn't have to be as confrontive with Rhode Islanders as Ellis may have to be with New Yorkers. Maladaptive cognitions seem to have been the key to this client's considerable distress, and after four sessions he is ready to terminate therapy after successfully completing a series of action steps. The client has some anxiety about terminating, because he has not yet moved into the maintenance stage, so the door is left open for the client to return for booster sessions if he begins to relapse in his ongoing efforts at self-change.

A cognitive therapist, concludes the observer—until the next session is underway. A 35-year-old salesman is expressing his anger at the therapist for having recommended sensate focusing as the first action step in treating an erectile dysfunction. The therapist should have known that such action wouldn't work. He should have known that the real problem was a lack of sexual desire for this particular partner. The therapist should have realized that the salesman was having difficulty being honest with his present partner lest he risk losing a relationship that was good in most ways except sex.

A novice therapist, concludes the observer—misled into premature action by the client's defenses. Out of fairness to the therapist, however, the therapist realized that the client had real trouble being honest and direct in his relationships, since the therapist had observed the client changing his story several times in just three sessions. As is often the case, the therapist recommended the action technique more for its diagnostic value than expecting it to work smoothly. Action techniques, like sensate focusing, can serve as projective devices, with clients varying tremendously in the way they experience and respond to the therapist's recommendations.

At least now the client was being direct and honest with the therapist. The client's individual therapy had helped him to be conscious of how he attempted to manipulate relationships through passive, dependent, and devious communications. He had done a lot of reevaluationg of his style of relating, and he seemed ready to take action at the interpersonal level. He appreciated that his present relationship was a good opportunity to begin to change his communication and control patterns. He planned to bring his partner to therapy the next session and risk rejection as he begins to be more open and honest with her.

What will the next session bring? There is often some anxiety and some excitement anticipating each session, especially when it is the first session with a new client. The tension increases when it becomes clear that the client is in the precontemplation stage. He is a mildly retarded, 28-year-old, unemployed jewelry worker who is facing court charges for molesting a 10-year-old girl. He knows he is in trouble with the law but he doesn't really know why he is in therapy. He had been in therapy briefly before, and it didn't seem to have any impact. His court counselor wants a psychological assessment to see whether therapy at any level might be of help.

A confused therapist, concludes the observer—he doesn't really know whether to intervene, let alone how to intervene with this highly resistant client. When in doubt rely on trying to form a working relationship and see whether the client can progress into contemplating change at any level. But be honest—recognize that he will continue to be resistant or will drop out if he feels that the therapist can't identify with a mildly retarded, unemployed jewelry worker who is facing court charges for molesting a 10-year-old girl. The therapist wishes for a moment that he didn't have a 10-year-old daughter.

Who have we next? A whole family coming down the corridor? A 38-year-old woman had originally come in for anxiety, depression, and other symptoms of psychological distress. She was having trouble coping with her adolescent son, and her second husband wasn't being much help. The most pressing family conflict revolved around moving, with mother and son having very strong feelings in opposite directions and with stepfather feeling caught in the middle. The session focuses on empathy training with mother being asked to communicate as fully as she can her son's feelings about moving and he in turn trying to communicate his awareness of his mother's feelings about moving.

A family therapist, concludes the observer—but only occasionally. Next is a longer-term client who would have to be observed across many sessions to appreciate how hard she has worked to facilitate changes at each level of her life. Her hardest struggle has been to accept herself, even though her parents had never really been able to accept that their fourth and final child was another daughter. It is holiday time, and she is experiencing a less frequent but still intense episode of distress. She weeps over how little she has achieved in life. She wasn't able to have a child; her hostile and hateful marriage has ended. So what if she has been able to complete graduate school? So what if she has a career? What has she achieved? Her therapist responds spontaneously, "Marie, what if a more important question in life is what have you experienced not what have you achieved?" She stops weeping. There is a long silence. Finally Marie says, "I never thought of life that way. That's really helpful. Thanks."

Twelve more clients constitute this therapist's current case load. If space permitted, descriptions of these clients would further illustrate the diversity of problems and patients that one eclectic therapist confronts. But most therapists work with quite a diversity of clients. The issue is not how diverse is our case load; the issue for eclectics is how diverse are our assessments of clients and our interventions with clients. If the problems of all patients are construed at the same level and if all patients receive similar interventions, then we do an injustice to the diversity of clients. We also do an injustice to the spirit of eclecticism. On the other hand, if we try to treat every client as entirely unique, we end up with no guidelines for our practice and no ability to transfer our training and our experiences from one case to the next. We can experience our work as fragmented and undirected. We are like circus clinicians who are always flying by the seat of their pants. The transtheoretical approach adopts a middle ground that we hope is diverse enough and yet systematic enough to do justice to both clients and clinicians.

A More Detailed Case Study

With the previous case reflecting some of the breadth of the transtheoretical approach, we will now describe in more depth the treatment of a psychologically distressed client. Tom was a 50-year-old schoolteacher who was referred for marital therapy by a colleague who had been working with Tom's wife, Barbara, in individual therapy for about a year. Barbara's therapist did not believe that Tom would stay in treatment for more than three sessions, even though he was quite distressed. Barbara's therapist actually thought that Tom needed individual therapy, but he agreed to go to therapy only if they went as a couple.

Barbara called to make the appointment and she communicated Tom's reluctance to enter treatment. Tom and Barbara were seen together in the first session, in part to assess both their problems and their ability to work together at the interpersonal level. The first issue focused mainly on Tom's resistance to being in therapy. Usually we begin therapy by talking about the problems that bring people to therapy. But the first problem at hand was the client's resistance to therapy. Confronting the problem directly communicates to the client that we are going to try to deal with problems in a straightforward and direct manner. It communicates that the therapist cares about the client's resistance and the client need not be defensive about it. It also communicates the therapist's hope that maybe there is something the client and/or therapist can do to make it easier for the client to be there. Many spouses have said that their partners would never come to therapy and if they did they wouldn't stay. And yet, Prochaska has found that almost all reluctant partners would come in for at least one session if the therapist asked, and most would continue in therapy.

Tom said, "I don't believe therapy is worthwhile. My wife has been going to therapy for a year, and she's still always lying and spending money like it's going out of style."

"Sounds like you might be angry at her therapist," the therapist responded.

"You're damn right! He just feeds into her wasting money," said Tom.

"Have you let him know you're angry?" the therapist asked.

"No, he doesn't want to talk to me," Tom said.

"Would you like me to let him know you're angry?" the therapist asked.

"Yeah, I would appreciate that," said Tom.

So we're off and running. Tom's resistance to therapy is being addressed, if only at the situational level. But at least he doesn't have to be defensive about his defensiveness. He may be able to experience the therapist as someone who cares about his defensiveness and is trying to understand it. He may, to his surprise, experience the therapist as being helpful both in dealing with his resistance as well as dealing with his anger.

At the same time, the therapist has to be concerned with Barbara's experiencing the therapist as Tom's ally. The therapist could have addressed Tom's anger toward his wife for what he labels "lying and wasting money." But this would have risked putting Barbara on the defensive, and if she counterattacked, the couple could slip into the blame game that involves partners quickly shifting from the offensive to the defensive position.

"It must be hard to have your husband accusing you of lying and wasting money." I said this to Barbara, knowing I was still risking the blame game but feeling that I wanted to empathize with her as well as with Tom. I also wanted to communicate that I appreciated that there are two sides to every marital conflict, and that her perspective was as important as Tom's.

These opening segments of therapy indicate that treatment usually begins immediately. There usually is not a formal assessment period, although assessment usually occurs right from the start. In the course of the first two therapy sessions, the following information was shared. Tom's mood was usually depressed; he couldn't relax; he was having trouble sleeping; he was irritable and often verbally abusive; he felt lousy about himself; and he was having trouble relating to his students, his colleagues, and the customers who sought his services in his after-school job. Tom's distress increased whenever he approached Barbara to be sexual and she refused, which happened at least once a day.

Barbara was really angry at Tom. She was angry about his constant accusations about her lying, spending money behind his back, and having affairs when she went out on Friday night with her women friends. She was angry about Tom's constant surveillance. He would check the phone bill to see whom she had been calling; he would open mail addressed to her to see what money she owed; and he would sometimes follow her out with her friends to see whether she was meeting other men. How could she want to make love, when they were so embroiled in a game of "Cops and Robbers"? Tom had coerced her into having sexual intercourse a couple of times, and she resented it.

Barbara also resented Tom's preoccupation with money. If he wasn't preoccupied about her spending money, he was preoccupied with his compulsive gambling. Tom denied that his gambling was a problem. Oh, it had been a problem in the past but never so bad that he couldn't get out of debt. But he had changed his behavior. He wasn't going to the track anymore, and he was limiting his gambling to $20 a week—mostly on the lottery and on nassaus while golfing with friends. But these were bets they could afford, said Tom. If they lost everything it would come to $1000 a year, and between the two of them, they were making over $80,000. Besides, he claimed to win more than he lost.

What is a therapist to believe? At worst we have a compulsive gambler and an obsessive and possessive lover married to a compulsive liar and an impulsive spender. We may have classic character disorders who have trouble managing their own lives let alone managing marriage effectively. Character disorders either don't stay in therapy or they stay forever.

We usually don't find such traditional diagnoses particularly helpful for most problems and most patients. Many of our diagnostic categories include some of the most damning attributions about people. Problems are attributed to deep-rooted pathologies that are rigidly resistant to change. Diagnoses all too often tell us why people won't change rather than how people might change.

From the transtheoretical perspective, it appeared that Tom was in the precomtemplation state in regard to most of his problems. The exception was his gambling, which Tom had changed on his own to controlled gambling. He appeared to be maintaining his controlled levels, although he showed signs of relapsing. For example, he displayed preoccupation with gambling and revealed considerable psychological distress, which tended to weaken his ability to maintain behavior changes on his own.

Barbara, on the other hand, appeared ready to take action. She had been contemplating making changes in her marriage for the past year in therapy. The problem was that the action she most likely was going to take was divorce. She didn't say this directly; she said she was coming to therapy to try to improve her marriage. All too often, clients mislead therapists into thinking they are doing marital therapy, when in fact they are doing divorce therapy. The problem is that research suggests that different approaches to marital therapy have a differential effect depending on whether the couple remains married or gets divorced (Cookerly, 1973). Out of six different modalities, conjoint interviews were the most successful for couples who remained married but produced the poorest outcomes for those who obtained divorces. Individual interviews, on the other hand, were worst for those remaining married but were second best for those who obtained divorces. So our approach to marital therapy should depend in part on whether a particular couple is heading for divorce or seeking to stay married.

Unfortunately, few couples present asking for divorce therapy. Most couples present asking for marital therapy. Assessing whether a couple is likely to be a divorce case rather than a marital case can make a considerable difference in therapeutic outcome. Elsewhere we present in detail the subtle and not so subtle signs of impending divorce that we use to assess a couple's case (Prochaska & Di Clemente, 1984).

In the present case, some of the obvious signs included the fact that Barbara had been contemplating divorce for some time. More important, she had told some of her family and friends that she was contemplating divorce. When people go public with their contemplations, they are moving much closer to action. Barbara had also lost her excess weight and engaged in some other self-improvement activities. Making oneself more marketable is often preparatory action for people heading for divorce. Barbara had also been in individual interviews for a year, with the theme being increased independence and autonomy.

Tom, on the other hand, was psychologically distressed. He had not been contemplating divorce although he knew that Barbara was. On the contrary, he was obsessed with trying to control Barbara's actions to prevent losing her. Tom was resistant to change, as if he knew the ultimate change in their marriage was going to be divorce.

Tom seemed to be distressed by the prospect of having the drastic change of divorce imposed upon him. The imposition of change is one of the most common causes of psychological distress. People who are pressured or pushed into resigning, retiring, moving, advancing, retreating, or making any other major unintended changes are much more likely to develop psychologically distressing symptoms. The more partners have divorce imposed on them, for example, rather than intentionally participating in the stages of divorce, the more psychologically distressed they are likely to become.

Psychological distress caused by imposed change is likely to lead to people resisting change. Change can be experienced as a threat, not an opportunity. People can struggle with all their energies to resist change. They defend against any awareness of needs to change as they dig more deeply into the precontemplation stage. They have trouble contemplating change as they become cognitively impaired by distress (Mellinger, Balter, Uhlenhuth, Cisin, Manheimer, & Rickels, 1983). They have trouble making decisions and trouble taking action, even action that could lead to self-enhancement.

What do we do when we have spouses in two different stages of change, which is common in marital therapy? What do we do when we have spouses in two different stages of divorce, which is even more common in divorce therapy? The most common pattern is to have one spouse in precontemplation and one who is ready for action, like Tom and Barbara. This is a difficult position for therapists to be in, because they are likely to be damned by one spouse for moving too quickly and damned by the other for moving two slowly.

When we are treating psychological distress precipitated by an impending and imposed divorce, we need to slow down the spouse who is ready for action and speed up the spouse who is resisting change. Usually it is easier to slow down partners who are initiating divorce. They usually initiate therapy, because, at some level, they recognize that their partners are too dependent on them and are vulnerable to becoming profoundly distressed by an impending divorce. They may only want to transfer the dependency onto the therapist, like leaving an unwanted baby in a basket at the doorstep of a home that is known to be warm and caring. Often, however, they have fantasies that their distressed partners may go crazy, become suicidal or homicidal, or be totally unable to function.

In part because they care and in part because they want to be able to reevaluate themselves as decent people after initiating a distressing divorce, most spouses will give the therapist some time to intervene. It certainly helps for the initiator to be made conscious of the stages of divorce and how divorce can be least destructive if both partners are ready for action at about the same time.

Barbara was willing to spend some time trying to resolve some of their interpersonal problems. The therapist made it clear that they were going to work at the interpersonal level to improve their relationship whether they stayed together or got divorced. Either way, they were going to have a long-term relationship, in part because they shared two lovely daughters.

The couple first needed to become more conscious of the interactive nature of their conflicts. Tom and Barbara agreed that their struggles over control were producing the most conflict. The therapist presented feedback about this conflict based on the therapist's assessment of what was going on at the interpersonal level. Tom's actions appeared to be based on his intention to keep the couple together. His actions were based on values of closeness and togetherness. Barbara, on the other hand, had developed an increased need for independence. Her actions were based on values of individualness and separateness.

The problem was that the more Tom tried to control their being together, the more Barbara felt a need to be apart. Barbara agreed. Conversely, the more Barbara pulled apart, the more Tom felt the need to control her to keep them together. Tom agreed. The needs and values that Tom was expressing set off opposite needs and values in Barbara.

So what was the cause of their problem? the therapist asked Tom. "Barbara's pulling away." What was the cause of the problem? Barbara was asked. "Tom's trying to control me." Round and round they went for several sessions as the complex concept of circular causality gradually sunk in. The blame game is based on our preference for linear causality—she acts and I react. Circular causality can help

couples appreciate that they both act and react—that their behavior is both a cause and an effect of their ongoing relationship.

"How do we break out of this vicious circle?" Tom and Barbara seemed to be asking as they went round and round, each trying to redefine their relationship in the preferred direction. Divorce is one way of bringing circles to a stop. Tom and Barbara were becoming more conscious of what they personally contributed to their control struggles. They were going beyond the blame game. They were also able to reevaluate the partner's behavior to some extent. Togetherness is somewhat more positive than dependence. Separateness is something different from selfishness. With the help of the therapist's minilectures based on his experience with family life education (Prochaska & Prochaska, 1982), Tom and Barbara were becoming aware that a more mature relationship includes both togetherness and separateness. They were taught that individuals mature in their relationships from dependence to independence to interdependence. Interdependence is the caring and sharing together of two independent individuals with separate identities.

The problem was that Tom was entirely in charge of togetherness and Barbara was standing just for separateness. They were, however, willing to risk acting differently. The therapist recommended that Tom be in charge of separate activities and Barbara be in control of shared activities. Tom was going to liberate himself from a vicious circle by acting more like Barbara, and vice versa. The longer they could continue such reversal of roles, the more they would condition themselves to respond with new alternatives.

This action worked for a while. Tom took charge of recording on the calendar Barbara's nights out with her friends and his golfing dates. Barbara recorded their dates together on the calendar and was in charge of initiating shared activities. They were communicating better and feeling better. Tom's chief complaint was that Barbara was not initiating any sex.

Because they were doing better, the therapist recommended that gradually getting involved in sexual relating could help them get over anxieties they might have about sexual performance. They had been avoiding sex for quite a while, and the first steps of sensate focusing (Masters & Johnson, 1970) might give Barbara, in particular, a chance to deal with her feelings about gradually getting close again. They agreed with the idea and agreed that they would start with light massage.

Tom came alone to the next session. "Barbara is not coming back again. She said she knows she just wants out of the relationship," he said. The therapist probably had made a mistake in too quickly encouraging the couple to move to action in their sexual relationship. After the session, the therapist called Barbara and expressed his concern that he might have made a mistake and inquired whether she would be willing to come in to talk about how she was feeling.

Barbara actually came in for a couple of sessions. She said that the only thing the therapist's recommendation had done was force her to realize that she just didn't want to be close to Tom anymore. For whatever the reasons, her feelings had changed. The fact that their relationship had improved somewhat made her even more aware that she just didn't feel the same about Tom. She still was concerned that Tom wouldn't be able to handle a divorce but she wanted out.

Tom was distressed but he wasn't devastated. Fortunately, therapy had become a place where he could be really open about his feelings. He wasn't all alone as he had feared. He allowed himself to relive the memories of losing his first love. He had felt more rejected then than he felt now. He had had so many regrets about not having tried harder in that relationship. But this time he had been trying.

Back then, he withdrew from everyone. He stayed in his room. He wasn't able to eat. He couldn't work. His parents were concerned but they left him alone.

No wonder he avoided contemplating divorce. He never, never wanted to go through such emotional hell again. He didn't think he would make it. He thought he couldn't handle another rejection. But he realized he didn't have to go through it alone this time. Not only was therapy available but he had other helping relationships. At school, for example, he had told the school psychologist that he was in therapy. His friend couldn't believe it—not Tom, who always kidded about psychology as witchcraft. But now, Tom could talk more openly and rely more on the social supports in his natural environment.

The therapist encouraged Tom to explore fully why that rejection as a young man had been so distressing. Eventually Tom focused on the rejection he had experienced from his parents. When Tom was about seven or eight, his parents had lost their business and didn't have the financial resources to take care of him. Tom had gone to live with an aunt and uncle who had no children. They weren't particularly loving, but they did give him a lot of money. He always had a roll of dollars on him and that gave Tom a lot of status among his peers.

After a couple of years, Tom's parents were on their feet again and were able to have him back. Tom recalled not wanting to go back. He didn't want to give up all that money. Tom had forgotten how rejected he had felt as a child. The therapist suggested that perhaps he had substituted the money for the love he had lost. Yes, maybe that was why money had come to mean so much to him. Maybe that was part of the reason he was preoccupied with money. Gambling was fun, but he also felt more lovable when he won. And when he lost? Well, maybe he was getting used to losing love.

After that early separation, Tom had closed off his relationship with his parents, or maybe it had always been too closed. The therapist took a lead from Bowen (1978) and encouraged Tom to act on his emerging feelings. He encouraged Tom to go back and talk to each of his parents individually about how they had experienced that time in their lives.

Tom's mother was especially pleased with the opportunity to talk. She had never told Tom how much it had hurt her to give him up and how much it hurt when he didn't want to return home. She felt that Tom was always angry at her after that. Maybe that was why she didn't reach out when Tom was distressed. Tom began to realize that his hurt and his anger had caused him to avoid close contact with others. But now Tom was risking new ways of relating—with his parents, his daughters, and his friends. He was communicating more spontaneously and openly. He felt more sensitive to the needs of others. He was asserting himself more at work without having to get angry. He was making many self changes after a total of 22 therapy sessions. But he was puzzled by his reluctance to take action and move out and get a place of his own. He and Barbara had been able to work out a pretty good divorce settlement on their own. But Barbara's divorce lawyer thought he could do a lot better for her, and Tom and Barbara quit communicating. Tom and Barbara were living in separate rooms, but Barbara really wanted Tom out of the house. She went so far as to break the zippers in his three new sets of trousers. She harassed him in other ways, but Tom wouldn't move.

He told himself that it was because he wanted to be close to his daughters, but he knew he was really afraid that Barbara might turn them against him. He also realized that he was still concerned about money and didn't want to spend the money on an apartment if he could help it. Furthermore, staying in the house was a safe way of expressing his resentment at Barbara for rejecting him. At a deeper level, Tom became aware that leaving his home stirred up painful feelings about when he had to leave his family's home. And at an intrapersonal level, Tom became aware that he really did have some unresolved dependency problems. He had, for example, never lived alone. He lived at home while going to college. He had gone from his parent's home to marriage with Barbara.

The therapist helped Tom to appreciate that moving out and living on his own was a maximum impact action that could facilitate further progress at each level of his life. At a situational level, Tom would be moving into an entirely new environment that would reflect the new era of his life. He would be free from all the conditional stimuli that elicited so many painful thoughts and feelings. At a cognitive level, Tom would be challenging his "awfulizing" tendencies that added to his distress, such as his belief that it was awful that he was the one to have to move when he didn't want the divorce in the first place (cf. Ellis, 1973).

At the interpersonal level, Tom could further let go of his desire to remain in control of his relationship with Barbara. As long as Barbara wanted him out and he refused to leave, Tom felt in control. But he could let go of this need to control and accept that Barbara was getting the house so he had to leave. At the family level, Tom was very tempted to move back with his parents. Moving on his own, however, would enable Tom to further separate from his parents without rejection or resentment. And at the intrapersonal level, Tom could experience himself as becoming more fully adult. He would be moving beyond dependence to independence and would be better preparing himself for an interdependent relationship.

Tom began to look for a place of his own. He quickly found a house that seemed perfect—a small, but charming house in the country not far from his school. The rent was right. There was privacy, and yet there were friends close by. The only problem was that it needed to be taken immediately and Tom still wasn't ready to move. But he took a lease on it anyway. After a couple of months more of encouragement in therapy and additional harassment at home, Tom was ready to leave his nest.

This was a major move in his life. It evoked a variety of countertransference feelings in his therapist, who felt like a parent watching his 50-year-old son going off to college. Would he be distressed by loneliness and homesickness or would he flap his wings and fly, enjoying his newfound freedom? Needless to say, Tom soared. He felt more fully connected to life than he had ever been. For the first time in his life he began to appreciate activities like concerts and plays. He asserted himself and found women responding rather than rejecting. Certainly he felt lonely at times, but never alone. He even felt a spiritual awakening for which his atheist therapist takes no credit whatsoever.

Therapy was already terminating when Tom met a special woman. Ironically, she too had just come out into the world in the past few years. She had hidden in a nunnery while Tom had hidden within himself and his home. She had had several years of therapy struggling with intrapersonal issues both before and after leaving the nunnery; Tom was terminating after nine months of therapy.

Tom had made a remarkable transformation from a distressed and defensive individual preoccupied with a small portion of his existence to a growth-oriented person able to function more freely and fully at each level of life. What process or processes account for such rewarding changes? First, Tom had been facing turning 50, and he probably had the benefit of developmental changes urging him on to a new stage of life. He also faced dramatic but distressing environmental

changes being imposed on him. Therapy had helped Tom shift from a resentful and resistant position in the precontemplation stage to becoming more conscious of and committed to the self-liberating qualities of intentional change. Tom, the gambler, would also attribute some of his good fortune to lady luck. The last time I talked to Tom, not only was he doing well with his woman friend, his family, his daughters, his friends, and himself; he also had just won $750 in the lottery two weeks in a row. Tom was on a roll!

RESEARCH ON THE APPROACH

Research from the transtheoretical approach has been process oriented primarily rather than outcome oriented. This is in part because too much of therapy research has been outcome oriented and has taught us too little about how change occurs in therapy. Research on the effectiveness of different therapy systems has revealed too little about what to do or how to be in therapy to facilitate change.

We also believe it is important to summarize some of our process research to illustrate how an integrative approach to eclecticism can lead to innovative programs of research. In the area of research, eclectics have too often been followers rather than innovators of new approaches to research. While most of the studies summarized in this section do not assess the effectiveness of the transtheoretical approach for facilitating change, they do assess the effectiveness of the transtheoretical approach for understanding change.

Research to date provides support for the assumption that there is a common set of change processes utilized by individuals attempting to overcome a variety of problem behaviors (DiClemente & Prochaska, in press; Prochaska & DiClemente, in press). A common set of change processes has been clearly identified across such diverse problem areas as psychic distress, smoking, and weight control (Prochaska & DiClemente, in press). In addition, important similarities and differences were discovered in how frequently these processes were applied for different problems and among diverse populations. With psychic distress, weight control, and smoking cessation, rank ordering of processes in terms of frequency of application was similar across problems. Helping relationships, consciousness raising, and self-liberation, for example, were the three top-ranking processes for self-changers, while reinforcement management and stimulus control were the lowest-ranked processes. However, significant differences in the absolute frequency of use did emerge. Individuals struggling to overcome psychic distress rely more on helping relationships and consciousness raising than they do for weight control. Conversely, weight control subjects rely more on self-liberation and stimulus control than do distressed individuals (Prochaska & DiClemente, in press).

The processes of change have also been examined in a number of studies using both psychotherapists and lay persons comparing self-change and therapy-assisted change. Highly trained psychotherapists committed to very different theoretical orientations differed significantly in the processes they emphasized in treating clients with psychic distress (Prochaska & Norcross, 1983). Cognitive-behaviorists, for instance, reported using counterconditioning and contingency control more than any other group, while psychodynamically oriented therapists used them the least, with eclectics and humanists in the middle. When it came to treating themselves for distress, on the other hand, no significant differences emerged for any process of change among the therapists of divergent theoretical orientations.

A similar pattern of results was found in other studies. When there are significant differences, therapy changers apply particular processes most often. Smokers in two well-known behavioral treatment programs were found to use consciousness raising, counterconditioning, contingency control, and stimulus control significantly more than self-changers (DiClemente & Prochaska, 1982). With a small sample of 15 therapy changers and 15 self-changers struggling with weight problems, we found that the therapy changers tended generally to use the change processes more, with one process, counterconditioning, being significantly different (Olcott, Prochaska, & Velicer, 1984).

A pivotal assumption of the transtheoretical approach is that the application of the processes is best understood in the context of the stages of change. In developing an instrument to assess the stages for clients entering therapy, four highly reliable and well-defined components emerged representing the precontemplation, contemplation, action, and maintenance stages (McConnaughy, Prochaska, & Velicer, 1983). These results were replicated with samples of psychiatric and alcoholic outpatients (McConnaughy, Prochaska, DiClemente, & Velicer, 1984; DiClemente & Hughes, in preparation). The only measure to predict progress over a four-month period, or rather lack thereof, was the stage of change profile, with precontemplators making the least amount of progress. For the alcoholics, the precontemplative profiles appeared to identify a more defensive group and a group who were discouraged about change (DiClemente & Gordon, 1984).

Research with smoking cessation and weight loss supports the contention that the importance of change processes varies with the stages of change (Prochaska & DiClemente, 1983; Prochaska, DiClemente, Norcross, & Guadagnoli, 1984). Processes tend to be utilized in a systematic manner as individuals progress from one stage to the next (DiClemente & Prochaska, in press). A cross-sectional analysis of the processes comparing 886 self-changers representing different stages of change found significant differences on 8 of the 10 processes (Prochaska & DiClemente, 1983). In a longitudinal analysis of subjects who progressed, regressed, and remained the same over a six-month period, discriminant functions predicted movement for the groups representing the precontemplation, contemplation, action, and relapse stages. Predictors included the 10 processes, two decision-making variables, and measures of self-efficacy and temptation, all variables that are open to change (DiClemente & Prochaska, in press). When more static variables such as age, education, smoking history, withdrawal symptoms, reasons for smoking, and health problems were used as predictors, the results were much less significant (Wilcox, Prochaska, Velicer, & DiClemente, in press).

Not only are people in different stages of change and using different processes during these stages, but they also attribute their problems to different levels of change. The levels of attribution and change (LAC) scale has been developed to assess 10 dimensions (Norcross, Prochaska, & Hambrecht, in press). The levels of change have been replicated on samples of college students, psychotherapists, and self-changers (Norcross, Prochaska, Guadagnoli, & DiClemente, 1984). The levels identified as most relevant for the transtheoretical model in these studies are situational difficulties, maladaptive cognitions, interpersonal conflicts, family/system conflicts, and intrapersonal conflicts.

The only outcome research to date on the transtheoretical approach involves our efforts to facilitate change with smokers. A transtheoretical action manual (TTT) has been tested in pilot studies with smokers, many of whom had not been able to quit on their own during the past two years. These pilot studies included a comparison of the action manual materials with the sophisticated American Lung Association (ALA) action manual materials, which have been accepted as the "gold-standard" manuals for smoking cessation (Glasgow & Rosen, 1978) under both self-administered (manual) and four-week therapist-administered (clinic) conditions. Comparable studies were conducted simultaneously in both Houston, Texas, and Rhode Island.

Results of these pilot studies are very encouraging. At the four-week posttest, the percentage of subjects who had taken action in the TTT clinic groups was much higher than in the ALA clinic groups (58% vs. 23%). At the six-month follow-up for these subjects, 17% of the TTT clinic subjects ($n = 4$) reported they were not smoking compared to only 3% ($n = 1$) of the ALA subjects. Similar six-month results were found in Rhode Island. Five of twelve subjects (42%) in the TTT clinic group were not smoking at six months compared to 1 of 16 subjects (6%) in the ALA group.

The self-administered manual studies also supported the TTT materials. Combining both locations, 42 subjects received the TTT manual and 42 subjects the ALA manual. At the four-week follow-up, only three TTT subjects and two ALA subjects reported quitting in the previous month. However, the delayed quitting effect was striking. At the six-month follow-up, 38% of the TTT manual subjects reported taking action in the previous month compared to only 17% of the ALA manual subjects ($X^2 = 6.00$, $p<0.01$). Neither group received materials to assist with maintenance, and sustained nonsmoking was limited for both groups.

Most of the research on the transtheoretical approach has been process rather than outcome oriented. Comparative outcome studies with a general psychiatric population have not yet been done, and much more needs to be learned about the effectiveness and efficiency of this approach. We have focused on processes and patterns of change as well as validation of the basic contructs of the model. Although outcome is important, we believe that research must continue to focus on understanding the basic structure of change to make intervention research more useful.

CLINICAL TRAINING

The transtheoretical approach began with a comparative analysis of the major systems of psychotherapy (Prochaska, 1984). Learning the transtheoretical approach would best begin the same way. *Systems of Psychotherapy: A Transtheoretical Analysis* provides a comparative theoretical analysis of the major therapy systems. It attempts to provide a synthesis both within each system and across the different systems. This book provides an integrative framework that highlights the many similarities of therapy systems without blurring their essential differences. Developing therapists are introduced to the diversity and complexity of alternatives that are available to therapists and clients alike. An appreciation is presented for the vitality and personal meaning that different therapeutic approaches can have for different clients and therapists. As the same complex client is analyzed from each therapeutic perspective, readers can appreciate the additional insights and treatment alternatives provided by each of the major therapies.

After being introduced to therapy from a relatively broad but integrative perspective, developing therapists should then throw themselves into learning specific therapy systems. Therapy systems can best be learned by bracketing one's skepticism and by temporarily accepting the system and the unique perspective it provides. A detached observer can always find fault with any system of thought. It is always easier to criticize than to create. The eclectic spirit, however, is to appreciate the best that each system has to offer and to appreciate what the best minds in

our field have created in an attempt to understand the complex conditions of clients and of change.

A problem, of course, is that there are more than 200 therapy systems (Parloff, 1980) and no clear criteria for choosing which systems to learn. The traditional eclectic position was that therapists had to learn every approach to therapy before they could be considered true eclectics (Thorne, 1973). The proliferation of therapy systems has made the traditional position impossible.

The transtheoretical approach advocates learning a minimum of one system for intervening at each level of change and at least one systematic aproach for applying each process of change. For the symptom/situational level, behavior therapy would be the system of choice. At the maladaptive cognitions level, rational emotive therapy is most widely used. No system has really emerged as the leading approach to interpersonal conflicts. Transactional analysis is probably the most complete system currently available for this level, but it can be rather difficult for therapists to obtain training in transactional analysis. At the family/systems level, Prochaska prefers Bowen's (1978) family/systems therapy while DiClemente recommends Minuchin's (1974) structural therapy. At the intrapersonal level, psychoanalytic therapies are the most fully developed and widely used alternatives.

In learning the preceding systems, therapists would also have learned how to use counterconditioning, stimulus control, contingency management, self-reevaluation, and consciousness-raising processes of change. Most of the systems also teach the development of a helping or therapeutic relationship. As indicated earlier, however, Rogers (1959) has been most systematic in his theoretical, clinical, and research work on helping relationships, and most therapists are likely to be familiar with Rogers' client-centered approach. Existential therapy has been the leader in understanding and applying personal choice as a critical change process and would provide therapists with alternatives for using both self- and social liberation. Cathartic therapies, like Gestalt therapy, provide the most intensive techniques for applying the process of dramatic relief.

From a transtheoretical approach, then, a more complete eclectic therapist would receive training in six to eight of the major systems of psychotherapy. Of course, the intensity of the training would vary, with some systems involving at least a year of study and supervision, whereas other approaches could be appreciated through independent reading and professional workshops.

For some therapists, learning six to eight approaches to therapy may seem overwhelming. Developing a more systematic and synthesized approach to eclectic therapy is certainly more demanding than just becoming an expert in one system. We expect that most experienced eclectic therapists probably have an adequate background in four or five therapy systems and would not need a great deal of additional training to develop a transtheoretical approach. Similarly, most developing therapists would prefer to learn a variety of systems, like behavioral, cognitive, systems, psychodynamic, and Gestalt therapy.

After therapists have achieved some proficiency in each of the recommended therapy systems, we would then recommend additional reading and training in the transtheoretical approach. *The Transtheoretical Approach: Crossing the Traditional Boundaries of Therapy* provides the most complete description available of how this approach is applied to some of the most common but complex clinical syndromes. Our own students also have available a year-long supervised practicum in the clinical psychology doctoral training program at the University of Rhode Island with Prochaska and a year-

long supervised practice in the psychology internship program at Texas Research Institute of Mental Sciences with DiClemente.

As part of their training, systematic eclectic therapists should have supervised clinical experience working with clients at each level of change. Ideally, this would include at least a semester-long practicum or internship rotation in behavior therapy, cognitive therapy, marital or couples therapy, family therapy, and psychodynamic therapy. We believe that intensive supervision with a small number of cases is preferable to brief supervision with a large number of cases. Once therapists develop their skills with a couple of clients, they can usually transfer their training to new cases. We do believe, however, that eclectic therapists should have been supervised with clients at each stage of change so that they have a clear sense of how clients in the precontemplation stage can differ from clients in the action stage. They need to learn from experience that processes that work so effectively with clients ready for action fail miserably with clients who have just begun to contemplate changing.

Research has found that experienced therapists who have had personal therapy think it is an important part of training, while those who have not had personal therapy do not believe it is so important (Norcross & Prochaska, 1984). Since both DiClemente and Prochaska have had personal therapy, it is not surprising that they value such experiences for training.

From a transtheoretical perspective, personal therapy would probably not be particularly important for therapists who know that they want to specialize in working at the symptom/situational level of change and/or the cognitive level. For therapists who want to be able to work across each of the levels, personal therapy that involves intensive self-exploration and self-understanding can be invaluable. Such therapy can help therapists appreciate how each of the levels of experience can contribute to their current functioning and malfunctioning. Personal therapy can clearly demonstrate how defenses tend to increase as the focus moves from more conscious and contemporary situations and cognitions to less conscious and more historical family and intrapersonal conflicts.

As part of clinical training, personal therapy can help developing therapists become more conscious of their defenses, their prejudices, and their problems that can interfere with working more effectively with a broad range of clients across a more complete range of conflicts. Therapy as part of training also enables experienced therapists to turn to their colleagues for professional help during periods of intense psychological distress that the vast majority of therapists experience a few times during their careers (Prochaska & Norcross, 1983).

Since the authors are both active researchers as well as active therapists, they appreciate how much research can enrich their practice as well as how much practice can enrich their research. For example, phenomena of the stages of change that emerged from our research on self-changers have been extremely helpful in assessing and intervening with clients at any level of change. On the other hand, as practicing clinicians, we know that changing troubled behavior is a complex phenomenon that cannot be adequately understood by simplistic research programs that attempt to study only one variable. As clinicians we are immediately skeptical of research that suggests that there are simple solutions to complex problems, such as research that suggests that most clients can resolve their problems in six or eight sessions of therapy.

Research experience is necessary for developing an integrative eclecticism that is data based. Research experience that is clinically relevant, such as small n therapy studies on the patterns of change over time, could certainly enrich a developing therapist's appreciation of the complexities of change from a transtheoretical perspective. Research as part of training would be a desirable, but not a necessary, experience for learning therapy from a transtheoretical approach.

An ideal training program would begin with a theoretical overview of the major systems of psychotherapy. Developing therapists would learn the transtheoretical framework and first see how it can help them appreciate both the common and the specific insights and interventions of leading systems of therapy. Ideally, fledgling therapists would then have an opportunity to observe specialists intervening with clients at each of the stages and levels of change. Therapists in training would then have a prolonged opportunity to immerse themselves in six to eight major systems of therapy. Preferably, the sequencing would follow the levels with individuals first training to intervene at the symptom and situational level. Such experiences would help therapists learn for themselves that a variety of real clients can indeed be helped at this level without symptom return. The trainees would then shift to the cognitive level and systematically learn how to understand and intervene effectively within this domain. The trainees would then progress to the interpersonal, systems, and intrapersonal levels. An advantage of such sequencing is that the trainees will already have had experience with less complex cases prior to taking on supervised experiences with conflicted couples, or entire families, or difficult character disorders.

Following training in the major systems of therapy, developing therapists would then have a year-long supervised practicum that would enable them to integrate what they have been learning. Such a practice would include training in assessing the stages, levels, and processes that are most relevant to particular clients.

Training would be given in applying the key level, shifting-levels, and maximum-impact strategies. Therapists would learn to appreciate the importance of helping short-term clients progress through one stage of change and be better prepared to continue to change on their own. Therapists would also learn to appreciate how longer-term therapy can help a variety of clients be able to live more freely and fully as they progress at each level of life. Finally, developing therapists would have the experience of failing to help some clients change, because for some problems and some people none of us know enough to be of help. It is likely that such experiences can motivate therapists to contribute in whatever ways they can to our clinical and empirical understanding of therapeutic successes and therapeutic failures.

FUTURE DIRECTIONS

Psychotherapy is probably 20 to 30 years away from its heyday. This prediction is based on what has been happening in biology and medicine for the past 30 years. As biology made major breakthroughs in understanding different levels of organisms, from basic genetic processes, to cellular processes, and to organ functioning, medicine has benefited immensely. The dramatic increases in basic knowledge of biological processes lead to equally dramatic increases in medicine's ability to apply this knowledge. Medicine has been experiencing a heyday, with the development of creative interventions ranging from genetic engineering to biochemical controls for diseased cells to transplants of entire organs. At the same time, many experts in medicine are beginning to recognize that there are serious limits to discovering biological cures for many of our major health problems. Medicine is beginning to recognize the need for people to make dramatic changes in their life-styles, if we are going to combat such frequent killers as certain cancers, heart disease, and other cardiovascular illnesses.

Fortunately, as society begins to turn more and more to behavior changes and life-style changes as the best preventions and interventions for many health problems, psychology is likely to replace biology as the most supported science, just as biology once surpassed chemistry. Psychology has already been making major strides toward understanding different levels of human behavior. The behaviorists are perhaps furthest along in understanding the situational and environmental controls of behavior. The interpersonal level of understanding human behaviors may be the least developed aspect of psychology and other social sciences. As more social scientists begin to study the dynamics of ongoing, intimate relationships, we can expect important, though delayed, increases in knowledge of dyadic behaviors. Systems scientists working with all forms of human organizations bring a rich array of analytical skills and tools that should contribute considerably to our understanding of families as key influences on human functioning. Ironically, the intrapersonal level has had one of the longest traditions of inquiry in psychotherapy, but does not currently receive adequate support from academic psychology. Just as cognition was recently rediscovered by academic psychology, so too can we expect more basic researchers to begin to rediscover the importance of understanding intrapsychic dynamics of human beings. The affective and irrational aspects of being human are all too often disowned by patients in psychotherapy and are all too often disowned by researchers in psychology.

The most important issue that eclectic therapists will need to address is how we can best apply the knowledge that we can expect to emerge from research on each of the basic levels of human functioning.

Psychotherapy practitioners and researchers are in a position to contribute to our knowledge of how change can best be facilitated in troubled situations, cognitions, interactions, systems, and intrapersonal dynamics. Eclectic psychotherapists are in a position to contribute to our understanding of how changes at one level can lead to changes at other levels, even though no direct intervention was made at the other levels. Eclectic psychotherapists are in a unique position to discover the best ways to integrate change processes that are derived from diverse therapy systems that are seen as inherently incompatible.

Eclectic therapists need to address the important issue as to whether they will be leaders toward a new era of more effective, efficient, and sufficient change or whether they will be followers of other orientations. Eclectic therapists in the past have contributed all too few theories, studies, and even techniques for advancing the field. There seems to have been something inherent in eclecticism that resulted in being led by more narrow but more innovative orientations. It is ironic, for example, that hundreds of studies have been completed on behavior therapy, which is favored by less than 10% of therapists (Prochaska and Norcross, 1983), while very few studies have been done on eclectic therapy, which is favored by one-third to one-half of all therapists.

But eclectic therapists might be confused about what to study. Eclecticism has been too fragmented, too asystematic, too vague, and too disorganized to study. As more systematic forms of eclecticism are created, eclectics will be able to evaluate which forms of eclecticism are most valid, most helpful for clients and therapists, most heuristic for researchers, and most effective for integrating the knowledge that comes from research on different levels of change.

To improve eclecticism we need comparative studies of our own to assess what advantages, if any, there are to adopting an atheoretical eclecticism, a technical ecleticism, or a synthetic eclecticism. Alternatively, should students and therapists be encouraged to take the easier alternative of becoming specialists in just one therapy system? Most eclectics, such as ourselves, believe there are real advantages to being eclectic, but we need to demonstrate empirically what those advantages are and how different forms of eclecticism vary in the degree to which they contribute to these advantages.

To improve eclecticism, we need to know much more about the processes and patterns of change. What techniques, for example, are best for applying each of the basic processes of change? Have interpretations been overused in the past, at the expense of confrontations and observations that may facilitate greater reliance on self-change and less reliance on therapy? What are the patterns of change that we can expect with different problems at different levels of change? Is it true, for example, that little change can be expected at the intrapersonal level when we are working with character disorders? Eclectic therapists could begin to chart the patterns of change that occur in both the problems and the processes involved with individual patients. Sharing these short-term and long-term patterns of change of individual patients, we could add substantially to our knowledge of how a broad range of clinical problems change or fail to change over time.

In what directions is eclecticism heading in the next decade? To address this question we shall draw upon a Delphi poll on the future of psychotherapy (Prochaska and Norcross, 1982). For the next decade we expect eclecticism to parallel the general trends predicted for psychotherapy in general. Translated into transtheoretical terms, the consensus of the 36 experts in this poll was that therapists will increase how often they work at the family/systems and interpersonal levels. They will also increase their work on the cognitive and situational levels but not on the intrapersonal level. Therapy will become more problem specific, briefer, and present centered. The emerging pattern of predictions was that psychotherapists' efforts at change will become more similar to self-change processes that are used by people in their natural environment.

The transtheoretical approach hopes to facilitate a movement toward integrating self-change and therapy change processes. We are working to create a more complete spectrum of change alternatives for specific problems that will range from people choosing to change entirely on their own to people choosing to rely on longer-term therapy. In between these alternatives, individuals could choose to use self-help materials based on the transtheoretical approach, correspondence courses that are more individualized and interactive according to the person's stage and level of change, and short-term therapy that is more personalized and individualized and enables clients to progress in therapy while learning a model of change that they can use on their own once therapy is over.

To aid therapists who are interested in maximizing the clients' two-thirds contributions to change, we are designing computer-assisted tests and aids that can be used both within and between therapy sessions. As therapy becomes briefer, we will need to maximize the efforts that clients make in the 99% of their working week that they are not in therapy. The computer-scored tests would help assess the stages and levels of clients. If the therapists and clients choose, the software programs would also be able to generate homework suggestions that clients could use for applying the processes of change that are being emphasized within the therapy sessions. The primary purpose of these computer programs will be to optimize cooperative efforts between what the client is intending to do and what the therapist is intending to do. For therapists and clients who are willing to share their results, these computer packages could also generate patterns-of-change graphs for a broad range of problems, patients, and psychotherapists.

Future directions also include considerably more work on developing the key level and maximum-impact strategies for intervening at different levels of change. This work will involve further development of the levels-of-change test for assessing the clients' problem levels. The more therapists are able to identify a key level that is involved in maintaining a client's problem, the more therapists will be able to effectively and efficiently use the limited time they have with clients.

One of our most creative challenges will be to develop the maximum-impact strategy for work with clients with multilevel problems. If clients know that therapeutic interventions or homework assignments have the potential for facilitating changes at the symptom/situational, cognitive, interpersonal, family/systems, and intrapersonal levels, we would expect clients to be willing to spend more time and energy on such therapeutic activities. The purpose here is to use our synthetic eclecticism to produce a synergistic effect that can help clients progress more fully at each level of change.

REFERENCES

Bandura, A. (1977). Self-efficacy: Toward a unifying theory of behavior change. *Psychological Review, 84,* 191–215.

Bandura, A. (1982). Self-efficacy mechanism in human agency. *American Psychologist, 37,* 122–147.

Bowen, M. (1978). *Family therapy in clinical practice.* New York: Jason Aronson.

Cookerly, J. (1973). The outcome of six major forms of marriage counseling compared: A pilot study. *Journal of Marriage and the Family, 36,* 608–611.

DiClemente, C. C., & Gordon, J. R. (1984). Stages of change in alcoholism treatment. A presentation at the Eighth Annual Alcoholism Conference—Current Issues in the Treatment of Alcoholism, El Paso, Texas, February 15–17.

DiClemente, C. C., & Hughes, S. (1985). Stages of change in alcoholism treatment: Measurement and profiles (In preparation).

DiClemente, C. C., & Prochaska, J. O. (1982). Self-change and therapy change of smoking behavior: A comparison of processes of change of cessation and maintenance. *Addictive Behaviors, 7,* 133–142.

DiClemente, C. C., & Prochaska, J. O. (In press). Processes and stages of change: Coping and competence in smoking behavior change. In S. Shiffman & T. A. Wills (Eds.), *Coping and substance abuse.* New York: Academic Press.

Ellis, A. (1973). *Humanistic psychotherapy: The rational-emotive approach.* New York: McGraw-Hill.

Glasgow, R. E., & Rosen, G. (1978). Behavioral bibliotherapy: A review of self-help behavior therapy manuals. *Psychological Bulletin, 85,* 1–23.

Goldfried, M. (1980). Toward the delineation of therapeutic change principles. *American Psychologist, 35,* 931–950.

Goldried, M. (1982). *Converging themes in psychotherapy.* New York: Springer Publishing Co.

Janis, I. L., & Mann, L. (1977). *Decision making: A psychological analysis of conflict, choice and commitment.* New York: The Free Press.

Lambert, M. (1983). *Psychotherapy and patient relationships.* Homewood, IL: Dow-Jones-Irwin.

Levinson, D., Dorrow, C., Klein, E., Levinson, M., & McKee, B. (1978). *The seasons of a man's life.* New York: Alfred A. Knopf.

Masters, W., & Johnson, V. (1970). *Human sexual inadequacy.* Boston: Little, Brown.

McConnaughy, E. A., Prochaska, J. O., & Velicer, W. F. (1983). Stages of change in psychotherapy: Measurement and sample profiles. *Psychotherapy: Theory, Research and Practice, 20,* 368–375.

McConnaughy, E. A., Prochaska, J. O., DiClemente, C., & Velicer, W. F. (1984). Stages of change, types of psychopathology, and progress in therapy. Manuscript under review.

Mellinger, G. D., Balter, M. B., Uhlenhuth, E. H., Cisin, I. H., Manheimer, D. I., & Rickels, K. (1983). Evaluating a household survey measure of psychic distress. *Psychological Medicine, 13,* 607–621.

Minuchin, S. (1974). *Families and family therapy.* Cambridge, MA: Harvard University Press.

Norcross, J., & Prochaska, J. (1983). Clinicians' theoretical orientations: Selection, utilization, and efficacy. *Professional Psychology: Research and Practice, 14,* 197–208.

Norcross, J., & Prochaska, J. (1984). Psychotherapist heal thyself: The self-initiated and therapy facilitated change experiences of mental health professionals (In preparation).

Norcross, J., Prochaska, J., Guadagnoli, E., & DiClemente, C. (1984). Factor structure of the levels of attribution and change (LAC) scale in samples of psychotherapists and smokers. *Journal of Clinical Psychology, 40,* 519–528.

Norcross, J., Prochaska, J., & Hambrecht, M. (In press). Levels of attribution and change scale: Development, validation and measurement. *Journal of Clinical Psychology.*

Olcott, P., Prochaska, J., & Velicer, W. (1984). Self change and therapy change approaches to weight control. Unpublished manuscript.

Parloff, M. (1980). Psychotherapy and research: An anaclitic depression. *Psychiatry, 43,* 279–293.

Prochaska, J. O. (1984). *Systems of psychotherapy: A transtheoretical analysis* (2nd ed.). Homewood, IL: The Dorsey Press.

Prochaska, J., & DiClemente, C. (1983). Stages and processes of self-change of smoking: Toward an integrative model of change. *Journal of Consulting and Clinical Psychology, 51,* 390–395.

Prochaska, J., & DiClemente, C. (1984). *The Transtheoretical approach: Crossing the traditional boundaries of therapy.* Homewood, IL: Dow Jones/Irwin.

Prochaska, J., & DiClemente, C. (In press). Common processes of change for smoking, weight control, and psychological distress. In S. Schiffman and T. Wills (Eds.), *Coping and substance abuse.* New York: Academic Press.

Prochaska, J., DiClemente, C., Norcross, J., & Guadagnoli, E. (1984). Processes and stages of self-change for weight control. Unpublished manuscript, University of Rhode Island.

Prochaska, J. O., DiClemente, C. C., Velicer, W. F., & Zwick, W. R. (1981). Measuring the processes of change used in smoking cessation. Paper presented at the Annual Meeting of the International Council of Psychology, Los Angeles.

Prochaska, J. O., & Norcross, J. C. (1982). The future of psychotherapy: A Delphi poll. *Professional Psychology, 5,* 620–627.

Prochaska, J. O., & Norcross, J. C. (1983). Psychotherapists' perspectives on treating themselves and their clients for psychic distress. *Professional Psychology: Research and Practice, 14,* 642–655.

Prochaska, J. M., & Prochaska, J. O. (1982). Dual-career families are a new challenge for spouses and agencies. *Social Casework: The Journal of Contemporary Social Work, 63,* 118–120.

Prochaska, J., Velicer, W., & DiClemente, C. (1984). Patterns of self-change in smoking cessation. Unpublished manuscript, University of Rhode Island.

Rogers, C. (1951). *Client-centered therapy.* Boston: Houghton Mifflin.

Rogers, C. (1959). A theory of therapy, personality, and interpersonal relationships, as developed in the client-centered framework. In S. Koch (Ed.), *Psychology: A study of a science, Vol. III: Formulations of the person and the social context.* New York: McGraw-Hill.

Sloane, R., Staples, F., Cristol, A., Yorkston, N., & Whipple, K. (1975). *Psychotherapy versus behavior therapy.* Cambridge, MA: Havard University Press.

Strupp, H. (1978). Psychotherapy research and practice: An overview. In Garfield, S., & Bergin, A. (Eds.), *Handbook of psychotherapy and behavior change.* New York: John Wiley & Sons.

Taube, C., Burns, B., & Kessler, L. (1984). Patients of psychiatrists and psychologists in office based practice: 1980. *American Psychologist, 39,* 1435–1447.

Thorne, F. (1973). Eclectic psychotherapy. In R. Corsini (Ed.), *Current psychotherapies.* Itasca, IL: F. E. Peacock.

Velicer, W., DiClemente, C., Prochaska, J., & Brandenburg, N. (1985). A decisional balance measure for predicting smoking cessation. *Journal of Personality and Social Psychology, 48,* 1279–1289.

Wilcox, N., Prochaska, J., Velicer, W., & DiClemente, C. (In press). Client characteristics as predictors of self-change in smoking cessation. *Addictive Behavior.*

CHAPTER 7

Functional Eclectic Therapy

Joseph T. Hart

BACKGROUND

Functional therapy is more than a hundred years old; it developed before both the psychoanalytic and the behavioral orientations. Before Sigmund Freud collaborated with Josef Breuer to publish his first partial statement of the theory and methods that led to psychoanalytic therapy, *Studies on Hysteria*, in 1895, the two major originators of functionalism —Pierre Janet in France and William James in the United States—had already published important clinical and theoretical books. (James' *The Principles of Psychology* was published in 1890 and Janet's publication on *The Mental State of Hysterics* in 1893.*)

An extremely important feature to recognize about functional eclectic therapy's history is that it *began* as an eclectic ori-

entation. In the late 1800s and early 1900s, James participated in what was known as the Boston School of Psychotherapy. The group included Morton Prince, J. J. Putnam, Hugo Munsterburg, Adolph Meyer, Boris Sidis, G. S. Hall, Josiah Royce, Isodor Coriat, August Hoch, and George Santayana. The historian Eugene Taylor commented on the eclectic attitude of the group:

The orientation of this "school" was by no means a carbon copy of James' ideas although James was undoubtedly a primary motivating force. Rather, the group as a whole reflected a very open-minded and eclectic attitude toward psychotherapy and the unconscious, focusing on the therapeutic process but drawing from widely diverse fields of philosophy, neurology, experimental psychology, psychic research, religion, and faith healing. (Taylor, 1980, p. 3)

Modern therapies are still trying to achieve the catholicism of the "open-minded and eclectic attitude" which characterized the Boston School a hundred years ago.

James' *Principles* began with this definition, "Psychology is the science of mental life, both of its phenomena and their

---

*This chapter concentrates on the contributions of William James. For a broader discussion of the historical background of functional therapy that includes more details about James' ideas as well as coverage of Pierre Janet, Trigant Burrow, Jessie Taft, Frederick Thorne, and others, see Hart (1983). For broader historical coverage of "functionalism" as a school of psychology consult Chapters 6, 7, and 8 of Schultz (1960).

conditions (James, 1890/1950, p. 1). By "phenomena," James meant "feelings, desires, cognitions, reasonings, decisions, and the like" and by "conditions," he referred to any influences that could alter the phenomena such as aging, drugs, sickness, excitement, exhaustion, competition, and repetition. He said that "the quest of conditions becomes the psychologist's most interesting task" (quoted in Allen, 1967, p. 3).

According to James' definition, the functional therapist must pay attention to feelings, desires, cognitions, reasonings, and decisions and to any conditions that cause problems of functioning. Furthermore, the functional therapist should attend to the clients' goals and consciously chosen plans and actions. *Any therapist who agrees with these basic points is starting from the framework of clinical functionalism.*

Emotion

The James-Lange theory of emotion is often mentioned in textbooks of general psychology. Unfortunately, the clinical significance of the theory is never discussed.

The famous, often-quoted passage from the *Principles* on emotions reads:

Our natural way of thinking about these coarser emotions is that the mental perception of some fact excites the mental affection called the emotion, and that this latter state of mind gives rise to the bodily expression. My theory, on the contrary, is that the *bodily changes follow directly the perception of the exciting fact, and that our feeling of the same changes as they occur is the emotion.* Common sense says we lost our fortune, are sorry and weep; we meet a bear, are frightened and run; we are insulted by a rival, are angry and strike. The hypothesis here to be defended says that this order of sequence is incorrect, that one state is not immediately induced by the other, that the bodily manifestation must first be interposed between and that the more rational statement

is that we feel sorry because we cry, angry because we strike, afraid because we tremble. (James, 1890/1950, Vol. 2, pp. 449–450)

James was concerned with three components of emotion: the perception, actions in response to the perception, and bodily feelings following the actions. James' theory is quite assimilable into later theoretical and research approaches, such as Schachter's (1966), which emphasize significance of set and setting in determining the perception of emotional arousal. His theory is also supported by the cross-cultural research on facial expressions that showed a uniformity of expressions across cultures for basic emotions such as happiness, sadness, anger, fear, surprise, and disgust (Ekman, 1971). James would say we see something sad, our facial expression shows sadness, and we feel sad. The clinical significance of his theory of emotion was elucidated by James in his 1894 article "What Is an Emotion?" James counseled,

If we wish to conquer emotional tendencies in ourselves, we must assiduously, and in the first instance cold-bloodedly, go through the *outward motions* of those contrary dispositions we prefer to cultivate. (p. 201)

Of course, this advice is very similar to what might be given by a modern cognitive behaviorist.

The important theoretical and clinical point is that feelings and emotions should not be considered apart from their expressions. The therapeutic target is not the feeling alone (as in extreme analytic existentialism) or the behavior alone (as in extreme behaviorism) but the percept-action-feeling unit. What James did was to define perception-expression-experience as the total *unit* of emotionality.

Whether the therapist is a cognitive behavior therapist applying systematic desensitization or a humanistic therapist who is reflecting feelings, both are working within the James-Lange model. Their common goals are (1) to help their clients understand how their actions are causing their discomfort and (2) to aid their clients to try new actions that will lead to new, more satisfying feelings. Most therapists attempt to get clients to change their actions, their perceptions, and their thoughts.

James' theory directly establishes why emotions and feelings are of such central importance in therapeutic work. It is *not* because they are especially dangerous or troublesome, as is popularly thought, but because *feelings can be used as conscious mediators of behavior and personality change.* In the percept-action-feeling sequence it is the feeling which most strongly rises to consciousness. To change the way they feel clients must notice which percepts and actions lead to which feelings. From there, new expressions and actions can be tried to develop, consciously, new feelings. Feelings provide the feedback that can lead to change. The percept-action-feeling unit is the original biofeedback machine.

Consciousness

Freud's name will be forever associated with the theory of the unconscious; James' special position in the history of psychology is his theory of consciousness.

Rychlak has commented on the importance of James' conceptualization of consciousness, with its *equal* weighting of thought and feelings, for humanistic therapists:

The intellectual list theorists have also taken the position that feelings do not enter into mentation, if indeed they exist at all. But for James, feeling relations are central to the course of thought. And here we observe a tendency that I think all humanists share, that is, to ascribe significance to something called emotion, feeling, or affection in human affairs. (Rychlak, 1978, p. 101)

Chapter 9 of James' *Principles* is titled "The Stream of Thought"; his choice of the stream metaphor conveys very well his emphasis on the affective in consciousness.

Consciousness, then, does not appear to itself chopped up in bits. Such words as "chain" or "train" do not describe it fitly. . . . It is nothing pointed; it flows. A "river" or a "stream" are the metaphors by which it is most naturally described. In talking of it hereafter, let us call it the stream of thought, of consciousness, or subjective life. (James, 1890/1950, p. 239)

The contemporary theorist Howard Gardner has stressed the significance of a theorist's choice of dominant metaphor:

The individual's sense of purpose—his goal-directedness—guides the choice of a whole set of enterprises and dictates, which to focus on at a given time, which to abandon, when to develop a new set of skills, and when to fall back on the tried and true ones. . . . A total system stems from the creator's affective life. (Gardner, 1982, p. 355)

The fundamental and crucial therapeutic significance of James' central concern with the stream of consciousness is his insistence that subjective knowledge is possible and useful. The functional technology of consciousness is so simple and basic that it is usually unstated. Let us here try to state the obvious: it is valuable for clients (1) to *report* on what they are experiencing subjectively, (2) to *include* not only thoughts but images and feelings in their reports, and (3) to *use* their insights to attempt to consciously change actions and personality patterns. Any therapist who adopts these a-b-c's of consciousness is working within the Jamesian framework of functional therapy.

Of course, James' theory did not say that everything was accessible to consciousness. Even so, James would certainly advise therapists to *first* attend to what clients can consciously report, *next* attend to what they experience on the fringes of consciousness, and only *then* attend to the inferred unconscious. These a-b-c's and 1-2-3's are quite different from the emphases and orderings that would be made by a psychoanalyst or behaviorist.

The Subconscious

For James what is vague, or on the fringe of consciousness, is precisely what leads to the development of consciousness: "It is, in short, the reinstatement of the vague to its proper place in our mental life which I am so anxious to press on the attention" (James, 1950, p. 254). For both therapeutic change and self-development, it is the sustained attention to the subliminal that leads to discoveries. Freud's basic rule of analysis is: say everything that comes to mind. James' basic rule could be phrased: pay attention to the gaps and seek to fill them.

James argues in the 1896 lectures that "we should broaden our notion of health instead of narrowing it" (Taylor, 1982, p. 164). He recognized that a mundane, seemingly adaptive life may be much less fulfilled and real than a life that is open to uprushes from the subconscious: "A certain tolerance, a certain sympathy, a certain respect, and above all a certain lack of fear, seem to be the best attitude we can carry in our dealings with these regions of human nature" (Taylor, 1982, p. 165).

For both James and Janet the subconscious or subliminal was an accessible psychic process. The most direct means of access was by attending to "gaps" in consciousness and by staying with "felt" tendencies to fill those gaps. This method is essential in almost every session of functional therapy.

The Self

James begins the chapter on "The Consciousness of Self" by defining the "con-stituents of the self": (1) the material self (the body, clothes, and physical possessions); (2) the social self (recognition given by friends and acquaintances); (3) the person's psychological faculties and dispositions; and (4) the pure ego (the central self or self of all other selves). These definitions of the self are essentially similar to those taken into account by most clinicians in a mental status examination. How does the person look? How is the person regarded by friends? What are the person's personality characteristics? And how does the person regard himself or herself?

On page 310 James comments on feelings of success and failure and provides a summary formula for evaluating the individual's self-confidence: self-esteem = success/pretensions. "With no attempt there can be no failure; with no failure, no humiliation . . . so our self feeling in this world depends entirely on what we *back* ourselves to be and do" (James, 1950, Vol.p, p. 310). He goes on to distinguish between the present self and the ideal or potential self and discusses the conflicts that develop between different self-concepts. In these formulations James can clearly be recognized as the precursor of modern formulations about self-concepts and their use in therapy by such theorists as Carl Rogers and George Kelly.

For James, the self is not an abstraction but a felt, bodily experience:

The consciousness of Self involves a stream of thought, each part of which as "I" can remember those which went before, and know the things they knew; and emphasize and care paramountly for certain ones among them as "*me*" and *appropriate to these* the rest. The nucleus of "me" is always the bodily experience felt to be present at the time. (James, 1950, Vol. 1, p. 400)

The Jamesian self is not fixed but changeable—and fragile. In James' theory the self must be constructed and maintained and is susceptible to aberrations. The stream of consciousness is a multiple stream, and it is possible for ongoing thoughts, feelings, and even actions to be dissociated from the person's central, conscious self.

Dissociation is not a rare condition. Anytime people are unaware of how they are feeling because they are "too busy," or "too tired," or "too worried," or in some other way occupied, a degree of dissociation exists. The first task of most therapy is to teach clients how to move from dissociated consciousness in which fringe thoughts, feelings, and images are ignored to an integrated consciousness in which gaps or dissociations are filled in with awareness.

MODERN FUNCTIONAL THERAPY

In functional therapy, *any* technique or idea is considered open for exploration; more important, no single role model is endorsed as the most appropriate one for the therapist-client interaction, and no single social context is considered the most desirable for therapeutic effectiveness. It is this extreme diversity of roles and structures, characteristic of Jamesian functionalism, which made it politically difficult for functional therapy to flourish. In the early 1900s when the professional identities of psychotherapists were being established, any therapy that could not be boxed, wrapped, and presented to other professions and to the public definitely and simply was politically disadvantageous. The dominant role models became the doctor-patient medical model, the scientist-practitioner applied scientist model, and the teacher-student counselor model.

The "eclectic attitude" is more important to emphasize than any special method or idea, or any particular role model. It is an attitude that does not always align itself easily with professional precepts about how a therapist should think and act. James sought to maintain the dialectic tensions between "tough-minded" and "tender-minded" evaluations, between philosophy and religion, and between science and art.

The eclectic therapist Frederick Thorne introduced a useful distinction between "case handling" and "psychotherapy." In handling a case, a professional might do any number of things—from testing to reeducation to setting up a supportive medication therapy program, and so on. None of these activities are necessarily related to particular psychotherapeutic theories. From a case-handling point of view it seems desirable for every therapist to be widely flexible. A therapist's range of choices would vary considerably depending on the context within which the client was seen. For example, a therapist working in a hospital will have a different range of case-handling choices from a therapist who works at a high school or a church or in a private practice in a small town or in a therapeutic community. Each different context sets up different case-handling possibilities. This sort of eclecticism might be called contextual eclecticism—therapeutic variety arises from the limits, demands, and possibilities of the settings in which therapeutic relationships are established.

It is sometimes difficult to separate contextual eclecticism from theoretical eclecticism. That is, the same therapist might do very different things in different settings. But because most therapists work within a limited range of settings, they experience a relatively limited set of demands and possibilities. It is often hard to tell whether a therapist is doing what he or she is doing because of the demand characteristics of the setting, or because of the theoretical ideas and methods brought to the setting.

In functional therapy, although anything may be used for *case handling* depending on the context, in *psychotherapy* some methods and ideas are used repeatedly; these are chosen on the basis of a guiding theory.

CLIENT ASSESSMENT

This will be a short section because, since functional therapists operate more from the humanistic-experiential model than from the clinical-medical model, very little emphasis is placed on testing and diagnosis as a guide to therapy.

On the other hand, when the practitioner is operating in the case-handling mode rather than as a psychotherapist, the full range of modern psychological, psychophysiological, and observational tools are used. In addition, considerable use is made of audiotaping, videotaping, and, more recently, microcomputer-aided client self-monitoring.

Clients are frequently encouraged to keep journals or therapy diaries. These are used more for guiding the therapy than are tests. When tests are used (such as the MMPI, the Meyers-Briggs, the TAT, the Millon Multiaxial Clinical Inventory, and the SCL-90), more attention is directed, in therapy, to elucidating the specific item responses than to the use of profiles or normative evaluations. Life area questionnaires are used to gain information about the client's background and about the positive and negative areas of functioning in the person's life. (See Hart, 1983, and Corriere & Hart, 1979, for samples of life area questionnaires.)

APPLICABILITY

Functional therapy is most applicable to the milder forms of psychological maladjustment in outpatient settings. Clients must be able to talk about their feelings, attitudes, and life-styles and must be capable of trying new ways of living to benefit from the functional approach.

When new clients are mainly in need of maintenance rather than experiential explorations and personality change, they are referred to other practitioners, or the therapist shifts to a case-handling mode rather than trying to implement the functional process. Similarly, clients in need of group support, milieu therapy, or institutionalization are referred to other settings. Functional therapy can be practical in several different delivery modes: short-term or long-term, group professional practice or individual practice, programmatically or session-by-session, and group therapy or individual therapy.

In general, clients who want specific symptom relief and nothing else or clients who want to change a specific behavior without wider experiential self-examination are not good candidates for functional therapy. They are referred to behavior therapists, hypnotherapists, or other more guided, directive approaches. Also, clients who desire a long-term exploration of their psychological development and of transference phenomena are referred to analysts. Cases of severe mood disorder or psychosis are typically referred for psychiatric chemotherapy.

THERAPY PROCESS

Functional therapists work with the same stuff of therapy as do most other therapists. Very few therapists of any persuasion actually live with their clients; therapy relies on *reports* about the person's life and on *observations* about how the client relates to the therapist. In a sense, therapy is a kind of story-telling activity—the client tells his/her story and the therapist, an audience of one, listens. Sometimes, the client shows or acts out the story and the therapist watches the play.

Occasionally, the narration and monologue will be replaced by real-life exchanges between the client and the therapist. But even this "couch theater" is a very tiny sample of the client's daily life. Given the artificiality of the basic therapeutic situation, it is not unexpected that therapists tend to work with highly selective samplings of the client's reports. It would be unbearably boring and unproductive if the client were truly to tell the therapist *everything*. At the extreme, clients would bring in 24-hour videotapes of every day of their lives, and they and their therapists would examine the tapes together. (In fact, in functional therapy, clients are often asked to tape-record samples of their interactions with people, which are then used in therapy sessions.)

In functional therapy, the selective focus is on emotional or feeling-toned events. Feelings are used as rough indicators of positive and negative functioning. Clients soon learn, as a rule of thumb, to report happenings that made them feel good or bad. Within the session itself the therapist listens to the client's report and observes the style of reporting. In tuning in to the person's stream of consciousness, the therapist pays special attention to gaps or discontinuities because these signal something on the fringes or borders of consciousness that is nonetheless affecting the conscious report. Gaps in what is said or expressed are just as important as what is expressed.

The Feeling Moment

Much of therapy revolves around "crises." Clients come to therapy because of external or internal crises that leave them feeling demoralized. The task of therapy is to help clients consciously cope with the crises; how to do this is subtle and demanding work. The twin dangers of covering over a crisis with false reassurances or with distracting involvements are matched by the double dangers of evoking more feeling or more responsibilities than the person can integrate.

According to James, intense emotion could accelerate the process of habit formation. Unfortunately, the habits engendered by intense emotion can be either good habits or bad habits. The real work of therapy is to sustain, and sometimes even to provoke, crises in order to undo old, bad habits and foster new, good habits.

Within a therapy session mini-crises can be evoked and resolved if the client and therapist attend to *feeling moments*. A potential feeling moment exists whenever the client or the therapist notices a mismatch between *what* is being said (the content) and *how* it is being said (the style). For the ordinary rule of conversation, which is "you must make social and intellectual sense," the therapy setting substitutes a new rule, "you must make emotional sense."

Ordinary conversation is designed to accommodate cognitive communication; speakers exchange information primarily and feelings secondarily. In therapy this is reversed: feelings are primary and information is secondary. That is why so much can take place in an hour. The therapist cares most about how the person experiences his/her life, not about obtaining a detailed record of what happened. Therapy deals with exemplary events, crises that teach.

A functional therapist teaches by noticing mismatches, selecting some to work with, and guiding a client to resolve a mismatch when it is brought into awareness. When therapists talk about "listening with the third ear" they are pointing toward feeling moments. In ordinary conversation we accept mismatches and gaps; in therapy we do not. Therapists use their special perceptiveness to help clients achieve emotional consistency (matching) and full expressiveness in place of emotional chopping, withholding, and inconsistency.

The functional tradition starts from the *visible* unconscious; it is the source of therapy's mini-crises. It is not necessary to infer the unconscious when gaps and mismatches are so easily and directly perceived. As James recognized, the basic in-session task of therapy is to elucidate the vague and fill in the gaps.

There is no presumption, within functional theory, that the content of a feeling moment is something that is repressed or suppressed. What is contained in a gap is unknown, and what will be revealed when a mismatch is redirected into a matched feeling expression is unpredictable. Whether a gap in consciousness represents an emergent feeling or a pushed-down feeling, or both, is not known until the feeling moment is completed.

Clients who cannot pay attention to feeling moments or who cannot learn to notice mismatches and work toward expressing fully what they feel and mean should be taught how to do so. If that is not possible, the therapist should switch into a case-handling mode and stop trying to apply functional therapy. Feeling moments are such critical basic events within the functional approach to therapy that no progress can be made unless the client can function to some degree at a level of awareness that is open to this kind of therapeutic intervention. Gendlin (1981) has devised a procedure called "focusing" which teaches clients to pay attention to gaps in their inner experience and to notice how those gaps are filled with shifts in feelings, thoughts, and images. The focusing method can be used for therapeutic purposes or as a method of meditation.

In functional therapy, focusing is taught to clients usually within the first two or three sessions. The client is taught what focusing is and how to do it. The major theme in the didactic sessions is to convey that "focusing is paying attention to what you are experiencing and how your inner experience changes moment-by-moment." A secondary theme is to point out a few feeling moments and to teach "feeling moments are times when your expressions and your experiences do not match, they are important events in therapy because they can be used as times for exploring changes." (See the programatic manual in Part IV of Hart, *Modern Eclectic Therapy*, 1983, pp. 228–236.)

The value of feeling moments is that they are manageable crises. They contain the ingredients that are often present in everyday interpersonal crises—emotion, lack of clarity, and an inability to communicate fully—but they are contained within the safety of the therapy mileu. The feeling expression that the therapist will help the client to achieve in order to match content with form will be a controlled or mock expression.

The therapy setting is a kind of stage on which crises and dramatic expressions of feelings can be acted out during a temporary suspension of the roles of ordinary life but the anger, frustration, sadness, despair, jubilation, and other feelings that are expressed are not completely real. For example, if a client expresses anger about a spouse who is not present, that expression may lead to an accurate matching of inner experience and outer expression, but the consequences are quite different than they would be if the spouse were present. Even direct expressions of feeling toward the therapist are bounded expressions. When the client says, "I could kill you. . . . I feel like ripping your head open," in most instances, both the client and the therapist know that this feeling expression is a mock expression; i.e., the action is not really intended to be carried out.

The Dynamics of Expression

Once feeling moments are pointed out, the therapist can use a variety of methods to reveal the emotional meanings that have not been fully expressed. Affective communications follow a different rhythm than ordinary social conversations. Unfortunately, the linguistics of affective communication are largely unknown. Any "principles" of affective communication are nothing more than guidelines. Therapists who work with feeling moments will find as much guidance from drama, poetry, rhetoric, film, and novels as from the scientific literature.

Nonetheless, here are a few general, tentative, empirical guidelines about how to work with expressions in order to reveal the emotional, preconscious meaning hidden within a feeling moment:

1. Vary the loudness of the expression; ask the client to repeat something louder or softer.
2. Vary the tempo of the expression; instruct the client to speak faster or slower.
3. Vary the emphases in the expression; ask the client to stress different words or different accents in the word.
4. Change the movements that accompany the expression; instruct the client to move faster, slower, more smoothly, more unevenly, and so on.
5. Change the position of the body; ask the client to assume different postures.
6. Change the direction of the delivery; have the client move closer, farther away, to the side, etc.
7. Repeat the expression; some expressions of feeling sound very different the fifth or tenth or twentieth time they are verbalized.
8. Substitute nonsense words or sounds and work with the dynamics of the sounds. This device can sometimes take the client completely away from words that do not fit the feeling. Once the feeling is clearly felt, new accurate words can be found to fit the emotional expression.

Although these speech dynamics are familiar to poets, songwriters, speechwriters, and advertisers, they are seldom taught directly to students of therapy. Even something as simple as an instruction to "repeat what you just said" can often yield very powerful emotional effects. Unfortunately, therapists and therapy supervisors often focus on understanding *cognitive* meanings rather than

emotional meanings. They apply the methods of scientific or literary analysis rather than the evocative methods of drama and art.

For example, if a client says, "I'm not really angry with her," and the therapist detects a mismatch between what is said and what seems to be felt, one typical direction of response would be to ask, "Are you really not angry?" or "Not angry?" or "What do you mean when you say you aren't really angry?" Even a reflection of feeling such as "You are saying you aren't really angry but there is something you feel" tends to keep the client at a cognitive level. In contrast, direct work with the dynamics of expression will lead more surely toward the feeling and not add irrelevant explanations. Instead, the submerged emotional expression can begin to surface.

Using Functional Dynamism to Work with Dreams, Fantasies, and Memories

So far, the functional therapist might be viewed as more of a drama coach or teacher than therapist. That impression is partly true because functional therapy does sound and look somewhat different from other therapies. However, the functional therapist also attends to the kinds of phenomena that are often taken as synonymous with therapy, namely dreams, fantasies, and memories, but does so in a special way. When a client relates a dream or a fantasy or a memory, the functionalist *first* examines the levels of functioning the client demonstrates and only then asks, "What does this experience mean?" For functional therapy, the primary meaning of an inner experience is in what it shows directly about the client's functioning. Inferences about symbolic meanings are used but are secondary to the first line of inquiry.

The small units of therapy interaction—feeling moments, gaps in consciousness, and expression dynamics—can be organized into larger units called dynamisms. By a "dynamism" is meant a variable personality characteristic related to emotional perceptiveness and expressiveness. A person's level of dynamism functioning can vary not only from situation to situation but from experience to experience.

Five personality dynamisms that have been identified as useful in therapy are:

1. The *feeling dynamism*, which refers to the individual's overall level of feeling or emotional tone.
2. The *activity dynamism*, which is the specific physical action the person makes in response to events and interactions.
3. The *clarity dynamism*, which refers to the person's level of awareness.
4. The *expression dynamism*, which concerns the extent to which the person verbalizes feelings and thoughts.
5. The *contact dynamism*, which relates to the person's involvements with other people.

(Research has demonstrated that these dynamisms can be reliably measured and applied to dreams, fantasies, and waking reports; also, improvement in therapy is correlated with higher levels of functioning on these dynamisms. See Karle, Corriere, Hart, & Woldenberg, 1980, and Hart, Corriere, Karle, & Woldenberg, 1980.)

Functional therapy teaches clients to evaluate dreams, fantasies, and memories according to these dynamisms. Specifically, clients are taught to ask:

"How expressive was I?"
"How active was I?"
"How clear was I?"
"How much feeling did I experience?"
"How much contact did I make with other people?"

The functional emphasis is on *how* people

dream or fantasize rather than on *what* they dream or fantasize about. Clients are also taught to look at consequences if dynamisms were to be changed. Specifically, "What would happen if you were . . .

more active?
more expressive?
more feelingful?
clearer?
or if you made more contact?"

Dreams are especially valuable in studying dynamisms because there is no stimulus pull and there are no outer distractions. The way a dreamer responds to feeling moments in dreams is largely self-determined. From the functional perspective, dreams can be used to show how much feeling awareness the dreamer shows and the ways the dreamer responds from feelings.

In the functional approach to dreams, the focus is on *how* the dreamer functions emotionally, not on the content of the dream or the interpretation of dream symbols. A functional dream analysis begins with the dreamer's self-assessment of how he or she functioned in the dream on the five dynamisms: expressiveness, clarity, feeling, contact, and activity. Then the dreamer considers which functional characteristics might be increased or decreased. Next, the dreamer looks at parallels between the dream profile and similar functional profiles from waking life. Functionalism stresses (1) the conscious meaning of the dream as the central meaning: (2) direct expression of feelings as primary and symbolic expression as secondary; and (3) a parallelism between waking function and dream functioning (in contrast to the compensation or safety valve hypotheses). To change dream functioning, the dreamer must change waking functioning.

Functional analysis of dreamer personality processes does not preclude interpretive analyses of what a dream means.

However, the functional preference for taking what is available to consciousness first and what is repressed or unconscious last is applied to dreams in the same way it is applied to fantasies, waking reports, and therapy experiences.

The Process of Reintegration

Therapy is difficult because clients are resistant to change and defensive about fully revealing their emotional thoughts and images. Therapy is also very difficult because people face real-life problems that are not easily solved. If it were not for defenses, resistances, and problems, therapy would be very easy. (But psychotherapy might not exist!) Going to a therapist would be similar to visiting an insurance broker; the client would walk in, describe the life changes he or she wanted to make, and then purchase the therapy plan that seemed to meet his or her needs.

It is sometimes possible to achieve a good deal of positive change by simply working from a fitness or growth model and ignoring areas of dysfunctioning. Dysfunctioning in one life area can be offset by improved functioning in other life areas. For example, mental problems that are exacerbated by a job layoff might be very much eased through direct vocational counseling or job placement.

The familiar distinctions between counseling and psychotherapy, short-term and long-term therapy, and supportive therapy versus depth therapy relate to the extent to which basic personality change is needed and attempted and the extent to which defenses, resistances, and dysfunctional life patterns are uncovered. A basic question is *when* must a therapist work directly with problems of dysfunctioning, resistances, and defenses? To state the question from the other end, *when* can a therapist simply concentrate on improving a client's functioning? The answer to

these questions requires specification of the process of personality growth and change. Then the answer becomes obvious—a therapist *must* work with dysfunctioning when clients are unable to make positive changes.

In functional theory, a four-step model of the growth or integration process is used to guide therapeutic interventions. When working with growth or integration steps, a therapist can ignore problems, symptoms, complaints, resistances, and defenses *unless* those dysfunctionings make it impossible for the client to carry out steps in the change process. In functional therapy, the therapist teaches the client about the four-step change model, and the therapist, when working on specific attempts to change, helps to make the client aware of each step in the process; this allows both the therapist and the client to know when a step is missing or incomplete.

The four steps or stages are: the *need* stage, the *choice* stage, the *action* stage, and the *image* stage. Moving through all four stages can take several days, weeks, or months, but the person who completes all four steps will have made a meaningful personality change.

The *need* step of the growth process involves helping the client isolate, recognize, and verbalize a need or want. The process of satisfying needs and wants is one of the main jobs of the personality. The personality is the bridge between the biological experience of the need and the actions that must be taken to satisfy the need. Clearly, needs and wants are different from problems. When a client makes the shift from stating needs as problems (which is a personal misapplication of the medical model) to a personal declaration of what he or she needs, significant room has been made for personality development.

The *choice* step of the process of integration is an extension of the recognition of needs and wants. Once a personal desire has been felt and stated, the client is encouraged to respond to his or her needs as an important reality. Choosing one's own needs requires an affirmation of inner-directedness. The person can't remain outer-oriented ("The world must [or won't] fulfill my needs"). A shift to an inner-orientation involves taking on responsibility for fulfilling one's own needs and wants as much as possible ("I can try to fulfill my needs"). All needs and wants are important; they all add to the ratio of positives to negatives in a person's life. The choice may be as small as "I want this and not that for dinner" or as large as "I want to feel more deeply with my wife." The therapist's task in this choice step is to help the person feel what it is like to affirm personal needs.

The *choice* step is followed by the *action* step. Once a person has admitted a need and chosen the need as a real value in his or her life, then new actions can be tried to fulfill that need. The therapist may teach the client how to behave in new or more functional ways, or may simply be a sounding board for the effectiveness of the ways that the client tries.

The last step in the growth process is the *image* step. Awareness of a new need, choosing that need, and acting to fulfill that need eventually will result in a new personality image. The new image (e.g., "I am a person who feels deeply with my wife") functions to integrate a great many experiences and actions. The person now conceives of himself and guides his life, when it is relevant, from this image. The new image replaces old images (e.g., "I'm too busy to feel much with my wife") and will self-define the person in a world that contains a multitude of possible wants, choices, actions, and images.

The complete four-step integration process (need-choice-action-image) will be repeated again and again throughout a person's lifetime. Because needs and wants change, no set of personality images can

be sufficient for a lifetime. The integration process goes on inside and outside the therapy situation. All that is unique to therapy is that therapists can directly and conceptually teach clients to be aware of the process. People are in the process long before they come to therapy and long after they leave it.

The first place to look for dysfunction is in failure to grow. Defensiveness or resistances are most clearly manifested when a person refuses to become aware of new needs and wants, or to choose them, or to act on them, or to change personality images to accommodate them. If the four-step integration process is conceptualized as a cycle going from needs and wants to choices to actions to images, then dysfunctioning consists of a reversal of the clockwise cycle to a counterclockwise cycle. Instead of choosing and acting from needs and wants, the dysfunctioning person begins to allow old images to dictate how he or she will act, what he or she will choose, and what needs and wants can be satisfied: images—to actions—to choices—to needs and wants. This means, in effect that only old needs and wants can be satisfied because the person's old images are determining actions, choices, and even the awareness of what is needed and wanted. Since it is extremely unlikely that old needs and wants will match current needs and wants, the person caught in a reverse cycle is bound to be dissatisfied but may not know why. Only awareness of how the old personality images are blocking the emergence of new awareness and functioning will lead to a clearing away of the block or resistance. It is at this stage, when old images effectively block the natural growth process, that therapists must shift from a growth model to a pathology model in their work.

Personality images may or may not match momentary feelings. If, during a therapy session, the therapist notices frequent mismatches between what a client expresses and what he or she seems to be experiencing, then the therapist may decide to counter the image that is sustaining the mismatch. For example, a woman whose self-image is that of a "loving wife" might be so inflexibly attached to her image that she maintains a "loving" demeanor even when she is obviously upset and angry about something her husband said to her. Her image acts as a defense or resistance to cover over the perception and expression of her underlying feelings. Defenses and resistances always function to substitute more accepable feelings and expressions (more acceptable to the personality image) for unacceptable feelings and expressions. In other words, defenses and resistances are substitutes consistent with the personality image but inconsistent with the feelings of the moment. With resistances, the substitution is more or less conscious: the person is *suppressing*. With defenses, the substitution is subconscious: the person is *repressing*.

The process of reintegration can involve four steps; however, not every step occurs every time. It is possible to go from step one to step four while skipping two and three. A full process of reintergration involves these four steps: counteraction, catharsis, proaction, and reintegration.

There are innumerable ways that a therapist can counteract an image that has become dysfunctional. The most straightforward way of proceeding is simply to point out the mismatch between the apparent feeling and what the client is saying: "Even though you are talking about loving your husband you look and sound angry." This kind of functional interpretation may well be resisted—"Well, I don't feel angry." The therapist can then work with the resistances, applying the same methods of working with expression dynamics and personality dynamisms that would be applied to an emergent image. Working with feeling moments is always dynamically the same whether the feel-

ings are suppressed, repressed, or merely unknown. For example:

T: Say that again only louder.
C: "I don't feel angry!"
T: Keep saying it, say it five times.
C: (Client repeats five times.)
T: Now imagine that you are saying that to your husband five times.
C: (Client repeats again but in a flat voice.)
T: Try saying, "I'll go flat to keep from being angry."
C: (She does and then she and the therapist talk about the process of "going flat," when it happens, and what it means.)

Counteraction takes place by the therapist instructing clients to increase or decrease personality dynamisms and dynamics of expression, often with reference to a defensive image. All resistances and defenses are maintained within a certain narrow set of expressive parameters. So the counteractive process, by not allowing these parameters to stay fixed, begins to undermine the image. When counteraction begins to occur, clients experience some stress. A kind of temporary disintegration takes place because the person starts to express things incompatible with the old image but does not yet have a new personality image to accommodate the new ways of functioning.

The counteractive step often leads to an emotional release. In this cathartic stage, the client expresses the emotions that have been held in by the old personality images (e.g., "I don't like being nice all the time . . . that's not love."). Sometimes the catharsis may be an extended abreactive catharsis in which the client reexperiences times in his or her past when the old image was instilled to block feelings. The skilled therapist can use this stage to help the client distinguish between the past environment that demanded the old images and the new environment that requires new images and new levels of functioning. The major requirement of the catharsis step is that the client maintain a real level of contact with the therapist sufficient to allow the exploration of times in the past when contact was missing or distorted.

In the proactive step, the client moves from a focus on reexpressing feelings that were blocked in the past to *the expression of similar or related feelings with the therapist in the present*. Here the client is helped to explore new feelings and develop new expression skills that eventually will lead to new personality images. At this stage the person who has just undergone a temporary disintegration has no idea whether the images and ways of behaving that are being given up will lead to something more satisfying. All that he or she knows is that the old way of being no longer seems to be enough.

In the final step of the reintegration process, the person ends up where he or she would have been all along if the old personality image had not distorted the individual's perceptions—at the top of the need-choice-action-image cycle. The person is now ready to start off open to new wants and needs that were blocked by the old image. The reason for calling this cycle a reintegration process is because it puts the person back into the cycle of integration. As a result of the controlled disintegration of a dysfunctional personality image, the person is now open to thinking, feeling, and acting in new ways.

It is important to emphasize that this process of reintegration is necessarily an emotional process. The feelings and emotions that emerge may be mild or intense, but they will be involving.

Another feature of reintegration is that the client experiences a kind of dual consciousness in which the sense of reality attached to the old image is suspended. This allows the person to experience the specific resistances and defenses attached to the old image without believing them in the same way they would be believed and acted on outside the therapeutic setting. A sort of play acting takes place during reintegration. By exaggerating the expression of the old image beyond its usual expression parameters, the person is actually freed from attachment to the image. Indeed, during counteraction and catharsis and proaction the person may experience how much self-inflicted distress comes from efforts to maintain the old personality image. In ordinary circumstances, the self-inflicted distress is hidden because the defense or resistance is not experienced in a concentrated way. When clients actually experience what their own resistances and defenses feel like, they are then much more willing to give them up.

The rather abstract terms counteraction-catharsis-proaction-reintegration were used to describe this four-step process because it is an artificial process. Although disintegration (both positive and negative) occurs outside the special circumstances of therapy, the full four-step process of positive disintegration would very rarely occur without the direction and presence of a therapist. The process of integration is described in simple, common terms (need-choice-action-image) because it occurs naturally and frequently in ordinary adult development. The full four-step process of reintegration that is described does not usually occur outside the therapeutic setting.

The role of emotion and feeling in therapy has not been generally understood. The idea that emotions are important because they are a cause of pathology is true but only partly true: the reason emotions *can be* a cause of pathology is that they energize or activate many other psychological functions (memory, action, perception, cognition, etc.) and lead to the reorganization of these functions. Emotions and feelings can be the source not only of pathology but of growth and creativity, not only defensiveness but the reversal of defensiveness.

The two fundamental reasons fixed images become dysfunctional and frustrating is because: (1) they fail to meet current needs and wants, and (2) fixed images tend to block the affective drive (the picture-symbol cognitive system overrides the affective system). In both creative development and therapeutic development there is a strong reliance on subconscious emotions and feelings to break through fixed symbols and pictures.

Historically, insanity and creativity often have been thought to be related. The reason for this basically false historical presumption is that both insanity and creativity are "disorders" of feeling. In one condition, insanity, the feelings serve mainly the negative disintegrative functions. In the other condition, creativity, feelings serve positive disintegration and integration. The historically intuitive linking of insanity and creativity is correct at one level but in error overall. So, too, are the analytic and humanistic theories about "regression in the service of the ego" and the creative use of "primary process" or "right-hemisphere" thinking. It is *not* imagery and spatial, nonsequential thinking that is primary; it is feeling. Feeling processes are more basic (both psychologically and physiologically) than cortical hemispheric functioning. That is why feeling-action functions can undercut, redirect, and unfix both pictures and thoughts.

What is unique about the therapeutic situation, in contrast to ordinary life, is that any complex emotion can be made into an action emotion simply by helping the client express what is usually left unsaid. This is done by helping the person express within different parameters of expression than are typical in ordinary life (it is here that the skillful use of expression dynamics becomes important). In effect, artists, writers, and scientists do the same thing when they are creating:

they fill in gaps and express beyond the usually accepted boundaries in their fields. All creativity works bisociatively at the level of feeling moments.

It is now possible to understand *why* the crucial step in all functional therapies is the facilitation of expression. By identifying feeling moments, using dynamics of expression, and shifting personality dynamisms, the functional therapist can move from the experiential mode to the expressive mode. This allows *any* feeling to become a participatory feeling. This step is crucial because it allows for bisociation. (See Koestler, 1964, p. 104.) By shifting from the cognitive mode to the feeling-action mode, the client is consciously moving to an underlying level of functioning that can disrupt fixed pictures, thoughts, feelings, and habits.

In creative endeavors in the arts and sciences the creative person uses an external medium of expression (painting, sculpting, mathematical symbols, etc.) to channel the bisociated insights. In therapy, the client talks to the therapist. What both domains have in common is the use of feeling functions as the level at which bisociation takes place to reorder and reorganize old pictures and symbols. To drastically reorganize at any level within the organism there must be a temporary shift to a lower, common level of organization. For both therapy and discovery, the medium of growth is in the feeling consciousness that underlies picture and symbol consciousness. Access to feeling consciousness is available simply by filling in feeling gaps—making vague and fleeting feelings into participatory feelings that are just as visible as laughter and crying.

The process of bringing incomplete feelings to complete expression is the same whether the therapist is dealing with defenses that hold back feelings or impulses that promote feelings. In both cases, the therapist applies the same skills: identifying feeling moments, varying expression dynamics, and shifting levels of the personality dynamisms. All these methods are designed to make partial and fragmentary feelings into complete participatory feelings that will, in turn, lead to new insights, pictures, choices, and actions, as well as a new openness to neglected needs and wants.

One of the side benefits of the linkage between the process of creativity and the process of therapeutic change is that the many techniques and programs that have been developed to facilitate creativity can be applied directly to the tasks of therapy. A second benefit is that clients can be taught to look upon therapy as an active, positive, creative process rather than a mechanical, medical, passive one. The growth of the self can be seen to resemble the growth of a novel, a song, or a poem.

*Purposiveness and Adult Growth**

Moments, crises, and expressions of feeling are hardly sufficient to sustain and

---

*Concerns about adult development and the growth cycle occupy a central place in the history of functional psychology beginning with the early formulations of James and Janet. The functional psychologist Jastrow wrote an early manual on psychological health in his book *Keeping Mentally Fit* (1928). The theme of fitness was extended by Thorne (1965) in his monograph on "Tutorial Counseling: How to Be Psychologically Healthy." The fitness motif was popularized by Corriere & Hart (1979) in their book *Psychological Fitness* and developed by Hart (1983, ch. 11), into a theoretical model for counseling, "Psychological Fitness: A Model for Personality Exercise and Change." More recently, this model has been applied to elementary and secondary schools as a way of teaching children and young people modes of personality fitness (see John Hart, 1985). The very crucial role of consciously acquired attitudes for psychoimmunization has been stressed by many authors, but it is still a wide-open area for research and for the development of self-care training programs. Silverman's book *Health Care and Consciousness* (1983) provides a provocative overview of the possibilities and directions of potential development in the health care field. For applications of the fitness approach to sports psychology, see Hart (1984).

organize personality change. Eventually in therapy, the crises of consciousness and feeling must arrive at some superordinate, real-life involvement that is personally meaningful. Inner meanings and outer meanings must come together. Self-improvement for the sake of self-improvement's is like a bird flying in a cage.

Crises are not phenomena restricted to therapy, nor are basic personality growth and change. Most people confront crises throughout their lives without benefit of therapeutic help or psychological knowledge. They cope with crises on their own and with the help of friends and relatives. It is really an open question as to how people recognize, understand, and use crises in their lives. Psychology has only begun to study the phenomena of adult life changes. Work by authors such as Sheehy (1981) and Vaillant (1977) suggests that some people do learn to creatively use crises for psychological development while others do not.

The medical sociologist Aaron Antonovsky in his book *Health, Stress and Coping* (1979) marshals evidence that some individuals show a stress-resistant attitude that allows them to cope with major problems and difficulties with relative success. Antonovsky described the common attitude or philosophy shared by these individuals as a *sense of coherence*, ". . . a pervasive, enduring though dynamic feeling of confidence that one's internal and external environments are predictable and that there is a high probability that things will work out as well as can reasonably be expected" (p. 10).

When these ideas are applied to therapy and the task of remoralization, therapeutic theories must be couched teleologically. The teleological model has been most insistently pressed upon psychology by the personality theorist Joseph Rychlak (1981):

If psychology were to adopt a concept of teleosponsivity, thereby bringing the final cause back into the description of human behavior, it would surely benefit the science of humanity in the long run. . . . Teleology was dismissed from traditional natural science for a good and proper reason. It was attributing unfounded and unprovable characteristics to natural phenomena, which were totally unnecessary to a scientific description of these phenomena. But psychology has been finding it quite impossible to capture all that there is to the human experience with teleology left out of the account. (p. 798)

Within the Jamesian view of psychology, it is an essential function of consciousness to supply a superordinate, guiding purpose to the individual's life. When this view is directly applied to therapy, the functional therapist is, at the very least, obligated to inquire about what dominant purposes or symbols the client is using to guide his or her life. Consciousness raising as a goal of therapy involves helping the individual to examine what makes life meaningful. A sense of coherence or purposiveness in one's life is the strongest counter to dissociation. Conversely, when a person is at odds with himself or herself, then dissociations of consciousness will occur frequently.

To the extent that the examination of a client's basic purposes can be explored within a technique, functional therapists not only utilize the analysis of the client's symbols and metaphors but also directly prompt clients to answer questions about:

"What is the meaning of your life?"
"What makes your life valuable?"
"What is the guiding purpose of your life?"
"What does your life symbolize?"

Both the answers that people give themselves and the activity of seeking answers are valuable therapeutic activities. One of the case studies that follows will illustrate the symbol-purpose technique.

CASE EXAMPLES*

Condensations of theory can be rather misleading; condensed theories like condensed soups need a few cups of common water added to be palatable. The preceding short summary of theoretical concepts necessarily stressed differences between functional theory and other theories. Eclecticism in practice makes therapists more alike than different. The case samples that follow will show that functional eclectic therapy shares many features with other orientations.

Both clients in the following cases were seen at a university counseling center; the case vignettes attempt to provide enough background information about each client to make the therapeutic interventions intelligible. The case outcomes were considered to be positive and fit within the methods and theory of functional therapy.

Within the framework of functional therapy a therapeutic intervention is evaluated as positive and critical if it: (1) helps the client to understand defensive, symbolic behavior; (2) helps the client to match expressions with feelings; (3) helps the client to shift from a lower level to a higher level of functioning in some important area of living; or (4) facilitates the recognition of gaps in consciousness and the filling in of those gaps.

---

*To read case samples of functional therapy drawn from a clinical private practice, consult Hart (1983). A postgraduate training program in functional therapy is offered through Hart and Associates in Los Angeles. Contact Dr. John Hart, Clinical Director, for information; training tapes and manuals are offered from the same site. Predoctoral internships in eclectic counseling are available at the Counseling and Testing Center of California Polytechnic University in Pomona, California. Consult the Fourth edition of C. H. Patterson's *Theories of Counseling and Psychotherapy* (1985) for a critical review of functional therapy which includes an evaluation of the fitness model.

The Case of Nora

Nora came to the counseling center because she was unable to finish term papers in two of her required courses. She wanted help to get over a "writing block." She appeared extremely depressed in the first interview; she had dark circles under her eyes, wrung her hands repeatedly, and sat slumped in the chair. She said that she was a married reentry student, 49 years old, majoring in teacher preparation.

It quickly became apparent that Nora's agitated depression had good cause: her oldest son had been shot and killed seven months earlier by the lover of the son's wife. Nora had efficiently taken care of all the details of the funeral and had been "the strong one in the family." She could not understand why she was still suffering so much from the pain of her son's death:

"It hurts too much."
"I've got to get over it."
"You can only care so much."

She cried often in the first interview but alternated between expressions of painful grief and emotionally flat statements about the need to get over her block and finish the papers: "I've got to get them done." She reported that her husband, Chuck, had gotten on with life and had "stopped putting things off."

In the first interview, the therapist mostly listened and gently encouraged Nora to express her grief, anger, and confusion: "Seven months isn't a long time. . . . The papers are not really important compared with the loss you feel. . . . Saying something once isn't enough, feelings aren't like statements about the weather, you need to repeat how you feel over and over." The therapist also learned that Nora was taking an antidepressant medication, prescribed by her family physician, on an "as-needed" basis.

Subsequent weekly sessions followed much the same pattern as session 1, with the therapist supporting the expressions of grief while Nora would alternately grieve deeply and then give herself admonitions to pull herself together, e.g., "I want to just close the door on it . . . crying won't bring him back." In session 3, Nora brought in a poem that she had written Steve, her son, and cried as she read each line.

The therapist recommended that Nora use biofeedback training to alleviate the tightness and coldness she often experienced. Nora began a series of sessions with the counseling center's biofeedback technician utilizing EMG, temperature, and GSR feedback. Usually, the one-hour biofeedback sessions preceded the therapy sessions. Nora did not experience quick results from the biofeedback training but persisted because she did not want to rely on medication for relaxation. Within three months she was able to use the biofeedback sessions to relax and feel less agitated, but she could not transfer the procedure into her daily life. Nonetheless, the biofeedback training was continued because the tension "timeouts" seemed beneficial, especially in relieving Nora's neck muscle pains. Also, there was some transfer from the biofeedback sessions to the therapy sessions that followed. Nora seemed able to start the therapy from a deeper feeling level; she less often stopped herself from matching expressions with feelings.

Statements such as, "Nothing changes the facts that are there, that are real" continued to punctuate Nora's therapy, but she seemed to let go of the punishing way in which she applied her self-criticism.

In session 10, a very critical point emerged. Nora asked, aloud, "Why me?" and "What matters?" "What's right?" She commented, "God plays favorites. Why can't I be a favorite?" In the next week's therapy, the therapist returned to these questions and asked Nora to answer them. At first, her answers were shallow and delivered with a shrug: "Why me?" and

"What matters?" "What's right?" She commented, "God plays favorites. Why can't I be a favorite?" In the next week's therapy, the therapist encouraged Nora to really ask herself the questions and to try answering in a way that made sense to her: "These are real questions. . . . You used to have answers but they don't work for you anymore. No one else can answer these questions except you, for you. . . . You could spend years asking and answering these questions, and that's all right."

Clearly, Nora was seeking a new view of life that could encompass the despair she felt and guide her to a meaningful way of living each day. The therapist in subsequent sessions continued to return to the questions Nora had posed and referred her to books on religious psychology such as *When Bad Things Happen To Good People* (Kushner, 1983), *Love Is Letting Go of Fear* (Jampolsky, 1979), and *Intersection and Beyond* (Howes, 1971). Nora was able at this point to talk about her son's death explicitly in relation to the history paper she was supposed to write. One textbook historical episode stood out for her; it described sheep slaughtered by a railroad labor gang. She felt that her son, Steve, had been slaughtered like a sheep. In the next meeting she said, "Your expectations change . . . hopes change" and went on to talk about how her new hopes and expectations weren't clear.

After six months of weekly one-hour sessions, Nora stopped coming to therapy for three months during the summer break. She felt well enough to be off medication and wanted to spend a lot of time with her three daughters and one daughter's new baby. It was made clear that she could call for an emergency session anytime, but she did not.

At the first session three months later, Nora spoke movingly and tearfully about her continuing grief. She also described a remarkable image of a fine crystal vase that could be dropped and would bounce without breaking or bumped and not shattered but then "break into pieces for no reason just while holding it in your hands." The therapist interpreted this symbol as: "That *is* how fragile you are. That is how fragile your life is." Nora: "You have to go on." T: "You have to choose how to go on."

Commentary. Is this progress? Nora has still not completed her term papers. Neither has she completed her grieving. But she does feel better about herself. She can say and believe, "I am a strong person. . . . I can feel as sad as I do about Steve and still go on." The therapy was much the same from day 1 to the last session, with the therapist listening, encouraging, and helping Nora to full expressions of feeling and with Nora going back and forth between feeling, questioning, and seeking a new perspective on her life. Is this therapy? Good therapy? Or is it applied philosophy? Moral theology? All that can be said for sure is that both the therapist and the client valued the time and experiences shared together. Nora was faced with the trials of Job: she answered fate's questions with courage and perseverance and by searching for new answers to old questions. Who could do more?

The Case of Richard

Richard, a 20-year-old sophomore transfer student, was referred for counseling by the director of housing. He was told, "Go see a counselor or move out of the dorms." Richard had been involved in several rowdy drinking incidents and had recently smashed his car into a tree while intoxicated. The car damages were $3,000.00; Richard's father was threatening to take the car away from him.

At the first session, Richard, "Call me Richie," was mainly concerned about not getting kicked out of the dorm and not losing his car. He was not happy to be seeing a counselor, "I've got to come and talk to you."

As Richard described his life, it became understandable that he might be testing limits since he was away from home alone for the first time and felt very adventurous about trying new things and meeting new people. He seemed to be drinking mainly to live up to a "playboy image' he had acquired in the dorms. For many of the other students Richie seemed rather sophisticated because he was from San Francisco, had worked in his father's successful restaurant for several years, and had traveled throughout Europe a number of times. He was also unhappy about staying at the university—it was too isolated from city life for him. He had chosen the university because of its hotel and restaurant management major but decided to return to school in the Bay Area as soon as possible.

In the second interview, Richie taught the therapist a game—flipping quarters into a jar like tiddly winks. "Quarters" was a bar game Richie had learned in his dad's restaurant and he was very good at it. The therapist shifted the game to nickels and pennies. While playing, the therapist and Richie did some problem solving and planning about how he could survive one more quarter without getting expelled and how he could reassure his father about his good intentions. After this session, Richie stopped coming to the counseling center except for "checkin" sessions every two weeks that lasted only 5 or 10 minutes. To give him something to talk about, he also took the Kuder-Richardson and Myers-Briggs Preference Indicator: the results were discussed in relation to his plans to take over his father's business after getting a business degree. Richie made it through the quarter with no further drinking incidents and transferred to the University of California, Berkeley.

The game of "quarters" (or "nickels") has not appeared in manuals of functional eclectic therapy. For this young man, who did not show any signs of psychopathology, it seemed to be the right method at the time. This case illustrates that deep therapy is not always the best therapy. Sometimes a counselor who acts as a bar man will do just fine.

RESEARCH

Only a few modern process and outcome investigations of modern functional therapy have been conducted. There have also been some analogue laboratory investigations related to concepts and methods used in the therapy.

Hart (1965) conducted a series of experimental studies on the feeling-of-knowing experience which demonstrated that feelings could be used as accurate monitors of gaps in consciousness. Marston, Hart, Hileman, and Faunce (1984) established a laboratory paradigm for the investigation of crying and demonstrated that crying in response to an emotional film had positive, cathartic effects.

A number of clinical studies on sleep and dreams have been conducted that demonstrate shifts in personality dynamisms (contact, expression, feeling, activity, and clarity) for experienced clients in functional therapy; these investigations confirm the parallelism hypothesis, i.e., that waking and dreaming levels of functioning change together as clients progress in therapy. [See Scott, Karle, Switzer, Hart, Corriere, & Woldenberg (1978); Karle, Hopper, Corriere, & Hart (1977); Karle, Hopper, Corriere, Hart, & Switzer (1977); and Karle, Hart, Corriere, & Woldenberg (1980).]

One outcome study used standardized tests to measure client changes in therapy (Karle, Corriere, Hart, & Klein, 1981). The Shostrom Personal Orientation Inventory (POI) and Eysenck Personality Inventory (EPI) were administered to 221 clients and 134 controls, compared over time. Results indicate significant shifts toward self-actualizing on the POI profile with increasing length of time spent in therapy. On the EPI there were significant increasing extraversion and decreasing neuroticism scores with longer exposure to therapy.

Several investigations have been conducted using physiological measures of tension reduction to measure changes in response to therapy sessions. Woldenberg, Karle, Gold, Corriere, Hart, and Hopper (1976) measured pulse, rectal temperature, and blood pressure before and after 13 individual therapy sessions with 19 new clients. Measurements were compared with those taken on 18 college students who participated in 13 model therapy sessions in which therapeutic activities were simulated. The therapy clients showed significant reductions in all parameters following the therapy sessions. No significant change was found for the control group's measures of tension. The results indicate that the activity of matching expression with feeling may bring about at least a temporary reduction in physiological tension.

In a follow-up investigation in "Maintenance of Psychophysiological Changes in Feeling Therapy" by Karle et al. (1976) five experienced clients were compared to five new clients. While both groups showed large drops in tension, as measured by the physiological indices, neither group could sustain the extremely relaxed state that immediately followed the therapy sessions. However, the more experienced clients evidenced a considerably lower level in every parameter throughout. The study suggested possible long-term effects from the therapy.

A related study by the same researchers (Karle et al., 1978), looked at POI, EPI, and psychophysiological measures in new clients (10 with less than six months in therapy), experienced clients (10 with one to two years in therapy), and very experienced clients (10 with over three years in therapy). Again, the POI results showed

increasing self-actualization with more time in therapy. The previous EPI results were not completely confirmed in this study; there was increased extraversion with more time in therapy, but neuroticism scores fluctuated from high to low and back up to a level between high and low for the three groups. The psychophysiological measures showed increases in the variability or oral and rectal temperatures and systolic blood pressure levels over increased time in therapy and reduced variability and mean of pulse. Maple (1976) interpreted these changes in terms of the motivation response as showing lower tension with greater physiological flexibility for advanced clients.

For a critical review of these psychophysiological research studies consult Pierce, Nichols, and Dubrin (1983); the authors also provide a general review of many research investigations focused on the use of emotional expression in therapy.

One more different area of research will be mentioned. Concerns about adult development and the growth process have occupied a central place in the history of functional therapy since the early formulations by James and Janet. (See Hart, 1983, Chapter 11 for a full discussion.) Recently, the psychological fitness model has been applied in elementary and secondary schools as a way to teach children and young people modes of positive personality change. John Hart (1985) found that students who were exposed to a six- to nine-week program of psychological fitness training showed significant improvements on self-rated self-esteem and decreased stress levels. This line of research is now being extended to colleges and counseling centers.

There is a need within functional therapy to move away from the group comparisons used in the previously discussed investigations. The individual case designs described by Barlow, Hayes, and Nelson (1984) would fit very well into the framework of functional theory and practice. This shift in research methodology would lead to more alignment between case studies and research studies and more rapprochement between research and training.

CLINICAL TRAINING

Most clients have in common what Dr. Jerome Frank (1983) has called "demoralization"; i.e., each person feels unsure about whether and how he/she can cope with life. (Richard was the least demoralized; Nora the most.) At the level of technique there is no common, prescriptive method that can be applied to every client. The antidote for demoralization is remoralization, but how to achieve that end is elusive and subtle. One necessary condition for remoralization is a raising of consciousness. Each client has to become aware of inner events or outer happenings, or both, which have remained vague and undefined. By increasing consciousness, a person is able to construct a new set of consciously chosen purposes. The next step in remoralization is to hold these purposes in mind while taking actions in line with them.

Therapy is much more art than applied science, with each therapy session more like the creating of music or painting or dance than like an engineering or medical procedure. Perhaps the most relevant framework for the evaluation of therapeutic case work would be an aesthetic framework rather than a scientific one. No one really believes that symphonies can be scientifically evaluated as to their musicality or that paintings can be usefully scrutinized in the same way that bridges and automobiles are stress tested. So why not take seriously the cliché that therapy is more art than science?

The consequences of an aesthetic approach to evaluating and teaching therapies would be: (1) styles and schools would be accepted as inevitable and desirable; (2) therapist training would concentrate on developing aesthetic sensitivity rather than scholarship or scientific skills; (3) the overall goal of therapy would be to achieve beauty, truth, and the good in a person's life. Clients and therapists would seek moral creativity in therapy sessions.

The demands of professionalization and licensing have pushed training of therapists very much toward the clinical-medical model. Functional eclectic theory does not fit this trend for two reasons: (1) functional therapy's broad range of legitimate role models includes, but does not overstress, the doctor-patient model; (2) functional therapy places more value on the humanistic, experiential, philosophical end of the therapy continuum than on the scientific, clinical, objective end.

The consequences for training are these: (1) counseling is more aligned, as a profession, with the functional therapy approach than are psychiatry and clinical psychology; (2) paraprofessional training by individuals with nontraditional backgrounds is welcomed; (3) training stresses the apprenticeship with an experienced therapist rather than academic coursework; and (4) insearch and case analyses are the main vehicles for training rather than research or course work.

What we seek in therapy is the development of what Howard Gardner has called "personal intelligences."

On the one side, there is the development of the internal aspects of a person. The core capacity at work here is *access to one's own feeling life*—one's range of affects or emotions: the capacity instantly to effect discriminations among these feelings and eventually, to label them, enmesh them in symbolic codes, to draw upon them as a means of understanding or guiding one's behavior. In its most primitive form, the intrapersonal intelligence amounts to little more than the capacity to distinguish a feeling of pleasure from one of pain and, on the basis of such discriminations, to become more involved in or withdraw from a situation.

At its most advanced level, intrapersonal knowledge allows one to detect and to symbolize complex and highly differentiated sets of feelings. . . . The other personal intelligence turns outward, to other individuals. The core capacity here is *the ability to notice and make distinctions among other individuals* and, in particular, among their moods, temperaments, motivations, and intentions. (Gardner, 1983, p. 239)

Within Gardner's theory of multiple intelligences, therapy can be seen as one way for individuals to develop their personal intelligences. The criteria that Gardner uses to evaluate aesthetic works can also be used to evaluate the way trainees use their feelings. The first criterion is the inclusion of "expressiveness" in one's artistic symbols or feelings. If a person uses the materials of a medium in such a way as to create something that is "lively," "sad," "angry," or "powerful," that person has provided a sign of aesthetic intelligence or personal intelligence. A second criterion, which Gardner terms "repleteness," involves the way that properties of the medium (or the feelings) are utilized. If a person can use materials—for instance, the lines of a drawing—in such a way that several aspects are significant (e.g. thickness, shape, shading, and uniformity of line), the person is exhibiting command over repleteness. Similarly, if a person can use words, sensations, postures, movements, thoughts, and images to express a feeling fully, that person is showing more personal intelligence than someone who is limited in the use of these psychological materials.* In this view, therapy becomes a human endeavor for the furthering of personal intelligences, for the understanding of symbols and consciousness, and for the development of a personal philosophy.

---

*Consult Gardner's *Artful Scribbles* (1980, p. 133) and also the philosopher Nelson Goodman (1968), who first formulated these criteria in *Languages of Art: An Approach to a Theory of Symbols.*

FUTURE DIRECTIONS

Among some eclectics (including some represented in this book) there is a pressure for synthesis and calls for the elimination or curtailment of schools. The functional philosophy is not aligned with such attitudes. Indeed, from the functional perspective's emphasis on diversity, it would be considered desirable if there were two thousand schools of therapy by the year 2000. Optimally, there should be more schools than the total number of therapists; that would mean that every therapist would establish several schools of therapy during his or her lifetime. At the extreme, perhaps there should be a new school of therapy created for every new client-therapist relationship!

An open-minded attitude that encourages variety is not incompatible with a serious search for guiding principles. However, the functional approach regards guiding principles in therapy as having the same status as principles in art, religion, philosophy, and education. Therapeutic guiding principles are *not* scientific, deductive, and testable generalizations. They do not even have the same status as principles from applied sciences such as engineering or medicine. Instead, therapy principles are heuristic guidelines—suggestions and recommendations to keep in mind when thinking about what happens in therapy. History indicates that we can never reach complete agreement on philosophical, artistic, religious, or therapeutic guidelines because of the many value choices that are possible. The question "What is best to do?" will always lead to a multiplicity of contrasting and conflicting answers.

If eclectic therapists can ever give up the one-sided identification with the medical and applied scientist models that are now dominating the field, we can hope that the therapist of the future will be more receptive to influences from religion, philosophy, the liberal arts, the fine arts, and the performing arts. It is highly doubtful whether this "future need" will soon become a clear direction within professional counseling and psychotherapy.

REFERENCES

Allen, G. W. (1967). *William James: A biography*. New York: Viking Press.

Antonovsky, A. (1979). *Health, stress and coping*. San Francisco: Jossey-Bass.

Barlow, D. H., Hayes, S. C., & Nelson, R. O. (1984). *The scientist practitioner*. New York: Pergamon.

Corriere, R., & Hart, J. T. (1979). *Psychological fitness*. New York: Harcourt, Brace, Jovanovich.

Ekman, P. (1971). Universals and cultural differences in facial expression of emotion. In J. K. Cole (Ed.), *Nebraska symposium on emotion*. Lincoln: University of Nebraska Press.

Frank, J. (1983). *Therapeutic components shared by all psychotherapies*. Cassette Recordings N. 1–113–81A & B). Alexandria, VA: Audio Transcripts, Ltd.

Gardner, H. (1980). *Artful scribbles*. New York: Basic Books.

Gardner, H. (1982). *Art, mind and brain*. New York: Basic Books.

Gardner, H. (1983). *Frames of mind*. New York: Basic Books

Gendlin, E. (1981). *Focusing*. New York: Bantam.

Goodman, N. (1968). *Languages of art: An approach to a theory of symbols*. Indianapolis: Bobbs-Merrill.

Hart, J. L. (1985). *Personality fitness for children and youth*. Unpublished doctoral dissertation, Dept. of Social Work, University of Southern California.

Hart, J. T. (1965). Memory and the feeling-of-knowing experience. *Journal of Verbal Learning & Behavior, 6*, 685–691.

Hart, J. T. (1983). *Modern eclectic therapy: A functional orientation to counseling and psychotherapy*. New York: Plenum.

Hart, J. T. (1984). Sports psychology. In R. Corsini (Ed.), *Encyclopedia of psychology*: Vol. 3 (pp. 358–359). New York: Wiley Interscience.

Hart, J. T., Corriere, R., Karle, W., & Woldenberg, L. (1980). *Dreaming and waking: The functional approach to using dreams*. Los Angeles: The Center Foundation Press.

Howes, E. B. (1971). *Intersection and beyond*. San Francisco: Guild for Psychological Studies.

James, W. (1894). What is an emotion? *Mind, 9*, 188–205.

James, W. (1950). *The principles of psychology*. New York: Dover.

Jampolsky, G. (1979). *Love is letting go of fear*. New York: Bantam.

Jastrow, J. (1928). *Keeping mentally fit*. New York: Greenberg.

Karle, W., Corriere, R., Hart, J., Gold, S., Maple, C., & Hopper, M. (1976). Maintenance of psychophysiological changes in feeling therapy. *Psychological Reports, 39*, 1143–1147.

Karle, W., Corriere, R., Hart, J., & Klein, J. (1981). The Personal Orientation Inventory and The Eysenck Personality Inventory as outcome measures in a private outpatient clinic. *Psychotherapy: Theory, Research and Practice, 18*(1), 117–122.

Karle, W., Corriere, R., Hart, J., & Woldenberg, L. (1980). The functional analysis of dreams: A new theory of dreaming. *The Journal of Clinical Psychology Monograph Supplement, 36*, 5–78.

Karle, W., Hart, J., Corriere, R., Gold, S., & Maple, C. (1978). Preliminary study of psychological changes in feeling therapy. *Psychological Reports, 43*, 1327–1334.

Karle, W., Hart, J., Corriere, R., & Woldenberg, L. (1980). A clinical illustration of a new theory of dreaming. *Psychology: A Quarterly Journal of Human Behavior, 17*(3), 3–9.

Karle, W., Hopper, M. Corriere, R., & Hart, J. (1977). The alteration of sleep patterns in psychotherapy. In M. H. Chase, M. M. Milter, & P. L. Walter (Eds.), *Sleep Research, 6*, 150.

Karle, W., Hopper, M., Corriere, R., Hart, J., & Switzer, A. (1977). Two preliminary studies on sleep and psychotherapy. *Physiology and Behavior, 19*, 419–423.

Koestler, A. (1964). *The act of creation*. New York: Macmillan.

Kushner, H. (1983). *When bad things happen to good people*. New York: Avon.

Maple, C. (1976). Psychophysiological changes in psychotherapy. Unpublished doctoral dissertation, School of Social Sciences, University of California, Irvine.

Marston, A., Hart, J. T., Hileman, C., & Faunce, W. (1984). Toward the laboratory study of sadness and crying. *American Journal of Psychology, 97*, 127–131.

Patterson, C. H. (1985). *Theories of counseling and psychotherapy*. (4th ed.). New York: Harper & Row.

Pierce, R., Nichols, M., & Dubrin, J. (1983). *Emotional expression in psychotherapy*. New York: Gardner Press.

Rychlak, J. (1978). The stream of consciousness: Implications for a humanistic psychological theory. In K. S. Pope & J. L. Singer (Eds.), *The stream of consciousness* (pp. 91–116). New York: Plenum.

Rychlak, J. (1981). *Personality and psychotherapy* (2nd ed.). Boston: Houghton Mifflin.

Schachter, S. (1966). The interaction of cognitive and physiological determinants of emotional state. In C. D. Spielberger (Ed.), *Anxiety and behavior*. New York: Academic Press.

Schultz, D. P. (1960). *A history of modern psychology*. New York: Academic Press.

Scott, R., Karle, W., Switzer, A., Hart, J., Corriere, R., & Woldenberg, L. (1978). Psychophysiological correlates of the spontaneous K-complex. *Perceptual and Motor Skills, 46*, 271–287.

Sheehy, G. (1981). *Pathfinders*. New York: Morrow.

Silverman, J. (1983). *Health care and consciousness.* New York: Irvington Publishers.

Taylor, E. (1980). Impact of the Jamesian unconscious on American social movements. Paper presented at the William James Symposium. American Psychological Association Convention. Montreal, Canada.

Taylor, E. (1982). *William James on exceptional mental states: The Lowell lectures.* New York: Charles Scribner's Sons.

Thorne, F. C. (1965). Tutorial counseling: How to be psychologically healthy. *Clinical Psychology Monograph, 20,* 1–157.

Vaillant, G. (1977). *Adaptation to life.* Boston: Little, Brown.

Woldenberg, L. Karle, W., Gold, S., Corriere, R., Hart, J., & Hopper, M. (1976). Psychophysiological changes in feeling therapy. *Psychological Reports, 39,* 1059–1062.

CHAPTER 8

Eclectic Time-Limited Therapy

Addie Fuhriman, Stephen C. Paul, and Gary M. Burlingame

BACKGROUND

The model of eclectic time-limited psychotherapy presented in this chapter was initially stimulated by pragmatic rather than academic or theoretical considerations. It was developed in a university counseling center in response to an incessant, growing client wait-list. The wait-list problem constituted a stressful situation for potential clients, staff members, and the agency. It was obvious that those in need of services were being neglected. Referring agencies, aware of the long wait-list, became reluctant to refer to the agency, and administrators, also aware of the problem, were pressing for a solution. Internally, therapists felt forced to work to a point of exhaustion or deny the existence of the wait-list. In addition, embarking on new programs that might improve staff morale seemed unjustifiable given the unmet direct service needs. The problem needed to be addressed before the staff became dysfunctional and the agency lost credibility in the community.

At a staff retreat held to consider the wait-list problem, unanimity of support was expressed for identifying and trying out possible solutions. Out of the brainstorming came the recommendation to examine the feasibility of a time-limited approach to treatment. The authors of this chapter agreed to carry out that examination.

The problem facing us was different than those typically encountered in academic settings. In academia, one most often develops methods based on theoretical foundations and then tests them in a suitable setting. In our situation, we found ourselves in an existing setting, needing to develop a theoretical foundation and method that would accommodate the circumstances.

The staff at the center was comprised of counseling and clinical psychologists, social workers, and psychiatrists who represent a wide variety of theoretical perspectives ranging from behavioral and analytic to eclectic. We needed to construct an approach to time-limited treatment that could, and would, be adopted by people operating from very different treatment perspectives. It seemed unlikely that an unfamiliar theoretical orientation could be imposed on members of the staff, and therefore, it seemed beneficial to find an approach that would allow individuals to draw from the strengths of their own theoretical viewpoints. The best solution appeared to be the introduction of a time-limited approach that allowed for eclectic application of various theoretical perspectives.

Our first task was to become familiar with the brief psychotherapy literature, and we began a thorough search in hopes that an eclectic brief model already existed. We were unable to locate such an approach. In fact, as Butcher and Koss (1978) have noted elsewhere, we found that no broad-based model of brief psychotherapy had been proposed to accommodate therapists working from diverse theoretical orientations. Rather, we found a number of theoretically specific approaches. The synthesizing work of Budman (1981) facilitated progress toward our own model by presenting several unifying elements that theoretically diverse models seem to hold in common. These elements included: (1) time limitation, (2) specific, restricted goals, (3) more directive therapeutic intervention, and (4) selection of appropriate clients. The idea of distilling critical elements to be superimposed on any theoretical perspective was attractive, and we subsequently drew heavily on those elements in constructing the eclectic time-limited therapy approach.

Given these seemingly critical, consistent elements, what was lacking was a skeletal framework to integrate the elements across the theoretical orientations of the staff. We selected the developmental model of the helping process outlined by Gerard Egan (1975), who views the progress of therapy in terms of a series of sequential, but flexible stages. The first stage involves therapist encouragement of client self-exploration. In the second

stage, a therapist adds his or her perspective to arrive at an integrative understanding of the problem. Problem-resolving actions are initiated and facilitated in the third stage of Egan's model. We overlaid the time-limited, unifying elements onto the stage model at the points we deemed most appropriate.

Once the eclectic approach was developed, our next task was to determine whether that model could be trained and subsequently adopted by the center staff. We were interested in determining the relative effectiveness of therapists having been trained over those not having received training and wanted to examine whether senior therapists and trainees would be equally amenable to training in the approach. In order to examine these questions, a study was designed to compare the time-limited therapy outcomes of three groups of randomly assigned senior staff and intern therapists who received (1) no training in the model, (2) minimal instruction via a manual, or (3) intensive didactic instruction and practice in model components.

The outgrowth of our efforts is a model of eclectic time-limited therapy (ETLT) which conceivably can be applied in a wide range of settings by practitioners operating within different theoretical frameworks. In that sense, it is an extremely eclectic model. Having been developed from an atheoretical perspective, it is also eclectic in that any number of theoretical perspectives can be applied within the treatment of a single client. The approach provides the basic time-limited framework upon or through which the individual therapist can apply his or her unique orientation.

THE APPROACH

The brief psychotherapy approach presented here combines the features of time-limited therapy and eclecticism in a way that is responsive to clinical issues. The model utilizes an eclectic point of view which accommodates a wide range of theoretical orientations. The brief therapy component provides a structured or programmatic means of responding in a way that efficiently utilizes resources of both therapist and client. The ubiquitous, increased need for services coupled with the continuing reduction of resources to respond to that need place a high priority on achieving cost-effective treatment. The approach is practical in that it economizes agency resources, rallies client resources, and accommodates the multidisciplinary and multitheoretical personnel residing within agencies.

In the development of the model, the press for both theoretical inquiry and practical implementation initially created a difficult dichotomy within which to specify the model building objectives. However, attention to both lines of thought strengthened the approach. It was successfully incorporated within an agency and evaluated in such a manner that theory was testable and implementation was still feasible. As a result, this time-limited, eclectic approach offered a bridge for dealing with research in a field setting. If it is possible to do research in the natural setting and thereby discover what is and is not effective regarding either eclecticism or short-term treatment, professionals can be in a better position to provide quality services and be assured that what they are doing can be evaluated, thus providing an empirical base for decision making.

Two strengths of this approach lie in its applicability to a variety of theoretical positions and its responsiveness to expressed client need. Because a clinician can incorporate this approach within his or her preferred theoretical position, it becomes extremely applicable to agencies staffed by professionals of diverse disciplines and theories. While therapists need not give up values they hold that emanate

from a particular theoretical framework, they do need to adapt their orientation to the constraints of the approach. The approach relies on specific, basic principles that can be taught but also takes advantage of a therapist's experience.

Another distinguishing feature is that ETLT emphasizes only the common components found in extant short-term therapy models. This is in contrast to other short-term therapy training programs that seem to emphasize the unique personality characteristics of the model author as much as the principles of short-term treatment espoused by the model. For instance, it is not uncommon to hear short-term therapy trainees identify themselves by the author they are attempting to "emulate" rather than the underlying principles used by the author. More specifically, we made the assumption that effective time-limited therapy primarily involves the integration of short-term therapy principles by the therapist into his/her own personality and therapeutic style rather than attempting to copy another short-term therapist's personality and therapeutic style. In addition, we thought that an undue emphasis on the unique personality variables of other short-term therapy training programs (e.g., Davanloo's confrontive style versus Malan's interpretive style) could backfire in our diverse agency; hence our emphasis on the core components of time-limited therapy.

The approach responds to increased need and decreased resources through a structure that is based on appropriate brief components. A review of the brief therapy literature revealed some treatment plans, but the few, well-developed programmatic examples encountered (Malan, 1976; Mann, 1973; Mann & Goldman, 1982; Reid, 1978; Sifneos, 1979) were theoretically bound (i.e., dynamic, behavioral). Eclectic time-limited therapy is sufficiently described that therapists have an idea of the objectives to be accomplished and the skills, attitudes, and behaviors that can be used in order to accomplish the objectives with the client. Training is detailed in a way that facilitates therapist learning of techniques that correspond to stated objectives. Finally, the approach is a complete entity that can be incorporated into an agency.

Central Principles of the Approach

The principles upon which this approach is based were drawn from eclecticism and time-limited therapy. We tried to identify those principles and themes that were consistently used across a variety of theories and models and that were applicable and operable in a brief time period. Attention was focused on identifying unifying concerns and common process elements described in the literature. As a result, the approach is distinguished by its capability to be applied across theories and its particular specification of therapeutic goals and objectives for each therapy session.

In order to ascertain the components underlying time-limited therapy, an extensive review of the brief literature was undertaken. From the literature, it was determined that brief models focused on an assortment of themes such as separation and individuation, dynamic conflict between present and past and unconscious and conscious, decisional conflict, and dysfunctional and maladaptive behaviors (Janis, 1982; Malan, 1976; Mann, 1973). However, there were also some common components and elements that were included across models.

The identification and incorporation of these common components into the model involved a team of investigators who collectively conducted the review of the literature. This team was composed of clinical and counseling psychologists, representing a variety of treatment orientations including behavioral, humanistic, existential, eclectic, and psychodynamic. The team

met weekly to review the literature with the purpose of synthesizing the short-term therapy strategies into a model that could and would be adopted by the multidiscipline, multitheoretical staff. The implications (i.e., theoretical and practical) for including each element within the proposed model of ETLT was thoroughly discussed with consensus among reviewers being a requisite before an element was accepted into the model. This process not only controlled for a particular theoretical orientation unduly biasing the development of the model, but also enriched the model development process because of the varied clinical viewpoints represented.

The final selection of brief components used in the ETLT approach was made based on the consistent and/or frequent occurrence of the component in the literature (whether implicit or explicit), its adaptability to implementation, and the ease of theoretical articulation and integration of the component. Further selection of components was accomplished in the training sessions by choosing a few to teach rather than many and by emphasizing the frequency of the use of these few in ETLT. Components were chosen to produce an approach in which a few client goals were addressed and accomplished rather than one in which many goals would be approached. In other words, we tried to identify those principles, themes, and skills that were used consistently across a variety of theories (thus having some consensual quality to them) and models that were applicable in a brief time period. Two additional reviewers (Budman, 1981; Butcher & Koss, 1978) (Table 1) illustrate some of the consistency found across brief models and the ETLT approach.

Conclusions drawn by these reviewers regarding the consistent elements of the brief models permitted us to see which elements had theoretical underpinnings and/or empirical support. Theoretical emphasis was found for the following ele-

TABLE 1
Common Components and Processes in Time-Limited Therapy

Budman	Butcher/Koss	ETLT Approach
Selection	Transference	Selection
Time	Interpretation	Time
Limited goals	Client expectations	Therapeutic focusing
Focused interviewing	Change under arousal	Client expectations
Present centeredness	Time limits	Therapeutic relationship
Therapeutic relationship	Directiveness	Therapist activity
Therapist activity	Behavioral practice	Emotional ventilation
Directiveness		Goal orientation
Therapeutic flexibility		Specific techniques
Client ventilation		
Rapid/early assessment		

ments: selection criteria, focusing, client/therapist relationship factors, and therapist activity. There were mixed theoretical speculations concerning the elements of time limits and client expectations in brief treatments. Empirical support was reported for the effects of time limits, client expectations, and the client/therapist relationship, while mixed empirical support was described for the impact of selection criteria, therapist activity, and emotional ventilation. Utilizing these conclusions, the ETLT approach includes four components seen as most relevant to time-limited therapy. The components of time (Lambert, 1979; Mann, 1973), expectation sharing (Butcher & Koss, 1978; Frank, 1974), and focusing (Balint, Orstein, & Balint, 1972; Malan, 1976) became the core process elements of the brief psychotherapy model. All three elements were then integrated through the fourth, the client/therapist relationship. It was also apparent from the literature that client selection was an important theoretical variable in brief treatment (Butcher & Koss, 1978). Thus, client selection also became a fifth element that was incorporated into the model.

Time. The literature on brief therapy reveals a variety of time restrictions on the length of therapy, ranging from one to 40 or more sessions having different goals and purposes (Bloom, 1980; Wolberg, 1980). Length of treatment was determined by focus or purpose of treatment and theoretical orientation. Wolberg (1980) distinguished among approaches based on their goal orientations and corresponding time limits. One to six session treatments focus most often on crisis issues, six to 25 sessions have a supportive, educational emphasis, and up to 40 sessions appear to be common among the extensive dynamic approaches. Mann (1973) described time developmentally, considering 12 sessions as an adequate therapeutic framework. Malan (1976) used time limits suggesting 20 to 30 therapeutic sessions depending on therapist experience. Butcher and Koss (1978) point out that currently just as many clinics emphasize one to six sessions as 10 to 25. Obviously, time restrictions may vary as a function of theory, purpose, or a pragmatic principle such as agency philosophy or practice (Gelso, 1982).

In addition to the specific intervention components, we thought it was important that therapists and clients realize that a time limit existed. By determining a conclusion point, the model would consider man's teleological nature, having the end in mind at the beginning of treatment (Mann, 1973). Thus, time was significant not only in reference to the amount of treatment, but as an intricate part of the treatment structure specifically evident in explicitly shared expectations. We wanted a sufficient amount of treatment time to facilitate movement, involvement, and action on the part of both therapist and client. It was equally important that the treatment be seen as a whole, compact, and nonfragmented unit with sufficient time to utilize the therapeutic relationship. We did not want "brief" to mean treatment that was disruptive, fragmented, or an experience that did not feel concluded. Faced with such a wide range of time limits (1 to 40), and wanting to differentiate between short-term therapy and crisis intervention models, we attempted to align the time limit with the typical treatment goals of our multidiscipline agency. The average length of individual treatment in the agency had been approximately 12 sessions over the preceding years. We assumed that this time limit would correspond with the typical treatment goals of the clinicians in the agency. This time frame was then matched with the literature, resulting in a 10-session time-limited therapy model which included an intake assessment (Sifneos, 1979) and a follow-up session (Bloom, 1980).

Undoubtedly, the application of the model in a different setting (i.e., differing theoretical orientations and treatment goals) might yield a different time limit. However, the basic processes emphasized in the model would remain intact and suggest a similar process for determining any variations in time limit. A final note regarding the time limit is that we request ETLT therapists to consistently respect the time-limited contract with the client. If additional treatment is deemed necessary, therapists are instructed to refer to another treatment modality (e.g., group or time-unlimited therapy) rather than violate the original time-limited therapy contract.

Expectations. Given the time restriction, it was thought that expectation sharing would create a greater likelihood of goal attainment through engendering openness and directness within the therapeutic alliance. The process also would engage the client in the therapeutic interaction as the client shares and responds to expectations. The sharing of expectations gives the client access to the future course of treatment and the means to be used to accomplish the purposes and objectives. It was thought that open expectation sharing could create an atmosphere of mutuality which could lead more effectively to the client's modeling of independence.

A review of those models that attempted to influence client expectations as an element of short-term therapy (e.g., Poey, 1972) indicated that a number of expectations had been addressed. Two types of expectation are evident in our approach: anticipations on the part of the therapist about the course or results of treatment and therapist anticipations regarding the roles of the client and therapist during treatment (Table 2). The role description expectations occur early in the therapy, specifically during the intake and first session. The expectations concerning the therapeutic process occur throughout the nine sessions and focus on discussion of therapy success, time limits, and client and therapist affect, behavior, and cognitions.

Focus. The component of focusing is developed in the model in two ways: focusing on the problem or concern of the client and focusing on the therapeutic process. Focusing on the process was expected to contribute to the quality of the therapeutic relationship because of its generative or catalytic capability. One example of focusing is the use of specifying, reflected in constantly moving from general to specific regarding the client problem, examples used, and interaction expressed. The therapist is trained to specify the problem in terms that make the resolution of the

TABLE 2
Definitions of Insession Expectancies

General expectancy definition: Verbal anticipations on the part of the therapist about the course or results of treatment, and/or the role of the client and therapist during treatment.

1. Therapy success: The therapist indicates that therapy will be useful and successful in dealing with client's problems.
2. Time limits: The therapist talks about the number of past and future sessions with the client.
3. Client affect: The therapist discusses how the client is likely to feel differently in, or as a result of, therapy.
4. Therapist affect: The therapist discusses how he/she may feel during the course of therapy.
5. Client behavior: The therapist discusses how the client is likely to behave differently in, or as a result of, therapy.
6. Therapist behavior: The therapist discusses how he/she may behave during the course of therapy.
7. Client cognition: The therapist discusses how the client is likely to think differently in, or as a result of, therapy.
8. Therapist cognition: The therapist discusses how he/she might share his/her thoughts during the course of therapy.
9. Client miscellaneous: An expectation that the therapist shares about the client's role in therapy that is not classifiable in the above categories.
10. Therapist miscellaneous: An expectation that the therapist shares about his/her role in therapy that is not classifiable in the above categories.

problem more likely. Shifts from "there and then" to "here and now" are encouraged. Directness and explicitness regarding the content and process of the therapeutic interaction also illustrate focusing. Directness is exemplified in such statements as, "Does what I have discussed match your expectations?" Personal responsibility is illustrated in statements such as, "I will actively participate, offering support, exploring areas of interest, etc." Focusing is also apparent in the continual review of the process describing what has happened, what the client and therapist want to happen, and how desired processes will take place.

The components of time limitation, expectation sharing, and focusing were selected on their own merits but were also utilized because of their potential interaction with each other. Focusing can stimulate work with a time limit and makes expectation sharing more explicit; expectation sharing specifies focusing and tempers and makes conclusion possible within the time restriction; and time restriction

creates an arena for expectation sharing and a continual impetus for focusing.

CLIENT ASSESSMENT AND SELECTION

A number of intrapsychic, behavioral, and interpersonal variables are used for client selection into ETLT. The primary aim of the selection guidelines in the brief treatment is not to prescribe the treatment to particular types of clients, but rather to set a *minimum* standard of functioning for the client who might benefit from a time-limited treatment modality. This minimum standard is set based on criteria drawn from the short-term therapy literature.

A second assessment and selection feature that is not explicitly dealt with in the approach involves matching the appropriateness of the therapist treatment orientation (e.g., cognitive behavioral, insight oriented) with the client's presenting complaint. This is not specifically addressed in the ETLT model due, in part, to the unique definition of eclecticism that the model espouses. The model was designed to apply short-term therapy principles to a multitheoretical and multidisciplinary group of clinicians where flexibility of approach was of prime value. Therefore, therapists are essentially left to their own discretion with respect to the efficacy of their particular orientation and set of intervention strategies for specific clients. Nevertheless, a few guidelines for matching clients to treatment are provided.

Pragmatically, in the agency where the model originated, a treatment of choice framework was used which included a wide range of potential developmental and remedial treatment offerings such as structured (assertiveness, communication skills, etc.) and open therapy groups; individual, couple, and family therapy; developmental workshops and classes (career planning, social skills training, etc.); and time-limited individual treatment. Undoubtedly, this array of service offerings affected the therapists' use and development of the model by having available

alternate treatments for clients not meeting the selection criteria.

The vehicle for gathering the necessary information is the initial assessment interview and the first "work" session. In these sessions, particular attention is paid to the inclusion and exclusion guidelines for ETLT (Table 3).

Some authors (Lambert, 1979; Small, 1979) have suggested that there are few, if any, a priori selection variables that demonstrate a "differential effectiveness [between] brief versus long-term psychotherapy" (Lambert, 1979, p. 19). We believe that selection guidelines are intuitively important to the type of therapeutic relationship deemed necessary in brief therapy and have some basis in predicting successful treatment outcome in general. Our choice of the selection guidelines corresponds as much with the type of process we believe important to create in ETLT as with attempts to capitalize on what the empirical literature suggested regarding potent predictors of psychotherapy outcome. The guidelines we chose represent a more conservative selection

TABLE 3
Brief Selection Form—Assessing for Brief Therapy: Minimal Criteria for Selecting Clients

Determine the presence or absence of each of the following characteristics on the basis of interview data (circle present or absent on each criterion):

A. Inclusion criteria

Present	Absent	1. The ability to form a satisfactory relationship(s) in the past or present.
Present	Absent	2. Evidence of good premorbid adjustment.
Present	Absent	3. The ability to establish an early and positive relationship with the therapists.
Present	Absent	4. The ability to arrive at a mutual set of therapeutic expectations.
Present	Absent	5. The ability to perceive a personal problem in a circumscribed manner and to remain focused in describing it.

B. Exclusion criteria

Present	Absent	1. Severely depressed, requiring medication.
Present	Absent	2. Anger as main effect.
Present	Absent	3. Acutely psychotic, or recent psychotic episode.
Present	Absent	4. Borderline personality disorder.
Present	Absent	5. Organic or psychotic disorder.

procedure than some short-term-therapy authors advocate (Malan, 1976; Wolberg, 1980).

The inclusion/exclusion criteria listed in Table 2 first address information relating to the clients' past and current functioning, as well as their response to the initial therapeutic encounter (i.e., intake and first work session). Past functioning is assessed by examining the premorbid adjustment of clients, including their ability to recall, with sufficient detail, a satisfactory relationship in the past. The criterion of premorbid adjustment parallels Axis V of DSM-III, which assesses occupational (or academic), leisure time, and social relation functioning. An overall Axis V rating of fair (4 or lower) in the recent past five years would meet our criteria for inclusion for adequate premorbid adjustment. In operationalizing these two criteria, Axis V of the DSM-III seems best suited for both a global and a generalizable set of criteria.

The importance of having a successful relationship in the past is underscored by Sifneos (1979), who suggests that having such a relationship portends a more productive therapeutic relationship. Having had such a relationship in the past may decrease resistance in therapy due to the fact that the client already has had a rewarding interpersonal experience. Because of this approach's interactional process, the likelihood of transferring learning to the "outside" and generalizing to like experiences is increased because the client has had similar experiences in the past. Sifneos further defines this criterion in terms of altruistic behavior where the patient reports a give-and-take relationship of some depth as opposed to "narcissism, passivity, dependence, sadomasochism, and acting out tendencies" (p. 29) in relationships that reflect an inability to interact in an interdependent fashion.

Another subset of selection criteria centers around the client's current function-

ing. The ETLT method essentially utilizes an exclusionary approach in dealing with the client's current level of functioning. This is in contrast to other short-term therapy approaches (Sifneos, 1979) where specific inclusion criteria regarding current client functioning are used such as adequate ego strength and intelligence. In part, we chose to use an exclusionary approach to guard against the increased probability of casualties in brief therapy (Lambert, 1979) based on high-risk clinical cases. On the other hand, an important by-product of this exclusionary approach is a fairly broad range of eligible clients. As can be seen from Table 3, disorders that are excluded from treatment involve the more severe psychopathologies including borderline personality, schizophrenic, organic mental, and psychotic disorders. In addition, disorders severe enough to require medication (e.g., major depression/recurrent:296.3x) are also excluded from treatment in this approach. Clients excluded on these criteria are referred to more appropriate treatments in the agency (long-term individual or group therapy, psychiatric consultation, etc.).

Given the exclusionary criteria for ETLT cited above, who is an appropriate client for this treatment approach? At present, this has been determined in two complementary ways. The client's initial response during the assessment interview has taken on a primary role in determining client-therapist and client-intervention match. Three specific inclusion criteria are used to assess client-therapist and client-intervention match during the initial interview. It should be noted that these inclusion criteria are conservative, in contrast to other short-term therapy approaches (e.g., Malan, 1976; Mann, 1973), and that the ETLT approach may be effective with a broader range of clients.

The client's ability to establish a positive relationship during the assessment interview is considered not only a good prognostic sign for client-therapist matching, but also a critical variable in ETLT, given the emphasis placed on beginning the "work" of therapy during the first session. A positive therapeutic relationship in relation to the client's perspective is most closely related to Strong's (1968) interpersonal influence variables (expertness, attractiveness, and trustworthiness), which have been consistently shown to be indicative of the client's response to the therapist. Although these are not formally assessed with Strong's counselor research form, the therapist is trained to be sensitive to these aspects of client perception. Relationship viability from the therapist's perspective is determined in response to the following question: "Can I work in a collaborative fashion with this patient?" This question covers concerns about whether the client is responsive to the therapist as a person and is psychologically minded enough to adopt the role of client as determined by the therapist's theoretical orientation. If the question is answered in the affirmative, then the guideline of positive therapeutic relationship is satisfied. If not, then the therapist is instructed to work with the client in some other treatment regimen.

The client's ability to arrive at a mutual and realistic set of expectations regarding the therapeutic encounter is also deemed important. In essence, the therapist assesses whether the client has unrealistically high expectations for therapy and also whether the defined role of client will be adopted. More specifically, five separate expectation statements for both therapist and client are delineated in the approach. Therapists are instructed not only to assess these initially but to incorporate the expectancies throughout therapy. If the client is unable to accept the treatment contract, then ETLT is seen as unsuitable.

The final inclusion guideline that is assessed during the initial interview is the ability of clients to perceive their presenting problem in a circumscribed man-

ner and to remain focused in describing it. Circumscription of presenting problem is determined by: (1) the pervasiveness of the disorder, e.g., is a great deal of the client's life becoming dysfunctional due to the disorder? (2) the acuteness of onset in contrast to chronic behavior patterns that have their origin in character disorders; (3) the ability of the client to engage the disturbing material both affectively and cognitively, and (4) the therapist's ability to develop a feasible treatment plan in working toward the consensual goals of treatment. Measures such as target complaints (Battle, Imber, Hoehn-Saric, Stone, Nash, & Frank, 1966) are excellent tools for determining the circumscription of a presenting complaint, or lack thereof, by virtue of the specificity required by the problem designation of these instruments. To a great extent, meeting this criterion (circumscribed focus) enables the therapist to engage in greater levels of therapeutic focusing.

Given the above-stated selection guidelines, a valid question is, what types of clients have been successfully treated with ETLT? At present, the diagnoses of clients treated have primarily included mild to moderate affective, anxiety, and adjustment disorders. A caveat with this population is that to a great extent, it was determined by the type of setting where ETLT therapists were trained and practiced (university mental health and counseling centers), which essentially parallels outpatient mental health facilities. Although extrapolations to other populations are possible, as yet, generalizations are only appropriate to these types of clients.

Assessment to Treatment Link

Although this approach calls for a separate assessment interview to determine client appropriateness, integration of assessment with treatment is accomplished in several ways. First, we suggest, if at all possible, that the assessment interviewer and therapist be the same person so that the link between assessment and treatment becomes a change of content only, and not of interviewers. If this is not possible, the next best strategy, given our training experience, is that the therapist carefully review the assessment interviewer's notes with the client so that treatment is clearly linked with what happened during assessment.

Second, we recommend that the therapist practice her/his particular orientation during an assessment interview to ascertain how the client will respond. In other words, if a therapist relies primarily on insight through catharsis, then focusing on the affect of the clients to ascertain their response to this approach is heartily encouraged. Some models of short-term treatment (e.g., Malan, 1976) use the client's response to frequently used interventions (e.g., trial interpretations) in the initial interview as an inclusion or exclusion criterion. Our position is to use this method to ascertain whether a working relationship can be established.

Finally, the generation and selection of goals in the assessment phase can and should guide the work of therapy in later sessions. A critical aspect of ETLT is rapid and early assessment so that the work of therapy is outlined early, even if this outline is incomplete. If established in this manner, the work of therapy is a direct extension of what were identified as goals during the assessment stage, thus allowing the therapist to actively engage the client around what seems to be the most troublesome symptoms in the first therapy session.

TREATMENT APPROACH

Therapeutic interventions that can be applied to ETLT are varied but require some integration with the core elements (time limit, expectations, therapeutic relationship, and focusing) that had been extracted from the brief therapy literature. It was important that (1) principles could be understood and applied; (2) interventions could be identified and described and were applicable to a variety of theoretical orientations; (3) there was efficacy across time-limited models (as indicated by the literature review) and general counseling/therapy skills; and (4) there was a good theoretical match with time-limited therapy.

The clinical setting that was used in the first application of the approach was a university counseling center. The approach was developed to fit an outpatient setting rather than inpatient or hospital settings, but may be applicable to those settings. The outpatient population of this agency is nested within a university community, and clients present a variety of concerns and issues. Symptoms range from mild anxiety to severe, but ambulatory disorders. Many clients present with concerns of identity, independence, and career choice. Others have problems resulting from absent or disruptive relationships, while others find themselves unable to succeed in their educational pursuits.

The approach relies on a nine-session, once-per-week treatment period with a tenth session follow-up two months after termination. Each session is based on the standard practice in the agency of the 50-minute hour. The format was designed to meet the accepted practice of the agency and to respond to the brief literature regarding length of time in treatment (Wolberg, 1980). The majority of the treatment decisions are negotiated by the therapist with the client. Fees, for example, are set according to a sliding scale but negotiated with the client. Most of the decision making is negotiated though the process of shared expectations, objectives, goals, and process. The treatment calls for only individual therapy, but it certainly is within the purview to include other options if they are deemed important. For example, there may be specific concerns or issues of the client that could better be dealt with concomitantly with marriage therapy, or participating in a group may well increase the transfer of learning occurring during the brief, individual therapy. Decisions can be made to economize by minimizing treatment more closely related to need, rather than "piling on" treatment modalities.

TREATMENT FORMAT

The model outlines the responsibilities and purposes of the therapist. In addition, suggestions are given regarding possible ways to share expectations, engage the client, and focus the discussion. The therapist is responsible for assessing the client's appropriateness for treatment. In addition, he or she creates the expectation for brief therapy and what it may or may not accomplish. The therapist describes and sets the therapist and client therapeutic roles and works toward the negotiation of those roles, as well as their implementation. He or she creates an atmosphere of openness, engagement, and mutuality which is conveyed through his or her attitudes, feelings, and behaviors. The therapist is responsible for focusing both on the problem and on the counseling process. The therapist initiates problem solving and engages the client as a participant in that activity. Throughout all the sessions, he or she supports, assists, and reviews the process with the client. The overall process goals of focusing and expectation sharing are carried by the therapist. As the components of expectation sharing and focusing are woven throughout the whole model, the therapist ensures their impact through continual intensifying and specifying.

The approach prescribes specific principles and therapist attitudes that are necessary in order to respond to those principles. Although there is some evidence (Burlingame, 1982) that suggests that therapists' attitudes toward ETLT might vary based on experience level and employment settings, we have not encountered attitudinal difficulties in our training experience with the ETLT model. The therapist is active and, in some ways, directive. He or she is engaged with the client continually through reflecting, questioning, structuring, specifying, and focusing. He or she provides direction for the process of the interaction. As Pope (1979) noted, higher therapist activity correlates with ease of communication and a synchronous increase in client verbal productivity. In a similar fashion, in a problem-solving focus mode of therapy, activity and directiveness may be a natural concomitant (Etzion, 1980). In ETLT, directiveness takes the general form of providing structure. The therapist does not necessarily interpret (in the analytic sense) client's thoughts and attitudes but takes a role of describing and focusing on the client's understanding and action, within the context of a therapist's particular theoretical orientation.

The client assumes responsibility for his/her own treatment in this model. The client is to share expectations concerning the therapist as well as his or her own role. In addition, he or she shares his or her goals, desires, and objectives concerning ways in which he or she expects to change and grow. It is also anticipated that he or she will determine possible actions to be taken during the week, attempt to take those actions, and then report the attainment or lack of success experienced during the week. This engages client and therapist in a joint venture in and out of the regular therapeutic hour. Through disclosure and involvement, the process of mutuality occurs and the client moves toward more independence and control over self. The client's involvement is evident not only during the session, but also outside the therapeutic hour as the client is engaged in action designed to lead toward change. Maintaining the focus during the session on what he or she plans to do and has done outside therapy is designed to reinforce and encourage him or her toward reaching the discussed goals.

Approach Outline

Structure is evident in ETLT in a variety of ways. The entire therapeutic experience is outlined in five stages comprised of 10 sessions (Table 4). A description of each stage of therapy is provided with objectives for each stage outlined. In the approach, the objectives are stated in objective language to avoid terms that have varied meanings in different theoretical orientations. Illustrative dialogue is given for each session that can be used or modified by the therapist. In addition, a training component is outlined for teaching therapists how to use the model within their own theoretical orientation. In many ways, the structure provided is somewhat like a skeletal framework. The outline provides the core around which a therapist can add and subtract theory and technique in order to respond to individual client needs and objectives as well as accomplish the model's objectives.

The brief psychotherapy program consists of an intake session and four distinct stages. The intake stage, or session 1, is devoted to exploration and assessment. During this first-hour interview, the therapist has two objectives: to determine the appropriateness of a brief therapy referral and to create an expectation for success.

The first treatment stage is titled "role description, rapport building, and problem specification." The therapeutic objectives of this session are: to describe and set the therapist and client roles, to create an atmosphere conducive to openness, engagement, and mutuality, and to focus on the problem(s) and further specify therapy objectives and outcome. It is during this stage that the therapist and client discuss how they are going to behave in therapy. Through this negotiating, the therapeutic relationship begins to emerge. Further discussion in this session is directed toward specifying the client's concerns and problems.

Stage II is comprised of two sessions in which to accomplish two objectives: to provide a context within which a client can expand his/her thinking and understanding of self and to facilitate the client's arrival at a commitment for change and to begin the process of adding specific solutions and actions. The principle governing the third session of "enhanced self-understanding and anticipated action" is an increased understanding of self, problems, and the environment that will lead to more effective action. During the fourth

TABLE 4
Brief Psychotherapy Program: Therapeutic Stages

INTAKE	STAGE I	STAGE II	STAGE III	STAGE IV
1st Session Exploration and assessment	2nd Session Role description, rapport building, and problem specification	3rd Session Enhanced self-understanding and anticipated action	5th Session Active coping	8th Session Pretermination
			6th Session Active coping	9th Session Termination
		4th Session Action planning	7th Session Active coping	10th Session Follow-up

session, "action planning," the therapist and client decide what they want to happen and how they are going to accomplish it.

Stage III includes three sessions, each designated as "active coping." The goals of these sessions are: to review the therapeutic progress, to identify and share insights resulting from the client's action, and to continue problem solving regarding new behaviors, attitudes, or actions. These sessions are characterized by "doing and reviewing."

Stage IV concludes the brief experience with three sessions, "pretermination," "termination," and "follow-up." The objectives of this stage are to provide closure and to review the therapeutic goals and progress and relate them to the client's future functioning. This final stage highlights and reinforces the process orientation of the brief model. By reviewing the progress to date, the client recognizes there is still work to be done, anticipates potential stresses, and determines strategies for dealing with increased independence. During the follow-up session, client and therapist review the goals of therapy and what has occurred since termination. The client can review the stress and success that he/she has had and discuss the effect of more independent functioning.

Treatment Issues

The therapeutic relationship is important in ETLT, particularly with respect to the client's involvement in that relationship. A number of interventions are used that will engage the client in the process of therapy as well as in his/her own growth. The process of sharing expectations contributes to the relationship by creating an atmosphere of mutuality that engages clients. Sharing the descriptions of the role expectations of both client and therapist also involves the client not only in the relationship but in the process as well. The therapeutic relationship is important from the initial contact with the client. During intake, the therapist is noting the client's past and present ability and/or willingness to engage in an intimate, mutual relationship. This, then, becomes part of the selection criteria. Not only is the relationship seen as a precondition for change, but it becomes a mechanism of change and is used throughout the therapeutic encounter.

The relationship is seen as particularly important owing to the time-limited element of this approach. Engaging the client through the discussion of the week's experiences and activities and relating those to the objectives reminds the client that his/her input is vital if effective therapy is to occur. Discussion of the week's events also integrates each session with the next and in-therapy time with outside-therapy experiences. It is hoped that the client's reviewing and linking will lead to client change and increased transfer of learning. The overall creation of an atmosphere that is conducive to openness, engagement, and mutuality provides a basis for a healthy, therapeutic relationship.

Generally, when resistances and blocks occur in therapy, the therapist responds to them with openness and forthrightness. In fact, resistance could well be the focal point of a session. The initial resistance will probably occur at the time of setting the commitment to the brief amount of time for therapy. Many clients arrive at therapy with the idea that they will be in treatment for a good length of time and may be concerned that 10 weeks will not be sufficient for them to change or for life to become better. This idea may be supported by the expectations that the therapists hold since there is some evidence that clients want less therapy than therapists expect (Cornfeld, Johnson, Spiegel, Whitaker, Wasserman, & Gelso, 1983). Most likely, few clients view therapy as solely a catalytic experience. Through the therapist sharing expectations and describing the process of brief treatment, the client gains more information and begins to understand his/her part.

Resistances may also occur as the therapist begins to share the expectations of therapist and client roles. In a similar manner to the prejudices clients may have as to the length of time in treatment, many think that in therapy the therapist will "do" something to them—they tell their story and the therapist will fix it up. While initially clients may resist the sharing of expectations, the invitation for them to be involved immediately and the respect the therapist shows for their contribution help modify attitudes and preset expectations. The initial, careful selection of clients reduces the likelihood of excessive client resistance. During intake, the sharing of expectations allows both therapist and client to understand the forthcoming process and helps the therapist be alert to possible client resistances to the therapeutic relationship and process, which can be used to select a client out of ETLT.

The ETLT approach describes therapist activity regarding self-disclosure. The therapist discloses a great deal concerning his/her expectations regarding self and the client's role in therapy. He/she is equally open concerning the therapeutic process and the objectives and discusses with the client his/her own assessment of progress in therapy. The approach does not dictate what or how much the therapist discloses about his/her personal feelings, attitudes, and behaviors other than those that relate to the sharing of expectations regarding the process of therapy.

A high level of activity is expected for the therapist and the client. The activity is illustrated through the structure of the approach as well as the specifying and focusing displayed by the therapist. There is a certain explicitness in the approach prescribing high engagement and involvement on the part of both therapist and client.

Basically, the therapist's role does not change throughout therapy. The therapist is active, open, involved, supportive, and engaged with the client in the process. Often in therapy, the mutuality aspect of the relationship between client and therapist increases, almost in a developmental fashion. In ETLT, mutuality and the value for it are built in from the beginning, the evidence for which can be seen in the sharing of expectations, the openness existing in the relationship, and the focusing on the process occurring between therapist and client.

Termination provides a good example of integrating the entire therapeutic process. It is discussed at the beginning of treatment, and the client is made aware when therapy will end, what will be done in order to arrive at that point, and how he or she is part of the process of change. Termination is highlighted in the final two sessions and alluded to in the middle sessions. The attention to termination is used to increase the intensity of the brief treatment time (Mann, 1973). The focus on termination illustrates the bringing together of time (past, present, future) in a way that allows the client to have more awareness and understanding of the process. Such understanding helps the client have more control in being able to transfer what he/she learns in therapy to other situations, thus ensuring a catalytic process in his/her future. There are times when termination at the end of the 10 sessions may not be appropriate and the client may well need increased time. The expectation is that, given the sharing of the process throughout treatment, both therapist and client are in a better position to determine future necessity or possibility.

There are a number of common, and some serious, errors a therapist can make in applying the eclectic brief model. Initially, it is apparent that many therapists hold attitudes and beliefs that are biased toward long-term treatment. These attitudes can affect the treatment that the therapist provides (Burlingame, 1982). Although therapists use their own theoretical orientation with this model, it is difficult for some therapists to incorporate the constraints of this format. Negative attitudes and biases toward short-term therapy (Gelso & Johnson, 1983) would probably interfere with therapist application of the time-limited model more than their attitudes toward eclecticism.

Similar problems attend the lack of expectation sharing. Many therapists lack experience in or hold negative or neutral values toward sharing expectations, particularly those describing the therapist role. Yet, it is through expectation sharing that the client becomes an active part of the process. The client first observes the therapist sharing expectations and then becomes involved in the exchange of expectations. It is the awareness of the process that also helps the client more effectively utilize the length of time in therapy. The reviewing of weekly and session activities also enhances the use of time and brings the client's past, present, and future into a more integrated whole.

The training is designed to help the therapist incorporate a variety of specific principles and attitudes that are prescribed in the model and that will ensure effective application. A portion of the training, both in principle and in structure, is designed to attend to treatment issues, particularly those involving therapist attitude and behavior. Through the training process, it is hoped that the therapist will become committed to behaving in ways that are consistent with the purpose and objectives outlined in the brief treatment.

MECHANISMS OF CHANGE

A description of the primary mechanisms of change in eclectic time-limited therapy is framed by the practitioner and what that clinician brings to the thera-

peutic enterprise. ETLT does not provide strict guidelines as to what is and is not an appropriate intervention. On the contrary, the model offers an opportunity for the therapist to carefully compare a number of interventions in an eclectic fashion against process parameters that have been either theoretically or empirically related to potent treatment effects in short-term therapy. This position is supported by the growing evidence that technique or specific intervention variables account for a very small portion of the outcome variance (Bergin & Lambert, 1978). Once again, this position illustrates the unique definition of eclecticism wherein process principles of short-term therapy are identified and emphasized rather than specific interventions or treatment approach. The application of eclectism resides in the therapist who uses specific process principles (e.g., therapeutic focusing) as touchstones to determine the appropriateness of particular interventions (e.g., historical-genetic insight versus interactional insight).

The primary vehicles of change reside in three complementary process principles of change: (1) the therapeutic relationship, (2) the level and consistency of therapeutic focusing both within and across sessions, and (3) the use of expectancies as a strategy to impact and shape the therapeutic relationship.

Therapeutic Relationship

The therapeutic relationship in the time-limited approach is defined as a case collaborative approach where mutuality of responsibility between the therapist and client is underscored. The optimal relationship dictated by the model is a horizontal relationship, in contrast to a top-down or vertical relationship. Vertical relationships typically define the therapist as a protaganist for change who incorporates compliance- or defiance-based interventions (Papp, 1983) as the primary motivating force behind movement in therapy, whereas the horizontal relationship emphasizes cooperation and mutuality.

The horizontal relationship in ETLT stresses mutual responsibility in the work of therapy. This relationship is a function of the type of client selected and the therapist acceptance and ability to work in this manner. Although a completely horizontal relationship is probably an unrealistic goal (Strong, 1968), this approach encourages a close approximation. Client variables contributing to such a relationship include satisfactory relationships in the past as well as the client's present ability to establish a positive relationship during the assessment interview. These demonstrate the requisite client skills necessary to participate in a horizontal relationship.

One therapist variable contributing to the development of this mutual relationship is the adoption of an attitude that encourages a client to "own" troublesome behavior or characteristics as a requisite for change. Yalom (1980) proposes a responsibility assumption principle in group therapy wherein the therapist creates a therapeutic environment in which "the members are the agents of change" (p. 240). This principle is similar to ETLT's intent to use client responsibility as a catalytic experience. If ETLT specifically, and short-term therapies in general, are catalytic rather than curative treatments and continued work is expected on the client's part after therapy is complete, then it behooves the therapist to inculcate an attitude of mutual responsibility for change. In essence, client interdependence is thought to encourage attributions of change being made to the client, in contrast to the therapist being considered the primary change agent. Given the catalytic nature of short-term therapy, this is deemed an essential component of the process.

On the other hand, this division of labor does not mean that the therapist is a passive participant in the therapeutic relationship. In discussing the therapist as a participant, Yalom (1980) stated that "therapist passivity may discourage the patient's assumption of responsibility . . . [while] excessive activity, either in the form of guidance or limit setting, may also interfere with the assumption of responsibility. . ." (p. 242). Short-term therapies are often framed as more active and directive treatments (Butcher & Koss, 1978). This is the stance adopted in the ETLT approach. High activity and directiveness may, at first, seem contradictory to a horizontal relationship. However, there is growing empirical evidence that optimal levels of therapist activity and directiveness result in the following flow of events: (a) clients perceive more active therapists as more empathic, (b) clients who view their therapists as more empathic talk more and become more involved in their own therapy; and (c) clients who perceive their therapists as empathic and who talk more fluently and who are more involved in their therapy experience therapeutic gain (Matarazzo & Wiens, 1977; Gelso & Johnson, 1983). If this flow is a characteristic process of short-term therapies, then the therapists who establish a close collaborative relationship with clients may be more active and directive; their clients, in turn, may become more involved and active in their own work of therapy.

In summary, the relationship dictated by the ETLT approach is a hortizontal relationship where mutual responsibility for the work of therapy is incorporated. This relationship may encourage higher client activity and involvement. The primary principle underlying this horizontal relationship is to decrease client dependence on the therapist as an agent of change and increase the client's self-reliance and attributions for change to self. The underlying caveat for the efficacy of this principle is client selection wherein clients who have the requisite life experiences to participate in this type of therapeutic encounter are engaged.

Therapeutic Focusing

The component of therapeutic focusing is one treatment process that has almost universal support across short-term models. Although terminology varies, the process of identifying a central focus early in short-term treatment and using this to guide intervention delivery is commonly shared across theoretical orientations. There is growing evidence that therapists who identify this focus early in therapy and then consistently center interventions throughout treatment around this focus have better treatment outcomes (Malan, 1976; Burlingame, 1983). Different terms and content areas have been the focus of short-term therapists (Bellak & Small, 1978; Mann, 1973; Reid, 1978). However, there is a uniformity across theoretical orientations with respect to the occurrence of focusing.

Therapeutic focusing in this approach consists of two related tasks. The first is the development of a focal aim (Balint, Ornstein & Balint, 1972), defined as the therapist's reformulation of the client's presenting complaints into a treatment hypothesis. This reformulation is a function of a therapist's own theoretical formulation and serves as the touchstone for therapeutic interventions. The second aspect of therapeutic focusing is therapist focality (Malan, 1976), which is defined as the therapist's ability to consistently center the majority of therapeutic interventions around the focal aim. A therapist who is highly focal is one who is active and directive concerning content specifically related to the focal aim of treatment.

Focal aim. Focal aim of therapy is essentially the therapist's conceptualization of the client's presenting complaint into a treatment plan which includes etiological considerations, as well as the instrumental, intermediate, and ultimate goals for treatment. A therapist selectively attends to client information about symptoms, the precipitating events that led the client to therapy, and related past events. Based on his or her theoretical orientation, a therapist then develops a case conceptualization or focal aim including probable etiological factors and necessary therapeutic steps required to remediate the problem behavior. Depending on the therapeutic orientation of the ETLT therapist, these may include any number of techniques. An example of focal aim process in a psychodynamic model of short-term treatment might involve a psychodynamic reformulation of the client's presenting complaints accompanied by considerations about the type of insight necessary for resolution of dysfunctional personal or interpersonal patterns (Malan, 1976; Binder, 1977). On the other hand, a social learning model of short-term therapy might involve a problem specification procedure and concomitant task development and analysis to resolve the psychosocial problems (Reid, 1978). Regardless of orientation, the ETLT approach suggests that the focal aim development process be expedited owing to the time-limited nature of treatment.

ETLT therapists are assisted in early focal aim development by applying three primary guidelines (Luborsky, 1984) for identifying and refining the focal aim in the beginning sessions of therapy. These include: (1) attention to redundancy of themes or issues that frequently appear during the early sessions of therapy, the assumption being that material central to the focal complaint will continue to arise in different contexts; (2) attention to themes or issues that frequently follow each other in time, the assumption being that this material is important in determining the breadth of the problem area; and (3) attention to shifts in affective or behavioral states that often parallel material for focal aim development, the assumption being that focal material is often associated with cathartic experiences. Therapists trained in ETLT are also encouraged to use these principles to check the efficacy of their interventions and the further refinement of focal aim.

A final consideration for focal aim development is to share that aim with the client. An effective procedure that has facilitated arriving at a consensually acceptable focal aim is to incorporate the use of a scale such as the target complaint inventory, which essentially operationalizes the work of therapy for the client.

Therapist focality. After focal aim development, the next related process principle stressed is consistent and frequent focusing throughout the subsequent intervention. There are two mechanisms for accomplishing therapist focality: direct and specific attention to the problem area and attention to the therapeutic relationship. The first corresponds to earlier descriptions of therapeutic focusing where the therapist is constantly moving from general to specific and "there and then" to "here and now" regarding the client's troublesome behavior. A method similar to the one used by Balint and his colleagues (1972) is incorporated in the training of ETLT therapists. Therapists review their interventions across an entire session with the following questions in mind: (a) What is my focal aim for this client? (b) What were the main trends and therapeutic interventions given? (c) What was the atmosphere in the interview for both the client and therapist? (d) What interventions were thought of but not given? (e) What are my own afterthoughts concerning the general theme of interventions? These questions are intended to prod therapists toward continual review of the general direction of their interventions and the subsequent impact on the

client, hence making adjustments based on client response.

The second mechanism intended to produce high levels of therapist focality is direct attention to the therapeutic process. Focus on the therapeutic process is considered to be a generative process wherein client knowledge is increased concerning the mechanisms of change contributing to improvement. We think that providing the client with knowledge and understanding of the mechanisms of change leads to greater client independence, resulting in the transfer of learning from the therapy hour to similar outside situations, thus resulting in a catalytic process. Focus on the process of therapeutic change provides clients with insight into how they are changing in therapy so that they can, in turn, transfer these principles to similar situations outside of therapy. The final step in this process is for the client to generalize these principles into problem areas having different content and context.

Insession Expectancies

The final mechanism of change is the incorporation of insession expectancies into the therapist's repertoire of interventions. This strategy was the most intrusive and detailed procedure in the training program. Therapists were asked to insert specific expectancy content within the therapeutic hour. These expectancies can be divided into two categories: (1) those pertaining to parameters of the treatment, and (2) those pertaining to the role of the client and therapist in treatment, or essentially, the role induction and explanatory statement about the treatment process.

The expectancies dealing with treatment parameters include the specific time limits of treatment as well as the likelihood of success in treatment. Expectancies concerning the time limits of treatment are essentially statements of affirmation ("you have been selected into a time-limited therapy modality because your problem seems best suited for this type of treatment") or landmarks ("this is our fifth session today and . . .") to remind the client of the temporal framework of treatment. This type of expectancy statement was included because of evidence (Young, 1977) that the introduction of the element of time in time-limited treatment, or time as structure, produces an increased expectancy for treatment gain equivalent to that realized across the remainder of therapy. These expectancies, in turn, are often related to positive treatment outcome (Young, 1977; Frank, 1974).

The treatment success expectancy ("given the strengths that you bring to therapy I believe that you can successfully work through your . . . in the following manner") essentially addresses Butcher and Koss's (1978) caution that time-limited treatments may be more susceptible to negative or unrealistic expectancy sets which can in turn become an obstacle for the client (i.e., discouragement when their unrealistic expectancies are not met). Therefore, it seems prudent to establish some initial expectancies regarding the time limit and type of treatment results to expect and to review them periodically throughout treatment in order to counteract these negative results.

The second category of expectancies centers on client and therapist role descriptions. These involve the therapist describing his or her typical affective, behavioral, and cognitive involvement in therapy as well as expectations of the client regarding affective, behavioral, and cognitive involvement. These descriptions are shaped by the therapist's theoretical orientation and vary by therapist. These role description expectancies are included for two reasons. First, role description methods that essentially prepare the client for therapy have been consistently shown to facilitate the development of the ther-

apeutic alliance (Heitler, 1976), which, in turn, results in keeping clients in treatment longer, thereby increasing the chances for successful resolution of client complaints. In addition, these are part and parcel of a number of short-term therapy models found in the literature. Second, we think consistent attention to these expectations provides further reinforcement for the case collaborative approach by reminding the client and therapist of their respective roles in treatment.

In summary, the collaborative therapeutic relationship, therapeutic focusing, and insession expectancies as mechanisms of change in ETLT are complementary and yet have been adaptable across a variety of theoretical orientations based on our training experiences in various settings. They, in essence, encompass many of the other common components of brief therapy models reviewed earlier while not dictating to the therapist precise behaviors and interventions.

CASE EXAMPLE

The case example presented here was selected from among the group of clients who had successful outcomes and who were treated by a therapist who had received both didactic training and practice in the use of the approach. The specific dialogue is drawn from in-therapy statements of both therapist and client. The following summary illustrates the way the approach was applied throughout the stages of therapy. It demonstrates the implementation of the key elements described earlier and the eclectic approach employed by the therapist in the context of the problem presented by the client.

Intake

The client presented in this case example was, at the time, a 23-year-old single male Caucasian near the end of his undergraduate education. The client's parents were in the process of divorcing, and he was living with his mother. This was his first experience with counseling or therapy of any type. The client identified a major concern in the area of heterosexual relationships. At the time of the initial intake interview, he reported having low self-esteem, which he related to being physically unattractive because of his overweight condition. He also indicated that he had been experiencing mild depression and difficulty concentrating on his academic work owing to the problems cited. The intake worker determined that the client met all the selection criteria for brief therapy. The therapist was a psychologist who had done therapy for approximately 18 years and who reported working from an eclectic orientation.

Stage I. Role Description, Rapport Building, Problem Specification

Stage I is extremely important, and much of the structure around the key elements suggested by the approach unfolds here. Rapport is built, the presenting problem is specified, and expectations concerning the roles of both the client and therapist are articulated. Early in the first session the therapist is expected to review the information gathered from the client during the intake session, clarifying any changes in the client's situation or discrepancies. At the same time, the therapist is reaffirming the suitability of the brief approach in light of the client's characteristics and presenting problem.

T: Well, I got the materials the intake worker worked on. You filled out earlier that you're a senior? Good academic standing now but have been on probation in the past? And social behavioral sciences? And you want to explore your feelings about yourself and others. The intake worker listed a couple of those . . . some self-esteem issues, relationship issues, some difficulty concentrating on academics because of that. I thought it would be useful if we could take just a minute and see if those are still what the issues are . . . if anything has changed at all.

C: I feel better than I did a couple of weeks ago. I feel like I'm over the problems I'm having but they keep recurring. And I know if I don't do something about it now, I know I'll just continue to have these problems.

T: So the immediate issues have kind of taken care of themselves. But . . .

C: A little bit.

T: Okay, a little bit. We'll talk more about that. But you want to get to the bottom of them so they don't keep coming up every so often.

C: Yeah. I really feel there are some things I have to work on because I keep having the same sort of patterns recurring.

T: Okay, help me understand what those are.

This particular dialogue exemplifies the importance of continuing to clarify and specify the presented problem, or focusing. As the therapist reviewed the material the client presented in the initial intake session, the vagueness of the depression he had reported in that session transformed into a set of specific possible sources which could be explored further.

T: The girl talked to you before Christmas and said that the relationship's going nowhere.

C: Yeah, yeah.

T: And your mother's brother killed himself.

C: Yeah.

T: And your mother was served the divorce papers.

C: And those three things were enough to really screw up a holiday.

T: They sure are . . . they sure are. Where are you now with the depression?

C: I feel pretty good. What I am more concerned about now is my inadequacies, or my self-esteem, or what it is that I haven't got that makes me not acceptable.

T: Okay.

C: To someone who I care about. And that I think is the biggest problem. The depression has kind of passed, and I'm not worried about that anymore. I feel pretty good, really. Things are going real well.

T: Okay. That's helpful. So the main focus is asking yourself, what is it about me . . .

C: Why I cannot continue any kind of a satisfying relationship. . . .

The therapist went on to examine each of the potential sources of the depression the client had presented. It became clearer that while several of the sources had stressed the client, he had either already managed them or was in the process of dealing with them. However, he was still very concerned about his inability to establish an intimate relationship. Once the presenting problem was clarified, the therapist reaffirmed the appropriateness of the brief treatment and outlined explicit expectations about how he and the client would work together.

T: And that is kind of perplexing for you and I'm sure . . . let me just kind of back up and put a direction. You know, as we've talked and pursued what was in the folder, I really do feel that a brief model is appropriate and that we can focus in. I would see myself being pretty active. And would see you being pretty active in the sessions. Maybe our deciding on some things for you to do outside the sessions, and we could come back and talk about it . . . some things to try. Kind of focusing in, what I want to do is just list the kind of complaints

that have us . . . kind of zero in and move pretty quickly because I see us being able to move that way and we can decide how many sessions we need, but I can see us doing that in relatively few sessions. . . .

The therapist spent a good deal of the remaining time in the session considering symptoms the client had reported during the intake. Those complaints included trouble with concentration and depression. It became clear that both symptoms were closely linked to the loss of the prospects of an important relationship the client had been developing and tied to a failure to establish intimate relationships. The client and therapist then arrived at a statement of their mutual goals for treatment. This reflects the mutuality and openness of the relationship throughout treatment.

C: Yeah, it's a complaint.

T: Okay, let's talk about what our goal will be, and let me talk about therapy. Our goal will be to keep those symptoms down [depression, concentration problems], to eliminate them, to establish the equilibrium which would mean you feel better about yourself or are feeling some confidence about being able to establish a . . .

C: Right, confidence about that . . .

T: . . . long-term relationship. And maybe understanding that and being able to increase your future coping. We'll talk about that . . . what goes on and what happens. And maybe suggest some things. Now, does that fit your expectations of counseling?

C: Yeah! I think that's what I am after . . .

Stage II. Enhance Understanding and Anticipate Action

Stage II really began in the first treatment session after the intake, and the therapist set to work exploring the agreed-upon problem area with the client. The timing of the beginning of this exploration can vary depending on the ease with which the problem is specified. During this phase of treatment, the purpose was to help the client examine his own understanding of the problem area. In this instance, the client began by talking about his view of what had occurred in a recent relationship. The therapist encouraged the client to explore that relationship and similar past unsatisfactory relationships.

T: So part of the issue is you really care about her, and how she feels about you is pretty important.

C: Right. I value her opinion because I see her as such a good person. I can't see any negatives. Even when I try, I can't. I think, "God, there's nothing wrong with her." Everything that she's done has been perfect. And she's treated me so well and everything. And I think that a person who has that many good qualities can't have anything wrong with them so it's got to be me. It's got to be something I'm doing. Plus the fact that I've had problems with this kind of relationship in the past . . .

T: Tell me about that.

C: Well, just people I've gone out with that I really thought that there was some potential for that kind of relationship, and I tried to get that sort of thing going and it didn't work.

The focus for treatment and the expectation regarding the time-limited nature of therapy are emphasized repeatedly over the course of sessions. During each of the subsequent sessions, the therapist begins the session by reviewing the progress up to that point and focusing on where he and the client are currently. At times, he states very explicitly how many sessions remain in order to keep the time limit clearly in mind.

T: Well, let's see. This is our fourth session. Uh, where do you see things?

C: I don't know. I feel better. I . . . I think it's coming from the fact that I'm trying to do something about a problem. Uh, I still don't really know what to do about it. But, . . .

The understanding of the presented relationship problem continues to expand as the therapist brings one component of his eclectic theoretical framework into play during Stage II. The therapist turns the client's attention to exploring the role of his need for control in both his recent relationship and other potential new relationships. It becomes evident that the client, owing to his insecurity, attempts to maintain that sense of control in an important relationship by trying to do and say things that will make women like him.

C: Yeah. Yeah. If I was really secure with myself, I would have told her what I was thinking. But I'm still . . . I don't know, I'm still, maybe have some insecurities. I have to be a little more happy with myself, than I am right now . . . .

T: Well, part of the reason you're not happy with yourself is because you don't say how you feel.

C: Right.

T: So, it's . . . it's kind of a spiral. I feel one down and I don't say anything about it, so I'm even further down.

C: Yeah. But that, I think that goes back to not wanting to say anything to make people dislike me. You know. I feel like I don't have my looks to go on, so I have to be real careful about what I say. So I don't always say what I'm feeling. I . . . you know, I'd like to think that I do, but I really don't sometimes.

T: Well, I think that's an important insight. And it may affect the depth of relationships.

C: Um hum.

T: You know, if you're responding in a careful, controlled, nonspontaneous way, uh, the relationship is not going to be as deep.

C: Um hum. That could be the whole problem then. That might be the reason for everything.

T: So instead of having you to respond to in a relationship, there is this careful, tentative, uh, pretty nice guy, but not quite real.

C: I might not be real open because I'm being too careful trying too hard to be liked, saying just the right things and not what I really want to say.

That theoretical tact is carried on into sessions 5 and 6 when the therapist begins to examine the relationships the client has with his father and mother. The client related a history of critical unacceptance with his mother that has intensified since the divorce and which he has dealt with by withdrawing from her and being gone from the home. The therapist offers an interpretation linking the relationship with other women to the one he has with his mother.

C: Yeah. I think I get a lot of . . . of negative comments from my mom. Not so much lately, but, you know, there are times when I have felt that nothing I could do could possibly be right. You know, and I had an accomplishment that I was really proud of, or something that I had really done right. And I was really happy with it and all she could do was just complain about it.

T: I . . . I wonder if that, the parallel you're drawing between your dad and mom, is almost like the parallel between your being at ease with men and women. With your buddies, your friends who are male, and with women.

C: That may have something [laughs] to do with it. But, uh . . .

T: You really are on edge with women as though, "Am I going to be all right?" "What I'm gonna do, is that going to be acceptable?" And that's what you're saying about your mother. That there were times that you felt like no matter what you did, it wasn't quite good enough or all right.

The therapist also helped the client to realize the angry and helpless feelings he has had about being caught in the middle of his parents' relationship struggle, yet being unable to break free of the financial or emotional dependency he has felt.

T: Maybe that's where the anger is. You know, I've been hearing a lot of anger . . .

C: Maybe that's it. I am mad because I have to depend on somebody else all the time. And, uh, I'm in no position to change that right now. You know, if I could . . . if I was out of school, and working on my own, I'd move out and I'd have my own money and I wouldn't worry about it. But right now I don't have any choice. So I have to live with it.

T: And it hurts.

C: Yeah. I just feel like there's nothing I can do.

T: Where's the pain coming from right now?

C: I don't know. I just feel really powerless.

T: Um hum.

C: Like I can't change the situation at home [begins to cry]. It's like there's nothing I can do. [Pause] So I just have to put up with it I guess. [Pause] I don't see it changing in the near future.

The approach suggests that there be a clear delineation of goals at the end of Stage II that results in the development of a mutually agreed upon action plan to be applied in Stage III. This step fosters both the collaborative nature of the relationship and the creation of a clear focus for treatment. This sequencing is seen as a tentative guide to the process and not a regimentation. In this case, as early as session 3, the therapist suggested that the client try out a dating situation in which he acted as himself. At this point, the therapist adopted a more task-oriented or behaviorally defined therapy style.

T: How about upending the expectancy and over the next couple, the next week or two, having a date, a new date with at least two different people, and keeping the cost to a minimum, and just saying, Hey, would you like to do something? And you go on saying, Here's what I would like to do tonight. Being able to say, you know, short on funds so we can't go to a fancy place, but how about grabbing a pizza and, stopping by a practice, or . . . 'cause what I'd like . . . what I'd like to see us do is . . . is getting to the point when you know, those first contacts are just as comfortable as the late ones. With the expectation that some of these people aren't going to enjoy that and I'm not going to enjoy some of these people. And, why not find out, you know, why play the game and then find out. Why not find out right away, and not feel like, you know, maybe you'll ask them out again, maybe you won't. But it's just a chance to . . . to get beyond that first-date jitters.

In session 6, the client is encouraged to approach his father about his feelings despite his fears that he may be rejected. The concerns about approaching the father are linked to hesitancy in being direct with women. Here the therapist helps prepare the client for an action by anticipating relevant concerns.

C: Well, I don't know. I'm angry at him, but I don't know what to tell him.

T: Maybe just that. And why.

C: Well if I tell him that and he decides he doesn't like what I've told him, I can't go to school or anything. I really don't think he'd ever do that, but . . .

T: So he's got all the power.

C: Um hum. He's in complete control.

T: You're afraid that if you tell him how you feel . . . that he won't be nice to you anymore.

C: Basically, yeah.

T: That's not unlike the feeling you're having with some of the women you're going out with. That if you didn't . . . do everything right their way, then they wouldn't like you.

C: Um hum. Yeah, that's true.

T: Maybe you could talk with him about that one, saying, "Now I have feelings, but I'm always afraid that if I told you how I felt that you'd kick me out."

C: Maybe I should talk to him.

Later in the same session the client agrees to take another step to improve his situation with his mother at home by helping her talk more with a neighbor.

T: You know, if there's anything specific I can think of that we need to, you know, maybe focus some more on is for you to be able to separate your mother's idiosyncrasies from you so that she doesn't hook you. So that you can just say, well, that's mom and, uh, either share how you're feeling or choose to feel differently. Just say that's her and I don't have to feel hooked, or I don't have to feel guilty or I don't have to feel mad.

C: I think it . . . idiosyncrasies would be better replaced by neuroses [laughs], you know. And there are some things that just drive me nuts about her. And I really wish she would talk to ———, talk to our neighbor. I really think she could use some . . . some counseling. Especially with this divorce thing.

T: Sounds to me like she could.

C: Yeah. Yeah, but trying to get her to go is like pulling teeth, you know.

T: Now is that something you can work on?

C: It . . . it is, I could work on it, yeah. I think I could work on it especially with the help of my neighbor.

T: Why don't you set that as a goal?

Finally, in the ninth session, the therapist returns to the list of initial target complaints. Once again, he identifies the focal issues and evaluates progress. The therapist acknowledges that they have not completed everything that the client needs to continue working on. He has fostered a more cooperative relationship throughout the sessions, and it seemed natural at the close of therapy for the client to assume personal responsibility for the future. The therapist reviewed the strengths he saw in the client. He also discussed his future plans and considered alternatives should those plans not work out. At the close of treatment, the client seems to have reduced the negative affect that brought him in. He also seems prepared to try out some coping on his own in the future in a more realistic way.

T: When we started out, we'd identified, as the target complaints, worrying about long-term relationships; concentrating on your studies; and not feeling so good about yourself. And we've talked about those and some other things, you know, that impacted on those. I'm wondering where you're feeling like you are now, with all of this.

C: I don't know. I just . . . you know . . . I don't have . . . it's the break so I don't have any study problems. And as far as long-term relationships go right now, I'm not interested, as, you know, I've come to the decision that that's not what I want right now.

T: Well, what are the areas that we haven't finished, and I think we both recognize we wouldn't finish with every-

thing. What we have to resolve here is for you, and one of them is wanting to be on your own more. More independent . . .

C: Um hum. Well, that's the result in a way that I didn't . . . it's not gonna happen right now. You know, there's no way I could do it—just working part time and . . . and having to go to school and everything. I couldn't swing it. So I'm just gonna have to live with that, for two years. . . .

C: It's something like I felt this is the way to go. And I really feel like it's helped. I think it's, you know, the problems I had, I don't have anymore. For whatever reason. I don't have them anymore.

T: And now if, you know on the issue about independence, getting out on your own, will come, when . . .

C: I really look forward to doing that. I just know that it's gonna be probably two years before I get to.

T: Yeah.

C: And so, it's not something I have to face right now. I think I'm capable of doing that, you know. I think I'm capable of handling all the little problems, and everything, but there are advantages to living at home, even once I start to work somewhere it might be a good idea to st . . . to stay at home for a while. To save a little money.

As the last segment of dialogue suggests, the client was feeling quite free of the symptoms he presented at the beginning of treatment. He was completely free of depression and had completed a good academic quarter in school. In fact, during the last session he discussed plans to pursue graduate work. The client reported that he felt a sense of resolve about his major, initial concern around his inability to maintain long-term relationships. By the end of treatment, he was clear about not being ready to pursue an extended involvement. The issue concerning the client's need to establish himself in an independent way with his parents, which arose during the course of the sessions, also seemed to reach some satisfying closure during therapy. The client recognized that until he completed his education he would need to postpone that important step toward being on his own. However, he had considered, and even tried out through homework assignments, efforts of resolving the relationship strains he felt with his parents. Both the therapist and the client were prepared for, and accepted in a cordial and mutual way, the end of treatment.

When we surveyed the client at the time of follow-up, the positive effects of treatment appeared to have been sustained. The satisfaction questionnaire indicated that the client was still very satisfied with the therapy he had received and that, in terms of the problems he had presented, there was no further need for counseling. He rated that he had made good progress toward meeting all of his therapy goals (50 to 75 percent) and that he felt very capable of continuing his progress toward those goals on his own. When asked to rate more specifically the target complaints he had initially listed, he reported a very slight problem severity in the areas of establishing a long-term relationship and concentrating on his academic work and only moderate problem severity in the area of his feelings about himself. In addition, the client appeared to be entirely symptom-free on the symptom checklist at follow-up. Taken in combination, these data suggest that the client had maintained the changes that he had attained by the end of treatment and that he felt quite capable of doing independently the work that remained.

RESEARCH ON THE APPROACH

We conducted a comprehensive research project in order to test the eclectic time-limited model. The efficacy of *planned* short-term individual psychotherapy is becoming a well-established empirical fact (Piper, Debbane, Bienvenu, & Garant, 1984; Johnson & Gelso, 1980). However, despite the increasing support for brief treatment, and the proliferation of models, there has been little systematic investigation into the training of therapists in these planned short-term treatment models or the impact of different training strategies on the therapeutic outcome.

The first major research purpose was to examine the relative outcomes obtained by experienced therapists and therapists-in-training using the time-limited therapy approach. Given that no significant self-reported attitude or skill differences concerning brief therapy were present among the therapists, we predicted that more experienced therapists would produce significantly greater improvement in clients than less experienced trainees. The second purpose was to examine the effects of different methods of training therapists in the time-limited therapy approach. While we expected that all training groups would show improvement from pretesting to posttesting to follow-up testing, we predicted that therapists who received the more intensive training would produce better client outcomes than their lesser trained or untrained counterparts. The outcomes that we measured to examine those predicted differences included attrition, symptom change, client goal attainment, and client satisfaction with treatment.

The client participants were selected during a structured intake interview which was administered to all counseling center clients by two postinternship doctoral students in clinical and counseling psychology. Minimal inclusionary criteria included the ability to form a therapeutic relationship, a circumscribed presenting problem, at least one successful past relationship, the ability to arrive at mutual expectations with the intake counselor, and a good premorbid history. On the other hand, clients were excluded if they were severely depressed or acutely psychotic, had a borderline personality, presented anger as the main affect, or held unrealistic expectations for therapy. Using these criteria, 26 male and 31 female university students and staff were selected and recruited to participate. The participants, who ranged in age from 18 to 43 years, were randomly assigned to the therapists in the three training conditions.

Six interns, with an average of 2.5 years of experience, and six senior therapists, averaging 9.2 years of experience, were randomly selected from the pool of volunteer psychologist and social work staff members. Among the selected therapists, cognitive behavioral, dynamic, humanistic, and eclectic treatment orientations were represented. Two interns and two senior staff therapists were randomly assigned to each of the three training conditions: (1) no training in the time-limited model, (2) didactic training only in the model, or (3) didactic training plus practice in applying the model. No restriction was placed on the theoretical orientations that the therapists applied during the course of treatment in any condition.

In keeping with recent recommendations (Bergin and Lambert, 1978), we attempted to approach the measure of change from several vantage points using multiple measures. Prior to assigning the case, the intake counselor completed a target complaint inventory (TC—Battle et al., 1966) and the Brief Hopkins Psychiatric Rating Scale (BHPRS—Derogatis, Abelhoff, & McBeth, 1977). At the end of the first session, the therapist completed TC and BHPRS ratings and the client completed the TC and the Hopkins Symptom Checklist (Derogatis, 1977). All sessions were audiotaped, and unobtrusive data including early terminations, no-shows, and missed appointments were recorded.

At termination, the therapist again rated the client on the TC and BHPRS,

and the client completed the SCL90R, the TC, and a questionnaire that measured satisfaction with treatment, the intake worker rated the client on a second set of the TC and BHPRS. Six months after the end of therapy, all clients were mailed copies of the TC, SCL90R, and the satisfaction questionnaire. Finally, after all the client data were collected, each therapist in the study was interviewed to gather self-reported information concerning his or her level of compliance, any demand characteristics he or she had experienced, and his or her perceptions of the process.

Thirty-eight of the initially selected cients completed therapy either by reaching the session number limit or by mutual agreement with their therapist that they had reached their goals even before arriving at the designated session number limit. Of 19 clients who left prematurely, nine reported that they were not satisfied with the treatment, six simply failed to arrive at scheduled sessions without explanation, and four were referred for what was determined to be a more appropriate treatment (e.g., marital therapy). Twenty-seven of the clients who completed treatment responded to the six-month follow-up instruments. This task of tracking staff and clients and gathering the needed data over time was an enormous undertaking in a very active agency.

Upon analysis,* as expected, we found that those clients who had been seen by more experienced therapists showed greater improvement across several of the outcome measures. The clients themselves reported more gain on the SCL90R and average TC score, and the experienced therapists likewise reported greater client improvement on their BHPRS and TC average ratings. Despite the fact that

---

*We examined the major questions addressed in the study with a 3 (training: NT, DT, D/PT) X 2 (experience: intern, senior staff) analysis of covariance using residual gain scores for each outcome measure as the dependent variables and the actual number of sessions attended as the covariate.

the predicted differences were not present for intake rater measures or follow-up data, there does seem to be evidence that suggests therapist developmental or experience level is a factor in eclectic time-limited therapy. As a result, the experience level of practitioners should be taken into consideration in future attempts to apply the eclectic time-limited model. These results are consistent with the findings of most of the research on the effects of experience in long-term therapy (Bergin & Lambert, 1978).

The analysis conducted to examine the differential effects of the three training procedures yielded mixed results. As predicted, we found a significantly higher level of attrition in the untrained therapist group than in the two trained groups. This finding suggests that the structure provided in the trained conditions may have served to hold clients in treatment longer. The implications are important for all treatment modalities. Attrition early in therapy renders moot the subsequent question of potential therapy effectiveness.

The analyses conducted on intake worker, therapist, and client instrument ratings yielded no significant differences across the three training groups. However, there were consistent trends toward significance on the client-rating data. Clients in the highly trained group reported higher client ratings on the TC at posttreatment and more improved SCL90R scores at follow-up.

The attrition findings offer one possible explanation for the lack of significant differences among the groups on the instruments. Those clients who remained in treatment in the no-training group may have been the more motivated and most likely to improve clients. The less motivated clients in the trained groups may have chosen to stay because of the heightened focus and structure they provided. If this were the case, then the outcomes of the trained groups reflect the presence of

the less motivated clients, while the no-training group outcomes do not. Obviously, this conjecture will require further exploration, but it does hold implications both for the value of the model and for general therapy outcome research if substantiated.

Other possible explanations for the lack of measured significant differences also exist. First, the study was based on a relatively small sample in each condition. Gelso (1982) has noted that it is very unlikely to obtain significant, between-group differences with samples this small. A third point that deserves mention is that while the two training groups received training that differed in terms of intensity, no attempt was made to compare the groups on any performance measures. Demonstration of the intermediate training effect would remove this possibility. Future training programs may want to examine objective criteria for skill acquisition and require attainment of those criteria.

CLINICAL TRAINING

We have had an opportunity to conduct a number of training sessions with practitioners from several disciplines, theoretical backgrounds, and levels of experience. Drawing from the training practices employed over the past few years, we will integrate those elements which our experience has taught us may be useful. This section will describe our view of how an ideal program and sequence of training in ETLT should be structured and presented.

Our own research on the application of eclectic time-limited psychotherapy with intern and senior therapists trained in the model indicated substantial differences in outcome based on level of experience. The senior therapists produced better outcomes consistent with findings from several long-term therapy studies (Parloff,

Waskow, & Wolfe, 1978). We have also trained practicum-level practitioners in the use of this approach. While we did not include practicum students in this study, our impression, based on training the approach in practicum courses, is that their outcomes would fall below those of both the senior therapists and interns because of their lack of both skill and theoretical content to superimpose on the bare bones of the stages of the approach. Training in the model may tend to improve the outcomes of therapists at all levels of training, but given the same training in the model, more experience results in improved outcome. The approach provides a basic framework to guide the brief therapy process, but relies heavily on the therapist to add the theory, technique, and personal elements that constitute the content of the process.

It does seem essential that the therapist, regardless of development, has basic therapy skills in his/her repertoire. We have drawn the sequence of the stages of our model from the work of Gerard Egan (1975). He has identified a number of helping skills he considers critical to each of the stages. Specifically, in the first stage of client self-exploration he emphasizes the skills of accurate empathy, genuineness, respect, and concreteness. During the integrative second stage of the process, Egan identifies a set of skills that include mutuality, advanced accurate empathy, self-disclosure, confrontation, and directness. Obviously, the skills Egan outlines still must be supplemented by the therapist's conceptual framework and change techniques.

Because this approach is atheoretical in nature, there really is no specific theoretical or treatment system background required. Rather, a therapist must have a personal frame of reference to overlay onto the model, and to the extent he or she has collected depth in one or more orientations, he or she will be better equipped to draw from those sources in

treatment. Likewise, the greater the exposure to a wide range of clients and client problem areas, the greater the set of background and experience resources that can be drawn upon. In a similar vein, any personal therapy or personal development work that the therapist has done to remove obstacles to his or her functioning effectively in the therapy process will certainly expedite the time-limited approach and avoid possible pitfalls that would interfere with the successful completion of therapy within the prescribed time limits.

There is another factor that appears to be an important predetermining condition for ETLT. Therapists from most disciplines and orientations are trained in certain approaches. They are accustomed to applying those approaches in an unrestricted and unstructured way. The model does impose some significant restraints on the practitioner. As a result, it is very important that potential users have attitudes that can accommodate a new approach. We found that some therapists in our study needed constant encouragement to stay with the model. One therapist, without announcing any concerns, simply practiced an entirely different approach. If the model is to be used in a uniform way in an agency, the attitudes of staff members have to be addressed and commitment is a very important consideration. It is our expectation that the approach will be implemented most effectively by therapists who adopt it with both an acceptance of its tenets and an optimism about its usefulness.

The actual training procedure might well vary depending on the type of application setting and the type of staff being trained. For purposes of describing an ideal training program, we will describe the training that we would apply in an outpatient setting like our own, staffed by senior personnel and advanced trainees. Our first step would be to present a rationale for time limited therapy to the entire staff. Following an open discussion of the advantages and disadvantages of such an approach, one of two tactics could be taken. Either interested, willing participants could be recruited to be trained in the model, or an extended commitment enlistment process could be undertaken until staff agree regarding commitment to time-limited therapy. In either case, we would recommend training a motivated and committed group.

The training procedure consists of applying a common sequential process to each of what we identify to be the key elements of each stage of the model. This process is carried out in a small group setting. (1) The initial phase of the sequence consists of a didactic presentation that outlines the purpose of the stage followed by an explanation of each of the key elements of the stage. (2) A pair of trainers model the application of key elements in the context of a representative case example or use videotape case examples. (3) The role play carried out by the trainers is discussed within the small group with a focus on understanding the techniques applied, considering the client's response, and anticipating personal problems applying to the element. (4) The participants then break into groups of three in which they practice the element, rotating through the roles of therapist, client, and observer and processing each rotation. (5) The total group then reconvenes to discuss special problems that arose in the triads and consolidate the concept. Each training session focuses on training one element and applying that element to the same case examples used throughout the training period.

The elements that are trained for each stage may be varied based on the strengths and weaknesses of the trainees. The Stage I elements we typically recommend training include role description, rapport building, and problem specification. The major elements of Stage II training are self-understanding enhancement techniques (including advanced accurate empathy, active interpretation, self-disclosure, immediacy, teaching, and confrontation) and action planning. In both the first and second stages, there is a training emphasis on expectation sharing and focusing. For Stage III practice, the focus turns to selecting and setting up actions, handling failures on the actions, and dealing with new issues that arise. Finally, training for Stage IV of the model revolves around termination, based on reviewing the process and accomplishments, recognizing unfinished work, anticipating future skills, and saying goodbye.

There seems to be a clear advantage to continuing the group meetings (on a case consultation basis) following the end of the training. The group provides a forum for discussing each individual's attempts in applying the model. The group can provide support and help troubleshoot as each member moves through the entire process. Through discussion and observing videotapes of sessions, individuals get useful feedback and the group benefits from expanded vicarious experience with a wider range of clients.

If the setting allows, it would be good to introduce an intermediate training step before therapists assume primary responsibility for a case. In that step, the trainee would sit in on a complete case with one of the trainers as a cotherapist. This method has been used at a practicum level and allows disinhibition and further modeling to occur. Increased reliance on the training can help a therapist exercise the brief treatment in a more effective manner. The training illustrates specific ways to practice different ways of intervening. The core components of expectation sharing and focusing are those areas in which the therapist is most likely to err. His or her neglect of specifying and directing will cause him or her to drift from the objectives of brief treatment, and time will be impacted negatively and will be too short to accomplish behavior or attitude change in the client, or to set in motion the catalytic process. In addition, the therapy may appear to lack integration and perhaps be fragmented, and closure will be difficult at the end of nine sessions. It may well be that the training is an attempt to influence the therapist's attitude and to provide a cognitive framework wherein the therapist can apply his/her theoretical orientation within a brief time period.

FUTURE DIRECTIONS

Eclectic time-limited therapy is a means of organizing time-limited elements in a way that provides an eclectic framework for the therapist. It was designed to be electic because there is eclecticism in the composite orientation of therapists in most applied treatment settings. The attempt was made to identify and use key elements that could be used in a thematic way with a particular client and across clients. The approach contains elements that are not new, but rather they have been combined in a fashion that permits their use in a limited time frame. Therapists who apply the model have to have previously been trained in conducting therapy, since this approach does rely on a therapist having basic helping skills and attitude.

There are a number of theoretical questions that still need to be addressed concerning the treatment. Up to this point, we have operated on the assumption that the approach could easily accommodate a wide range of theoretical perspectives and could be applied eclectically. Therapists were trained and said they adopted the approach, but it remains unclear in what way the approach was specifically applied.

The question of the efficacy of the inclusion and exclusion criteria remains. It is assumed that the treatment is suited for particular types of clients who meet the specific inclusionary and exclusionary screening criteria. This may or may not be a valid range of restriction for applying the model. It could be too restrictive or too broad. In addition, the question of the use of the model in other agencies or settings has not been addressed although it has been alluded to by Gelso (1982) in reference to the time component. He suggests that time limits be established that are viable both clinically and practically. Thus, the specific time limit could vary among different agencies.

The question of the use of ETLT in combination with other forms of treatment needs some attention. For example, use of the approach may be dependent on what other treatment alternatives are available. It may well be that this approach could serve as treatment prior to more extended treatment and have specific, positive effects; feasibly, it could be used as a termination strategy concluding a long-term therapeutic experience.

This approach was designed for use in an individual therapeutic format; it may be applicable to group therapy as well. Some adaptations may need to be included, particularly regarding the time element, as the increased number of group clients sharing expectations, reporting on activity during the week, etc. may require more specific structure on the part of the therapist. Nonetheless, the elements relate to group as well as individual therapy and may be applicable in that format.

Regarding the training component of the approach, it seems reasonable to conclude that experienced therapists may not need training in theory or technique to supplement the application of key elements of time-limited therapy. Those with less general and basic training in therapy (i.e., interns, residents, and practica students) may require specific training in the application of the key elements plus aid with basic counseling skills, theory, or technique. Thus, training in the approach may depend on the experience level of the therapist.

The issue of therapist commitment to applying the approach needs to be seriously considered. Training in the use of the approach has evolved since the first application. A greater emphasis on therapist attitude toward brief therapy and commitment to the key elements may be required. Therapist drift from the application of the elements may need to be a central focus of future training. Therapists seemed less concerned that they were restricted in applying their own theoretical orientation. If they felt constrained, it was not evident from the follow-up interview or from the transcripts. Research on the approach uncovers some questions that need further attention. Although there were no differences in therapist attitudes toward brief therapy, there was at least one therapist who either did not value it or who, for some reason, did not follow through. It may be that the instrument describing attitude was not sensitive enough to discriminate or that the social desirability of having positive attitudes toward brief therapy impacted therapist response.

Adherence to the key elements is another issue raised by the research. At this point, it is unclear whether or not, or to what extent, therapists attended to the core elements and emphasized the catalytic orientation of this process. We are currently analyzing the transcripts in order to correlate focusing and expectation sharing with outcome, which will help answer part of the question, but we have not made an attempt at this point to determine therapist adherence to the approach or the deviation from the principles and key elements outlined in ETLT that may have occurred. It is important to know what specifically in the approach makes a difference.

The importance of using unobtrusive measures is illustrated by the study on the time-limited approach. Although there were no differences on the outcome measures, there was a significant difference among clients who left treatment early, with more clients terminating early in the untrained therapist group. There is some indication that these clients left dissatisfied as more of them returned to the center to try again. Unobtrusive measures can tell us something about what we do not know, although they are not sufficient to tell us all that we need know.

We began the chapter narrating why and how we got involved in time-limited therapy using an eclectic approach. We close the chapter by asking ourselves, would we do it again? The answer to the question seems clearer but more complex. Both time-limited therapy and eclecticism warrant continued use and study, but understanding the specifics of each, the integration of the two, and the application to a varied population requires further understanding and substantiation. Eclectic time-limited therapy holds promise for effectively responding to client needs; fulfilling that promise awaits further focus and elaboration.

REFERENCES

Balint, M., Ornstein, P., & Balint, E. (1972). *Focal psychotherapy*. London: Tavistock Publications.

Battle, C., Imber, S., Hoehn-Saric, R., Stone, A., Nash, E., & Frank, J. (1966). Target complaints as a criteria for improvement. *American Journal of Psychotherapy, 20*, 184–192.

Bellak, L., & Small, L. (1978). *Emergency psychotherapy and brief psychotherapy* (2nd ed.). New York: Grune & Stratton, 1965.

Bergin, A. E., & Lambert, M. (1978). The evaluation of therapeutic outcome. In S. Garfield & A. Bergin (Eds.), *Handbook of psychotherapy and behavior change*. New York: Wiley.

Binder, J. (1977). Models of focusing in psychoanalytic short-term therapy. *Psychotherapy: Theory, Research & Practice, 17*, 52–62.

Bloom, B. (1980). Social and community interventions. *Annual Review of Psychology, 31*, 111–142.

Budman, S. (1981). *Forms of brief therapy*. New York: Guilford.

Burlingame, G. (1982). *Clinician attitudes toward brief and long-term psychotherapy*. Unpublished manuscript.

Burlingame, G. (1983). *Therapist content focus and specificity in brief therapy*. Dissertation, University of Utah, Department of Educational Psychology.

Butcher, J., & Koss, M. (1978). Research on brief and crisis-oriented therapies. In S. Garfield & A. Bergin (Eds.), *Handbook of psychotherapy and behavior change*. New York: John Wiley.

Cornfeld, J., Johnson, D., Spiegel, S., Whitaker, J., Wasserman, D., & Gelso, C. (1983). Duration expectancies and client satisfaction with time limited counseling. In C. Gelso & D. Johnson (Eds.), *Exploration in time-limited counseling and psychotherapy*. New York: Teachers College.

Derogatis, L., Abelhoff, M., & McBeth, C. (1977). Cancer patients and their physicians in the perception of psychological symptoms. *Psychosomatics, 7*, 35–46.

Derogatis, W. (1977). *SCL90 Administrative, scoring and procedure manual*. Baltimore: Clinical Psychometrics.

Egan, G. (1975). *The skilled helper: A model for systematic helping and interpersonal relations*. Monterey, CA: Brooks/Cole Publishing Company.

Etzion, D. (1980). Consultants involvement and its convergence in consultant-client verbal interaction. *Journal of Counseling Psychology, 27*(1), 1–8.

Frank, J. (1974). Therapeutic components of psychotherapy. *Journal of Nervous and Mental Disease, 159*, 325–342.

Gelso, C. (1982). *Eclectic brief psychotherapy: Theory, training, application and evaluation*. Paper presented at the Nineteenth Annual Convention of the American Psychological Association. Washington, DC.

Gelso, C., & Johnson, D. (1983). *Explorations in time-limited counseling and psychotherapy*. New York: Teachers College, Columbia University.

Heitler, J. (1976). Preparatory techniques in initiating expressive psychotherapy in lower-class unsophisticated patients. *Psychological Bulletin, 83*, 339–352.

Janis, I. (1982). *Counseling on personal decisions*. New Haven, CT: Yale University Press.

Johnson, D., & Gelso, C. (1980). The effectiveness of time limits in counseling and psychotherapy: A critical review. *The Counseling Psychologist, 9*(1).

Lambert, M. (1979). Patient characteristics and their relationship to outcome in brief psychotherapy. In T. Sloane & F. Staples (Eds.), *Brief psychotherapy*. Philadelphia: Saunders Company.

Luborsky, L. (1984). *Principles of psychoanalytic psychotherapy*. New York: Basic Books.

Malan, D. (1976). *The frontier of brief psychotherapy*. New York: Plenum.

Mann, J. (1973). *Time limited psychotherapy*. Cambridge, MA: Harvard University Press.

Mann, J., & Goldman, R. (1982). *A casebook in time-limited psychotherapy*. New York: McGraw Hill.

Matarazzo, J., & Wiens, A. (1977). Speech behavior as an objective correlate of empathy and outcome in interview and psychotherapy research. *Behavior Modification, 1*(4), 453–480.

Papp, P. (1983). *The process of change*. New York: Guilford Press.

Parloff, M., Waskow, I1, & Wolfe, B. (1978). Research on therapist variables in relation to process and outcome. In S. Garfield & A. Bergin (Eds.), *Handbook of psychotherapy and behavior change*. New York: Wiley.

Piper, W., Debbane, E., Beinvenu, J., & Garant, J. (1984). A comparative study of four forms of psychotherapy. *Journal of Consulting and Clinical Psychology, 52*(2), 268–279.

Poey, K. (1972). A study of the effects of patient-therapist expectancies regarding short term therapy on therapeutic outcome. *Dissertation Abstracts, 32*, 9B, 54–56.

Pope, B. (1979). *The mental health interview*. New York: Pergamon Press.

Reid, W. (1978). *The task centered system*. New York: Columbia University Press.

Sifneos, P. (1979). *Short-term psychotherapy and emotional crisis*. Cambridge, MA: Harvard University Press.

Small, L. (1979). *The briefer psychotherapies (2nd ed.)*. New York: Brunner/Mazel.

Strong, S. R. (1968). Counseling: An interpersonal influence process. *Journal of Counseling Psychology, 153*, 215–224.

Wolberg, L. (1980). *Handbook of short-term psychotherapy (2nd ed.)*. New York: Thieme-Stratton.

Yalom, I. (1980). *Existential psychotherapy*. New York: Basic Books.

Young, D. (1977). Time-limited psychotherapy: The effect of the time factor on patient expectations. *Dissertation Abstracts, 37*, 7B, 3639–3640.

CHAPTER 9

A Structural–Phenomenological Approach to Eclectic Psychotherapy

Stephen Murgatroyd and Michael J. Apter

BACKGROUND

In a valuable contribution to the literature on eclectic psychotherapy, Dryden (1984) suggests that a critical issue facing eclectic psychotherapists is that of therapist decision making. A central part of this issue concerns the basic decisions that therapists make when choosing interventions they consider to be appropriate, given both the presenting problem and their own hypothesis about the meaning of that problem for the client. As Cornsweet (1983) has observed, the problem is that many therapists have an unclear theory of therapy. Their eclecticism is not founded upon a thoroughgoing understanding of the way in which therapy has an impact on individuals. Such therapists lack insight into their own motivations for using particular forms of therapy, and they remain unclear about the structural

qualities of their work in relation to their clients' presenting problems.

In this chapter the "theory of psychological reversals" is used to illustrate an integrative and systematic theory of therapy, the general approach being known as *structural phenomenology* (Apter, 1981, 1982). This chapter builds on and develops earlier contributions to the literature on psychotherapy by the present authors and their co-workers (see Apter & Smith, 1979a, 1979b; Blackmore & Murgatroyd, 1980; Murgatroyd, 1981; Murgatroyd & Apter, 1984).

Reversal theory was originally developed by Apter in consultation with Smith in a child guidance clinic and adult psychiatric practice over a number of years. It began as a concern to explain the problematic and paradoxical behavior of children in therapy and developed into a general theory of motivation and personality which has come to be seen as of value in a variety of psychological settings. A recent collection of papers devoted to the development of the theory (Apter, Fontana, & Murgatroyd, 1985) includes contributions from researchers in such varied areas as psychophysiology, educational psychology, psychometrics, sports psychology, comparative religion, personality theory, and social psychology. The theory is therefore much more than a theory of psychopathology or a theory of therapy, although these are becoming central concerns. For a detailed account of the theory readers are referred to Apter (1982).

REVERSAL THEORY

The basic assumption of reversal theory is that behavior, including "symptoms," can only be understood if the structure of the phenomenological field of the person is taken into account. It is for this reason that the orientation has become known as *structural phenomenology*. (The term *phenomenological field* implies the totality of an individual's experience at any given moment in time—his/her sensations, emotions, thoughts, and so on.) What the approach does is to identify certain recurring mental states, which are described in structural terms, and to explain the way in which transitions occur between these states over time. At one level, therefore, the theory bears a certain formal resemblance to other approaches based on the idea of distinctive modes of being, such as transactional analysis (Berne, 1964) and the configurational analysis of Horowitz and his co-workers (Horowitz, 1979) —although the way in which this basic idea is understood and worked through is different in each of these cases.

Homeostasis and Bistability

In order to understand the way in which reversal theory conceives of the dynamics of change in mental life, it is necessary to see how it goes beyond the concept of homeostasis and how, in doing so, it marks a break with most other general theories of motivation. A homeostatic system is one in which one or more of its variables is maintained within certain preset limits. The range of values of the variable specified can be thought of as the *preferred state* of the system, and since a homeostatic system is one which tends to oppose any movement away from the preferred state, this state can come to be regarded as the stable state of the system. Every major theory of motivation, including those of Freud, Perls, Hull, and Lewin, could be said to assume that a person is homeostatic in this sense. For example, Hull's drive reduction theory proposed that people constantly seek to maintain a low level of drive since the preferred state is relaxation and this is equated with low drive. Similarly, one of the most influential theories of motivation in recent years—the theory of "optimal arousal" originally due to Hebb (1955)—proposes that at all times the person will seek to maintain arousal at an intermediate preferred level so as to maintain homeostatic balance.

Yet not all psychologists have been satisfied with the explanation of motivated action in terms of homeostasis. Frankl (1969), Maslow (1954, 1971), and Charlotte Buhler (1959) have all offered detailed critiques of the construct in relation to motivation, especially when applied to the practice of therapy. Indeed, each of these authors suggests that homeostasis is a sign of disorder rather than emotional health.

An alternative to homeostatic systems are a class of more complex systems known as *multistable systems*. The common characteristic of such systems is that they have more than one, and perhaps many, preferred stable states of the variables which the system regards as central. A particular type of multistable system is the *bistable* system in which there are two preferred states between which the system will "choose" at any given moment in time. One example of such a system would be a light switch, its two stable positions being "on" and "off" with all intermediate positions between these two opposing ones being regarded as unstable.

Reversal theory begins with a rejection of homeostatic models of the person, such as those advanced by Freud, and suggests instead that human motivation is best understood in terms of bistability. Though this is a technical issue (see Apter, 1982, Chapter 2), it can be understood through the idea that mental states are arranged in pairs of opposites and the person switches between one or other of the states within a pair with some regularity. Each such pair of states is regarded as a polarity and constitutes a bistable system in itself. All that follows stems from this idea.

Metamotivational States

Consider a person going to a drama therapy group: the behavior is drama therapy activity, the person's goal is self-understanding. There are two ways in which the person can experience the relationship between goal and behavior here. In one of these the goal (self-understanding) is in the foreground and the behavior (drama therapy) is the background. This may occur if the drama therapy activity holds some special significance—the person finds some symbolic meaning in a routine and works it so as to exhaust this meaning for him. In this case the behavior is chosen to suit the goal. The alternative way of experiencing this same situation is for the behavior to be in the foreground and the goal in the background. In this case, the goal is no more than an excuse to perform the behavior—the person may find some drama routine pleasurable and wish to sustain it solely for this reason.

Behaviors are therefore engaged in primarily because they lead to the achievement of some goal or because they are intrinsically satisfying in themselves. The differences between these two activities are not about the goals or the means themselves; rather, they are about the way in which these motives and activities are structured, interpreted, and organized within experience; they can therefore be referred to as *meta*motivational states or modes. The theory of reversals proposes that there are a number of pairs of metamotivational states which display polarity at this level, with one metamotivational state (e.g., conformity) being paired with another (e.g., negativism) to provide the alternative frames of mind within which the person can view his/her actions. For each of these pairs of metamotivational states individuals will always be experiencing one or the other state at a given moment in time during waking life; they will also switch or *reverse* between the two states with some regularity, if they are psychologically healthy.

Three pairs of metamotivational states —the *telic/paratelic, negativism/conformity*, and *mastery/sympathy pairs*—have been identified and interpreted within the theory. The characteristics of these are summarized in Table 1, which shows that the drama therapy example just used is an illustration of the difference between telic and paratelic metamotivational states, the pursuit of the goal of self-understanding being a telic mode and the pursuit of pleasure a paratelic mode. At any given moment in waking life a person's individual experience will be characterized by a subset of three of these six states—i.e., one from each pair.

In order to provide some concrete details about the way in which each of these states functions to govern experience and activity, Table 2 presents an account of the activities of one client during one morning. It should be noted that the comments in the diary reflect the client's

TABLE 1
Three Pairs of Metamotivational States

TELIC	PARATELIC
The person is serious-minded, planning-oriented, and seeks to avoid arousal.	The person is playful, prefers to be spontaneous, is "here and now" oriented (pursues goals only insofar as they add to the immediate pleasure of a situation), and prefers high arousal.
NEGATIVISTIC	CONFORMIST
The person feels a need to act against a salient pressure that is felt to be imposed from the outside.	The person feels a need to conform to a salient pressure that is felt to be imposed from the outside.
SYMPATHY	MASTERY
The individual feels a need to be sympathized with by the other with whom he/she is interacting, and transactions are experienced as involving "giving" or "receiving."	The individual feels a need to dominate or control the other with whom he/she is interacting, and transactions are experienced as involving "taking" or "yielding up."

TABLE 2
Diary Extract from a Client

Diary	Comment
Couldn't sleep very well . . . John had made love to me the night before and I had found it . . . well, unbearable. He didn't notice (well, I don't think he did), and I faked coming . . . but I didn't sleep for thinking that he's bound to realize that I am not enjoying sex with him as I used to.	Remembers conformist feelings in a telic state
Got up at 7:30 and had a shower . . . it felt good just being there under the hot jets of water . . . normally I shower very quickly and am out, but today I took almost 15 minutes under the water . . . I just forgot about the time.	Paratelic experience
8:00 a.m. John was out to work already—I was glad I didn't have to talk to him about last night . . . the more I think about it the more serious it seems . . .	Negativism
I put some Mozart on the stereo and found myself becoming absorbed in the music until the haunting part of the music, when I began to feel that it was about me and John.	Paratelic turning to telic as she connects the music to her own problems
Around 10:30 I thought to myself that I would get out of my feeling blue by going to spend some money—something I rarely do. I went downtown intending to buy a skirt . . .	Negativism
I had seen one I liked and had priced it against similar models in other stores. When I got there I found myself buying on impulse.	Indicates earlier telic orientation Paratelic
What should have cost $36 ended up costing me $122—John will be angry when he finds out that I've spent so much on clothes. As if I didn't have enough to worry about!	Paratelic experience turns to telic when connected to John

thoughts about the predominant state at the time, i.e., the one state of the three operative at that time which most contributed to his own understanding of his own experience. This diary example suggests that reversals between metamotivational states can occur with some regularity and over short time periods. Clinical observations by Blackmore and Murgatroyd (1980) suggest that they can also be sudden and unexpected. They document the case of a young girl (aged six years) who dramatically and frequently reversed between serious and purposive activity (telic) to disruptive and sensation-seeking activity (paratelic-negativism) during the course of a typical school day.

In fact, reversal theory identifies three classes of inducing agents in relation to the process of reversal: (1) *contingent events*, in which some feature of the person or the environment changes in such a way as to trigger a reversal, e.g., experiencing the effect of some drug or being attacked by one's spouse; (2) *frustration*, in which the needs of the person in one metamotivational state are not being satisfied and the frustration builds up to a point when a reversal occurs; and (3) *satiation*, as the period of time spent in one metamotivational state increases so the person becomes increasingly sensitive to environmental or internal cues to other reversal-inducing agents (e.g., frustration and contingent events) to the point at which a reversal can occur. Indeed, eventually satiation will bring about a reversal even in the absence of other factors. Each of these three factors interact with each other in a facilitative or inhibitory way to determine whether or not a reversal will occur at a particular moment in time.

Telic and Paratelic States

In the development of the theory particular attention has been paid so far to the telic and paratelic metamotivational states. The first point to emphasize about them is that the terms *telic* and *paratelic* refer to states and not traits. Thus, as we have seen, an individual can be said to be experiencing the phenomenological field in a telic state at one moment and in a paratelic state at another. Although there is strong evidence that individuals have an innate tendency to be in one of these states rather than another—a person can be said to be telic or paratelic dominant —this tendency to spend more time in one state does not preclude the person from experiencing his/her phenomenological field in the opposite state from time to time and cannot therefore be regarded as a trait in the conventional sense.

Defining the telic and paratelic metamotivational states, Apter (1982) says:

The telic state is defined as a phenomenological state in which the individual is primarily oriented towards, or feels the need to be primarily oriented towards, some essential goal or goals. The paratelic state, in contrast, is defined as a state in which the individual is primarily oriented towards, or feels the need to be primarily oriented towards, some aspect of his continuing behavior and its related sensations (p. 47).

The word "telic" is derived from the Greek word "telos," meaning a goal or an end. The phrase "primarily oriented towards" is meant to imply that the feature of experience concerned is the focus of conscious attention rather than at the fringes of such attention—the goal is the figure in the case of the telic state and the behavior is the ground, whereas in the paratelic state the opposite is the case. Thus a reversal can be seen as a kind of "figure-ground" reversal that involves the whole of the person's phenomenological field.

Remembering that each of the metamotivational states with which reversal theory is primarily concerned is defined phenomenologically, it follows that goals are also defined in terms of the phenomenology of the person. Thus goals in the telic state are goals which that individual regards as essential. Goals which the person regards as essential at one time (e.g., securing social status) may not be seen as essential by others or by the same person at some other time. A person in the paratelic state may also claim to be pursuing some goal, but the function of the goal in this state is quite different: it is an excuse to pursue some activity or a device for structuring and enhancing that activity, rather than being a fundamental reason for pursuing an activity which, after all, is not essential.

Although the defining quality of the telic and paratelic states concerns the relationship in experience of means and ends, these two states turn out to have other distinctive features related to the "seriousness" of the telic state and the relative "playfulness" of the paratelic state. These characteristics cannot be described fully here (but see Apter, 1982, Chapter 3). One feature that does need to be understood, however, concerns the opposite ways in which arousal is experienced in each state. In the telic state the preference is for low arousal, with high arousal being experienced as anxiety and low arousal as pleasurable relaxation. Thus, if a goal increases in its importance or a barrier seems to be preventing goal achievement, anxiety will be felt; if a goal is achieved, low arousal will be experienced as pleasant relaxation. In contrast, the paratelic state involves the person interpreting arousal differently: the intensity of an activity is likely to be greater if arousal levels are high and this high arousal is experienced as "thrilling" or "exciting"; a low level of arousal will be experienced as "boredom." So the relationship between arousal, on the one hand, and hedonic tone (pleasure/displeasure), on the other, is opposite in each case.

It will be noted from these comments that reversal theory differs substantially from optimal arousal theory. It will also

be appreciated that a reversal occurring from one metamotivational state to another will change the meaning given to the experience of arousal and not necessarily the level of arousal itself: there are always two ways of interpreting arousal in experience.

A related proposition in reversal theory is that emotions of all kinds, not just anxiety, that are experienced as highly arousing will be felt as unpleasant in the telic state. However, introspection will suggest that there are occasions when normally unpleasant emotions (e.g., anger, guilt, fear) are actually experienced as pleasant. For example, one enjoys some unpleasant emotions when watching a horror film or play. Feelings of guilt may also contribute to the pleasures of such activities as overeating, flirting, excessive drinking, and speed driving. How, then, does reversal theory account for such paradoxically pleasant emotions? It does so by postulating that all highly arousing emotions which are experienced as unpleasant in the telic state can be experienced in some form in the paratelic state and (providing a reversal to the telic state does not occur) will be experienced as pleasant in this state. What appears to happen to such "negative" emotions as guilt, anger, fear, hate, or horror is that a paratelic "frame" is put around them so that they can be experienced playfully, and the high arousal they generate is thus felt as pleasant. When such a reframing occurs, the resulting emotions are referred to within the theory as "parapathic emotions."

There is much more to reversal theory than it has been possible to indicate here. For one thing, we have concentrated on the telic and paratelic pair of metamotivational states to the exclusion of other pairs postulated within the theory. Even here, we have presented a "bare-bones" picture of these two states and have left much to be explained. Second, there has been no direct reference to other concepts in the theory, such as tension and synergy.

Third, there has been no reference to supporting psychometric, psychophysiological, phenomenological, and experimental studies (but see below), so some aspects of the theory may seem arbitrary or doctrinaire. Nonetheless, the points developed here are central to an understanding of the key features of the theory which apply to the practice of eclectic therapy.

THE APPROACH TO THERAPY

The value of reversal theory as a basis for eclectic therapy is that it provides a structure within which the motives of both clients and therapists can be understood. Using reversal theory, it is possible to interpret the client's presenting problem in structural and phenomenological terms, to examine alternative courses of intervention in a way which attends to their likely impact on the clients' motivational experiences, and to evaluate therapy in terms of its structural impact. All this needs to be done within a phenomenological framework which assumes: (a) that clients are inherently inconsistent in their experiences because of reversal, but that this inconsistency is patterned in some way; (b) that the specific presenting problem the client brings to therapy is a symbol of an underlying structural problem in experience; and (c) the therapist's own interventions must be seen to be concerned with both the presenting problem and the underlying motivational experience of the person.

The concept that a presenting problem, such as anxiety or a neurotic disorder, needs to be understood in terms of its origins in the structure of experience suggests that there are specific structural disturbances which the therapist needs to attend to. In a recent development of reversal theory (Murgatroyd & Apter, 1984) four specific structural disturbances have been identified. These are: (1) *reversal in-hibition*—when the person displays a relative inability to reverse between metamotivational states with the consequence that the person is "stuck" in one state for most of the time; (2) *inappropriate reversal*—when the person experiences reversal between one metamotivational state and another at times when such reversal is inappropriate; (3) *socially inappropriate behavior*—when the behaviors a person engages in satisfy felt needs in a particular metamotivational state but which are regarded as socially inappropriate or unacceptable; and finally, (4) *temporally inappropriate behavior*—when the achievement of satisfactions in one state makes reversal more difficult or makes the achievement of satisfaction in the same or alternative state less likely in the future.

Instances of problems 1 and 2 are easy to think of. For example, chronic anxiety is clearly a case of reversal failure, with individuals experiencing their actions and social events from within the telic state and finding all arousal anxiety provoking. Similarly, phobias involve, as well as suddenly increased arousal in certain specific situations, an inappropriate reversal into the telic state on these occasions so that arousal rather than excitement is experienced. Problems associated with category 4, structural disturbances, may be more difficult to imagine, so we now provide some examples. A person may avoid anxiety in the telic state by refusing to put him/herself into a situation in which such anxiety might occur or in which he/she might fail in some way. The result is that, though he/she avoids anxiety, he/she also fails to engage in a task which may subsequently be useful to the later experience of life (van der Molen, 1985). A second example is that of a telic-dominant person who plans his/her life ahead in such rigid detail and commits him/herself to such serious goals that the chances of spending significant amounts of time in the paratelic state are substantially reduced. In a rather different way, a paratelic-dominant person may engage in activities which have many short term "payoffs" in the sense of thrills or sensations, but which turn out to be damaging to longer-term interests—drug abuse, gambling, and promiscuity may all be examples of this.

This fourfold classification of presenting problems constitutes the basis for all subsequent intervention in structural phenomenological eclectic psychotherapy. The task of the helper becomes one of changing the structural basis of the person's motivational processes—the aim is not simply to treat anxiety or a phobia, for example, but to enable the person to develop different ways of experiencing his own motivations.

Equally important to the approach is the way in which it permits the therapist to view interventions in terms of their likely structural impact. Rather than suggest new therapeutic interventions, this approach to therapy provides criteria by which the therapist can make decisions about which intervention to use. The question the therapist needs to ask when considering an intervention is, "In what way does this intervention seek to affect the structure of the person's experience?" This question has many subquestions: Will it facilitate a reversal between one metamotivational state and another and, if so, which states? Will it make the person more aware of the social impact of his actions? Will the intervention change the way in which arousal is experienced? A later section of this chapter will explore the precise way in which the therapist examines his/her options within this approach.

PATIENT ASSESSMENT

When a person presents for therapy, the first task of the therapist is to seek to understand the phenomenological field of the person. This is required both in relation to the presenting problem *and* in relation to the person's normative experience of his own behaviors and actions. To do this requires the therapist to develop considerable skills in empathy. In addition, the therapist needs to establish not only what the phenomenological field is like in terms of the fabric of experience (i.e., the emotional and cognitive contents of experience) but also what the structure of that experience is like. He needs to explore such questions as, How often does reversal occur between metamotivational states? What are the predominant metamotivational states in this person's experience? To what extent can the presenting problem be tied to the structure of his experience? How do the three reversal-inducing agents (contingency, frustration, and satiation) operate for this person? To what extent is this person aware of the structure of his own experience? These issues need to be explored in a climate of empathy, warmth, and genuineness (Rogers, 1957) and in a way that ensures that the therapist is keeping track of the phenomenological quality of these data.

In pursuing this route of establishing the phenomenological field and its structure we have found the headings used by Lazarus (1976) for case history taking to be especially helpful. Specifically, we explore with patients their behavior, affective states, sensations, imagery, cognitions, interpersonal relations, and drug-taking behavior. In collecting patient data of this kind the aim is always to illuminate the phenomenal field and its underlying structure. Under each of these headings (abbreviated to BASIC I.D.) we examine: (a) the reversal processes that characterize the patient's daily life; (b) the way in which he cognitively appraises his own psychological processes; (c) the dominance of one metamotivational mode or cluster of modes over others; (d) the interrelationship between modes for this person; (e) the precise "fabric" or content of the modes, to see whether the modes commonly utilized by the person have an associated image or action example which the therapist can make use of; and (f) the experience of previous helper behavior in terms of the modes and structures of experience.

As part of this process there are three assessment devices that we sometimes use. The first is a standarized measure of telic dominance known as the *Telic Dominance Scale*, developed by Murgatroyd and his co-workers (Murgatroyd et al., 1978). This provides an indication of the extent to which an individual can be said to be telic or paratelic dominant in terms of three dimensions: seriousmindedness, planning orientation, and arousal avoidance. An evaluation of the value of this instrument will be found in Murgatroyd (1985). A second instrument has been developed which looks at the current state of the person in terms of the telic/paratelic polarity; known as the *telic state measure*, this instrument provides a basis of assessing the degree to which a person is experiencing tension as well as the current mode. Full details of this state measure are given in Svebak and Murgatroyd (1985). The third device developed for assessing the client's operative state is to ask him to describe in detail his experience of the previous day and to describe what he hopes the next day will be like. Svebak and Murgatroyd (1985) have shown that a trained interviewer can discern the dominance of the person and his current state from a study of the grammar, syntax, and content of their answers to these seemingly simple questions (see also Murgatroyd, 1985). Such devices are useful only when it is thought that the telic or paratelic states need to be better understood for a particular person—other measures are in development that will examine the mastery/sympathy and negativism/conformity states.

Apter and Smith (1979a) and Murgatroyd and Apter (1984) have shown that

it is possible to apply the structural analysis of experience to individuals or families. There is little work done as yet that shows the applicability of assessment methods to psychotic clients, however.

The purpose of all assessment work, whether by interview, the collection of BASIC I.D. data, or the use of instrumentation, is the same: understanding the underlying structural disturbances of the client. Simply diagnosing the presenting problem does not tell us about the way this problem is experienced and interpreted by the person in need.

TREATMENT APPLICABILITY

The structural phenomenological approach to psychotherapy has been used in a variety of treatment settings. These include a child guidance clinic (Apter & Smith, 1976), counseling in a school setting (Blackmore & Murgatroyd, 1980), family therapy (Apter & Smith, 1979a), sex therapy (Apter & Smith, 1979b), crisis counseling (Murgatroyd, 1981), and adult psychotherapy (Murgatroyd & Apter, 1984). In addition, the value of reversal theory for a structural phenomenological approach to developmental therapy has also been examined (van der Molen, 1985).

Most of this work has been undertaken with individuals or subgroups of families or with children. Some of the work has been with special populations, such as prisoners receiving psychotherapy or patients experiencing some crisis while hospitalized. None of the work has involved patients diagnosed as psychotic—emphasis has been on the neurotic disorders (though, of course, structural phenomenology, having its own taxonomy of client-presenting problems, makes little use of the labeling of the various kinds of neurotic disorder).

Though some of the crisis work developed and described by Murgatroyd (1981) has been extremely brief—no more than

10 hours—most of the therapeutic applications of structural phenomenology have taken some time, notably 26 sessions over a two-year period. Much depends on the nature of the presenting problem and its structural origins. Work is in an early stage of development, and it is not yet clear whether this time period can be reduced.

All counseling and psychotherapy offered within this framework develops from a clear contracting between the therapist and client. In part this is because the therapy involves going beyond the presenting problem and into the structure of experience and in part because those of us involved in developing this work have a belief in contracting with our clients (see Murgatroyd, 1985). Contracts help to specify the nature of the problem, delineate the role of the client and the therapist, and provide a framework for evaluation of progress within an agreed time frame.

TREATMENT INTERVENTION AND STRATEGIES

The essential task of therapy in this approach is to affect the underlying structure of motivated experience. This is undertaken through a number of phases in therapy. These are: (a) assessment, (b) climate setting, (c) choice of strategy and contracting, (d) treatment programs, and (e) assessment and evaluation.

We have already described some of the features of assessment. We emphasize again that the purpose of the assessment process is not to establish the precise nature of the presenting problem but rather to understand the way in which this presenting problem arises from within the structural features of the client's experience of the phenomenal field. Thus the therapist is seeking to assess the extent to which the presenting problem can be understood in terms of one or other of the four kinds of structural disturbance described earlier (i.e., reversal inhibition, inappropriate reversal, socially inappropriate behavior, and temporally inappropriate behavior). Most often, assessment activity and climate setting are linked in this approach. Thus, brief biographies, accounts of daily experience, and some art drawing of the way in which a person experiences various features of the phenomenal field (especially giving emphasis to opposite experiences of the same phenomena) are used as part of the assessment and climate-setting process. Climate setting can also be done through small-group work (we have sometimes involved clients in small groups so as to assess the ability of clients to reverse in social conditions), especially groups that use some of the drama techniques developed and described by Johnstone (1981).

This climate-setting period, which can last between four and seven sessions, needs also to be used by the therapist to establish the likely structural impact of any interventions that he/she might choose to use. In addition, this period establishes the dominant modes within which therapy is likely to take place (i.e., in terms of the metamotivational states of the person) and thus helps to establish the appropriateness of humor, role play, drama therapy, and many other therapeutic interventions from which the eclectic therapist may wish to choose.

Following the climate-setting period, the therapist needs to contract with the client for change by declaring the rationale behind the planned intervention. This period requires the therapist to have made a decision as to the most appropriate course of action for this particular client, given the structural disturbance.

Different therapeutic interventions have different impacts on structural disturbance. What is more, the same intervention will have different kinds of impact in different cases. For example, both paradoxical intention and exaggeration (a standard Gestalt technique) can be used as devices for unblocking inhibited reversal. We have also shown that some of the drama improvisation techniques elaborated by Johnstone (1981), when adapted to the client's own circumstance, can facilitate reversal between the telic and paratelic states or the negativistic and conformist states. Effective interventions aimed at facilitating appropriate reversals appear to have two main origins, though they are not restricted to these sources. These are: (1) social skills training, especially in anger reduction which can be regarded as a special form of negativistic to conformist state reversal (see Novaco, 1973), and (2) cognitive-behavioral techniques. Of particular value in facilitating paratelic to telic reversal in these circumstances has been shame-attacking exercises derived from RET in which the *in vivo* behavior of the client is set at an extreme and is progressively "hyped."

In considering techniques that are fruitful in reducing the extent to which current behavior, though appropriate to the current metamotivational state, inhibits subsequent reversal, techniques derived from reality therapy and decision making are especially productive. In addition, rational-emotive imagery has also been found to be useful in encouraging clients to reflect on the alternatives to their current behavior in a way that does not "close down" subsequent action opportunities.

These illustrative examples of therapy choices are intended to show that the rationale for a decision to use an intervention is based on its probable structural impact on the person in need. That is, structural phenomenology requires the therapist to address the question "how will a specific intervention affect the underlying structural qualities of this person's experience while at the same time attending to the presenting problem?" throughout the course of therapy.

This period of deciding on an intervention and implementing it via a contract leads naturally to the change process in therapy. Throughout the period of strategy implementation the therapist needs to address a number of basic questions continually. These include: (a) Is this therapy enhancing this person's ability to reverse and/or unblocking a blocked reversal? (b) Is this intervention making reversals more appropriate in terms of their timing? (c) Does this intervention enhance the quality of action the person engages in so as to provide "better" satisfactions within the particular mode? (d) Does this intervention reduce the extent to which a typical behavior engaged in by the client impairs subsequent reversal? There are further questions about the process of therapy that the therapist needs to ask. These include: (a) To what extent does the intervention require the person to be in a particular state at the time of the intervention and how can I achieve this state? (b) To what extent does the success of this intervention depend on social support of the phenomenological field of the person and its structure? (c) What are the likely effects of an intervention aimed at affecting one pair of metamotivational modes (i.e., telic/paratelic) upon the other modes (i.e., mastery/sympathy, negativism/conformity)? The precise nature and importance of these questions will become clearer in the case study to be presented below.

The most serious error that can be made by the therapist during this stage is to fail to understand correctly the meaning of the presenting problem in terms of its origins in structural disturbance, for example, deciding that something is an inappropriate reversal when it is in fact a failure to reverse. For this reason we suggest that the therapist behave as a scientist and seek to establish a hypothesis as to which one of the four categories of structural disturbance is associated with the presenting problem of the person and then test this hypothesis against available data provided both by the patient and by the process of therapy itself.

Termination of therapy occurs once the contract has been achieved or earlier if the patient and therapist are able to discern clear changes in the way in which the person experiences the phenomenal field. In achieving termination we have found it helpful to engage in some psychoeducational activity designed to teach some of the concepts from reversal theory so as to increase the extent to which the person recognizes his/her own experiences and their meaning. In addition, we have frequently had to overcome some barriers to change and development through termination work. Of particular importance here is the social expectation of consistency in behavior, a belief that we suggest is irrational and not supported either by the client's own daily experience or by the data collected by those of us engaged in the study of structural phenomenology. This psychoeducational activity has been found useful in ending therapeutic contracts.

THERAPIST BEHAVIORS

A number of the comments made so far suggest that the therapist needs to be: (a) highly empathic, so as to be able to discern both the fabric and structure of the client's experience; (b) able to act in a scientific way so that he can discern both the structural nature of the client's presenting problem and the probable structural impact of his own behavior; and (c) able to act as a teacher of structural concepts in a simple and direct way. In this section we briefly examine some other qualities which therapists need to bring to their work with clients.

Because this approach does not involve the development of new techniques of therapy but instead seeks to provide a new classification of existing techniques in terms of their structural impact, the therapist needs to have a wide knowledge and range of skills in the practice of a variety of interventions. To some extent, this will need to be a knowledge and experience that permit therapists to divorce the practice of a particular skill (e.g., Gestalt dreamwork) from its origins in a particular theory so that they are able to see the relevance of a particular therapeutic activity to the structural disturbance the client is experiencing.

Therapists also need to understand their own reversal processes and be able to experience their phenomenal field in the various ways outlined at the beginning of this chapter. For example, if the therapist is able to reverse between the telic and paratelic states with some regularity and is able to enjoy the experience of both states, then he/she is more likely to be able to encourage normal reversal than a therapist who is stuck in the telic state. Furthermore, the use of some techniques, such as paradoxical intention, requires the therapist to work at times within the paratelic mode, since substantial amounts of humor are required to render such an intervention effective (Frankl, 1969). Not all therapists will be effective in the use of this technique since it requires rapid reversal between the telic and paratelic state; indeed, some therapists feel themselves unable to utilize humor at all in their therapeutic work (see Kubie, 1971).

Structural–phenomenological eclectic therapists need to be able to vary their treatment strategies to meet the specific needs of clients. Thus therapists will sometimes develop a directive approach which distances themselves from the client, while at other times they will use high levels of self-disclosure and physical contact (through drama work, massage, or dynamic meditation) so as to engage the client in a direct discovery of the similarity between the structural phenomenological experiences of the therapist and his own. In deciding which level of involvement to choose, the therapist bears in mind the probable impact on the structural features of the person's presenting problem.

MECHANISMS OF CHANGE

The processes of therapy outlined briefly here are intended to lead to changes in the way in which people in need experience their own motivation and hence their own actions. This is the task of therapy, a task we have referred to as affecting the underlying structure of motivated experience.

Therapy involves the use of one or more of four general categories of intervention. These are: (1) *blocking of normal transactional patterns through which the person interprets his/her motives*—interrupting the client's normal thinking pattern, the normal way in which he seeks to obtain feedback from others and the normal way in which he seeks to be consistent; (2) *emphasizing differences and inconsistency in his/her own experience*—rather than avoiding these issues, the therapist is seeking to show how inconsistency in experience and differences in experience illuminate the underlying structure and uses this knowledge to promote and secure change; (3) *developing inner conflict and resolve*—encouraging clients to see themselves as working in and between alternative modes of experience (i.e., reversing between opposing polarities in relation to metamotivational states) and seeking to find ways of regulating or structuring this inherent inconsistency; and (4) *enacting or facilitating the opposite modes of experience*—enabling clients to experience, in the safety of therapy, those features of their experience which they have been denying, repressing, or misusing. Each of these types of intervention has the effect of increasing the arousal the person ex-

periences in therapy, and this, in turn, provides an opportunity for the therapist to witness and then utilize the three reversal-inducing features—satiation, frustration, and contingency—as therapeutic devices.

This "grand" classification of therapeutic strategies (derived from Minuchin, 1974) says nothing about the tactics of change which the therapist might use. (A strategy is distinguished from a tactic here in the same way as such a distinction would be used in the context of a strategy game: strategy refers to the overall aim and tactics to the way in which such an aim might be achieved through a specific maneuver). Tactics are many and varied and can be derived from any of the existing schools of therapy with which the therapist is familiar. The choice of tactic relates to the strategy the therapist is pursuing *and* to the therapist's hypothesis about the nature of the structural disturbance he/she is seeking to affect.

Though there have been no clinical trials as yet, it is our view that the critical features of successful therapy within this approach are: (a) the ability of the therapist to communicate accurate empathy; (b) the ability of the therapist to act as scientist in the testing of a structural–phenomenological hypothesis; (c) the ability of patients to permit themselves to disclose and experience their inconsistency and to reflect on themselves at the metalevel; and (d) the "correctness" of the choice of intervention by the therapist given the client and the structural disturbance which the client presents.

In that this approach is phenomenological the therapy proceeds by using a great deal of insight, but the therapy is also structural in its origins, so insights become hypotheses to be tested against both client-generated data and the evidence of therapy itself. Change arises when the climate of therapy permits the client to experience and understand appropriate reversal.

CASE EXAMPLE

The following case study illustrates treatment within a structural phenomenological approach to therapy. Sally (aged 30) was diagnosed by the psychiatrist who referred her for psychotherapy as suffering from frequent anxiety attacks of an agoraphobic type, with an overlay of depression. The psychiatrist had himself been treating her for two years with minor tranquilizers and had observed little improvement. Indeed, at the time of referral she was experiencing a particularly bad period, and her anxiety attacks had become even more frequent than they had been at the outset of treatment. The psychiatrist's case notes disclosed that her marriage to a bank teller was not consummated for a number of years, largely owing to her fear of sex, but that this problem had been overcome some years previously through sex therapy, and her sexual relationship with her husband was now satisfactory. At the time of referral she had a son aged four.

At the first interview the client revealed herself to be an intelligent and articulate young woman with a pleasant, outgoing personality and a sense of humor. She reported that she suffered from panic attacks which could occur at any time of the day but which, she claimed, were particularly likely to occur outside the home, for example, while shopping. These attacks were so severe that she felt she was going mad whenever they occurred. The effect of the feeling of possible madness and the fear of attack now acted to keep her housebound, going out only when her husband accompanied her.

During the first weeks of therapy, which was conducted on a weekly basis, she was asked to note in detail the situations in which her panics arose so that any structural pattern could be discerned. These situations turned out to be far more varied than she had herself fully realized. They included not only those situations in which she was in public places (e.g., in crowded shops or on public transport) but also situations occurring in her home, such as: being involved in an argument with a neighbor who called, starting to make love to her husband, getting angry at her son, watching an especially exciting program on television, telling a joke to a friend, listening to a relative's problems, and being visited by a friend toward whom she felt some sexual attraction. Although there is no obvious connection in terms of the content of these experiences, the connection made by the therapist was that each of these events occurred at points when there was a sudden increase in her experience of arousal (or "felt arousal" as it is termed within reversal theory).

A number of different techniques were used by the therapist to gain insight into the phenomenological field that Sally was experiencing. These techniques included: (a) the use of the third-chair technique, in which she was asked to describe herself from the outside as if sitting in a third chair in the interview room, which showed that she was afraid of being overwhelmed by her own sexuality; (b) looking at her dreams using dreamwork techniques derived from Gestalt work, which showed that the theme of being overwhelmed by her emotions was prevalent—a typical dream involved being caught on the seashore by a rising tide and being unable to escape; and (c) the "magic money game" from reality therapy in which she was asked to list the experiences she would most like to buy with some magic money —her choices were to visit Paris on a conventional sightseeing tour or to fly all over the world (especially on fast jets) giving instructions to others and feeling in control of the situation. The aim of these activities, apart from aiding in the climate-setting phase of therapy, was to establish a clearer basis for the therapist's understanding of the phenomenological field of this client and to enable him to make an accurate assessment of the underlying structural disturbance that she was experiencing.

Her scores on the *Telic Dominance Scale* indicated that she was paratelic dominant. Her subscale scores on this instrument turned out to be very revealing: she was highly paratelic dominant on the serious-minded and planning-orientation subscales (i.e., her natural tendency was to be highly playful and spontaneous), but her scores on the arousal avoidance subscale were definitely within what would normally be regarded as the telic-dominant range. This suggested that she sought the satisfactions of the paratelic state without the experience of high arousal.

In structural phenomenological terms the therapist hypothesized that this client's problem could be defined as follows. Although paratelic dominant, and therefore in the normal way of things likely to get herself frequently into high arousal situations because these are experienced as pleasurable and exciting, she tended to experience sudden increases in felt arousal as involving a loss of control and therefore as threatening. The experience of such a threat led her to switch into the telic state in which high arousal is experienced as anxiety. Thus, her presenting problem was located in an inappropriate reversal disturbance. She was certainly not "stuck" in the telic mode, being paratelic dominant, nor was she stuck in the paratelic mode, since her panic attacks arose from her experiences in this mode and her subsequent reversal from it. The problem was that she reversed into the telic state at times when she should have been enjoying, in a nonthreatening way, the high arousal that her situation was helping to generate. Thus, the situations in which panic attacks occurred were all situations which, had she been in the paratelic state for the duration of the activity, would have produced pleasurable excitement: sexual activity, an animated discussion at a party, watching an exciting film, and so on. She was now so used to inappropriate

reversal that this in itself had become a problem: she now feared the inappropriate reversal so much that it was almost certain to take place whenever excitement was suddenly felt. As far as her depression was concerned, this appeared to be of the boredom type. That is, in the paratelic state she tried to avoid rather than seek out arousing situations with the result that she spent long periods in a state of paratelic low arousal (boredom). Each time she sought to overcome her boredom-depression by engaging in some activity likely to lead to excitement—going shopping, flirting, telling jokes, having an argument—reversal would occur and she experienced anxiety rather than excitement. The consequence was alternation between long periods of boredom-depression and periods of acute anxiety.

This analysis immediately revealed why the use of tranquilizers over a period of years had been so ineffective, indeed why they might even have been counterproductive. By helping to lower arousal levels during everyday life, they simply contributed to the boredom depression. In addition, they were not strong enough to overcome the acute anxiety fostered by the panic attacks themselves.

The therapist, having shared this interpretation with the client, decided to focus his attention on the acute-anxiety episodes, since if these could be overcome there would be little need for the client to avoid arousing situations and the boredom-depression would dissipate of its own accord. This interpretation of the client's problem and the decision to focus treatment in this way gave rise to a number of different treatment options. These included: (a) lowering the level of arousal during an anxiety (panic) attack so that relaxation would be felt rather than anxiety; or (b) overcoming the threatening feeling of loss of control associated with sudden surges of felt arousal in an attempt to prevent inappropriate reversal taking place; or (c) providing techniques for bringing a reversal back into the paratelic state at the beginning of a panic attack, so that high arousal could be experienced as excitement rather than anxiety.

Of these three treatment options, the first and the third are obviously mutually exclusive, while the second strategy could be applied in combination with either. In the case of each of these strategies, a number of different intervention tactics could be pursued. Although a number of quick relaxation techniques were taught early in therapy as a means of providing symptom relief, the detailed understanding of the phenomenological field of the person strongly indicated the preference of the second and third strategies being used in combination. This decision was also informed by the work of Heide and Borkovec (1983), which showed that some clients find relaxation stressful, and the therapist's assumption that this is the case with paratelic-dominant subjects. Furthermore, the use of relaxation techniques would be inappropriate to the behaviors the client wished to be able to engage in when the panic attacks occurred, e.g., sexual activity, engaging in sports, or watching an exciting adventure movie. For these reasons a number of the arousal-reducing techniques employed in the treatment of anxiety (e.g., biofeedback, meditation, massage) were deliberately excluded. In addition, *in vivo* desensitization was excluded since this necessarily involved seeking to reduce arousal levels actually experienced; the therapist in this case sought to change the way arousal was experienced *not* the level of arousal.

During the next 18 months the therapist actively pursued a number of tactics aimed at implementing the second and third treatment options described above. As each tactic was employed, the therapist examined its impact on the structural disturbance the client had presented and sought to evaluate his hypothesis concerning the nature of this client's inap-

propriate reversal. Throughout this time, therapeutic encounters occurred once each month. On each occasion, the nature of her structural disturbance was explained to Sally, since it appears that clients respond well to explanations that remove some of the mystery from their motivational experience.

Several techniques were used in the attempt to inhibit inappropriate reversal whenever Sally become highly aroused. One of these was to try to take advantage of her strong sense of humor (humor being a paratelic emotion—see Apter, 1982). By helping her see the ridiculous side of her reactions to arousing situations, the therapist was able to encourage a cognitive reappraisal of these situations as less threatening than they had hitherto been. In particular, she was asked to play-act herself during therapy and to exaggerate her reactions (a standard Gestalt and drama therapy technique). One session involved a role reversal between herself and the therapist, with Sally taking the part of the therapist and the therapist playing the role of Sally in as exaggerated and as humorous a way as he could. A second technique concentrated on her continuing problems with her sexuality. Although she did now have intercourse with her husband occasionally, she still tended to avoid sexual encounter with him for fear of a panic attack. She was therefore advised to use some of the Masters and Johnson techniques of sensate focusing and nondemand pleasuring. She was also encouraged to masturbate (which she reported that she had rarely done) so as to be able to experience high arousal in a situation she controlled. Though much of this work was intended to reinforce earlier sex therapy activity, it was undertaken within a different orientation. Instead of seeking to reduce arousal the therapist sought to find conditions in which arousal could be experienced differently. While the techniques may appear behavioral here, their utility derived from the fact that the therapist presented them as a way of creating "safe" excitement.

To enable Sally to reverse into a paratelic state whenever the beginning of a panic attack occurred, the therapist used a number of tactics. The most successful involved the therapist seeking to change the meaning of the arousal experienced. Instead of encouraging her to feel excitement rather than anxiety, the therapist encouraged her to feel angry, the initial aim being to break the normal transactional pattern of arousal always being experienced as anxiety. This was first used in a therapy session in which the therapist feigned disinterest and became unsympathetic, suggesting that Sally was self-centered and just looking for sympathy and attention. As a result, she became angry. Afterward the therapist explained what he was doing and why he was doing it. In reflecting on this process, Sally said that she had recognized the play acting that was going on and had enjoyed it for much of the time. At the end of this session she felt "on top of the world." The next week she telephoned to say that the depression had lifted and she had had no panic attacks for a week, though both later began to return. What seems to have happened was that Sally experienced her anger in the paratelic state as a form of parapathic emotion (see above), which, because it was a highly arousing emotion experienced in the paratelic state, she was able to enjoy. This had demonstrated to her that her life could be more than an alternation between anxiety and boredom, that a fuller emotional life was possible, and that high arousal was fun and could be enjoyed.

It has been suggested that this treatment initiative can be conceptualized in purely behavioral terms as a form of reciprocal inhibition which utilizes counter-conditioning and response prevention. This is indeed the case if just this segment of therapist behavior is taken in isolation from its other features and if the therapy

was to end there. However, these behavioral interventions were utilized to illuminate the underlying structural features of the client's phenomenological field. Indeed, some time was spent on each occasion the client and therapist met exploring the structural meaning of these experiences.

Such engineered arguments as described above were used occasionally in therapy sessions, as were guided daydreams. The latter were used to evoke a variety of emotions associated with high arousal, including anger. But anger was the emotion that Sally found she could enter into with most ease whenever she experienced a panic attack. For some reason, the induction of the negativistic metamotivational state (which converts anxiety into anger) seemed to make it easier for Sally to remain in or return to the paratelic state. She was therefore advised to role-play anger on a daily basis as a homework assignment. What she was to do was to retire to her bedroom for 20 minutes or so after her husband had gone to work and think of things that made her angry, all the time clenching her pillows while making angry facial expressions. Although initially embarrassed by this, she soon achieved proficiency in this task.

The crucial question was whether Sally could experience the parapathic emotion of anger during a panic attack. She was instructed to attempt to do so whenever she felt a panic attack beginning. If she was at home, she was to go to her bedroom and "act angry" in the way in which she had role-played. If she was in a public place and unable to obtain privacy, she was to "think angry" and clench her fists as hard as she could. If she could not summon up an object to be angry about (e.g., a remark, a gesture, a failure to act) then she was to be angry about the panic attack itself. Initially Sally reported difficulty in doing this, but gradually she was able to develop the skill of being able to do this. As her confidence increased, not only could she bring her panic attacks under control sooner, even stopping them in their tracks, but the attacks themselves seemed to be occurring less frequently. Though there were to be periods of achievement and failure in this time, progress was gradual but sure.

During this treatment phase Sally's husband was invited to meet the therapist so that his support for the treatment program could be secured. This was becoming increasingly necessary since Sally wondered what would happen if he discovered her play-acting in the bedroom or "looking odd" in some public situation. In fact, he was not only supportive, but offered his active help, for example by role-playing arguments with Sally from time to time and even doing so, if this would be helpful, during a panic attack.

Finally, Sally was taught some of the skills necessary for her to be more assertive, argumentative, and "difficult" in everyday life situations. She was also encouraged to develop a social activity program, going out more with her husband and rekindling interests in sports and dancing.

During this phase of therapy Sally became pregnant and gave birth to a second son. This naturally made much of the treatment program difficult to follow, especially late in the pregnancy and directly after the birth of her son. Despite this natural disruption, she was still able to follow the main lines of treatment and found that the attacks, when they did occur, were now manageable. After an 18-month treatment period, it became possible to discontinue regular therapy sessions and to move to a more demand-responsive therapy contract. In fact, over the next two years (i.e., up to the time of writing this chapter) Sally has requested a meeting approximately every two and a half months, indicating the successful nature of her treatment.

Although we may suppose that a number of the tactics used in the pursuit of the overall strategy contributed to the outcome, the anger promotion tactic was the most significant. The possible reasons for its effectiveness are as follows: (a) experiencing anger with some regularity broke up the normal transactional pattern that Sally used to process her experience; (b) since Sally was playing an active part in determining what emotion she would experience under certain conditions, she felt more in control of her emotional life in general; (c) since anger is easier to act out and display than anxiety (for Sally), the anger routine she developed gave her something to "do" with her emotions; (d) the intervention showed her that she did not have to experience anxiety when she experienced high arousal; and (e) Sally learned to discriminate more finely between anger in the telic state and anger as a parapathic emotion, thus permitting her to feel more in control of her emotions and more able to understand and enjoy her emotional experiences.

The result of the intervention was that Sally reversed more regularly between the telic and paratelic states and was able to do so more appropriately than was hitherto the case. In addition, she was also able to induce reversal under certain conditions (notably from the telic to the paratelic state) or to inhibit inappropriate reversal under certain conditions (especially during a sudden surge of felt arousal). Furthermore, this intervention program broke the vicious circle of fearing a panic attack so strongly as to guarantee such an attack occurring—Sally now is angry with the attacks and anger does not induce anxiety for her.

At the point of referral, Sally had been experiencing a panic attack once every day or two, with smaller feelings of anxiety being prevalent each day. Depressive feelings permeated her life. All this was happening despite (or in part because of) her regular use of tranquilizers. At the time of writing, and despite a major family crisis (the suicide of a relative), the situation has improved considerably. Generally, Sally is free of panic, although a flurry of attacks has occurred three times over the last year. She now leads a full and normal life, going shopping regularly, visiting with neighbors, being active in sports. Although she continues to keep her tranquilizers in her purse, she has taken a tablet only on extreme occasions since the treatment phase of therapy began. Her depression has returned on one or two occasions, usually associated with a particularly heavy period. Furthermore, the quality of her sexual relationship with her husband has also improved. All of this may not constitute a complete "cure," but it does represent a substantial improvement.

The reader will have noticed traces of many different kinds of therapeutic intervention including: cognitive reappraisal, rational-emotive therapy, Gestalt therapy, logotherapy, psychodrama, and behavioral techniques. The tactics were selected as part of a strategy and the strategy was decided following a clear understanding of the nature of the client's structural disturbance.

RESEARCH ON THE APPROACH

Unlike many approaches to eclectic psychotherapy, the structural phenomenological approach is based firmly on a particular and detailed psychological theory—the theory of psychological reversals. Since it is so difficult to assess directly the effectiveness of a particular eclectic orientation over and above the effectiveness of particular intervention tactics used (and no such outcome research has yet been completed in relation to structural phenomenology), such a relationship to a psychological theory presents in principle a great advantage. It means that if the underlying theory can be tested, it is possible in this way to bring empirical evidence to bear on the general therapeutic approach involved. Thus, data that support the theory—for example, experimental or psychometric data—*ipso facto* may also be taken to support the rationale for therapy. In the case of structural phenomenology, then, the question arises as to whether and how far the theory of motivation and personality on which it is grounded is in fact supported by evidence.

This is not the place for an extended review of all the research completed to date which is relevant to reversal theory (but see Apter, 1984, and Apter, Fontana, & Murgatroyd, 1985). In his introduction to the theory, Apter (1982) cites over 170 previous studies in such areas as personality, motivation, cognition, and social and comparative psychology which illuminate the way in which this theory can be integrated with a range of existing data from other sources.

One of the main ways in which reversal theory per se has been investigated is through the development of psychometric and psychophysiological measures. The *Telic Dominance Scale* has been used for a variety of purposes, experimental and applied, in many countries and is available in translation in a number of languages. Other scales measuring negativism and mastery dominance are in an advanced stage of development. The data derived from these measures are reported more fully in Murgatroyd (1985).

Svebak and his co-workers in the psychophysiology laboratories at the University of Bergen have thoroughly investigated the psychophysiological nature of the telic and paratelic states. In a series of reports (Svebak, 1982, 1983, 1984, 1985; Svebak, Storfjell, & Dalen, 1982; Svebak & Murgatroyd, 1985) it has been shown that the telic and paratelic states are not just motivational constructs but have a demonstrable biology of their own—the physiology of the person differs between these two states. These findings are discussed in detail in Svebak (1985).

There are, as yet, no direct studies of the therapeutic practices of structural phenomenological psychotherapy within an eclectic tradition.

CLINICAL TRAINING

There are no specific programs for clinical training in structural phenomenological eclectic psychotherapy, though a number of workshops have been held in various countries, and courses in reversal theory have been taught at universities in Canada, Britain, Belgium, and Norway. This section will therefore briefly examine the ingredients that would be needed to make such training worthwhile.

There are three: (1) a knowledge of the place of metamotivational systems in the psychology of well-being; (2) a knowledge of phenomenological methods and procedures for understanding the phenomenal field and its structure when looking at a person's experience; and (3) an ability to interpret the structural qualities of different therapeutic interventions. These three ingredients require trainees to do more than understand the basic themes and ideas of the various schools of thought within psychotherapy (e.g., Gestalt, behavioral, psychoanalytic). Indeed, rather than see specific tactics derived from such approaches as specific to them, the trainee needs to examine tactics as being open to use in a variety of situations provided that their structural qualities are fully understood. That is, the use of a specific intervention tactic needs to be seen as divorced from its origins so that its phenomenological properties and its abilities to affect the structure of experience can be better understood. For example, the therapist needs to be encouraged to regard techniques as being appropriate to different kinds of intervention; thus what might be appropriate for encouraging a paratelic to telic reversal may well be inappropriate for encouraging a reversal in the other direction. The same techniques can also be seen to produce different results when applied to the different kinds of structural disturbance a patient can experience.

This idea is radical: it suggests that trainees need to develop a mastery and competence in the use of skills and the ability to examine the likely and actual structural impact of such interventions without the need to associate the methods with their theoretical origins.

The second radical idea here is that trainees need to develop skills in phenomenological methods—case study, observational work, participant observation, introspection, structure, frame, and network analysis. Rather than seeing these as learning tasks associated with research, evaluation, and assessment, these topics need to be studied as basic tools for understanding the phenomenal field of the person in need. Indeed, these so-called qualitative "research tools" need to be regarded as tools for researching the quality and structure of the client's motivational experience.

The final point we wish to make about training concerns therapists' own understanding of their motives during the therapeutic contract. A therapist who is locked in one state and is unable to reverse is hardly going to be able to facilitate a reversal by another person; equally, a patient who is predominantly paratelic and seeks to become more telic will not be helped by a therapist who makes extensive use of humor, games, and excitement-drama in his work. Therapists must therefore have a thorough knowledge of their own styles and limitations and must also be able to reflect upon the processes they use in therapy with the same clarity as they are able to reflect upon the processes used by their clients. This requires supervision and training using observational screens so that the therapist can obtain feedback as to the structure of the therapeutic process itself.

FUTURE DIRECTIONS

After a long period of increasing proliferation and fragmentation within the field of psychotherapy, we appear to have reached a period when the beginnings of genuine integration and synthesis can be discerned. In this respect, this volume represents a major attempt at integration and a hope for the future.

It is the belief of the present writers that one of the most important requirements, if this process is to continue, is for the development of a conceptual framework into which different therapeutic strategies and tactics can be fitted and, without prejudice, compared and contrasted with each other. Another way of putting this is to say that what is needed is a "meta" language for describing the means and ends of the variety of therapeutic practices now available. Such a language should be inclusive rather than exclusive; it should provide the user with an ability to talk about conscious and unconscious processes; it should be as concerned with behavior as it is with mental life; it should concern social and familial processes just as much as individual psychological processes. In addition, such a metalanguage should not favor one school of therapeutic thought over another. This probably also means that this language should not have developed out of one of these schools but should have a fresh origin neutral to existing systems. At the same time, such a metalanguage should not disguise the real differences between the existing schools of thought. Indeed, only through the use of such a neutral metalanguage will it be possible to see what the real differences between approaches actually are, without being distracted by questions of style or terminology.

We see structural phenomenology based on the theory of psychological reversals as the beginning of the development of such a metalanguage. It is not the only contender in providing such a language, as

a number of other contributions to this volume testify, but does have many features to commend it, as you will now have seen.

There are many ways in which this approach needs to be developed if its full potential as a rationale for eclectic practice is to be realized. Unconscious processes may need to be taken into account far more than they have been; social and political factors that impinge on the phenomenological field of the client may need to be understood in these terms; consideration will need to be given to psychotic disorders as well as those examined here; more attention will need to be given to the mastery/sympathy and the negativism/conformity pair of metamotivational states if the theory is to be more widely understood and applied in therapy. Nevertheless, we believe that structural phenomenology is among the broadest, most systematic, and most rapidly developing approaches to eclectic therapy at the present time. It holds promise for the development of dialogue through a metalanguage between therapies which have hitherto been antagonistic forms of therapeutic practice. At least, we feel optimistic and we are not alone in our confidence in reversal theory (Hetherington, 1983).

REFERENCES

Apter, M. J. (1981). The possibility of a structural phenomenology—The case of reversal theory. *Journal of Phenomenological Psychology, 12*(2), 173–187.

Apter, M. J. (1982). *The experience of motivation—A theory of psychological reversals.* London: Academic Press.

Apter, M. J. (1984). Reversal theory and personality—A review. *Journal of Research in Personality, 18,* 265–288.

Apter, M. J., Fontana, D., & Murgatroyd, S. (Eds.). (1985). *Reversal theory—Applications and developments.* Cardiff: University College Cardiff Press and NJ: Lawrence Erlbaum.

Apter, M. J., & Smith, K. C. P. (1976). Negativism in adolescence. *The Counsellor,* Nos. 23–24, pp. 25–30.

Apter, M. J., & Smith, K. C. P. (1979a). Psychological reversals—Some new perspectives on the family and family communication. *Family Therapy, 8*(2), 89–100.

Apter, M. J., & Smith, K. C. P. (1979b). Sexual behaviour and the theory of psychological reversals. In M. Cook & G. Wilson (Eds.), *Love and attraction: An international conference*. Oxford: Pergamon.

Berne, E. (1964). *Games people play*. New York: Grove Press.

Blackmore, M., & Murgatroyd, S. (1980). "Anne" the disruptive infant. In S. Murgatroyd (Ed.), *Helping the troubled child—Interprofessional case studies*. London: Harper and Row.

Buhler, C. (1959). Theoretical observations about life's basic tendencies. *American Journal of Psychotherapy, 13*, 561–581.

Cornsweet, C. (1983). Nonspecific factors and theoretical choice. *Psychotherapy: Theory, Research and Practice, 20* (3), 307–313.

Dryden, W. (1984). Issues in eclectic practice of individual psychotherapy. In W. Dryden (Ed.), *Individual psychotherapy in Britain*. London: Harper and Row.

Frankl, V. (1969). *The will to meaning—Foundations and applications of logotherapy*. New York: E. P. Dutton.

Hebb, D. O. (1955). Drives and the CNS (Conceptual Nervous System). *Psychological Review, 62*, 243–254.

Heide, F. J., & Borkovec, T. D. (1983). Relaxation-induced anxiety/paradoxical anxiety enhancement to relaxation training. *Journal of Consulting and Clinical Psychology, 51* (2), 171–182.

Hetherington, R. (1983). Sacred cows and white elephants. *Bulletin of the British Psychological Society, 36*, 273–280.

Horowitz, M. (1979). *States of mind—Analysis of change in psychotherapy*. New York: Plenum Press.

Johnstone, K. (1981). *Impro—Improvisation and the theatre*. London: Methuen.

Kubie, L. (1971). The destructive potential of humor in psychotherapy. *American Journal of Psychiatry, 127*, 861–866.

Lazarus, A. (1976). *Multi-modal behavior therapy*. New York: Springer.

Maslow, H. H. (1954). *Motivation and personality*. New York: Harper and Row.

Maslow, A. H. (1971). *The farther reaches of human nature*. New York: Viking.

Minuchin, S. (1974). *Families and family therapy*. London: Tavistock.

Murgatroyd, S. (1981). Reversal theory—A new perspective on crisis counselling. *British Journal of Guidance and Counselling, 9* (2), 180–193.

Murgatroyd, S. (1985). The nature of telic dominance. In M. J. Apter, D. Fontana, & S. Murgatroyd (Eds.), *Reversal theory—Applications and developments*. Cardiff: University College Cardiff Press and NJ: Lawrence Erlbaum.

Murgatroyd, S. (in press). *Counselling and helping*. London: The British Psychological Society and Methuen Books.

Murgatroyd, S., & Apter, M. J. (1984). Eclectic psychotherapy—A structural phenomenological approach. In W. Dryden (Ed.), *Individual psychotherapy in Britain*. London: Harper and Row.

Murgatroyd, S., Rushton, C., Apter, M. J., & Ray, C. (1978). The development of the telic dominance scale. *Journal of Personality Assessment, 42*, 519–528.

Novaco, R. (1973). *Anger control—The development and evaluation of an experimental treatment*. Lexington, MA: D. C. Heath.

Rogers, C. R. (1957). The necessary and sufficient conditions of therapeutic personality change. *Journal of Consulting Psychology, 21*, 95–103.

Svebak, S. (1982). *The significance of motivation for task-induced tonic physiological changes*. Doctoral dissertation, University of Bergen, Norway.

Svebak, S. (1983). The effect of information load, emotional load and motivational state upon tonic physiological activation. In H. Ursin & R. Murison (Eds.), *Biological and psychological basis of psychosomatic disease: Advances in the biosciences*, Vol. 42. Oxford: Pergamon.

Svebak, S. (1984). Active and passive forearm flexor tension patterns in the continuous perceptual-motor task paradigm: The significance of motivation. *International Journal of Psychophysiology, 2*, 167–176.

Svebak, S. (1985). Psychophysiology and the paradoxes of felt arousal. In M. J. Apter, D. Fontana, & S. Murgatroyd (Eds.), *Reversal theory: Applications and developments*. Cardiff: University College Cardiff Press and NJ: Lawrence Erlbaum.

Svebak, S., & Murgatroyd, S. (1985). Metamotivational dominance: A multi-method validation of reversal theory constructs. *Journal of Personality and Social Psychology, 48* (1), 107–116.

Svebak, S., Storfjell, O., & Dalen, K. (1982). The effect of a threatening context upon motivation and task-induced physiological changes. *British Journal of Psychology, 73*(4), 505–512.

van der Molen, P. (1985). Learning, self-actualisation and psychotherapy. In M. J. Apter, D. Fontana, & S. Murgatroyd (Eds.), *Reversal theory: Applications and developments*. Cardiff: University College Cardiff Press and NJ: Lawrence Erlbaum.

CHAPTER 10

An Eclectic Family Therapy

Lawrence C. Grebstein

Family therapy is an approach to psychotherapy that emphasizes the importance of the family in the therapeutic process. Unlike individual psychotherapy, which sees symptom formation primarily as a function of the individual person's intrapsychic dynamics and/or learning experiences, family therapy evolved out of a systems orientation. Contemporary family therapy is based on the dual theoretical assumptions that disruptions in the family system can be a *cause and/or effect* of individual symptomatology. Although present approaches to family therapy differ in theoretical emphasis and techniques, all the major theories share the belief that the family unit is the focus for therapeutic intervention. In fact, this is probably the only thing that family therapists have in common. Family therapy is still a widely adverse field. As Gurman and Kniskern (1981, p. 819) note: "Family therapy is unified only in a belief that relationships are of at least as much importance in the behavior and experience of people as are unconscious events."

Family therapy is still in its early stages of development, having begun as a separate discipline in the 1950s. Most approaches to family therapy reflect the ideas of their founders and are usually based on clinical work rather than research. As Hansen and L'Abate (1982) point out, most theories of family theory are rooted in one of three major antecedents: humanism, psychoanalysis, or behaviorism. However, many of the approaches to family therapy use similar interventions, reflecting a greater amount of overlap or eclecticism in technique than in theory. A recent study of practicing family therapists (Green & Kolevzon, 1982) found that more of them have an eclectic orientation than allegiance to any one approach. In this study, which surveyed over 1000 family therapists, 231 respondents were classified according to their approach. Of this group, approximately 38% were *eclectic*, 28% represented the *communications* approach, 18% followed the *structural/strategic* approach, and 16% were systems advocates.

The data from this study are not the only sign that electicism in family therapy is becoming more prominent. More formal eclectic models which integrate the theories and techniques of family therapy are being published with increasing frequency (Doherty & Colangelo, 1984; Grunebaum & Chasin, 1982; Pinsof, 1983). In a recent discussion of the value of integrating approaches to family therapy, Lebow (1984) indicates that the debates among proponents of various approaches are now being replaced by attention to the similarities among diverse schools of family therapy.

This chapter will present an eclectic approach to family therapy which combines elements of several contemporary systems. It is not intended to serve as a unique, original, or formal model of eclectic family therapy. Rather, it represents an example of how electicism is used in the professional life of a practicing family therapist. Other authors (Haley & Hoffman, 1967; Haley, 1976; Minuchin & Fishman, 1981) have described a variety of family therapy techniques. Much of the material in this chapter overlaps information presented by these authors and others, even though they are not generally labeled as eclectic family therapists. This chapter does not attempt to provide an all-inclusive review of the literature on eclectic family therapy. It is an attempt to describe how I select from the various theories and techniques of family therapy and to present the rationale for these choices.

BACKGROUND

A family of four is seated around a kitchen table having supper. The family consists of a father, mother, and two sons, ages seven and 16. The family is involved in the usual and uneventful small talk that goes on during meals. The conversation begins to get heated when the topic turns to money and quickly escalates into a loud quarrel between the husband and wife. It frightens the younger son to hear his parents argue because they seldom do. The mother is an outgoing, nurturant, and emotionally expressive woman. The father is a hard-working, kind, and quiet man. They ordinarily treat each other with consideration, caring, and respect. But when they argue, it all changes. They trade taunts and insults in loud and angry voices. It is more than the little

boy can stand. He quietly slips away from the table and goes and sits on the stairs leading to the second floor, out of sight of the rest of the family. Here he listens to the argument and weeps quietly, expressing his pain and the pain of his family. After a short time, his absence is noticed, and his mother finds him on the stairs. She asks him why he is crying. He tells her he can't stand it when she and Daddy fight like that. She tells him not to be upset, that mommies and daddies argue now and then, but that they aren't really mad at each other. It does not make sense to him how they can yell at each other like that and not be angry, but he says nothing because they have stopped fighting. She makes him laugh with a joke and coaxes him back to the table with the promise that they won't argue any more.

Family therapists will recognize that the little boy in this illustration was playing the familiar role of the "parental child." A parental child engages in behavior usually expected of the adults or parents in the family, such as breaking up fights or holding the family together. It has been suggested that parental children grow up to become family therapists. In this case it is apparently true. I was that seven-year-old boy. It was at that point, when I learned that I had the power to stop my parents from arguing, that I became a family therapist, even though I would not complete my formal education and training until many years later. In fact, it was only after I had been practicing family therapist for a number of years that I was able to make the conscious connection between my role as a parental child in my family of origin and my decision to become a family therapist.

In retrospect, I recognize that the background for this approach evolved from certain experiences I had both prior to becoming a psychologist and early in my professional career. These experiences impressed upon me the important influence the family can have on the behavior of any of its members and the necessity of including the family in therapy in order to both change and maintain change in individual persons. Three experiences stand out in my memory as being especially significant in shaping my development as an eclectic family therapist.

First, prior to becoming a psychologist, I learned to be an effective confidante, go-between, and peacemaker for my parents during and after their infrequent but awful arguments. The incident described above is my clearest recollection of a specific incident but is representative of the role I would play in the family until I left home. This role was in part situationally determined. My older brother left home to go to college (3,000 miles away) when I was 11, leaving me as the only other person in the household besides my parents and the beneficiary of the parental child role.

A second incident occurred when I was working as a counselor at a summer day camp. I noticed that one of the children in particular got along fine during the day but would often return the next morning in a belligerant, irritable, and cranky mood. One day I asked this youngster why he came to camp every morning in such a lousy mood. His answer suggested that his home life was undoing much of the positive impact of camp. It was not a startling revelation to learn that his family life was affecting him adversely. What impressed me was the dramatic change in his behavior from when he arrived in the morning to when he left in the afternoon. It was clear from what he described that the positive support, encouragement, and compliments he received from his peers and counselors at camp was being replaced by blame, criticism, and punishment at home.

The third incident occurred during play therapy with an adolescent boy who had been referred to the local community mental health clinic because he was terrorizing the classroom. Psychological testing of the youngster had revealed that underneath his "tough guy" facade was an insecure and inept boy with little self-confidence and low self-esteem. One of the major goals in therapy was to give him the opportunity to be successful at some activity other than mischief with the hope that this would help raise his level of self-esteem. To accomplish this goal, we had been playing a game of skill in competition with each other. After several attempts, he beat me and went home feeling triumphant. He returned the following week with a chip on his shoulder and acting once again in a hostile and belligerent manner. After several attempts on my part to find out what caused the sudden change in his behavior, he gave me the explanation. His alcoholic father had been home the night of his victory, one of the father's infrequent evenings at home. When my client proudly informed his father of his accomplishment, his father replied: "You couldn't beat anybody at anything. The doc must have let you win!" I now understood the reason for the boy's sudden change back to his old behavior. I also saw the power of the family. In one sentence, a father was able to undo months of psychotherapeutic work.

The point of these examples is to indicate that eclectic family therapy developed out of my growing realization of the importance of the family in influencing the behavior of its members, an attempt to understand my clients, and my desire to be more effective in my therapy with them. The eclecticism evolved out of the dual realization that no one theory is adequate for understanding all the problems within families and no one therapeutic approach is adequate for dealing with them.

My introduction to formal training in family therapy came relatively late in my professional development. Although the idea of dealing with the entire family appealed to me even before becoming a psychologist and I consulted with parents in my predoctoral training at a child guidance clinic, the notion of working with an entire family together on a continuing basis did not occur to me until I attended a workshop on family therapy with Walter Kempler, a California-based psychiatrist. I was spending my sabbatical leave at the University of Bergen, Norway, and Kempler was invited to present a weekend workshop on family therapy by a group of Norwegian psychotherapists who were interested in advancing their knowledge of psychotherapy. Kempler is a well-known experiential-Gestalt family therapist who was living in Oslo, Norway at the time. His approach in the workshop was unusual and engaging. He made a few comments about the importance of working with the whole family, particularly of direct emotional engagement and confrontation by the therapist, and stated that his approach was best illustrated by example. He then showed us a videotape of a family therapy session with himself as a therapist.

Kempler is a charismatic and powerful therapist whose work with families is both impressive and provocative. I was awed and frightened by his clinical skill and courage in confronting people and issues in the family. His level of emotional self-disclosure and directness went beyond anything I or the other workshop participants had experienced. When we asked how we could achieve comparable impact, Kempler indicated that there were no shortcuts. You had to be there yourself. The result was that the rest of that workshop and a follow-up workshop several months later became marathon personal growth groups for us led by Kempler. The workshops had a profound and powerful effect on me, personally and professionally. They were the single most important factor in my decision to become a family therapist.

When I returned to the United States, I became a "self-taught" family therapist in which I combined work with families with reading and periodic workshops on different family therapy approaches. More extensive formal training did not come until my next sabbatical leave, which I spent as a fellow in family therapy and family research at the Center for Family Research with David Reiss, Peter Steinglass, Steven Wolin, Marion Usher, and their colleagues, taking seminars, doing research, and working with families under supervision. During that year, I read Epstein and Bishop's newly published article on the McMaster model of family functioning. This work, with its emphasis on practical problem solving, closely fit my own beliefs about working with the family. While I was away, Epstein and Bishop came to Rhode Island, so that when I returned, I was able to join Nathan Epstein's supervision group for approximately two years and learned his approach of problem-centered systems therapy with families.

THE APPROACH

The basic reason for adopting an eclectic approach to psychotherapy is to find an effective intervention for the presenting problem. The clinician with a large repertoire of theory, assessment techniques, and intervention tactics has a greater knowledge base for understanding clinical problems and a wider range of choices of treatment options. My style of eclectic family theory emerged from a background rich in theory, research, and clinical technique that I have attempted to integrate in a continuing effort to understand and help a variety of families. The approach is rooted in the hypothesis-testing model of the experimental psychologist and the observational-inferential model of the clinical psychologist. Conceptually, it draws heavily on neo-Freudian psychoanalytic theory, especially that of Sullivan and Horney, humanistic psychology, phenomenology, social learning theory, and social psychology. Technically, the assessment and intervention strategies combine elements of client-centered, behavioral, experiential, and problem-solving approaches. Within family therapy, the model draws most heavily from the work of Bowen, Minuchin, Epstein and Bishop, Kempler, and Satir. Their specific contributions will be described in greater detail later in the chapter.

The cornerstone of my approach is the belief that psychotherapy can be a significant and useful adjunct to life, but it cannot serve as a substitute for life. The purpose of any psychotherapy is to help people live their lives more effectively. I believe the therapist can best accomplish this by helping the family to accept responsibility for its actions, by keeping the therapy relevant to their values, goals, and desired changes, and most of all, by keeping therapy brief. In families where there is no agreement about values and acceptable behavior, achieving some sort of consensus or acceptable compromise may become a goal of therapy. The therapist must have sufficient life experience and professional knowledge to understand the family and a large enough repertoire of intervention skills to be able to help the family achieve its goals. The psychological concept of individual differences, so well established in the study of personality, exists for families as well. No two families are exactly alike. The popular phrase "different strokes for different folks" reflects the need for an eclectic family therapy.

Eclecticism offers a number of advantages to the family therapist. The primary advantages are flexibility, adaptability, and diversity. An eclectic approach allows the family therapist to choose from existing theories, research, and clinical information to provide a broad knowledge base for dealing with families that vary in geographic, socioeconomic, ethnic, and religious backgrounds; developmental stages; problem-solving styles; and other factors. Similarly, electicism gives the family

therapist a wider choice of intervention strategies and techniques from which to choose. This is important at this particular stage of development in the history of family therapy. Family therapy, if not in its infancy, is still in childhood. Available research on process and outcome, while encouraging, is still minimal (Gurman & Kniskern, 1981; Pinsof, 1983). It would be premature at our present state of knowledge to conclude that any one approach for dealing with families has demonstrated its superiority.

The disadvantages of an eclectic approach are the potential for confusion and uncertainty, especially for the inexperienced therapist. A danger is that the therapist can become overwhelmed by too many choices. Anyone who has ever tried juggling can appreciate the difficulty of doing family therapy in comparison with individual therapy. With each added ball, the juggler's task becomes more difficult. With each added person, the therapy becomes more complex. With each additional approach, the therapy becomes even more complicated. Doing family therapy requires amassing and integrating a considerable body of knowledge, including: factors affecting individual personality development, psychopathology of adults and children, family developmental stages, parenting skills, group dynamics, and systems theory. In addition, the therapist must have personal skill in relating to persons of vastly different ages, from young children to grandparents. Eclecticism demands that the clinician thoroughly digest different approaches to family therapy and make some attempt to find how each can contribute. It is important to choose carefully and selectively so that the final result is a cohesive and integrated approach, rather than a random assortment of ideas or hodgepodge of different techniques. This requires more than just conceptual knowledge of different approaches. It requires thoughtfulness. Developing an eclectic approach to family therapy that fits the therapist takes time. It cannot be rushed or hurried.

The successful eclectic family therapist, like the experienced individual or group therapist, is not one who always knows what to do in a given situation. Expertise is not defined by having all the answers. The expert is one who recognizes options for trying different interventions and has criteria for evaluating whether the therapeutic tactics are working. Much of the work in successful psychotherapy is not done during the psychotherapy session. It is done between the sessions when the therapist has the opportunity to digest the contents of the session, think about what is going on and what needs to be done, and makes plans for future interventions. This is especially true in family therapy because of the large amount of therapeutic material to process. The specific form of eclectic family therapy to be presented here combines different theories and techniques. The therapeutic process is seen as consisting of several simultaneous dimensions, including (1) the theoretical orientations the therapist uses to understand both the family's dynamics and the psychological functioning of the individual family members; (2) technical factors, such as specific tactics used in assessment and therapy; (3) therapist variables, such as the extent and style of the therapist's use of self in the interview; and (4) situational or practical considerations that impact on the family therapy process.

THEORETICAL CONSIDERATIONS

At the core of all family therapy is the belief in the reciprocal interaction that exists between an individual and the family. I find *family systems theory* as developed by Murray Bowen (Bowen, 1976; Kerr, 1981) to be most useful for under-standing the relationship between individual personality functioning and family dynamics and for understanding the historical development of family relationships. The *structural family therapy* approach developed by Minuchin (1974) provides a framework for organizing present family dynamics into clear and distinct constructs. The structural approach is especially useful for helping the family therapist solve one of the practical problems of family therapy: how to organize and keep track of all the specific and complex interactions that take place in a family.

In dealing with families, therapists are presented with a tremendous amount of data and isolated bits of clinical information. Theory is important in providing guidelines for what data to collect and how to integrate it in a meaningful way. Important questions to be considered by the therapist include: In what ways did the client's family of origin contribute to the etiology of the presenting problems or current situation? How is the family presently contributing to the maintenance of alleviation of the problem? Are the presenting problem(s) highly influenced by family factors or are family influences minimal? Have there been significant events in the family's history that might be related to the current problems?

TECHNIQUE

In discussing therapeutic technique, it is important to recognize the difference between therapeutic interventions at different levels. For example, Epstein and Bishop (1981) differentiate *micromoves*, the specific intervention tactics used by the therapist, from *macromoves*, which define the major stages of treatment. Skill level interventions are not unique to any form of family therapy. There are a large number of therapeutic tactics which can be employed equally well by family, group, individual, or marital therapists. These include interventions such as modeling, interpreting, inquiring, reinforcing, and a number of other specific therapeutic actions. If use of different therapeutic techniques was the only criterion used for judging eclecticism, then most of the major contemporary family therapy approaches would have to be labeled eclectic. For example, Minuchin and Fishman (1981) have compiled a lengthy and detailed list of specific family therapy techniques which are not restricted to structural family therapy.

An effective eclectic family therapist not only has a large repertoire of specific intervention skills but is able to organize and conceptualize the process of therapy into definable stages and areas of family life requiring alteration. My own approach combines a wide variety of different tactics ranging from highly structured behavioral techniques, such as modeling and behavioral rehearsal (role playing), to very unstructured interventions, such as experiential confrontation. In general, I combine the practical problem-solving focus of Haley (1976), the interpersonal interaction of the structural approach (Minuchin, 1974; Minuchin & Fishman, 1981), and the problem-centered orientation of Epstein and Bishop (1981), which encourages the family to actively serve in defining and solving its own problems in collaboration with the therapist, who functions as an informed guide.

In choosing among the wealth of available techniques, the eclectic therapist can be guided by questions such as: What technique offers the greatest chance of achieving the particular goal being addressed? What techniques can the family accept and respond to? What tactics can the therapist use comfortably? Is the therapist skilled and experienced in the use of a particular intervention? Is there clinical and/or research data which suggest that specific techniques may or may not be effective with the problem(s) at hand?

THERAPIST VARIABLES

The therapist's use of self is a controversial variable. While family therapists tend to agree on the importance of the therapist's use of self as an important instrument for assessing family process, they disagree markedly on how the therapist should act in the session. The disagreements primarily involve how active the therapist should become with the family. As a group, family therapists tend to be more active than individual therapists because the nature of family therapy requires more activity on the part of the therapist to maintain control of a session that includes several people. However, there is still considerable variability, with some therapists being more charismatic and others advocating more low-key styles. Similarly, from the standpoint of emotional development, schools of thought range from those advocating a close and affiliative relationship (changing the family from within) to those suggesting a more distant and emotionally disengaged approach (changing the family from without).

What distinguishes the eclectic therapist from the noneclectic therapist is the ability to change styles to fit the family rather than vice versa. Many families seeking help, like individual clients, already think or feel there is something wrong with them. They do not need the additional feelings of inadequacy that can result from incompatibility with the therapist. Therapists can ask themselves: Can I appreciate this family's pain? Does my own life experience enable me to understand their problems? Am I behaving in ways that they can understand and accept? An eclectic approach utilizes the full range of therapist behavior depending on the family, clinical context, and nature of the problem. More specific guidelines for therapist behavior will be discussed later in the chapter.

SITUATIONAL FACTORS

The final set of factors that influence the therapeutic process are the situational constraints and/or practical considerations accompanying the therapy. These include issues such as: whether or not the family has come for therapy voluntarily or under duress (such as court mandated), whether the family recognizes that there is a justifiable need for the referral or is there to satisfy an external referring agent (e.g., school guidance counselor or pediatrician), or whether the family is being seen in conjunction with inpatient treatment (for medical or psychological problems) of one of its members or is being seen on an outpatient basis. All these factors have an effect on the therapist's approach to dealing with the family.

The eclectic family therapy approach presented here is based on combining elements of several existing schools of family therapy with theory and interventions taken from areas of psychology outside of family therapy. The approach fits into what Weiner (1983) has labeled a *complementarity stance*, in which the clinician tries to draw from different theories and methods. The model can be characterized as *synthetic* (Goldfried, 1981; Prochaska & DiClemente, 1984), to the extent that different theories are integrated, and *committed* (Prochaska, 1984), to the extent that it is concerned with finding the most effective ways to do psychotherapy. It is basically a clinically based system which relies heavily on the therapist's knowledge, experience, skill, and judgment. The fundamental beliefs of the system apply to family therapy but are not limited to family therapy. At the core of the system is a basic belief in the importance of the therapist's honesty, commitment, willingness to practice what he/she preaches (modeling), and willingness to self-disclose.

ASSESSMENT PROCEDURES

Family assessment from an eclectic perspective is an extensive and thorough procedure which involves obtaining information about family systems and the persons in the family. As in individual therapy, family therapists of different orientations vary not only in how an assessment is made but in the amount of importance attributed to assessment. A basic belief of the model being presented here is that a thorough and detailed assessment is an essential prerequisite for successful therapy. This section will describe several assessment techniques that can be used to determine the extent and nature of the problems in the family, whether treatment is needed, and what therapeutic procedures to use.

Nathan Ackerman, one of the founding fathers of family therapy, states that the assessment of family problems occurs at three levels: the family level, the individual level, and at the point of interaction between the family and individual. A thorough assessment involves obtaining information about a number of variables, including: specific family conflicts; the nature and effectiveness of the family's methods of coping with conflict; verbal and nonverbal communication patterns; the overt and covert expressions of emotion in the family; the extent of agreement or disagreement about important family issues, such as values and acceptable behavior; and differences between the family's potential and actual functioning (Ackerman, 1958, 1966).

In keeping with these suggestions, the family assessment process to be described here includes obtaining information about the nature of the referral problem and any other problems that exist in the family; a three-generational family history and significant prior events; current family functioning on a number of relevant dimensions; interaction patterns among family members; and specific behavioral goals and changes that the family, or any of its members, would like to make.

The assessment of a family begins on the telephone at the time of the initial referral. The first decision to be made is who to include in the first interview. Some family therapists insist that all persons living in the present household be included in the first interview, while others will work with part of the family. Although there are clinical and theoretical rationales offered for different choices about who to include, there is no research evidence to suggest that any one approach is best. My own preference is to ask that the entire family be present for the first interview. This request often flushes out family problems that might not otherwise be mentioned, at least initially. The following case illustration provides an example of how this can occur.

A woman called requesting help for her 16-year-old daughter whom she described as acting out in a variety of ways, such as poor behavior in school, violating curfews, drinking, and other unacceptable behavior. When I asked her to bring in the rest of her family, she said she would be glad to bring her other two children but that her husband would not be able to make it because he was a commercial fisherman who was often at sea for three or four days at a time. I stated that my schedule was flexible and she could call me when she knew he would be in port. She made some other excuses which I countered. Finally, she stated (in what sounded like a tone of exasperation), "I might as well tell you that my husband is an alcoholic, and I don't think he'll come in." To which I replied, "Then why are you referring your daughter?" The conversation ended when I told her I would be happy to see them if she could get the whole family to the inter-

view. A couple of weeks later I saw the family, including the father, for an initial interview.

In this case, the mother's desire to exclude the husband from the interview reflected both the reality of the family situation (the husband was rarely at home) and, as was confirmed later, her reluctance to stay married to him. This is not an atypical situation. Frequently parents refer a symptomatic child when the child's behavior may be an expression of difficulty in some other family subsystem, such as the marriage. This is supported by research which indicates that referral to a child guidance clinic is primarily a function of parental reactions (Shepard et al., 1966). Gurman and Kniskern (1978) review additional research which suggests that focusing on the child alone is insufficient and troubled children often reflect troubled marriages. It has been my experience that parents most often object to bringing in young children, particularly if they are not involved in the presenting problem. Ironically, the children are often the most helpful in revealing what is going on in the family.

The first part of the initial family assessment interview is what Haley (1976) has described as the social stage and involves introductions and the usual greeting rituals. When this is completed, the therapist moves on to more specific assessment techniques. While family therapists may vary in how long they allow the family to "chitchat," it is at the point when the social stage has been completed that family therapists are likely to use assessment procedures reflecting different theoretical systems or clinically based preferences. I favor a comprehensive assessment which includes four main components: (1) a detailed description of the family's presenting problem(s); (2) a family history, including a genogram (Guerin & Pendagast, 1976); (3) a thorough assessment of the family's current functioning on a number of basic parameters using the McMaster model (Epstein, Bishop, & Levin, 1978; Epstein & Bishop, 1981); and (4) observing family interaction patterns from the viewpoint of structural family theory (Minuchin, 1974).

It is important to point out that it is not always possible or necessary to do such an extensive or detailed assessment. The assessment process can be modified in accordance with the circumstances of the presenting problem, specific characteristics of the individual family, and clinical judgment of the therapist. The process described below is a model for a comprehensive assessment which incorporates aspects of several major schools of family therapy. It is designed to obtain a thorough and multidimensional assessment of the family.

The assessment interview begins with introductions of all family members present. My own style is to introduce myself individually to everyone in the family, including the children, and shake hands with each person. In the case of preverbal youngsters or infants, I often make some sort of additional contact. The point is to communicate to the family that all of its members are important. After introductions, I ask the family what their understanding is of the purpose of the visit. This allows any misconceptions to be brought out into the open and clarified.

The substance of the assessment begins with a request for a description of the presenting problem. As Haley (1976) has noted, this serves several purposes. It informs the family of a shift from the social stage of the interview to the business at hand and sets an appropriate tone for the remainder of the interview. It reassures the family by indicating the therapist's willingness to understand and deal with the family's troubles in an immediate, direct, and forthright manner, even though asking about problems may raise the family's anxiety level. It is important to observe who takes the initiative in presenting the problems and whether there is agreement or disagreement about the problems among the different family members. Regardless of who makes the initial presentation, the therapist should ask every family member attending the session for his or her opinion about the problems in the family before ending any discussion of the presenting or other problems.

The next phase of the initial assessment involves either taking a three-generational family history using a genogram (Guerin & Pendagast, 1976) or assessing the family's current functioning based on the McMaster model (Epstein, Bishop, & Levin, 1978). The order in which this is done varies with the particular family. One of my main objectives during the assessment is to keep the level of anxiety or threat as low as possible. This is in keeping with Harry Stack Sullivan's (1954) belief that patients are anxious enough when they come for therapy, and there is no justifiable excuse for a therapist to intentionally raise a person's anxiety level. A second objective is to have the interview make sense and appear relevant from the family's perspective. Both the genogram and McMaster assessment tend to be non-threatening procedures which complement each other and can be used interchangeably. The genogram is a structured family history, usually covering three generations, which provides a diagram of the "family tree" and chronology of significant life events. It is especially useful for discovering potentially "toxic" events in the family's history, such as deaths, divorces, and "nervous breakdowns." The genogram is based on Bowen's (1976) theory that the effects of major losses and other significant events can be transmitted across generations if not adequately dealt with by the family, thus creating the potential for developing significant family psychopathology. The following case illustration provides a good example of how a genogram can reveal clinically significant material from the past that might not otherwise surface.

A mother called requesting an appointment because she was concerned about the recent "unusual" behavior of her son, a man in his early twenties. She stated on the phone that she did not think he would come in voluntarily. An initial family session was scheduled and was attended by the entire family, except for the son, who refused to come to the interview. After obtaining a complete description of the parents' concerns, which were supported by an older sibling, a genogram was done. The genogram disclosed that the oldest son had been killed a few years earlier in a tragic accident while still in his twenties. The son had been outstanding in a number of ways and had been expected to join his father in the family business, eventually taking it over. The family's ethnic background attaches great significance to the role of the eldest son. The father was a self-made man with a good business. His eldest son had adopted many of his father's values, and the two of them had been very close.

After learning of the son's death, the therapist directed a series of specific questions to the father about how he had coped with his son's death. The questions constituted both a standard assessment for signs of clinical depression and a general assessment of the father's functioning. The father's answers clearly suggested that he had many of the symptoms of a serious and long-standing depression. This man, who had been a vigorous, energetic, and hard-working man for all of his adult life, described a pattern of withdrawal, loss of interest in work and community affairs, low energy, sadness, and unresolved grief. It is interesting to note that the changes had been sufficiently gradual and subtle so that the man had little awareness of his depression. The therapist ended this part of the assessment by commenting that the father had apparently put his own life on hold since the death of his son. The assessment then turned to finding out how the death had affected the other family members. It was discovered that the youngest son's symptoms began to appear about a year after his brother's death. At the next interview, the father spontaneously reported that he had thought a lot about what the therapist had said. He stated that he now realized this was true and that it was time to "bury his son" and get on with the business of living.

This case illustrates two important points: first, how a genogram can be used to uncover important clinical information from the past that might not otherwise be revealed, at least initially; second, that the processes of assessment and therapy are interwoven. Although assessment and therapy can be conceptually separated, they are often intertwined in actual practice. Therapy begins during the assessment phase, and assessment continues throughout therapy as the clinician gathers new information about the family.

Just as it is important to obtain a detailed family history, it is equally important to assess current family functioning. The McMaster model of family functioning (Epstein, Bishop, & Levin, 1978; Epstein & Bishop, 1981) is a comprehensive system for obtaining a detailed description of the family's current functioning. The McMaster model is based on the study of nonclinical families (Epstein, Sigal, & Rakoff, 1962) and provides a structured and thorough way of exploring the family's present behavior. It is very useful for revealing not only areas of dysfunction but also family strengths and competences which can be used as a basis for future interventions. The method is straightforward, widely applicable to a variety of problem families, and particularly useful for inexperienced family therapists because of its clear and structured procedures.

The assessment phase consists of four stages: orientation, data gathering, problem description, and compilation of a problem list. In the *orientation stage*, as noted earlier, the family is informed of the purpose of the interview, and any problems or misunderstandings they have are clarified. The *data-gathering stage* is the focus here and consists of obtaining information about the problems in the family and current family functioning in six areas: problem solving, communication, affective responsiveness, affective involvement, behavior control, and roles. *Problem solving* refers to the family's usual way of resolving both instrumental (task-oriented) and affective (feeling-related) problems. *Communication* involves assessing the family's style of exchanging information. Particular emphasis is placed on exploring communication patterns along the parameters of clear versus masked communication and direct versus indirect communication. *Affective responsiveness* is the capacity for the family members to respond emotionally to each other. Assessment on this dimension involves clinical judgments about the range, appropriateness, and degree of emotional expression and experience in the family. A closely related but separate dimension is *affective involvement*, which refers to the extent to which family members value, care for, and show interest in each other. A family can range from overly close, enmeshed relationships (symbiotic involvement) to detached, distant, uninvolved relationships. *Behavior control* describes the methods a family has for monitoring the behavior of its members. The means of discipline used by the parents is an example of behavior control. *Roles* are the "recurrent patterns of behavior by which individuals fulfill family functions" (Epstein & Bishop, 1981, p. 466). The assessment of roles provides useful information about how the household is run, divisions of labor, and task assignment. While all of these dimensions provide important and useful information about the family, roles are especially sensitive to the many changes that have occurred in families as a result of recent social changes, such as two-career marriages, divorce, and single parenting. The dimensions are not only useful for the information they provide, but the specific questions associated with each of the dimensions often "stir up" interesting family interactions which provide additional information about family interactions.

The *structural* approach to family therapy (Minuchin, 1974), unlike the two previous approaches, does not have a formal assessment procedure which is separate from the process of therapy. This approach places more emphasis on the ongoing interactive process of assessment and therapy in which the family therapist observes various aspects of family interaction and conceptualizes them in structural terms. Family structure refers to the repetitive or characteristic organization of the family interaction patterns. Family structure is defined in terms of various subsystems through which the family functions. Subsystems can be based on function, generation, or interest. For example, typical family subsystems include the spousal subsystem, sibling subsystem, and parental subsystem. These subsystems operate according to unwritten "rules" which affect who participates in the subsystem and how the subsystem operates within the family. These "rules" serve as *boundaries* which describe how the family subsystems interact. For example, boundaries can be rigid, in which case the persons are distant from each other and the subsystems impervious. Families with authoritarian parents have rigid boundaries. At the other extreme are enmeshed boundaries in which there is no separation of subsystems. Incest families are prototypes of enmeshed families. Well-functioning families tend to be characterized by clear boundaries, in which the subsystems are appropriately separate and allow for reciprocal influence and interaction. The structural approach is useful in family assessment by providing a conceptual framework for classifying and summarizing complex family interactions.

Additional specialized assessment procedures may be used when the situation calls for them. For example, if the referral problem relates to the sudden or unexpected death of a child, a special assessment scale such as the SIDS (sudden infant death syndrome) family adjustment scale (May & Breme, 1982) may be a useful adjunct. Other specialized assessment scales or structured interview formats can be incorporated as needed. It is important to point out that the eclectic family clinician must be familiar with relevant information about a variety of specific clinical phenomena as well as having a knowledge of general assessment procedures. Issues such as serious physical illness, death, child or spouse abuse, geriatric problems, and physical handicaps often require knowledge about the particular problem as well as about family dynamics.

A careful assessment is an important first step in dealing with a family. It is often a lengthy and time-consuming procedure but can ultimately shorten the total length of time needed for treatment by extracting the essential issues. If properly done, it can help the clinician determine whether therapy is needed, whether the family is amenable for treatment, or whether some other procedure is indicated. Unlike individual assessment, less attention is paid to diagnosis, particularly in terms of individual symptomatology. One reason for this is that the systems approach is to some extent incompatible with an emphasis on individual symptoms. More important, the assessment should provide information about the family's strengths and deficiencies, its need and desire for treatment, and its suitability for family therapy. A detailed assessment is the essential first step in formulating a viable treatment plan. If the therapist fails to do an adequate assessment, therapy may begin prematurely or be conducted in a manner that is unacceptable to the family. It is important to determine in the beginning, insofar as possible, what a family needs and wants, rather than to forge ahead and discover in the middle of therapy that the goals of the family and therapist are at odds. The model presented here incorporates aspects of three of the current approaches in a manner that is complementary and pro-

vides more information than any one of the systems by itself.

TREATMENT

Eclectic family therapy is as much a conceptualization as it is a combination of techniques. What distinguishes family therapy from individual psychotherapy is the inclusion of family members other than the symptom bearer in the therapy sessions, at least in spirit. In some situations and in some approaches to family therapy, family members may not attend the actual therapy sessions but their ghosts are always there. The family is included in the therapy even when their bodies are absent. The eclectic family therapist operates at the conceptual and technical levels simultaneously. Conceptually he or she chooses theories, models, or explanations that best fit a particular clinical situation. Technically, he or she chooses intervention strategies that are most likely to alter the designated problem behavior. In the case of the committed professional eclectic family therapist, these choices are not whimsical, random, or exclusively intuitive or spontaneous. Rather, they are based on a firm knowledge of family therapy technique and theory, research findings, and clinical experience. In successful family therapy, as in competent individual or group therapy, much of the therapist's work in therapy is done between sessions in the form of thinking and planning. This is especially important in eclectic family therapy where the combination of ideas and techniques from different approaches requires careful integration and cohesion if it is to work.

TREATMENT APPLICABILITY

Although there are individual differences of opinion among family therapists as to what kinds of clinical problems are most effectively dealt with through the use of family therapy, there are no diagnostic groups that are excluded a priori. This is especially true when family therapy is used as a collateral or adjunctive treatment in addition to being used as a primary treatment. In the formative years of family therapy, during the 1950s and 1960s, research on the relationship of family factors to schizophrenia was a major interest (Bateson et al., 1956; Bowen, 1960; Haley, 1959, 1965; Jackson, 1960; Jackson & Weakland, 1959; Laing & Esterson, 1964, 1967; Lidz, 1958; Wynne et al., 1958; Wynne & Singer, 1963). Finding a cure for schizophrenia was the original goal of many of the founders of the family therapy movement. However, the application of family therapy has grown well beyond its origins, and serious psychopathology is no longer the only criteria for the use of family therapy.

Common sense, supported by increasing amounts of research and clinical experience, suggests that any problem affecting one member of a family will have an impact on the rest of the family. Physical illness, loss of a job, loss of a friend or a lover, or a psychologically diagnosable disturbance are all examples of problems that can have profound effects on an individual. And anyone who has ever lived in a family knows that when one person is "bummed out," for whatever reason, the other people in the household are affected by it. Family therapy recognizes this fundamental fact and accepts it as a basis for therapeutic intervention, if, in fact, psychotherapy is needed.

With the increase in the lay public's awareness of family therapy in recent years, particularly among the middle class in the United States, more prospective clients are calling and requesting family therapy at the time of the initial contact. In my own clinical experience, the most frequent single problem that motivates the request for family therapy is genera-

tional conflict between adolescents and their parents. This is expressed in a variety of ways, including: power struggles over autonomy; parental feelings of ineffectiveness regarding discipline; disputes about household tasks and responsibilities; disagreements about choice of friends, social activities, or clothing styles; unacceptable sexual behavior; drug and alcohol use; and traditional adolescent-parent battles. An interesting paradox is that while adolescent problems are the most common complaint of parents requesting family therapy, an almost equally frequent occurrence is the threatened refusal of the adolescents to participate. The next most frequent request for family therapy is for problems with preadolescent children, usually behavior problems at home and/or in school.

Any discussion of the applicability of eclectic family therapy has to differentiate family therapy as defined by *concept* and family therapy as defined by *technique*. Conceptually, family therapists differ in their beliefs about which family subsystem (e.g., marital or sibling) may be the most important causal element in the development of clinical problems, whether individually based symptoms are a *cause* or an *effect* of problems in the family system, and whether or not family problems reflect disturbances in the family system. Not all family therapists embrace systems theory. For example, Nathan Ackerman, who many persons regard as one of the most important figures in the development of family therapy, did not believe that systems theory could be successfully applied to family dynamics (Ackerman, 1972).

Technically, family therapists can be distinguished by how they work. Family therapists have been somewhat flippantly categorized as belonging to one of two schools: the "all-together-nows," who insist that all members of the family attend the therapy or there is no therapy, and the "we'll take whoever comes" school. The latter group, as their label suggests, try to get the entire family to attend but do not insist on it as a precondition for therapy and will in fact work with family subgroups or even individuals. However, it is important to emphasize, as Kerr (1981) has noted, that family therapy is not distinguished by how many people are in the room but by the way in which the therapist thinks about the problem.

An eclectic family therapist does not adhere a priori to any one particular approach, but makes choices about attendance, technique, and theory in keeping with the individual clinical situation. Therapy sessions with a given family may consist of the entire family or any combination of family members, including extended family, such as grandparents, aunts, uncles, and live-in lovers. The therapist may combine different theories to understand a case or may choose a single theoretical framework for an entire case. In treating a case, the therapist may include a variety of techniques, such as interactional, behavioral, paradoxical, strategic, or problem-solving tactics, or stay within one particular framework.

Decisions about which specific therapeutic interventions should be used are usually made on the basis of what the therapist knows. This knowledge is based on training in particular approaches, prior clinical experience, familiarity with research findings, and borrowing relevant theory, techniques, and approaches from other areas of applied psychology (e.g., group dynamics). When the therapist is not aware of any intervention of known utility, decisions about what to do are usually made on the basis of clinical intuition or trial and error. Hopefully, the latter occurs infrequently. A major reason for adopting an eclectic approach is that it increases the therapist's repertoire of interventions.

Family therapy is not appropriate when: (1) the family cannot be together in the same room; (2) the family *does not want* to resolve its problems as a family unit; or (3) the therapist decides that it may be more effective and/or expedient not to use family therapy. These different situations are perhaps best illustrated through clinical examples.

The first case involves a middle-aged woman who was brought, against her will, by her husband and eldest married daughter to an outpatient clinic following an apparent psychotic episode. The precipitating incident occurred earlier that day when she began shouting obscenities at and physically attacking other customers at the local supermarket. When I tried to interview the family, it was extremely difficult. The woman would constantly interrupt and contradict, challenge and dispute whatever her husband and/or daughter said and launch into verbal tirades. She threatened never to speak or have any contact with either of them again once she was released from treatment. It is interesting to note that in the middle of one of these outbursts she reached over, touched me on the knee, and said with lucidness and compassion: "You poor young man, I feel badly that you have to listen to all this. I know you're trying to help and I'm not really mad at you." When I separated her and talked with her alone, she showed none of the agitation or rage that characterized her behavior in the family interview. However, as soon as I brought her family back into the room, she would explode into her uncontrollable fits of anger.

This clinical vignette is an example of a family that cannot be together. The amount of disruption that occurred when I tried to conduct a conjoint interview was too much for me to control. While this is sometimes an issue of therapist skill and/or experience, in other cases there is simply too much family disorganization either at a particular time or in general to allow conjoint family therapy to proceed.

An example of a family *not wanting* to resolve its problems through family therapy is illustrated by the following situation.

The family consisted of a mother and three daughters, two teen-agers (aged 16 and 18) residing in the home and one older daughter in her twenties who lived out of the home. The presenting problem was poor school attendance and minor acting out by the middle daughter. The first assessment session revealed that there were a variety of problems in the home centering around conflict and bickering between the two teen-agers and a general breakdown in the mother's ability to control the household.

This case was being treated using the problem-centered systems approach (Epstein & Bishop, 1981) in which the family contracts to work on a specific problem list. Therapy consists of having the therapist assign homework tasks which the family can do to facilitate the resolution of the problems. If the family fails to do the homework, this leads either to outside consultation and/or termination. In this case, one goal of therapy was to resolve the bickering and increase communication between the two teen-aged daughters. They had been assigned a homework task of having one five-minute conversation with each other for each of five days before the next therapy session. The first week this was assigned, they did not do it and had a variety of excuses. The second week they modified the task and had one conversation for 30 minutes, rather than the prescribed five conversations for five minutes each. Since this was not the first homework assignment they failed to complete as designed, this led to a discussion of the original contract and their motivation for therapy. The family clearly stated that they had come to realize that they did not want family therapy and were more interested in finding ways to separate from each other and be more independent rather than learning to get along better. So family therapy ended.

The question of when family therapy is not indicated or appropriate is a difficult one to answer because the whole point of eclectic family therapy is that it allows the therapist maximum flexibility to include a variety of techniques within the family therapy. This flexibility goes beyond simply varying who attends the actual sessions and includes the incorporation of specific interventions, such as behavioral techniques, within the therapy. In some instances, such as drug and alcohol addiction, psychosis, serious physical illness, and delinquency, hospitalization or incarceration of the identified patient may be necessary. In these instances family therapy is primarily utilized as an adjunctive treatment in which the patient may or may not be included in the family sessions. In other cases individual therapy sessions on a regular or intermittent basis may be included along with the family therapy. Minuchin (1974) points out that one of the most common mistakes inexperienced family therapists make in working with disturbed children is that the individual needs of the child are neglected because of the emphasis on the family. Very often disturbed children require individual psychotherapy along with the family therapy.

Sometimes families are not available as a result of distance or death. This does not preclude a family therapy approach. If, in the judgment of the therapist, unresolved family issues are involved, this can be accomplished by using the "coaching" techniques of Bowen (1976, 1978) in which a person is seen individually but is helped to differentiate from his/her family of origin. In the final analysis, the question of when another form of therapy and/or another therapist should be utilized is a clinical judgment that is determined primarily by the willingness of the therapist to honestly evaluate the effectiveness of the treatment and accept the need for a change in treatment strategies and/or therapists. In some instances, the appropriate decision may be that no psychotherapy will be helpful and treatment is not indicated.

TREATMENT STRUCTURE

Eclectic family therapy can be applied in any setting but is most typically used on an outpatient basis, in either private practice, mental health clinics, or other human service agencies. The physical characteristics of the room in which the therapy is conducted are important. The best room is one that has been set up as a comfortable living room with both separate chairs and at least one couch included. In addition to helping put the family at ease, this arrangement allows the therapist to assess existing family relationships through seating patterns and to alter structural relationships in the therapy by changing seating relationships. For example:

A family consisting of a depressed, seriously ill father, a strong, martyrlike mother, and an uninvolved 12-year-old daughter had seated itself with the mother between the father and daughter. The mother dominated the conversation during the session. At one point, the father was talking about his waning will to live, nodded toward his daughter, and stated that she was the only reason he did not kill himself. The mother interrupted and tried to say something in behalf of the father. The therapist's intervention was to have the daughter change seats and sit next to her father, on the side away from her mother. He then instructed the father and daughter to discuss their feelings about his living or dying. With an outpouring of tears, the daughter exclaimed: "I don't want you to die, Daddy!" For all practical purposes, it was the first thing she had said in the entire interview.

Seating placement is important for assessment as well as intervention. It is important to see who chooses to sit together on the couch in distinction to choosing individual chairs. Does the family argue over preferred seats or take them easily? Are seats assigned by a parent or chosen freely? Do the family members remain in the same seats for each session or do they move around? These are just some of the questions that can be answered if the room is properly designed and furnished.

It is also important, particularly during the early or assessment stage of therapy, to visit with the family in their own home. Home visits provide a wealth of information about the family that might not be readily obtainable from office visits and also help establish the therapeutic relationship by indicating the therapist's commitment to the family and willingness to visit with them on their "home turf." It is a well-known fact in competitive athletics that teams often play better at home than away. Similarly, families often feel more comfortable in their own home and are more likely to behave in ways which are more representative of their characteristic functioning. Obviously, home visits are not always easy or practical to make and may be particularly difficult from an economic viewpoint in private practice because of the greater amount of time involved. Nevertheless, home visits can provide a valuable addition to the therapist's understanding of the family, reveal strengths that might not otherwise be apparent, and help develop the therapist's relationship with the family. Consider the following illustration:

A middle-aged man brought his much younger wife into therapy because he felt she drank too much alcohol. The initial session was stormy and characterized by the husband's criticism of the wife's functioning and by the wife's denial, her anger at being identified as the "sick one," and her feelings that the therapist was probably on the same "side" as her husband because he was a man and of the same religious and cultural background as the husband. After several sessions, a visit was scheduled for the couple's home. The therapist noticed, to his surprise and in contrast to the husband's criticism, that the home was well kept and well organized and the couple's two children, who were not at the earlier sessions, obviously had a good relationship with their mother. The wife took pride in her housekeeping and felt much more secure in her own home. As a result, she was much less defensive and less irritable. She served coffee and home-baked pastry, which gave the therapist the opportunity to compliment her. The wife did in fact drink too much. The home visit was useful in obtaining a more accurate assessment of her strengths than the husband had presented and in being able to use these strengths as a basis for designing future therapeutic interventions.

Unlike individual therapy, family therapy is often difficult to conduct in the traditional "50-minute hour." This is particularly true during the assessment stage when it is necessary to collect a lot of information. Also, if adolescent or teen-age children are involved and/or both parents are working, finding a common time to meet can be a major problem. For these reasons, many family therapists schedule visits less frequently and of longer duration. In my own private practice, I try to schedule families once a week initially to establish continuity but often shift to every other week after treatment is underway. The typical session is 75 minutes, but flexibility is the rule here as well. I rarely continue sessions for more than two hours but on unusual occasions have had sessions go on for as long as four hours (when relatives came from long distances and/or the session was designed to deal with a specific issue that could be resolved in a single session). At the other extreme, I have met with families for as little as 15 minutes in the termination phases of therapy where the sole purpose was to follow up on the family's progress. Family crises, on the other hand, may involve more frequent contact until the crisis is resolved. Issues such as frequency and length of sessions are usually negotiated with the family and are determined by the particular characteristics of each family's situation. The length of treatment is unlimited and varies with the clinical facts of each case but in general tends to be short term, between 10 and 15 sessions for the active phase of therapy. Often there are spaced follow-up sessions to monitor the family's progress.

INTERVENTION STRATEGIES

As noted earlier, the model of eclectic family therapy being presented here combines existing techniques and theories both from within family therapy and from other therapeutic modalities. The choice of particular techniques is based on the clinical repertoire of the therapist, what clinical experience and research has demonstrated to be effective, and, in the absence of such data, what appears to make logical and common sense in the context of existing theory and the clinical problem. At present there is little research evidence available to support matching of specific therapeutic approaches with particular problems. Selection of a specific technique must be done primarily on the basis of theory and clinical judgment.

Based on the clinical and research literature and my own clinical experience, it appears that different approaches may lend themselves better to different problems. For instance, family systems theory and therapy (Bowen, 1976, 1978; Kerr, 1981) is effective for dealing with issues of autonomy and separation of individuals from their family of origin; functional family therapy (Barton & Alexander, 1981) and behaviorally oriented family therapy (Patterson, 1971, 1976) are useful for delinquent and acting-out behavior in children and adolescents; structural family therapy (Minuchin, 1974; Minuchin, Rosman, & Baker, 1978) has been used successfully with some psychosomatic problems in the family; strategic and communication-based systems of family therapy (Haley, 1972, 1976; Watzlawick, Weakland, & Fisch, 1974; Satir, 1967; Satir, Stachowiak, & Taschman, 1975) are useful for dealing with communication problems in the family; paradoxical approaches have been applied to schizophrenic families by the Milan group (Selvini-Palazzoli, 1978) and to rigid families by the Rome group (Andolfi et al.,

1983); and problem-centered system therapy (Epstein & Bishop, 1981) is appropriate for short-term therapy with functioning families that have specific problems. Most of these and other approaches to family therapy have been developed as general approaches to family therapy rather than specific treatment formats for particular problems.

Eclectic family therapy consists of developing a familiarity with these and other major systems and integrating them for use with different problems. This can be done in one of two ways. First, the clinician can select a particular method or approach to use with a given family. Second, the different methods and conceptualizations can be combined for use with the same family to deal with different problem areas. When the second approach is taken, the therapist must be careful not to jump around or change so much that the family and the therapist end up confused. While the therapist may choose a particular intervention based on its apparent clinical utility, sometimes the most effective interventions are unintentional. Serendipity not only is a well-established basis for discovery in science but occurs in therapy as well. With perhaps greater frequency than I would like to acknowledge, clients will report that a particular comment I made in the previous session was especially helpful or thought-provoking or unsettling. When I ask them what it was, I sometimes discover that I have no conscious memory of the particular intervention.

There is no specific basis for matching families and therapists in eclectic family therapy. The only requirement is that the therapist have sufficient clinical experience for dealing with the expressed problem and the therapist can form enough of an empathic relationship with the family to minimize any value judgments that might interfere with treatment. The life experience of the therapist is probably more of an issue in family therapy than it is in individual therapy. I can remember once early in my career as a therapist, before I was married and had children, being asked by a frustrated father if I had children following what must have appeared to him as an insensitive intervention. My answer was something to the effect that I did not have children of my own but that my clinical experience with children made up for my lack of experience in raising them. Now that I have children, I do not believe that any more. It is more difficult for therapists without children to be effective family therapists and for single persons to be effective marital therapists. Not having the requisite life experience can limit the therapist's capacity for empathy, accurate understanding, and realistic interventions.

Successful therapy does require that the therapist have credibility in the eyes of the family, and this can be established in a variety of ways, sometimes unexpected. I was once called by a mother for help with her suicidal son because she had heard that I was "athletically oriented" and she thought this would be an important factor in dealing with the case. The issue was that her son, who had a chronic illness that sometimes affected his coordination, was being neglected and harassed by his high school coach and some teammates. My "athletic orientation" originated from the fact that I coached recreational youth soccer in the community as a hobby, and the referring physician had informed the mother of this. One of the advantages (or disadvantages) of practicing in a small community is how knowledge of one's nonprofessional characteristics can affect perceived professional competence.

Recently, the question of specific matching of therapist and clients has become more of an issue. For example, issues such as the suitability of heterosexual therapists for gay clients and same-sex versus different-sex therapist and client are receiving more attention. These issues can be extended to family therapy as well. For example, can nondivorced therapists deal sensitively with reconstituted families? Probably the best solution to questions of relationship compatibility at the present time, if they exist for either the therapist or the family, is for them to be fully discussed in the initial stages of therapy. In beginning with a new family in therapy, part of my orientation is to inform them that the assessment phase is a mutual one in which the family and I will evaluate our potential for relating and working together.

Eclectic family therapy, because of the integration of different approaches and techniques, requires the therapist to help the family maintain a clear focus. In keeping with the model established by Epstein and Bishop (1981), I believe in clarifying the nature and stage of the therapy so that the family not only knows what is going on but consents to the process in advance. This is done not only through an initial orientation but through periodic reorientations whenever a different stage of therapy (i.e., assessment, contracting, treatment, or termination) is entered. Through these orientations, the family is kept apprised of what will be happening and what to expect during each stage of therapy. This facilitates a cooperative working relationship between therapist and family. This is not to say that each time the therapist plans on introducing new techniques that he or she announces it to the family and explains its purpose. But whenever necessary, the therapist should clarify not only the stage of therapy, but the general procedures and their objectives.

Engagement is both one of the most difficult and important aspects of family therapy. As noted earlier, some families specifically seek out family therapy. However, many persons call for appointments not expecting to be asked to bring in the

rest of the family. Generally, I use the common-sense rationale that there are at least two sides to every story as the basis for including additional family members and as a way of engaging the family. I usually acknowledge very early that conflict and disagreement is inevitable and goes on in most families, and that it is natural to believe that your own perspective is the correct one. My experience has been that a straightforward, matter-of-fact, and comfortable explanation of the rationale of family therapy is sufficient to engage most families even though they may be initially anxious because of the unfamiliarity of the procedure. Candid acknowledgment of the problem(s) in the family and empathic identification of the family's discomfort and pain are additional ways of engaging the family.

A problem for all therapists is what to do when you are stuck. This usually means the therapist does not know what to do in a given situation or the family is reluctant to go along or participate for some reason. This latter situation is often described as "resistance." Although resistance is a phenomenon universal to all psychotherapy, it is particularly likely to occur in family therapy because, as Anderson and Stewart (1983) have pointed out: "Since most families present with one symptomatic member, other family members may fail to see the relevance of involving the whole family, or fear that requests for such family involvement amount to the therapist's blaming them for their problem member's difficulties" (Anderson & Stewart, 1983, p. 2). Anderson and Stewart (1983) suggest a number of specific ways of both anticipating and overcoming resistance. The general approach I adhere to in dealing with problem behavior in therapy is to recognize it, identify the behavior in question for the family without necessarily defining it as resistance, and try to obtain an understanding of what is motivating the behavior. When this is accomplished, clues are often provided as to how best to deal with the situation. When all else fails and I am truly stuck, I say this to the family. This usually stimulates some reaction that helps therapy to proceed.

THERAPEUTIC ERRORS

Eclectic family therapy, like all eclectic psychotherapy, is a process of educated trial and error. It attempts to find the best fit between therapeutic interventions and clinical problems. It is this very search for the most effective interventions which can lead to the most common errors. This can result in choosing techniques on a purely spontaneous basis without sufficient attention paid to how the particular intervention fits into the overall treatment plan. Another common error is for the therapist to change tactics too quickly or too frequently. This is most likely to occur with difficult families, with inexperienced therapists, and with therapists who have low frustration tolerance or excessively high needs for achievement.

Mistakes in therapy are inevitable. Yet some therapists worry that if their clients discover they are imperfect, their therapeutic effectiveness will be diminished. Although it may be true that some clients want to perceive their therapists on a pedestal, my own view is that the most serious technical error a therapist can make is to deny or cover up errors. This is especially true in family therapy where the therapist is often dealing with several persons simultaneously who are in conflict. Often there is no one way of doing things that will satisfy everyone, and willingness to compromise is essential for success.

One of the main advantages of the eclectic approach is the availability of a variety of theories and techniques. It is important that an eclectic therapist not be too facile in their use. Eclectic thera-

pists must resist what Kaplan (1967) has called "the law of the instrument." In its simplest form, this law states: "If you give a small boy a hammer, it will turn out that everything he runs into needs pounding" (Kaplan, 1967, p. 325). Similarly, eclectic therapists must resist the indiscriminate use of their tools.

THERAPIST BEHAVIORS

The therapist's role in eclectic family therapy is analogous to the guide used in mountain climbing. The therapist serves as a consultant about which problem to tackle first, what are the best paths to take, and how to prepare for the journey. But, as in mountain climbing, the family members do their own hiking. If they get tired or overwhelmed, they can stop and rest. The therapist does not attempt to carry them up the mountain, but helps them figure out the way and leads them on their journey. Sometimes families choose to climb mountains that the therapist may feel they are unable to climb. It is important for the therapist to point this out. Only an incompetent or irresponsible guide would take someone on a journey he was unable to master.

The therapist's tasks are to observe, understand, design intervention strategies, help the family implement them, and lead the family during the sessions by serving as a model. The family's task is to actively participate in the process, experiment with new ways of relating, and practice agreed-upon homework assignments. In eclectic family therapy, the process is not limited to the therapy sessions. As much work is done between sessions as is done during the sessions. Homework assignments are often designed by the therapist and family in collaboration in order to facilitate the process of change and problem resolution.

It is not possible in the limited space

here to delineate a "cookbook" of eclectic therapist behaviors. On the contrary, to attempt this would be to contradict a basic tenet of the approach outlined here: namely, that the essence of eclectic family therapy is for the therapist to be able to choose conceptions and interventions that best fit the individual clinical situation. However, there are some guidelines that can be established.

First, do not make assumptions. All families are unique, despite whatever apparent similarities they may have to other families. Just as individuals resent being categorized or stereotyped, so do families.

Second, do not go too fast. It is easier to eat quickly than to digest quickly. Meaningful therapy is based on the completeness of the digestion process, not the speed of the consumption process. This is particularly true in family therapy where one is dealing with the collective digestion process of several persons simultaneously. In teaching family therapy to inexperienced persons, I use the "traffic light" concept of therapeutic behavior. When things are flowing smoothly, this is like a green light and the therapist can proceed without hesitation. When in doubt, for whatever reason, this is like a yellow light and the therapist should slow down and proceed with caution. When something happens to create therapeutic uncertainty, this is like a red light, and the therapist should stop and assess the situation carefully before proceeding.

Third, do not be afraid to acknowledge mistakes or uncertainty. Most people coming for therapeutic help are not perfect and often are relieved to discover the therapist is not perfect. Success in therapy is not based on the therapist's never being wrong but on his/her willingness to recognize and acknowledge mistakes and unproductive gambits and to correct them. More than one client family has commented to me that one of the aspects of therapy they found most reassuring and

helpful was my ability to laugh at myself and my willingness to share my own uncertainties and mistakes, both in therapy and from my own family life.

Fourth, be as honest and direct as possible in your communications with the family. In discussing patterns of communications within families, Satir (1972) distinguishes four types of communications that are characteristic of persons when they are under stress and feel their self-esteem is threatened. These patterns are placating, blaming, computing, and distracting. These kinds of communications are more likely to exist in unhealthy or troubled families than in well-functioning families. A fifth type of communication, which Satir (1972) labels "leveling," occurs when all parts of the message—facial expression, voice quality, body language, and words—are consonant. Leveling occurs when self-esteem is not threatened and the relationships are easy, free, and honest. According to Satir, only the leveling type of response has the capacity to "heal ruptures, break impasses, or build bridges between people" (Satir, 1972, p. 73). Leveling is difficult to achieve and requires honesty and courage. It cannot be faked. As Satir states: "Being a leveler enables you to have integrity, commitment, honesty, intimacy, competence, creativity, and the ability to work with real problems in a real way" (Satir, 1972, p. 77). What Satir has called leveling, I call "talking straight" and believe it is one of the most important functions of the therapist. By using leveling kinds of communications, the therapist is able to model the very behavior he or she is trying to help the family develop.

The fifth and final guideline for therapist behavior is based on the therapist's unique position as an outside person who joins the family. Probably the most important function that the therapist can serve is to share with the family in as honest and direct a manner as possible his/her experience of what it is like to be in the family. This often is done with a particular family member in response to specific behavior. Consider the following illustration.

A mother called requesting help for her 15-year-old son who had become increasingly belligerent, uncooperative, and disrespectful. However, for the two weeks immediately prior to her call, he had stopped talking altogether and had been totally silent in the house. I told her I would be happy to see her son if she would bring the rest of the family as well. She objected to bringing her 10-year-old son and could not see how he could contribute to the therapy. We discussed this briefly, and she reluctantly agreed to bring him. I met with the mother, father, and four children, aged 20, 15, 14, and 10. From the outset of the session, the mother was difficult to deal with. She attempted to monopolize the session and acted in a demanding, controlling, and antagonistic manner to the rest of her family. On several occasions, I tried unsuccessfully to stop her from talking in order to direct questions to other family members. Each time, she would interrupt and try to take over the conversation despite my hand signals to her and repeated requests to not interrupt. Finally, in exasperation after another interruption, I turned to her and said in a loud and firm voice: "Look, I've asked you several times now to please not interrupt so others in the family could have a chance to talk. I'm fed up with your constant interruptions. Now just sit there and shut up and I'll tell you when you can talk." Now, everyone in the family was silent. But I noticed a slight smile on the face of the identified patient, and in a few minutes he began to talk. Apparently, he now felt "safe" enough to express himself since someone had finally neutralized his mother's power. Two other points of interest occurred during this session. First, the husband later complained that he could not have a meal in peace because of his wife's incessant chattering and complaining. To which she replied, "If I talk too much, why don't you just tell me to shut up like the doctor did!" Second, the 10-year-old started to weep during the session and said his tears were because he thought his older brother hated him because he always teased him and hit him. This turned

out to be an important issue that no one in the family was aware of. It would not have come out had the mother not brought her youngest son to the session.

I typically do not tell people to shut up in therapy; this was probably the only time in my professional life I have ever done it. However, that spontaneous act represented exactly how I was feeling at the moment and how the rest of the family often felt around the mother. The son's "symptom" of silence was his attempt to counter the mother's excessive control, dominance, and self-centeredness. My outburst expressed the family's collective frustration.

This case illustration is an example of the therapist's use of self to create and provide therapeutic movement. Kempler (1973, pp. 72–73) states that for a remark to be therapeutic, four conditions must be met:

1. There must be a struggle.
2. The other—the listener—must be significant.
3. The words must be the right words.
4. The words must ride on the crest of the corresponding affect.

Kempler (1981, p. 8) describes experiential therapy as characterized by "exploration, experiment, and spontaneity." The experiential encounter is the essence of the therapist's contribution to family therapy, and the therapy session is a "laboratory in which we have new experiences" (Kempler, 1981, p. 8). The therapist's task is to encourage an atmosphere in which the verbal exchanges between participants are accompanied by a flow of the underlying feelings. "I encourage this atmosphere by doing it, being it, and sometimes by exploring verbally my difficulty in doing it—not by talking about (broadcasting or announcing) this desired atmosphere" (Kempler, 1981, p. 8).

Although I agree with Kempler's emphasis on the importance of therapist spontaneity and honesty, this must be tempered with restraint and occur in a supportive context. Previous research (Strupp, Fox, & Lessler, 1969; Truax & Carkhuff, 1967) indicates that therapist qualities of warmth, acceptance, understanding, attentiveness, and respectfulness are important ingredients in successful psychotherapy. I agree with Yalom (1975, p. 113) who, in describing the behavior of the group therapist, states:

The leader sets a model of interpersonal honesty and spontaneity; however, he keeps in mind the current needs of the members and demonstrates behavior which is congruent with the development stage of the group. Total disinhibition and unrestrained expression of all feelings is no more salubrious in therapy groups than in other forms of human encounter and if faithfully enacted may lead to ugly, purposeless, destructive interaction, such as Albee portrays in *Who's Afraid of Virginia Woolf.* The therapist must set a model which includes responsibility and appropriate restraint as well as honesty. The concept of the totally analyzed therapist who experiences no destructive feelings and fantasies toward his patients is, in my experience, illusory. But the judicious use of the leader's own feelings is an invaluable part of his armamentarium.

This active and direct use of self, especially when it involves the therapist's communication of his/her own feelings, is in marked contrast with the therapeutic behavior used in two of the other main components of the eclectic approach described here. Both the Bowen and Epstein and Bishop approaches discourage the active communication of therapist affect for different reasons. In the Bowen approach, the therapist's role is to serve as a "coach" to the family and deemphasize the role of emotionality, not only for the therapist but for the clients as well. In fact, even direct interactions between clients are discouraged in favor of directing all communication to the therapist so that emo-

tional arousal can be minimized. This is consistent with the main theoretical orientation of Bowen that excessive emotionality causes a lack of individual differentiation and contributes to triangulation in relationships, both of which are the exact opposite of the goals of therapy and of healthy functioning. Epstein and Bishop's approach places the emphasis on family problem solving. Therapist self-disclosure and emotional responsiveness are minimized. As Kantor and Neal (1985) point out, a pivotal difference among modern family therapy approaches represents the types and amount of distance that the therapists should establish between themselves and their clients. It is a challenge for eclectic family therapists to find ways of integrating and resolving these wide differences of opinion.

The issue of therapist self-disclosure, emotional responsiveness, and directness of confrontation is complex and not easy to describe succinctly. Previous research on encounter group therapy (Lieberman, Yalom, & Miles, 1972) has demonstrated that most therapeutic casualties occur with "charismatic" therapists. In emphasizing the importance of therapist honesty, straight talk, and the experiential encounter, I do not intend to advocate reckless or insensitive behavior on the part of the therapist or satisfaction of the therapist's narcissistic needs at the expense of the family. Spontaneous confrontation must always occur in the context of support and astute clinical judgment about what the situation and participants can tolerate. My own style is frank, open, direct, and self-disclosing in terms of giving feedback about my own internal reactions when I think it can be "heard" by the family. It is always offered in the service and spirit of therapeutic benefit. At times, however, when the "yellow" light is on, there is risk involved since it is not clear what the impact of the feedback is likely to be. A colleague of mine characterizes marital relationships as being of two kinds: low risk, low gain and high risk, high gain. Similarly in therapy, the amount of gain is often tied to the amount of risk the therapist and the family are willing to take. This is very difficult to assess or make statements about apart from a specific clinical situation. The important point is that the therapist's behavior be within acceptable limits to the family or the family will probably not stay in therapy.

MECHANISMS OF CHANGE

Any discussion of mechanisms of change in family therapy must be considered largely hypothetical or speculative at this time because of either the lack of research or inconsistency of findings on specific change factors. However, clinical observation and some research does suggest some variables that may contribute to the change process. It will remain for future research to either confirm or disconfirm these variables or suggest additional ones.

To begin with the simple and obvious, having the family together contributes to the family's change in therapy. Gurman and Kniskern (1981) state that the inclusion of both spouses, particularly the father, has a powerful effect on treatment outcome. These same authors also note that there are limited data that a few markers of family interaction style are associated with positive outcome. The specific factors they identify are: low authoritarianism, openness to disagreement, low coercion and competitiveness, and low role traditionality.

Some ideas about the mechanisms of change in family therapy can be gleaned from an analysis of group therapy. As Yalom (1975) points out, the group resembles the family in many ways, and group and family therapy can be considered as highly similar processes. Yalom (1975) describes 12 "curative" factors in group

therapy that overlap significantly with factors identified by Corsini and Rosenberg (1955). The curative factors described by Yalom (1975) are: the installation of hope, universality (realization that one is not alone in having problems), the imparting of information (this includes specific skill training and didactic information), altruism (the results of being helpful to others), development of socializing techniques, imitative behavior, interpersonal learning, group cohesiveness, catharsis, and existential factors (which represent several issues, such as responsibility, basic isolation, and recognition of mortality). It is interesting to note that one of the curative factors is identified as the corrective recapitulation of the primary family group, a factor that is one of the basic goals of family therapy.

In one of the few discussions of eclectic family therapy described in the literature, Grunebaum and Chasin (1982) present a model for integrating present approaches to family therapy. Their approach, like the one presented here, is a synthetic model which emphasizes the complementarity and integration of existing systems. According to them, all family therapy techniques can be classified into three primary mechanisms of change: *understanding, transformation, and identification.*

Understanding includes the interpretation of historical material, clarifying current interaction, and encouraging intimate disclosure with the purpose of increasing the family's knowledge of the origin and nature of its current difficulties. Specific techniques used within this approach include family pictures, diaries, role-play reenactments of prior events, videotaped replays of therapy sessions, family sculpting, and other creative techniques designed to increase the family's understanding of its past or present behavior.

Transformation involves the therapist's strategic direction of the family with the goal of modifying and correcting its dysfunctional behavior and structure. Examples of transformation-based techniques are overt directives, such as task prescription, or covert directives, such as paradoxical instructions.

Identification refers to those approaches where the therapist attempts to change the family by serving as a living model, designing and participating with the family in emotional experiences in order to facilitate new identifications and to alter existing or old destructive loyalty bonds and introjects. Specific techniques used within this approach include a variety of therapist behaviors, such as playful antics, designed to alter family behavior or bringing into the therapy sources of early identification, such as parents or grandparents.

Grunebaum and Chasin (1982) recommend that in order to be effective, the techniques used in each of these approaches should be consistent with the principles that underlie the corresponding ways of learning. For example, therapists using approaches based on understanding should be engaging and clear teachers. Techniques involving transformation require that the therapist pay close attention to motivation, reinforcement (reward and punishment) contingencies, and family members' cooperation. When identification is the primary mode, the therapist must pay attention to the kind of model he or she is setting for the family. While family therapy approaches tend to use primarily one of these categories of change mechanism, family therapy can utilize all three, and an eclectic approach, in fact, does.

The study of therapist variables and change in psychotherapy is primarily associated with the measurement of improvement or deterioration. As Gurman and Kniskern (1978, 1981) point out, there is ample clinical and empirical evidence that negative changes occur in both family and marital therapy. While family therapy in general or specific family therapy approaches in particular cannot be identified at this time because of the lack of controlled studies, Gurman and Kniskern (1981) suggest that the similarity of findings with previously documented work in individual and group therapy indicates the kind of family *therapist* who is likely to induce negative therapeutic effects. Such a therapist is characterized by poor relationship skills, directly attacks highly sensitive family issues early in therapy, provides little structure or support for the family in therapy, and fails to intervene in or interpret family confrontation. Their capsule description is highly similar to some of the concerns discussed in the last section.

In a study of families who terminated or continued in therapy, Shapiro and Budman (1973) found that the only factor which differentiated continuers and terminators was the therapist's activity level. Over two-thirds targeted their therapist's activity level as making a positive contribution to their therapy. Pinsof (1983), in his review of family therapy process research, concludes that the research focusing on the family therapist behavior has not produced "a clear or consistent body of substantive findings" (Pinsof, 1983), p. 714).

Research evidence about the mechanisms of change in family therapy is limited and inconclusive at this time. The major conclusion, which must be documented with future research and clinical observation, is that change in therapy is a function of both the techniques used by the therapist and the client(s) readiness to change. Existing clinical and research data suggest that a variety of factors contribute to change in therapy. Eclectic family therapy, by utilizing a combination of a variety of mechanisms of change, increases the likelihood of therapeutic success.

CASE EXAMPLE

The following case illustrates the use of brief eclectic family therapy with a patient presenting with symptoms of anxiety and depression or psychological distress. The patient was self-referred and seen in an outpatient clinic associated with a medical school in a large city. The family was seen for a total of 15 sessions.

Presenting Problem

The patient was a 37-year-old black woman, Mrs. R., who was accompanied to the initial interview by her husband. Mrs. R.'s presenting complaints included difficulty in concentration and memory; irritability and "jumpiness"; loss of interest in leisure activities such as reading and television; sleep difficulties, both falling asleep and remaining asleep; and a significant lowering of her sexual drive. Mrs. R. dated the onset of these symptoms to her recovery from open-heart surgery for replacement of a defective valve two years earlier. Further questioning revealed that she had problems in getting along with her eight-year-old daughter and that the conflict between them had been increasing in both frequency and severity.

Family Constellation and History

The family consisted of Mrs. R., who worked as an accountant technician prior to her illness; her husband, a 32-year-old black man who worked as a truck driver; Mary, Mrs. R.'s eight-year-old daughter from a previous marriage which ended in divorce; and Jane, aged 22 months, a child of the present marriage. Mrs. R. was the middle child of three. Her mother died of kidney disease when Mrs. R. was three years old. Her father was still alive, remarried, with three additional children, one of who died at age 24. Mrs. R. had an older sister, aged 39, a younger brother,

35, a stepsister, 28, and a stepbrother, 24. Mr. R. was the second youngest of seven siblings, of whom one was deceased. He was unable to give the names and ages of all of his surviving brothers and sisters. Both his mother and father were deceased. His mother died of heart disease at age 59, when Mr. R. was 27. His father died of cirrhosis of the liver when Mr. R. was 22. Mrs. R. stated that she was very upset by the death of her younger stepbrother but denied any other problems in her family of origin. Similarly, Mr. R. stated there were no problems related to his family of origin. Both Mr. and Mrs. R. stated that they came from very strict homes and were worried that they were too lenient with their own children.

Assessment

Mr. and Mrs. R. were seen together and separately in the first interview. This interview consisted of obtaining a description of the presenting problems and taking a genogram and family history. Two additional assessment interviews included the two children. These interviews were used to obtain more information about the family's current functioning and problems. The assessment followed a modified version of the McMaster model and used structural concepts as a basis for organizing the observed family interactions. These sessions were videotaped.

Mental Status and Impressions

Both Mr. and Mrs. R. were neatly dressed and well groomed at the time of the initial interview. They were well oriented in all spheres and did not indicate any unusual ideation, hallucinations, or other signs of serious psychopathology. Despite her complaints of low energy and depressive symptoms, Mrs. R. was energetic, active, animated, and impressed me as a highly intelligent woman with considerable insight and sensitivity. Mr. R. was more restrained and less verbal than his wife but also impressed me as a thoughtful, sensitive, and caring man. Mary, the oldest child, was initially inhibited and shy. She exhibited several signs of anxiety and tension including rocking in her chair, restlessness, and irritability. She would frequently interrupt her mother when she disagreed with her and showed a low tolerance for criticism. This was expressed in the form of sulking, pouting, and being short-tempered with her younger sister. Jane, the youngest, was a highly energetic child who would run around the room trying to become the focus of attention. Despite their obvious annoyance at her antics, neither parent was able to set limits with her very effectively, although they both tried. Collectively, the family all showed a "short fuse" with regard to tolerating frustration and inhibiting anger. They were all easily annoyed by each other and quick to express it. Mr. R. was physically affectionate with Jane and more willing to interact with her spontaneously. It was clear that Mary was the more neglected and scapegoated child and was in more open conflict with both parents, although it came out in different forms. She would actively challenge and disagree with her mother whereas she would respond to her stepfather by withdrawal and giving him the "silent treatment." Despite these problems, it was clear that this was a basically competent family with a number of strengths, both individually and collectively, and that they had the potential for much better functioning as a family unit.

Formulation and Treatment Plan

The problems in this family were perceived as existing in three primary areas: *relationships, parenting, and couple issues*. In the area of relationships, Mrs. R. was overinvolved with Mary, and much of their conflict had to do with her trying to control Mary's life. Mrs. R.'s self-perception was that of a dominant and controlling woman who was often in conflict with others. She did not like this quality in herself and saw her daughter Mary as being "just like me." Mr. R. was underinvolved with Mary. There was a lot of sibling rivalry between the two youngsters with Mary feeling that she was loved less than her younger stepsister and was often unjustly blamed for problems caused by her sister. There were also residual effects of Mary's feelings of loss related to her mother's long absence from the home during her hospitalization. A goal of therapy was to bring these issues out in the open and alter the ways in which the family members perceived and related to each other. Specifically, the goals were to establish more distance between Mrs. R. and Mary and to bring Mr. R. and Mary closer together.

With regard to *parenting*, the situation was one of Mrs. R. ineffectively using authoritarian methods to get Mary to behave differently primarily with regard to homework and eating. Mr. R. adopted a more laissez-faire attitude and left all the parenting and discipline to Mrs. R. The goals in this area were to help Mary take more responsibility for her own weight control and homework and to teach her and her mother how to communicate about these topics with less friction. A second goal was to help both parents be less indulgent of Jane and help them to set more effective limits and to blame Mary less for the problems in the house.

The *couple* issues were increasing difficulties in intimacy and sexual behavior, differences of opinion with regard to Mr. R.'s success at work and his ability to effectively assert himself with his superiors, and unresolved differences in values. A goal of therapy was to identify these issues, point out how the feelings related to them were being displaced onto the children, and explore possible ways of resolving these problems. Since it was known from the beginning of therapy that the therapist would not be available to the family for more than six months, the couple issues were deferred for possible treatment with a different marital therapist once the other family issues were resolved.

Interventions and Strategies

The initial strategy was to eliminate the scapegoating of Mary and to help her to feel more loved and appreciated. The ice was broken between Mary and Mr. R. early in therapy when the therapist asked Mary what she liked about Mr. R. and she responded: "He's got style!" Mr. R. was surprised to hear that she had any positive feelings about him and was obviously pleased. He then expressed some of his positive feelings about her. A major thrust of the early therapy sessions was to increase the parents' awareness of the sibling rivalry and to get them to give Mary more attention by reading her stories, spending time with her when Jane was asleep, and kissing her goodnight. Modeling was used in the therapy sessions, and I would spend time talking to Mary, playing with her, showing interest in what she was doing, and, on occasion, taking her on my lap and hugging her so that her stepfather could see how to relate to her.

The conflict areas between Mrs. R. and Mary were dealt with by role-playing meals and Mrs. R. helping Mary with her homework. Role reversal, didactic instruction, negotiating skills, and other behavioral tactics were used to alter these problems. Similarly, a variety of educational and behavioral techniques were used to help Mary deal with her overeating. These included having her list what she ate and decide which foods to eliminate or reduce. The general strategy was to turn over control of these functions from Mrs. R. to Mary herself so that there was

less conflict and Mary could have more control and autonomy over her life. This was extended to other conflict areas such as amount of TV time. Mary and her mother responded very well to these interventions, and conflict between them was quickly reduced.

The success of these practical interventions helped to establish my credibility and set the stage for the next major phase of therapy, which was to deal with the unresolved issues of anxiety and abandonment related to Mrs. R.'s long absence from the home during her surgery. Mary vividly talked about the fear, sadness, and nightmares she had experienced while her mother was in the hospital. Neither parent had any awareness of these feelings and had never discussed them with Mary. This was very significant because Mrs. R. had to be hospitalized for additional tests for two weeks during the therapy. Her parents were more sensitive to some of Mary's fears and could deal with them better. It turned out that both Mr. and Mrs. R. also had considerable anxiety about her hospitalization which they had never discussed openly. Mary served as a catalyst for them to discuss their own feelings.

The final phase of therapy consisted of exploring some of the unresolved marital issues and making specific plans for addressing these in marital therapy. The children were not included in these sessions. Specifically, the issue of how Mrs. R.'s tendency to dominate and control affected their relationship was explored along with how Mr. R.'s passivity complemented her style. They became more aware of the parent-child quality of their relationship and of the mutual feelings of resentment that this generated.

Outcome

The family therapy was terminated after 15 sessions, three beyond the original therapy contract. At the time of termination, most of the child-related issues had been successfully resolved, and Mrs. R.'s original symptoms of anxiety and depression had greatly subsided. The couple was much more aware of continuing unresolved issues between them and expressed a willingness and eagerness to resume in marital therapy with a new therapist following a (summer) vacation.

RESEARCH ON THE APPROACH

Winston Churchill's famous words are particularly applicable here: "The simple words are the best and the short words the best of all." This section will be short and simple. Outcome research on family therapy is a rapidly expanding field. In a recent article on the state of the art (Simon, 1983), Gurman indicates that close to 500 family therapy outcome studies have been published since 1970, when there were essentially none. Many fewer studies have been done on family therapy per se. Although the number of studies is increasing rapidly, there is still a dearth of research. Research on this particular model of eclectic family therapy is nonexistent. Only two studies have been published comparing different types of family therapy in which at least one of the types is considered "eclectic" (Alexander & Parsons, 1973; Klein et al., 1975), and the second study was a follow-up of data obtained in the first.

The research that has been done on family therapy is promising. As reported by Gurman and Kniskern (1978, p. 835), "every study to date that has compared family therapy with other types of treatment has shown family therapy to be equal or superior." Gurman and Kniskern's (1978) analysis of family therapy outcome studies indicated that 73% of family cases improved and 27% did not improve. Family therapy is clearly alive and well and in the process of being thoroughly investigated.

FUTURE RESEARCH

Probably the most compelling clinical argument for the use of eclectic family therapy is that an increase in the clinician's repertoire of techniques will be associated with an increase in clinical effectiveness. This belief needs to be empirically verified by controlled studies. We need more research comparing different approaches and more studies on what kinds of clinical problems respond best to which kinds of family therapy. This research could help establish a firm basis for an eclectic model by identifying the most effective components of family treatment. A related area of needed research involves comparative outcome studies of different eclectic approaches on comparable clinical problems. In order to do this research, clear eclectic models have to be established, taught, and followed consistently. This is no small task. It is a difficult but important area of research to pursue. Until the alleged clinical superiority of the eclectic approach can be empirically verified, it retains the status of a belief, not a fact.

CLINICAL TRAINING

Many years ago I was asked to introduce a visiting faculty member who was renowned for her teaching skills and had won a national award as the outstanding teacher in her discipline. She was going to lecture on effective teaching and learning. There was a good-sized audience in the room but not large enough to fill the auditorium. So prior to beginning my introduction, I asked the students in the back rows to move closer to the front. She began her lecture by pointing out how I had violated one of the basic tenets of effective learning by asking the students to move. In a nice and noncritical manner, she pointed out that each person learns in his or her own way. Some people learn better if they have "space," and they do not like being up front or close to the teacher. Others do better in the front row. By asking people to move, I may have inadvertently moved people out of a comfortable space to an uncomfortable one, possibly interfering with their learning efficiency.

That lesson proved invaluable. To this day I don't know if that visiting lecturer was right or not, but the point sensitized me to the importance of individual differences in learning. I typically begin therapy supervision by asking the supervisee how he or she learns best. What is interesting is how often the person is surprised by this question and does not have an answer easily available, even though he or she is already highly educated and has spent many years in school.

Family therapy training has come out of the woodwork. One recent estimate I read stated that there are currently about 1500 different training programs at family institutes and other training agencies available in the United States and abroad. Clearly, there is no shortage of training opportunities. In the midst of all this diversity, it is difficult to come up with a model that is either original or unique. The point is that there is not a "best way" to teach or learn family therapy. There are a number of processes that I have found useful and will describe them.

First, there is no agreement about how to train people as family therapists. This is particularly relevant to the training of eclectic family therapists since two of the major approaches I have presented as part of my own approach have diametrically opposing ideas. For example, as Liddle (1982a) points out, Bowen trainees are expected to work on their own emotional functioning by successfully completing family-of-origin work during their training. At the other extreme, the structural and strategic schools clearly deemphasize and devalue family-of-origin work and put more emphasis on learning skills for working with families through live su-

pervision. As I see it, it is not a matter of either-or. Family therapy trainees can learn assessment and intervention skills *and* work on their own unresolved issues from their family of origin. However, it is important that the two processes not get mixed up. One does not want to do therapy in order to get therapy, although in training the line between personal therapy and supervision is sometimes a fine one.

Clinical training in eclectic family therapy requires the mastery of knowledge and skills in several reas. These include: conceptual knowledge of family life and family behavior; conceptual knowledge of the major family approaches; specific training in family assessment and therapy skills with ongoing supervision through live monitoring and/or videotape replay; and awareness of one's own emotional vicissitudes with regard to family issues. Although it is possible to learn the conceptual information in a relatively short period of time (e.g., a semester or academic year), it takes a longer time to digest and integrate the different approaches in a meaningful way. I think it is a mistake to try to teach several different techniques simultaneously or in rapid sequence. Learning to be comfortable with a family and get through an interview is difficult enough without trying to juggle a number of partially understood techniques. I like introducing novices to the practice of family therapy by using the problem-centered systems approach of Epstein and Bishop (1981). This is a practical, straightforward, and structured approach which spells out the procedures in specific and sequential detail. Consequently, it provides a clear map to persons who are traveling in unfamiliar terrain. Later, after persons have some experience with families and feel comfortable conducting an interview, other approaches can be presented and assimilated.

Although the theory of the different approaches to family therapy can be learned purely in the classroom and apart from practice, technique cannot be learned without application. Structured learning experiences, including role playing and the presentation of information specific tactics, are useful ways of introducing inexperienced persons to family therapy. Very often inexperienced students have fantasies about anxiety-provoking situations. Candid discussion of these situations, options for responding, and role-playing the situations often helps to reduce the anxiety and prepare the therapist for the actual sessions. Similarly, discussion of detailed goals in therapy and ways of attaining them is useful in teaching how to develop specific treatment plans.

A prerequisite for successful learning of family therapy is the willingness to expose oneself to observation and feedback. Family therapy makes use of live supervision and videotape replay as training techniques more than any other form of therapy with which I am familiar. I don't know whether this is a function of the greater openness of family therapists or the fact that family therapy happened to come into being at a point in time coinciding with the availability of the technology. In any case, this close scrutiny often creates undue anxiety for trainees. Most of my own experience is with doctoral students in clinical psychology, who, by virtue of their career goals, have a high achievement motive. Videotaping and live observation reveals all of one's imperfections. Since family therapy training often occurs in the context of other work in which performance is closely scrutinized and the perceived consequences of an unfavorable evaluation are of great concern, the notion of exposing oneself so directly can be very anxiety provoking and needs to be overcome. The best way to overcome the fear of therapeutic drowning is to jump in and swim while a lifeguard is watching. Discussion of the issues, reassurance, and guidance on the part of the supervisor can help, but in the final analysis one has to

get on the bicycle and ride, even after falling off publicly. I try and expose my own uncertainties through both discussion and videotapes of my own imperfect sessions with emphasis on my own uncertainties and mistakes. The goal of therapy training is to help someone become effective, not perfect or narcissistically exhibitionistic of one's great talents. Showing demonstration tapes of highly skilled therapists doing their best work is also of questionable didactic value for inexperienced therapists who often despair of their own skills by comparison. These tapes are more appropriate for the more experienced therapist who can focus on the nuances of technique and appreciate the work of master clinicians without feeling inadequate.

An issue that often evokes strong feelings among graduate students is whether research training should be required for therapists. Most clinically oriented students I have known, regardless of their discipline, question the value of research design and graduate statistics courses for preparing them to help people. I think all clinicians should have research training and all researchers should have clinical training. Clinical work and research each give different but equally important perspectives required to increase knowledge. Clinicians without any training in hypothesis testing, notions of validity and reliability, or other basic concepts of disciplined inquiry will be unable to question and evaluate the work or effectiveness of their interventions. Similarly, researchers with no practical knowledge of the difficulties, challenges, or problems of clinical work will find it hard to design research that is meaningful and ultimately useful. With the knowledge explosion in the mental health field and the accompanying specialization, it is becoming increasing difficult to separate research and applied skills in many areas. When I was a freshman in college, I was failing a course in mathematical logic. I ended up setting a tutor who was a senior mathematics major with very high grades. One day while we were chatting, I learned that he was planning on going to law school. How was a mathematics background relevant to law school? I asked. He explained that being a good lawyer required the ability to think precisely and logically (a quality I was obviously having trouble mastering), and mathematics provided the best training in logical, disciplined, and systematic problem solving. Like the lawyer and mathematician, family therapists and researchers may share more in common that is apparent on the surface. Both are trying to solve problems and proceed like good detectives, looking for valuable clues and trying to integrate them in a way that suggests a solution to the problem at hand.

One interesting question is who can do family therapy. Luthman and Kirschenbaum (1974) state that ". . . not everyone likes to do family therapy; some are not qualified to do family therapy, and others find that the active use of self required by the method does not fit their personalities" (p. 209). Their experience in training family therapists has indicated that family therapy, unlike individual therapy, requires an active and aggressive use of self and that persons who like family therapy and continue to do it are more outgoing, aggressive, and extroverted. I think the issue of personal style is less important than another characteristic they emphasize: namely, the commitment of the individual to remain open to his/her own emotional blocks in the training and treatment process. They feel that if an individual is unwilling to consider the feedback of the supervisor and group and explore emotional blocks that may occur in treatment, then the person is not a suitable candidate for further training.

This is an issue that is not limited to family therapy training. The problem is often one of differing perceptions or values. Unfortunately, emotional blocks are often not readily perceived by the person

with the block, making the issue a difficult one for the supervisory and learning process. Requiring personal therapy is one way of ensuring that persons become sensitive to their emotional blocks. I have serious reservations about such a requirement since there are other ways to obtain and maintain openness. Certainly personal therapy is one way to accomplish personal growth, but I question its value if it is not sought voluntarily.

An interesting question for training is whether or not family therapy training should come before or after other forms of therapy training. Some persons believe that a systems orientation is so different from the traditional individual models of diagnosis and treatment that it is hard to develop a true systems approach after being exposed to individual approaches. Although I agree with the difficulty of developing a true appreciation of systems thinking, it is not impossible to develop. As I noted at the beginning of this chapter, my own introduction to formal training in family therapy came rather late in my professional career. My earlier training did not interfere with my learning of family therapy. On the contrary, my existing knowledge and experience made it easier to learn a new approach because I had a foundation upon which I could build. A good family therapist, like any good clinician, needs to know a lot about a lot of things.

A number of years ago Jay Haley visited the university where I was teaching. He attended an informal seminar with the clinical faculty and doctoral students and discussed the now famous project at the Philadelphia child guidance clinic in which persons selected from the unemployed were given the same family therapy training as the psychiatric residents and clinical psychology interns. He described how judges could not differentiate these persons from the more formally trained therapists on the basis of observing videotapes of their therapy. Needless to say, this was quite provocative to everyone listening. "If this is true," asked one graduate student, "what can you say about the many years of formal education required in the training of psychiatrists and psychologists?" "About the best thing I can say about it," replied Haley, "is that it ages them!"

The issue of learning specific therapy systems apart from an eclectic approach is an important question. I think specific therapy approaches should be learned first, but no one approach should be learned exclusively. This is especially true in family therapy. For one thing, as noted earlier, only a few models of eclectic family therapy have been published. Also, as Liddle (1982b) notes,

. . . having most therapists believe they should immediately be capable of skillfully combining several therapeutic approaches in a unified, consistent, and effective way would be akin to believing that most cooks can, after a few cooking lessons, be gourmet chefs. Systematic eclecticism, or the orderly application of theory and technique from differing but compatible schools of thought, cannot be taken as a simple task. (p. 246)

The process of learning, assimilating, and combining family therapy approaches into a workable eclectic model is a gradual and time-consuming task which requires practice, patience, practice, experimentation, practice, reflection . . . and more practice.

A DESIRABLE TRAINING PROGRAM

Earlier in the chapter I indicated that one of the most serious errors a clinician can make is to try to be or appear perfect. It would be a clear violation of this belief to try to describe an ideal or perfect training program for eclectic family therapy. Hence, I shall present the basic components for what I am calling a desirable training program.

The basic didactic element in an eclectic training program should consist of the ingredients (theoretical constructs and techniques) of the particular form of eclecticism, a specific format for combining these variables, and the rationale for their selection, combination, and use. Family therapy is still at the stage of development where models of eclecticism are just beginning to appear, and these models tend to be informal, idiosyncratic, and developed on an ad hoc or as-needed basis by the individual clinician. It is still rare as far as I can tell for students to be taught eclectic approaches to family therapy (or perhaps to any form of therapy) in the training stage. A desirable eclectic training program would teach the eclectic system rather than leave it to be evolved by the therapist.

The specific components would involve didactic instruction in relevant information, research, theory, technique, and supervised practice, both preparatory and with clients. The knowledge base would consist of presenting relevant information about the following: (1) family systems theory; (2) some of the major theoretical approaches to family therapy; (3) information about family life, such as developmental stages, ethnic and sociocultural differences, family crises, and other salient issues; (4) didactic instruction in assessment and therapy procedures; exploration of one's own family of origin; (5) role playing and other rehearsal-type procedures to develop facility and comfort in the application of the methods prior to seeing families; and (6) "hands-on" practicum training with carefully selected families under close supervision, including videotape and live supervision (direct observation at the time of the therapy).

Within this general format emphasis should be placed on finding meaningful ways of organizing the eclecticism, such as indicating which techniques work best with certain problems, situations, or types of families. It is here that information from research which on the surface may appear unrelated to clinical application can be useful. For example, in almost all forms of therapy, family therapy included, emphasis is placed on the importance of establishing a relationship or engaging the client(s). One of the ways of engaging clients is for the therapist to both act and present information in ways that are compatible with the individual's or family's system of processing information. Riess (1981) has done research establishing that families can be categorized into three types based on the ways in which they process information or what can be loosely called family "cognitive styles." If a therapist knows about these styles, they can serve as a useful guide for selecting ways of relating to the family which will be compatible with their own ways of organizing their experiences of the world. This can help the therapist to "make sense" to the family and facilitate the engagement and therapeutic process.

Any effective family therapy training program should combine elements of theory and practice. For the inexperienced therapist, too much emphasis on theory divorced from actual contact with families can lead to hollow intellectualizations. Too much emphasis on practicum training without a conceptual map can result in the mindless application of techniques. A desirable program provides some theory, followed by supervised practical experience, accompanied and followed by more discussion of theory. There is nothing like seeing families to help make abstract concepts more understandable. Typically, the eclectic therapist is like the diner at the buffet table of an unfamiliar cuisine, picking and choosing what looks good. In the approach to training I am suggesting, the diner would be presented with a predetermined assortment of dishes from the buffet table chosen by an experienced maître d' who would explain the rationale for the particular choice and be able to answer questions as to why some of the other enticing dishes were not selected. Later, after the diner was more familiar with the food, he or she could select dishes with greater confidence and knowledge.

FUTURE DIRECTIONS

Family therapy has been in a rapid stage of development and expansion in the 30 years since its beginning. There has been a productive and prolific outpouring of theories, techniques, and research. It is time now to begin to examine the current state of our knowledge and begin to refine the state of the art. This is the opportune time to apply eclecticism to family therapy. There are several ways in which this can be accomplished.

Since eclecticism is based on combining aspects of different approaches, we should begin to examine overlap and duplication and see what are the truly independent ideas in the various theories. What I am suggesting is a sort of conceptual factor analysis. The purpose of this would be to develop eclectic theories based on concepts from existing theories which would truly enhance each other, and, at the same time, reduce redundancy. In keeping with this needed theoretical development, there should be a greater integration of existing research and information about families with knowledge of the research findings and theories from other relevant disciplines, such as social psychology, sociology, and anthropology. For example, theory and research in areas such as small-group dynamics and attitude change has great applicability for family assessment and family therapy.

Perhaps no other field of therapy has involved so much openness in terms of therapeutic exposure by both trainees and supervisors. In my own graduate training, the opportunity to watch a supervisor actually do therapy was rare. In six years of graduate school, I only had the chance to see one supervisor work with a patient, and he was not affiliated with the university where I received my training.

However, as two recent articles (Roberts, 1983; Beroza, 1983) suggest, the emphasis on live supervision and maximum exposure is not without its problems. We need to learn more about the most effective ways to train people to become family therapists.

The teaching and supervision of eclecticism in family therapy requires study, development, and greater emphasis. This can be accomplished, as was suggested earlier, by having the teachers of family therapy present an eclectic model and, most important, the rationale for their selection and inclusions of its components. It is the rationale behind the model which will allow its exponents the basis for evaluating it and testing it clinically, empirically, and logically.

In a recent article, Lebow (1984) discussed the merits and pitfalls of integrative and eclectic approaches to family therapy. Many of his ideas overlap comments I made earlier, but they are worth repeating. He believes that the advantages of an integrated eclectic approach include: having a broad theoretical base upon which to draw, greater flexibility for individualized treatment, applicability to a broader range of clients, combining the best parts of different approaches, promoting objectivity in selecting interventions, and permitting the relatively easy addition of new techniques. The potential dangers are lack of a sound theoretical basis, a lack of consistency, excessive complexity, and the encouragement of premature closure to theory development. Lebow's arguments appear sound and persuasive. In this chapter, I have tried to demonstrate how the beginnings of such a model can be applied.

The eclectic model of family therapy described in this chapter was developed out of my own experience as a clinical psychologist and family therapist. It represents a combination of ideas and techniques that I feel are important, useful, and distinct but complementary. But it is based primarily on my own clinical experience and belief system. It has not been tested in part or whole by research. Future eclectic models should be less experientially and intuitively based. They should evolve, insofar as possible, out of validated clinical trials and be confirmed by controlled research.

REFERENCES

Ackerman, N. (1958). *The psychodynamics of family life*. New York: Basic Books.

Ackerman, N. (1966). *Treating the troubled family*. New York: Basic Books.

Ackerman, N. (1972). The growing edge of family therapy. In C. Sager & H. Kaplan (Eds.), *Progress in group and family therapy*. New York: Brunner/Mazel.

Alexander, J., & Parsons, B. (1973). Short-term behavioral intervention with delinquent families: Impact on family process and recidivism. *Journal of Abnormal Psychology, 81*, 219–225.

Anderson, C. M., & Stewart, S. (1983). *Mastering resistance: A practical guide to family therapy*. New York: Guilford Press.

Andolfi, M., Angelo, C., Menghi, P., & Nicolo-Corigliano, A. M. (1983). *Behind the family mask: Therapeutic change in rigid family systems*. New York: Brunner/Mazel.

Barton, C., & Alexander, J. F. (1981). Functional family therapy. In A. S. Gurman & D. P. Kniskern (Eds.), *Handbook of family therapy*. New York: Brunner/Mazel.

Bateson, G., Jackson, D. D., Haley, J., & Weakland, J. (1956). Toward a theory of schizophrenia. *Behavioral Science, 1*, 251–264.

Beroza, R. (1983). The shoemaker's children. *Family Therapy Networker, 7*, 31–33.

Bowen, M. (1960). A family concept of schizophrenia. In D. D. Jackson (Ed.), *The etiology of schizophrenia*. New York: Basic Books.

Bowen, M. (1976). Theory in the practice of psychotherapy. In P. Guerin, Jr. (Ed.), *Family therapy: Theory and practice*. New York: Gardner.

Bowen, M. (1978). *Family therapy in clinical practice*. New York: Jason Aronson.

Corsini, R., & Rosenberg, B. (1955). Mechanisms of group psychotherapy: Processes and dynamics. *Journal of Abnormal and Social Psychology, 51*, 406–411.

Doherty, W. J., & Colangelo, N. (1984). The family FIRO model: A modest proposal for organizing family treatment. *Journal of Marital and Family Therapy, 10*, 19–30.

Epstein, N. B., & Bishop, D. S. (1981). Problem-centered systems therapy of the family. In A. S. Gurman & D. P. Kniskern (Eds.), *Handbook of family therapy*. New York: Brunner/Mazel.

Epstein, N. B., Bishop, D. S., & Levin, S. (1978). The

McMaster model of family functioning. *Journal of Marriage and Family Counseling, 4,* 19–31.

Epstein, N. B., Sigal, J. J., & Rakoff, V. (1962). Family categories schema. Unpublished manuscript.

Goldfried, M. R. (1981). On the history of therapeutic integration. *Behavior Therapy, 13,* 572–593.

Green, R. G., & Kolevzon, M. S. (1982). Three approaches to family therapy: A study of convergence and divergence. *Journal of Marital and Family Therapy, 8,* 39–50.

Grunebaum, H., & Chasin, R. (1982). Thinking like a family therapist: A model for integrating the theories and methods of family therapy. *Journal of Marital and Family Therapy, 8,* 403–416.

Guerin, P. J., Jr., & Pendagast, E. G. (1976). Evaluation of family system and genogram. In P. J. Guerin, Jr. (Ed.), *Family therapy: Theory and practice.* New York: Gardner.

Gurman, A. S., & Kniskern, D. P. (1978). Research on marital and family therapy: Progress, perspective, and prospect. In S. L. Garfield & A. E. Bergin (Eds.), *Handbook of psychotherapy and behavior change.* New York: Wiley.

Gurman, A. S., & Kniskern, D. P. (1981). Family therapy outcome research: Knowns and unknowns. In A. S. Gurman & D. P. Kniskern (Eds.), *Handbook of family therapy.* New York: Brunner/Mazel.

Haley, J. (1959). The family of the schizophrenic: A model system. *Journal of Nervous and Mental Disease, 129,* 357–374.

Haley, J. (1965). The art of being schizophrenic. *Voices, 1,* 133–142.

Haley, J. (1972). *Strategies of psychotherapy.* New York: Grune & Stratton.

Haley, J. (1976). *Problem-solving therapy.* San Francisco: Jossey-Bass.

Haley, J., & Hoffman, L. (1967). *Techniques of family therapy.* New York: Basic Books.

Hansen, J. C., & L'Abate, L. (1982). *Approaches to family therapy.* New York: Macmillan.

Jackson, D. D. (1960). *The etiology of schizophrenia.* New York: Basic Books.

Jackson, D. D., & Weakland, J. (1959). Schizophrenic symptoms in family interaction. *Archives of General Psychiatry, 1,* 618–621.

Kantor, D., & Neal, J. H. (1985). Integrative shifts for the theory and practice of family systems therapy. *Family Process, 24,* 13–30.

Kaplan, A. (1967). A philosophic discussion of normality. *Archives of General Psychiatry, 17,* 325–330.

Kempler, W. (1973). *Principles of gestalt family therapy.* Oslo, Norway: A. S. Joh. Nordahls Trykkeri.

Kempler, W. (1981). *Experiential psychotherapy within families.* New York: Brunner/Mazel.

Kerr, M. (1981). Family systems theory and therapy. In A. S. Gurman & D. P. Kniskern (Eds.), *Handbook of family therapy.* New York: Brunner/Mazel.

Klein, N., Alexander, J., & Parsons, B. (1975). Impact of family systems intervention on recidivism and sibling delinquency: A study of primary prevention. Paper presented at the Western Psychological Association, Sacramento, CA.

Laing, R. D., & Esterson, A. (1964). *Sanity, madness and the family,* Vol. 1: *Families of schizophrenics.* London: Tavistock.

Laing, R. D., & Esterson, A. (1967). Families and schizophrenia. *International Journal of Psychiatry, 4,* 65–71.

Lebow, J. L. (1984). On the value of integrating approaches to family therapy. *Journal of Marital and Family Therapy, 10,* 127–138.

Liddle, H. A. (1982a). Family therapy training: Current issues, future trends. *International Journal of Family Therapy, 4,* 81–97.

Liddle, H. A. (1982b). On the problem of eclecticism: A call for epistemologic clarification and human scale theories. *Family Process, 21,* 243–250.

Lidz, T. (1958). Schizophrenia and the family. *Psychiatry, 21,* 21–27.

Lieberman, M. A., Yalom, I. D., & Miles, M. B. (1972). *Encounter groups: First facts.* New York: Basic Books.

Luthman, S. G., & Kirschenbaum, M. (1974). *The dynamic family.* Palo Alto, CA: Science and Behavior Books.

May, H. J., & Breme, F. J. (1982). SIDS family adjustment scale: A method of assessing family adjustment of sudden infant death syndrome. *Omega, 13,* 59–74.

Minuchin, S. (1974). *Families and family therapy.* Cambridge, MA: Harvard University Press.

Minuchin, S., & Fishman, H. C. (1981). *Family therapy techniques.* Cambridge, MA: Harvard University Press.

Minuchin, S., Rosman, B. L., & Baker, L. (1978). *Psychosomatic families.* Cambridge, MA: Harvard University Press.

Patterson, G. R. (1971). Behavioral intervention procedures in the classroom and in the home. In A. E. Bergin & S. L. Garfield (Eds.), *Handbook of psychotherapy and behavior change.* New York: Wiley.

Patterson, G. R. (1976). The aggressive child: Victim and architect of a coercive system. In E. J. Mash, L. A. Hamerlynck, & L. C. Handy (Eds.), *Behavior modification and families.* New York: Brunner/Mazel.

Pinsof, W. M. (1983). Integrative problem-centered therapy: Toward the synthesis of family and individual psychotherapies. *Journal of Marital and Family Therapy, 9,* 19–36.

Prochaska, J. O. (1984). *Systems of psychotherapy: A transtheoretical analysis* (2nd ed.). Homewood, IL: Dorsey Press.

Prochaska, J. O., & DiClemente, C. C. (1984). *The transtheoretical approach: Crossing the traditional boundaries of therapy.* Homewood, IL: Dow Jones-Irwin.

Riess, D. (1981). *The family's construction of reality.* Cambridge, MA: Harvard University Press.

Roberts, J. (1983). The third tier: The overlooked dimension in family therapy training. *Family Networker, 7,* 31, 60–61.

Satir, V. (1967). *Conjoint family therapy.* Palo Alto, CA: Science and Behavior Books.

Satir, V. (1972). *Peoplemaking.* Palo Alto, CA: Science and Behavior Books.

Satir, V., Stachowiak, J., & Taschman, H. A. (1975). *Helping families to change*. New York: Jason Aronson.

Selvini-Palazzoli, M. (1978). *Self-starvation: From individual to family therapy in the treatment of anorexia nervosa*. New York: Jason Aronson.

Shapiro, R., & Budman, S. (1973). Deflection, termination and continuation in family and individual therapy. *Family Process*, 12, 55–67.

Shepard, M., Oppenheim, A., & Mitchell, S. (1966). Childhood behavior disorders and the child guidance clinic: An epidemiological study. *Journal of Child Psychology and Psychiatry*, 7, 39–52.

Simon, R. (1983). The state of the art. *Family Therapy Networker, 7*, 17–25.

Strupp, H., Fox, R. E., & Lessler, K. (1969). *Patients view their psychotherapy*. Baltimore: Johns Hopkins Press.

Sullivan, H. S. (1954). *The psychiatric interview*. New York: Norton.

Truax, C., & Carkhuff, R. (1967). *Toward effective counseling and psychotherapy*. Chicago: Aldine Press.

Watzlawick, P., Weakland, J., & Fisch, R. (1974). *Change: Principles of problem formation and problem resolution*. New York: Norton.

Weiner, I. B. (1983). Theoretical foundation of clinical psychology. In M. Hersen, A. S. Kazdin, and A. S. Bellack (Eds.), *The clinical psychology handbook*. New York: Pergamon Press.

Wynne, L. C., Rickoff, I. M., Day, J., & Hersch, S. I. (1958). Pseudomutuality in the family relations of schizophrenics. *Psychiatry, 21*, 205–220.

Wynne, L. C., & Singer, M. T. (1963). Thought disorder and family relations of schizophrenics. I: A research strategy. II: A classification of forms of thinking. *Archives of General Psychiatry, 9*, 191–206.

Yalom, I. D. (1975). *The theory and practice of group psychotherapy*. New York: Basic Books.

CHAPTER 11

Eclectic Casework

Joel Fischer

The winds of change are blowing on social casework. Since the earliest days of the profession, most caseworkers tended to approach knowledge development for practice in more or less unsystematic, haphazard, and uncritical ways. Criteria for knowledge selection were either vague, undefined, or, when they were available, unrelated to the empirical status of the knowledge. Such criteria included the comfort of the practitioner with new knowledge, the prestige of the proponent of new knowledge, or consensus among experts or peers. Part and parcel of this era was an inability of caseworkers to demonstrate their effectiveness in empirical research (Fischer, 1973, 1976).

But the last decade or so has seen major changes in the world view of many caseworkers, changes that have been described elsewhere as—in Kuhn's (1970) terms—revolutionary (Fischer, 1981). There appears to be a paradigm shift underway in casework involving a movement toward more systematic, rational, and empirically oriented development, selection, and use of knowledge for practice with a concomitant increase in practice effectiveness (Reid & Hanrahan, 1982). For want of better terminology, it appears

as though casework is moving toward the development of a practice that could be called scientifically based. This development in social work, or at least its potential, is one that has also been noted by a number of other authors (Mullen, 1978; Thomas, 1977; Reid, 1978; Hepworth & Larsen, 1982; Gambrill, 1983; Wodarski, 1981; Bloom, 1975; Briar, 1978).

WHAT IS SOCIAL CASEWORK?

Casework is a branch of the social work profession, the branch that provides the individualized, individualizing, case-by-case services of social work. Caseworkers operate in a broad range of settings—from general and psychiatric hospitals to clinics, family service, and child care agencies to schools, rehabilitation centers and prisons. In fact, social workers provide the bulk of the clinical services in the mental health clinics in the United States (Goleman, 1985).

Often, caseworkers work in collaboration with other professionals, and in many instances, their assignments are identical (as in providing direct clinical services in outpatient clinics). Thus, there is often considerable overlap among the practices of caseworkers and other professionals, especially in the area of direct, therapeutic work with clients. Indeed, it is just such overlap, including the accumulated evidence showing no interprofessional differences in terms of views and attitudes toward clients or in outcome, that has led Giannetti and Wells (1985) to the suggestion that all of the psychotherapeutic professions may be engaged in a uniform enterprise (Henry, Sims, & Spray, 1971).

The commonalities among professions when engaged in providing a direct service or interpersonal influence role strongly suggest the need to be aware of knowledge from any source that can lead to greater effectiveness in practice, whether that knowledge is developed inside or outside a given profession. Thus, when practitioners from across the professions are engaged in common activities (e.g., therapeutic work with a depressed or highly anxious client), it is crucial for them to utilize the best, most effective knowledge available, no matter who has developed that knowledge.

On the other hand, this is not to say that there are not a number of differences among the professions with regard to training, interests, societal mandate, and spheres of functioning. Caseworkers operate from a far broader base than the field of psychotherapy provides. Caseworkers provide a wide range of services and function in a variety of roles other than the clinical or psychotherapeutic role. At the core of this functioning is a commitment not only to the individual, but also to the social and physical environments in which individuals function. It is this interaction between people and environments which is at the heart of social work concerns and provides a perspective for understanding the distinctive tasks and functions of social work: helping people cope with impinging environments and attempting to improve environments. Thus, in addition to a clinical or thera-

peutic role, caseworkers will provide concrete services, act as advocates for their clients, serve as brokers or mediators, and engage in social action to affect legislation and organizational or governmental policies.

However, since this book is concerned with psychotherapeutic services, this chapter will focus only on that role of caseworkers, with the understanding that many of the principles (e.g., of knowledge selection) apply to other casework roles even though some of the actual practice techniques may not.

CASEWORKERS AND ECLECTICISM

Most caseworkers report that they are "eclectic," selecting that as their own description of their orientation, because they claim allegiance to more than one theory, or because their actual practice activities are not necessarily constrained by adherence to only one theoretical orientation (Jayaratne, 1978, 1982; Cocozzelli, in press). However, it is not at all clear that even those caseworkers who consider themselves to be eclectic use any systematic criteria to select their approaches in practice or that the use of two approaches of undemonstrated or questionable effectiveness is necessarily any better than use of just one approach of undemonstrated effectiveness. The real task of the eclectic practitioner is to be both systematic and empirically oriented in his/her selection of knowledge for practice, unhampered, to the extent possible, by the narrowness and biases of adherence to one particular school, cult, or theoretical orientation.

BACKGROUND

Eclectic casework—to the extent that it is an increasing phenomenon in social work—arose out of a recognition in the early 1970s that traditional approaches to practice simply were not providing persuasive evidence of their helpfulness to clients. There were, as of the mid-1970s, no controlled studies providing a clear demonstration of the effectiveness of any form of social casework, regardless of the practice approach, or client population, or problem (Fischer, 1976). At the same time, an increasing number of studies were appearing in the literature of allied professions, particularly clinical psychology and counseling, suggesting that several techniques were available that had accumulated a considerable body of evidence of effectiveness. It was these two strands—lack of evidence of effectiveness from within casework and evidence of effectiveness from several other sources —that were the initial impetus to begin the process of trying to develop an approach that can integrate the best knowledge the clinical helping professions have to offer.

THE APPROACH

The very nature of eclecticism—the fact that its components are selected from a variety of sources—mitigates against a tightly knit, integrated conceptual framework. It would be easy to see how some of the virtues of an eclectic approach —especially its potential effectiveness for practice—might be sacrificed for the sake of neatness, the attempt to fit all components into as nice a meta- or quasi-theo-

retical framework as possible. A key argument of this chapter, however, is that effectiveness in practice is the ultimate—in fact, the only—criterion for judging the success of an eclectic approach, and that a demonstrably effective technique cannot be ignored simply because it does not seem to fit within the "conceptual framework" of someone or other's brand of eclecticism. (It is not difficult to imagine "an eclectic approach" become just another cult.)

On the other hand, there are some areas, both conceptually and in practice, that suggest eclecticism need not be an unsystematic collection of a little bit of this and a little bit of that, but can become a rigorous, rational, and systematic approach to practice in its own right.

Knowledge Characteristics

There are two broad classes of knowledge potentially available to practitioners: causal/developmental knowledge and intervention knowledge (Fischer, 1978). Figure 1 illustrates the relationship between these two knowledge areas.

Causal/developmental knowledge is by far the largest area of knowledge in the social and behavioral sciences. This is the bulk of knowledge developed in anthropology, psychology, sociology, and much of psychiatry and social work. Causal /developmental knowledge essentially focuses on explanations geared toward understanding the development of human

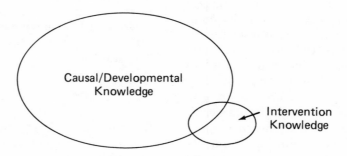

Figure 1. Areas of knowledge and their relationships.

behavior (adaptive and maladaptive). To the extent that this knowledge has many implications for practice, it is in helping the practitioner understand *why* an individual (or other client system) developed as he or she did, providing at least part of the knowledge base of the assessment process.

The other area of knowledge, intervention knowledge, focuses on the question "What can be done to modify a given situation or problem?" Intervention knowledge is used to prescribe principles and procedures for inducing change.

As can be seen in Figure 1, there is some overlap between these areas, for example, in use of knowledge where understanding specific developmental considerations is a precondition (or provides specific guidelines) for intervention. But as Figure 1 also is intended to suggest, there are areas of intervention knowledge that are independent of causal/developmental knowledge. Perhaps even more important, there often is a lack of recognition of the real and important differences between these two areas of knowledge.

For many years in social work, caseworkers have attempted to use causal /developmental knowledge as a substitute for intervention knowledge, ignoring the fact that causal/developmental knowledge describes and explains only problem development. Thus, caseworkers became far more sophisticated in their diagnostic/ assessment knowledge than in their intervention knowledge. This, in turn, led to a pervasive assumption in casework that understanding a problem somehow led almost automatically to the problem being changed.

But understanding is not helping. An entirely different set of principles and techniques is necessary in order to have specific guidelines for changing problems. Thus, major schools of casework developed with almost no attention to techniques: prescription of specific step-by-step procedures a practitioner could implement in

practice (see, e.g., Roberts & Nee, 1970).

It seems clear from the plethora of research that will be cited later in this chapter that intervention knowledge can lead to effective practice independent of knowledge about the "cause" of problems. This does not mean, however, that intervention knowledge is applied haphazardly or unsystematically. It does mean that there are a variety of sources from which intervention knowledge may be derived ranging from theories or systems of psychotherapy or behavior change to techniques derived inductively from empirical research and/or clinical observation. The nature and extent of intervention knowledge can vary greatly, from elaborate principles explaining how behavior changes to comprehensive frameworks describing the therapeutic process.

But it appears as though there is one irreducible minimum, or *sine qua non*, for intervention knowledge, a minimal floor beyond which intervention knowledge cannot go without losing its identity as intervention knowledge. That minimum level is the need for specific *techniques*: step-by-step procedures for guiding and inducing change with clients. Techniques are the expression in action and in a precise form of what the practitioner should actually do in a given situation and with a given client or problem. It is these techniques that form the core of eclectic practice.

Intervention Knowledge and Theory

A key point of this chapter is that intervention knowledge for an eclectic approach can be derived from a variety of sources, including, but not limited to, theories, or systems, of intervention. Such systems can range from comprehensive and expansive general systems prescribing a whole range of techniques to midrange and low-range theories focused on fewer phenomena. Indeed, it is tempting to consider limiting one's approach to techniques derived from only one system, especially if that system begins to accumulate a large number of positive research findings (e.g., behavior therapy). This is due to a variety of reasons including the facts that there is a certain security for the practitioner in the neatness of a more or less integrated system, and use of one system allows for the development of orderly and consistent ways of observing and explaining the relationships among a variety of events. A single system or theory can be useful, a clear way of observing, understanding, planning, implementing intervention, and predicting results.

On the other hand, there are several problems in devoting allegiance to particular systems:

1. Because of their more or less comprehensive nature, it is difficult to adhere to more than one or two theories at best.
2. Clinging to one theory may not only be not useful, it may lead to inaccurate or incorrect predictions and weak or ineffective interventions.
3. Clinging to the tenets of one system often channels the perceptions of adherents into narrow perspectives leading practitioners to try to force a number of significantly different people, problems, and events into an incompatible jell.
4. People and their problems are simply too complicated for the use of only one approach to resolve all problems.
5. No single perspective or theory has produced successful empirical results regarding all the problems that practitioners face. Indeed, as will be discussed later, empirical evidence appears to be scattered among several approaches.
6. Theories are too complicated to be validated in toto. At best, selected techniques can be validated.
7. The fact that there are so many competing casework, psychotherapy, and counseling theories—some estimate several hundred—suggests both that they all cannot be equally valid and that none has achieved sufficient documentation to stand alone as the only effective approach, thereby commanding universal acceptance by virtue of the weight of evidence.
8. There seem to be so many possibly valid principles from a range of different systems explaining behavior change that it seems as though ". . . the best strategy . . . would be to consider the hypothesis that different kinds of responses may be governed by different principles and may require different procedures for their modification" (Ford & Urban, 1963, p. 345).
9. Finally, relying exclusively on one or two theories as integrating bases for practice often precludes the systematic, objective examination of other approaches, even when positive evidence from these approaches becomes available. Theories become the master of the practitioner rather than the guide to practice, producing cults and schools and a faith in one's own theory that ignores rational decision making. Thus, the literature becomes filled with attacks and rejoinders as adherents of one approach attack adherents of other approaches while blissfully ignoring the deficiencies in their own approach. For example, now that the vituperation between psychoanalysts and behaviorists seems to have died down, a whole new generation of vituperation has developed involving advocates of behavior therapy, quasibehavior therapy, cognitive therapy, cognitive behavior therapy, multimodal therapy, and various eclectic therapies (see, e.g., Wilson, 1982). It is not infrequent to see these exchanges almost devoid of any reference to evidence of effectiveness.

In all, then, it appears not only unnecessary to think in terms of a unitary theoretical perspective as a guide to practice, it appears unwise as well. There is just too much evidence from too broad a range of approaches to make any other conclusion reasonable. Now this is not to say that there are not advantages to being guided by a theory in the *development* of techniques, nor is it to deny the possible value of knowledge about theoretical principles that might underlie techniques so they won't be applied blindly. But it is to say that for the *practitioner,* the evidence seems to point to the need to possess a framework for practice that utilizes the best knowledge available from a variety of different sources or, specifically, the development of an eclectic approach to practice.

Eclecticism Defined

The dictionary definition of eclecticism is ". . . not following any one system as of philosophy, medicine, etc., but selecting and using whatever is considered best in all systems" (*The American College Dictionary*, 1957, p. 381). Eclectic casework practice, then, consists of a variety of intervention techniques, derived from a number of different sources, including those that may appear to be incompatible on the surface, in large part on the basis of demonstrated effectiveness. These techniques would be applied with people and problems where the evidence indicates that such application has a substantial chance to produce successful outcome. The goal of this eclectic approach is to be outcome-oriented, and to be empirically based to the extent possible, and grounded in the use of interventive techniques that are developed and/or adapted through a process of rigorous and systematic testing, implementation, and retesting.

The eclectic approach is atheoretical for all the reasons described earlier. Rather than attempting to integrate a variety of presumably different intervention theories, or even principles derived from theories, the focus of integration is on techniques, with primary emphasis on those techniques that have been shown in empirical research to enhance the effectiveness of practice.

Essentially, eclecticism refers to a commitment to being guided in practice by what works, a commitment that takes precedence over devotion to any theoretical orientation. Thus, the practitioner can be divorced from any theoretical orientation currently in vague. But eclectic practice requires the ultimate in flexibility and open-mindness on the part of practitioners. They cannot afford to become complacent and satisfied with any one approach or any one technique no matter how efficient and effective it appears to be at a given time. This is because the knowledge used at any point in time will almost inevitably change as new research invalidates old. Thus, eclectic practice requires a continuing critical evaluative stance by practitioners and actually calls for far more work and a higher degree of competence than more narrowly or rigidly conceived practice.

It would be easy for practitioners to adopt systematic eclecticism as a slogan and to pay lip service to this rigorous form of practice, while at the same time continuing traditional practices. This does in fact appear to be happening in a large proportion of situations where caseworkers claim they are indeed eclectic and will use a variety of techniques based on whatever will help the client, as noted in the research on caseworkers' practice orientations reviewed earlier in this chapter. But the approach to eclecticism described here, rooted in empirical evidence whenever possible and requiring a large expenditure of time to become familiar with developments in the literature, goes beyond catch phrases and requires a restructuring of practice from its philosophical and epistemological bases to the nature of day-to-day contact with clients.

Eclecticism is not a disordered conglomeration of disparate methods thrown together into an expedient potpourri (Wolberg, 1966). Nor is eclecticism inevitably intellectually barren because there are no consistent rules to guide thoughts or action (Wolpe, 1969). Instead, eclecticism involves the selection from varied sources and studied amalgamation of intervention techniques of demonstrated effectiveness that can be used compatibly and in ways that support each other. These different techniques in implementation complement each other and serve to buttress weaknesses in the individual systems from which they were derived. Furthermore, even though the synthesis may seem harmonious at any given time, it is subject to constant study and reorganization as new techniques with evidence of effectiveness become available (Wolberg, 1966).

Now, the fact that there are literally hundreds of clinical approaches available poses some problems for eclectic practice. Is it possible to ". . . know all there is to be known about everything" (Thorne, 1973, p. 450)? Obviously, this is a patently impossible task. More important, it is not necessary. Eclecticism is not a camouflage for some mushy supertheory that attempts to integrate every approach merely because the approach exists. A wide variety of approaches do have to be studied, however, through systematic analysis to determine whether they do in fact offer the promise of adding effective techniques to the eclectic practitioner's repertoire. Furthermore, it is obvious that not all approaches have something to offer in terms of demonstrated success with particular problems. As will be demonstrated in the next section, the task of narrowing down the variety of available approaches is not only crucial, it becomes possible by using preselected criteria for evaluation, most particularly empirical evidence of the availability of effective techniques. In this way, several hundred approaches can quickly be narrowed down to only a handful that claim empirical evidence of effectiveness.

Eclectic practice is not a grab bag of procedures selected without a consistent underlying rationale. Nor does the eclectic practitioner utilize a "shotgun approach," blindly trying one technique, then another, until finally one "works." Nor is the eclectic practitioner a "Jack-of-all-trades, master-of-none," knowing a little about a good deal but a great deal about very little.

The fact is that an eclectic practitioner as described here uses specific principles to guide the selection of techniques for practice in a way that far exceeds the rigor that could be expected from adherents to any unitary practice orientation. Furthermore, the heart of eclectic practice is sensitive and accurate assessment of the individual case/situation with the goal of selecting the best possible techniques. These techniques are selected on the basis of familiarity with the practice and research literature with an eye to answering the following question: What technique is effective with what kind of problem with what client in what circumstances?

Indeed, the eclectic practitioner can and should be as highly trained in the use of a single technique as are practitioners whose training is *only* in that school *if* skill in use of that single technique is warranted by the evidence. The eclectic must have optimal levels of competence in the use of those techniques whose merit has been determined by other than blind faith or the fact that they are part of one's own theory. Eclectic practitioners can be judged not on how much they know of one approach but by a much more crucial criterion—how effective they are in helping clients.

Selecting and Integrating an Eclectic Approach

The most obvious questions that arise in considering the use of knowledge derived from a variety of divergent sources are, first, what guidelines are there for selection of that knowledge, and, second, how can this material be integrated for practice in a meaningful way?

Eclecticism is an attempt to bring order and systematization to the selection of approaches for practice. Clear, specific criteria are delineated against which any system can be evaluated. New approaches are carefully elaborated and assessed in relation to each other and to their potential use with clients. The criterion of effectiveness is given top priority. The special order and efficiency that is best produced by being systematic, and which is at a premium for the busy practitioner, is maintained and enhanced.

However, while the selection of knowledge for practice can appear relatively clear-cut, it could seem that practitioners would still have on their hands only a jumble of techniques without a real way of integrating them.

In fact, some form of integration of knowledge for practice is crucial so that the practitioner can systematically go about his or her business. Otherwise he or she would be left with a number of presumably contradictory techniques and an inability to figure out what technique to implement with what problem.

There are several ways in which practice is integrated in an eclectic approach. One is through a systematic client-problem-situation assessment, the purpose of which is to identify just what techniques to use in what situation. The second is through development of a systematic framework spelling out the process of practice in a way that adds a considerable amount of systematization. Both areas will be discussed in subsequent sections.

The third approach to integration is on a broader level and consists of the very guidelines used to select any given piece of knowledge for practice. This is an atheoretical integration grounded in certain values and propositions that cut across theoretical domains. Each criterion provides an aspect of philosophical, conceptual, or empirical evidence for use (or nonuse) of a given technique. It is these criteria that are used not only to evaluate and select different techniques, but also as principles of integration, producing a variety of techniques that all have been judged and can be compared on common dimensions.

There are several dozen criteria that actually can be used to evaluate any system of intervention (Fischer, 1971). The key ones will be summarized here.

At the broadest level, in making selections from among various options for practice and in integrating those options into a practice framework are preeminent ethical considerations. The first principle involves the extent to which use of a given technique is congruent with the values of social work: respect for the dignity and worth—or, more appropriately, the humanity—of every person. Second, in actual application, a technique can be evaluated as ethically suitable if its use does not demean (and, one hopes, enhances) the dignity and individuality of the persons involved and can be implemented in a way congruent with the values of clients and practitioners.

Another major dimension for use in both selection and integration is related to the area of concern of casework as described earlier: the interactions between people and their environments. This includes not only the behavior of individuals as they attempt to cope with life tasks and environmental demands, but the resources available in the environment that play a part in every person's development. Thus, a key dimension for selection and integration of knowledge for eclectic practice is the extent to which that knowledge is concerned with social functioning and the way people and systems interact.

Another criterion for selection and integration for practice lies in the extent to which knowledge deals with interventive practices (rather than purely casual /developmental understanding), either indirectly in presenting assessment guidelines that lead to selection of the appropriate technique with a given client, or directly in that the knowledge itself consists of a specific intervention technique.

These practice techniques are prescriptive guidelines—step-by-step procedures for implementation by the practitioner that allow him/her to induce change in the client or relevant environmental system. These techniques can deal with extinguishing or decreasing unwanted behavior, thoughts, feelings, or activities, or increasing desired behavior, thoughts, feelings, or activities. Either way, it is the specific techniques themselves which are at the heart of eclectic practice. (Indeed, without specific techniques to implement, it would be difficult to engage in *any* type of practice, let alone eclectic.)

The last, and perhaps most important, criterion for evaluating, selecting, and integrating knowledge for eclectic practice is the extent to which there is some degree of empirical validation of successful intervention with clients when techniques are implemented. When research establishes the efficacy of a technique, it must be a primary candidate for adoption, whatever its theoretical or professional point of origin.

A number of implications stem from major reliance on research. Obviously, there are numerous levels of research ranging from simple single-case designs to complex factorial designs with random assignment and controls. Thus, it is crucial to be able to evaluate the rigor and generalizability of a given study, as well as to be particularly concerned with the replication of results.

Second, even assuming two techniques have equivalent amounts and quality of evidence, there are other criteria by which to decide which techniques should be implemented in a given case. These criteria include: which is most efficient, is one less aversive to the client or practitioner, is the practitioner more competent at using one, does one have clearer guidelines for implementation, and is one more appropriate to (or designed for) this particular type of problem?

A third major implication arises from using research as a guide to selecting and integrating practice. Presumably, the studies upon which a judgment is made to select a technique also illustrate the conditions under which the technique is successfully used. This, in turn, has the makings of a very explicit client/problem typology which would demonstrate the kinds of problems and clients for whom a given technique has been and could be applied effectively. Thus, the practitioner in a sense "starts" with techniques (rather than any preset diagnostic categories), knowing the kinds of problems that respond to those techniques and developing a typology of techniques that are selected in practice according to evidence as to which problems respond best. Combination of several techniques, then, can supply not only a complementary range of intervention procedures, but a range of problem/situation configurations where the techniques can be most effectively applied. The goal, of course, is the maximum in technical flexibility for the practitioner in response to potential client problems.

It is important to note here that this empirically based model of eclectic practice is only a goal. It is unlikely that every technique in the practitioner's repertoire will be totally validated or that every problem faced in practice will have a validated technique. Practice is too complicated for that. And since no techniques claim 100% effectiveness in all cases, there will always be some clients who need new techniques or different combinations, or whom we simply do not have the knowledge to help. On the other hand, this empirical model seems a worthy goal to aim for, since the more closely we approach it, the better off our clients will be.

Now, absence of empirical validation does not automatically render a technique useless (unless, perhaps, it is being suggested as an alternative to a technique that does have empirical evidence of effectiveness). This is because a number of other criteria are available to assess knowledge for practice, particularly when empirical evidence is lacking. Thus, an approach might be assessed as to the clients and problems for which it is intended, the extent to which a technique is specified in step-by-step fashion, the internal consistency of a technique, the expected results, its ethical ramifications, and so on. In some situations and in the absence of research evidence to the contrary, such a technique might be the intervention of choice in a given situation. In the absence of research showing any other techniques to be effective with the problem, that technique might very well be the best for that problem at that time.

Ultimately, what is sought is a careful piecing together of a number of analytical dimensions. When a number of techniques can be evaluated as satisfactory by the variety of criteria described here, and can be seen to complement each other on the basis of some clearly defined prescriptive statements for use with a range of clients and problems, then some degree of integration for practice can be demonstrated to have occurred.

TREATMENT APPLICABILITY AND STRUCTURE

Eclectic casework—and, for that matter, most eclectic approaches to therapeutic practice—is comprised of a range of techniques selected from a number of approaches that, on the surface at least, may seem somewhat disparate. For this very reason, it is difficult to concisely describe all dimensions of the approach such as those situations and clients for whom the approach is most relevant and the "typical" setting, frequency, and duration of the sessions. However, it is possible to say this: the components of this approach—as will be delineated in this chapter—have been used successfully with individuals, couples, and families along the full range of human functioning. Client problems with which some of these techniques have been successfully used range from the most severe dysfunctions, such as chronic mental illness, "autism," and "retardation," to moderate and mild problems, such as speech anxiety in college students. The only limits of an eclectic approach such as this one are the limits prescribed by the outcome research. These techniques are most appropriately used where there is evidence of effectiveness of their application.

Similarly, although many of these techniques have been used in relatively brief, 8-to-12-session contacts, no specific time limits or frequency of sessions that applies to all of them has been validated in research. The key here, perhaps, is that the eclectic approach described in this chapter is a highly structured one involving use of contracts; clear specification of goals, client tasks, and practitioner activities; and careful monitoring and evaluation of progress. This type of structure and feedback makes it less necessary to specify in advance how many sessions will be necessary since there is less danger than with more conventional, open-ended practice that client contacts will be interminable.

However, most eclectic caseworkers attempt to specify with their clients some time limits in advance, if only to emphasize the importance of hard work together and to enhance expectations of success and any possible goal gradient effect. These time limits can be renegotiated if more time is needed and there is a reasonable expectation that the extra time will lead to greater success.

COMPONENTS OF AN ECLECTIC APPROACH

The essence of an eclectic approach to practice is *flexibility*. It is very possible, and even likely, that what appears to be a key ingredient of an eclectic approach at one time may be replaced at a later time because of new empirical evidence. Thus, not only might it be difficult to spell out every technique of an eclectic approach at a given time, but the relevance of such explication probably will be diminished in the future by shifts in the evidence generated by empirical research.

Nevertheless, an eclectic approach to practice that does not include a clear delineation of its components truly would be irrelevant lip service to a noble but unreachable goal. The purpose of this section is to examine some of the key components of an eclectic practice as of the mid-1980s, with the important caveat that the practitioner must not become wedded to any of these ingredients as though they were engraved in stone. What follows, then, is an attempt to provide an overview of what appears to be the best the literature has to offer at a particular time.

There seem to be four major "thrusts" in the clinical literature where the bulk of the evidence of effectiveness is contained. Brief overviews of these four areas will be presented. This will be followed by a delineation of several specific techniques and technique packages that have been derived from these four areas and that meet, in varying degrees, the criteria that were described earlier in this chapter.

Core Ingredients

The four major areas to be described here include: (1) the use of structure, (2) behavior therapy, (3) cognitive therapy, and (4) the interpersonal skills of empathy, warmth, and genuineness.

There are several reasons for selecting these four major areas as the core ingredients of an eclectic approach at this time. First, as noted previously, the bulk of the empirical evidence on clinical practice is concentrated in these four areas. This is not to say that all techniques in all four areas have been validated or even have been studied. Nor is it to say that there are not scattered findings throughout the literature about individual techniques from other areas that may be effective. But it is to say that all four of these areas have accumulated a fair to substantial amount of empirical evidence attesting to the effectiveness of some of their techniques. And it also appears that no other areas in the literature seem to come close to any of these four regarding the amount of evidence they have accumulated. Thus, these four areas appear to be the primary candidates from which judicious selection of techniques for practice can be made.

Second, all these areas contain specific guidelines for implementation of techniques or associated procedures so that it is clear what the practitioner should be doing when he or she is faced with a particular client, problem, or situation. The clarity of these techniques is also crucial for conducting evaluations of their effectiveness in empirical research.

Third, work in all these areas has been conducted with a wide variety of clientele, ranging from nonverbal, low-income clients to middle- and upper-class clients. Similarly, all four areas have been applied with a relatively wide range of problems. Thus, there seems to be a fair amount of generalizability across all four areas.

Structuring

Structuring is an umbrella term covering a variety of discrete principles and techniques that have appeared in the literature, but which do have one common thread: they all add some degree of "structure" to practice. Structuring is considered a critical variable for practice for one major reason: most research that has compared any form of structured with unstructured practice has concluded that structuring is as effective as and frequently more effective than unstructured practice. Indeed, the apparent potency of structuring has led some psychotherapy researchers to believe that structuring is the underlying reason for any approach to practice that demonstrates its effectiveness.

Structuring involves essentially two levels, a general orientation to practice and a range of specific techniques. At the most general level, structuring emphasizes careful planning, specificity, and systematic use of variables designed to influence or change the problem/situation. At a more specific level, a number of techniques or programs have been found either to enhance effectiveness or at least to contribute to added structure in practice. These include the following:

1. Role induction interviews: structuring and clarifying the intervention process and associated expectations prior to onset of intervention (Parloff and Wolfe, 1978).
2. Use of specific and precise goal setting.
3. Use of contracts between practitioner and client.
4. Use of time limits, particularly when no other major aspect of structuring is present (Reid & Shyne, 1969; Wattie, 1973; Shlien et al., 1962; Muench, 1964; Beck & Jones, 1973; Gordon & Gordon, 1966; Phillips & Wiener, 1966; Blenkner et al., 1964; Luborsky et al., 1975; Butcher & Koss, 1978).
5. Use of several techniques to enhance client expectations (Lick & Bootzin, 1975; Frank, 1972; Coe & Buckner, 1975; Fish, 1973; Murray & Jacobson, 1978).

6. Use of homework and task assignments (Reid, 1978; Martin & Worthington, 1982; Shelton & Levy, 1981).
7. Use of a variety of findings from social psychological research (Strong, 1978; Goldstein, 1980; Goldstein & Simonson, 1971; Feld & Radin, 1982).
8. Use of a number of techniques to enhance generalization or transfer of change and maintenance effects (Goldstein & Kanfer, 1979; Karoly & Steffen, 1980).

Behavior Therapy

Although social workers for some time were not convinced of the value of behavior therapy for their practice, there is some evidence that this no longer is the case (Thyer, 1983). Social workers increasingly are recognizing the compatibility of behavior therapy with social work philosophy and goals, particularly the shared view of the importance of the interactions between people and their environments.

Behavior therapy has a number of distinct advantages for eclectic practice, including:

1. Availability of several dozen specific intervention techniques, each of which includes clear procedural guidelines for implementation (Bellack & Hersen, 1985).
2. A clear relationship between assessment and intervention (that is, the end result of assessment is a clear prescription regarding which technique(s) should be selected.
3. Development of a number of techniques focused specifically on social-environmental change, a practice that is at the core of the social work perspective.
4. A number of specific techniques and programs for training caretakers in the natural environment (e.g., parents, teachers, etc.).

5. Consistent evidence of effectiveness
—several hundred controlled, experimental studies, several hundred single case designs showing the relationship between application of a technique and client change, and a number of comparative studies showing that one or another technique of behavior therapy is as effective as or more effective than other approaches (Kazdin & Wilson, 1978; Rachman & Wilson, 1980; Rimm & Masters, 1979; Gambrill, 1977; Turner et al., 1981; Hersen et al., 1975–1984; Franks & Wilson, 1973–1984).

It is important to note here that evidence on effectiveness varies tremendously from technique to technique in behavior therapy, ranging from well over 125 controlled studies on one technique alone (systematic desensitization) to few, if any, controlled studies attesting to effectiveness of other techniques. On the other hand, many behavior therapy techniques do show limited evidence of effectiveness but, perhaps more important, are constructed in such a way as to permit evaluation of effectiveness.

Cognitive Change Techniques

The third area in which evidence of effectiveness is rapidly accumulating is comprised of several different techniques that have an important common dimension: they focus on changing cognitive patterns or ways of thinking that are dysfunctional for the client and/or the client's environment. This area illustrates the importance of practitioners being attuned to new developments: just about all the research on cognitive change has been conducted since 1970, a relatively recent period of time.

Cognitive change techniques are focused on a variety of areas of cognition and related affective and behavioral responses. These include changing miscon-ceptions, unrealistic expectations, and dysfunctional self-statements; systematic approaches to problem solving and decision making; and applications in self-control or self-change approaches (Beck, 1976; Raimy, 1975; Mahoney, 1974, 1978; Meichenbaum, 1977; Emery et al., 1981; Janis, 1982; Beck et al., 1979; Ellis & Grieger, 1977). While the evidence on cognitive techniques is not nearly as impressive as the accumulated evidence on behavior therapy, the increase in studies and positive findings since the 1970s suggests that this is a field that will continue to grow in importance.

In fact, perhaps the major trend in clinical practice today is the convergence among cognitive and behavioral techniques (the techniques of self-instruction training and stress-inoculation training [Meichenbaum, 1977] are prime examples). This has produced what amounts to a new field: cognitive-behavior therapy (or cognitive-behavior modification), and a good deal of positive evidence has been generated from this confluence of two major streams of work in clinical practice (Meichenbaum, 1974; Foreyt & Rathjen, 1978; Kendall & Hollon, 1979; Franks et al., 1982; Wilson et al., 1984.)

Interpersonal Skills of Empathy, Warmth, and Genuineness

The fourth area for consideration for eclectic practice is directly related to the fact that the eclectic practitioner must be more than a technician or an automaton, blindly applying techniques without considering the important issues of the essential humanity of the relationship between practitioner and client. No school of therapy or theoretical orientation argues that practice is applied outside of an interview and relationship between practitioner and client. (As one group of noted behaviorists, after a careful examination of their own program, has stated, "Many clinical colleagues have told us all along that the 'relationship' is an essential component of any therapy. We are now convinced that they are right" Philips et al., 1973, p. 76). This points to the desirability of developing a relationship that will do as much as possible to enhance the interactions between client and practitioner.

To be optimally effective, it appears as though practitioners must succeed in at least two areas: (1) they must create those personal conditions which establish a relationship of trust, caring, and acceptance between themselves and their clients, and thereby increase their clients' amenability to therapeutic influence; and (2) in the context of these conditions, they must employ a technology or program involving a variety of techniques to influence their clients in desired directions (Bergin & Strupp, 1972). It is in this context that the interpersonal skills of empathy, warmth, and genuineness appear to be central.

Although the evidence here is neither as elegant nor as consistent as in the other areas, there does appear to be sufficient evidence to suggest that these communication skills are important for effective practice (Marshall et al., 1982; Truax & Mitchell, 1971; Carkhuff & Berenson, 1976; Parloff & Wolfe, 1978; Mitchell et al., 1977). The key to this approach is the development of scales to measure the communication of empathy, warmth, and genuineness (plus several other interpersonal dimensions; Carkhuff, 1969). This allows for these interpersonal skills to be observed, evaluated, and taught, with a fair amount of evidence now accumulated that they can be successfully learned in courses focusing on structured, step-by-step, experiential training (Marshall et al., 1982; Gantt et al., 1980).

These interpersonal skills can be viewed as the foundation of an eclectic approach, providing the crucial interviewing and relationship skills that influence the effective implementation of techniques. In fact, there is a body of several experimental studies showing that practitioners who demonstrate higher levels of one or more of these interpersonal skills are more effective than practitioners with lower levels in their use of a number of specific techniques (Dowling & Frantz, 1975; Morris & Suckerman, 1974a, 1974b; Cairns, 1972; Harris & Lichenstein, 1971; Mickelson & Stevic, 1971; Vitalo, 1970; Namenek & Schuldt, 1971; Naar, 1970; Bergin, 1969; Wandersman et al., 1976; Goldstein, 1976; Curtiss, 1976; Gold, 1976; Ricks et al., 1976).

Techniques for Eclectic Practice

The heart of eclectic practice is, of course, what the practitioner does. And the most important activity of the practitioner is the implementation of techniques. Techniques are step-by-step procedures used by the practitioner to induce and guide change. To the extent possible, the techniques are selected so as to be problem-specific and, one hopes, known to be the best possible intervention with a particular problem, client, and situation at that particular time.

There are several criteria that might be used in selecting a technique in practice to be used with a given problem:

1. Relative effectiveness compared to no treatment and/or other techniques—the paramount consideration.
2. Relative efficiency—the amount of time and energy required for use.
3. Resources available, including people who may be necessary to implement the procedures (e.g., in parent training), cost of implementation, and availability of time and materials.
4. Type of problem—if the practitioner's goal is to increase the occurrence of some behavior or activity, one would try to locate a technique designed to increase (and not decrease) that category of behavior or activities.

5. Design of the technique—some techniques are specifically designed to deal with the exact problem the practitioner is facing.
6. Clarity—wherein the operations to be used in implementing a technique are clearly spelled out.

In actual practice, it is rare for only one technique to be used with a particular problem. Most often, techniques are combined in programs or packages that have a broader effect than implementation of just one technique. Following, then, are several techniques and technique packages that were selected for two major reasons: (1) they have accumulated a substantial amount of empirical evidence of effectiveness with one or more problems; and/or (2) with a modicum of evidence, they are specifically designed to deal with certain problems that the other techniques listed do not successfully address.

Although this listing is not intended to be exhaustive, the techniques and technique packages that best appear to meet those criteria as of the mid-1980s are the following:

1. Assertion training and social skills training (Curran & Monti, 1982; Bellack & Hersen, 1979). These technique packages have been used successfully with a wide range of skill deficits in populations that range from severely disturbed psychiatric patients to unhappy marital couples (Twentyman & Zimering, 1979).
2. Contingency management (Rimm & Masters, 1979). A "catchall" term for a whole variety of operant techniques to both strengthen or maintain desired behaviors and weaken or decrease undesired behaviors, these techniques and packages include reinforcement, punishment, extinction, time out, the token economy, overcor-

rection (Foxx & Bechtel, 1982), and others. Contingency management has been used successfully with almost all imaginable populations including children and adults, individuals, couples, and families, and with the most moderate to the most severe of problem behaviors (Bellack & Hersen, 1985).
3. Systematic desensitization (Wolpe, 1982). A technique for decreasing maladaptive anxiety, most successfully used when the anxiety is related to relatively specific stimuli, systematic desensitization has been the subject of more controlled investigations than any other therapeutic technique—well over 125—and has been found to be effective with a wide range of anxiety disorders (Walker et al., 1981).
4. Behavioral contracting (Kirschenbaum & Flanery, 1983). Although largely associated with contingency management, the use of contracting has received a fair amount of independent evidence of effectiveness in use with several problem populations and with individuals, families, and couples.
5. Problem solving (D'Zurilla & Nezu, 1982). Although the accumulated evidence is somewhat weak, and a number of problem-solving packages are available, the evidence is encouraging enough to suggest the importance of providing clients with an overall, step-by-step framework to aid in solving problems and making decisions. A framework that seems particularly useful is the one developed by Janis & Mann (1977).
6. Self-instruction training (Meichenbaum, 1977; Cormier & Cormier, 1985). A package essentially combining cognitive and behavioral techniques, self-instruction training has accumulated some 50 controlled stud-

ies showing it to be effective with several disorders including problems of impulsive children and public speaking and test anxiety (Rachman & Wilson, 1980).

7. Stress-inoculation training (Meichenbaum, 1977; Cormier & Cormier, 1985). Another combination of cognitive and behavioral techniques, stress-inoculation training, though not as extensively studied as self-instruction training, has been successfully used with problems involving interpersonal and general anxiety and stress and anger control (Novaco, 1979).

8. Cognitive restructuring (Goldfried, 1979; Ellis & Grieger, 1977). Although cognitive restructuring comes in a variety of packages (see Cormier & Cormier, 1985, for an excellent synthesis), it appears to be an important intervention for dealing with problems where the assessment suggests that unrealistic expectations, misconceptions, or dysfunctional self-statements may be at the root of those problems.

9. Modeling and participant modeling (contact desensitization) (Rimm & Masters, 1979; Cormier & Cormier, 1985; Walker et al., 1981). Modeling, and its many variations including contact desensitization, has been found to be an effective package in and of itself and in combination with other techniques for both increasing positive behaviors and activities and decreasing negative behaviors and activities. The population modeling has been applied with ranges from the slightly to severely impaired and includes behavioral, cognitive, and affective (decrease in anxiety) outcomes.

10. Covert sensitization (Cautela, 1967; Rimm & Masters, 1979). Although the evidence on covert sensitization is not extensive (Kazdin & Smith,

1979), there does seem to be enough to suggest that covert sensitization might be useful, in combination with other techniques, in decreasing unwanted sexual behaviors, alcohol abuse, smoking, and overeating. In particular, covert sensitization is one of the few techniques that addresses some of these problems without resort to electrical or mechanical devices or chemical aids.

11. Covert positive reinforcement (Kazdin & Smith, 1979; Walker et al., 1981). A limited amount of research suggests that covert reinforcement can be effective in modifying negative self-statements, test anxiety, weight control, certain specific animal phobias, and attitude change. This is a technique which is readily adaptable to use with other techniques in more broadly based intervention programs.

12. Covert modeling (Kazdin & Smith, 1979; Cormier & Cormier, 1985). Covert modeling has been shown in some studies to be as effective as live modeling, but with a very limited range of problems, essentially involving fear and lack of assertiveness. Once again, it is a technique that can readily be combined with others.

13. Exposure and response prevention (Mathews et al., 1981; Marshall et al., 1979). A relatively new technique package, exposure has been found to be effective in a number of studies with problems involving simple and social phobias, agoraphobia, and compulsive rituals (Foa & Steketee, 1979; Brehony & Geller, 1981).

14. Thought stopping (Rimm & Masters, 1979; Cormier & Cormier, 1985; Walker et al., 1981). Thought stopping is one of the few available techniques designed specifically to deal with problems involving obsessive thoughts that the client cannot control. Although the controlled evidence

is insubstantial, there appears to be enough case study evidence to suggest that thought stopping might be included as one component in a broader intervention program.

15. Habit reversal (Azrin & Nunn, 1977, 1982; Turpin, 1983). This technique is specifically designed to overcome a variety of specific undesired habits such as tics, nail-biting, and hair pulling (trichotillomania). Although the number and quality of studies available are not impressive, habit reversal does appear to be a promising way of dealing with a variety of specific problems that most other techniques do not address.

It is probably obvious that just about all of the techniques described here have their roots in cognitive and/or behavioral formulations. The reason is simple: no other approaches or theoretical orientations have described their techniques in such specific fashion, allowing for clear evaluation, and then carried out the literally hundreds of studies that document the effectiveness of these techniques, especially in a way that they can be isolated and examined as independent entities. Indeed, some of the individual techniques described here have often been compared in controlled research to entire systems of therapy and found as effective or more effective (Kazdin & Wilson, 1978). Thus, this clarity and subsequent evaluation allow one to be able to distinguish between legitimate therapeutic procedures and fads.

Another advantage of this clarity of description involves ease of training. When step-by-step procedures are specified, learning how to use the techniques becomes a much easier task. The vagaries of trying to operationalize and implement complicated systems of intervention simply become unnecessary. Indeed, each one of the techniques and technique packages

described here has been placed into a common format using step-by-step flowcharts. Two examples of these flowcharts are reproduced here as Figures 2 and 3, one of a technique with relatively few steps—self-instruction training—and the other of a more complicated technique—assertive training. Whenever possible, the flowcharts for these techniques were designed to follow the format in Cormier & Cormier (1985), a book that has been found to be the most useful in helping graduate students learn these techniques.

Although only 15 techniques were described here, in fact, when the several techniques of contingency management and the variations of other techniques (e.g., different types of modeling) are explicated, the 15 techniques expand to over 25. Moreover, many of these techniques can and have been used not only with individual clients but with couples and families as well. Used together—and with a foundation in the interpersonal skills and structuring procedures described earlier —these techniques can provide an integrated and comprehensive approach to practice that at the present time appears to have the best chance of optimizing our effectiveness with our clients.

Common Characteristics of Techniques

Although the variety of techniques described here may appear disparate on the surface, it is possible that there are some characteristics that cut across many of them, thereby accounting for some degree of their success. Although this section is speculative, based on reviewing the research on techniques and attempting to categorize them regarding their commonalities and differences, it does seem that the most effective techniques have certain ingredients in common. These are described here mainly as hypotheses for future research on identifying the effective

SELF-INSTRUCTION TRAINING

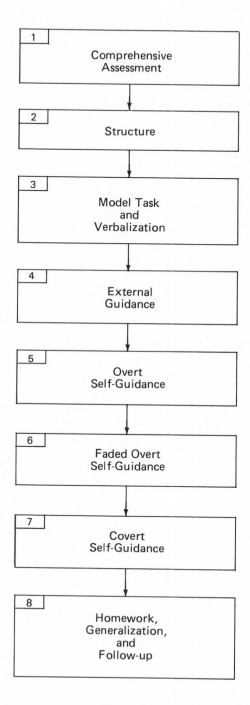

Figure 2.

components of techniques. This scheme also has heuristic effects in that it serves as a handy vehicle for teaching practitioners. In essence, students are urged to examine their practice to ensure that as many of these ingredients as possible are present as they implement any given technique. Thus, the following is what might be proposed as some common characteristics of effective technique implementation:

1. Structure. Provide a verbal set including a rationale for use of the technique and an explanation of what is to be done, and enhance positive expectations of success.
2. Modeling. Demonstrate to the client what you want the client to do.
3. Extensive rehearsal and practice. It is almost impossible to expect a client to be successful at implementing the practitioner's ideas in real life unless he/she has practiced them—over and over again—with the practitioner.
4. Graduated steps. With few exceptions, it is better to move slowly rather than too quickly. This means, for example, moving from confronting low-anxiety-eliciting situations to increasingly higher-anxiety-eliciting situations. It also means use of shaping—moving from less to more complicated objectives.
5. Provide feedback. It is a good idea to try to provide your client with gentle and constructive suggestions on what to change or try next as you progress in your rehearsal.
6. Coping thoughts. Prepare the client with what to say to himself/herself when preparing for, confronting, or successfully completing an assignment.
7. Praise and positive reinforcement. Not only can the client's efforts be enhanced by praise from the practitioner, but praise and positive rein-

ASSERTIVE TRAINING

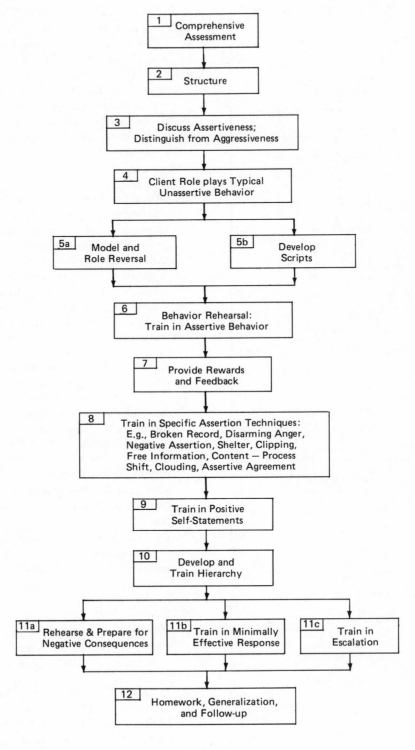

Figure 3.

forcement from other sources (or self-reinforcement) should be built into the client's program whenever possible.

8. Homework and task assignments. It is crucial to give the client homework to try out in real life each part of what the practitioner and client have worked out in their contacts (Martin & Worthington, 1982).

9. Exposure. Increasing the time of the client's exposure to anxiety-producing events—in real life or in imagination—leads to optimal reduction in that anxiety.

10. Transfer of learning. It is absolutely critical that an entire phase of the intervention process be devoted to ensuring that therapeutic gains are maintained, both in direct practice with the client and in training others in the environment to support and reinforce those gains.

ASSESSMENT

The core of eclectic practice involves conducting an adequate assessment. It is through the assessment that the eclectic practitioner makes a judgment as to which technique to implement. As noted earlier in this chapter, one key factor in this assessment is being aware of what techniques work best with what problems (or, at least, were designed to be used with a given problem), so that the assessment can be clearly geared toward making that decision a rational one.

Although space limits the amount of detail that can be provided about assessment, some general principles can be described here. In essence, assessment for eclectic practice contains ingredients similar to those described across a broad range of theoretical orientations. The basic purpose is to provide detailed information that will lead to the establishment of specific goals, a strategy of intervention, and

selection of specific intervention techniques. The purpose of assessment is not understanding for the sake of understanding; if the assessment does not lead the practitioner to select specific intervention techniques, the assessment probably has been inadequate.

The focus of assessment is on evaluating what is to be changed, what factors are maintaining or controlling the problem, what resources are necessary to bring about change, and what problems might result from bringing about change. Past factors need not be ignored, but the sole purpose of this information would be to shed light on current conditions (e.g., it would be important to know what efforts in the past have been made to deal with the problem). It is difficult, if not impossible, to take overt interventive action on past variables (Fischer, 1978). Similarly, the goal of assessment is not to assign diagnostic labels (although sometimes these are required by the system in which a practitioner works).

There are, at the broadest level, only a limited number of ways of collecting information for an assessment. For most situations, an eclectic practitioner will prepare an assessment package that would consist of all of these, using a multimethod approach such as that described by Nay (1979). The specifics (e.g., a questionnaire) may change depending on the problem, but if the practitioner uses several methods, he or she is more likely to produce well-rounded and informative assessments.

The major data collection methods include interviews, questionnaires and other structured instruments, and direct observations. A range of references are available describing all of these in great detail (Haynes & Wilson, 1979; Haynes, 1978; Kendall & Hollon, 1981; Cone & Hawkins, 1977; Barlow, 1981; Mash & Terdal, 1981; Hersen & Bellack, 1981; Ciminero, 1977; Sundberg, 1977).

Some general principles of assessment

that can be used as guides are the following:

1. Use more than one data collection system.
2. Be sure to obtain a relevant sample of people, events, and activities.
3. Collect information on people and environments, assessing the way people interact with the various systems that affect them (families, peers, organizations, communities, and so on).
4. Conduct a force-field analysis in which you specifically delineate the forces that might aid or restrain change (Brager & Holloway, 1978).
5. Answer specific "what" questions (rather than "why" questions) (what is a person doing that is of concern, under what conditions does it occur, what are the effects of those activities, what does the client expect, and so on), being as specific as possible in identifying relevant variables.
6. Focus on variables that can be affected, rather than those that have only vague and perhaps inaccurate explanatory value.
7. Develop an integrative formulation (Siporin, 1975) that takes into account all of the above and that is written in terms relevant to selecting intervention techniques, specifically, pinpointing necessary areas of change and indicating the direction of these changes, whether they be to maintain, increase, or decrease some behavior, cognitions, activities, or other dimensions. Some eclectic practitioners also use additional guidelines to help in this process such as Lazarus' (1981) BASIC I.D. formulation to be sure that all aspects of functioning are covered and techniques are selected for each problem area.

Once all this is accomplished in a time period that, depending on the case, may run from less than an hour (with a client in crisis) to several sessions, it still remains for the practitioner to be able to select the correct techniques. Here is where knowledge of the available techniques is so crucial, and where the practitioner must formulate a typology linking specific problems to specific interventions. An assessment that concludes the problem is "anxiety" is not enough. The type of anxiety determines the choice of intervention technique based on prior evidence of effectiveness, and to some extent, the only way this can be done is if the practitioner knows what technique is effective with what type of anxiety (Goldfried & Davison, 1976). So, for example, if the anxiety can be traced to a specific stimulus situation, the technique of choice might be systematic desensitization or exposure (in the case of certain phobias). If the anxiety is a result of skill deficits, social skills or assertive training might be called for. If the anxiety is maintained by the client's dysfunctional verbalizations, cognitive restructuring might be the intervention of choice. If the anxiety seems to be a general, free-floating anxiety, then cognitive restructuring, or, secondarily, stress-inoculation training, might be called for. For problems due to speech and communication anxiety, the practitioner might choose systematic desensitization or self-instruction training. For stress and anger control, stress-inoculation training might be the intervention of choice. And if the anxiety appears to be the result of an untenable environment, the practitioner has the choice of helping the client cope with it using one of several techniques for decreasing anxiety as described previously, helping the client try to change that environment through social skills or assertive training, or attempting to change the situation himself or herself or help remove the client from it.

As can be seen, an adequate assessment requires a combination of assessment skills along with knowledge of the effects of a wide range of intervention techniques.

RESEARCH AND EVALUATION

It is difficult to see how eclectic practice or any other form of practice can be considered as sufficient without some form of systematic evaluation being considered part of the process. Although human service practitioners traditionally either have been reluctant to evaluate their practice or simply did not possess the requisite skills, there is now an evaluation technology available that can be built right into practice with each case and that can be used no matter what the theoretical orientation or types of techniques of the practitioner (Bloom & Fischer, 1982). This technology has important advantages for practice: it can be used by the practitioner with each case, it can be used to evaluate outcome, and it also allows the practitioner to monitor progress so that he or she can make changes in the intervention program if necessary.

There are several more or less interchangeable terms for this technology: single-case design, single-system design, time series research, idiographic research, single N and/or single-subject design, and so on. All of these names basically refer to a practice-oriented approach to evaluation wherein the individual, couple or family is viewed as a single unit and data are collected on client progress over time. Since the literature on this topic has developed extensively in recent years, it is not necessary to go into detail about this evaluation process here (Barlow et al., 1984; Kazdin, 1982; Bloom & Fischer, 1982; Jayaratne & Levy, 1979; Hersen & Barlow, 1976).

Boiled down to its essence, this form of evaluation has four key components:

1. Specification of the problems to be changed;
2. Finding a way to measure the problems;
3. Systematic collection of information on the problem over time, preferably in-cluding a baseline of information prior to intervention and using a planned format or design; and
4. Clearly identifying an intervention program, no matter what type of techniques the practitioner is using, that can be distinguished from the baseline/assessment phase.

Although these steps seem rather simple, they *are* the core of this form of evaluation. Of course, each of these steps bears considerable elaboration such as the different types of measures available, how to use the measures, how to organize and implement the variety of designs, how to analyze the data, and so on. This type of information can be found in the references cited previously.

Obviously, the point here was not to review this methodology in depth, but to emphasize its importance to eclectic practice. If anything, eclectic practice can be characterized as an attempt to integrate research and practice. Use of systematic case evaluations is one of the key trademarks of practitioners who really are serious about enhancing the effectiveness of their practice.

A FRAMEWORK FOR PRACTICE

The framework presented here is an attempt to integrate, structure, and systematize the process of eclectic practice, and to highlight the interrelationship between practice and research in the overall process. A number of features characterize this framework, in the way they illustrate, or attempt to enhance, eclectic practice:

1. *Empirically based.* To the extent possible, this framework attempts to enhance development of an empirical base for practice. This actually has two meanings here. The first is the use of the results of research to inform prac-

tice, as in the selection of techniques. The second is in careful and systematic evaluations of the effects of intervention. This framework includes the specific steps of evaluation as parts of the steps of practice.

2. *Eclectic.* This framework is based on the assumption that the knowledge base of practice is both pluralistic and eclectic. It is pluralistic in the sense that the knowledge is derived from many sources. It is eclectic in that only the best available knowledge is selected from those sources. Eclecticism means using clear, precise, systematic criteria to select knowledge. In particular, this relates to the empirical base of practice in that, whenever possible, practice consists of a variety of techniques selected largely on the basis of evidence of effectiveness and applied with people and problems where the evidence indicates that such application has a good chance of producing a successful outcome. Of course, it is not always possible to achieve this ideal with every problem. But as an organizing principle of practice, it seems a worthwhile goal to shoot for. More concretely, this framework is intended to apply whatever the theoretical orientation, methods, or approach of the user.

3. *Systematic.* This framework is an attempt to systematize practice. This means clearly identifying the various phases of practice and organizing them into a step-by-step sequence that appears to offer a good chance of enhancing both effectiveness and efficiency. In fact, one of the most important characteristics of practice is being systematic: in how goals are identified, in how intervention techniques are selected, in how outcome is monitored. It also appears to make sense to try to organize the diverse activities of practice into a logical sequence that runs from

initial contact to termination and follow-up.

Although the process of practice is described here as a sequence of phases, this is not meant to prescribe a rigid, lock-step approach to practice. For example, depending on the problem or situation, the length of time for any phase could vary considerably, the phases could overlap, or a phase might not occur at all. Indeed, despite the fact that a number of phases are described, the essence of practice using this framework still must be flexibility: selecting what is done on the basis of a specific client-problem-situation configuration, individually tailored to the needs of a particular case. These are less formal steps in the process than aspects of the process that are likely to take place at some point. Thus, an attempt to organize that process may bring some order and direction into the subtleties and contradictions of real-life practice. Importantly, this framework has been found to be a very useful teaching device for new practitioners providing them with an anchor as they learn how to engage in practice.

4. *Accountable.* This framework is an attempt to add to our accountability as practitioners. It brings the entire process of practice out into the open for careful scrutiny by anyone concerned. It allows for an organized sequence of activities that can be specified and taught. It points out and builds into practice the necessity for carefully evaluating results with every case.

5. *Way of thinking.* This framework is intended to illustrate and/or enhance, perhaps more than anything else, a way of thinking about practice: systematic, data-based, outcome-oriented, flexible, depending on the needs of the client, empirically based, and up to date with the relevant literature. All of this is grounded in the ethics and

values—the scientific humanism —which underlie the philosophy and practices of the helping professions.

The framework is comprised of five major phases and 18 steps, each of which is divided into component parts. The framework is called the PRAISES model, with PRAISES being an acronym for the five major phases (Table 1). Because of space limitations, only the outline and flowchart (Figure 4) of the framework can be presented here. Despite the fact that it looks like a General Motors wiring diagram at first glance, the flowchart on closer examination consists simply of the varied aspects that constitute the flow of eclectic practice.

TABLE 1
The PRAISES Model

Phase I. *PR*e Intervention
  1. Evaluate the context
  2. Process the referral
  3. Initiate contact
  4. Structure

Phase II. *A*ssessment
  5. Select problem
  6. Conduct assessment
  7. Collect baseline information
  8. Establish goals

Phase II. *I*ntervention
  9. Develop intervention plan
  10. Develop evaluation plan
  11. Negotiate contract
  12. Prepare for intervention
  13. Implement intervention

Phase IV. *S*ystematic *E*valuation
  14. Monitor and evaluate results
  15. Assess and overcome barriers
  16. Evaluate goal achievement

Phase V. *S*tabilize
  17. Stabilize and generalize changes
  18. Plan follow-up and termination

CASE EXAMPLE

The following case example (from Fischer, 1978) illustrates a number of aspects of eclectic practice. The entire process is grounded in the relationship —communication of empathy, warmth, and genuineness—and moves through several stages from initial exploration and structuring to selection and implementation of the technique to evaluation.

The client, Dean, 23 years old, has told the practitioner he wants to change his orientation from homosexual to heterosexual. Dean is obviously experiencing tremendous conflict over his homosexual orientation. He has been struggling with his problem over a year but has not sought any professional help until now. He begins hesitantly; he has let very few people in on the secret that he is "a homosexual." The practitioner recognizes Dean's tentativeness. He acknowledges how hard it must be for Dean to express himself about the problem, and how especially frightening it must be to do so with a stranger. The practitioner demonstrates to the client the kind of caring, respect, and nonjudgmentalness that Dean has not encountered before; the practitioner demonstrates also that he understands. Gradually, Dean realizes that this is a person who will not look with horror or shock at his behavior, and also that the practitioner is a person who will not plunge immediately into inappropriate advice giving ("So why don't you go out more with women?"). Gently the practitioner encourages Dean to explore the nature of the problem and his feelings about it.

Dean discloses numerous reasons for wanting to change: social pressure, the fear of being stigmatized as "abnormal," of being considered just a freak; the fear that his future employment possibilities will be limited; the fear of other people's reactions to learning he's gay; the fear of not being able to find personally mean-

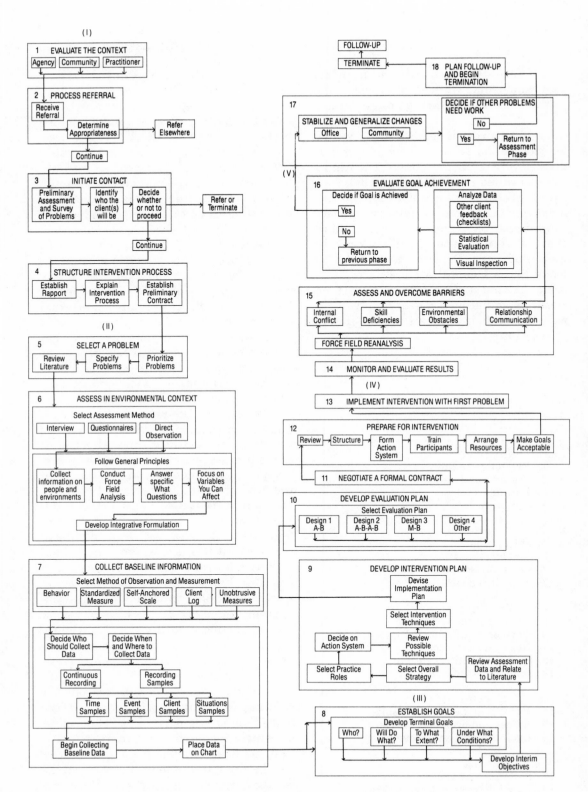

Figure 4. PRAISES model: A framework for eclectic practice.

ingful, fulfilling, and lasting homosexual relationships.

The practitioner probes beneath the surface of these reasons. Dean is filled with anger at the lack of society's understanding of the homosexually oriented. Dean has tried dating women as a way of overcoming his attraction to men. That did not work: while he can be attracted to women, he says, he still is more attracted to men. His rage at his situation leaves him feeling hopeless and depressed, with feelings of being an unworthwhile person. He feels trapped in his situation—unable to "come out of the closet" except with a few of his closest friends, yet unable to change his own homosexual tendencies. The practitioner also acknowledges with Dean the pervasive fear Dean is experiencing over his situation, afraid to move in any direction, afraid of what might happen if he does. The early sessions are difficult ones for Dean, but as the practitioner moves with him, he increasingly realizes the practitioner is someone who cares and who can be trusted.

Gradually, and very tentatively, the practitioner begins to draw connections, to examine patterns in Dean's life. The practitioner notes, on the basis of what Dean has said, that in many situations in Dean's life he appears to be afraid to make changes, to take action. New situations particularly tend to paralyze Dean; the practitioner also helps Dean think about the possible analogy between other new situations and the newness of his relationship with the practitioner. As the practitioner probes at higher levels of empathy, and as Dean becomes more trusting and more comfortable, he helps Dean uncover and express some of his deepest fears about being homosexually oriented. He also confronts Dean on many apparent discrepancies. For example, a key discrepancy is that all the reasons Dean cites for wanting to change seem related to external pressures and that Dean may not have

committed *himself* to the change. Dean has never said he really wants to change because it is what he truly and deeply desires. Most of his reasons for wanting to change are to avoid external pressures. But Dean actually views himself as, and deeply identifies with, being homosexually oriented.

Dean only gradually begins to deal with the fact that another alternative to changing his sexual orientation may be open to him. That alternative is to accept the fact of his homosexual orientation and to accept himself as he is. Part of this also is to learn to deal with the outside pressures that he experiences as overwhelming.

Gradually, always tentatively, the practitioner pushes Dean to deal with his situation—and with himself—in more honest terms. Dean finally admits that he really does not want to change his sexual orientation, but that, on the other hand, he does not know how to live with it either. But some of the anger—generated by the helplessness of being caught in what appeared to be a hopeless situation—already is diminishing as Dean increasingly reveals and understands more of himself. Dean begins to deal with himself in a more honest way than he ever has before.

The practitioner and Dean examine the alternatives: (1) stay in the closet and keep his homosexual preferences to himself; (2) come out of the closet and learn to deal with himself and his environment in constructive and comfortable ways; or (3) attempt to change his sexual orientation and become heterosexual. The practitioner promises his support and help no matter which of the three Dean selects.

Dean chooses. He wishes to remain homosexually oriented and despises the idea of keeping it secret. He therefore no longer wishes it to be a secret. The general goal Dean and the practitioner agree on, then, is to remain homosexually oriented and to learn to deal comfortably with it. Several subobjectives include learning how to tell people and handle their reactions comfortably, how to deal with current and future employers without undue anxiety, and how to develop better skills in relating to other homosexually oriented men.

Dean says that he finally realizes how tied up he has been over this decision and that finally deciding makes him feel as though a giant burden has been lifted from his shoulders. He feels less and less depressed as he begins to see that he is not helpless in the situation, that there is hope.

The practitioner strongly supports these changes. But he also cautions that while making the decision was a crucial step—more, that it added directionality to Dean's life and to Dean's efforts at helping himself—making the decision in the office is different from being able to carry out the consequences in real life. Dean readily acknowledges this; he knows there is much more work ahead.

The practitioner and Dean set up a multifaceted program. Indeed, one part of the action program is the deepening of the relationship between Dean and the practitioner, who unconditionally demonstrates caring and regard for Dean. Dean begins to learn that he is indeed a person deserving of high self-esteem.

The practitioner also consults community resources and locates at a clinic a group run specifically for homosexually oriented men struggling with crises similar to Dean's. This is offered as an additional support to Dean, and Dean readily accepts.

Dean has a variety of fears which the practitioner attacks in two ways: by setting up a program to deal specifically with the anxiety, and by setting up a program to deal specifically with the behaviors in which Dean must engage in the natural environment.

Together with Dean, the practitioner designs a systematic desensitization package focused around Dean's fear of criticism and ridicule. Items on the hierarchy, organized from lesser to greater fear stimuli, deal with many of the situations in which Dean would or could possibly find himself, including telling his employer about his homosexual activity.

At the same time as the desensitization program is being implemented, the practitioner and Dean implement a social skills and assertive training program. Using modeling, behavior rehearsal, feedback, and reinforcement, Dean is trained in a variety of behaviors needed to engage in satisfying interpersonal situations. These behaviors include revealing to others his homosexual orientation and dealing with a variety of reactions (positive and negative), and social skills training to compensate for Dean's discomfort with and apparent lack of knowledge about how to relate to other young adults, both men and women. Dean is given structured homework assignments on a graduated basis according to the amount of difficulty with which he is prepared to deal.

Throughout this stage, the program is carried out in the context of continuing communication of empathy, warmth, and genuineness from the practitioner. This includes social reinforcement, praise, and encouragement when progress is made or when efforts in the direction of progress (e.g., attempting new behaviors) are made. It includes support and help when Dean expresses fears or questions about the direction of the program. It includes being especially sensitive to Dean's behaviors and feelings during interview sessions and, at one point, temporary suspension of implementation of one of the techniques to discuss and deal with a crisis Dean was experiencing.

The practitioner has selected several measures to evaluate progress, including Dean's own reports of how he is doing —subjectively and in terms of behaviors accomplished. The measures include the Fear Survey Inventory (Wolpe, 1973), a measure of assertiveness (Rathus, 1973), and a measure of self-esteem (Hudson, 1982), which is administered to Dean once a week. In addition, behavioral measures are used including tape recordings of the number of Dean's positive self-references during randomly selected interview sessions and a self-report measure of actual approach behaviors with other young adults comparing baseline with intervention and postintervention frequencies.

After about three months, and at the conclusion of most of the action programs (Dean chose to remain in the group at the clinic), Dean's increasingly self-assured demeanor, his obvious behavioral changes in the environment, and his own pleasure in what he termed "the new me" indicated that the intensive stages of intervention could be terminated. Comparisons on all measures showed improvement; particularly dramatic was the improvement in Dean's overall self-assuredness and in the measure of self-esteem. He did, indeed, seem like a new man. Dean reported satisfactory social contacts and the ability to deal comfortably with others' reactions when he told them about his sexual orientation. Dean noted proudly that the surest sign that he was "ready" was that he had finally told his boss "his secret," prepared for the worst. The reaction of his boss was to shrug his shoulders and say, "Nobody's perfect!"

The practitioner and Dean planned some follow-up, with formal dates for contact over the next six months arranged in advance. It was an emotional leave-taking, as Dean, shaking his head when he left, commented, "I can't believe I'm the same person who sat here so tormented only three months ago."

CLINICAL TRAINING

Because eclectic casework is essentially an evolving system, and because it has not been uniformly accepted as the optimal system in social work as a whole, it is dif-

ficult to specify all the parameters of effective clinical training. This is especially hampered by the fact that there is as yet no clear empirical evidence that caseworkers using this system are more effective than caseworkers using any other system.

However, it is possible to speculate about some aspects of training that would prepare practitioners to utilize an eclectic model. All of this must be viewed from the perspective that training for the degree of master of social work is essentially a two-year program, and that there are a number of competing (and legitimate) educational concerns within the MSW curriculum.

The typical MSW curriculum is comprised of five parts: courses in research, social policy, human behavior and the environment, social work practice, and two to three days of practicum experience for the entire two years. To produce the optimally functioning eclectic practitioner within that period of time would require the entire two years to be devoted to clinical training for eclectic practice. Since this essentially is impossible and may be undesirable as well (as mentioned earlier, social workers operate from a far broader base than therapeutic or clinical practice alone), the most efficient use of the time that is available in the two years would include the following:

1. Research courses including courses aimed at stimulating the practitioner's interest in and skill at assessing the research literature to form a basis for selecting empirically based techniques plus at least one course on single-system design teaching students how to monitor and evaluate their own practice.
2. Practice courses of three types. The first type would provide students with a conceptual model such as described in this chapter along with a practice framework such as the PRAISES model,

including assessment skills. The second type would be courses devoted to reviewing major approaches to casework, counseling, and therapy. The third type would be courses organized around learning of specific techniques such as described here, with the understanding that students will need to keep abreast of the literature and new developments in the field.

3. Practicum experience where students are guaranteed the opportunity to implement a range of the techniques learned in class with actual clients.

In fact, such a curriculum is available at the University of Hawaii and a few other schools of social work in the United States. It is hoped that future research will validate the effectiveness of both this type of training and its impact on clients.

FUTURE DIRECTIONS

Eclectic casework practice is a development geared toward enhancing the overall effectiveness of practice. Although there is no evidence as yet as to the effectiveness of eclectic caseworkers versus any other type of practitioners, the indirect evidence on effectiveness can be derived from the fact that the bulk of eclectic practice is comprised of use of a variety of techniques that, in their own right, have been shown to be effective. Moreover, eclectic practice is an attempt to systematize and objectify practice and calls for greater discrimination in the selection of knowledge than was true in the past and for a higher degree of professional responsibility in trying to ensure that what we do does indeed work. Eclectic casework practice maintains the profession's intrinsic humanistic orientation while focusing increased attention on sharpening and refining the technology the practitioner uses.

The eclectic caseworker is someone who

might be considered the new breed of social worker, the scientific practitioner. This is a social worker who: (1) systematically evaluates and monitors progress with each case; (2) grounds practice to the extent possible in empirically based knowledge, particularly the numerous available intervention techniques for which there is evidence of effectiveness, and uses those without such evidence only with due caution; and (3) has the skills and attitudes to be able and willing to keep learning and searching for new and more effective approaches to intervention.

The future of eclectic practice promises to be an exciting one. There is some evidence from informal contacts among social work faculty that the core ingredients of eclectic casework are being taught at an increasing number of universities. But a number of largely empirical issues need to be addressed:

1. What is the optimal training arrangement for eclectic caseworkers and can generalization to actual practice after graduation be attained?
2. Is the PRAISES model or any other integrative framework essential to the success of eclectic practice?
3. Is there a need—and can it be empirically assessed—for developing a more unified theoretical framework for integrating the variety of techniques of which eclectic casework is comprised?
4. And, most important, does eclectic casework really make a difference? Will future research clearly establish that practitioners using eclectic casework are more effective than practitioners using any other form of practice?

REFERENCES

Azrin, N. H., & Nunn, R. C. (1977). *Habit control*. New York: Simon & Shuster.
Azrin, N. H., & Nunn, R. C. (1982). Habit reversal: A method of eliminating nervous habits and tics. *Behaviour Research and Therapy, 11*, 619–628.
Barlow, D. H. (Ed.) (1981). *Behavioral assessment of*

adult disorders. New York: Guilford.

Barlow, D. H., et al. (1984). *The scientist practitioner.* New York: Pergamon.

Beck, A. T. (1976). *Cognitive therapy and the emotional disorders.* New York: International Universities Press.

Beck, A. T., Rush, A. J., Shaw, B. F., & Emery, G. (1979). *Cognitive therapy of depression.* New York: Guilford.

Beck, D. F., & Jones, M. A. (1973). *Progress on family problems.* New York: Family Service Association of America.

Bellack, A. S., & Hersen, M. (Eds.). (1979). *Research and practice in social skills training.* New York: Plenum.

Bellack, A. S., & Hersen, M. (Eds.). (1985). *Dictionary of behavior therapy techniques.* New York: Pergamon.

Bergin, A. E. (1969). A technique for improving desensitization via warmth, empathy and emotional re-experiencing of the hierarchy event. In R. Rubin & C. Franks (Eds.), *Advances in behavior therapy, 1968* (pp. 117–130). New York: Academic.

Bergin, A. E., & Strupp, H. H. (1972). *Changing frontiers in the science of psychotherapy.* Chicago: Aldine-Atherton.

Blenkner, M., et al. (1964). *Serving the aging: An experiment in social work and public health nursing.* New York: Community Service Society.

Bloom, M. (1975). *The paradox of helping: Introduction to the philosophy of scientific practice.* New York: Wiley.

Bloom, M., & Fischer, J. (1982). *Evaluating practice: Guidelines for the accountable professional.* Englewood Cliffs, NJ: Prentice Hall.

Brager, G., & Holloway, S. (1978). *Changing human service organizations: Politics and practice.* New York: Free Press.

Brehony, K. A., & Geller, E. S. (1981). Agoraphobia: Appraisal of research and a proposal for an integrative model. In M. Hersen et al. (Eds.), *Progress in behavior modification,* Vol. 12 (pp. 1–66). New York: Academic Press.

Briar, S. (1978). Toward the integration of practice and research. Paper presented at NASW Conference on the Future of Social Work Research, San Antonio, October, 1978.

Butcher, J. N., & Koss, M. P. (1978). Research on brief and crisis-oriented psychotherapies. In S. L. Garfield & A. E. Bergin (Eds.), *Handbook of psychotherapy and behavior change* (2nd ed.) (pp. 725–768). New York: Wiley.

Cairns, K. (1972). Desensitization and relationship quality. Unpublished master's thesis, University of Calgary, Alberta, Canada.

Carkhuff, R. R. (1969). *Helping and human relations,* Vol. 2. New York: Holt, Rinehart, & Winston.

Carkhuff, R. R., & Berenson, B. (1976). *Teaching as treatment.* Amherst, MA: Human Resources Development Press.

Cautela, J. R. (1967). Covert sensitization. *Psychological Reports, 20,* 459–468.

Ciminero, A. R. (Ed.). (1977). *Handbook of behavioral assessment.* New York: Wiley.

Cocozzelli, C. L. (In Press). The theoretical orientation of clinical social workers: Ideology or pragmatism? *Journal of Social Service Research.*

Coe, W. C., & Buckner, C. G. (1975). Expectation, hypnosis, and suggestion methods. In F. H. Kanfer & A. P. Goldstein (Eds.), *Helping people change* (pp. 393–432). New York: Pergamon.

Cone, J. D., & Hawkins, R. P. (Eds.). (1977). *Behavioral assessment.* New York: Brunner/Mazel.

Cormier, W. H., & Cormier, L. S. (1985). *Interviewing strategies for helpers* (2nd ed.). Monterey, CA: Brooks/Cole.

Curran, J. P., & Monti, P. M. (Eds.). (1982). *Social skills training.* New York: Guilford

Curtiss, S. (1976). The compatibility of humanistic and behavioristic approaches in a state mental hospital. In A. Wandersman et al. (Eds.), *Humanism and behaviorism: Dialogue and growth* (pp. 235–252). New York: Pergamon.

Dowling, T. H., & Frantz, T. T. (1975). The influence of facilitative relationship on imitative learning. *Journal of Counseling Psychology, 22,* 259–263.

D'Zurilla, T. J., & Nezu, A. (1982). Social problem solving in adults. In P. C. Kendall (Ed.), *Advances in cognitive-behavioral research and therapy,* Vol. 1 (pp. 201–274). New York: Academic Press.

Ellis, A., & Grieger, R. (Eds.). (1977). *Handbook of rational-emotive therapy.* New York: Springer.

Emery, G., Hollon, S. D., & Bedrosian, R. C. (Eds.). (1981). *New directions in cognitive therapy.* New York: Guilford.

Feld, S., & Radin, N. (1982). *Social psychology for social work and the mental health professions.* New York: Columbia.

Fischer, J. (1971). A framework for the analysis of clinical theories of induced change. *Social Service Review, 45,* 440–454.

Fischer, J. (1973). Is casework effective? A review. *Social Work, 18,* 5–20.

Fischer, J. (1976). *The effectiveness of social casework.* Springfield, IL: Charles C Thomas.

Fischer, J. (1978). *Effective casework practice: An eclectic approach.* New York: McGraw-Hill.

Fischer, J. (1981). The social work revolution. *Social Work, 26,* 199–207.

Fish, J. M. (1973). *Placebo therapy.* San Francisco: Jossey-Bass.

Foa, E. B., & Steketee, G. S. (1979). Obsessive-compulsives: Conceptual issues and treatment considerations. In M. Hersen et al. (Eds.), *Progress in behavior modification,* Vol. 8 (pp. 1–53). New York: Academic Press.

Ford, D., & Urban, H. (1963). *Systems of psychotherapy.* New York: Wiley.

Foreyt, J. P., & Rathjen, D. P. (Eds.). (1978). *Cognitive behavior therapy.* New York: Plenum.

Foxx, R. M., & Bechtel, D. R. (1982). Overcorrection. In M. Hersen et al. (Eds.). *Progress in behavior modification,* Vol. 13 (pp. 227–288). New York: Academic Press.

Frank, J. D. (1972). *Persuasion and healing* (2nd ed.). Baltimore: Johns Hopkins.

Franks, C. M., & Wilson, G. T. (Eds.). (1973–1984). *Annual review of behavior therapy*, Vol. 1–9. New York: Guilford.

Franks, C. M., Wilson, C. M., Kendall, P. C., & Brownell, K. D. (Eds.). (1982). *Annual review of behavior therapy*, Vol. 8. New York: Guilford.

Gambrill, E. D. (1977). *Behavior modification: Handbook of assessment, intervention, and evaluation.* San Francisco: Jossey-Bass.

Gambrill, E. (1983). *Casework: A competency-based approach.* Englewood Cliffs, NJ: Prentice-Hall.

Gantt, S. et al. (1980). Paraprofessional skills: Maintenance of empathic sensitivity after training. *Journal of Counseling Psychology, 27,* 374–379.

Gianetti, V. J., & Wells, R. A. (1985). Psychotherapeutic outcome and professional affiliation. *Social Service Review, 59,* 32–43.

Gold, G. H. (1976). Affective behaviorism: A synthesis of humanism and behaviorism with children. In A. Wandersman et al. (Eds.), *Humanism and behaviorism: Dialogue and growth* (pp. 253–264). New York: Pergamon.

Goldfried, M. R. (1979). Anxiety reduction through cognitive-behavioral intervention. In P. C. Kendall & S. D. Hollon (Eds.), *Cognitive-behavioral interventions* (pp. 117–152). New York: Academic Press.

Goldfried, M. R., & Davison, G. C. (1976). *Clinical behavior therapy.* New York: Holt, Rinehart and Winston.

Goldstein, A. (1976). Appropriate expression training—humanistic behavior therapy. In A. Wandersman et al. (Eds.), *Humanism and behaviorism: Dialogue and growth* (pp. 223–234). New York: Pergamon.

Goldstein, A. P. (1980). Relationship-enhancement methods. In F. H. Kanfer & A. P. Goldstein (Eds.), *Helping people change* (2nd ed.) (pp. 18–57). New York: Pergamon.

Goldstein, A. P., & Kanfer, F. H. (Eds.). (1979). *Maximizing treatment gains: Transfer enhancement in psychotherapy.* New York: Academic Press.

Goldstein, A. P., & Simonson, N. (1971). Social psychological approaches to psychotherapy research. In A. E. Bergin & S. L. Garfield (Eds.), *Handbook of psychotherapy and behavior change* (pp. 154–196). New York: John Wiley.

Goleman, D. (1985, April 30). Social workers vault into a leading role in psychotherapy. *The New York Times,* pp. C1, C9.

Gordon, R., & Gordon, K. (1966). Is short-term psychotherapy enough? *Journal of the Medical Society of New Jersey, 63,* 41–44.

Harris, D. E., & Lichenstein, E. (1971). The contribution of non-specific social variables to a successful behavioral treatment of smoking. Paper presented at the Annual Meeting of the Western Psychological Association, San Francisco, April 1971.

Haynes, S. N. (1978). *Principles of behavioral assessment.* New York: Gardner.

Haynes, S. N., & Wilson, C. C. (1979). *Behavioral assessment.* San Francisco: Jossey-Bass.

Henry, W. E., Sims, J. H., & Spray, S. C. (1971). *The fifth profession.* San Francisco: Jossey-Bass.

Hepworth, D. H., & Larsen, J. (1982). *Direct social work practice.* Homewood, IL: Dorsey.

Hersen, M., & Barlow, D. H. (1976). *Single case experimental designs.* New York: Pergamon.

Hersen, M., & Bellack, A. S. (Eds.). (1981). *Behavioral assessment: A practical handbook* (2nd ed.). New York: Pergamon.

Hersen, M., et al. (Eds.). (1975–1984). *Progress in behavior modification,* Vol. 1–16. New York: Academic Press.

Hudson, W. W. (1982). *The clinical measurement package.* Homewood, IL: Dorsey.

Janis, I. L. (Ed.). (1982). *Counseling on personal decisions.* New Haven: Yale.

Janis, I. L., & Mann, L. (1977). *Decision-making.* New York: Free Press.

Jayaratne, S. (1978). A study of clinical eclecticism. *Social Service Review, 52,* 621–631.

Jayaratne, S. (1982). Characteristics and theoretical orientations of clinical social workers: A survey. *Journal of Social Service Research, 4,* 17–30.

Jayaratne, S., & Levy, R. (1979). *Empirical clinical practice.* New York: Columbia University Press.

Karoly, P., & Steffen, J. J. (Eds.). (1980). *Improving the long-term effects of psychotherapy.* New York: Gardner.

Kazdin, A. E. (1982). *Single-case research designs.* New York: Oxford.

Kazdin, A. E., & Smith, G. A. (1979). Covert conditioning: A review. *Advances in Behavior Research and Therapy, 2,* 57–98.

Kazdin, A. E., & Wilson, G. T. (1978). *Evaluation of behavior therapy: Issues, evidence, and research strategies.* Cambridge, MA: Ballinger.

Kendall, P. C., & Hollon, S. D. (Eds.). (1979). *Cognitive-behavioral interventions: Theory, practice, and procedures.* New York: Academic Press.

Kendall, P. C., & Hollon, S. D. (1981). *Assessment strategies for cognitive-behavioral interventions.* New York: Academic Press.

Kirschenbaum, D. S., & Flanery, R. C. (1983). Behavioral contracting: Outcomes and elements. In M. Hersen et al. (Eds.), *Progress in behavior modification,* Vol. 15 (pp. 217–275). New York: Academic Press.

Kuhn, T. S. (1970). *The structure of scientific revolutions* (2nd ed.). Chicago: University of Chicago Press.

Lazarus, A. A. (1981). *The practice of multi-modal therapy.* New York: McGraw-Hill.

Lick, J., & Bootzin, R. (1975). Expectancy factors in the treatment of fear: Methodology and theoretical issues. *Psychological Bulletin, 82,* 917–931.

Luborsky, L., Singer, B., & Luborsky, L. (1975). Comparative studies of psychotherapy. *Archives of General Psychiatry, 32,* 995–1008.

Mahoney, M. J. (1974). *Cognition and behavior modification.* Cambridge, MA: Ballinger.

Mahoney, M. J. (1978). Cognitive and self-control therapies. In S. L. Garfield & A. E. Bergin (Eds.), *Handbook of psychotherapy and behavior change* (pp. 689–722). New York: Wiley.

Marshall, E. K., Kurtz, P. D., et al. (Eds.). (1982).

Interpersonal helping skills. San Francisco: Jossey-Bass.

Marshall, W. L., et al. (1979). The current status of flooding therapy. In M. Hersen et al. (Eds.), *Progress in behavior modification*, Vol. 7 (pp. 205–275). New York: Academic Press.

Martin, G. A., & Worthington, E. L. (1982). Behavioral homework. In M. Hersen et al. (Eds.), *Progress in behavior modification*, Vol. 13 (pp. 197–226). New York: Academic Press.

Mash, E., & Terdal, L. (1981). *Behavioral assessment of childhood disorders.* New York: Guilford.

Mathews, A. M., et al. (1981). *Agoraphobia: Nature and treatment.* New York: Guilford.

Meichenbaum, D. (1977). *Cognitive-behavior modification.* New York: Plenum.

Mickelson, D., & Stevic, R. (1971). The differential effects of facilitative and nonfacilitative behavioral counselors. *Journal of Counseling Psychology, 18*(4), 314–319.

Mitchell, K. M., Bozarth, J. D., & Krauft, C. C. (1977). A reappraisal of the therapeutic effectiveness of accurate empathy, non-possessive warmth, and genuineness. In A. S. Gurman & A. M. Razin (Eds.), *Effective psychotherapy: A handbook of research* (pp. 482–502). New York: Pergamon.

Morris, R. J., & Suckerman, K. R. (1974a). The importance of the therapeutic relationship in systematic desensitization. *Journal of Consulting and Clinical Psychology, 42,* 148.

Morris, R. J., & Suckerman, K. R. (1974b). Therapist warmth as a factor in automated systematic desensitization. *Journal of Consulting and Clinical Psychology, 42,* 244–250.

Muench, G. (1964). An investigation of time-limited psychotherapy. *American Psychologist, 19* (abstract).

Mullen, E. J. (1978). The construction of personal models for effective practice: A method for utilizing research findings to guide social intervention. *Journal of Social Service Research, 2,* 45–64.

Murray, E. J., & Jacobson, L. I. (1978). Cognition and learning in traditional and behavioral therapy. In S. L. Garfield & A. E. Bergin (Eds.), *Handbook of psychotherapy and behavior change* (2nd ed.) (pp. 661–688). New York: Wiley.

Naar, R. (1970). Client-centered and behavior therapies: Their peaceful coexistence: A case study. *Journal of Abnormal Psychology, 76,* 155–160.

Nameneck, A. A., & Schuldt, W. J. (1971). Differential effects of experimenters' personality and instructional sets on verbal conditioning. *Journal of Counseling Psychology, 18,* 173–176.

Nay, W. R. (1979). *Multimethod clinical assessment.* New York: Halsted.

Novaco, R. W. (1979). Cognitive regulation of anger and stress. In P. C. Kendall & S. D. Hollon (Eds.), *Cognitive–behavioral interventions* (pp. 241–286). New York: Academic Press.

Parloff, M. B., & Wolfe, B. E. (1978). Research on therapist variables in relation to process and outcome. In S. L. Garfield & A. E. Bergin (Eds.), *Handbook of psychotherapy and behavior change*

(2nd ed.) (pp. 233–282). New York: John Wiley.

Phillips, E. L., et al. (1973). Behavior shaping works for delinquents. *Psychology Today, 7,* 75–79.

Phillips, E. L., & Wiener, D. (1966). *Short-term psychotherapy and structured behavior change.* New York: McGraw-Hill.

Rachman, S. J., & Wilson, G. T. (1980). *The effects of psychological therapy* (2nd ed.). New York: Pergamon Press.

Raimy, V. (1975). *Misunderstandings of the self.* San Francisco: Jossey-Bass.

Rathus, S. A. (1973). A 30-item schedule for assessing assertive behavior. *Behavior Therapy, 4,* 398–406.

Reid, W. J. (1978). *The task-centered system.* New York: Columbia University Press.

Reid, W. J., & Hanrahan, P. (1982). Recent evaluations of social work: Grounds for optimism. *Social Work, 27,* 328–340.

Reid, W., & Shyne, A. (1969). *Brief and extended casework.* New York: Columbia.

Ricks, D. F., Wandersman, A., & Poppen, P. J. (1976). Humanism and behaviorism: Toward new syntheses. In A. Wandersman et al. (Eds.), *Humanism and behaviorism: Dialogue and growth.* (pp. 383–402). New York: Pergamon.

Rimm, D. C., & Masters, J. C. (1979). *Behavior therapy: Techniques and empirical findings* (2nd ed.). New York: Academic Press.

Roberts, R. W., & Nee, R. (Eds.). (1970). *Theories of social casework.* Chicago: University of Chicago Press.

Shelton, J. L., & Levy, R. L. (1981). *Behavioral assignments and treatment compliance.* Champaign, IL: Research Press.

Shlien, J., et al. (1962). Effects of time limits: A comparison of two psychotherapies. *Journal of Counseling Psychology, 9,* 31–34.

Siporin, M. (1975). *Introduction to social work and practice.* New York: Macmillan.

Strong, S. R. (1978). Social psychological approach to psychotherapy research. In S. L. Garfield & A. E. Bergin (Eds.), *Handbook of psychotherapy and behavior change* (pp. 101–135). New York: John Wiley.

Sundberg, N. D. (1977). *Assessment of persons.* Englewood Cliffs, NJ: Prentice-Hall.

Thomas, E. J. (1977). The BESDAS model for effective practice. *Social Work Research and Abstracts, 13,* 12–17.

Thorne, F. C. (1973). Eclectic psychotherapy. In R. Corsini (Ed.), *Current psychotherapies* (pp. 445–486). Itasca, IL: F. E. Peacock.

Thyer, B. A. (1983). Behavior modification in social work practice. In M. Hersen et al. (Eds.), *Progress in behavior modification*, Vol. 15. New York: Academic Press.

Truax, C. B., & Mitchell, K. M. (1971). Research on certain therapist interpersonal skills in relation to process and outcome. In A. E. Bergin & S. L. Garfield (Eds.), *Handbook of psychotherapy and behavior change* (pp. 299–344). New York: Wiley.

Turner, S. M., Calhoun, K. S., & Adams, H. E. (Eds.). (1981). *Handbook of clinical behavior therapy.* New York: Wiley.

Turpin, G. (1983). The behavioral management of tic disorders: A critical review. *Advances in Behavior Research and Therapy, 5,* 203–245.

Twentyman, C. T., & Zimering, R. T. (1979). Behavioral training of social skills: A critical review. In M. Hersen et al. (Eds.), *Progress in behavior modification,* Vol. 7 (pp. 319–400). New York: Academic Press.

Vitalo, R. (1970). Effects of facilitative interpersonal functioning in a verbal conditioning paradigm. *Journal of Counseling Psychology, 17,* 141–144.

Walker, C. E., Hedberg, A., Clement, P. W., & Wright, L. (1981). *Clinical procedures for behavior therapy.* Englewood Cliffs, NJ: Prentice-Hall.

Wandersman, A., Poppen, P., & Ricks, D. (Eds.). (1976). *Humanism and behaviorism: Dialogue and growth.* New York: Pergamon.

Wattie, B. (1973). Evaluating short-term casework in a family agency. *Social Casework, 54,* 609–616.

Wilson, G. T. (1982). Clinical issues and strategies in the practice of behavior therapy. In C. M. Franks et al. (Eds.), *Annual review of behavior therapy: Theory and practice,* Vol. 8. New York: Guilford.

Wilson, G. T., Franks, C. M., Brownell, K. D., & Kendall, P. C. (Eds.). (1984). *Annual review of behavior therapy,* Vol. 9. New York: Guilford.

Wodarski, J. S. (1981). *The role of research in clinical practice.* Baltimore: University Park Press.

Wolberg, L. (1966). *Psychotherapy and the behavioral sciences.* New York: Grune & Stratton.

Wolpe, J. (1969). Presidential address, second annual meeting of the Association for the Advancement of Behavior of Therapy. In R. Rubin and C. Franks (Eds.), *Advances in behavior therapy, 1968.* New York: Academic Press.

Wolpe, J. (1973). *The practice of behavior therapy.* New York: Pergamon Press.

Wolpe, J. (1982). *The practice of behavior therapy* (3rd ed.). New York: Pergamon.

CHAPTER 12

Eclectic Psychotherapies:
A Critique of Leading Approaches

Windy Dryden

To attempt a comprehensive critique of the approaches to eclectic psychotherapy presented in this volume would require an entire separate text. Since space is limited, I will discuss the major strengths and weaknesses of each approach from a decision-making perspective. I will thus consider how helpful each approach is in providing practitioners with detailed criteria for making appropriate clinical decisions.

I have read many texts on psychotherapy and have been disappointed by the majority of them. It seems to me that psychotherapists have, in general, been relatively unsuccessful in communicating what guides them in the practice of their work. And yet this is precisely the quality that eclectic psychotherapists need to demonstrate if their readers are to fully understand their approaches. Thus, to say "I am an eclectic psychotherapist" tells us nothing; to say "I am an eclectic psychotherapist combining psychoanalytic and behavioral approaches tells us a little more, but we are still basically in the dark concerning the guiding principles of the practitioner's approach. To say "I am a multimodal therapist" or "a transtheoretical therapist" or a practitioner of any other type of eclectic therapy outlined in this volume again tells us yet a little more about the person's work, but unless certain points are *clearly* communicated, the reader is still left with more questions unanswered than answered. Labels are no substitutes for clarity!

With this caveat in mind, I will first outline a decision-making framework that has helped me to bring some order to the written work of my colleagues, before addressing myself to the task at hand. My hope is that this framework will help readers to appreciate the extent to which my colleagues have been successful in communicating clearly the principles that guide them in making informed decisions in their work as eclectic psychotherapists.

THERAPEUTIC DECISION MAKING

Every therapist of whatever persuasion is faced with making a myriad of different decisions at various levels in the practice of psychotherapy. Perhaps one of the attractions of aligning oneself with one of the many *distinct* therapeutic systems that currently exist is that a prescribed framework is available to help the therapist make such decisions. It is certainly a comfort to know, as one trainee psychoanalyst once put it, that "you are doing the right thing even though the patient isn't improving." Eclectic psychotherapists do not have such sources of comfort readily at hand, unless, of course, the eclectic approaches to psychotherapy outlined in this volume in turn become prescribed therapeutic systems.* And yet if eclectic psychotherapists are to make effective therapeutic decisions, they must have at their disposal frameworks to help them do so. My central point here has been made by Norcross in Chapter 1: Facing eclectic therapists is the challenge to "operationalize fully treatment procedures and to concretize, as much as possible, therapists' decision-making processes" (p. 20). It will thus be a major theme of this chapter to determine to what extent my colleagues have responded to this challenge.

As mentioned previously, eclectic psychotherapists are faced with making a myriad of different decisions at different levels of analysis, from selecting organizing frameworks that guide their practical work (at the most abstract level) to making specific responses to immediate client material (at the most concrete level).

At the most abstract level, eclectic psychotherapists are guided by theoretical considerations *even if they deny that they have theoretical allegiances*. Lazarus, a technical eclectic, has acknowledged this in his chapter: "Every practitioner has, at the very least, an implicit theory that determines how he or she conceptualizes

problems and that influences his or her choice of techniques" (p. 67). Cornsweet (1983) has argued that a theory in psychotherapy is "primarily a model, a way of structuring and understanding a complex set of phenomena. It provides the clinician, in particular, with a framework from which to view the patient and with a rationale for intervention" (p. 308).

Taking Cornsweet's statement as a starting point, I recently argued that

... therapists cannot help but be theoretical in that (a) they structure what they observe, and (b) this structuring is based on explicit or implicit assumptions which influence their actions to some degree. Thus therapists who claim to be atheoretical and conduct therapy in a highly individualistic, eclectic fashion are in fact probably operating from an implicit, informal set of beliefs; while therapists who choose not to understand why client problems develop or why therapeutic techniques work and merely use those techniques that are deemed to be effective are, as Cornsweet (1983) has shown, operating from a radical empirical theory which operates on observational data alone. (Dryden, 1984a, p. 354)

Many eclectic therapists have, perhaps understandably, eschewed theory construction since the task probably involves the development of what Beutler calls a "superordinate" theory. In his chapter, Beutler argues that "if eclectic psychotherapy is to be effective, it must provide a *sound theory* to direct the modification of procedures in accordance with defined patient characteristics" (p. 96, emphasis added). For Beutler a superordinate theory "must facilitate communication ... must be able to describe and encompass therapeutic change agents from diverse points of view ... and must provide a focus of treatment" (p. 97). It thus behooves my colleagues to clearly specify the nature of their superordinate theory and upon what epistemological foundations such theory rests.

Since psychotherapy is, according to

---

*One of the dangers inherent in the production of this volume.

Beutler, a process of persuasion, eclectic psychotherapists who do not pay attention to possible inconsistencies in their implicit theories run the risk of unwittingly "persuading" their clients to adopt a set of incoherent, contradictory beliefs with all the incumbent dangers that this entails.

A useful organizing framework thus has to serve eclectic therapists on three major criteria. First, as Beutler has noted, it has to be communicable and comprehensible. Second, it has to reduce the risk of the communication of inconsistent messages to clients. Third, and most important, it has to have clinical utility; i.e., it has to help eclectic therapists make sense of what would otherwise be an overwhelming mass of data, while showing due regard for the complex nature of interacting clinical variables. It should not oversimplify matters. Such a framework must, at least, help readers understand why therapists intervene in different ways with different clients at different stages in the change process. It has to account for the reasons why therapists choose to see clients in different therapeutic arenas, and it has to specify the different ways in which therapists develop and maintain effective therapeutic alliances with their clients. An organizing framework must, then, provide practitioners with helpful criteria for the execution of sound clinical decisions in what Frances, Clarkin, and Perry (1984) have called the practice of "differential therapeutics." This point requires amplification.

First, when a client consults a therapist, the latter has to decide whether to see that person in one of a number of therapeutic arenas (Dryden, 1984b), i.e., individual therapy, couple therapy, family therapy, or group therapy. The therapist also has to decide how seriously to take the client's preferences in this matter. Eclectic approaches to therapy have to specify criteria concerning what constitute sound clinical decisions on this issue. An excel-

lent example of an eclectic approach to psychotherapy that does just this is to be found in Frances, Clarkin, and Perry (1984). In addition, the eclectic approach should ideally specify criteria concerning movement between arenas and concurrent use of multiple arenas.

Second, eclectic therapists have to make a number of important decisions concerning the establishment and maintenance of effective therapeutic alliances with their clients. Eclectic approaches should thus preferably offer a way of conceptualizing the therapeutic alliance so that decisions to establish different kinds of alliances with different clients can be clearly understood.

Third, an eclectic approach needs to offer a comprehensive *and* clinically useful framework to account for client variation. The fact that clients do differ from one another is obviously a truism and one that does not, by itself, suggest guidelines for differential therapeutics. What are needed are clear criteria concerning the fundamental ways in which clients differ from one another which also provide a link between assessment and treatment. In addition, the approach needs to argue why these particular criteria have been chosen over competing criteria.

Fourth, to be truly useful, client variation postulates need to interact with a variety of treatment postulates. The latter need to take into account the fact that interventions can be conceptualized at a variety of levels. Eclectic approaches need to provide guidelines that demonstrate variation at each level. Thus, these guidelines must suggest ways in which therapists are to vary their interactive style, their use of therapeutic strategies, and their choices of therapeutic methods and techniques (which are the means of implementing these strategies). If certain styles, strategies, and techniques are not to be employed, reasons have to be put forward for their omission. Most important, these guidelines need to be combined with the client variation postulates discussed previously.

Fifth, eclectic approaches should take into account the fact that therapeutic processes change over time. The authors need to specify not only how these changes are conceptualized but also how they interact with the client variation and treatment variation postulates discussed previously.

It should be noted that, at this early stage of the development of the eclectic therapies, it is unlikely that any one approach will score highly on all these criteria. However, it is my contention that such strengths are to be found among the approaches featured in this volume and that in true eclectic fashion these approaches have much to learn from one another.

MULTIMODAL THERAPY

Arnold Lazarus developed his multimodal approach to eclectic therapy primarily as a result of becoming dissatisfied with, first, behavior therapy and subsequently cognitive-behavior therapy. He cogently argues that a comprehensive approach to eclectic psychotherapy has to take into account seven fundamental modalities of human experience. Lazarus argues, correctly in my view, that therapists' clinical work is founded on specific theories that determine the manner in which they conceptualize clients' problems and how they construe human change processes. In his chapter, he notes that multimodal therapy "rests primarily on the theoretical base of *social learning theory* ... but draws also from *general system theory* ... and *group and communications theory*. ... These theoretical systems blend harmoniously into a congruent framework" (pp. 67–68). However, while he has outlined the theoretical foundations of multimodal therapy in skeletal

form, he does not show clearly, in his chapter, how these three theoretical systems blend harmoniously into a congruent framework. This perhaps constitutes one of the major weaknesses of multimodal therapy as it now exists.

However, when assessment of client problems is considered with respect to the practice of therapy, the strengths of multimodal therapy as an eclectic approach emerge. Client variation is determined through rigorous analyses of comprehensive modality profiles. Here therapists attempt to determine clients' strengths and deficits on each of the seven modalities of human experience that constitute the BASIC I.D. Indeed, multimodal therapists often undertake second-order BASIC I.D. assessments when appropriate. These often yield subtle differences between clients who may present with overtly similar clinical problems. In addition, clients are deemed to be "structurally" different. Such differences emerge when multimodal therapists construct structural profiles focusing particularly on the degree to which clients rely on each of the seven modalities in conducting their lives. A further way in which the multimodal approach demonstrates attention to client variation is in its application of a method called "tracking." Here Lazarus argues that clients who may experience similar clinical problems may differ markedly in the order in which their modalities are "fired." Thus, a client with a CISB firing order is deemed to differ quite markedly from a client who has an ISBC firing order. As we shall see, these differences have important implications for the sequencing of treatment interventions.

Having demonstrated clearly how clients vary from a multimodal perspective, Lazarus proceeds to show how such assessments structure the practice of psychotherapy. Initially, "technique selection commences with the most obvious and logical procedures" (p. 77). It is apparent from his chapter that, in this respect, Lazarus is clearly guided by the empirical literature on the efficacy of specific techniques for specific psychological problems and that he favors techniques that are closely associated with social learning theory. For example, techniques designed to alleviate marital problems are derived from treatment methods closely allied to social learning approaches to marital therapy. What is not so clear in this respect is when Lazarus might use techniques derived from general systems theory and communications theory —theoretical perspectives that, Lazarus argues, also feature in the theoretical underpinnings of multimodal therapy.

As noted previously, a particularly elegant feature of multimodal therapy concerns the way in which multimodal therapists determine the order in which therapeutic techniques are applied with different clients. Thus, employing the "tracking" procedure, multimodal therapists would treat a client who has an ISBC firing order with techniques in the order in which the person's modalities are fired (i.e., imagery, sensation, behavior, and cognition). Lazarus' hypothesis is that treatment thus properly sequenced will be more effective than treatment where such sequences are random. It is to be regretted that to date Lazarus has been unable to attract funding to carry out systematic research on multimodal therapy since, although these guidelines are intuitively sensible, empirical confirmation of such hypotheses is yet to come.

While multimodal therapy, as outlined in Lazarus' chapter, does provide clinicians with a great deal of assistance in choosing among different techniques and their orderly sequence, Lazarus has not, to date, given equal attention to the selection and ordering of different therapeutic "strategies." At present, strategy selection is implicit in multimodal therapy, and yet it would strengthen the approach for this issue to be made more explicit.

Lazarus does give careful attention to therapist-client matching, particularly as it pertains to therapist style and client expectations for therapy. One of the major purposes of initial sessions in multimodal therapy is to enable therapists to answer two questions: (1) Am I the best therapist for this particular client? and (2) Which particular therapeutic style should I emphasize in my initial interactions with this particular client? Thus, multimodal therapy, particularly at the beginning of therapy, does advocate sensitive attention to therapeutic alliance issues, especially as they refer to the "bond" dimension (Bordin, 1979). However, it is less clear from Lazarus' chapter what factors clinicians need to take into consideration concerning what may occasion appropriate shifts in therapeutic style. Here, Lazarus argues that therapists should initially follow fairly closely the client's "script" concerning expectations, while subsequently developing a therapeutic style that appears to be more suitable for the client's problem. With regard to therapist-client matching, Lazarus argues that therapists whose structural profiles, for example, reveal especially high ratings on the cognitive and behavioral modalities may have problems understanding clients who score highly on the affective and imagery modalities. This is plausible and suggests very important areas for empirical inquiry. On a similar theme, Lazarus argues, later in his chapter, that questions concerning degrees of appropriate therapeutic involvement with clients can be answered with recourse to "countertransference" factors. It would be helpful if Lazarus, who is very explicit on other clinical topics, could be more specific on this important issue.

In his chapter, Lazarus does not address himself to the important issue of therapeutic arena selection. Thus, it is not clear what guides multimodal therapists in their decisions concerning what may be the most appropriate therapeutic arena to work in with different clients at the outset of therapy and when arena changes are suggested. It is also not clear how multimodal therapists vary their therapeutic approach with different clients over time. I believe that multimodal therapy could be considerably enhanced by applying Prochaska and DiClemente's suggestions on this particular issue. While Lazarus outlines specific mechanisms of change, it is difficult to pinpoint how he applies his conceptualizations in therapeutic practice. Indeed, my suggestion is that his schema here could form the foundation upon which the issue of differential selection of therapeutic strategies may be based. On the other hand, Lazarus does present clear guidelines to help therapists who struggle to appropriately respond to instances of "therapeutic resistance."

In conclusion, it is apparent that, from a decision-making perspective, multimodal therapy has many strengths as an eclectic approach. These concern the specification of client variation, how such variation informs choice of therapeutic techniques, the close attention paid to how best to meet clients' expectations at the beginning of therapy, and the appropriate choice of initial interactive styles with clients. Future developments in multimodal therapy could usefully lead to the following: more explicit guidelines being made available for the selection of appropriate therapeutic arenas and movements between arenas; more attention being paid to therapeutic strategies and how these may suggest therapeutic methods; the mechanisms of change being given a more central role in the approach, particularly to facilitate work linking strategy selection to technique selection; and finally, more explicit attention being paid to the issue of how the practice of multimodal therapy changes over time and what occasions such changes.

SYSTEMATIC ECLECTIC PSYCHOTHERAPY

Larry Beutler's approach to eclectic psychotherapy is based on interpersonal influence theory, an organizing framework chosen by him according to his own personal preferences. This is an important point to bear in mind while considering approaches to eclectic psychotherapy, since it is unlikely that all psychotherapists will adopt a commonly agreed superordinate theory to guide their eclectic endeavors. I personally find Beutler's choice of interpersonal influence theory "persuasive," which, to some degree, reflects my own initial background in social psychology. However, I know that a number of eclectically orientated clinicians have been dissatisfied with Beutler's work precisely because he has chosen interpersonal influence theory as his organizing framework. This is due to the distaste such clinicians have for the view that psychotherapy is basically a process of "persuasion." It may well be then that interpersonal influence theory is not "neutral" enough to provide an adequate common language for the eclectic psychotherapies. Indeed, it is unlikely that any current theory could meet such a criterion.

Despite the concern I have about the appeal of interpersonal influence theory as an organizing framework, I consider that Beutler has made a promising start in developing an approach to eclectic psychotherapy which succeeds in providing clinicians with clear decision-making guidelines. Thus, Beutler has selected a number of dimensions along which clients are deemed to vary. He argues that symptom complexity, coping style, reactance level, and focal theme can be combined to suggest "therapeutic menus" for use by eclectic clinicians with different clients. In doing so he puts forward a number of testable propositions which will hopefully stimulate much-needed research.

Beutler makes a number of suggestions

about how formal assessment procedures can help clinicians make appropriate judgments concerning where particular clients stand on the four client dimensions. These assessments then form the basis for the development of treatment plans tailored to the different needs of different clients. These suggest the employment of (a) appropriate therapeutic strategies (namely, insight enhancement, emotional awareness, emotional escalation, emotion reducing, behavioral control, and perceptual change); (b) specific techniques that may implement such strategies; and (c) an appropriate therapeutic style which in particular takes into account the client's reactance level.

In contrast to Lazarus, Beutler does pay particular attention to therapeutic strategies. At present, his statements concerning therapeutic strategies and techniques are aimed at the cognitive, affective, and behavioral modalities. In addition, although Beutler argues that psychotherapists need to take into account the fact that different therapeutic styles, strategies, and techniques will be employed at different times as clients vary across salient dimensions, he argues that similar criteria which guide the choice of these interventions at the outset of therapy will also apply at all other points in therapy. While this may be true, Prochaska and DiClemente argue most persuasively that therapists need to take various processes and stages of change into account when making clinical decisions, and incorporating their work into his schema could aid the development of Beutler's future work.

While Beutler notes that the concepts of systematic eclectic psychotherapy have been applied primarily to individual therapy, he argues that "there is no reason why they cannot be applied to group or family treatment" (p. 113). However, he goes on to say that at the current status of knowledge "the concepts of eclectic psychotherapy would probably be best suited to those group and family exchanges in

which the therapist functions individual-to-individual" (p. 113). This statement would not satisfy the majority of group and family therapists, particularly those who apply a systems perspective to their work. Perhaps in order not to alienate such practitioners, Beutler argues that it is possible to incorporate concepts of systems theory into the general persuasion framework to make it more applicable to the arenas of group and family therapy, although he does not outline specifically how this might be accomplished. It is apparent, then, that further work needs to be done to determine how the persuasion framework would incorporate concepts of systems theory to enable practitioners of systematic eclectic psychotherapy to make the same refined decisions in group and family therapy that Beutler has shown can be made in the practice of individual therapy.

Concerning the management of the therapeutic alliance in systematic eclectic psychotherapy, Beutler puts forward the point made previously by Lazarus that eclectic psychotherapists had better fulfill clients' initial treatment expectations in order to sustain them through these initial stages of therapy. He argues that similarity in demographic attitudes and intellectual strivings at the outset of therapy are important and that these (among others) help to sustain the therapeutic bond and to enable dissonance induction to occur—a major goal of systematic eclectic psychotherapists.

It is apparent, then, that Beutler's approach to eclectic psychotherapy scores highly on the criteria advanced by the decision-making perspective that has been chosen as the focal point of this chapter. However, although Beutler's approach has been well received in the literature, certain people (e.g., Auerbach, 1984) have questioned whether the client dimensions chosen by him are in fact the best available. Indeed, my own view in this respect is that the dimension of cognitive complexity might be of additional value here. However, other eclectic therapists could well make similar claims for other dimensions. Future research should be directed toward the study of the clinical utility of competing dimensions. This is not to detract from Beutler's work, which is in many ways a model for the development of future eclectic endeavors.

GARFIELD'S ECLECTIC APPROACH

Sol Garfield's claim for his own eclectic approach to psychotherapy is modest. He acknowledges at the outset of his chapter that he does not have a clearly organized system of therapy and calls his approach atheoretical. Indeed, he refers to it as "an empirically oriented eclectic approach emphasizing common therapeutic variables" (p. 139). Given that I am employing Cornsweet's (1983) view that a theory is a way of structuring and understanding a complex set of phenomena, it is clear that Garfield's approach to eclectic psychotherapy is guided by two major sets of principles: (1) empiricism and (2) integrationism. In addition, I sense an inconsistency in Garfield's chapter. Thus, he states, "No systematic research has been conducted on this approach" (p. 157), and yet he argues that his expectation is that "empirical evidence should be provided in support of a given clinical or therapeutic procedure" (p. 132). Indeed, it is ironic that a man who is widely respected for his writings on the psychotherapy research literature has not himself experimentally tested his own eclectic approach to therapy.

Perhaps the major strength of Garfield's approach to eclectic psychotherapy is that he shows clearly that there are common factors that span the extant different approaches to psychotherapy. However, it is unclear from Garfield's chapter how clinicians can employ such knowledge to try to effect different treatment plans with different clients. Garfield himself speculates that "perhaps some of the common factors are more important for particular disorders than for others" (p. 160), but he does not elaborate on this particular theme. Thus, it appears that the common factor framework that Garfield makes the pivotal point of his eclectic approach is helpful in that it encourages clinicians to synthesize such factors from the research literature, but it is at present of little *practical* use in a clinical setting in helping therapists make informed clinical decisions. It is not true to say that Garfield fails to give any guidance on this issue. For example, he argues "when a patient is in a state of tension or turmoil, the opportunity to fully confide and express one's feelings and emotions to a trusted therapist may lead to strong emotional discharge with positive consequences" (p. 150). However, as Garfield himself acknowledges, "it is difficult to spell out what the relative contribution of the various hypothesized therapeutic variables actually are" (p. 148).

Unlike Lazarus and Beutler, for example, Garfield does not offer a systematic scheme whereby clients are shown to vary across different dimensions. Thus, although Garfield argues that "the therapist usually cannot follow one specific set of procedures for all patients even if they appear to have similar diagnoses. Rather the therapist has to continually evaluate and reevaluate the client and the process of therapy, selecting procedures that appear useful and discarding ones that do not appear to be aiding the progress of therapy" (p. 145), he offers little guidance concerning what constructs he uses to implement such decisions. For example, when discussing the role of hope in the therapeutic process, Garfield argues that "hope . . . helps to foster the possibility or release of a number of other potentially therapeutic variables. Which ones come into play in a particular instance depends to some extent on the particular client and his or her problems" (p. 149). Perhaps because very little research has been carried out on this particular point, Garfield is reluctant to specify further which particular therapeutic variables interact with particular clients. Indeed, he is very careful not to make speculations in the absence of empirical data. In taking such conservative position, therefore, Garfield, given the present state of knowledge, must inevitably obfuscate rather than clarify.

What does seem to characterize Garfield's approach is a lot of clinical good sense based on his many years of experience as a therapist. This is particularly true in the area of the therapeutic alliance, and it is clear that here Garfield's approach is dominated by the consideration of maintaining cooperative therapeutic alliances where clients are given a good deal of choice concerning the content and direction of therapy sessions. However, Garfield does not consider the point which Lazarus, for example, makes concerning the fact that different therapeutic relationships are formed in different ways and that although some clients may prefer an informal therapeutic relationship, others may prefer a more formal one.

Other lacunae in Garfield's approach as demonstrated in his chapter concern the choice of therapeutic arenas in which to work and what might lead clinicians to suggest changes of therapeutic arenas to their clients. In addition, although Garfield lists "time" as a mechanism of change, he does not clearly show how therapists' interventions might change with different clients at different stages in the therapeutic process.

In summary, it appears that an eclectic approach to psychotherapy which is guided by reference to empiricism and common therapeutic factors is helpful in synthesizing clinical material but is not helpful at the moment in enabling clinicians to make important clinical decisions concerning the practice of differential therapeutics.

THE TRANSTHEORETICAL APPROACH

The transtheoretical approach to eclectic psychotherapy emerged from James Prochaska's own survey of different theoretical approaches to psychotherapy (cf. Prochaska, 1984). This survey spawned his desire to understand how people change both as a result of their own efforts and as a response to psychotherapy. This desire has led to an impressive series of research studies being conducted which has found that people utilize a variety of *processes* of change and can be reliably located at different *stages* in the change process. In addition, Prochaska and DiClemente (this volume, Chapter 6) argue that therapeutic interventions can be targeted at various *levels* of change. Thus, transtheoretical therapists are guided in their decision making by a three-way interaction: levels of change × stages of change × processes of change. Moreover, this framework helps therapists to avoid making clinical errors. For example, therapists who follow it are unlikely to implement therapeutic procedures that are more appropriate at one stage of change when clients are in another stage of change. Such an error is frequently made with clients who are at the precontemplation stage of change. Prochaska and DiClemente argue that therapists need to show a genuine interest in the welfare of such clients while respecting their right not to change. In addition, Prochaska and DiClemente argue that it is important for therapists not to use intrusive interventions with clients who are in the contemplation stage of change. Such clients require a great deal of patience on the part of their therapists who can best facilitate a move to the action stage by helping clients weigh up the advantages and disadvantages of change.

It is apparent that the 10 processes of change described by Prochaska and DiClemente are closely related to the level of therapeutic intervention known as therapeutic strategies, i.e., that level which falls between theoretical considerations at the abstract level and therapeutic techniques at the concrete level (Goldfried, 1980). However, a beneficial addition to Prochaska and DiClemente's analysis would be a rigorous consideration of the indications and contraindications for using specific techniques to implement each therapeutic strategy. While transtheoretical therapists are given much guidance concerning which therapeutic strategy (or process) to implement with a particular client, they are not currently given much help in selecting specific techniques best designed to implement such strategies with different clients.

Prochaska and DiClemente also put forward a hierarchy of levels of change (symptom/situational → maladaptive cognitions → current interpersonal conflicts → family/systems conflicts → interpersonal conflicts). It is important to acknowledge that Prochaska's research team has not at the moment conducted much empirical work on these levels of change and that their hierarchy appears to rest on certain assumptions that some therapists would not share. For example, cognitive therapists would question their notion that the level of maladaptive cognitions is in fact "higher" than the intrapersonal level. Indeed, this hierarchy reminded me of the model of the mind put forward by psychoanalytic therapists, where intrapersonal problems are considered to be "deep" problems. Such therapists criticize cognitive therapists for intervening at the more "superficial" level of maladaptive cognitions.

At present, then, Prochaska and DiClemente's hierarchy may not serve as a very effective common language. Future work here might involve (a) greater specification of what constitutes intrapersonal data and how these differ from the level of maladaptive cognitions; and (b) removal of the value-laden notion of hierarchy. However, their research-based work on the stages and processes of change appears more promising in providing such an appropriate common language. While it is clear that the work on levels of change requires a good deal more refinement, as outlined previously, the inclusion of this particular dimension is obviously important. For example, it helps alert therapists to look for the "key" level at which therapeutic endeavors can best be focused. Prochaska and DiClemente also make the important point that, for some clients, interventions must be geared at all levels of change, i.e., the maximum impact level. In light of these statements I was confused to read that "in the transtheoretical approach we prefer to intervene initially at the symptom/situational level because change tends to occur more quickly at this more conscious and contemporary level of problems and because this level often represents the primary reason for which the individual entered therapy" (p. 168). While this has some face validity, it seems to be at variance with Prochaska and DiClemente's statements concerning the importance of focusing therapy at the "key" level of change. It is also at variance with their emphasis on therapists' working at the level of change desired by their clients.

The transtheoretical framework is particularly useful in helping therapists to develop and maintain effective therapeutic alliances with their clients. Prochaska and DiClemente advocate that therapists explain to clients about the various stages of change and help them to determine which stage best approximates their own situation. Psychotherapists are then urged to "join their clients" at this particular stage in therapy and implement initial interventions accordingly. In addition, therapists are urged, quite correctly in my view, to undertake a thorough assessment of those processes of change that clients have already *unsuccessfully* initiated so that therapists do not needlessly cover unproductive ground with their clients.

Prochaska and DiClemente's framework is particularly helpful in facilitating clinicians' decisions concerning appropriate choices of therapeutic arena. Information gained from assessments of levels, processes, and stages of change is combined to guide clinicians on this point. Thus, with an alcoholic client who is at the precontemplation stage of change a therapist might decide to work at a family level of change to facilitate the client's movement from precontemplation to contemplation stage by working in a family setting and using the family to apply the consciousness-raising process of change.

I have already mentioned that a possible shortcoming in the transtheoretical approach is its apparent failure to incorporate therapeutic techniques into its superordinate framework. That therapists are not given much guidance concerning which particular interactive styles to employ with different clients constitutes another weakness. Here, for example, Prochaska and DiClemente could well utilize Beutler's level of reactance dimension to help therapists determine how directive to be at various points in the therapeutic process. At present, all Prochaska and DiClemente say on the issue of style is that therapists should adopt the style of consultants. They do not consider under what conditions such a style may be inappropriate.

While Prochaska and DiClemente are unusually helpful in offering dimensions to explain client variation in terms of processes, stages, and levels of change, they are less helpful in accounting for differences in clients' personality, degree of symptomatology (cf. Beutler's dimension of symptom complexity), and predominant defenses. This is not to say that they ignore such considerations—indeed, they do

not. However, my point is that these dimensions of client variation need to be more explicitly incorporated into their framework.

I also consider that Prochaska and DiClemente would do well to incorporate Lazarus' BASIC I.D. schema into their work. At present their levels of change can be viewed as an attempt to utilize some of the modalities outlined in the BASIC I.D., but this attempt is less systematic than that of Lazarus. For example, Prochaska and DiClemente do not appear to distinguish between cognitive and imaginal modalities and do not refer to the sensation modality featured in Lazarus' framework.

In conclusion, although there are several lacunae in Prochaska and DiClemente's system, they cannot be criticized too much in this regard, since they have, in a short period of time, conducted pioneering research into the stages and processes of change that both clients and nonclients use in their endeavors to overcome their psychological problems. In this respect, they have made an extremely important contribution to eclectic psychotherapy and one which I predict will become one of the major foundations of future eclectic work.

FUNCTIONAL ECLECTIC THERAPY

Joseph Hart's approach to eclectic psychotherapy is based on the functional theory of William James. Given the Jamesian theory of emotions, particular attention is placed on the ways in which clients express themselves. This theory argues that when we see something sad, our facial expressions precede rather than follow our feelings of sadness. In addition, according to James (quoted in Hart), "What is vague, or on the fringe of consciousness, is precisely what leads to the development of consciousness" (p. 204). This particular tenet suggests that therapists pay attention to and help clients pay attention to various gaps in their consciousness. One of the fundamental tasks of functional eclectic therapists is to help clients fill in these gaps by attending to "feeling moments." Here Hart argues that "a potential feeling moment exists wherever the client or the therapist notices a mismatch between *what* is being said (the content) and *how* it is being said (the style)" (p. 207).

According to the functional eclectic framework, clients become disturbed because they perpetuate outmoded and unhelpful personality images which then determine how they act. These actions in turn determine their choices, which then influence their needs. It is another major task of functional therapists to help clients to counteract their outmoded personality images by helping them to become aware of the mismatches between *what* they say and *how* they say it. When done productively, this facilitates a constructive catharsis which leads to a proactive step where clients are "helped to explore new feelings and develop new expression skills that eventually will lead to new personality images" (p. 214). In doing so, clients are helped to enter a reintegration process, through which they end up "where he or she would have been all along if the old personality image had not distorted the individual's perceptions—at the top of the need-choice-action-image cycle. The person is now ready to start off open to new wants and needs that were blocked by the old image" (p. 214).

While Hart has outlined a full description of the application of Jamesian theory to the practice of a particular approach to psychotherapy, it is difficult for me, at this time, to conclude that Hart has been successful in establishing an *eclectic* approach to psychotherapy, i.e., one based on helping therapists to intervene in different ways with different clients at different times in the therapeutic process. However, the rudiments of such an eclec-

tic approach certainly do exist in Hart's chapter. His counteraction-catharsis-proaction-reintegration schema is helpful in suggesting an order to the therapist's strategies. However, at present, he does not clearly indicate which particular therapeutic techniques may be used with different clients at each stage of this process. Hart's need-choice-action-image-schema, which represents stages clients should go through in order to profit from psychotherapy, loosely parallels Prochaska and DiClemente's stages of change schema (i.e., precontemplation-contemplation-action-maintenance). However, the major difference here is that while Prochaska and DiClemente have validated their work by studying both "self-changers" and "therapy changers," Hart relies on functional theory in order to guide his endeavors. While Prochaska and DiClemente have carried out research to help therapists make accurate assessments locating clients at particular stages of change, Hart, as far as I am aware, and as far as he made clear in his chapter, has not done so.

Hart also does not clearly indicate how clients vary according to functional eclectic therapy. Again, the seeds of a helpful schema of a client variation are present. For example, Hart describes a number of personality dynamisms which could, with further work, serve as a base upon which clients could be deemed to vary. Having outlined such a schema, Hart would then need to carefully indicate how therapists could intervene in different ways with clients who vary according to this "personality dynamisms" framework. Another way that Hart could help therapists to understand client variation would be for him to elaborate upon his distinction between clients who are suitable for psychotherapy and those who are suitable for "case handling." At the moment Hart says, "Clients who cannot pay attention to feeling moments or who cannot learn to notice mismatches and work toward expressing fully what they feel and mean should be taught how to do so. If that is not possible, the therapist should switch into a case-handling mode and stop trying to employ functional therapy" (p. 208). This statement needs to be considerably amplified if it is going to be helpful to therapists attempting to apply functional eclectic therapy.

Hart does not convincingly outline a schema where clients are deemed to differ along important dimensions and so does not offer a helpful decision-making framework for therapist intervention in this respect. Perhaps one of the reasons for this is Hart's preference for the realm of drama and art rather than the realm of scientific analysis. Hart's chapter left me with the impression that functional eclectic therapists rely very much on intuition. And yet if intuition is going to be clinically helpful it is incumbent on such therapists to attempt to articulate what guides them in their intuitive decisions.

Hart also does not discuss clearly how best to create and maintain different therapeutic alliances with different clients and what may guide functional eclectic therapists in their choices of appropriate therapeutic styles and therapeutic arenas with different clients at different times in the therapeutic process.

Reading Hart's chapter after I had read the chapter by Fischer served as a potent reminder that we should refer to eclectic *approaches* to psychotherapy rather than *the* eclectic approach (cf. Norcross, Chapter 1). Indeed, it is difficult to envision Hart and Fischer agreeing on which epistemological base might best guide the development of eclectic approaches in the future. Where Fischer, together with Lazarus and Garfield, looks to the empirical literature of psychotherapy as a guide, Hart would be more likely to turn to the fields of art and drama. Also, any dialogue between Hart and Fischer would come to an end as soon as Hart would try to convince Fischer that blocked growth rein-

tegration does require a double-minded, fixed-unfixed bisociation activity to move beyond the dysfunctional image toward receptivity to new images. This unfortunately is not the kind of common language that serves to encourage productive communication among eclectic psychotherapists. However, if Hart is prepared to better integrate the artistic and scientific perspectives on psychotherapy, then we can look forward to future developments in his work that will more clearly aid eclectic psychotherapists in their clinical decision-making endeavors.

ECLECTIC TIME-LIMITED THERAPY

Eclectic time-limited therapy (ETLT) was developed by Addie Fuhriman and colleagues mainly for pragmatic purposes, to enable a university counseling center to more effectively meet the needs of its client population and to enable therapists from different orientations to better communicate with one another. Thus, ETLT can be used as an integrative model in that it appears to draw on key features from various different approaches to time-limited psychotherapy. In doing so, it provides therapists with an acceptable common language. The ETLT model outlines in a given sequence various stages of short-term therapy where different therapeutic strategies are clearly delineated at each stage. The model rests on adequate assessment where clear inclusion and exclusion criteria are delineated.

However, no dimensions of client variation are put forward, and therefore it is difficult to understand how the model can be applied in different ways with different clients. As noted previously, while the model does clearly outline different strategies to be used at different stages, it appears as if each therapist is given an open brief concerning how to implement these strategies. However, in being given this wide brief, therapists are again not guided in how they can employ the model in different ways with different clients.

At this point it is worth noting that eclectic approaches which do not put forward dimensions of client variation are precisely those which are most vague in providing therapists with clear guidelines concerning how to intervene in different ways with different clients at different stages. Indeed, Fuhriman, Paul, and Burlingame note that "basically, the therapist's role does not change throughout therapy" (p. 240). It is possible to argue that the inclusion-exclusion criteria employed in ETLT actually partial out much of the variance due to client differences to the extent that the model is applicable to a restricted range of clients. However, it is not clear from reading the authors' chapter whether this speculation is warranted and, if so, what are the salient core dimensions of client variation which remain.

The model does, however, specify clear guidelines for the development and maintenance of appropriate therapeutic alliances. Indeed, this is one of the major strengths of the model. It stresses the importance of the development of a collaborative relationship, although clients who are not able to use such a relationship are in fact selected out. ETLT therapists strive to develop a "horizontal" relationship with their clients and try to develop a climate where therapists and clients share a mutual responsibility for therapeutic work. At the early stage of ETLT, the therapist focuses on the client's treatment expectations and seeks to develop positive anticipations concerning each participant's role. Therapeutic goals are established by use of a treatment plan that represents the therapist's conceptualization of the client's presenting complaint. Once this plan has been established, it appears that a considerable amount of the therapist's activities is founded on work that implements this "focal aim." ETLT therapists

are advised to focus on both problem areas and salient processes of therapy and are urged to deal with therapeutic resistance in an open and forthright manner. As mentioned earlier, guidelines for intervention are based on the use of clearly described strategies at different stages in the therapeutic process. However, in their keenness not to alienate any of the therapists in their team and in trying to ensure that all therapists of different orientation can use the model, Fuhriman et al. do not show clearly why their model is an eclectic one in the sense of providing clear guidelines for therapeutic decision making concerning the development of what Beutler calls "therapeutic menus." The authors say that "the application of eclecticism resides in the therapist who uses specific process principles (e.g., therapeutic focusing) as touchstones to determine the appropriateness of particular interventions (e.g., historical-genetic insight versus interactional insight)" (p. 241). Unfortunately, they do not give any examples to illustrate their point, and they fail to provide clear guidelines that explain how particular cases are handled.

When choices of therapeutic arenas are considered, Fuhriman et al. say that "this approach was designed for use in an individual psychotherapeutic format; it may well be applicable to group therapy as well" (p. 257). However, no guidelines are proposed concerning which clients may benefit from group ETLT. It is apparent that work needs to be done in the application of a model to different therapeutic arenas and in the development of criteria concerning which clients may be appropriate for different arenas.

In summary, Fuhriman et al.'s model represents an integrative type of eclecticism which has been specifically applied to time-limited psychotherapy arising out of pragmatic need. As such, it shares the strengths and weaknesses of an integrative approach. Its major strength is that it enables therapists of different orientations to work on a common project by applying their own particular ways of working to an integrative framework couched in an acceptable common language. However, its major weakness is that it provides very few guidelines concerning how the model can be differentially applied with different clients. It does not then, give therapists who are already eclectic in their orientation an organizing framework for making clinical decisions, particularly at the level of technique. The model is similar to that outlined by Garfield and shares similar strengths and weaknesses. As a creative and sensible response to a pressing clinical service problem, it is exemplary. As a framework to enable eclectic therapists to make informed clinical decisions on the basis of matching therapeutic strategies and techniques to the treatment needs of different clients, it is presently in an embryonic stage of development.

A STRUCTURAL–PHENOMENOLOGICAL ECLECTIC APPROACH

Stephen Murgatroyd and Michael Apter utilize the theory of psychological reversals (Apter, 1982) as a superordinate framework to help eclectic therapists make effective clinical decisions. This theory draws on phenomenology, structuralism, and cybernetics and has been applied to other areas of psychology as well as to psychotherapy. Much of their work depends on the existence of three pairs of metamotivational states which are bipolar in nature and which clients are deemed to switch between. In their chapter, Murgatroyd and Apter place most emphasis on the telic/paratelic pair of states, and, indeed, much of their work in both psychology and psychotherapy has been focused on this pair. Nonetheless, they propose three pairs of metamotivational states as a framework to help therapists

understand client variation. An advantage of this framework is that it is one which emphasizes states rather than traits and can account for "nontypical" behavior of clients. It thus can help therapists take into account both clients' dominant state and their situational state in planning therapeutic interventions.

When describing psychological disturbance, Murgatroyd and Apter use the "language" of reversal theory. They argue that psychological disturbance occurs when there is: (a) reversal failure, (b) inappropriate reversals, (c) reversal-potential inhibition, and (d) socially inappropriate behavior. However, what they do not do—apart from briefly in their case study—is to present detailed information whereby clinicians can make finely tuned distinctions between these four indications of disturbance. Thus, it is particularly difficult to fully judge the adequacy of their framework as a basis for helping therapists make clinical decisions. However, like Beutler, although in a less complete way, they do outline the rudiments of a taxonomy of intervention tactics which is based on some of these four indications of psychological disturbance. Thus, they outline various techniques that can (a) promote reversal between two states so as to unblock inhibited reversals; (b) facilitate appropriate reversals, in particular those between paratelic to telic states; and (c) reduce the extent to which clients engage in behaviors which, though appropriate to their current operative state, inhibit a subsequent reversal. It would be helpful if they elaborated on this schema and outlined a taxonomy of intervention tactics for each of the three pairs of metamotivational states. Nevertheless, their framework certainly allows for this future development.

A particular strength of Murgatroyd and Apter's work is their point that eclectic therapists should take into account the structural implications of therapeutic strategies and techniques. Thus, when employing a particular strategy or technique, Murgatroyd and Apter encourage clinicians to ask themselves, for example, whether it is designed to alleviate reversal failure or to promote an appropriate reversal. But they do not apply this important point to the issue of appropriate timing of such interventions. Thus, unlike Prochaska and DiClemente in particular, they have little to say concerning the practice of their form of eclectic psychotherapy over time. One would expect this to be another future development of their work. However, what I particularly like about their approach is that by outlining a taxonomy of interventions that takes into account the structural implications of particular strategies and techniques, they help clinicians to detect which state "a client may be in at any particular time." This is especially helpful in providing aid to clinicians in their moment-to-moment clinical decision making. However, I would like to have seen more discussion on the question of assessment of metamotivational states, particularly with reference to how this is done in the therapeutic situation. Nonetheless, their framework does allow for this, and again one would anticipate that this will be a future development of their approach.

Another positive feature of Murgatroyd and Apter's approach is that they go further than most other theorists in discussing not only the question of helping clinicians to choose among different therapeutic techniques to achieve a particular therapeutic goal, but also the issue that different productive goals may be possible for a particular client. Thus, the goals of relaxation and of experiencing high arousal as excitement may both be possible for a particular client. Unfortunately, Murgatroyd and Apter do not outline criteria to help clinicians to determine when one particular strategy may be chosen rather than the other.

Although their framework for the practice of differential therapeutics is still to some degree in an embryonic stage, Murgatroyd and Apter have made an encouraging start, and it is possible to anticipate future important work which hopefully will enable Murgatroyd and Apter to do the following:

1. Outline clear criteria for the assessment of structural disturbance, i.e., help clinicians to clearly distinguish among reversal failure, inappropriate reversals, socially inappropriate behavior, and reversal-potential inhibition.

2. Outline a taxonomy of intervention tactics for each of the three metamotivational states that are presently referred to in the theory which can be used to help clinicians remedy these structural disturbances.

3. Outline particular interventions and their alternatives for complex problems where more than one structural disturbance exists and which implicate more than one pair of metamotivational states.

4. Present clear guidelines concerning how clinicians might vary their therapeutic style with different clients, with particular reference to each of the three pairs of metamotivational states as they may be manifested in clients' behavior in therapy sessions. In addition, clear guidelines should be proposed concerning the "level" of therapists' involvement with different clients at different times in the therapeutic process. At present, Murgatroyd and Apter's comments and suggestions on this particular point are rather vague and not clinically helpful.

5. Provide a taxonomy of "climate-setting activities" for use in therapy sessions with clients in each of the three pairs of metamotivational states. This is a particularly fascinating aspect of Murgatroyd and Apter's approach and one

which is not discussed to the same degree by any of the other contributors to this volume.

6. Incorporate the seven triggers of structural disturbance outlined in the case study, i.e., frustration, satiation, contingency, fear of noncompletion, threats to self-esteem, threats from the behavior of others, and perceived intrinsic threats of a situation, and integrate these with the other elements in the theory to suggest a comprehensive framework of differential intervention.

At present, although Apter's (1982) theory of psychological reversals has stimulated a good deal of research in a short period of time, much of this research has been undertaken outside of the discipline of psychotherapy. Validational studies are needed, particularly those which investigate the link between structural disturbance and more traditional measures of psychological disturbance. In addition, Murgatroyd and Apter need to show that alleviation of structural disturbance is correlated with the alleviation of psychological disturbance. From a more clinical perspective, I hope that Murgatroyd and Apter will address more fully than they do at present the issue of how structural-phenomenological eclectic therapists may utilize the three pairs of metamotivational states to develop individualistic therapeutic alliances with their clients based on assessment of these metamotivational states. Of particular interest here would be suggestions to enable therapists to maintain productive alliances with clients who switch between states at different times in therapy sessions. Also, Murgatroyd and Apter currently do not fully discuss the issue of how their framework may help clinicians to make important clinical decisions concerning appropriate choices of therapeutic arena. They have made a start here by looking at contingent events and their effect on move-

ment between telic and paratelic states, but this work needs to be amplified.

In conclusion, I find sufficient potential in Murgatroyd and Apter's work to suggest that future developments may provide clinicians with a most helpful framework to facilitate decision making. At present, however, although they have made an impressive beginning, their work is very much in an embryonic stage and needs to be viewed as such. And yet, given the fact that Murgatroyd and Apter are prolific workers, I confidently expect that their future work will help realize their theory's potential in the field of eclectic psychotherapy.

ECLECTIC FAMILY THERAPY

In his chapter Lawrence Grebstein outlines an eclectic approach to family therapy that is based on a number of different conceptual theories and on the work of a number of family therapists. Although Grebstein gives plausible reasons why he has drawn on these theoretical and technical sources, it is possible to imagine another eclectic family therapist giving equally plausible reasons for drawing on a different set of sources. Grebstein's explanations, in this volume, tend in the main to be based on personal reasons rather than on sound epistemological ones.

So far in this chapter, I have noted that an eclectic approach needs to specify dimensions along which clients are deemed to vary in order to provide clinicians with clear guidelines for making clinical decisions. Extrapolating this viewpoint to the present approach, I think it is important for an eclectic family therapist to clearly outline salient dimensions along which families are deemed to differ. Although Grebstein states that "no two families are exactly alike" (p. 286) and although he outlines clearly the assessment procedures he uses in the practice of eclectic family therapy, his approach is presently lacking in this respect. He does not suggest guidelines that family therapists can employ in selecting the most appropriate therapeutic strategies and techniques for use with different families. Grebstein himself argues that "an eclectic approach allows the family therapist to choose from existing theories, research, and clinical information to provide a broad knowledge base for dealing with families that vary in geographical, socioeconomic, ethnic, and religious backgrounds; developmental stage; problem-solving styles; and other factors" (p. 286). Given the current status of family therapy, it is perhaps unfair to expect Grebstein to outline clearly such a framework. However, as we shall see, he does recommend particular family therapy approaches for particular problems.

Grebstein proposes two major ways of proceeding eclectically in family therapy. "First, the clinician can select a particular method or approach to use with a given family" (p. 300). It is here that Grebstein is at his most specific in outlining different approaches to different family problems. Thus, he notes that the following approaches can be used with the following problems:

Family systems theory and therapy . . . is effective in dealing with issues of autonomy and separation of individuals from their family of origin; functional family therapy . . . and behaviorally oriented family therapy . . . are useful for delinquent and acting-out behavior in children and adolescents; structural family therapy . . . has been used successfully with some psychosomatic problems in the family; strategic and communication-based family therapy . . . are useful for dealing with communication problems in the family; paradoxical approaches have been applied to schizophrenic families by the Milan group . . . and to rigid families by the Rome group . . . and problem-centered systems therapy . . . is appropriate for short-term therapy

in functioning families that have specific problems" (pp. 299–300).

Grebstein's second approach to eclectic family therapy occurs when "different methods and conceptualizations can be combined for use with the same family to deal with different problem areas. When this second approach is taken, the therapist must be careful not to jump around or change so much that the family and the therapist end up confused" (p. 300). Unfortunately, since Grebstein does not outline clear criteria to help family therapists make important decisions concerning the selection of appropriate therapeutic strategies and therapeutic techniques to deal with different families, his approach may not rescue the eclectic family therapist from such confusion. However, the suggestions that Grebstein makes when describing the practice of differential family therapy, the first type of eclecticism, may provide the nucleus for a transition to the second type and constitute a fruitful area for future development. This will be particularly true if Grebstein can isolate the *specific factors* that make particular approaches to family therapy effective with the groups outlined. If this can be achieved, particular strategies and techniques may be recommended for use rather than entire approaches.

Grebstein notes that "it is not possible in the limited space here to delineate a 'cookbook' of eclectic therapist behaviors" (pp. 302–303). The guidelines that he does offer in this respect are: (1) do not make assumptions; (2) do not go too fast; (3) do not be afraid to acknowledge mistakes or uncertainty; (4) be as honest and direct as possible in your communications with the family; (5) share with the family in as honest and direct a manner as possible (your) experience of what it is like to be in the family. Although these are helpful pieces of therapeutic wisdom, they are insufficient to form the basis of an organizing framework for the practice of an eclectic family therapy.

While Grebstein does not explain how his chosen theories and approaches can be incorporated into a coherent whole, he does state that doing so may lead to problems. Thus, he notes that the active, direct use of self advocated in Kempler's model of family therapy is in stark contrast to the approaches of Bowen and Epstein and Bishop, which actively discourage the communication of therapist affect. Unfortunately, Grebstein does not suggest possible solutions to this potential obstacle to integration.

Grebstein outlines three primary mechanisms of change that can be used to classify family therapy techniques. These three mechanisms are understanding, transformation, and identification (see Grebstein's chapter for a more extended description of these change mechanisms). While noting that eclectic family therapists can utilize all three change mechanisms, Grebstein does not elaborate on this theme and explain how they can be used, when in the change process, and with which families. In this respect, Grebstein, like Garfield, does not show how knowledge of change mechanisms can be used to form the basis of a framework of clinical decision making.

When referring to the practice of family therapy over time, Grebstein notes that Prochaska and DiClemente's work can be applied to family work, but once again he does not specify how this may be done in practice. Thus, his statement "eclectic family therapy, by utilizing a combination of a variety of mechanisms of change, increases the likelihood of therapeutic success" (p. 307) must be viewed skeptically against this backdrop.

Grebstein is clearer when outlining the criteria for when family therapy is not appropriate—when (1) the family cannot be together in the same room; (2) the family does not want to resolve its problems

in the family unit; or (3) the family decides that it may be more effective and/or expedient not to use family therapy.

In all other circumstances it appears that Grebstein favors the use of family therapy. Although it is too early to expect this, it is desirable that a comprehensive approach to eclectic therapy should clearly specify the advantages and disadvantages of each therapeutic arena. To what extent we can realistically expect this from any one eclectic approach to therapy is debatable since it may be that the majority of eclectic therapists favor one modality over others. It will be interesting to see whether the future developments in eclectic psychotherapy will spawn different eclectic approaches for use in different therapeutic arenas or whether a superordinate theory which clearly delineates appropriate criteria for the assignment of cases to appropriate therapeutic arenas will emerge.

In summary, I have been quite critical of Grebstein's approach to eclectic family therapy. I have done so because it does not meet most of the criteria suggested by my decision-making framework. However, it is important to note that he has been brave enough to make a start in an area where less courageous individuals have feared to tread.

ECLECTIC CASEWORK

Throughout his chapter, Joel Fischer reminds the reader that effectiveness should be the guiding principle underpinning the eclectic therapies. He argues that an eclectic approach to psychotherapy has to be based on therapeutic techniques, a level which best reflects what practitioners actually do in therapy. He urges clinicians to become familiar with the research literature on the efficacy of techniques and then to apply what "works." In this respect, Fischer is most similar in his perspective to Lazarus, who also favors a technical eclecticism. However, Lazarus is more willing than Fischer to use techniques that have been insufficiently studied (e.g., imagery techniques and sensation-based techniques). Also, in expounding his BASIC I.D. framework, Lazarus has put forward a schema to help therapists make sense of important differences between clients—a perspective not currently present in Fischer's approach.

In his appraisal of the research literature, Fischer argues that "there seem to be four major 'thrusts' . . . where the bulk of the evidence of effectiveness is contained" (p. 330). These are the use of structure, behavior therapy, cognitive therapy, and the interpersonal skills of empathy, warmth, and genuineness.

It is interesting to speculate whether all eclectically oriented practitioners who have the adequate skills to appraise the research literature would identify the same four thrusts. Indeed, other contributors to this volume appear to read the research literature in different ways. For example, Beutler notes that while "over 80% of the literature on psychotherapy theory is devoted to specific technologies and procedures, most of the effectiveness of psychotherapy can be attributed to factors that are common across approaches and that characterize most effective therapies in suitable conditions" (p. 94). In his introductory chapter, Norcross quotes Lambert (1979, 1983) and Smith, Glass, and Miller (1980) in noting that less than 10% of outcome variance is generally accounted for by technique variables. Thus, while Fischer's view that therapists pay attention to the cardinal value of effectiveness is laudable, apparently different criteria are being applied to the research literature, and equally distinguished writers come to very different conclusions.

I am reminded here of an important published debate between Ellis (1979) and, among others, Mahoney (1979) and Meichenbaum (1979), where Ellis begins by putting forward a remarkably large

and seemingly impressive number of studies in support of the effectiveness of rational-emotive therapy (RET). In their rebuttals both Mahoney and Meichenbaum question (a) much of the evidence that Ellis puts forward and (b) the conclusions that he makes based on these findings. It is apparent, then, that Fischer is far more impressed with what the research literature has to say on the effectiveness of therapeutic techniques than are Beutler and Norcross. I have discussed this issue at length because Fischer's reliance on the efficacy of techniques is central to his eclectic approach.

Fischer urges readers to study the research literature on techniques while keeping in mind the conditions under which these techniques have been studied. He argues that such consideration would lead to the development of explicit client/problem typologies which "would demonstrate the kinds of problems and clients for whom a given technique has been used and could be applied effectively" (p. 328). It would have been helpful here if Fischer had provided examples of technique-client/problem typologies to show how such matching procedures can be used in practice. Indeed, such information would have helped me to appraise better the utility of Fischer's framework in providing practitioners with a coherent and helpful decision-making schema for effective intervention. In the absence of any such schemata, Fischer, in his chapter, does not outline meaningful dimensions of client variation although he does suggest that the development of such dimensions (or, in his terms, typologies) constitutes an important task for eclectic psychotherapists.

Fischer views the interpersonal skills of empathy, warmth, and genuineness (one of his four "strands") as "the foundation of an eclectic approach providing the crucial interviewing and relationship skills that influence the effective implementation of techniques" (p. 333). However, unlike Beutler and Lazarus, who argue that it is important for therapists to vary their style of participation with different clients, Fischer does not address the important issue of variability of therapeutic style. Nor does he deal with the point cogently argued by Beutler that some clients, particularly those whose sense of autonomy is easily threatened by therapist structuring and directiveness, are better served by therapists who emphasize a less directive and structured approach. Although it may be true that, in general, therapist structuring is more frequently effective with the majority of clients than lack of therapist structure, an effective framework of eclectic psychotherapy should ideally be equipped to deal with key important exceptions, as Beutler seems to do on this particular issue. Fischer's approach would benefit from further enquiry into those dimensions where therapeutic alliance issues become particularly salient.

Fischer's focus on the "technique" level of intervention leads him to neglect, along with Lazarus, the intermediate level of therapeutic strategies. Goldfried (1980) has argued that focusing on therapeutic strategies may facilitate the collaborative efforts of therapists from different persuasions to develop a common language and to promote an exchange of ideas. In addition, he argues that if therapists think in terms of strategies, they can then see more clearly that different techniques may be employed to implement a single therapeutic strategy. Although Fischer does outline a number of behavioral and cognitive techniques, his schema would be more useful from a decision-making perspective were he to provide a matrix of technique-strategy links.

Fischer, correctly in my opinion, argues that assessment of client problems is a core activity of eclectic psychotherapists. He considers that an effectively conducted assessment will suggest particular techniques and failure to do so means that the

assessment has probably been inadequate. However, Lazarus, who basically shares Fischer's emphasis on technical eclecticism, is more flexible on this point. Lazarus is less focused on techniques than Fischer and, for example, would be prepared to adopt a nondirective therapeutic *style* if this seemed to be indicated by *his* particular approach to assessment. In addition, Lazarus' assessment procedures appear to pay far more attention to clients' expectations than do Fischer's.

Fischer's framework does not meet two other important criteria suggested by a decision-making framework perspective on eclectic psychotherapy. First, Fischer does not specify clearly when the different therapeutic arenas are indicated in the treatment of different clients at different stages in therapy. Second, he does not consider the important point, emphasized particularly by Prochaska and DiClemente, that the tasks of psychotherapists appear to vary *over time* and that different strategies and techniques may be used on different occasions in the change process. It is possible that Fischer considers that the volume of research emanating from Prochaska's laboratory is not yet sufficient to qualify as a major strand. Indeed, one of the dangers of Fischer's overreliance on major trends emanating from the research literature is that it may take a long time for new developments to be integrated into his schema.

In summary, Fischer's chapter serves as a salutary reminder that eclectic therapists need to take into account the concept of effectiveness in the development of eclectic approaches to psychotherapy. However, it was noted that different authorities appear to make different interpretations of this current literature. Perhaps as a result of his reliance on the present state of empirical research, Fischer appears to be more conservative than, for example, Beutler, Prochaska and DiClemente, Lazarus, and Murgatroyd and Apter in suggesting new frameworks that will assist clinicians to intervene differentially in the change process. Moreover, while the frameworks elaborated by those just listed do suggest testable propositions that might advance the field, Fischer presents an overly cautious approach to the development of eclectic psychotherapy. However, if Fischer is prepared to draw more from the work of this eclectic colleagues, without sacrificing his concern for effectiveness, then we can expect important future work from him.

CONCLUDING COMMENTS

All contributors are to be acknowledged for publicly presenting their embryonic approaches to scientific scrutiny. As I have noted, each approach has its strengths and deficiencies, and the main purposes of the present critique are to present a balanced view of each approach and to point to possible future developments for these approaches, in particular, and for eclecticism, in general. In this chapter I have stressed that if the eclectic approaches described in this volume are to have maximum impact on the field, they will have to offer clinically useful frameworks which therapists can apply in practice. It is for this reason that I have employed a decision-making perspective in this critique. It is too early to expect any one eclectic system to meet all the criteria outlined at the beginning of this chapter, and certainly conventional therapy systems fare poorly in this regard. An encouraging start has been made considering that the development of eclectic psychotherapy is still in its infancy.

I conclude with an interesting observation. There is little evidence at present that the contributors to this part of the volume (including the above-mentioned) are drawing upon one another's work to a significant degree. This surprises and troubles me. It is important that the pi-

oneers of eclectic psychotherapy *demonstrate* an eclectic attitude (i.e., willingness to draw upon diverse sources) among their own ranks. Otherwise they will act as poor role models and increase the chances that schools of eclectic therapy will proliferate in the future. If this happens, the nettle will not have been grasped! However, one of the goals of this volume is to facilitate communication among eclectic psychotherapists so that they can draw upon what is best in their respective approaches and thus advance the development of this exciting new field.

REFERENCES

Apter, M. J. (1982). *The experience of motivation: A theory of psychological reversals.* London: Academic Press.

Auerbach, A. H. (1984). Ideas whose time has come. *Contemporary Psychology, 29,* 456–457.

Bordin, E. S. (1979). The generalizability of the psychoanalytic concept of the working alliance. *Psychotherapy: Theory, Research and Practice, 16,* 252–260.

Cornsweet, C. (1983). Nonspecific factors and theoretical choice. *Psychotherapy: Theory, Research and Practice, 20,* 307–313.

Dryden, W. (1984a). Issues in the eclectic practice of individual therapy. In W. Dryden (Ed.), *Individual therapy in Britain* (pp. 341–363). London: Harper & Row.

Dryden, W. (1984b). Therapeutic arenas. In W. Dryden (Ed.), *Individual therapy in Britain* (pp. 1–22). London: Harper & Row.

Ellis, A. (1979). Rational-emotive therapy: Research data that support the clinical and personality hypotheses of RET and other modes of cognitive-behavior therapy. In A. Ellis & J. M. Whiteley (Eds.), *Theoretical and empirical foundations of rational-emotive therapy* (pp. 101–173). Monterey, CA: Brooks/Cole.

Frances, A., Clarkin, J., & Perry, S. (1984). *Differential therapeutics in psychiatry.* New York: Brunner/Mazel.

Goldfried, M. R. (1980). Toward the delineation of therapeutic change principles. *American Psychologist, 35,* 991–999.

Lambert, M. J. (1979). *The effects of psychotherapy.* St. Albans, VT: Eden Press.

Lambert, M. J. (Ed.). (1983). *Psychotherapy and patient relationships.* Homewood, IL: Dow Jones-Irwin.

Lazarus, A. A. (1981). *The practice of multimodal therapy.* New York: McGraw-Hill.

Mahoney, M. J. (1979). A critical analysis of rational-emotive theory and therapy. In A. Ellis & J. M. Whiteley (Eds.), *Theoretical and empir-*

ical foundations of rational-emotive therapy (pp. 177–180). Monterey, CA: Brooks/Cole.

Meichenbaum, D. (1979). Dr. Ellis, please stand up. In A. Ellis & J. M. Whiteley (Eds.), *Theoretical and empirical foundations of rational-emotive therapy* (pp. 174–176). Monterey, CA: Brooks/Cole.

Prochaska, J. O. (1984). *Systems of psychotherapy: A transtheoretical analysis* (2nd ed.). Homewood, IL: Dorsey Press.

Smith, M. L., Glass, G. V., & Miller, T. I. (1980). *The benefits of psychotherapy*. Baltimore, MD: Johns Hopkins University Press.

PART III

Concepts, Research,

and Directions

CHAPTER 13

Eclecticism in Psychotherapy: Underlying Assumptions, Problems, and Trade-offs

Stanley B. Messer

Surveys of clinical and counseling psychologists conducted over the past two or three decades have consistently revealed that from 30 to 50% of the respondents regard themselves as eclectic in their practice of psychotherapy (Garfield & Kurtz, 1976, 1977; Kelly, 1961; Norcross, this volume; Smith, 1982). Some of these therapists were eclectic in the sense of applying different approaches to different clients, and I shall refer to them as "selective eclectics." Others combined several theories, approaches, or aspects in one psychotherapy, and I shall call them "integrative eclectics." Assessing the results of his survey, Smith (1982) concludes that "the days of individual schools in counselling and therapy are drawing to a close." Eclecticism, it seems, is on the rise

(Brabeck & Welfel, 1985; Dimond, Havens, & Jones, 1978; Goldfried & Newman, this volume).

Along with such empirical surveys affirming the popularity of eclectic practice have come books, articles, conferences, and workshops whose purpose has been to further the cause of eclecticism or psychotherapy integration. Representative books include those of Beutler (1983), Garfield (1980), Goldfried (1982), Lazarus (1981), Marmor and Wood (1980), Palmer (1980), and Wachtel (1982). In such an atmosphere of cooperation and willingness of former adherents of one camp or another to beat their spears into pruning hooks, and to graft branches of one theory or therapy onto another, the critic's job is not easy. Nevertheless, as every horticulturalist knows, a graft does not always take, and even when it does, a superior result is not always achieved. This metaphor notwithstanding, I do not intend to

The author acknowledges the suggestions made by Louis Sass, Arnold Lazarus, Sandra Harris, and Cyril Franks on an earlier draft of this chapter.

present a polemic on the liabilities of eclecticism in therapy. Rather, I take the view that assessment of the value of eclectism depends both on the vantage point from which one approaches it and on one's attitude about the possibilities within that particular vantage point.

In this chapter, I will present several different, largely independent perspectives on eclecticism, each of which can be evaluated on its own particular merits. I will examine first the basic claims and goals of eclecticism, namely, the formulation of a system of psychotherapy that is: (a) more comprehensive and (b) more adequate than our current psychotherapies. Are such claims justified? Next I will discuss three philosophical notions that aid our understanding of the motives that fuel eclecticism. The first is the concept that underlying the appearance of diversity and contradiction in the world is a basic unity. When we organize data at a superordinate level, say the integrative eclectics, apparent contradictions disappear and the integrated fabric of knowledge emerges.

A second motive, one that drives what I have referred to above as selective (versus integrative) eclecticism, is the idea that we do not merely discover what is already present in nature but, rather, we create our categories and impose them on the world. That is, there are different ways of construing our observations of human behavior, each having a certain legitimacy. As a result, the selective eclectic advocates the use of different approaches for different clients, compared with the integrative eclectic who proposes a single, comprehensive, adequate, and unified therapy for all clients. A third motive sparking eclecticism is the belief that we can share a common language in psychology, that our diversity of theoretical and ideological terms can be relinquished in favor of a neutral language form. Is this really possible?

The third topic is a consideration of how

each psychotherapy embodies a vision of life of mythopoetic proportions. The literary forms described include the tragic, romantic, ironic, and comic, and the systems of therapy to which they are applied include psychoanalysis, behavior therapy, and humanistic therapy. This forms a backdrop to consider both the prospects and problems of eclecticism as a function of the change in visions of reality that eclecticism necessarily brings about.

The fourth section takes up the issue of what constitutes evidence or knowing in different therapeutic frameworks. The empirical/experimental method is contrasted with the hermeneutic mode of truth seeking. The ways in which this split creates certain potential obstacles to eclecticism are discussed. Finally, how the value framework of therapists affects their attitude toward eclecticism is briefly considered since, in the final analysis, it is they who must implement the eclectic therapy.

BASIC CLAIMS OF ECLECTICISM

Comprehensiveness

Eclectic theories of therapy claim to be more comprehensive than existing theories.* Regarding this claim of widened scope, it is hard to see how an eclectic theory of therapy can be more comprehensive than psychoanalytic or social learning approaches. Each of the latter encompasses explanations of, and techniques for, changing the widest possible range of thought, affect, and behavior. This point can be illustrated by the diversity of subject matter in the recent *Annual of Psychoanalysis*, Volume 10 (Pollack, 1982).

---

*This section will focus more heavily on the theory of eclectic therapy than on its practice. However, I agree with Simon's (1974) statement that "every available therapeutic method has its own theoretical base" (p. 137), thereby emphasizing their mutual influence and interconnectedness.

In this single average-sized volume, there are articles employing psychoanalytic theory to account for the dream, affect, self-esteem regulation, the effects of psychotherapy, the enduring appeal of Peter Pan, the psychic tribulations of being an immigrant, and the way nostalgia is conveyed in the form, structure, and content of Charles Ives' music (Messer, 1984a). Similarly, the *Annual Review of Behavior Therapy*, Volume 8 (Franks, Wilson, Kendall, & Brownell, 1982) evaluates the application of behavioral techniques and their underlying theories to disorders ranging from A (autism) to V (vomiting) and to therapeutic techniques from A (aversion therapy) to Z (zen meditation). The wide acceptance of psychoanalytic and behavioral theory and therapy is, in part, due to their ability to help clinicians and scholars understand and cope with the typically confusing complexity of human behavior.

In addition, the elasticity of these theories is such that they continually expand their purview to encompass findings and ideas from related fields, which is necessary for them to remain viable. A current example in behavior therapy is its struggle to come to grips with the strong experimental evidence for "knowing without awareness" or unconscious processes (Marcel, 1983; Shevrin & Dickman, 1980). Two well-known cognitive behavior therapists, Meichenbaum and Gilmore (1984), argue that cognitive events, processes, and structures each imply an unconscious domain that cognitive behavior therapists must take into account. Thus, in a general sense, eclecticism is continuously preempted, at least in the theoretical realm, by the slow but steady absorption by current theories of ideas from competing theories and adjacent realms.

Adequacy

The second major claim of eclecticism is that it produces a better, more adequate

theory of therapy than provided by existing ones. Thus, eclectics frequently say that they take what is best from each existing theory or therapy or what they hold in common (see chapters by Garfield, Lazarus, and Prochaska & DiClemente, this volume). We are immediately faced with a problem. On what basis shall it be decided what is best to borrow from each theory or therapy? In their survey of eclecticism, Garfield and Kurtz (1977) found that there were 32 different theoretical combinations used by 145 eclectic psychologists blended in individually unique ways. Commenting in a more recent paper on this finding, Garfield (1982) quite wisely states that "in the absence of clear guidelines, theoretical or otherwise, possibly more procedures were used than were necessary, and perhaps the most efficient and effective procedures were not always utilized. Unfortunately, we have no data on this matter, but only conjecture" (p. 613). I would add that it is not only data that are lacking but, typically, a set of rules that specify what should be incorporated into a particular eclectic therapeutic system. (Several of the approaches in this volume, it should be noted, do provide such rules, e.g., Beutler, Prochaska & DiClemente). In the absence of such rules of inclusion, eclecticism must rely on the personal preference of the eclectic selector—with all the pitfalls that such an *ad hoc*, common-sense approach entails. As others have noted:

There is a persistent danger that being eclectic will justify a superficial, chaotic approach in which practitioners fly by the seats of their pants. (Norcross, this volume, p. 20).

The typical eclectic therapist chooses his or her methods, therapies, and techniques largely on the basis of subjective appeal. (Lazarus, 1981, p. 4)

One such result may be confusion and, in many cases, lack of effectiveness. To put the matter in the most pessimistic light:

No synthetic combination of the legs of one specimen and the wings of another will ever move except as their fabricator pushes them about with his tweezers. (Pepper, 1942, p. 112)

Furthermore, by fostering eclecticism, we lose our grip on the nomological net and the structural corroboration that adherents of a standard theory/therapy build up over time. Through bootstrapping, facts and validated hypotheses in one area of the theory lend confirmation to other parts of it. This skein of observation, fact, and theory is rent asunder by the combining of bits and pieces, parts and processes, which is characteristic of integrative eclecticism. Almost none of the eclectic systems presented in Part II of this volume can offer empirical validation of its total package. Each has to begin again to provide corroboration of its unique blend of elements.

But, wait, some eclectics may respond. Surely one theory is more adequate in some areas and another in different areas, and therefore, for practical purposes, they should be combined. For example, existential–phenomenological theory deals with concepts of human dignity and freedom more satisfactorily than does behaviorism, while behaviorism offers a more cogent account of superstitious behavior. This, indeed, may influence our decision in practical situations in choosing a clinical approach with an individual client. But for purposes of the present argument, it should be noted that Skinner's debunking of the notions of dignity and freedom from a behavioral standpoint is not without value or adherents. Behaviorism contains an impressive web of interlocking corroborative evidence that does not allow us to dismiss readily its spread to other areas. It is the essence of a good theory of therapy to explain as much as possible within its chosen domain. Even where current explanations are at the moment weak, we cannot be certain that it will not eventually come up with a satisfactory

understanding or view of such phenomena. It is for reasons such as these that Wilson (1982a, 1982b), referring to the search for consensus, advises behavior therapists to devote their energies "to developing replicable, testable, and effective methods of therapeutic change within the social learning framework of behavior therapy and invite other theoretical orientations to do the same" (1982a, p. 327).

PHILOSOPHICAL CONSIDERATIONS

Different forms of eclecticism are related to certain philosophical attitudes which are rarely, if ever, recognized or acknowledged by psychologists. In this section I will offer a brief exposition and critique of three philosophical positions that seem to fuel the drive to eclecticism. I will try to show that integrative eclecticism is closest to the philosophical belief called organicism; that selective eclecticism views the process of knowledge acquisition as discovery rather than invention; and that eclectics conceive of the (questionable) possibility of a language of description that is neutral and therefore acceptable to proponents of different therapies.

Eclecticism and Organicism

In a far-reaching philosophical treatise, Pepper (1942) spells out four "world hypotheses" into which all explanations are said to fall: mechanism, contextualism, formism, and organicism. Each has a root metaphor that provides the basic analogy by which we can get a grip on that world hypothesis. Thus, for *mechanism*, the root metaphor is the machine. In psychology we embrace mechanism when we conceive of psychological data as consisting of individual, independent parts or pieces existing in a spatiotemporal configuration, and which are governed by a set of universally valid laws. The British empiricists Locke, Berkeley, and Hume are most closely connected with this tradition insofar as they emphasized the existence of separate ideas that get linked up by the process of association. Behaviorism falls within the mechanistic world hypothesis.

Contextualism, unlike mechanism, is synthetic rather than analytic. The root metaphor is the historical event as seen within a setting or context. An act or event is explained by revealing the specific relationship it bears to other events occurring in its psychosocial sphere. The point is not to integrate all events in the field, nor to presume that there are timeless laws governing the data, but, rather, to limit the explanation to the specific domain and time period studied (White, 1973). "The quality of an event is the fused qualities of its strands, and the qualities of its strands come partly out of its context" (Pepper, 1942, p. 249). That is, unlike the case in mechanism, there is no separation of detail from context. Psychobiography is contextual in that it stresses the uniqueness and individuality of its subject matter. The phenomenological approach is contextualist, too, in its emphasis on a description of the lived world of experience with full allowance for detail embedded in context.

A third world hypothesis is *formism*, whose root metaphor is similarity. It seeks classes of things or events whose similarity to or difference from others can be described. "The formist considers an explanation to be complete when a given set of objects has been properly identified, its class, generic and specific attributes assigned, and labels attesting to its particularity attached to it" (White, 1973, p. 14). In psychology when we set about to construct a personality typology, such as Jungian archetypes, or a stage theory that presupposes ideal forms, such as Piaget's, we are encountering formism.

Finally, *organicism* is the most integrative world hypothesis within which a phil-

osophical (versus pragmatic) eclecticism can find a home. The organicist believes that in the world, we encounter fragments of experience—such as observations of a school of therapy; these appear with certain connections which then inevitably encounter contradictions, gaps, or opposition from other fragments of experience—such as the observations of other theories of therapy. The various fragments have a tendency to be resolved by incorporation into an organic whole which, all the while, was implicit in the fragments and which transcends the previous contradictions by means of a coherent totality (Pepper, 1942, p. 283)—or, we might say, by an integrative eclecticism. By organizing the data at a higher level, the appearance of conflict is dissolved into the reality of the organic whole. Progress is achieved by including more and more of the fragments into a better integrated whole.

In terms of integrating parts of one therapy with parts of another the eclectic, like the organicist, would argue that the apparent contradictions were never really contradictions because they vanish when the eclectic system is constructed (e.g., see Garfield; Hart; Murgatroyd & Apter; and Prochaska & DiClemente, all in this volume; also, Wachtel, 1977). Nothing is lost in such a system because it takes in all the pieces of one therapy and joins them to another. Individual pieces get aggregated into wholes that are greater than the sum of their parts.

Closely linked to the idea of organicism is the belief in the unity of knowledge. Some scholars proceed from the premise that unity of knowledge is possible because "the connections were really there all the time, working in nature. . . . There was nothing to do but let them come together. . . . These are immediately discoverable in observation. . . ." (Pepper, 1942, p. 292). Now, if this is the case, we have a powerful argument in favor of integrative eclecticism: in joining parts of different theories or therapies, we are contributing to that unity which is, in fact, the natural order of the psychological (and physical) universe. Within psychology, the most articulate spokesman for this viewpoint is Arthur Staats (1983), who argues that our field is in a crisis of disunity and that a unified science of psychology is now possible and desirable. He has suggested "that psychology marshal itself toward establishing an interest in such unification which will demand development of the need for unified theory and of methods for creative, unified theory" (Staats, 1981, p. 253). In the therapeutic realm, Goldfried (1980) has made the same claim—that the different schools of psychotherapy in fact share a commonality of viewpoint beneath the surface diversity. Norcross (this volume, p. 8) applauds eclectic therapists who recognize how differentiated parts of psychotherapy can be organized and integrated into the whole at a higher level and who appreciate the unity and complexity achieved thereby. By referring to such therapists as having "successfully reached the summit," in effect he is strongly endorsing the value of unity.

If the reader is persuaded that there is an affinity between integrative eclecticism and organicism, he or she should note that, in Pepper's scheme, it is only one of four world hypotheses. In fact, behaviorism, psychoanalysis, and existential-phenomenology are not basically organicist in outlook, which is to say that philosophical eclectics share one particular philosophical outlook on the best way to view psychological data, while adherents of specific schools of therapy prefer others. Consciously or otherwise we operate within a particular world view, but tend to lose sight of the existence of other, equally viable alternatives. In psychology, at the current time, we are in no position to judge in a once-and-for-all fashion which world hypothesis is best. It can be argued that what *is* best at present is the contin-

ued existence of a dynamic tension among these models, or what Royce (1982) might call "constructive dialectics," rather than a unimodal organicist view.

Perspectivism

The counterpart to the unity/discovery model and, hence, to an integrative eclecticism is that psychology, by its very nature, is pluralistic and "is not a single or coherent discipline but rather a collectivity of studies of varied cast. . . . Paradigms, theories, models (or whatever one's label for conceptual ordering devices) can never prove pre-emptive or preclusive of alternate organizations" (Koch, 1981, p. 268). There is no single truth to discover. Similarly, Royce (1982) argues that psychology is conceptually pluralistic, multiworld-view, and multitheoretical.

In discussing these issues in the context of the integratability of the therapies, Schacht (1984) sees the pluralistic view of psychology as related to the idea that we do not merely discover what is inherent in nature but *invent* our categories and theories and view nature through them. For Gergen (1982) this dichotomy is captured by a comparison of exogenic with endogenic thinking. In the latter, "recordings of reality are not so much correct or incorrect as they are creations of the observer. . . . *Multiple interpretations of experience are usually held to be both legitimate and desirable*" (pp. 176–177; emphasis added). Schacht (1984) points out that "the pluralistic position cherishes contradictions as spurs to the creation of knowledge and as antidotes to the suffocating intellectual effects of an *a priori* assumption of unity" (p. 125). Insofar as efforts at eclecticism lead to a truly new and creative theory of therapy, such efforts are to be valued (see Murgatroyd & Apter, this volume, as an example). But insofar as they attempt merely to summarize and unify current therapies, they may tend to stultify, not enrich, our discipline.

Given that different ways of conceptualizing reality are always possible and even desirable from the perspectivist standpoint, there will continue to be several extant theories of therapy. Rather than choose to practice within one, as single-minded therapists do, or to unite them, as integrative eclectics do, selective eclectics take a bird's-eye view of the therapies and are prepared to use any that seem suited to the purpose at hand. Of course, one can also be a hybrid eclectic, e.g., selective in practice but single-minded in theory (see Lazarus, this volume).

The Myth of a Common Language

There is a recognition among those attracted to eclecticism that therapists with different theoretical outlooks use different psychological languages. If a truly eclectic therapy is to be proposed and developed, how are the different languages to be joined? If the phenomenologist uses terms like "the phenomenal sense of self," the psychoanalyst, "projection of mental representations onto others," and the behaviorist, "conditioned stimuli and responses," how are we to understand each other and develop a common framework? The suggestion made by some is that we abandon our familiar language communities and develop a genuinely "neutral metalanguage" (Murgatroyd & Apter, this volume, p. 280) or "a superordinate language system to facilitate communication both between clinicians and researchers and among theoreticians" (Beutler, this volume, p. 94). Others suggest that we agree to speak in the vernacular or, in order to encompass experimental findings, that we adopt the language of experimental cognitive psychology (Goldfried, 1979, 1983; Goldfried & Newman, this volume; Ryle, 1978; Sarason, 1979). Goldfried (1983) suggests that such a language offers us

"a set of relatively neutral concepts, having a minimal theoretical superstructure, [one that is] closely related to the kinds of phenomena that we all see in our clinical work" (p. 103). Implicit in this proposal is the idea that one language of description is really as good as another and what is important is that we agree to employ it for the sake of a rapprochement among the different therapies. It presumes the possibility of a psychological Esperanto that would draw the world of psychotherapy closer together.

But is such a proposal possible or desirable? Even within established sciences such as physics there are specialized subfields employing different languages suited to their own purposes. "In practice, despite all pressures toward conformity, scientists even in the same field, speak slightly different dialects" (Keller, 1985, p. 136). Are cognitive concepts and language with their own unique set of suppositions and presuppositions and their own theoretical superstructures and substructures any more neutral than those of phenomenology, behaviorism, or psychoanalysis (Messer, 1984b)? I believe not. While terms like "script" or "schema" may not carry the same negative connotations for behavior therapists as "unconscious fantasy," or the same negatively conditioned association for psychoanalysts as "behavioral chain," they are not in any absolute sense neutral terms, *nor can they be.* Whether we recognize it or not, as psychologists we are always viewing phenomena from one angle or another, none of which is ever free from theoretical bias. "We have not yet a language which will serve as a permanent neutral matrix for formulating all good explanatory hypotheses, and we have not the foggiest notion of how to get one" (Rorty, 1979, p. 348).

It follows, then, that "in psychology we must have *many* language communities: Many subgroups of individuals equipped with diverse stocks of discriminations and differently specialized sensitivities. By *definition*, we must have a greater number of language communities in psychology than perhaps in any other field of inquiry currently institutionalized" (Koch, 1964, p. 28). The meanings of terms only make sense by virtue of their interrelations to other terms within a broad context. Even a staunch behavior therapy advocate like Cyril Franks (1984) makes the point that a term like "symptom substitution" has meaning within a psychoanalytic context but not for a behaviorist who may use the term "response substitution." Are they the same? According to Franks, "the difference between symptom substitution and response substitution is far more than semantic. Each has a specific contextual meaning and intimately interwoven series of conceptual linkages that make the two notions incompatible. Each becomes logically meaningful only within its own context" (p. 238). It seems that the logical positivist's dream of a neutral data language has been largely abandoned.

In a sense, the emergent viewpoint is a version of the Whorfian hypothesis: what we perceive around us and how we perceive it are a function of the language we employ. There is no bedrock language of definitions to which we can point and nod in agreement. The particular sensitivities of the observers will determine the extent to which high interobserver agreement is possible. There is no immaculate perception! In the phraseology of the modernist writers, we do not speak language; language speaks us. Beutler, Goldfried, Ryle, and others are right in one sense: we are prisoners of language. But they are wrong in thinking that escape from that prison is possible.

VISIONS OF REALITY: MYTHIC FORMS

Every system of psychotherapy contains a certain underlying thematic structure which embodies its way of viewing life's possibilities. Although there are different ways of classifying such therapeutic outlooks, I have found one scheme to be particularly useful. It was developed by the literary critic Northrop Frye (1957, 1965) to categorize different genres or mythic forms in literature and was subsequently applied by Roy Schafer (1976) to psychoanalysis. The four visions are called the romantic, the ironic, the tragic, and the comic. Meir Winokur and I have employed Frye's taxonomy to spell out the contrasting visions of reality in psychoanalytic therapy and behavior therapy (Messer, 1983; Messer & Winokur, 1980, 1984). In the present context the formulation will be elaborated and extended to include the most popular humanistic forms of treatment, which typically stress self-actualization and fulfillment. After illustrating the intersection of each of these therapeutic categories with the four visions, I will discuss the possibilities and the difficulties of psychotherapeutic eclecticism that such a framework reveals.

The Romantic Vision

From the romantic viewpoint, life is an adventure or quest in which the person as hero transcends the world of experience, achieves victory over it, and is liberated from it. "It is a drama of the triumph of good over evil, of virtue over vice, of light over darkness, and of the ultimate transcendence of man over the world in which he was imprisoned by the Fall" (White, 1973, p. 9). The romantic vision emphasizes exploration and conquest of the unknown, the mysterious, the irrational. It is more the world as we would like it to be than the world as we find it.

Humanistic therapists, such as Maslow (1971) and Rogers (1961), view life primarily as an adventuresome quest. In emphasizing peoples' potential for continued psychological growth, their willingness to take risks, and the ability to self-actualize, humanistic therapies are operating with a romantic outlook. Rogers, in fact, claims that we are born with an "organismic valuing" process that allows us to appreciate and strive for that which is life-enhancing.

The romantic vision idealizes individuality and what is "natural" (Schafer, 1976). To express oneself freely, spontaneously, and impulsively is prized. In a strongly romantic spirit, those therapies considered part of the human potential movement stress "doing one's own thing," acting naturally, and being authentic. Similarly, they advocate the pursuit of a unique life-style and the continuous search for self-realization.

Psychoanalytic therapy also partakes of the romantic vision but with a different emphasis. In stressing exploration of the unconscious, of the irrational and the unknown, psychoanalysts are influenced by the romantic attitude. Psychoanalysis is also viewed as a journey, a quest for redemption. The therapeutic process encourages a regression away from everyday reality and into the world of dreams, free associations, and fantasies. Unlike humanistic therapy, however, it envisions more obstacles *en route* and is much less optimistic about the possibilities for ultimate self-actualization and liberation. Nor does it value as strongly as some humanistic therapies acting "naturally" and what it might term narcissistically.

In contrast to both the psychoanalytic and humanistic therapies, the behavior therapies are much more reality-oriented and practical than they are romantic. While behavior therapists may have an attitude of curiosity and openness to the unexpected and the unknown, exploration of irrational fantasies is not encouraged in behavior therapy. Rather, problems are operationally defined, carefully measured on objective scales, and pragmatically treated. In some forms of cognitive behavior therapy, for example, irrational

thoughts are disputed rather than explored and understood (e.g., Ellis & Grieger, 1977). Since there is no objective, rational reason for clients needing to be perfectionistic or to be liked by everyone, the therapist wants to disabuse them of these irrational ideas. The romantic notion of the quest—so prominent in psychoanalytic and humanistic therapy—is almost entirely absent in behavior therapy.

The Ironic Vision

The ironic attitude is the enemy of romance. It is an attitude of detachment, of keeping things in perspective, of recognizing that there is another side of the coin. It challenges our beliefs, traditions, and (romantic) illusions. Like the tragic vision, it emphasizes the inherent difficulties of human existence, the impossibility of mastering the world and even of truly knowing its mysteries.

"The ironic perspective in analytic work results in the analysand's coming to see himself or herself as being less in certain emotional respects than was initially thought—less, that is, than the unconscious ideas of omnipotence and omniscience imply" (Schafer, 1976, p. 52). Interestingly, humanistic therapy is linked in a dialectical fashion to psychoanalysis in that it results in clients seeing themselves and life's possibilities as *more* than they initially thought.

Psychoanalytic therapists adopt the ironic attitude in therapy when they take a position of relative detachment (Stein, 1985). They do so in order to detect the flip side of the client's utterances and behavior—the hidden meaning, contradictions, and paradoxes—how cheerfulness may cover sadness, and well wishing, murderous thoughts. By contrast, in their therapeutic demeanor, behavior therapists and humanistic therapists are more likely to be friendly, self-disclosing, transparent, and affectively expressive, which may lessen the possibility of discerning irony. Behavior therapists are also more likely to accept client complaints at face value including their stated therapeutic objectives (Wilson & O'Leary, 1980), and humanistic therapists tend to accept most client feelings as authentic expression. It is the essence of the ironic posture to take nothing for granted, and in this sense, such accepting attitudes are a breach of the ironic position.

The Tragic Vision

The tragic and ironic visions are linked insofar as they both include a distrust of romantic illusions and happy endings in life. Furthermore, they are reflective in attitude whereas the romantic and comic views are more action oriented. Tragedy, however, unlike irony, involves commitment. In a tragic drama, the hero has acted with purpose and, in so doing, has committed, at least in his/her mind, an act causing shame or guilt. He/she suffers by virtue of the conflict between passion and duty and, after considerable inner struggle, arrives at a state of greater self-knowledge. What interests us in the work of the tragic poet "is the glimpse we get of certain profound moods of inner struggles. Now, this glimpse cannot be obtained from without" (Bergson, 1937/1956, p. 167). Such a mode of knowing may be contrasted with "the kind of observation from which comedy springs. It is directed outwards" (Bergson, 1937/1956, p. 169).

In the tragic vision the limitations in life are accepted—not all is possible, not all is redeemable, not all potentialities are realizable. The clock cannot be turned back, death cannot be undone, man's nature cannot be radically perfected. Tragedy "requires one to recognize the elements of defeat in victory and of victory in defeat; the pain in pleasure and the pleasure in pain; the guilt in apparently justified action; the loss of opportunities entailed by

every choice and by growth in any direction. . . ." (Schafer, 1976, p. 35).

Among the three major therapeutic orientations, the humanistic therapies are most dyssynchronous with the spirit of tragedy. In viewing people as fundamentally good, innocent, and unfallen (e.g., Rogers, 1961), the beliefs of humanistic therapy fly in the face of the tragic vision. To espouse the view that all the potentialities of human beings are in the service of maintaining and enhancing life falls squarely within the romantic and not the tragic mode. To encourage risk taking without taking cognizance of the potentially dire consequences is to operate within the comic not tragic perspective. To posit an inborn "striving toward superiority or perfection" (Adler, 1927) or to emphasize the possibility of "unselfish love" and "unbiased understanding" (Maslow, 1962) is to accentuate the romantic and to downplay the tragic. For both Rogers and Maslow, if the environment provides love, respect, and acceptance, along with satisfaction of basic physiological needs, that is enough for the natural unfolding process of self-actualization to take place (Maddi, 1980). Transposing this principle to psychotherapy, the therapist's warmth, genuineness, and unconditional positive regard are considered enough for therapy to progress.

Psychoanalysis, more than humanistic or behavior therapy, falls within the tragic vision. Man is viewed as caught within early fixations which themselves are subject to repression and thus beyond his ken. The fixations result from our sexual and aggressive nature and the conflicts such a nature gives rise to, conflicts from which we never can be entirely free. The psychoanalytic therapist recognizes "that suffering while learning and changing cannot usually be avoided, nor can the analysand realize himself or herself most fully and resume growth in the absence of adversity and deprivation" (Schafer, 1976, p. 42). Even then, the kind of reconciliation that occurs at the end of a psychoanalytic therapy is not unmixed joy and happiness. It is a fuller recognition of what one's struggles are about, the conditions of life one must work within. These conditions "set the limits on what may be aspired to and what may be legitimately aimed at in the quest for security and sanity in the world" (White, 1973, p. 9).

Behavior therapy has a far less somber outlook than psychoanalysis, and the kind of hope for cure it holds out is greater. Its emphasis on learning through modeling and reinforcement, direct and vicarious, allows for greater optimism regarding people's ability to change. Similarly, cognitive behavior therapists, in focusing on the correction of irrational cognitive constructions and attributions, imply a malleable and improvable subject. In Ellis's rational-emotive therapy, however, there is a recognition of people's need to accept imperfections and limitations, which is compatible with the tragic vision. That it differs from the full tragic vision is apparent from Hyman's (1957) statement on the tragic hero's situation: a person is locked in struggle with "inner forces of evil and must win through to some private redemption and true-seeing by means of his own suffering" (p. 169). In behavior therapy, by contrast, the client is helped to feel better or to change his behavior or thoughts rather than to reach an inner reconciliation based on self-knowledge.

The Comic Vision

Whereas in tragedy things go from bad to worse, in comedy the direction of events is from bad to better or even best. True, there are obstacles and struggles in a comedy, but these are ultimately overcome, and there is a reconciliation between hero and antagonist, between the person and his or her social world. Harmony and unity, progress and happiness prevail. For this reason, dramatic comedies often end with festive celebrations. Note that the conflicts portrayed in a comedy are between people and the unfortunate situation in which they find themselves, and not the kind of inner struggles or implacable oppositions encountered in dramatic tragedy.

In behavior therapy, too, conflict is often ascribed to external situations or forces which can be mastered through application of behavioral principles. Behavior therapists are not as interested as psychoanalysts in their clients' internal struggles but more in the direct alleviation of suffering and a rapidly achieved positive outcome. A phobia of crossing bridges, or a complaint of lack of assertiveness, is approached head-on with a spirit of optimism and laboratory-tested techniques from the behavioral repertoire. By contrast, struggles over separation issues symbolically expressed in difficulty crossing a bridge, or over fear of aggressive impulses in the unassertive client, are explored by the psychoanalyst not only with the goal of their remediation (psychoanalysis does have some comic thrust), but with the view that increased consciousness of one's condition is itself worthwhile.

Humanistic therapies do not strive for happy endings in quite the way behavior therapies do, nor are they as basically contemplative about inevitable warring and discordant factions of the mind as is psychoanalysis. But they do emphasize the substantial possibilities for gratifying impulses which Ernst Kris (1937) has described as an essential aspect of the comic view. For them, a freer, more joyful, laughter-filled existence is attainable. Our fondest hopes and daydreams can be achieved. The true self one comes to know in a humanistic therapy is not one fraught with struggle, nor is it one seeking reduction of tension, but rather it is an authentic self, free of conditions of worth, in touch with its natural, organismic valuing, and satisfied with life's enormous possibilities for self-enhancement. Insofar as the humanistic therapist's job is to penetrate the false self, and reveal the good, innocent, unfallen romantic beneath, it partakes of the comic vision.

Eclecticism and the Visions of Reality

Certain changes that have come about over time in each of the three psychotherapeutic modes, or changes that have been recently proposed, bring about a certain degree and kind of therapeutic eclecticism. Such modifications, however, involve alterations in the therapies' visions of reality. An examination of these modifications in light of the visions can provide us with a framework for understanding the impact of such eclectic shifts on the basic outlook of these psychotherapies.

Psychoanalytic therapies. I have characterized psychoanalytic therapy as more heavily informed by tragic, romantic, and ironic visions than by the comic vision. Certain variants of psychoanalytic theory and therapy, however, decidedly shift the balance in the direction of the comic vision as do certain recent trends in psychoanalysis itself. The neo-Freudians and the ego-psychologists, for example, deemphasize the relentlessness of biologically given drives; the former stress the power of cultural and societal forces or current, external life situations in distorting personality development and functioning, whereas the latter grant more ability to the ego to control the drives and to foster an adaptive, more conflict-free existence. In psychoanalytic therapy there has been a deemphasis on offering interpretations leading to insight (Appelbaum, 1981) in favor of the provision of a corrective emotional experience (Malan, 1976), a holding environment (Winnicott, 1965), empathy (Kohut, 1977), and a real relationship (Roland, 1967; Tuttman, 1982). Running

through all of these notions is the hope and belief that one can, in some way, make up for early deprivation and can enhance the person's positive mental representations of self and other through the healing power of the relationship. In Adelson's (1954) words, "We don't try to kill the weeds; we feed the clover and hope that *it* will kill the weeds." In both ego and self-psychoanalytic theory and therapy, then, there has been a relative shift from the tragic view with its emphasis on purpose (an intentional shameful act), passion (suffering), and perception (self-knowledge) to those possibilities which fall within the comic perspective: harmony, happiness, and health.

In a sphere of psychoanalytic therapy known as short-term or time-limited, a focus is established at the outset and concrete goals are set, thus delimiting the purview of the therapy (see Fuhriman, Paul, & Burlingame, this volume; Rasmussen & Messer, in press; Winokur, Messer, & Schacht, 1981). In so doing, the romantic vision—with its emphasis on a time-unbounded journey into the unknown—is curtailed in favor of a pragmatic problem-solving approach (psychoanalytic style), which again is more comic in outlook than romantic. Integrative therapies have been proposed in which action-oriented techniques supplement psychoanalytic exploration (Feather & Rhoads, 1972; Rhoads, 1984; Wachtel, 1977, 1984). This entails a shift in the direction of meeting problems head-on, by diminishing anxiety or enhancing assertiveness. In this respect the ironic view of enhancing multiple meanings and taking a relatively detached view is traded off for a more comic view involving pragmatic action, social adjustment, and enhanced comfort.

The behavior therapies. Behavior therapy was characterized as falling more squarely within the comic vision than within the other three visions. Recent changes in emphasis within behavior therapy, however, can be seen as broadening its vision of life. In the area of assessment, there is a greater interest in going beyond the presenting complaint as the necessary focus of treatment. For example, Fishman and Lubetkin (1983), both behavior therapists, write that "many practicing behavior therapists are too wedded to the *prima facie* problems that clients bring to therapy. . . . In a sense, the manifest problem serves as a cover for a more severe problem" (p. 27). And Woolfolk and Richardson (1984) portray the effort of behavior therapists to remain within their rationalist and pragmatic framework even while challenging their clients' goals and striving to establish a therapeutic dialogue. In viewing their clients' goals as having meaning beyond the obvious, they are adopting the ironic attitude in therapy.

In behavior therapy, both in theory and in practice, a major change has been the development of cognitive approaches with an emphasis on concepts like attribution, expectancies, plans, schemas, and scripts (Mahoney & Arnkoff, 1978; Meichenbaum, 1977). This has led to a relatively greater interest in cognitive conflict which is within the tragic mode. An even more dramatic change is behavior therapists' attention to unconscious processes and to the role of affect, including its link to cognition. "Cognitive behavioral therapy proposes that if one wishes to change the depressed individual's behavior (or for that matter the behavior of any individual), there is a need to develop an awareness of unconscious maladaptive thoughts and feelings and their effects on behavior" (Meichenbaum & Gilmore, 1984, p. 278).

In an AABT panel (1983) on relations among cognition, emotion, and behavior, Gal, Lang, Matthews, and Rachman each emphasized the primacy of emotion and the need for behavior therapists to pay closer attention to it. Elsewhere, Lang (1979) has proposed that behavior change "depends not on simple exposure to fear stimuli, but on the generation of the relevant affective cognitive structure, the prototype for overt behavior which is subsequently modified into a more functional form" (p. 501). As behavior therapists involve themselves more and more in their clients' subjectivity and their irrational, affect-laden cognitions, and as they come face to face with cognitive conflict, they necessarily partake of the romantic and tragic visions.

Humanistic therapies. Humanistic therapy continues to view people in process-oriented terms such as "exchanging," "emerging," "unfolding," and "flowing" (Cochrane & Holloway, 1974) and to uphold the romantic vision. There is an even greater emphasis in humanistic theory now than in the past on subjectivity and on "man as an active seeker of stimulation and novelty; an organism that seeks the assimilation of new experience" (Wexler & Rice, 1974, p. 17). While the theory has been broadened and deepened by the inclusion of cognitive concepts and information-processing language (Wexler, 1974), there is no apparent shift in its basic vision of reality. Even though the therapy now allows for interpretation as well as reflection (Ivey & Simek-Downing, 1980), for more self-disclosure by the therapist, stressing a more collaborative participation by both client and therapist (Boy & Pine, 1982), accurate empathy remains the *sine qua non* of at least client-centered therapy. In fact, one branch of the humanistic approach, transpersonal psychology, is even more romantic in perspective than its progenitor. The "transpersonal level refers to psychotherapeutic goals which are spiritually oriented toward ultimate reality . . . unity on the human, universal, or cosmic plane in which he [the client] experiences a transcendence of his ego boundaries into a universal consciousness" (Karasu, 1979, p. 559).

Trade-offs in the Service of Eclecticism

The variants of psychoanalysis such as ego psychology, neo-Freudianism, and brief dynamic therapy bring psychoanalytic therapy closer in its outlook and practice to both behavior therapy and humanistic therapy, and it thereby becomes more eclectic in the integrative sense of the term. Whether or not this is viewed as desirable depends on the relative value one places on the particular blend of the four visions. In emphasizing sociocultural influences and the power of the ego versus the immutable drives, and the curative power of the client-therapist relationship versus self-knowledge through interpretation, the full force of the tragic viewpoint is muted. In recommending action versus psychic exploration, the ironic vision is tempered by closing off avenues to further and deeper meaning and intention. And, in setting goals and a focus in advance, the romantic vision is curtailed. In short, there is no free lunch, which anyone with a tragic view of life would be quick to point out.

Behavior therapy has become more comprehensive or eclectic by bringing cognitive, affective, and even unconscious factors into its purview. By so doing, it reduces its appeal of clearly measurable goals and specifiable environmental triggers. The attractiveness of eliminating problems like phobias, compulsions, or headaches in a rather straightforward way is traded off for a more complicated and subjective view of client problems. Not all behavior therapists agree that such an eclectic shift is necessarily for the better (e.g., Ledwidge, 1978; Wolpe, 1976).

In viewing the three modes of therapy together, it seems that both behavior therapy and psychoanalytic therapy have become more humanistic in outlook, whereas humanistic therapy has deepened and refined its concepts even while remaining basically romantic in both its theory and therapeutic process. It is probably true

that humanistic therapy has had more impact on behavior therapy (e.g., Curtiss, 1976) and on psychoanalytic therapy (e.g., Appelbaum, 1979; Stolorow, 1976) than it has been influenced in any fundamental way by them. Thus, it can be said that humanistic therapists have been willing to forego the potential advantages of an eclectic vision. They have not compromised on their strong allegiance to the romantic vision but instead have concentrated on developing even further within that vision.

THE DEBATE OVER EVIDENCE

In almost every one of the chapters in Part II of this volume, a strong value is placed on empirical research in determining what shall be included in an eclectic therapy (see, e.g., Fischer, Chapter 11). The alternative in the minds of several authors (e.g., Garfield, Chapter 5; Lazarus, Chapter 3) seems to be reliance on unsupported speculation and conjecture. This empirical/experimental method of truth seeking, which psychologists have adopted from the natural sciences, relies heavily on observation, laboratory studies, elementism, and objectivism (Kimble, 1984; Krasner & Houts, 1984). Findings are typically context-free and presumably lead to universal, nomothetic laws. Psychologists who espouse this view would probably be those who accept the possibility of a neutral data language for psychology. They would also tend to be less interested in the visions of reality embodied in psychotherapy than in empirical findings on process and outcome.

While valuing the contributions made by empirical studies, I would argue that the criterion of truth that guides them is not the only one possible (Messer, 1985; Messer & Winokur, 1984). Whereas the experimental approach is referred to as paradigmatic and logicoscientific (Bruner, 1984), and as leading to historical truth or empirical truth, the alternative typically leads to what is variously called narrative truth (Bruner, 1984; Sherwood, 1969; Spence, 1982), hermeneutic-dialectical truth (Barratt, 1976, 1984), or, in Bruner's (1984) words, "truth-likeness" or "verisimilitude." It comes in the form of good stories, believable historical accounts, and a good narrative fit. It stresses meaning of experiences and their interpretation. Rather than seeking generality, it opts for a full account of uniqueness, of "personal events in their full comprehensible richness" (Bruner, 1984, p. 8).

How are we to judge the adequacy of a narrative? Sherwood (1969) offers three criteria. To satisfy the first, self-consistency, the general statements made must be consistent with each other. The second, coherence, requires a fit between parts of the narrative and the whole, that the narrative hangs together by virtue of its resolving the apparent incongruities in the text to be understood. The third, comprehensiveness, is the extent to which the narrative account covers the ground; e.g., the various portions of a case history are all included in the account. As should be apparent, this method is akin to textual interpretation employed in history, literature, and biblical exegesis. It is hermeneutic in that it involves meaning, interpretation, and disciplined subjectivity more than fact, explanation, and strict objectivity.

While the above account of the distinction between these two ways of knowing is necessarily brief, it is sufficient to make the following point. Insofar as eclectic therapy systems place sole value on behavioral science criteria for truth, it will be exceedingly difficult for them to incorporate psychoanalytic and phenomenological/existential approaches. As Franks (1984) has stated in regard to behavior therapy, "For data to be acceptable they must conform to the hypothetico-deductive or some related methodology of the behavioral scientist . . . it is conformity to

a generally accepted set of rules that constitutes one essential unity of contemporary behavior therapy" (pp. 233–234). Many of the contributors to this volume seem to hold a similar view of what kind of data can be relied on. Thus, the insights of the psychoanalytic and phenomenological/existential approaches tend to be underrepresented in their eclectic systems.

Is it possible to accept both modes of knowing and, therefore, to include both sets of criteria? Franks' response is a categorical no:

It needs to be reaffirmed, that the fact that such alternative intellectual styles cannot be ruled out is no reason for behavior therapists to abandon their conviction that, for behavior therapy to progress, it is an objectivist methodology that is most likely to yield fruitful results rather than an alternative system or some form of integration of the behavioral and psychoanalytic approaches. (p. 237)

Nevertheless, others do see a complementarity of these two modes of truth seeking:

Psychology needs to incorporate both modes of discourse, and hermeneutics can make a substantive and essential contribution to the understanding of human systems. I can readily accept Apel's (1967) argument that the human sciences should involve an interplay between hermeneutic-dialectical and naturalistic discourse, that is, in another sense between hermeneutics and empirics. These approaches should be complementary. (Barratt, 1976, p. 473)

Similarly, Blight (1981) argues, "We must give up the view that science seeks verified, ultimate explanations while the humanities settle for mere conjecture. On the contrary, all knowledge is conjectural and permanently so" (p. 191). The implementation of this complementarity remains to be accomplished, but if and when it is achieved, the prospects for eclecticism, at least among certain therapies, will brighten.

THE VALUES OF THE THERAPIST

The distinction between a hermeneutic and natural science approach to the data of therapy may also constitute a therapist's epistemological preferences, which in turn have an impact on their attitude toward psychotherapeutic eclecticism. That is, by virtue of their strong allegiance to a particular way of knowing, many therapists will reject eclecticism. For example, Schacht and Black (1985) compared the epistemological commitment of behavioral and psychoanalytic therapists using the psychoepistemological profile developed by Royce and Mos (1980). It yields the relative standing of subjects on the variables metaphorism, empiricism, and rationalism. (Metaphorism resembles the hermeneutic approach insofar as it involves testing of one's beliefs in terms of the way in which they fit into meaning structures. It emphasizes analogical reasoning and the construction of meaning rather than observation *per se*.) Eighty-six percent of the psychoanalytic therapists showed a profile with metaphorism as the highest score, which was significantly higher than the 33% attained by the behavior therapists. Behavior therapists had somewhat higher mean rationalism scores and were much more likely than psychoanalysts to rate empiricism as their preferred way of knowing (36% versus 6%). Similarly, in comparing the values of behavioral scientists with those of nonbehavioral scientists in psychology, Krasner and Houts (1984) found the former to endorse quantitative, empirical, and objectivist approaches to the study of human behavior, whereas the latter endorsed humanistic and subjectivist approaches.

As Sundland (1977) has documented, and Norcross (1981) has pointed out, "clinical investigators have repeatedly encountered numerous and predictable differences in both the activities and beliefs of therapists of differing theoretical orienta-tions" (p. 1544). Grebstein (this volume, p. 314) suggests, for example, that family therapy compared to individual therapy requires a therapist who is more outgoing and extroverted.

The studies cited are meant merely to illustrate that many therapists will probably remain strongly attracted to a specific way of knowing their clients, to specific visions of reality, and to specific values. For them, eclecticism will hold little attraction. Others—perhaps those whose value system, personality structure, or epistemological stance are more fluid (or who are more flexible, as Lazarus points out in his chapter)—will be more comfortable integrating features of more than one therapy without feeling they are violating deeply held philosophical outlooks. It is interesting to note that in the study by Schacht and Black (1985), behavior therapists were more evenly distributed among the three epistemological styles than the psychoanalytic therapists, suggesting, perhaps, their greater openness to eclecticism in therapy.

CONCLUDING COMMENTS

None of the analyses of the basic assumptions, problems, or visions of eclecticism presented in this chapter is meant to imply that some degree of eclecticism in practice is not desirable. It is. For purposes of validating theories of therapy, however, the intrusion of foreign elements breaks up the structure of corroboration. Kuhn (1977) makes a similar point in distinguishing between the basic scientist and applied scientist, whose "decision to seek a cure . . . must be made with little reference to the state of the relevant science" (p. 236). Pepper (1942) contends that in the interest of intellectual clarity we want our theories pure and not eclectic. In matters of practice, we want to be able to draw upon any theoretical ideas or techniques that are backed by evidence and are potentially useful. We want to be rational and reasonable, not dogmatic. This is best exemplified in the work of Lazarus, who borrows freely from a diversity of sources in the service of an efficacious therapy.

Nevertheless, we may ask: what should be the proper degree of eclecticism to introduce into practice? For some of the very reasons set forth above, this will remain a subject of debate. Some will see the resulting eclectic therapy as more comprehensive and adequate, but others will protest that it is no more so than a present, existing therapy. Where some will see virtue in the expansion of the visions of reality in an eclectic therapy, others will see an abrogation of the purer vision of its progenitors. There are those who will find intellectual satisfaction in the steps taken toward a unified theory of therapy, and others who will protest that such a view is neither possible nor desirable. While some will embrace a diversity of methods to obtain corroborating evidence, others will remain wedded to a particular philosophy of science. And, finally, whereas some therapists by virtue of their personal dispositions, beliefs, ways of knowing, and visions of reality will embrace full eclecticism, others will stick closer to a favored outlook even while slowly incorporating into it some diverse elements from the panoply of existing therapeutic approaches.

REFERENCES

Adelson, J. (1954). *Freud in America: Some observations.* Paper presented at the meeting of the American Psychological Association.

Adler, A. (1927). *The practice and theory of individual psychology.* New York: Harcourt, Brace, & World.

Appelbaum, S. A. (1979). *Out in inner space.* Garden City, NY: Anchor/Doubleday.

Appelbaum, S. A. (1981). *Effecting change in psychotherapy.* New York: Jason Aronson.

Association for Advancement of Behavior Therapy Meetings (1983, December). Symposium on *The relationships between cognition, emotion, and behavior: Implications for treatment.* Washington, DC.

Barratt, B. B. (1976). Freud's psychology as interpretation. In T. Shapiro (Ed.), *Psychoanalysis and contemporary science,* Vol. 5 (pp. 443–478). New York: International Universities Press.

Barratt, B. (1984). *Psychic reality and psychoanalytic knowing.* Hillside, NJ: The Analytic Press.

Bergson, H. (1937). Laughter: An essay on the meaning of the comic. In W. Sypher (Ed.), *The meaning of comedy.* Garden City, NY: Doubleday, 1956.

Beutler, L. E. (1983). *Eclectic psychotherapy.* New York: Pergamon Press.

Blight, J. G. (1981). Must psychoanalysis retreat to hermeneutics? Psychoanalytic theory in light of Popper's evolutionary epistemology. *Psychoanalysis and Contemporary Thought, 4,* 147–205.

Boy, A. V., & Pine, G. J. (1982). *Client-centered counseling: A renewal.* Boston: Allyn and Bacon.

Brabeck, M. M., & Welfel, E. R. (1985). Counseling theory: Understanding eclecticism from a developmental perspective. *Journal of Counseling and Development, 63,* 343–348.

Bruner, J. (1984, August). *Narrative and paradigmatic modes of thought.* Paper presented at the meeting of the American Psychological Association, Toronto, Ontario.

Cochrane, C. T., & Holloway, A. J. (1974). Client-centered therapy and Gestalt therapy: In search of a merger. In D. A. Wexler & L. N. Rice (Eds.), *Innovations in client-centered therapy.* New York: Wiley.

Curtiss, S. (1976). The compatibility of humanistic and behavioristic approaches in a state mental hospital. In A. Wandersman, P. Poppen, and D. Ricks (Eds.), *Humanism and behaviorism: Dialogue and growth.* New York: Pergamon Press.

Dimond, R. E., Havens, R. A., & Jones, A. C. (1978). A conceptual framework for the practice of prescriptive eclecticism in psychotherapy. *American Psychologist, 33,* 239–248.

Ellis, A., & Grieger, R. (1977). *Handbook of rational-emotive therapy.* New York: Springer.

Feather, B. W., & Rhoads, J. M. (1972). Psychodynamic behavior therapy. *Archives of General Psychiatry, 26,* 496–511.

Fishman, S. T., & Lubetkin, B. S. (1983). Office practice of behavior therapy. In M. Hersen (Ed.), *Outpatient behavior therapy: A clinical guide.* New York: Grune & Stratton.

Franks, C. (1984). On conceptual and technical integrity in psychoanalysis and behavior therapy: Two fundamentally incompatible systems. In H. Arkowitz and S. B. Messer (Eds.), *Psychoanalytic therapy and behavior therapy: Is integration possible?* New York: Plenum Press.

Franks, C. M., Wilson, G. T., Kendall, P. C., & Brownell, K. D. (1982). *Annual review of behavior therapy,* Vol. 8. New York: Guilford.

Frye, N. (1957). *Anatomy of criticism.* Princeton: Princeton University Press.

Frye, N. (1965). *A natural perspective: The development of Shakesperean comedy and romance.* New York: Columbia University Press.

Garfield, S. L. (1980). *Psychotherapy: An eclectic approach.* New York: Wiley.

Garfield, S. L. (1982). Eclecticism and integration in psychotherapy. *Behavior Therapy, 13,* 610–623.

Garfield, S. L., & Kurtz, R. (1976). Clinical psychologists in the 1970's. *American Psychologist, 31,* 1–9.

Garfield, S. L., & Kurtz, R. (1977). A study of eclectic views. *Journal of Consulting and Clinical Psychology, 45,* 78–83.

Gergen, K. J. (1982). *Toward transformation in social knowledge.* New York: Springer-Verlag.

Goldfried, M. R. (1979). Anxiety reduction through cognitive-behavioral intervention. In P. C. Kendall & S. D. Hollen (Eds.), *Cognitive-behavioral intervention: Theory, research, and procedures.* New York: Academic Press.

Goldfried, M. R. (1980). Toward the delineation of therapeutic change principles. *American Psychologist, 35,* 991–999.

Goldfried, M. R. (Ed.). (1982). *Converging themes in psychotherapy.* New York: Springer.

Goldfried, M. R. (1983). A behavioral therapist looks at rapprochement. *Journal of Humanistic Psychology, 23,* 97–107.

Hyman, S. E. (1957). Psychoanalysis and the climate of tragedy. In B. Nelson (Ed.), *Freud and the twentieth century.* New York: Meridian Books.

Ivey, A. E., & Simek-Downing, L. (1980). *Counseling and psychotherapy: Skills and practice.* Englewood Cliffs, NJ: Prentice-Hall.

Karasu, T. (1979). Toward unification of psychotherapies: A complementary model. *American Journal of Psychotherapy, 33,* 555–563.

Keller, E. F. (1985). *Reflections on gender and science.* New Haven: Yale University Press.

Kelly, E. L. (1961). Clinical psychology—1960. Report of survey findings. *Newsletter, Division of Clinical Psychology,* Winter, 1–11.

Kimble, G. A. (1984). Psychology's two cultures. *American Psychologist, 39,* 833–839.

Koch, S. (1964). Psychology and emerging conceptions of knowledge as unitary. In T. W. Wann (Ed.), *Behaviorism and phenomenology.* Chicago: University of Chicago Press.

Koch, S. (1981). The nature and limits of psychological knowledge: Lessons of a century qua "Science." *American Psychologist, 36,* 257–269.

Kohut, H. (1977). *The restoration of the self.* New York: International Universities Press.

Krasner, L., & Houts, A. C. (1984). A study of the "value" systems of behavioral scientists. *American Psychologist, 39,* 840–850.

Kris, E. (1937). Ego development and the comic. In *Psychoanalytic explorations in art.* New York: International University Press, 1952.

Kuhn, T. S. (1977). *The essential tension: Selected studies of scientific tradition and change.* Chicago: University of Chicago Press.

Lang, P. J. (1979). A bio-informational theory of emotional imagery. *Psychophysiology, 16,* 495–512.

Lazarus, A. A. (1981). *The practice of multimodal therapy.* New York: McGraw-Hill.

Ledwidge, B. (1978). Cognitive behavior modification: A step in the wrong direction? *Psychological Bulletin, 85,* 353–375.

Maddi, S. R. (1980). *Personality theories: A comparative analysis.* Homewood, IL: Dorsey.

Mahoney, M. J., & Arnkoff, D. B. (1978). Cognitive and self-control therapies. In S. L. Garfield & A. E. Bergin (Eds.), *Handbook of psychotherapy and behavior change* (2nd ed.). New York: Wiley.

Malan, D. H. (1976). *The frontier of brief psychotherapy.* New York: Plenum.

Marcel, A. J. (1983). Conscious and unconscious perception: An approach to the relations between phenomenal experience and perceptual processes. *Cognitive Psychology, 15,* 238–300.

Marmor, J., & Wood, S. M. (Eds.). (1980). *The interface between the psychodynamic and behavioral therapies.* New York: Plenum.

Maslow, A. H. (1962). Some basic propositions of a growth and self-actualization psychology. In *Perceiving, behaving, becoming: A new focus for education.* Washington, DC: Year book of the Association for Supervision and Curriculum Development.

Maslow, A. H. (1971). *The farther reaches of human nature.* New York: Viking.

Meichenbaum, D. (1977). *Cognitive behavior modification.* New York: Plenum.

Meichenbaum, D., & Gilmore, J. B. (1984). The nature of unconscious processes: A cognitive-behavioral prospective. In K. Bowers & D. Meichenbaum (Eds.), *The unconscious reconsidered.* New York: Wiley.

Messer, S. B. (1983). Integrating psychoanalytic and behavior therapy: Limitations, possibilities and trade-offs. *British Journal of Clinical Psychology, 22,* 131–132.

Messer, S. B. (1984a). A psychoanalytic smorgasbord. *Contemporary Psychology, 29,* 128–129.

Messer, S. B. (1984b). A review of M. R. Goldfried's *Converging themes in psychotherapy. Child and Family Behavior Therapy, 6,* 83–85.

Messer, S. B. (1985). Choice of method is value-laden too. *American Psychologist,*

Messer, S. B., & Winokur, M. (1980). Some limits to the integration of psychoanalytic and behavior therapy. *American Psychologist, 35,* 818–827.

Messer, S. B., & Winokur, M. (1984). Ways of knowing and visions of reality in psychoanalytic therapy and behavior therapy. In H. Arkowitz & S. B. Messer (Eds.), *Psychoanalytic therapy and behavior therapy: Is integration possible?* New York: Plenum Press.

Norcross, J. (1981). All in the family? On therapeutic commonalities. *American Psychologist, 36,* 1544–1545.

Palmer, J. E. (1980). *A primer of eclectic psychotherapy.* Monterey, CA: Brooks/Cole.

Pepper, S. P. (1942). *World hypotheses: A study in evidence.* Berkeley: University of California Press.

Pollack, G. (Ed.). (1982). *Annual of psychoanalysis,* Vol. 10. New York: International Universities Press.

Rasmussen, A., & Messer, S. B. (In press). A comparison and critique of Mann's Time-limited Psychotherapy and Davanloo's Short-term Dynamic Therapy. *Bulletin of the Menninger Clinic.*

Rhoads, J. M. (1984). Relationships between psychodynamic and behavior therapies. In H. Arkowitz and S. B. Messer (Eds.), *Psychoanalytic therapy and behavior therapy: Is integration possible?* New York: Plenum Press.

Rogers, C. (1961). *On becoming a person.* Boston: Houghton-Mifflin.

Roland, A. (1967). The reality of the psychoanalytic relationship and situation in the handling of transference resistance. *International Journal of Psychoanalysis, 48,* 504–510.

Rorty, R. (1979). *Philosophy and the mirror of nature.* Princeton, NJ: Princeton University Press.

Royce, J. R. (1982). Philosophy issues, division 24, and the future. *American Psychologist, 37,* 258–266.

Royce, J. R., & Mos, L. P. (1980). *Manual: Psycho-epistemological profile.* University of Alberta Center for Advanced Study in Theoretical Psychology, Alberta, Canada.

Ryle, A. A. (1978). A common language for the psychotherapies? *British Journal of Psychiatry, 132,* 585–594.

Sarason, J. G. (1979). Three lacunae of cognitive therapy. *Cognitive Therapy and Research, 3,* 223–235.

Schacht, T. E. (1984). The varieties of integrative experience. In H. Arkowitz and S. B. Messer (Eds.), *Psychoanalytic therapy and behavior therapy: Is integration possible?* New York: Plenum Press.

Schacht, T. E., & Black, D. A. (1985). Epistemological commitments of behavioral and psychoanalytic therapists. *Professional Psychology, 16,* 316–323.

Schafer, R. (1976). *A new language for psychoanalysis.* New Haven: Yale University Press.

Sherwood, M. (1969). *The logic of explanation in psychoanalysis.* New York: Academic Press.

Shevrin, H., & Dickman, S. (1980). The psychological unconscious: A necessary assumption for all psychological theory? *American Psychologist, 35,* 421–434.

Simon, R. M. (1974). On eclecticism. *American Journal of Psychiatry, 131*(2), 135–139.

Smith, D. (1982). Trends in counseling and psychotherapy. *American Psychologist, 37,* 802–809.

Spence, D. P. (1982). *Narrative truth and historical truth.* New York: W. W. Norton.

Staats, A. W. (1981). Paradigmatic behaviorism, unified theory, unified theory construction methods, and the Zeitgeist of separation. *American Psychologist, 36,* 239–256.

Staats, A. W. (1983). *Psychology's crisis of disunity: Philosophy and method for a unified science.* New York: Praeger.

Stein, M. H. (1985). Irony in psychoanalysis. *Journal of the American Psychoanalytic Association, 33,* 35–57.

Stolorow, R. D. (1976). Psychoanalytic reflections on client centered therapy in the light of modern conceptions of narcissism. *Psychotherapy: Theory, Research and Practice, 13,* 26–29.

Sundland, D. M. (1977). Theoretical orientations of psychotherapists. In A. S. Gurman and A. M. Razin (Eds.), *Effective psychotherapy: A handbook of research.* New York: Pergamon.

Tuttman, S. (1982). Regression: Curative factor or impediment in dynamic psychotherapy? In S. Slipp (Ed.), *Curative factors in dynamic psychotherapy.* New York: McGraw-Hill.

Wachtel, P. (1977). *Psychoanalysis and behavior therapy: Toward an integration.* New York: Basic Books.

Wachtel, P. L. (1982). What can dynamic therapies contribute to behavior therapy? *Behavior Therapy, 13,* 594–609.

Wachtel, P. L. (1984). On theory, practice and the nature of integration. In H. Arkowitz and S. B. Messer (Eds.), *Psychoanalytic therapy and behavior therapy: Is integration possible?* New York: Plenum Press.

Wexler, D. A. (1974). A cognitive theory of experiencing, self-actualization, and therapeutic process. In D. A. Wexler and L. N. Rice (Eds.), *Innovations in client-centered therapy.* New York: Wiley.

Wexler, D. A., & Rice, L. N. (1974). *Innovations in client-centered therapy.* New York: Wiley.

White, H. (1973). *Metahistory.* Baltimore, MD: Johns Hopkins University Press.

Wilson, G. T. (1982a). Clinical issues and strategies in the practice of behavior therapy. In C. M. Franks, G. T. Wilson, P. C. Kendall, and K. D. Brownell, *Annual review of behavior therapy,* Vol. 8 (pp. 305–345). New York: Guilford Press.

Wilson, G. T. (1982b). The psychotherapy process and procedure: The behavioral mandate. *Behavior Therapy, 13,* 291–312.

Wilson, G. T., & O'Leary, K. D. (1980). *Principles of behavior therapy.* Englewood Cliffs, NJ: Prentice-Hall.

Winnicott, D. W. (1965). *The maturational processes and the facilitating environment.* New York: International Universities Press.

Winokur, M., Messer, S. B., & Schacht, T. (1981). Contributions to the theory and practice of short-term dynamic psychotherapy. *Bulletin of the Menninger Clinic, 45,* 125–142.

Wolpe, J. (1976). Behavior therapy and its malcontents. II. Multimodal eclecticism, cognitive eclecticism, and "exposure" empiricism. *Journal of Behavior Therapy and Experimental Psychiatry, 7,* 109–116.

Woolfolk, R. L., & Richardson, F. C. (1984). Behavior therapy and the ideology of modernity. *American Psychologist, 39,* 777–786.

CHAPTER 14

Possibilities and Promises of Eclecticism

Edward J. Murray

This chapter is written as a reflection on the contributions to Part II of this volume and as a personal statement about the possibilities of therapeutic eclecticism. First, I will comment on the phenomenon of eclecticism as it appears today in the real clinical world as well as in the pages of this volume. Then, I will comment on some of the models that appear to be emerging in the writings of eclectic therapists. Finally, I will comment on the role of traditional orientations versus the newer models and on the possibility of integrating diverse orientations, with special emphasis on the issues raised by Messer in Chapter 13.

ECLECTICISM

Can Creeping Eclecticism Be Stopped?

In the thirties, a survey of British psychoanalysts by Glover (1940) revealed that these practitioners who, presumably, had been similarly trained were astonishingly variable in their techniques. They varied not only in minor details of treatment but in the content and nature of interpretations, the use of reassurance in dealing with anxiety, adherence to the rules of free association and abstinence, and many other features of treatment.

Ever since reading Glover's book, I have had an image of thousands of psychotherapists sitting in their lonely offices, doing all sorts of things, ostensibly in the name of psychoanalysis or humanism or behaviorism, that bear only a negligible connection to the theory these therapists espouse. I believe that therapists adapt therapeutic techniques to their clients and to their own personalities. Some may feel a little guilty about doing so. Some try to justify their innovations within their theoretical systems. But really they are closet eclectics.

I can remember the moment that I became a closet eclectic. Years ago, I was working at a clinic and was assigned a court-referred exhibitionist. In spite of the nature of the referral, we were able to establish a good therapeutic relationship and proceeded with dynamic psychotherapy, the approach that I had been taught and had been using with some degree of success. Although the therapy went well, the client began taking small chances in exhibiting himself. Finally, he came in one day and reported an incident that could have led to his arrest. This alarmed me.

At that point, I intervened in a way that I had never done before and had never heard of. In fact, I was not even aware of what I was going to do until the moment it came out of my mouth. I asked the patient if he fully realized what could happen if he were caught again. I painted a vivid picture of what could happen to a meek sex-offender if he were sent to an overcrowded state prison. He was visibly shaken and I felt terribly guilty. Nevertheless, the behavior stopped abruptly and did not recur in the ten years that I followed his case. Later, I saw him and his wife in straightforward marital therapy, which also helped ease his tensions.

How did I deal with my guilt? I came out of the closet and contacted a colleague who worked in a special unit for sex offenders. I told him what I had done and he smiled. He said that they did that sort of thing all the time and felt it was necessary. I never again felt constrained by a single approach. I also learned to consult with colleagues who were more knowledgeable about special populations than I was to find out what techniques they found most useful.

Actually, it was in research contexts that I really became convinced that eclecticism was creeping onward. First, as an NIMH consultant, I became aware of the problems in evaluating the efficacy of various forms of therapy. Researchers found it necessary to write therapy manuals in an effort to establish some consistency among clinicians within a given therapeutic condition. Even then it was necessary to monitor the therapists to prevent "therapy drift." The therapists had a tendency to use techniques that were not an official part of their treatment package; sometimes they would even "drift" into the techniques of the comparison treatment!

I was able to see this problem even more clearly in a current research project in which I am a co-principal investigator. The project involves a comparison of structural family therapy and individual psychodynamic therapy for emotionally disturbed, pre-adolescent, school-age children. At the beginning of the project we were concerned about keeping the two treatments as "pure" as possible. We met with the therapists to set up guidelines for each treatment and immediately encountered resistance because the therapists felt we were restricting them. For example, we originally thought that the psychodynamic therapists should only see the child so as to avoid overlap with the family modality. It soon became apparent that contact with the mother was an extremely important part of psychodynamic therapy so we agreed that the therapist could see the mother for five minutes at the end of each session provided that the interaction with her was dynamically oriented. The family therapists felt that any technique was permissible as long as it was used in a structural framework. They finally agreed not to use techniques that would obviously overlap with the dynamic treatment, such as dealing with the unfinished family of origin issues of the parents. Therapists in both groups wanted to have extensive contact with the schools but agreed to limit this for research purposes.

As the project progressed, we monitored the therapists for drift and were generally successful. The most interesting observation during this phase, from my point of view, was that one of the therapists in each condition used or encouraged behavior modification techniques, such as parental reinforcement systems. We had not anticipated this development because such techniques are not usually associated with either psychodynamic or structural family therapy.

What I have concluded from all of this is that there is a strong push toward eclecticism that is difficult to stop. Psychotherapists feel constrained when asked to use "pure" techniques because in their usual practice they are eclectic in varying degrees. I imagine that, in their daily practice, clinicians run up against problems, just as I did with the exhibitionist, and "invent" a technique. Now, there are so many workshops, books, and tapes around that therapists pick up techniques and incorporate them in their work, either explicitly or implicitly. Making this process more explicit could lead to a more systematic eclecticism.

Systematic Eclecticism

Although a general trend toward eclecticism may be creeping along, there are many disadvantages to such an implicit and disorganized process. For one thing, clinicians rarely learn from one another's experiences. For another, it is difficult for researchers or the public to evaluate the product. Finally, eclecticism impedes the fostering of an open-minded attitude in students, because they still believe most therapies are "pure."

The explicit eclectic approaches described in this book—by some of the foremost exponents of eclecticism—represent a quantum step forward. They epitomize the combination of techniques and theories from different traditions and demonstrate that such combinations make clinical sense. They demonstrate vividly that eclecticism need not be a random administration of whatever techniques the clinician comes upon. Rather, there appears to be a combination of a limited number or groups of techniques applied in an orderly fashion to clinical problems.

In general, the eclectic therapists in this volume recognize the importance of non-specific factors in therapy, as well as of establishing a therapeutic alliance. For example, Lazarus (Chapter 3) evaluates client expectations about therapy and tries, at least initially, to meet them. Beutler (Chapter 4) emphasizes the compatibility between the therapist and client, seeing it as an important determinant of the therapist's persuasiveness. Garfield (Chapter 5) talks about developing trust on the part of the client. Fuhriman and colleagues (Chapter 8) include as major components in their approach rapport-building and role descriptions. Fischer (Chapter 11) explicitly includes the interpersonal skills of empathy, warmth, and genuineness. Clearly these eclectic therapists have learned from Jerome Frank and Carl Rogers.

On the other hand, these eclectic therapists uniformly depart from many traditional practices in therapy. There is considerably more structure than in client-centered therapy, with the therapist playing a more active role. Almost no use is made of transference interpretations, the hallmark of psychoanalytical therapy. Historical material is not usually emphasized and, when it is, it is more likely to be handled with gestalt or similar techniques, as illustrated by Garfield and Lazarus. These eclectic therapists appear, therefore, to reject the more passive stances of the psychoanalytic and client-centered approaches. A good therapeutic relationship is seen as essential to therapeutic progress, but it is neither a sufficient condition, as it is in client-centered therapy, nor is it the main vehicle of change, as in psychoanalytic therapy. These eclectic therapists are active doers; sometimes they seem impatient. They are a long way from the leisurely "listening with the third ear" atmosphere that prevailed years ago.

None of the foregoing is meant to imply that client-centered or psychoanalytic techniques are not used. Lazarus reports, for example, that with some clients, at some times, he would be described as a reflecting Rogerian. Garfield uses catharsis and empathy. Hart (Chapter 7) uses catharsis for dealing with old experiences. Prochaska and DiClemente (Chapter 6) help clients discriminate between the events of childhood and present-day reality. Beutler makes perhaps the greatest use of psychoanalytic concepts and techniques. For example, he locates a dynamic conflict and recognizes resistances. However, he handles these areas differently with different people. In general, these eclectic therapists differ from the systematic client-centered and psychoanalytic therapists in not relying exclusively on one group of techniques for all clients at all times.

The eclectic group represented in this volume make much use of behavioral techniques such as relaxation, biofeedback, social-skill training, desensitization, counter-conditioning, modeling, rehearsal, stimulus control, and contingency management. There is no doubt but that they have been influenced heavily by the behavior therapy movement. One can see the influence of Wolpe, Bandura, Skinner, and others very clearly. Nevertheless, these eclectic therapists differ from traditional behavior therapists in that, except for a few very specific symptom problems, they do not rely on behavioral methods entirely. They combine these methods with techniques derived from the client-centered and psychodynamic traditions. More significantly, they combine them with cognitive techniques. They are a long way from "the therapist as a reinforcement machine."

The cognitive revolution in behavior therapy is well-known and its effects are clearly shown in the contributions in this volume. Lazarus was a pioneer in this movement within behavior therapy. He uses misconception corrections and views cognitive change as a basic process. Fuhriman and associates count cognitive therapy as one of their four major components.

Techniques include changing misconceptions, challenging dysfunctional self-statements, problem solving, decision making, and self-control. Murgatroyd and Apter (Chapter 9) specifically mention stress inoculation, rational-emotive methods, and cognitive-behavioral techniques. Imagery is used by Lazarus, Hart, and others. Hart also makes use of dreams but in a cognitive rather than dynamic manner. Clearly, eclectic therapists have learned from Ellis, Beck, Meichenbaum, and even Perls.

Family therapy, which represents a different modality and tradition, needs a special word. Grebstein (Chapter 10) mentions three groups of techniques: understanding, including historical interpretation, family pictures, role playing, and videotape replays; transformation, including task prescription, altering reinforcement contingencies, and paradoxical instructions; and identification, including role modeling, sharing emotional experiences, and playful behavior. Although these groups of techniques represent different models of family functioning and treatment, Grebstein recommends an eclectic family therapy that makes use of techniques from all of them. My own observations would confirm this point of view; family therapists make use of an incredible variety of techniques.

In conclusion, no one can doubt the reality of eclectic therapy used in a systematic and, apparently, effective way. But what is the system? How do you know when to use what? To many outsiders, and certainly to the beginning therapy students, it all seems chaotic and capricious. Indeed, many eclectic therapists insist on flexibility and creativity. In spite of this characteristic, eclectic therapy is used systematically. The secret is that each eclectic therapist has developed a model of personality functioning, dysfunctioning, and change. Some are more complete and explicit than others. Next, we will turn to these models.

Eclectic Models of Dysfunction

I thought of titling this section: "Models of Psychopathology" but I realized that it would be out of keeping with the spirit of the eclectic therapists, who prefer models of growth, learning, and functioning. Thus, it seems more appropriate to think in terms of a model of dysfunction. Furthermore, the emphasis in all these eclectic models is on interpersonal problems and problems of self-concept, very much related to social development and functioning. Purely intrapsychic processes, if indeed such exist, play little role in these models. And the eclectic therapists see biological factors as coming into play in certain conditions.

Lazarus is one of the therapists who is most explicit in specifying the sources of dysfunction. They can be summarized as: (a) conflicting feelings and reactions; (b) informational problems, including misinformation and skill deficits; (c) maladaptive habits; and (d) interpersonal disturbances, such as overdependency or hostility. I would imagine that most of the conflict has to do with interpersonal problems and that most of the informational problems have to do with social interaction. Thus, except for specific habit symptoms, such as tics and smoking, the model of dysfunction is basically interpersonal. Disturbances in cognitive processes and behavior are related to disturbed feelings, all in a social context.

Lazarus breaks down the processes into his BASIC-ID formulation. Affect occupies a central role in this model but cannot be influenced directly. Affect can be indirectly influenced, aroused, or decreased by cognition (including imagery), sensations, and behavior. Affect, in turn, can influence cognitions, sensations, and behavior. Thus, we have a model of reciprocal causation. In his diagnostic procedures, Lazarus tries to locate the most problematic area (e.g., frightening imagery). An important individual differ-

ence variable is the "firing order" of the various processes. For example, he says that some people have an Image–Thought–Behavior pattern, others have a Thought–Image–Behavior pattern, and so forth. When this pattern has been tracked properly the order of use of techniques follows.

Beutler starts from a somewhat more psychodynamic model, but not a drive-oriented one. For example, he stresses attachment types as a source of dysfunction, with a special emphasis on dependency and autonomy. Defenses are seen as ways of avoiding anxiety or achieving interpersonal goals. The "defense" may include acting out and thus require control or inhibition of some sort and require cognitive and behavior change. It seems to this observer that Beutler has departed from a truly psychodynamic model of dysfunction and moved toward an interpersonal approach, leaving a lot of room for cognitive and behavioral changes as opposed to the traditional emphasis on unconscious motivation.

Hart's model is explicitly derived from James's theory of emotion. Percepts and actions are the determiners of emotion. Emotional change, according to James, requires changing actions, particularly the bodily expression of affect. James also emphasized the exploration of conscious thoughts and images in dealing with emotions, particularly those concerning the self. For Hart, the important thing is the perception-expression-experience unit that needs to be considered in making emotional changes. Clients are taught to focus on feeling moments and to express their experience behaviorally as fully as possible. Five aspects of experience that can be discerned are feeling, activity, conscious clarity, verbal expression, and social contact. Apparently, deficits or problems in one or more of these areas indicate specific techniques. For example, a grieving mother is first encouraged to express feelings and then make cognitive corrections; a problem drinker with a "playboy" image is given reality therapy; other cases are given supportive case management. It is interesting to note that, while they differ on other matters, both Hart, originally a client-centered therapist, and Lazarus, originally a behaviorist, come to similar conclusions about the need to change affect through cognitive and behavioral changes.

A new theory of motivation and emotion is proposed as a framework for eclectic psychotherapy by Murgatroyd and Apter. These authors replace the common homeostatic notion with the idea of the organism seeking two stable states at both ends of a continuum. Thus, a sensation seeker may also seek quiescence at times. Three pairs of states are described: serious–playful, conforming–resisting, and dominance–dependence. Client problems revolve around reversing between different states and therapeutic techniques follow from the nature of the problem. Thus, social-skills training would be employed with an anger-control problem to facilitate reversal to a conforming state. Again we have the same emphasis on cognitive and behavioral techniques to produce affective change by these phenomenologically oriented therapists.

Some eclectic therapists specifically reject an explicit model of dysfunction. For example, Fischer distinguishes between causal–developmental knowledge and intervention knowledge, maintaining that we do not need to have knowledge about the cause of a problem to know how to intervene. So, too, Hart rejects an explicit model of dysfunction in favor of a growth model. On the basis of an extensive knowledge of the research literature, Garfield rejects the need for client assessment or clinical diagnosis. Nonetheless, these therapists seem to operate on the basis of implicit models of dysfunction that do not seem much different from the other eclectic therapists.

A model that is rather different from most of the others is the eclectic family approach of Grebstein (Chapter 10). All family therapists believe that individual dysfunction can be understood only in the context of the family system in which it exists. Individual problems such as cognitive distortions and behavioral deficits are recognized, but they are always seen in a family context.

Eclectic Models of Change

Several eclectic therapists use models that emphasize the process of change. One of the more elaborate of these is Prochaska and DiClemente's model of four stages of change:

1. *Precontemplation*, before the person thinks of wanting or needing change
2. *Contemplation*, in which the person starts deciding to change
3. *Action*, in which the person makes the changes
4. *Maintenance*, which is self-explanatory.

The important idea here is that different therapeutic techniques—even different systems—may be most useful at different stages. None of the techniques are useful in the Precontemplation stage, which is something to keep in mind. The techniques most useful during the Contemplation stage are those that raise consciousness, such as self-evaluation, bibliotherapy, and educational efforts. During the Action phase a helping relationship, behavioral methods designed to enhance self-efficacy, and contingency management are most useful. Maintenance even more strongly requires behavioral methods such as stimulus and control counter-conditioning. Much of Prochaska and DiClemente's work has been with clients wanting to change a symptom or situation such as stopping smoking. The model does seem to favor this type of problem.

Prochaska and DiClemente have extended their analysis to problems that occur at more complex levels. For example, intrapersonal conflicts might be treated initially with psychoanalytic therapy and, later, with existential or gestalt therapy. Interpersonal conflicts might start out with Sullivanian therapy and end up with couples communication training. Family conflicts might start out with strategic family therapy and then shift to structural family therapy. Although these ideas need more development, they suggest how techniques can be selected on the basis of stage of change and level of problem complexity.

Hart also stresses stages of change. The Need stage involves clarifying what the client wants. The Choice stage involves teaching the client how to behave. The Image stage is concerned with developing a long-lasting change in self-perception. There are obvious parallels with the transtheoretical model.

Beutler offers a process model of change. It draws from theories of social influence and persuasion. He uses a variety of cognitive, gestalt, and behavioral techniques. The key concept is dissonance induction, which is used in three ways. First, therapists may create dissonance in clients by pointing out inconsistencies in their attitudes or beliefs. Dissonance is uncomfortable and motivates change. Second, there may be dissonance between clients' attitudes and the therapists' attitudes. Beutler creates dissonance rather directly as a means, for example, of promoting his belief in autonomy over conformity. He is clearly not a shy therapist. The third area in which dissonance is used is in pointing out or demonstrating inconsistencies between belief, feeling, and behavior. Beutler also uses social psychological concepts such as social power and reactance to elaborate on the model.

In an interesting effort to develop an overall framework for a counseling center with therapists of different theoretical persuasion, Fuhriman and associates came up with a change model that everyone could live with. The first stage involves rapport building, role description, and specifying problems. The second stage emphasizes enhanced self-understanding and anticipated action with a lot of direction, confrontation, and therapist self-disclosure. The third stage involves trying out new behavior. The center emphasizes time-limited therapy so a Maintenance stage is not included but would not be inconsistent.

Garfield places a great deal of emphasis on the relationship between the therapist and client in the change process. At the beginning of treatment he relies on open discussions of problems and the expression of feelings. Later, he uses a variety of cognitive and behavioral techniques, depending on the individual needs of the client.

The main characteristic of these change models is that they tend to divide therapy into two main phases. In the first phase, after a therapeutic alliance is established, cognitive–emotional work of some sort is emphasized. This work may range from expressing feelings to changing a philosophy of life. Second, the cognitive–affective phase is followed by an action phase, which may involve everything from social-skills training to assigned tasks.

Conclusions

The models developed by these eclectic therapists have several important features. First, the models have very little to do with developmental processes. True, Lazarus assumes social learning antecedents to disturbed functioning, and Beutler takes off from the general idea of attachment difficulties, but these considerations have little to do with the actual therapy process. There is no detailed exploration of the past, although past figures may be conjured up in the gestalt manner to finish off some piece of business. Fischer is the most explicit in rejecting the need for a developmental model in order to devise a therapeutic model of change. But we are in the here and now. I think that a developmental basis must be organized eventually.

Second, these models deal directly with conscious experience as a major topic. I believe that this is an important advance. Thoughts and images are of central importance; they are not seen just as clues to the unconscious where the real action lies. So, too, consciousness is not rejected in favor of overt behavior. Thoughts and images are seen as keys to emotional reactions. Indeed, these eclectic therapists have a strong cognitive flavor. At the same time, increasing awareness of cognition, affect, and behavior is important.

Third, these eclectic models are very behavioral in the active change phase of therapy. Most of the behavior therapy techniques get a good play. However, behavior change is used in a context of decision and choice by the client. There is very little of the flavor of doing something to a client, of *making* the behavior change. Thus, we have a more humanistic behavior change emphasis.

The fourth characteristic of these models is that they include, to a greater or lesser degree, a consideration of the individual personality characteristics of the client. Techniques are modified depending on coping styles, primacy of imagery or thoughts, and level of emotionality. Perhaps the most consistent trend is for a distinction between clients who present with a great deal of emotionality and require some sort of quieting or relaxing techniques and those who need to have affect aroused.

All told, the models revolve around the connections between cognition, affect, and behavior. They are not always clear and

precise about how this system works but the message is obvious that entering this system and altering it is what therapy is all about. I believe that a generic model along these lines can be developed and will advance integration and systematic eclecticism.

THEORETICAL ORIENTATIONS

In the contributions of the eclectic therapists in this volume, theoretical orientations play a relatively small role. Lazarus, of course, comes from a behavioral tradition, but aside from a tie-in with social learning theory and a respect for empirical research, there is very little left of behaviorism, as it is usually understood. Beutler seems to have come from a psychodynamic background, but aside from the theme of dependence–autonomy and the classification of defenses as internal or external, there is little left of the psychoanalytic tradition. Hart shows the influence of the humanistic tradition, but it seems to have lost the hard edge of movement I remember from the sixties. Grebstein is clearly from the family tradition but has rejected the extremist positions in that area.

Yet, in the mental health world at large, theoretical orientation still looms as a major issue. When our graduate students interview for internships, they are always asked, "What is your theoretical orientation?" I find that parties at conventions are usually composed of people with a common theoretical orientation. People are comfortable with shared belief systems, a common language, and their own historical heritage. Dissonance is uncomfortable but, as Beutler maintains, it may be important for growth. In this section, I will examine the two main theoretical orientations, the psychodynamic and the behavioral, with a view toward understanding the basic differences and the possibilities of integration. Then, I will address some of the philosophical issues that have been raised by Messer (Chapter 13).

The Psychodynamic Orientation

The first psychological book I read, as an adolescent, was Brill's (1938) translation of *The Basic Writings of Sigmund Freud*, and I was enthralled. As I recall, I started smoking a pipe and analyzing my friend's dreams. I believe the book had a great deal to do with my becoming a psychologist. Like Wachtel (1977) I have a great deal of affection for this rich clinical tradition, and I was hurt when it was so vigorously attacked by the behavior therapists. At the time, it seemed to me that the psychoanalytic tradition encompassed all the clinical wisdom in the world.

Slowly, though, I came to realize that I could not accept the essence of Freud's theory—the idea that most of human behavior was determined by a seething mass of unconscious libidinal instincts and savage destructive urges that could be only defended against or sublimated and were relatively little influenced by the social environment. Freud's ideas underwent some change, but even in his last book (1949/1940) he stresses, as the primary determinants of personality development, the innate strength of the various instincts with environmental or "accidental" experiences playing a minor role.

I am not repelled by this theory on aesthetic or moral grounds. Indeed, I actually believed it for a while, when I was very young. I rejected the theory because it corresponded neither to clinical experience nor to empirical evidence. The people I saw clinically seemed to be grappling with problems of self-esteem related to their early social experience. Defenses seemed to be related more to threats to self-esteem than to instinctual energies. An important influence was the obligatory, fifties-

era five-year analysis I underwent. Only my analysis was with a Sullivanian, so I realized that the rich clinical tradition was not tied exclusively to Freud's theory. Meanwhile, I searched in vain for empirical support for Freud's theory. Recently, I read an extremely sympathetic review of the evidence for Freud's theory by Fischer and Greenberg (1977). I was struck by the fact that none of the evidence really supported the kernel of Freud's theory. For example, while there is good evidence for oral and anal personality types, there is virtually no evidence that these types are related to psychosexual development. They might better be labeled dependent and rigid personality types. Thus, the real clinical wisdom in these descriptions is obscured by the language of libido.

The whole history of the psychoanalytic movement can be read as an attempt to get out from under this cross of libido. The great dissidents like Adler, Horney, and Sullivan developed alternative, interpersonally oriented theories. Even Freudian insiders, from Erikson (1963) to Kohut (1977), have developed theories that do not depend on libidinal instincts. These theorists, however, often suffer the excessive burden of trying to cast their ideas in the language of libido and, somehow, of reconciling them with Freud's theory. Sometimes, they remind me of liberal Protestant ministers who try to preach the essence of their religion while picking their way through ancient dogmas and biblical fables.

Today, most clinicians who identify themselves as psychodynamic appear, implicitly or explicitly, to have adopted an interpersonal theory. This trend can be seen most clearly in the writings of psychologists like Breger (1974), Wachtel (1977), and Schafer (1976). In fact, Schafer, among others, makes the point that Freud himself operated at two levels: the familiar level of libidinal instincts and a more down-home, experiential analysis of human problems. Like Wachtel (1983), I believe that the interpersonal dynamic orientation offers a much better opportunity for integration than the libidinal one.

The interpersonal dynamic orientation does retain some of the essential features of the basic psychoanalytic position. Perhaps the most important belief is that behavior, in all of its forms, is purposive, although the individual may not be aware of the purposes, particularly defensive purposes. Motivation may be unconscious. However, motives are not instinctual energies; rather, they are concerned with handling threats to self-esteem and maintaining significant human relationships. The belief that most problems originate in early family relationships is pretty generally accepted, but it plays a less important role in the actual conduct of therapy than is often assumed. The emphasis is on current relationships—with the existing family, with friends and business associates and, above all, with the therapist. However, in some forms of interpersonal therapy, the analysis of the therapeutic relationship is not important; analysis of the client's social relationships is emphasized (Klerman, Weissman, Rounsaville, & Chevron, 1984). Thus, the interpersonal dynamic orientation is considerably more compatible with therapeutic modalities like marital, group, and family therapy.

In spite of all these considerations, I can see how implausible the possibility of integration seems to a behaviorally oriented person like Yates (1983b). He cannot see how someone can accept the general psychodynamic view of development without also accepting the implication that successful therapy must resolve the underlying conflict, thus denying the possibility that direct behavioral interventions may be successful. Let me try to answer this very profound point. First of all, I agree with Yates in reference to Freud's basic model. Insight and sublimation seem to be the only paths to the resolution of infantile conflicts. But, as I have tried to show, an interpersonal dynamic model

that emphasizes behavioral change has taken its place. Let us see how this works.

Two good examples of the latter-day dynamic approaches are the short-term therapeutic packages offered by Luborsky (1984) and Strupp and Binder (1985). They talk about identifying a "core-conflictual relationship" or a "dynamic focus". In essence, these refer to patterns of attitudes and behavior, learned in the early family situation, that persist in the present and have maladaptive consequences. The "dynamics" refer to the repetitive cycle of maladaptive behavior leading to confirmation of expectations and then more maladaptive behavior. I once heard Strupp describe a man who repeatedly came late to work. The man was constantly criticized by his boss, which confirmed the man's belief that authority is nonsupportive and hostile. How does the clinician deal with such a problem?

The interpersonal approach is to watch the same behavior develop in therapy (the transference) without the negative consequences (controlling countertransference). Strupp's patient came to therapy late, and Strupp pointed this out without being critical. He also drew a parallel between what the man was doing in therapy and what he was doing with authority figures. Strupp does not emphasize the past, but a parallel could also be drawn with the pattern the man probably developed with his father. The thrust of the therapy would be a corrective experience that would teach the man that authority is not always malevolent but can be provoked into retaliation by one's behavior. Longer term dynamic therapy might dwell more on the past, but even here the trend is away from historical reconstruction —increasingly recognized as impossible to achieve accurately—and more toward the understanding of current interactions.

The same problem could be approached with a cognitive–behavioral therapy. Thoughts and images about authority could be identified along the lines of "Authority figures are always hostile" or "Authority figures should love me in spite of what I do." These assumptions could be challenged or tested with behavioral experiments. The man could be taught social skills, like responsible assertiveness. There is little evidence available now as to which approach might be more effective. It is even possible that one approach would be better with some clients, the other approach with other clients.

Furthermore, the two approaches might be combined in the same case. I am on a cognitive-behavior therapy kick right now, but I often find opportunities to use "transference interpretations." For example, I recently saw a young woman who was very dependent on her father. Even when she had car trouble, she turned it over to her father, who took care of it. The result was that she never learned how to deal with a garage. About a month after therapy began, she brought in a copy of her health insurance plan, something I had a vested interest in. It was quite complex, and she handed it over to me. I began reading it and then realized what was happening. I laughed and said, "Look, I'm behaving just like your father!" She grimaced and snatched it back, but the point was made. Here, too, there is no evidence that combining techniques is advantageous; such a combination might even dilute the effectiveness of each technique. However, I see no *theoretical* reason for not combining these techniques if there is a common goal, such as fostering more independent behavior.

Integration is much more feasible when there is some agreement on the nature of the problem. I suspect that there would be a general consensus about the interpersonal problems just described. But not all problems are interpersonal, and one of the serious drawbacks of the psychodynamic approach is a tendency to view all problems as symptoms of some sort of unconscious conflict. Yates (1983a) is absolutely on target in questioning the dynamic interpretation of stuttering, tics, enuresis, and other problematic behaviors. They are better viewed as habits, often with a physiological basis. The dynamic interpretation of autism as due to "cold" parents caused a lot of pain before autism was recognized as organic in origin. I can hardly imagine anything more futile than approaching toilet training in mentally retarded children from a dynamic, interpersonal position. Clearly, the excesses of the dynamic approach need to be curbed. Again, it boils down to a definition and understanding of the nature of the problem.

The Behavioral Orientation

Another great tradition is the behavioral one, which I also cherish and respect. Nearly all of my academic training was in the behavioral tradition. I was an animal experimenter for eight years, running hundreds of rats and pigeons in learning experiments. My training started at Columbia University in the forties, when almost the entire undergraduate curriculum was organized around Skinner's radical behaviorism. We were imbued with the exhilarating feeling that we were pioneers in the development of a truly scientific psychology. I am still appreciative of the wealth of knowledge about learning and motivation that has come out of the behavioral tradition, as well as the impetus that tradition gave to the development of behavioral techniques.

In some ways, I view Watson the same way I view Freud. Both are great historical figures who advanced the field immeasurably but whose specific ideas have been superseded. At the time Watson introduced behaviorism, psychology was mired down in an excessive and sterile introspection. Mentalism in all its forms was the enemy; only the observable was a proper subject for science. The purest of the behaviorists, the Skinnerians, carry on this tradition. Sometimes, the extreme behavioral position is described as "black box" psychology. I have had many frustrating conversations with radical behaviorists about this issue. As an undergraduate at Columbia, I once had to answer a test question, "What does the term 'anxiety' add to our understanding of behavior?" Full credit was given if the answer was the single word "Nothing." Later, I heard Richard Solomon, one of our most distinguished animal experimentalists, use the term "anxiety" in a colloquium talk. A group of very behavioristic graduate students snickered and asked him if he really thought that the word meant anything. He answered with something like, "Oh, grow up!"

No one who has lived through the birth of the behavior therapy movement is unfamiliar with the black-box stance. There is no underlying neurosis, only symptoms to be removed. Somehow, the issue of the disease model of dysfunction became fused with the question of whether people had thoughts and feelings that might be related to their behavior. Behavior was seen as determined entirely by immediate environmental events. The laws of operant and classical conditioning were deemed sufficient to explain behavior. Sometimes, this approach led to dramatic successes, particularly with regressed mental hospital inmates and children who were difficult to manage. Sometimes this approach led to dangerous and ludicrous interventions, such as using cigarettes to reinforce depressed inmates for smiling. Just recently, I heard a behaviorist describe a treatment for obesity that consisted of reducing the reinforcement value of food by mixing it with excrement. He did have a rather high drop-out rate!

Messer and Winokur (1980) are completely correct in characterizing the radical-behaviorist orientation as having extraspective, objective, and realistic perspectives on reality. The real problem

with this orientation is the exclusive use of this type of perspective. An objective perspective can be a very useful way of approaching a problem at times. Sometimes, in doing marital or family therapy, it is very helpful to ignore what is being said and to observe how the people behave toward each other or even how they sit in relation to each other. I would go so far as to say that any psychotherapist who could not adopt an objective perspective periodically is not a very good clinician. I would also say that a psychotherapist who could not adopt a subjective perspective would have to limit his or her practice to nonverbal organisms. The ability to shift from one perspective to another greatly enhances the understanding of a person.

Several years ago I was seeing a woman who was intellectually very sophisticated and who loved psychodynamic explorations of herself and her children. The only problem was that her children were almost completely out of control. This woman would take them to a supermarket and then seethe when they ran up and down aisles, knocking over rows of cans. She would explode at them when she got home. I suggested that she was using an ineffective behavior control method and might try operant conditioning. She bridled at the idea that she was using any kind of "control" method and recoiled at the very thought of using a behavioral technique. First, I had to explore her subjective view of the meaning of control and her belief that love should be enough. Then she began examining what she was actually doing, such as buying ice cream cones for them after the supermarket trips regardless of their behavior. Ultimately, she was able to make the ice cream cones contingent upon good behavior and gained control. Both she and I had to take objective and subjective perspectives on the problems.

Actually, subjective phenomena, such as thoughts and feelings, were never completely eliminated from behaviorism. Watson even tried to photograph thought (i.e., tongue movements). Behavior therapists like to refer to the last chapter of Skinner's *Science and Human Behavior* (1953) where he gives official sanction to the study of "private events." The main fear of radical behaviorism seems to be a return to a subjectivism that implies a noncorporeal substance, like the soul, that is not subject to natural laws. If you can get over this phobia, it is possible to conceive of a psychological science that encompasses everything that dynamic, humanistic, and existential therapists view as important.

It is ironic that, just as the behavior therapy movement was getting underway, the field of learning was undergoing a major change—the cognitive revolution! The nature of this change and its implications for therapy have been described in more detail elsewhere (Murray & Jacobson, 1978). I was lucky enough to study with two very farsighted men, John Dollard and Neal Miller, who went far beyond the learning theories of their day to include thought and emotion, even psychodynamics, in their analysis of psychotherapy. Probably, I am an eclectic today because of their vision of an integration of learning theory, psychoanalysis, and social science.

Since that time, the changes in conceptions of learning, motivation, and emotion have been staggering. While the early behavior therapists were using simple conditioning procedures, learning theorists were developing increasingly sophisticated information-processing models. Important topics today include the relationship between memory and feeling, self-control processes, the development of cognitive structures, and even imagery, the very target of Watson's rebellion. Bandura's (1969) social learning theory has probably had the greatest clinical impact. His concepts of observational learning, self-efficacy, and reciprocal causation lead

to a model of man that is quite compatible with ideas of self-concept, interpersonal relationships, and personal responsibility. The change here is as fundamental as the shift from instincts to interpersonal relationships in the psychoanalytic tradition.

On the clinical level, what has emerged is the cognitive–behavioral approach. It is interesting that Lazarus builds his system around the various "faculties" that are now included: sensation, perception, cognition, imagery, and affect, as well as behavior. The work of Ellis and Beck, once rejected by the behaviorists, has been integrated in the work of cognitive-behaviorists like Meichenbaum (1977), Mahoney (1974), Goldfried (1982) and many others. Clearly, the cognitive–behavioral approach incorporates both subjective and objective perspectives.

I started using a cognitive–behavioral approach because, for some reason, I had a string of very depressed clients. I did not find the dynamic approach very helpful, particularly the assumption that depression was retroflexed anger. Examining developmental issues seemed futile, even dangerous, in the face of active suicidal threat. I found Beck's (1976) approach much more useful and got as much training in it as I could. Eventually, I began using cognitive–behavioral techniques with most clients. I start with the client's immediate conscious experience. I examine the client's thinking very carefully for content, most of which has to do with problems of self-esteem and interpersonal relations. I help the client become more aware of automatic thoughts, thinking errors, and underlying assumptions. I believe that I am getting deeper into the inner meaning of the client's existence than I ever did before. Then, I try to help the client challenge and change his or her belief system through behavioral experiments and improved reasoning. I do not impose my "objective" view of reality on a client, but I try to get him or her to develop a less distorted and self-defeating view of reality. I see clients who have had severe childhood deprivations and who have experienced very traumatic losses. I also see some clients who are dying. I do not avoid the tragedy that is in life, but I do try to help clients stop destroying what meaningful life they can have.

Messer and Winokur (1980) take the behavioral movement to task for not having a developmental theory to account for the interpersonal and other problems that they deal with. To a large extent, this has been true even for cognitive–behavioral therapists. Partly, this lack is due to the pressure to deal with immediate issues as well as the conviction that childhood reconstruction is not necessary. Recall that Karen Horney and other interpersonal dynamic therapists felt the same way. Personally, I find that clients often are helped with a short review of their past lives, particularly if they come to understand where some of their distorted views originate. These developmental excursions are pretty much the same as those done by interpersonal dynamic therapists.

Wachtel (1977) has suggested that interpersonal dynamic developmental theories may provide the understanding needed to make coherent cognitive–behavioral interventions. In fact, some cognitive–behavioral theorists have begun to address these issues. For example, Guidano and Liotti (1983) have tried to relate a cognitive–behavioral conception of clinical disorder to the developmental theories of Piaget and Bowlby. Certainly, the behavioral movement, with its emphasis on learning, should not be antithetical to a developmental approach.

Thus, I see the cognitive–behavioral approach as increasingly compatible with the interpersonal dynamic approach. I see these two modern versions of the two great traditions as complementing one another and providing a basis for technical eclecticism. The promises of eclecticism are greater applicability of a variety of tech-

niques to client problems with a less rigid reliance on single techniques. Nonetheless, there are still many problems in achieving integration. Next we will turn to some of the philosophical issues involved.

Philosophical Issues

In a stimulating analysis, Messer and Winokur (1980) and Messer (Chapter 13, this volume) take the position that there are such profound philosophical differences between the psychodynamic and behavioral positions, as well as the humanistic and other positions, that true integration is difficult if not impossible. Yates (1983a), writing from a behavioral viewpoint, generally concurs with this analysis. On the other hand, I have taken issue with the necessary connections between these philosophical positions and specific therapy techniques (Murray, 1983).

Messer and Winokur (1980) state that psychoanalytic therapy uses introspective, subjective, and idealistic perspectives, whereas behavior therapy uses extraspective, objective, and realistic perspectives. I would agree that, historically, this has been a real difference. The radical behaviorists could still be described as having extraspective, objective, and realistic perspectives. However, as I have tried to show in the last section, behaviorally oriented therapists and theorists have been steadily moving away from such perspectives. The newer cognitive–behavior therapies clearly include introspective, subjective, and idealistic perspectives. To use Rychlak's (1981) terminology, the cognitive–behaviorists have become more Kantian. What could be more Kantian than believing that it is not the actual situation that causes distress but the view one takes of it? I was pleased to note that Messer (Chapter 13) recognizes this change. On the other hand, psychoanalysis is not purely introspective, subjective, and idealistic. Freud was an astute observer of nonverbal behavior. Indeed, his hypothesis about the unconscious was based, in part, on observing discrepancies between what people said and what they did. Rychlak describes Freud, Adler, and Jung as using a mixture of Kantian and Lockean models. In the preceding section I have tried to illustrate the advantages of being able to use both subjective and objective perspectives in clinical work.

Messer and Winokur (1980) make a fascinating use of dramatic metaphor to describe four visions of reality: comic, romantic, ironic, and tragic. Psychoanalysis leans heavily on the romantic, ironic, and, especially, tragic visions. The comic vision is present but to a lesser degree. On the other hand, behavior therapists have a primarily comic vision. These visions of reality are of mythic proportions and have profound impact on therapeutic techniques.

Recently, I have begun to question the strength of the associations between these differing visions of reality and specific theoretical orientations. I have constructed a questionnaire that incorporates items taken directly from Schafer (1976) and Messer and Winokur (1980) to represent comic and tragic visions of reality, judging these two to be the most crucial. In a pilot study (Murray, 1985), I administered this questionnaire to a group of graduate students who were evenly divided between psychodynamic and behavioral orientations. Both groups endorsed the comic items and rejected the tragic items. In an ongoing study, I administered the questionnaire to experienced therapists who were asked to identify themselves as psychodynamic, behavioral, humanistic, or none of these. The preliminary results of this study show that all four groups endorsed the comic items at about the same level. The comic vision seems quite prominent in the thinking of psychodynamic therapists.

There was more variability in response to the Tragic but still the means indicated

that in general, all four groups tended to reject this view. About a quarter of the psychodynamic group could be classified as tragic and the rest as rejecting the tragic vision. Furthermore, there were a couple of people in each of the other groups who could be classified as having a tragic vision.

It seems, then, that some psychodynamic therapists have a tragic vision but many do not. I am not sure what differentiates these psychodynamic therapists, and clearly more data are needed. What is clear to me is that a person does not have to have a tragic vision of life in order to do psychodynamic therapy. If this belief is borne out, it seems to me to remove one of the impediments to integration and eclecticism.

I was pleased to note that Messer (Chapter 13) perceived some shifts in visions of reality in the writings of different theorists. For example, he notes that the neo-Freudians and the ego psychologists, as well as time-limited psychodynamic therapists, seem to be shifting away from the tragic, ironic, and romantic visions toward the comic vision. So, too, he sees some minimal shift on the part of behavior therapists toward the tragic, ironic, and romantic visions. I believe that these shifts are consonant with my analysis in the preceding two sections on changes within each theoretical orientation. I also believe that the shifts represent some convergence of opinion about the nature of the problems people bring to us.

Messer (Chapter 13) also raises some profound issues about the nature of truth and science as they are viewed by people with different theoretical orientations. Space does not permit the thorough discussion that these issues deserve, but I would like to make a few comments. Over the years, I have had the opportunity to discuss some of these issues with prominent and genuinely gifted scientists, including two Nobel prize winners. One of the Nobel prize winners, a biologist, told me that he had repeatedly nominated Freud for the prize but did not prevail. The other person, a physicist, when asked about the legitimacy of nonexperimental data, answered that "You use anything you can get." I was struck by the open-mindedness of these truly great scientists and could not help but contrast them with some of the narrow-minded psychologists I have known. I have long argued for a creative combination of clinical and experimental research in psychology (Murray, 1961).

Great scientists pursue an idea, a vision of reality, if you will. At the outset, at least, they are open, inquiring, and creative as they formulate their theory. If they have a good enough theory, they gain adherents and establish a paradigm that brings together many observations in different areas. But then a strange thing happens! The theory coalesces into a set of what Lakatos (see Guidano & Liotti, 1983) calls hard-core metaphysical assumptions that are resistant to direct test and invalidation. This hard-core belief system is surrounded by a protective belt of secondary assumptions that can be adjusted to accommodate discrepant data but whose real purpose is to protect the core beliefs. The research programs generated by the theory are designed to extend it in a somewhat aggrandizing manner. The sentimental view of scientists trying to disprove their own theories does not conform very much to reality.

I saw this process occurring with Clark Hull's hypothetico–deductive behavior theory. I lived through it and was part of it. We could always find a way to preserve the drive-reduction hypothesis. I believe the same thing is true of Freud's theory. After reading Fisher and Greenberg (1977), in which the evidence seemed to me to be preponderantly negative or inconclusive, I was astounded to find that the authors believed Freud's basic assumptions were confirmed. These theories never seem to die a natural death. My most important

scientific mentor, Neal E. Miller, used to say that the only way to kill a bad theory was to construct a better one.

As a theory ages, the older adherents become more protective but the younger disciples become increasingly dissatisfied. I think this is what is happening in the field of therapy-based personality theories. The process runs parallel to the movement toward psychotherapeutic eclecticism.

I do not think that classical behavior theory and classical psychoanalytic theory can be integrated in any meaningful sense, I agree with Messer that taking terms out of these complex theoretical contexts leads to confusion and distortion. I think that both of these theories need to be killed. Remember, the only way to kill a theory is by constructing a better one.

What is to take place of these grand old theories? The interpersonal approach and the cognitive–behavioral approach offer possibilities for integration at the clinical level. They also offer better conditions for communication among therapists because the concepts are not so abstract and rigid. However, true integration requires a coherent theoretical structure, which does not yet exist. We are still waiting for our theoretical integrator. In the meantime, the best we can do is live in a state of irony and behave pragmatically.

CONCLUDING COMMENTS

As we have seen, eclecticism seems to be progressing whether we like it or not. People are actively pursuing an eclectic course. The allegiances to the old orientations seem to be fading. I cannot see the tide turning back the other way. I am excited about the possibilities.

To begin with, we have the possibility of improving therapeutic services. The question of the efficacy of psychotherapy is at center stage right now. Third-party payers are not impressed with what we have done so far. The use of techniques that fit the particular client, problem, and situation may result in an improved product. Naturally, such an improvement has to be documented and evaluated.

Another exciting aspect of the eclectic movement is that it is not developing into a loose assembly of random techniques without a theoretical structure. People active in this area are developing their own models because the traditional orientations have not proven adequate. Furthermore, these models parallel developments in general psychology, particularly the study of cognition and affect, so that the dream of an applied field based on scientific psychology, broadly conceived, may be a reality some day. I look forward to developmental and social psychology having a greater impact on psychotherapy.

None of this enthusiasm is meant to imply that eclectic therapeutic models are satisfactory as they now stand. They tend to be incomplete and untested. They need to be pitted against each other and evaluated. As it is, there is some danger that each eclectic therapist will develop his or her own school: multi-model therapy, reversal therapy, functional therapy, family therapy, and so on. The only way I know to prevent such a development is to maintain a cooperative research spirit in the hope that eventually a better, comprehensive model will emerge.

The future of an integrated, eclectic approach might be helped if eclectic therapists exercised restraint in their claims. One way to do this now is to develop models for delimited populations and problems that could later be integrated into a comprehensive model. For example, the model of Prochaska and DiClemente seems to fit problems of breaking addictions better than anything else. Grebstein's family model fits disturbed families best. Others seem to fit the young adult with autonomy and identity problems best.

One of the strengths of the behavioral movement was the use of "packages" for specific problems such as public speaking anxiety. Some psychodynamic packages for short-term therapy have appeared recently. I believe that more complex packages can be developed for more complex problems using a combination of techniques. In fact such packages are emerging for the treatment of problems such as agoraphobia, eating disorders, and depression. I think that therapists who have a lot of experience with specific client groups may be able to suggest eclectic packages for borderline, passive-aggressive, and other difficult personality types. So, too, there might be different eclectic family packages for acting-out adolescents, schizophrenics, and psychosomatic children. These packages should be flexible and based on all the clinical and experimental research available.

Theoretical orientations still exert a major influence in the field. Traditions are important to people, but I think that *some* people can come to appreciate the traditions of others. Obviously some people never will. As a more adequate scientific basis for therapeutic techniques emerges, the older orientations will decline in importance. As therapists experiment with techniques from alien traditions, they may become committed to an eclectic, integrative orientation. Where there was conflict, let there be reason!

REFERENCES

Bandura, A. (1969). *Principles of behavior modification.* New York: Holt, Rinehart and Winston.

Beck, A. T. (1976). *Cognitive therapy and the emotional disorders.* New York: International Universities Press.

Breger, L. (1974). *From instinct to identity.* Englewood Cliffs, NJ: Prentice-Hall.

Brill, A. A. (Ed.) (1938). *The basic writings of Sigmund Freud.* New York: Modern Library.

Erikson, E. H. (1963). *Childhood and society* (2nd ed.). New York: W. W. Norton.

Fisher, S., & Greenberg, R. P. (1977). *The scientific credibility of Freud's theories and therapy.* New York: Basic Books.

Freud, S. (1949/1940). *An outline of psychoanalysis.* New York: W. W. Norton.

Glover, E. (1940). *An investigation of the technique of psycho-analysis.* London: Bailliere, Tindall, & Cox.

Goldfried, M. R. (Ed.) (1982). *Converging themes in psychotherapy.* New York: Springer.

Guidano, V. F., & Liotti, G. (1983). *Cognitive processes and emotional disorders.* New York: Guiford Press.

Klerman, G. L., Weissman, M. M., Rounsaville, B. J., & Chevron, E. S. (1984). *Interpersonal psychotherapy of depression.* New York: Basic Books.

Kohut, H. (1977). *The restoration of the self.* New York: International Universities Press.

Luborsky, L. (1984). *Principles of psychoanalytic psychotherapy.* New York: Basic Books.

Mahoney, M. J. (1974). *Cognition and behavior modification.* Cambridge, MA: Ballinger.

Meichenbaum, D. (1977). *Cognitive behavior modification.* New York: Plenum Press.

Messer, S. B., & Winokur, M. (1980). Some limits to the integration of psychoanalytic and behavioral therapy. *American Psychologist, 35,* 818–827.

Murray, E. J. (1961). The integration of clinical and experimental approaches to the science of psychology. *Proceedings, New York State Psychological Association,* 13–19.

Murray, E. J. (1983). Beyond behavioural and dynamic therapy. *British Journal of Clinical Psychology, 22,* 127–128.

Murray, E. J. (1985). Florida Area Regional Report. *Society for the Exploration of Psychotherapy Integration Newsletter, 3,* 8–9.

Murray, E. J., & Jacobson, L. I. (1978). Cognition and learning in traditional and behavioral therapy. In S. L. Garfield & A. E. Bergin (Eds.). *Handbook of psychotherapy and behavior change* (2nd ed.). New York: Wiley.

Rychlak, J. F. (1981). *Introduction to personality and psychotherapy.* Boston: Houghton Mifflin.

Schafer, R. (1976). *A new language for psychoanalysis.* New Haven: Yale University Press.

Strupp, H. H., & Binder, J. L. (1985). *Psychotherapy in a new key.* New York: Basic Books.

Skinner, B. F. (1953). *Science and human behavior.* New York: Macmillan.

Wachtel, P. L. (1977). *Psychoanalysis and behavior therapy.* New York: Basic Books.

Wachtel, P. L. (1983). Integration misunderstood. *British Journal of Clinical Psychology, 22,* 129–130.

Yates, A. J. (1983a). Behavior therapy and psychodynamic psychotherapy: Basic conflict or reconciliation and integration? *British Journal of Clinical Psychology, 22,* 107–125.

Yates, A. J. (1983b). Reply. *British Journal of Clinical Psychology, 22,* 135–136.

CHAPTER 15

Training Eclectic Psychotherapists

Malcolm H. Robertson

Goldfried and Newman (Chapter 2) have traced the history of the convergent trend in psychotherapy and have documented the theoretical and empirical support for therapeutic integration. Norcross (Chapter 1) has cited evidence of a growing practitioner preference either to develop an eclectically based approach, or at least to enrich an already-established psychotherapy system with theoretical and empirical contributions from other systems. These authors present a convincing case that eclecticism is not an adversarial position vis à vis the professional establishment, a potpourri of techniques, an anti-scientific mindset of "Well, let's try this and see if it works, and if it doesn't, well . . . ," or even a *single* therapy. As the authors of the chapters in Part II of this volume clearly show, the eclectic movement includes several carefully formulated and systematically applied therapies.

On the other hand, it is apparent that research on the effectiveness of eclectic psychotherapy, and training in eclectic therapy, have lagged behind eclectic practice and eclectic theory development. As Norcross notes, research studies, with few exceptions, do not delineate the applica-

tion of an eclectic therapy sufficiently to allow a valid comparison with other systems with respect to differential effectiveness. As a psychotherapy trainer, I have observed that graduate programs by and large are not responsive to the experiences of many practitioners. Often, clinicians become eclectic in practice, if not in theory, as a result of pragmatic considerations, therapeutic serendipity, or freedom from earlier academic pressures to bend to a doctrinaire position. Quite frankly, many of us who are trainers teach students pretty much the way we were trained, and most of us were not trained to be eclectic therapists. We may have been exposed to lectures and readings on different systems, but invariably the emphasis was on differences rather than on commonalities across systems. We might even have had the luxury of selecting a preferred orientation from among faculty of differing theoretical persuasions but for better or worse we had to (or thought we had to) live with the choices we made.

In several respects, the current climate of training is conducive to the trend toward a convergent or integrative approach. First, APA accreditation policy, although it allows graduate programs to promote competence in a single system, requires broad-based training. Second, state licensure policy, at least in some states (e.g., Michigan), requires exposure to a wide range of therapeutic approaches. Finally, the steadily growing influence of third-party payers has given training programs a decidedly pragmatic hue, in which therapeutic efficiency and effectiveness are placed ahead of therapeutic allegiance or personalities.

Although graduate programs have started to heed the trend toward convergence and integration, there is a paucity of published studies on systematic training in eclectic psychotherapy. For this reason, I have organized the present chapter as follows. First, I briefly review the current status of conventional training, with implications for training eclectic therapists. Next, I compare and contrast the training proposals that the authors in Part II of this volume have presented. I also include a description of my training program at Western Michigan University. Then, in the concluding portion of the chapter, I present an overview of eclectic psychotherapy training, the advantages, limitations, and promising developments.

CRITIQUE OF CONVENTIONAL TRAINING

At least eight studies since 1975 have underscored the inadequacy or irrelevancy of clinical training with respect to preparing graduate students to be competent practitioners (Kalafat & Neigher, 1983). Rachelson and Clance (1980) surveyed members of the APA's Division of Psychotherapy to determine their attitudes toward the training standards set forth by the Division's Curriculum and Consultation Committee. Respondents thought highly of the proposed standards, which they hoped would be swiftly implemented. On balance, however, graduate-level training was perceived to be a useful

but small part of the process of becoming a psychotherapist.

An early survey of the APA's Clinical Psychology members found close to 80% expressing some degree of satisfaction with graduate training. Practitioners generally gave lower ratings than did academicians/researchers (Garfield & Kurtz, 1976). For the most part, critical comments concerned the insufficient time allotted to training in clinical skills. The authors summed up the respondents' recommendations with the statement: "More clinical experience under supervision of experienced clinicians" (p. 6). A later, follow-up survey found that practitioners were more satisfied with their internships than were researchers or academicians, and approximately 20% of the respondents had very favorable attitudes toward training (Norcross & Prochaska, 1982b). Most of the critical comments centered on deficiencies in clinical-skill training and on the need for additional practica, more supervision by experienced clinicians, and greater exposure to diverse theoretical orientations.

Although surveys vary in the number of respondents who report satisfaction with different components of training (e.g., courses, practica, internship), the consistent recommendation is to place more emphasis on the teaching of clinical skills and the provision of competent supervision for the practice of those skills. As Robertson (1984) notes: "Psychotherapy training in an academic environment is often just that—academic—long on teaching by exposition and short on teaching by practice" (p. 209). The rapid rise of professionally oriented training programs and schools of professional psychology clearly signals the need for more clinical and less scientific training, and for sustained contact with clinically competent faculty who are rewarded for teaching competence rather than solely for scientific productivity.

The implications for eclectic psychotherapy training are as follows. First, in order to select change strategies common to most current systems and to choose interventions on the basis of proven effectiveness instead of theoretical derivation, students must become familiar with diverse theoretical orientations, as well as with research findings on the efficacy of specific interventions for particular disorders. Second, a key principle of eclectic therapy, to tailor an intervention strategy to a client's personality and problem, must be learned experientially in clinical facilities that provide a wide range of clients and problems. Third, if students are to learn by doing, they must have access to clinically competent supervisors who can teach from their experience and train by their example.

In the following sections, specific aspects of conventional training are reviewed. The next section addresses the issue of theoretical orientation.

Theoretical Orientation

Reviews of psychotherapy outcome research have consistently reported minimal evidence for the differential effectiveness of competing theories for most psychological disorders (Bergin & Lambert, 1978; Imber, Pilkonis, & Glanz, 1983; Parloff, 1980; Smith, Glass & Miller, 1980). Korchin and Sands (1983) state that the search for common properties in differing theoretical positions reflects (1) the consistent finding that no one theory is uniformly more potent than any other; (2) the increased pressure for accountability and demonstrated cost-effectiveness; and (3) an emerging rapprochement among contending schools of therapy.

Although a survey of practicing therapists by Norcross and Prochaska (1983) found theoretical orientation to be a significant factor in the therapists' practice, clinical experience emerged as the single most influential factor in adopting a the-

ory of therapy, a finding that the authors note has been reported in earlier studies. Norcross and Prochaska also report that in general practitioners were highly satisfied with their chosen orientation, although an earlier study of practitioners by Garfield and Kurtz (1977) found less satisfaction with theoretical orientation.

A reasonable conclusion is that a theoretical orientation that derives from and is congruent with clinical practice will be highly valued. Whether theoretical orientation significantly improves therapeutic effectiveness is still a moot point. In fact, being thoroughly grounded in the principles of one theory has lost much of its former luster, because theoretical differences are not linked consistently to differences in psychotherapy outcome. Drawing on a sterling track record of research and scholarship, Strupp (1978) concluded that the therapist's personhood is far more relevant than theoretical orientation, philosophy of life, values, or conception of psychotherapy; furthermore, he suggested that general clinical skill is more important than theoretical orientation or even specific techniques.

From a different perspective, Adams (1984) singled out two negative consequences that theoretical orientations have on the education and training of professional psychologists. First is that faculty assume a role of proselytizing in addition to educating and training. Second, the APA's accreditation policy allows training programs to be established in terms of a preferred theoretical orientation rather than a basic theory of normal and abnormal behavior. An implicit point in Adams' critique is that scientific inquiry may be vitiated by preferential research treatment of a particular theory.

In addition to the deficiencies noted by Adams, an unswerving commitment to a single theoretical orientation poses a major obstacle to the advancement of psychotherapy training. The promulgation of an orientation is often fueled by strong emotions and personal needs. To para-phrase a comment by Nick Hobbs, when emotion is invested in a theory, the theory becomes a personal mystique. Too often an adversarial stance develops—a circling of the covered wagons—in which propo-nents of the orientation adopt a protective posture and invest their energies in de-fending rather than challenging the sta-tus quo. An unfortunate consequence is that leaders and followers share the same blindspots, and as Goldfried (1980) points out, they fail to understand and appreci-ate alternative conceptualizations and in-terventions.

By contrast, a major goal of eclectic therapy training is to acquire a working knowledge of several viable systems in order to identify their particular strengths, to discern the similarities in their pur-ported differences, and to discover how diverse theories can supplement and com-plement each other in clinical practice. A necessary step in the implementation of this goal is for students to be able and willing to examine how well each psy-chotherapy system has stood up under sci-entific scrutiny. In the next section the contribution of research training to the education of eclectic therapists is ad-dressed.

Research Training

As might be expected, few writers now-adays argue that one needs research training or clinical research competency to become an effective practitioner. The consensus is that clinicians should be trained to be "consumers of research" (Peterson, 1976) rather than doers of re-search. Students must be knowledgeable about research and its contribution to practice. They must be able to evaluate research studies, and more important, to transfer research knowledge to practice.

Frank (1984) has argued that clinical psychologists who are interested in re-search and teaching differ from clinical psychologists who are interested in clini-cal practice in terms of abilities, interests, personality, and cognitive style. Clinical practice and clinical research necessitate different attitudes, talents, and interests.

Garfield (1981) acknowledges the need for clinical research to advance the field, but not the need to be trained in research per se because research training has not been demonstrated to improve therapeu-tic effectiveness. Norcross and Prochaska (1982a) conclude that 10% to 15% of the respondents in their survey of Division 12 (Clinical) produce 40% of the published work, although nearly 90% report having published at least one article during their careers. The authors hope to put to rest the stereotype of the average clinical psy-chologist who never does research and who never publishes. Interestingly, Bar-low (1981) reports that behavioral thera-pists, who might be expected to reflect faithfully the scientist–practitioner model, are no more inclined to integrate clinical research into their practice than are non-behavioral clinicians. As an aside, Barlow quotes a statement by Matarazzo:

Even after 15 years, few of my research find-ings affect my practice. Psychological science per se doesn't guide me one bit. I still read avidly, but this is of little direct help. My clin-ical experience is the only thing that has helped my practice to date. (originally in Ber-gin & Strupp, 1972, p. 340)

If the consensus is that graduate pro-grams should indeed train students to be "consumers of research" rather than doers of research, then eclectic psychotherapy training must help students to develop what Goldfried and Newman (Chapter 2) refer to as "a respect for research evidence and an openness to anything that can be clinically effective." In addition to form-ing an unbiased attitude of "letting the chips fall where they may," training fac-ulty must present a persuasive argument that knowledge of research findings can and does improve therapeutic competence. Otherwise, as future practitioners, students will pay only lip service to the value of research as a source for achieving a more clinically effective and efficient therapy. Another implication concerns a central goal of eclectic therapy, which Norcross (Chapter 1) describes as "the optimal match among the intervention, and the patient, the problem, and the setting." We must communicate clearly to students that the goal is not who is right, but what is right for which client, with which disorder. That goal, moreover, will require the collaborative efforts of theoreticians, researchers, and practitioners.

A topic in which the collaborative efforts of theoreticians, researchers, and practitioners have been evident is the differential contribution of relationship skills and intervention skills to psychotherapy outcome. In the next two sections, I present an overview of the topic and suggest how it bears on eclectic therapy training.

Relationship Skills

More than technique variables, the personal characteristics of the therapist and of the client and the quality of their therapeutic relationship have been singled out as the critical variables that contribute to the positive outcome of psychotherapy (Bergin & Lambert, 1978; Frank, 1979; Lambert & Bergin, 1983; Smith, Glass, & Miller, 1980; Strupp & Hadley, 1979).

Over the past five to ten years considerable research effort has been invested in determining how the therapeutic relationship specifically contributes to therapy outcome, and in identifying the essential therapist characteristics that facilitate an effective relationship. Korchin and Sands (1983) contend that if the relationship engenders faith and trust in the client, then a positive therapeutic "climate" is established, at which point the

therapist can implement change methods common to all therapy systems. Frank (1981) and Lazarus (1980) also underscore the importance of the relationship as a means to inspire faith, hope, and trust in the client. In a review of the essential therapist characteristics that facilitate an effective relationship, Patterson (1984) states emphatically: "The evidence for the necessity, if not the sufficiency, of the therapist conditions of accurate empathy, respect or warmth, and therapeutic genuineness is incontrovertible" (p. 437). In addition to genuineness, Garfield (1981) identifies therapist's sensitivity to client's welfare, tolerance for stress, self-awareness of needs and limitations, and objectivity.

To conclude, eclectic training programs should note the consensus that until technical skills can be demonstrated to be more potent than, and independent of, the therapist's personal qualities, training programs should give students the opportunity to develop effective interpersonal skills (Lambert & Bergin, 1983). Besides conventional academic criteria, students should be selected for their self-awareness, empathy, compassion, breadth of interpersonal relationships, and tolerance for human diversity. Furthermore, evaluation of progress in training must include, in addition to intervention competence, the interpersonal skills needed to develop and maintain a facilitative relationship, and to confront and resolve impasses in the therapeutic relationship.

Let us turn now to intervention competence. The next section summarizes the position of those who assign a major role to technique variables in therapy outcome.

Intervention Skills

Not everyone agrees that the primary determinant of therapy outcome is the quality of the client–therapist interaction. For example, Telch (1981) argues strongly that techniques or interventions are more potent than the relationship or the therapist's interpersonal skills. Polemics aside, an important thrust in psychotherapy research is identification and development of specific intervention procedures.

In summarizing the results of the Vanderbilt study (Strupp & Hadley, 1979), Lambert and Bergin (1983) report that interventions positively related to therapy outcome are those that facilitate client–therapist communication, maintain a current time focus, and enable the client to talk freely about feelings and life experiences. Korchin and Sands (1983) identified several effective interventions that are used in varying degrees by all therapy systems: persuasion, suggestion, affective arousal, different forms of learning, promoting self-exploration and self-understanding, constructive feedback, practice/rehearsal, and creating opportunities for successes within and outside of therapy.

Several writers have urged the adoption of programmatic formats, or "manual-guided" therapies, as an effective and efficient method to acquire an intervention repertoire (Ford, 1977; Kalafat & Neigher, 1983; Schacht, 1984). Four examples are Beck's Cognitive Therapy, Luborsky's Supportive–Expressive Therapy, Weissman's Interpersonal Therapy, and Strupp and Binder's Time-limited Dynamic Psychotherapy. The advantages are that manual-guided teaching formats specify the interventions to be learned, provide an instructive demonstration of how to apply the interventions, and establish specified, acceptable levels of performance for trainees. The major objective of the programmatic, skill-based training is to set the stage for trainees to conduct the interventions in a clinical facility.

A central feature of eclectic therapy practice is "to select what works best." Within the training setting, students must be presented with a theoretical rationale for which interventions work best with

which client disorders; a clear demonstration of how interventions are set up, conducted, and terminated; and finally, supervised practice of the interventions.

Summary of Relationship and Interventions Skills

A strong consensus exists that training should address both interpersonal and technical skills. Garfield (1981) captures the essence of the consensus by stating that "both skill and personality variables are important and so nothing is gained by emphasizing one over the other" (p. 183). Therefore, the charge for eclectic programs is to design training experiences for students that blend personal and professional growth. Students may then learn to combine relationship-building skills that foster trust, hope, and a sense of self-efficacy in clients with technical skills needed to match intervention strategies to clients' personalities, problems and environmental resources.

A potent source of growth in both relationship and intervention skills is the interaction between a supervisor and a supervisee. The next section underscores the importance of supervision as a teaching technique.

Supervision

Despite the key position that supervision occupies in psychotherapy training, it has not drawn as much theoretical and empirical attention as other psychotherapy issues (Lambert, 1980; Schaefer, 1981; Schmidt, 1979). In training programs, supervision is a critical link between the didactic learning that takes place in formal coursework and the experiential learning in clinical practica. The tutorial format individualizes and personalizes the trainee's learning of therapeutic interventions, relationship skills, and ethical sensitivity.

Regardless of the supervisory model (e.g., psychoanalytic, cognitive–behavioral, process-oriented), or the supervisory modality (e.g., one to one, cotherapy, group), there is a consensus that supervision should provide a professional growth experience, rather than personal therapy. The latter is best arranged by the trainee independent of the training program (Hess, 1980; Sank & Prout, 1978; Schaefer, 1981).

Several studies have examined the effectiveness of the supervisory process from the supervisee's frame of reference. Both the number of supervision hours and the number of supervisors correlate positively with supervisees' self-ratings of competency (Bradley & Olson, 1980). Highly valued by supervisees are a supervisor's commitment to supervision and willingness to be observed doing therapy (Nelson, 1978). Frank, objective discussion of conflicts, in particular those involving the trainee's personality style, facilitates conflict resolution (Moskovitz & Rupert, 1983).

Too often, supervision is defined narrowly (case conference or consultation) and confined to the later stages of training (practicum and internship). A broader perspective is needed, one in which supervision begins with the student's entry into a program and continues throughout the program, and is an integral part of the making of a psychotherapist. A promising example is an eclectic model of supervision that includes a year-long developmental sequence of individual and group supervisory experiences (Yogev, 1982). The first stage is to assist the supervisee to internalize the therapist role and to differentiate it from the student role. In the second stage the supervisee acquires and masters varied intervention skills through didactic sessions, observation, sitting in on therapy sessions, and role-playing therapist behaviors. The third stage provides in vivo practice and evaluation of progress combined with training on how to monitor and modify feelings, thoughts, and actions that interfere with therapy progress.

Although personal therapy ought not to be a part of the supervision process, opinion is divided over whether provision for personal therapy is a necessary or even desirable component of a program. The following section speaks to this issue and its feasibility for eclectic training.

Personal Therapy

The issue of personal therapy as an important component of training is still unsettled. Although Wampler and Strupp (1976) cite conflicting evidence on the importance of personal therapy to becoming a competent therapist, they conclude that personal therapy contributes to the preparation of the therapist for first-rate professional work, and that first-hand experience with one's own dynamics is one of the best, if not the best, guarantors of high quality professional work. Sank and Prout (1978) acknowledge the lack of data in support of the positive effect of personal therapy on therapeutic competence. However, they contend that being in the client role is worthwhile in and of itself, presumably because the client role gives an important perspective on the therapeutic relationship that cannot be acquired in the role of the therapist.

In a survey of the APA's Clinical Psychology members, Norcross and Prochaska (1982b) report that two-thirds of the respondents had had personal therapy and of these, 80% stated that personal therapy is an important or very important prerequisite for therapy training. In an earlier survey of practitioners, Kelly, Goldberg, Riske, and Kilkowski (1978) found that of those who had had personal therapy, approximately one-third gave as their reason the wish to become more competent professionals.

Whether or not personal therapy should

be a part of one's therapy training, many practitioners do obtain therapy in their postgraduate years and, in retrospect, state that it should be a part of one's training as a practitioner. There are really two issues here. First, some trainees must be encouraged by training faculty to arrange for personal therapy so that they can overcome personal obstacles in working with certain client disorders and coping styles. The second and larger issue is role familiarity. As noted in the sections on relationship skills and intervention skills, the quality of the client–therapist relationship is crucial to therapy outcome. Furthermore, it is the therapist who has primary responsibility for ensuring a quality relationship. In my judgment, an experiential familiarity with the client role is a decided advantage in learning how to initiate and maintain a therapeutically productive interaction, as well as knowing at what point the relationship has served its purpose. With that in mind, an eclectic training program that provides a hands-on experience in both therapist and client roles will strengthen students' relationship skills and thereby increase their therapeutic effectiveness.

The next section presents an overview of group and marital/family modalities in therapy training. It examines eclectic therapy training in particular.

Group, Couple, and Family Modalities

Within the last decade, psychotherapy training has expanded from the pursuit of competence with a dyadic model to incorporating didactic and experiential training in group, couple, and family modalities (Goldenberg, 1983; L'Abate, Berger, Wright, & O'Shea, 1979; Zohn & Carmody, 1978). The trend to broaden the student's psychotherapy education with exposure to more complex modalities parallels the increased use of more complex modalities by practicing therapists. At least among clinical psychologists, individual therapy remains the most frequently employed treatment modality. Nevertheless, in a recent study (Norcross & Prochaska, 1982a), over half of the respondents indicated they are actively engaged in marital and family therapy, and group therapy accounted for as much therapy time as did behavior modification.

Although professional psychology training programs that include theory and methods of group and marital/family modalities have been increasing in recent years, the number is small (Carmody & Zohn, 1980; Framo, 1979). For the most part, the demand for training is met by the proliferation of postgraduate workshops and institutes.

Typically, group and family therapy trainers emphasize small-group experiential learning and closely supervised practice with both simulated and "live" client groups and families. Framo (1979) points out that didactic training ought to be directed toward learning about ethnic family cultures, changing roles, and alternative family/marital life styles, as well as ecological systems surrounding the family. He favors group supervision with close attention to group process, so that trainees can blend group therapy with family therapy training.

The challenge for eclectic therapy training in group and marital/family therapy is twofold. First, we must identify commonalities across group theories (e.g., psychoanalytic, psychodrama, transactional analysis) and across marital/family theories (e.g., communications, structural, behavioral), and then operationalize a common set of change principles for supervised practice with groups or families. Second, we must provide trainees with a conceptual framework within which clinical decisions can be made in terms of when to intervene with which modality or modalities and in what sequence.

In the final section of this review of current psychotherapy training, the status of program evaluation is summarized and the relevance for eclectic training is noted.

EVALUATION OF TRAINING PROGRAMS

Reviews of training have not been encouraging (Ford, 1979; Kalafat & Neigher, 1983; Matarazzo, 1978). Training is provided in diverse settings with a variety of techniques, but with little formal evaluation of programs that claim to teach complex therapy interventions. Frequently lacking in evaluation studies are reliable and valid methods (e.g., rating scales with interjudge agreement and stability values, pre–post comparisons of behavior samples, outcome measures from trainees' clinical cases) to appraise training performance and to relate training to later job performance (Edelstein, 1985; Ford, 1977; Peterson & Bry, 1980). Regrettably, most of the traditional or conventional components of psychotherapy training, including selection criteria, do not correlate significantly with therapeutic effectiveness (Garfield, 1981; also Chapter 2, this volume).

Most APA-approved clinical psychology doctoral programs employ some type of training evaluation, and the majority use multiple sources of evaluation data. Informal, qualitative evaluation (e.g., personal impressions, reputations) were used most frequently, and formal, quantitative comparison data (e.g., pre–post comparisons) were obtained least frequently (Norcross & Stevenson, 1984). Cited as obstacles to improve evaluation were lack of personnel, time restraints, and inadequate evaluation measures. In psychology training clinics, 61% used quantitative evaluation of training, whereas the remaining 39% reported no systematic evaluation procedures. The authors (Stevenson & Norcross, 1985) conclude that training

evaluation is less well developed than treatment evaluation and, for the most part, is limited to a combination of supervisors' and supervisees' evaluations.

To ensure ongoing, systematic evaluation of training programs in relation to their stated goals, many writers urge the adoption of competency-based criteria or peer review procedures. Peer review procedures and competency-based criteria may accomplish several objectives. They may (1) assist students in improving their skills; (2) prepare for later credentialing; (3) increase their future accountability; and (4) safeguard the welfare of the public (Cohen, 1983; Stricker, 1984). Fantuzzo (1984) describes a specific competency-based training model to determine minimal competency for practice as well as evidence of the effectiveness of psychotherapy. The acronym for the model is MASTERY: "M" designates mastery of prerequisite knowledge; "A" means assessment of skill competency; "S" refers to setting minimal competency standards; "T" equates training with competency; "E" stands for evaluation of trainees' understanding of ethical and legal issues; "R" designates reassessment of skill level; and "Y" indicates yielding to continuing education.

With respect to the issue of continuing education, the rapidly expanding base of professional knowledge, combined with standards for licensure, makes it imperative that the newly degreed psychotherapist begin a continuing education program upon graduation. Lifetime education should be an important goal in training and professional practice, and a commitment to continuing education is a sure means of fostering and maintaining public confidence (Vitulano & Copeland, 1980).

PROPOSALS FOR ECLECTIC PSYCHOTHERAPY TRAINING

This section summarizes suggestions and recommendations made for eclectic psychotherapy training by the authors of the nine chapters in Part II of this volume. Explicit proposals are made in the six chapters by Beutler; Fuhriman, Paul, and Burlingame; Garfield; Grebstein; Lazarus; and Prochaska and DiClemente. For the three chapters by Fischer, Hart, and Murgatroyd and Apter, I have taken the liberty of inferring what the authors' recommendations might be. The authors' training proposals are compared in terms of six questions to which they were asked to respond.

Learning Therapy Systems Before or After Eclectic Training

The authors' proposals suggest a consensus for learning specific therapy systems before, rather than after, developing an eclectic approach.

Garfield, Grebstein, and Lazarus would provide a breadth of exposure to therapy systems in order to examine points of convergence and divergence as well as to determine each system's empirically demonstrated contributions. For Garfield, the goal would be to develop a repertoire of clinically effective interventions. Lazarus would require, in addition, an in-depth familiarity with one system that would serve as a theoretical framework within which to implement the multimodal therapy model. Grebstein would require a conceptual knowledge of family life and family behavior.

Prochaska and DiClemente have a more detailed proposal. In addition to introducing students to a broad but integrative perspective on current systems, they would require didactic and experiential knowledge of six to eight systems in preparation for learning transtheoretical eclecticism, that is, a knowledge of at least one system in order to intervene at each level of change, and of at least one system in order to apply each change process.

Instead of exposing students to a wide range of interventions from diverse systems, Beutler would train students to be competent with a few interventions of demonstrated relevance and effectiveness for his six categories of therapeutic goals.

Because of the atheoretical nature of their model, Fuhriman, Paul, and Burlingame conclude that diversified exposure to therapy systems might be helpful but would not be a prerequisite for learning eclectic, time-limited therapy.

Although three authors do not address the issue, we may conclude that familiarity with varied systems would help students acquire "the best obtainable knowledge" (Fischer) or would assist students in developing a common or "meta" language for synthesizing common properties of systems (Murgatroyd & Apter). Hart would probably want students to be familiar with the evolution of functional eclectic therapy and with his integration/reintegration model.

Prior Competence in Some/Many/All Systems

Competence in *all* systems would have been likely before 1950, probable before 1960, possible before 1970, and impossible after 1970. As several of the authors point out, the proliferation of therapy systems over the past 10 to 15 years rules out anyone being a competent practitioner for all systems. With respect to competence in *many* systems, several of the authors hedge their bets, but basically the jury is still out on this part of the question.

When we get down to the question of competence in *some* systems, most of the authors have a clear position. The most ambitious one is that of Prochaska and DiClemente, who ask for clinical competence (as opposed to conceptual knowledge) in six to eight therapy systems prior to learning transtheoretical eclecticism. Next come Lazarus, Grebstein, and Fuhriman, Paul, & Burlingame. Lazarus expects competence in one theoretical system in preparation for learning multimodal therapy. Grebstein has students acquire competency in one of the less complex family therapy systems (e.g., Problem-Centered Systems approach) before attempting to develop an integrative/eclectic system. To learn their eclectic, time-limited model, Fuhriman, Paul, and Burlingame would require clinical experience with an approach that incorporates basic helping skills.

On the other hand, Garfield states that no prior competence in any system is needed before becoming a "true eclectic therapist." I don't have a clear picture of Beutler's position except that he expects trainees to acquire competence with several change procedures and is still examining the question of how much competence in how many systems can reasonably be expected.

Fischer, Hart, and Murgatroyd and Apter do not speak directly to the issue, but I gather Fischer expects a modicum of competence in assessment, therapeutic, and evaluative skills; that Murgatroyd and Apter would require a working knowledge of Reversal Theory as the first step in the implementation of structural–phenomenological therapy; and that Hart would recommend established competence in an experientially based mode of therapy.

Amount and Type of Clinical Experience

I believe that all the authors want students to have a closely supervised clinical experience over an extended period of time with a variety of clients and modalities.

Garfield, and Prochaska and DiClemente specify a one-year practicum followed by a year-long internship. For Garfield, the two-year sequence would consist of supervised experience in applying both general change procedures common to most systems and specific procedures designed for particular problems. Progress is evaluated in terms of client change, and

a certain level of competence is required for completion of training. For Prochaska and DiClemente, students would gain experience in the differential application of well-known change processes to each problem level and within each stage of therapy. Progress would be evaluated in terms of demonstrated skill in working with each problem level within each therapy stage.

Although a time period is not specified, the proposal of Fuhriman, Paul, and Burlingame would establish a two-stage sequence in which competence in basic counseling or helping skills would precede supervised practice in conducting an eclectically based therapy within a time-limited format. The purpose of supervision is to assist therapists in adjusting their approach to the eclectic time-limited therapy model.

Beutler's proposal incorporates a competency-based clinical experience in which trainees' progress is evaluated in terms of specified levels of performance. A critical function of supervision is to ensure that trainees adhere to the change procedures which the treatment plan specifies.

A competency-based model is implicit in Lazarus's proposal. Moreover, Lazarus believes that a competency-based model is best implemented through apprenticeship with a therapist who has expertise in the theory and methods in which the trainee is seeking competence.

My impression is that Fischer, Hart, and Murgatroyd and Apter would devote considerable training time to supervised practice and evaluation of a wide range of eclectic interventions. The supervised practice and evaluation would be incorporated within the PRAISES model (Fischer), Reversal Theory (Murgatroyd and Apter), or the Integration /Reintegration model (Hart).

Grebstein responds to the question of amount and type of clinical experience in the context of family therapy training. Clinical experience would begin with practice of eclectic interventions with simulated families, progress to assessment and initial interventions with "live" families, and culminate in closely supervised intervention work with real families over an extended period of time.

Importance of Personal Therapy

The question of personal therapy is not addressed by either Fischer or Murgatroyd and Apter. Beutler does not speak directly to the issue, but his emphasis on developing a range of interpersonal styles in order to achieve compatibility with a variety of client interpersonal styles suggests a training component that fosters personal growth.

Garfield and Lazarus stress selection of students who have the interpersonal skills and overall maturity that is associated with suitability for therapeutic work. Personal therapy is always an option for a trainee who later encounters personal obstacles in adjusting to therapeutic work.

Prochaska and DiClemente, as well as Fuhriman, Paul, and Burlingame, take the position that voluntary personal therapy can strengthen the trainee's practice of therapy by eliminating defensive reactions and personal blindspots. In addition, Prochaska and DiClemente recommend personal therapy for trainees who wish to work with clients across all problem levels, in particular those levels that require self-exploration and self-understanding.

Grebstein states that openness and modifiability are requisite personal qualities for trainees intent on becoming family therapists, and voluntary personal therapy is a viable means to develop and strengthen those qualities. Personal therapy should be especially helpful for some trainees in understanding how their own family experiences create obstacles in working with certain kinds of family relationship problems.

Insofar as the goal of Hart's experientially based therapy is to have "access to one's feeling life" and to develop "the ability to make distinctions among other individuals" with respect to their psychological qualities, it is reasonable to have personal growth experiences (e.g., personal therapy) as an integral component of training.

Requirement of Research Experience

There is some variation among the authors in their qualified support for research training. Beutler, Garfield, Lazarus, Fischer, and Murgatroyd and Apter believe that research experience prepares trainees to be critical consumers of research, that is, to communicate effectively with clinical researchers, evaluate research findings with rigor and objectivity, and translate research findings into practice. Additionally, Beutler would encourage students to conduct research on how to match patients and therapists, and patients and interventions, in order to strengthen their understanding of systematic eclectic therapy.

Grebstein, Hart, and Prochaska and DiClemente propose that research activities have a specific focus, that is, that trainees acquire the requisite skills to evaluate how well they achieve the specific therapeutic goals set for each client. Grebstein concludes that a practitioner needs a researcher's perspective for an objective appraisal of therapy, just as a researcher needs a practitioner's perspective in order to do meaningful clinical research. Prochaska and DiClemente stress that clinically relevant research training will strengthen both theory and application of eclectic therapy. Hart's preference for an aesthetic rather than a scientific orientation suggests a less systematic and rigorous evaluation of therapy than the other authors advocate. Fuhriman, Paul, & Burlingame imply that the purpose of research training is to acquire flexibility in conducting therapy and an openness and willingness to experiment with other approaches.

Ideal Program and Sequence of Training

Only Prochaska and DiClemente and Fuhriman, Paul, and Burlingame spell out a sequence of training. Certainly, the proposal of Prochaska and DiClemente is ideal, but it is not easily attainable. Briefly stated, the sequence would unfold as follows:

1. Didactic learning of current systems within a transtheoretical framework
2. Observational learning in which competent therapists demonstrate transtheoretical eclecticism
3. Extended, experiential learning of six to eight systems
4. Two years of supervised experience in conducting transtheoretical eclecticism with a variety of clients and therapeutic modalities

The critical and not easily attainable step is acquiring competence in six to eight systems. The proposal of Fuhriman, Paul, and Burlingame is also ideal, but it is more practical to implement. Within a small-group format of trainees and trainers, their eclectic, time-limited therapy model would be learned in sequential phases:

1. Didactic presentations
2. Demonstration/modeling by trainers
3. Simulated therapy in which trainees rotate roles of client, therapist, and observer
4. Clinical experience, first by doing cotherapy with an experienced therapist, and then by taking primary responsibility for conducting therapy

The proposals of Lazarus and Garfield are similar in that both stress trainee selection that assesses personal suitability for therapy training. In addition to a solid grounding in psychology as a science and as a profession, students would have a broad-based exposure to current systems, which for Lazarus would include multimodal therapy. However, the major portion of training would be supervised experience in conducting and evaluating eclectic therapy with a variety of clients in different clinical settings. Lazarus favors an apprenticeship type of supervised experience, while Garfield prefers a combination of group and individual supervision.

Although Beutler and Grebstein do not respond explicitly to this question, a proposal for ideal training is implicit in their responses to the preceding questions. Beutler envisions a competency-based program that specifies criteria for satisfactory performance of a diversified group of change procedures designed to implement his six categories of therapy goals. The training model would be that of a "personal scientist," who assists clients in developing a scientific view of cause and effect in their behavior. An implicit requirement is that trainees first learn to be personal scientists in relation to their behavior as therapists. An important aspect would be skill in matching the therapist's interpersonal style and interventions to the client's interpersonal style and problems. For family therapy training, Grebstein suggests the following sequence: didactic learning of current family therapy systems, as well as acquiring knowledge about family life and development; experiential learning, for example, roleplaying interventions with simulated families, self-exploration and self-understanding of the trainee's family of origin; and closely supervised therapy with "live" families.

Although the other authors do not address the issue of training directly, I suspect that Fischer would train "scientific practitioners," whose therapy practice would be eclectic, systematic, empirically based, and accountable; that Hart would design a practitioner-oriented program that accepts and values different schools and styles of therapy, and encourages aesthetic sensitivity instead of a scholarly/scientific attitude; and that Murgatroyd and Apter would train students in structural–phenomenological therapy, both as a conceptual framework and as a mode of practice.

To conclude, all the authors reflect the open-mindedness of an eclectic orientation, and endorse the value of being sufficiently knowledgeable about current therapy systems to appreciate their common properties and the specific contributions of each system. The assumption is that a student's familiarity with current systems is a necessary step in the application of a systematically formulated eclecticism, whether it be an already developed eclectic model or one of their own. Explicitly or implicitly, all the authors would have trainees learn an eclectic model that is theoretically and empirically defensible, and sufficiently flexible to allow for modification and improvisation. The above points are compatible with the earlier reviewed literature on training.

The consensus on research training is that it is desirable but not necessary. Yet, an important component of training is to teach students to be critical consumers of the research literature. Personal therapy is also viewed as desirable—i.e., it contributes to therapeutic proficiency—but not as a prerequisite for becoming an effective therapist. To varying degrees, the authors support attention to personal growth and to the development of interpersonal skills in order to relate effectively to a wide range of client personalities. The above points are also consistent with the general literature on training.

Considerable importance is given to developing competency with interventions that have proven effectiveness in relation to commonly held therapy goals. The shift from the study of theory to closely supervised practice with interventions is clearly evident. All the authors support training that integrates assessment with psychotherapy, although some are explicit about the hand-in-glove fit between assessment/diagnosis and therapy. Finally, the authors are clearly responsive to the current emphasis in the literature on accountability, and the conscientious application of evaluation procedures both to training programs and to clients of trainees.

ECLECTIC TRAINING: A CASE ILLUSTRATION

Several recommendations presented by the authors in Part II of this volume are being implemented in a training program at Western Michigan University, e.g., teaching interventions rather than theories, learning by doing, emphasizing personal growth (Robertson, 1984). In preparation for practicum and internship, I expose graduate students to a wide range of therapeutic modalities and interventions by means of a four-course sequence of individual, group, marital, and family therapy. In the proverbial nutshell, the therapy model for the four courses can be described as experientially oriented (present-centered with an emphasis on emotions); radically eclectic (interventions selected from current therapy systems); flexibly structured (agenda tailored to client, session, and stage of therapy); time-adjusted (tentative time limits correlated with progress reviews); contractually based (between-session assignments); and thematically focused (problems conceptualized as recurring affective–cognitive–behavioral patterns for which goals are derived and interventions are chosen). The role of a therapist is fourfold: interpersonal model, conceptualizer of information, change agent, and professional friend.

Although some theory and research are taught through lecture and assigned reading, the main activity in each course is supervised practice of interventions with individuals, groups, couples, and families. In each course students are divided into training groups whose group leaders have completed the four-course sequence with distinction and have demonstrated leadership qualities. In the individual and group courses, the practice sessions are "live," in that the student–client deals with genuine issues in his or her life. In the marital and family courses, simulated couples and families are used.

The trainees learn and practice two types of skills: interpersonal and technical. The same interpersonal skills are used in each modality and include: cognitive clarification, empathic responding, relevant self-disclosure, nonjudgmental confrontation, selective probes, and planning–prioritizing–implementing alternative coping behaviors. The technical skills are interventions selected for each modality; for example, guided imagery and behavior rehearsal for the individual modality; structured feedback and two-chair dialogue, for the group modality; communication exercises and negotiating/contracting tasks, for the couple modality; sculpting and doubling, for the family modality. Both types of skills are explained and demonstrated by the author prior to the practice sessions.

Practice sessions are audiotaped and observed by the author, group trainer, and group trainees who are not in the client or therapist role. After each session, the therapist receives oral and written feedback from the client(s) and observers and integrates the written feedback with information obtained from the audiotape replay. Based on the first-session feedback from client(s), peer observers, group trainer, and author, therapists prepare a treatment plan that is evaluated in terms of a prescribed format as well as the therapist's adherence to the plan in subsequent sessions. Near the end of each course, trainees prepare a written self-assessment of professional and personal growth gained from their roles as therapist, client, and training group member. Trainees receive written feedback on the self-assessment from the author and group trainer. Ethical and legal issues are addressed both in the didactic sessions and as these issues arise during the therapy sessions.

Personal growth is addressed in the written self-assessment, in personal conferences with the author and group trainer, in spontaneous feedback from group trainees, and in the context of the client role. In addition, before beginning family therapy practice sessions, each trainee does a family-of-origin drawing and a family genogram that are presented and discussed within the training group.

Although formal assessment methods are slighted, trainees are sensitized to the gathering and conceptualization of client data through the treatment plan and as an integral part of ongoing therapy. Recently, the author has introduced an eclectically based framework for assessment and treatment planning described by Hulse and Jennings (1984). Beginning with the client's statement of the presenting problem, assessment is made according to the following categories: expectation, motivation, maturity level, cognition, affect, behavior, environment, health, and communication style. Based on each category and the interaction between the categories, a problem conceptualization is formulated and then related to a personality theory, a theory of psychotherapy, and a theory of psychopathology.

Regardless of the modality, the most difficult issues for the trainees are those described by Sank and Prout (1978):

- Transference/countertransference
- Client problem that is alien to the life experience of the therapist
- Therapist values that are incompatible with client values
- Moral/ethical sensitivity to certain interventions
- Similarity between client and therapist with respect to personal problems and coping styles

Both written feedback from the trainees (anonymous) and the observations of the author and group trainers are used to evaluate and modify the training program. Although it is not a substitute for supervised practicum or internship, the course sequence bridges the gap between classroom study and the later performance of psychotherapy in a practicum or internship setting.

CONCLUDING COMMENTS

In this final section I will try to give the reader a sense of the chapter by delineating advantages, problems, limitations, promising trends, and challenges for eclectic psychotherapy training.

Advantages of Eclectic Training

Eclectic therapy training has several distinct advantages. To begin with, it is sensitive to and congruent with the current *Zeitgeist*. Faced with a glut of therapies and a proliferation of innovative techniques, along with mounting social–economic–political pressures for accountability, an increasing number of practitioners are responding with treatment approaches that combine conceptual breadth with pragmatic intervention strategies (see Goldfried & Newman, Chapter 2, this volume; Norcross, Chapter 1, this volume; Smith, 1982).

Another advantage is that eclectic training supports and promotes a spirit of collaboration, in which the efforts of theoreticians, researchers, and practitioners potentiate each other in seeking what works best for clients and patients. Still another advantage offered by eclectic training is the fostering of a progressive, apolitical perspective in which improvisation is actively sought, and in which negative outcome findings have an instructive value in highlighting aspects of eclectic theory and application that need to be improved. On the other hand, these advantages must be weighed against some very real problems.

Problems of Eclectic Training

A major problem is the lack of a practical educational strategy to enable students to acquire competence in several current psychotherapy systems and to maintain that competence after completion of training. Only Prochaska and DiClemente (Chapter 6, this volume) envision a training program in which achieving competence in several major systems is considered feasible. The other authors in Part II of this volume propose either competence in one psychotherapy system that encompasses diversified interventions, or the development of broad-based change strategies that subsume specific, problem-focused interventions. Realistically, faculty and trainees in professional psychology programs have only so much time and energy available to cover basic and applied coursework, recommended cognates, practicum/internship, comprehensive exams, and research requirements.

Another problem has to do with the plethora of published reports on innovative techniques and new applications of established interventions, which makes the task of deciding how many and which interventions to teach a formidable one, even for committed eclectic trainers. With this problem and the preceding one, we need to remind ourselves that we can only provide a solid base for a lifelong process of becoming a "true eclectic therapist."

Still another problem is how to train students to operationalize clinical decision making within an eclectic framework (e.g., tailoring interventions to clients' personalities and problems; choosing when and where to splice in group or marital/family modalities).

Limitations of Eclectic Training

In addition to the problems just discussed, we have also to contend with several limitations. Not the least of these is a scarcity of training faculty who are committed to and competent in the theory and practice of integrative–eclectic psychotherapy. Too often, therapy trainers (and I have to include myself) teach eclecticism in the form of value *statements* instead of value *actions*. It is to be hoped that we will not transmit this limitation to the next generation of eclectic therapy trainers.

Another limitation is the scarcity of both research findings on the effectiveness of eclectic psychotherapy as compared with other approaches and empirically based comparisons among alternative forms of eclectic therapy. A related limitation is the absence of training evaluation that combines formative and summative criteria (Levy, 1983). Invariably, evaluation studies are designed to assess program outcome, without provision for ongoing, systematic quality control.

A potential limitation is that an eclectic therapy system, like other systems in the formative stage of development, may be diverted from its primary mission by a preemptive need to proselytize; students are especially susceptible to the strains of the pied piper. The worst-case scenario

would be for eclecticism to splinter into competing camps, each asserting its prior claim to be more truly and faithfully eclectic than the others. Inevitably, defections and deviations would surface in protest to the restrictions imposed by doctrinaire eclecticism, followed then by the birth of noneclectic therapy which, through theoretical mitosis, would produce competing noneclectic therapies. But I think we have learned our lesson too well to allow that prospect to become a reality.

Promising Trends

Despite current problems and limitations, there are encouraging signs. First, the trend to establish eclectic therapy training programs is gathering momentum, as evidenced in the training proposals of the nine authors in Part II of this volume. The translation of eclectic theory and practice into training is taking place, and there seems to be no lack of a receptive and responsive constituency.

Second, the increased number of publications and organizations that reflect the current interest in psychotherapy convergence and integration (see Goldfried & Newman, Chapter 2; Norcross, Chapter 1) attests to the relevance of eclectically based training programs.

Third, to paraphrase from another context, the practice of psychotherapy has become too important to be left to the professionals. It is not everybody's business, but it is a "big business," and we have become accountable to many external sources for continued financial, social, and political support. With a shorter history and less excess theoretical baggage than other therapy systems, integrative–eclectic therapy is uniquely positioned to meet the demand of consumers, consumer-advocates, and the public at large for a treatment approach that is comprehensible, relevant, and cost-effective.

Challenges for Eclectic Training

These promising developments also pose significant challenges for eclectic therapy training. As noted by several writers (see Goldfried & Newman, Chapter 2; Murgatroyd & Apter, Chapter 9), a common language is a pressing need. For training programs a common language would serve three purposes. It would (1) facilitate collaboration among theoreticians, among researchers, and among practitioners, as well as intergroup corroboration among these three groups; (2) create a conceptual tool for distilling and refining what Wachtel (1977) identifies as a therapeutic "underground" of clinical wisdom; and (3) provide students with a communication base for accessing divergent therapy systems.

Another challenge follows from the consensus that the quality of the therapist–client relationship is crucial to psychotherapy outcome. In my judgment, progress in understanding, predicting, controlling (and teaching) effective client–therapist interaction lags behind progress in developing problem-focused interventions and techniques. Still another challenge is to extend our knowledge of integrative –eclectic therapy within a dyadic modality to group, couple, and family modalities.

In conclusion, the ultimate challenge is to present trainees with a convincing demonstration that, as Norcross states in Chapter 1 of this volume, "the strengths of systematic, eclectic psychotherapy lie in their ability to be taught, replicated, and evaluated."

REFERENCES

Adams, H. E. (1984). The pernicious effects of theoretical orientations in clinical psychology. *The Clinical Psychologist, 37*(3), 90–93.

Barlow, D. H. (1981). On the relation of clinical research to clinical practice: Current issues, new directions. *Journal of Consulting and Clinical Psychology, 49*, 147–155.

Bergin, A. E., & Lambert, M. J. (1978). The evaluation of therapeutic outcomes. In S. L. Garfield & A. E. Bergin (Eds.), *Handbook of psychotherapy and behavior change* (2nd ed.). New York: Wiley.

Bergin, A. E., & Strupp, H. H. (1972). *Changing frontiers in the science of psychotherapy.* Chicago: Aldine-Atherton.

Bradley, J. R., & Olson, J. K. (1980). Training factors influencing felt psychotherapeutic competence of psychology trainees. *Professional Psychology: Research and Practice, 11*, 930–934.

Carmody, T. P., & Zohn, J. (1980). APA-approved group treatment internship training opportunities: Present status and future directions. *Professional Psychology: Research and Practice, 11*, 213–219.

Cohen, L. H. (1983). Document-based peer review in a psychology training clinic: A preliminary report of a statewide program. *Professional Psychology: Research and Practice, 14*, 362–367.

Edelstein, B. A. (1985). Empirical evaluation of clinical training. *The Behavior Therapist, 8*(4), 67–70.

Fantuzzo, J. W. (1984). Mastery: A competency-based training model for clinical psychology. *The Clinical Psychologist, 37*(1), 29–30.

Ford, J. D. (1977). Training in clinical psychology: A reappraisal based on recent empirical evidence. *The Clinical Psychologist, 30*(3), 14–15.

Ford, J. D. (1979). Research on training counselors and clinicians. *Review of Educational Research, 49*, 87–130.

Framo, J. L. (1979). A personal viewpoint on training in marital and family therapy. *Professional Psychology: Research and Practice, 10*, 868–875.

Frank, G. (1984). The Boulder Model: History, rationale, and critique. *Professional Psychology: Research and Practice, 15*, 417–435.

Frank, J. D. (1979). The present status of outcome studies. *Journal of Consulting and Clinical Psychology, 47*, 310–316.

Frank, J. D. (1981). Reply to Telch. *Journal of Consulting and Clinical Psychology, 49*, 868–875.

Garfield, S. L. (1981). Critical issues in the effectiveness of psychotherapy. In C. E. Walker (Ed.), *Clinical practice of psychology.* New York: Pergamon.

Garfield, S. L., & Kurtz, R. (1976). Clinical psychologists in the 1970s. *American Psychologist, 31*, 1–9.

Garfield, S. L., & Kurtz, R. (1977). A study of eclectic views. *Journal of Consulting and Clinical Psychology, 45*, 78–83.

Goldenberg, H. (1983). *Contemporary clinical psychology* (2nd ed.). Monterey, CA: Brooks/Cole.

Goldfried, M. R. (1980). Toward the delineation of therapeutic change principles. *American Psychologist, 35*, 991–999.

Hess, A. K. (1980). *Psychotherapy supervision: Theory, research, and practice.* New York: Wiley.

Hulse, D., & Jennings, M. L. (1984). Comprehensive

case conceptualization in counseling: A visual integrative technique. *Professional Psychology: Research and Practice, 15*, 251–259.

Imber, S. D., Pilkonis, P. A., & Glanz, L. (1983). Outcome studies in psychotherapy. In C. E. Walker (Ed.), *The handbook of clinical psychology: Theory, research, and practice* (Vol. 1). Homewood, IL: Dow Jones-Irwin.

Kalafat, J., & Neigher, W. D. (1983). Can quality survive in public mental health programs? The challenge for training. *Professional Psychology: Research and Practice, 14*, 90–104.

Kelly, E. L., Goldberg, L. R., Riske, D. W., & Kilkowski, J. M. (1978). Twenty-five years later. *American Psychologist, 33*, 746–755.

Korchin, S. J., & Sands, S. H. (1983). Principles common to all psychotherapies. In C. E. Walker (Ed.), *The handbook of clinical psychology: Theory, research, and practice* (Vol. 1). Homewood, IL: Dow Jones-Irwin.

L'Abate, L., Berger, M., Wright, L., & O'Shea, M. (1979). Training family psychologists: The family studies program at Georgia State University. *Professional Psychology: Research and Practice, 10*, 58–65.

Lambert, M. J. (1980). Research and the supervisory process. In A. K. Hess (Ed.), *Psychotherapy supervision: Theory, research and practice*. New York: Wiley.

Lambert, M. J., & Bergin, A. E. (1983). Therapist characteristics and their contribution to psychotherapy outcome. In C. E. Walker (Ed.), *The handbook of clinical psychology: Theory, research and practice* (Vol. 1). Homewood, IL: Dow Jones-Irwin.

Lazarus, A. A. (1980). Toward delineating some causes of change in psychotherapy. *Professional Psychology: Research and Practice, 11*, 863–870.

Levy, L. H. (1983). Evaluation of students in clinical psychology programs: A program evaluation perspective. *Professional Psychology: Research and Practice, 14*, 497–503.

Matarazzo, R. G. (1978). Research on the teaching and learning of psychotherapeutic skills. In S. L. Garfield & A. E. Bergin (Eds.), *Handbook of psychotherapy and behavior change* (2nd ed.). New York: Wiley.

Moskowitz, S. A., & Rupert, P. A. (1983). Conflict resolution within the supervisory relationship. *Professional Psychology: Research and Practice, 14*, 632–641.

Nelson, G. L. (1978). Psychotherapy supervision from the trainee's point of view: A survey of preferences. *Professional Psychology: Research and Practice, 9*, 539–550.

Norcross, J. C., & Prochaska, J. O. (1982a). A national survey of clinical psychologists: Characteristics and activities. *The Clinical Psychologist, 35*(2), 1, 5–8.

Norcross, J. C., & Prochaska, J. O. (1982b). A national survey of clinical psychologists: Views on training, career choice, and APA. *The Clinical Psychologist, 35*(4), 1, 3–6.

Norcross, J. C., & Prochaska, J. O. (1983). Clinician's theoretical orientations: Selection, utilization,

and efficacy. *Professional Psychology: Research and Practice, 14*, 197–208.

Norcross, J. C., & Stevenson, J. F. (1984). How shall we judge ourselves? Training evaluations in clinical psychology. *Professional Psychology: Research and Practice, 15*, 497–508.

Parloff, M. B. (1980). Psychotherapy research: An anaclitic depression. *Psychiatry, 43*, 279–293.

Patterson, C. H. (1984). Empathy, warmth, and genuineness in psychotherapy: A review of reviews. *Psychotherapy: Theory, Research, Practice, and Training, 21*, 431–438.

Peterson, D. R. (1976). Is psychology a profession? *American Psychologist, 31*, 572–581.

Peterson, D. R., & Bry, B. H. (1980). Dimensions of perceived competence in professional psychology. *Professional Psychology: Research and Practice, 11*, 965–971.

Rachelson, J., & Clance, P. R. (1980). Attitudes of psychotherapists toward the 1970 APA standards for psychotherapy training. *Professional Psychology: Research and Practice, 2*, 261–267.

Robertson, M. (1984). Teaching psychotherapy in an academic setting. *Psychotherapy: Theory, Research, Practice, and Training, 21*, 209–212.

Sank, L. I., & Prout, M. F. (1978). Critical issues for the fledgling therapist. *Professional Psychology: Research and Practice, 9*, 638–645.

Schacht, T. E. (1984). Toward a rational clinical training system. *The Clinical Psychologist, 37*(1), 26–27.

Schaefer, A. B. (1981). Clinical supervision. In C. E. Walker (Ed.), *Clinical practice of psychology*. New York: Pergamon.

Schmidt, J. P. (1979). Psychotherapy supervision: A cognitive-behavioral model. *Professional Psychology: Research and Practice, 10*, 278–284.

Smith, D. S. (1982). Trends in counseling and psychotherapy. *American Psychologist, 37*, 802–809.

Smith, M. L., Glass, G. V., & Miller, T. I. (1980). *The benefits of psychotherapy*. Baltimore, MD: Johns Hopkins Press.

Stevenson, J. F., & Norcross, J. C. (1985). Evaluation activity in psychology training clinics: National survey findings. *Professional Psychology: Research and Practice, 16*, 29–41.

Stricker, G. (1984). Clinical training and accountability in service delivery. *The Clinical Psychologist, 37*(1), 27–28.

Strupp, H. H. (1978). The therapist's theoretical orientation: An overrated variable. *Psychotherapy: Theory, Research, Practice, and Training, 15*, 314–317.

Strupp, H. H., & Hadley, S. W. (1979). Specific versus nonspecific factors in psychotherapy: A controlled study of outcome. *Archives of General Psychiatry, 36*, 1125–1136.

Telch, M. J. (1981). The present status of outcome studies: A reply to Frank. *Journal of Consulting and Clinical Psychology, 49*, 472–478.

Vitulano, L. A., & Copeland, B. A. (1980). Trends in continuing education and competency demonstration. *Professional Psychology: Research and Practice, 11*, 891–897.

Wachtel, P. L. (1977). *Psychoanalysis and behavior*

therapy: Toward an integration. New York: Basic Books.

Wampler, L. D., & Strupp, H. H. (1976). Personal therapy for students in clinical psychology: A matter of faith? *Professional Psychology, 7,* 195–201.

Yogev, S. (1982). An eclectic model of supervision: A developmental sequence for beginning psychotherapy students. *Professional Psychology: Research and Practice, 13,* 236–243.

Zohn, J., & Carmody, T. (1978). Training opportunities in group treatment methods in APA-approved clinical psychology programs. *Professional Psychology: Research and Practice, 9,* 50–62.

CHAPTER 16

Implications of Psychotherapy Outcome Research for Eclectic Psychotherapy

Michael J. Lambert

Research into the effects of therapy now spans a 50-year period. The results of this research, as well as the process of engaging in research, have had a modest impact on the practice of psychotherapy. This impact ranges from the clearer specification of treatment methods in the behavior therapies and person-centered therapy to the identification of treatment methods that are harmful to particular clients. Psychotherapy research will undoubtedly continue to play a role in the development of clinical methods, intervention strategies, and theory development. This chapter focuses on the implications of psychotherapy research for the practice of eclectic psychotherapy. First, several controversial issues, such as the general effects of therapy, are addressed. Then the factors that have been identified as causing therapeutic improvement are discussed. Finally, directions for future research are suggested.

RESEARCH AND THE EFFECTS OF THERAPY: GENERAL ISSUES AND QUESTIONS

This *Handbook* and the many therapy systems highlighted herein are evidence of the growing trend toward eclectic practice. For many reasons, this is an exciting development in the field of psychological interventions. In the first place, eclectic therapies, in general, are very friendly toward research. Eclectic therapy, like psychotherapy research, is preoccupied with practical results—with what is most helpful. Thus the eclectic therapist, like the psychotherapy researcher, maintains a commitment to the pursuit of data wherever they lead, unencumbered by conceptual, doctrinal, or prior professional commitments. Perhaps psychotherapy research has at last found in eclecticism the longed for broad base needed for the integration of research findings. Psychotherapy research may make its strongest contribution to practice in eclectic approaches that combine diverse techniques and concepts into a comprehensive and pragmatic approach to treatment that avoids strong allegiances to narrow theories or schools of thought. There appears to be a natural compatibility and affinity for research in many eclectic approaches, especially in systematic eclecticism. The most likely consequence of this compatibility will be the development of more balanced treatment approaches. The emergence and impact of eclectic approaches through the 1980s may be seen as not only an integration of treatment strategies but as an integration of diverse research findings. What are the implications of psychotherapy research for eclectic therapies? What problems does this research pose?

Figure 1 is an illustration of what empirical studies suggest about psychotherapy outcome. Figure 1 is based on reviews of psychotherapy outcome research (Lambert, Shapiro, & Bergin, 1986). This research literature is extensive, covering decades, and diverse in that it deals with a large range of adult disorders and a variety of research designs, including naturalistic observations, epidemiological studies, comparative clinical trials, and

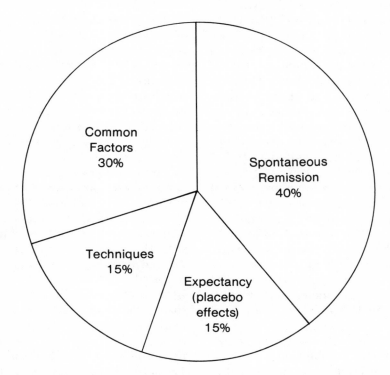

Figure 1. Percent of improvement in psychotherapy patients as a function of therapeutic factors.

a) *Spontaneous Remission*—Those factors that are a part of the client, such as ego strength (and other homeostatic mechanisms), and part of the environment (such as fortuitous events, social support) that aid in recovery regardless of participation in therapy.

b) *Placebo Effects*—That portion of improvement that results from the client's knowledge that he/she is being treated and from the differential credibility of specific treatment techniques and rationale.

c) *Common Factors*—Include a host of variables that are found in a variety of therapies regardless of the therapist's theoretical orientation: empathy, warmth, acceptance, encouragement of risk taking, etc.

d) *Techniques*—Those factors unique to specific therapies, such as biofeedback, hypnosis, systematic desensitization.

experimental analogues. However, no statistical procedures were used to derive the percentages that appear in Figure 1, which appears more precise than is warranted. The figure, nevertheless, conveys several of the conclusions to be drawn in this chapter.

Conclusion 1: A substantial number of outpatients improve without formal psychological intervention. The first conclusion apparent in psychotherapy research is that a portion of patients improve spontaneously without the benefit of psychotherapy. The available literature on spontaneous improvement using any of the research methods currently available to us has been summarized elsewhere (Lambert, 1976; Bergin & Lambert, 1978). The studies reviewed are the best this area has to offer in answer to the question of spontaneous remission rates. The data include subjects who had minimal treatment but not extensive psychotherapy as well as subjects who were, for the most part, untreated. The median spontaneous remission rate for all available studies was 43%, with a range of 18% to 67%. This figure is far from the original estimate of two-thirds suggested by Eysenck (1952) and presently supported by Rachman and Wilson (1980). The figure of 43% represents a rough estimate of spontaneous remission; however, it is an average figure that obscures considerable variation. The evidence reviewed suggests that rates vary from 0% to 90% at follow-up and that very low rates of spontaneous remission do not necessarily mean that the course of treatment will be long and difficult. Thus, low rates do not invariably lead to low predictions of success with treatment. Also, high spontaneous recovery rates for a particular disorder do not always imply that patients referred for treatment will recover quickly.

In general, it seems that the number of organ systems involved in a disorder; the length of time the disorder has persisted; the presence of an underlying personality disorder; and the nature, strength, and quality of social supports, all have a marked effect on spontaneous improvements (Lambert, 1976; Andrews & Tennant, 1978). There would also appear to be differential rates of improvement within the general category of neurosis. There is some evidence to suggest that these rates vary as a function of diagnosis, with depression having the highest remission rates followed by anxiety and hysterical, phobic, obsessive–compulsive, and hypochondriacal disorders (Schapira, Roth, Kerr, & Gurney, 1972).

In addition to diagnosis, it appears that subgroups of neurotics can be identified by the course their problems take. In one of the more well designed studies of spontaneous remission, Mann, Jenkins, and Belsey (1981) studied the twelve-month outcome of 100 neurotic patients attending general practice in England. These researchers were interested in identifying subgroups of neurotics who showed (*a*) a chronic course with no remission, (*b*) an intermittent course, or (*c*) a course marked by rapid recovery without recurrence. The patients were sampled from medium-sized market towns and identified as neurotic by their general practitioners (GPs) as well as a psychiatrist, following screening with the General Health Questionnaire. The patients, 72 women and 18 men, represented a range of ages (15–65 +) and were diagnosed as having anxiety neurosis/phobic neurosis (33%), depressive neurosis (38%), physical disorder of psychogenic origin/tension headache (17%), insomnia (5%), or other condition (6%). The selection procedure was used to make the sample studied representative of the kinds of neurotic patients consulting GPs in England as a whole. Patients were assessed in a post-psychiatric interview, aimed at diagnosis and ratings of stress and social support.

In addition, each time patients consulted a GP, status ratings were made.

The outcome of each patient was classified by two methods: (*a*) "caseness" at follow-up according to interview rating; (*b*) pattern of disorder: Improved, Variable, or Chronic. For example, for those classified as Variable a typical report was "Patchy progress with no sense of overall improvement. There is evidence of remission of symptoms over the year."

Of the 100 cases originally studied, 93 could be successfully followed up. Of these, 79% had shown at least some improvement and 52% were no longer considered "cases" by the end of the year. However, examining the pattern of disorders over the year, the results are perhaps a little less promising. Of the 93 patients, 22 (24%) were classified Improved, 48 (52%) had shown a variable course, and 23 (25%) had shown a chronic course.

It should be noted that although, on the whole, patients did not have formal psychotherapy, 9 were referred for psychotherapy and 52 received psychoactive drugs during the period. The patients also visited the doctor more than the average caseload patient. In trying to identify the variables that predict outcome, Mann et al. (1981) found that in addition to the initial severity of symptoms, the quality of social life and of marital and family life were significant factors in predicting outcome.

The substantial limitations of the research on spontaneous remission have been elaborated on elsewhere (Lambert, 1976; Rachman and Wilson, 1980). Despite these limitations, it is apparent that a number of patients improve without treatment and that the average proportion of those who improve substantially is well below the two-thirds estimate originally made by Eysenck (1952). This is especially true of patients with multiple organ system involvement, a prior history of problems, and an underlying personality disorder. Fortunately treatments (including behavioral treatments) do not need to surpass a two-thirds improvement rate to be considered more effective than the homeostatic mechanisms and fortuitous events that, with the passage of time, bring about improvement. Patients undergoing treatment with psychotherapy should, in general, be expected to surpass the 40% figure unless they are a special subsample of those whose cases are especially complex, with a chronic course. The existing large number of controlled research studies permits a more exact comparison of treated and untreated cases; thus, comparing treated persons with baseline or spontaneous remission estimates is no longer as important as it once was.

Conclusion 2: Psychological treatments are in general beneficial. A wide variety of treatment methods have been empirically tested in controlled outcome studies. Tests of these methods have usually been undertaken by advocates of a particular school of therapy. Ordinarily, however, particular systems of therapy are developed and advocated long before empirical evidence supports their use. As a result we have today perhaps as many as 250 therapies (Herink, 1980), most of which have not been tested. Nevertheless, most of the major therapeutic systems have been tested empirically in controlled research. This research has led to one basic conclusion: Psychotherapy, in general, has been shown to be effective. Positive outcomes have been reported for a wide variety of theoretical positions and technical interventions that have a long history of empirical investigation and support. Much of this research has been summarized in past reviews (Lambert, Shapiro, & Bergin, 1986; Bergin, 1971; Bergin & Lambert, 1978; Meltzoff & Kornreich, 1970) and in recent meta-analytic summaries (Smith, Glass, & Miller, 1980; Andrews & Harvey, 1981; Shapiro & Shapiro, 1982). These reviews represent outcome literature on literally thousands of patients and hundreds of therapists across the western world. The reviews represent data on mildly disturbed persons with specific limited symptoms as well as on severely impaired patients whose disorders are both personally intolerable and socially dysfunctional. The data average changes in these patients across diverse and comprehensive measures of improvement that include a variety of perspectives of importance to patients, patients' families, mental health professionals, and society in general.

A summary of meta-analytic studies of psychotherapy outcome research comparing, for the most part, untreated and treated patients is presented in Table 1.

As can be seen from Table 1, the average effect associated with psychological treatment approaches one standard devia-

tion unit. The first application of meta-analysis to psychotherapy outcome (Smith & Glass, 1977; Smith, Glass, & Miller 1980) addressed the general question of the extent of benefit associated with psychotherapy and found an average effect size of 0.85 standard deviation units over 475 studies comparing treated and untreated groups. This implies that, at the end of treatment, the average treated person is better off than 80% of the untreated sample. By the standards developed by Cohen (1977) for the quantitative evaluation of empirical relations in behavioral science, this is a large effect. The results of a meta-analysis suggest that the assignment to treatment versus control conditions accounts for some 10% of the variation among individuals assessed in

TABLE 1
Meta-Analytic Reviews and the Effects of Therapy

	Patient Diagnosis	Number of Studies	Effect Size
Smith, Glass, & Miller (1980)	Mixed	475	.85
Andrews & Harvey (1981)	Neurotic	81	.72
Landman & Dawes (1982)	Mixed	42	.90
Prioleau, Murdock & Brody (1983)	Mixed	32	.42[a]
Shapiro & Shapiro (1982)	Mixed	143	1.03
Nicholson & Berman (1983)	Neurotic	47[b]	.70
Andrews, Guitar & Howie (1980)	Stuttering	29	1.53-1.65[c]
Blanchard et al. (1980)	Headache	35	% improvement[d]
Quality Assurance Project (1982)	Agoraphobia	25	1.20[c]
Quality Assurance Project (1983)	Depression	200	.65
Steinbrueck, Maxwell, & Howard (1983)	Depression	56	1.22
Dush, Hirt, & Schroeder (1983)	Self Statement Modification	69	.74
Miller and Berman (1983)	Cognitive/Behavior Therapy	38	.83
Stein & Lambert (1984)	Professional vs Paraprofessional	28	.00
Wampler (1982)	Marital Communication	20	.43
Asay, Lambert, Christensen, & Beutler (1984)	Mixed Mental Health	9[e]	.82[c]

[a]Psychotherapy vs. placebo
[b]Number of comparisons
[c]Based on pre–post gains rather than control group comparison
[d]Improved 40–80% in psychological treatments and 20–40% in placebo controls
[e]Number of mental health centers studied

a typical study. Smith, Glass and Miller (1980) illustrated the clinical meaning of this effect size by contrasting effect sizes derived from therapy outcome studies to those achieved in other situations. For example, in elementary schools the effects of nine months of instruction in reading is about 0.67 standard deviation units. The increments in mathematics achievement resulting from the use of computer-based instruction is 0.40 standard deviation units.

The effect sizes produced in psychotherapy can also be compared to those derived from the use of psychoactive medication. For example, Andrews found that treatments of agoraphobics involving graded exposure produced a median effect size of 1.30, whereas antidepressant medication produced an average effect size of 1.10 (Quality Assurance Project, 1982). With depression, the effect sizes produced for antidepressants ranged from 0.81 to 0.40, depending on the type of antidepressant and on patient population. Thus, the effect sizes produced through the application of psychotherapies are typically as large as or larger than those produced by a variety of methods typically employed during medical and educational interventions.

Although the aforementioned data provide one way of examining the effects of therapy and psychosocial treatments on symptoms and adjustment, effect sizes are an abstraction. There is a need to move from the abstraction of an effect size back to the clinical significance of changes summarized in the effect-size statistic. Rosenthal (1983) recognized the need for making effect size more intuitively appealing and suggested that an effect size could be re-expressed as a comparison of the percent of cases considered improved versus the percent of cases considered unimproved. The expression of the 10% figure mentioned by Smith, Glass, and Miller (1980) and noted above, when transformed into percent of persons improved, is illustrated in Table 2, adapted from Rosenthal (1983).

Although researchers and clinicians alike are tempted to minimize the importance of an effect size that accounts for only 10% of the variance, Table 2 clearly shows that it is absurd to label as trivial or modest an effect that is equivalent to increasing a success rate from 34% to 66%. The magnitude of effects demonstrated from research on psychotherapy can be easily calculated and expressed by using the Binomial effect-size display suggested by Rosenthal (1983). This type of data more clearly represents the social importance of treatment procedures. Another method of converting effect-size data into more clinically meaningful statistics was reported by Asay, Lambert, Christensen, and Beutler (1984) in their study of community mental health center clients. In

TABLE 2

The Binomial Effect Size Display for a Correlation Between Assignment to Treatment and Therapeutic Outcome of 0.32[a]

	Treatment Outcome		
Condition	Percent Improved	Percent Not Improved	Sum
Treatment	66	34	100
Control	34	66	100
Sum	100	100	200

Source: Adapted from Rosenthal (1983).
[a]That is, when 10% of the variance is accounted for.

this study the average effect size for the 2,405 clients (seen at nine different locations and exposed to a wide variety of treatments) was 0.92. If one sets a cut-off score of 0.50 effect size as the defining point for considering people truly improved (a rather conservative figure), 66% of the cases may be considered improved, 26% unchanged, and 8% worse. Thus, the effect size can be used to estimate improvement rates.

It is important to reiterate that the changes occurring in patients as a result of therapy are neither trivial nor just cold statistics; rather, they are substantial. A considerable number of people who might be classified as "cases" before treatment would be considered enough improved to no longer be so classified following treatment, although the exact proportion who leave the ranks of the dysfunctional is open to interpretation (Jacobson, Follette, & Revenstorf, 1984). Research on psychotherapy outcome suggests that patients with a variety of problems are helped by many methods that may have been put to the empirical test. The results of psychotherapy outcome research by no means suggest, however, that every participant gains from treatment to a clinically meaningful extent. The results are also compatible with the suggestion some clients may deteriorate during therapy (Lambert, Bergin, & Collins, 1977).

Implication 1: To the extent that eclectic therapies actually do take the best (more effective) methods/interventions from other therapies, they should prove to be as least as effective as non-eclectic treatments that are supported by research and certainly more effective than no-treatment controls. Unfortunately this implication of psychotherapy research has not as yet been put to an adequate empirical test. It has not proved easy to identify the salient techniques from across schools. Thus, a great deal of agreement has not been reached with regard to which treatment

techniques are most effective and which should be chosen for incorporation in eclectic practice. Reviews of eclectic practice tend to support this conclusion. Garfield and Kurtz (1976), Larson (1980), and Norcross and Prochaska (1982) all suggest that there are many kinds of eclectic combinations and that there is great diversity in the techniques selected as "most beneficial" by eclectic therapists. Despite lack of agreement, systematic eclectic approaches that draw heavily on traditional, dynamic, humanistic, and cognitive–behavioral schools would appear to rest on a strong empirical base.

The idea of placebo controls was borrowed from medicine, where the effects of an active chemical agent were contrasted with a pharmacologically inert substance. This contrast makes good sense in medicine, allowing attributions of success to pharmacological agents rather than psychological agents. It makes less sense, however, when extended to psychotherapy research where the effects of treatments and placebos depend upon psychological activity and psychological mechanisms. In psychological treatments the placebo construct has taken on a variety of meanings. For example, Rosenthal and Frank (1956) defined a placebo as an intervention that is therapeutically inert from the standpoint of the *theory* of the therapy studied. As Critelli and Neumann (1984) have pointed out, a problem with this definition is that "virtually every currently established psychotherapy would be considered inert, and therefore a placebo, from the viewpoint of other established theories of cure" (p. 33), making this definition of placebo highly unstable.

In addition, placebos have also been labeled as "nonspecific" factors. This conceptualization, however, raises serious questions about the definition of "nonspecific." For example, once a "nonspecific" is operationally defined, does it then fall outside the domain of a placebo effect? We favor the term "expectancy control" as the most useful definition of a placebo in studies of the psychological therapies. Expectancy controls are those dimensions of the treatment setting that are modified to give the patient the impression that they are receiving a treatment. They are present in placebo control manipulations as well as in bona fide treatments. Some factors included in this term might be false biofeedback, expectations for improvement, persuasion, and attention. These variables should not be viewed as theoretically *inert* nor as *trivial*; indeed, they are a central core of psychological treatments and play an active role in patient improvement (see Critelli & Neuman, 1984, and Wilkins, 1984, for a further discussion of this issue). In addition to expectancy variables and related placebo mechanisms, psychological therapies and many so-called placebo control conditions also contain "common factors." These common factors (to be discussed later) are present in a wide variety of therapies and include such variables as therapist empathy, acceptance and warmth, and therapist encouragement and support.

Common factors and placebos play a central role in the evaluation of psychotherapies. The most effective therapies should be recommended for patients whether their effects are the result of specific techniques, common factors, or placebo mechanisms. Psychotherapy research is often designed to find effects that are incremental to common factors and placebo effects. And, in interpreting this research, it is important to keep in mind that failure to find incremental effects (effects beyond those attributable to common factors and placebo effects) for a specific therapy is not a finding that argues against the efficacy of psychotherapy. It is rather a finding that suggests that the therapy's additive effectiveness has not been demonstrated. This is a critical point because research that is aimed at discovering the incremental effects of therapy has been misinterpreted as suggesting

that therapies are ineffective (e.g., Prioleau et al., 1983; Shepard, 1984) and that therapists are placebologists (Bloch & Lambert, 1985).

Empirical research suggests that patients in placebo control groups typically show greater improvement than patients who are assigned to a wait-list or no-treatment control group. For example, Smith, Glass and Miller (1980) estimated the effect size for placebo controls (that often included common factors as well) to be 0.56. And the partial reanalysis of subsets of the Smith, Glass and Miller data by Andrews and Harvey (1981), and Landman and Dawes (1982), found similar effect sizes (0.55 and 0.58, respectively). This research clearly shows that a variety of methods used as placebo treatment (relaxation, discussion groups, pseudodesensitization, minimum contact attention controls, etc.) yield substantial effect sizes.

The results of several other meta-analytic reviews suggest a similar finding. The Quality Assurance Project (1983) suggested that the placebo effect with depressed patients (measured from pre-test to post-test rather than in relation to no-treatment controls) was 1.07, in contrast to the psychotherapies that achieved an effect size of 1.72. The estimate of improvement in cases of headache by Blanchard et al. (1980) showed the average improvement rate was 35.3% for psychological placebos, and 34.8 for medication placebos, in contrast to an average improvement rate of 60% for psychological treatments. Miller and Berman (1983) found a mean effect size of 0.71 for placebo treatments but found them to be less effective than the purportedly active treatments with which they were compared.

Support for the conclusion that psychotherapy is more effective than placebo can also be found in research studying the durability of treatment effects. Expectancy manipulations should not produce changes that are as enduring as improvement that increases patients' coping skills, a goal of most psychotherapies. If the results of therapies were relatively short term, then they would seem more consistent with a placebo explanation.

Psychotherapy outcome research shows that some control patients improve with the passage of time, that a variety of placebo control procedures produce gains that exceed those in no-treatment controls, and that psychotherapies produce gains that exceed those obtained through the use of placebo controls. Psychotherapists are much more than "placebologists." As noted earlier, however, an important aspect of all therapies is the hope they engender in patients with low morale and dysfunctional symptoms. That many psychological methods offer common factors—such as respect, reassurance, support, modeling, encouragement of risk taking and mastery efforts—is not to suggest that the gains made during treatment are superficial and temporary, but rather that psychotherapists often achieve their effects through psychological mechanisms.

Implication 2: In contrast to purely verbal approaches, the use of specific techniques by many eclectic therapies should enhance their effectiveness through the restoration of morale. Most eclectic therapies, especially technical eclectic systems that present a treatment with high credibility and a reasonable rationale, will be very powerful in mobilizing placebo effects.

Conclusion 3: A variety of factors common across therapies account for a substantial amount of improvement found in psychotherapy patients. Before turning to the contribution of specific techniques, it is important to note the major contribution of therapeutic factors that appear across most psychotherapies (see Figure 1). These so-called common factors may account for most of the gains that result from psychological interventions. It is important, therefore, to note that eclectic

therapies intentionally incorporate many widely accepted qualities of other therapies that are considered essential for therapeutic improvement. What are these common factors, and what empirical support has been found to support their contribution to therapeutic outcome?

Common factors can be conceptualized in a variety of ways. To clarify the differences between them, we have grouped them into Support, Learning and Action categories. These categories were chosen to represent a possible developmental sequence that is presumed to operate in most psychotherapies. The developmental sequence is at least partially mediated through factors common across therapies. The developmental nature of this sequence presumes that the supportive functions precede changes in beliefs and attitudes, which precede attempts to encourage action by the patient.

A variety of common factors attributable to the therapist, therapy procedures and the client are listed in Table 3. As already mentioned, these factors would seem to operate most potently during the process of therapy. Together they provide for a cooperative working endeavor in which the patient's increased sense of trust, security, and safety, along with decreases in tension, threat, and anxiety, lead to changes in conceptualizing his/her problems and ultimately in acting differently by refacing fears, taking risks, and working through problems.

Several studies emphasize the importance of many of these common factors. Among the common factors most frequently studied have been those identified by the client-centered school as "necessary and sufficient conditions" for patient personality change: accurate empathy, positive regard, nonpossessive warmth, and congruence or genuineness. Virtually all schools of therapy accept the notion that these or related therapist relationship variables are important for significant progress in psychotherapy and, in

TABLE 3

A Sequential Listing of Factors Common Across Therapies that Are Associated with Positive Outcomes

Support Factors	Learning Factors	Action Factors
Therapist warmth, respect, empathy, acceptance, genuineness	Insight	Encouragement of facing fears, taking risks, & mastery efforts
	Rationale	
	Cognitive learning	
Positive relationship	Changing expectations for personal effectiveness	Reality testing
Reassurance		Modeling
Identification with therapist	Self-acceptance	Practice
Structure		Working through
Trust		
Catharsis		
Release of tension		

fact, fundamental in the formation of a working alliance (Lambert, 1983).

Studies showing both positive and equivocal support for the hypothesized relationship have been reviewed elsewhere (cf. Levant & Shlien, 1984; Patterson, 1984; Gurman, 1977; Lambert, DeJulio, & Stein, 1978; Mitchell, Bozarth & Krauft, 1977). Reviewers are virtually unanimous in their opinion that the therapist–patient relationship is critical; however, they point out that research support for this position is more ambiguous than was once thought. Studies using client-perceived ratings of the relationship factors, rather than objective raters, obtain consistently more positive results, but the larger correlations with outcome are often between client process ratings and client self-reports of outcome. Nevertheless, there is considerable support for the positive effect these attitudes have on clients.

For example, Miller, Taylor, and West (1980) investigated the comparative effectiveness of various behavioral approaches aimed at helping problem drinkers control their alcohol consumption. Although the focus of the study was on the comparative effects of focused versus broad-spectrum behavior therapy, the authors also collected data on the contribution of thera-

pist empathy to patient outcome. One finding—surprising to the authors and important for our discussion—was the discovery of a strong relationship between empathy and patient outcome obtained from the six-to-eight month follow-up interviews used to assess drinking behavior. Therapist rank on empathy correlated ($r = 0.82$) with patient outcome, thus accounting for 67% of the variance on the criteria. These results argue for the importance of therapist communicative skills even with behavioral interventions. They were also presented in a context where variations in specific techniques did not prove to have a similar powerful effect on outcome.

Another approach in understanding the contribution of the therapist to effective outcome has involved the use of behavioral or adjective checklists filled out by clients following their therapeutic contacts. Lorr (1965), for example, had 523 psychotherapy patients describe their therapists on 65 different statements. A subsequent factor analysis identified five factors: understanding, accepting, authoritarian (directive), independence-encouraging, and critical–hostile. Scores on these descriptive factors were correlated with improvement ratings, with the result that client ratings of understanding and accepting correlated most highly with client- and therapist-rated improvement.

In a more recent study, Cooley and Lajoy (1980) attempted to replicate the Lorr study. In addition, they studied the relationship between therapist ratings of themselves and of outcome, as well as the relationship of discrepancies between patient and therapist ratings and outcome ratings. The patients were 56 adult community mental health outpatients who had been treated by one of eight therapists at the clinic.

As with the Lorr study, patient ratings of therapist understanding and acceptance correlated most highly with client-rated outcome. On the other hand, when self-ratings of therapist attributes were compared to therapist-rated patient outcome, the correlations were insignificant, suggesting that therapists did not perceive their personal attributes as a factor influencing therapeutic outcome.

Patients frequently attribute their success in treatment to personal qualities of the therapists. That these personal qualities bear a striking resemblance to each other across studies and methodologies is evidence that they are highly important in psychotherapy outcome. This notion was also emphasized by Lazarus (1971) in an uncontrolled follow-up study of 112 patients whom he had seen in therapy. These patients were asked to provide information about the effects of their treatment and the durability of improvement, and their perceptions of the therapeutic process and characteristics of the therapist. With regard to therapist characteristics, those adjectives used to describe Lazarus most often were sensitive, gentle, and honest. Patients clearly felt the personal qualities of the therapist were more important than specific technical factors, about which there was little agreement.

In their study comparing behavioral and more traditional insight-oriented therapy, Sloane et al. (1975) reported a similar finding and elaborated upon the place of therapist variables in positive outcome. Although they failed to find a relationship between judges' ratings of therapists' behavior during the third therapy session (on empathy) and later outcome, they did find that patients tended to emphasize the personal qualities of their therapists as causing personality change. These authors administered a 32-item questionnaire four months following treatment. The items included statements descriptive of both behavior therapy techniques (e.g., training in muscle relaxation) and dynamic therapy techniques (e.g., explaining the relationship of one's problem to early life events). In addition, some characteristics thought to be common in all forms of therapy were included. Each item was rated on a five-point scale.

Surprisingly, perhaps, the successful patients in both therapies placed primary importance on more or less the same items. In fact, 70% or more of the successful patients listed the following items as "extremely important" or "very important" in causing their improvement:

1. The personality of the therapist
2. His helping you to understand your problems
3. Encouragement to gradually practice facing the things that bothered you
4. Being able to talk to an understanding person
5. Helping you to greater self-understanding

None of the items regarded as "very important" by the majority of either patient group described techniques specific to one therapy (although item 3 is, in general, approached more systematically in behavior therapies). The foregoing studies suggest that, at least from the patient's point of view, effective treatment was due to factors associated with relationship variables, self-understanding, and active involvement.

The notion that common factors are important in producing positive outcomes is also supported by the failure to find differential outcomes in studies that compare therapies that use highly divergent techniques. This finding has been documented in several reviews (Bergin & Lambert, 1978; Luborsky, Singer, & Luborsky, 1975).

Typical of research in this area is a recent comparative study reported by Pilkonis, Imber, Lewis, and Rubinsky (1984), who compared the outcome of patients undergoing individual, group, or conjoint psychotherapy. For an average of 27 sessions, 64 outpatients were assigned one of these treatment modalities offered by experienced private clinicians. This study is probably the first simultaneous comparison of these commonly used treatment modalities. The therapists were nine (three for each modality) M.D. or Ph.D. level practitioners with at least seven years of post-doctoral experience, who were either dynamic or humanistic in orientation. The patients were diagnosed as neurotic or personality disordered, willing to participate in conjoint therapy if required, and living with another adult who would agree to act as an informant in the study.

The outcome of the study at termination and follow-up was based on a variety of measures tapping global and specific improvement as well as dimensions that were thought to be most likely to change in a particular treatment modality. Thus, a scale measuring self-awareness/self-exploration (thought to be a primary target of individual therapy), scales tapping interpersonal anxiety and control in interpersonal relations (thought to be affected by group therapy), and a scale aimed at tapping the family climate and ability to solve problems (thought to be sensitive to conjoint therapy) were given to all patients in this study. Data regarding outcome were collected from the patient, a significant other, and the therapist.

The results of this study showed little unique effect of treatment modality on patient outcome. Despite the fact that patients improved on 14 of 15 measures during the treatment period, and maintained these gains during the 8-month follow-up, effects could not be attributed to therapeutic modality. There were clear indications, however, that outcome was affected by patient social class, by degree of disturbance, and by individual differences between the therapists.

Although the results do not reflect a comparison of therapist theoretical orientations, they favor an interpretation of slight effects for treatment techniques and processes related to very different treatment approaches. A common-factor explanation seems to be most defensible.

Similar conclusions can be drawn from several other areas of well developed research. An area that has seen extensive experimental analysis of treatment effectiveness via dismantling studies that attempt to sort out the unique contribution of specific techniques is the cognitive–behavioral approach to depression. A series of studies was based on Rehm's (1977) self-control formulation of depression, whereby depressed persons are viewed as manifesting maladaptive self-monitoring, self-evaluation (including self-attribution) and self-reinforcement behavior. Encouraging results were obtained by Fuchs and Rehm (1977) and Rehm, Fuchs, Roth, Kornblith, and Romano (1979), for the treatment as a whole. However, when broken down into constituent components in a study by Rehm, Kornblith, O'Hara, Lamparski, Romano, and Volkin (1981), the results did not favor the additive effects of specific procedures. Surprisingly, the self-evaluation and self-reinforcement components were found to add little or no additional efficacy to the impact of self-monitoring alone. A subsequent study by Kornblith, Rehm, O'Hara, and Lamparski (1983) included a didactic condition lacking the instigational push of homework assignments, in addition to the full treatment, a condition lacking only the self-reinforcement element, and an active control treatment—problem-oriented psychodynamic group psychotherapy. All four treatments were equally effective, and the authors of this very carefully conducted and well-reported study were driven by their findings to ponder anew the commonalities among seemingly diverse treatments of depression:

Looking across cognitive and behavioral therapy procedures for treating depression generally, it is apparent that these packages have at least three important characteristics in common. First, they each present a concrete rationale. This rationale includes a vocabulary for describing and defining the problems of depression in ways that may be very new to participants. Rationales also provide a vocabulary for describing the mechanisms of change. Second, all of these therapy programs are highly structured. They provide clear plans for producing change in a logical sequence of steps. Third, all of these programs provide feedback and support so that participants can clearly see changes in their own behavior and are reinforced for these changes. . . . Research . . . needs to look more closely at characteristics of packages such as these, rather than merely at details of procedure or abstract differences in underlying theories. (p. 525)

Kornblith et al., (1983) suggest that even their group psychotherapy control condition, by virtue of the problem-oriented approach it followed, was an active, problem-solving process aimed at the current life situation of each participant, using problem-solving techniques such as redefining the problem and listing alternatives.

Similar conclusions were reached by Zeiss, Lewinshohn, and Munoz (1979). These authors compared interpersonal-skills training, a reinforcement-theory program to increase pleasant activities and the enjoyment of potentially pleasant activities, and a cognitive approach to the modification of depressive thoughts. They found that all treatments were associated

with reduction in depression, without any differential changes specific to aspects of the patient's problems targeted by the three treatments. Zeiss et al. (1979) note the improvements also recorded by the waiting list group and cite Frank's (1974) demoralization hypothesis as the most parsimonious explanation for the results. These researchers suggest that the impact of treatment was due to the enhancement of self-efficacy via training self-help skills, thus increasing expectations of mastery and perception of greater positive reinforcement as a function of the patient's greater skillfulness. Therefore, the common components of therapy for depression emerge as important. On the other hand, it should be noted that the experience level of the therapists was not high (counseling psychology graduate students and M.A.'s), and there was no monitoring of the therapists' contributions to therapy; thus treatment delivery according to the design is not assured. In addition, patients' and therapists' perceptions of curative factors were not studied, so that the attribution of causality to them is purely hypothetical.

Despite the importance to outcome of the therapeutic relationship and other common factors, it is becoming increasingly clear that the attributes of the patient, as well as the therapist, play an important part in creating the quality of the therapeutic relationship and in determining the outcome of the psychotherapy. Strupp (1980a, 1980b, 1980c, 1980d) reported a series of case studies in which two patients were seen by the same therapist in time-limited psychotherapy. In each case, one of the patients was seen as having a successful outcome, whereas the other was considered to be a treatment failure. These case reports were part of a larger study that used extensive outcome measures and an analysis of patient–therapist interactions during the process of therapy. In each instance the therapist was working with college males who were suffering from anxiety, depression, and social withdrawal. Although each therapist was seen as having good interpersonal skills, a different relationship developed with the two patients. In all four cases the patients who had successful outcomes appeared more willing and able to have a meaningful relationship with the therapist, whereas the patients who did not do well in therapy did not relate well to the therapist and had a tendency to keep the interaction at a more superficial level.

In Strupp's analysis, the contributions of other therapists remained relatively constant throughout therapy, and the difference in outcome could be attributed to patient factors, such as aspects of the patients' personality make-up, including ego organization, maturity, motivation, and ability to become productively involved in therapy. Strupp (1980b) adds:

Given the "average expectable" atmosphere created by a person functioning in the therapeutic role, that is, a person who is basically empathic and benign, the key determinants of a particular therapeutic outcome are traceable to characteristics of the patient that have been described: If the patient is a person who, by virtue of his past life experience, is capable of human relatedness and therefore is amenable to learning, mediated within that context, the outcome, even though the individual may have suffered traumas, reverses, and other vicissitudes, is likely to be positive . . . if, on the other hand, his early life experiences have been so destructive that human relatedness has failed to acquire a markedly positive valence, and elaborate neurotic and characterological malfunctions have created massive barriers to intimacy (and therefore to "therapeutic learning"), chances are that psychotherapy either results in failure or at best in very modest gains. (p. 716)

In their study of transference interpretations in psychoanalysis and psychotherapy, Luborsky, Bachrach, Graff, Pulver, and Christoph (1979) discuss relationship factors in terms of the patient's experiencing a helping relationship. In their view, the experiences of a helping relationship may be a function of the "object relations repertoire" that the patient brings to treatment, or of the therapist's ability to impart that experience to the patient, or some combination of the two. In considering the impact of the therapeutic relationship on outcome, these authors hypothesized that the patient's ability to experience a positive along with a negative component of helping relationships may be necessary for the patient to derive benefit from interpretations. Following this line of reasoning, the therapeutic relationship, as defined by the involvement of both therapist and patient, has a major impact on the acceptance of in-therapy interpretations and on the outcome of therapy itself.

Implication 3: Eclectic treatments should not only concentrate on integrating specific techniques but emphasize the application of factors common across therapies. These common factors are those that are embodied in the bonding and intimacy of a healthy human relationship as well as those that lead to cognitive reconstruction or learning mediated by the human encounter (self-acceptance), and those that are a part of encouraging autonomy and action. An over-emphasis on "using the best techniques" could result in a failure to foster and use the general factors that are central in therapies that work.

Fortunately there is considerable evidence that many eclectic approaches (cf. Garfield; Beutler; Fuhriman, Paul, & Burlingame; Lazarus; and Prochaska & DiClemente, all in this volume) are highly sensitive to the importance and pragmatics of common factors. Nevertheless, it is disheartening to note that some eclectic approaches seem to ignore the overwhelming evidence that favors the interpretation that many of the fundamental effective ingredients of psychotherapy consist of factors inherent in the style, attitudes and values of the therapist. To the extent that eclectic therapies merely embrace the use of multiple techniques to the exclusion of common factors, such therapies can be expected to fail to achieve results superior to traditional therapies.

Conclusion 4: Specific techniques can be selected on the basis of their peculiar effectiveness. As suggested by Figure 1 (p. 437), some of the improvements made in patients during psychological intervention are the result of specific techniques and interventions. Given the improvement that results from homeostatic mechanisms, fortuitous events, social supports, expectations, and common factors, there is, in general, little room for clear demonstration of the power and differential impact of specific techniques. Nevertheless, there is some evidence for the usefulness of particular methods with particular problems. We will now review the empirical status of some of these methods.

Traditional reviewing procedures of comparative studies have not resulted in conclusions that favor the superiority of a particular therapy across the broad categories of anxiety, depression, and interpersonal problems to which they have been applied (Meltzoff & Kornreich, 1970; Luborsky, Singer, & Luborsky, 1975; Bergin & Lambert, 1978). The newer quantitative reviews based on meta-analysis have been more likely to reflect small differential outcomes, albeit with little consistency. The results of these reviews have been summarized by Lambert, Shapiro, and Bergin (1986) with the conclusion that there are few clear, replicated instances of differential outcome. For example, Smith, Glass, and Miller (1980), based on their review of over 450 studies, concluded that differences among therapies were slight or non-existent. However, this finding was reached only after the relatively large effect sizes that had been

reported for the behavior therapies were reduced because they were based on dependent measures that were judged to be reactive to experimental demand characteristics.

Data from several additional meta-analytical reviews—Shapiro and Shapiro (1982); Nicholson and Berman (1983); Dush et al. (1983); Miller and Berman (1983); and the Quality Assurance Project (1983)—tend to yield a small but consistent advantage for cognitive and behavioral methods over traditional verbal and relationship-oriented therapies. However, the strength of this conclusion is limited by the shortcomings of data aggregation techniques and the nature of past research. There are reasons, therefore, to believe in both the theory of equal effects of therapies and the notion of superior effects of cognitive and behavior therapies.

For instance, a problem in most of the comparisons in meta-analytic reviews is that they are cross-study comparisons in which behavior therapy in one study is compared with verbal therapy from another study. In this situation, many variables besides treatment modality also differ across studies, making these comparisons less conclusive than comparisons in which the compared treatments are offered *within* a given study. Thus, the most important comparisons in meta-analytic reviews are those revealed from within-study comparisons. These studies are much more likely to hold numerous variables constant while comparing one type of therapy with another. The data from within-study comparison suggest some advantage for cognitive and behavioral therapies over dynamic–humanistic ones.

To examine this issue more carefully, let us consider Shapiro and Shapiro's (1982) extensive meta-analysis, which focused exclusively on studies comparing two or more active treatments with control conditions. In consequence, their data contained more replicated comparisons between treatment methods than found in the Smith et al. (1980) review, and permitted more definitive statements concerning the comparative efficacy of treatments. Based on an examination of 143 studies, Shapiro and Shapiro (1982) found that cognitive and various behavioral treatments yielded more favorable outcomes (1.00 and 1.06 effect sizes, respectively) than other treatments with which they were compared, whereas dynamic and humanistic therapies tended to yield inferior outcomes (effect size 0.40).

Like Smith et al., however, Shapiro and Shapiro also attributed the larger effect sizes to strong biases in the behavioral and cognitive literature toward analog studies, mild cases, and highly reactive criteria. They stated that the treatments and cases studied were unrepresentative of clinical practice but very representative of the simple experiments on those techniques that are frequently conducted in university settings.

Again, these criticisms have validity, but they can be overdone in a way that does not do justice to cognitive and behavioral interventions. The verbal therapies, with presumably clinical populations, did not fare well in this analysis. And breakdowns of the outcome tables showed large effect sizes across different symptoms and levels of severity for behavioral and cognitive methods.

An interesting sidelight of the Shapiro and Shapiro report was the finding of a significantly larger effect size for cognitive therapy over systematic desensitization. This conclusion has, however, been challenged by yet another meta-analyses.

Miller and Berman (1983) compared behavior therapy with other therapies, mainly behavioral. They defined cognitive behavior therapy in terms of a rationale requiring patients to examine maladaptive beliefs, recognizing that such treatments vary in the extent of behavioral techniques employed, and omitting the therapies based only on the repetition of self-statements. The review was limited to patients with so-called "clinical complaints," excluding artificially induced problems such as the ability to keep one hand in a bucket of ice water. They did not exclude students with relatively minor, albeit non-artificially induced, problems such as test and public speaking anxiety; indeed 23 of the 48 studies included in the review were of student volunteers rather than self-referred clients. The procedures followed were quite similar to those of Smith et al. (1980) except that the *study* rather than the individual measure of effect was used as the unit of analysis, and cognitive behavior therapies that differed in their emphasis on behavioral techniques were accorded their own effect sizes within an analysis contrasting such treatments.

In comparisons with untreated groups, cognitive behavior therapies secured a mean effect size of 0.83 post-treatment (38 studies) and 0.63 at follow-up (18 studies). Untreated group data were obtained by pooling all control groups after a preliminary analysis of 15 studies that used both waiting list and placebo control groups had revealed similar effect-size estimates in comparisons with the two types of control groups. Comparisons with other therapies yielded a differential effect size of 0.21 at the end of treatment (36 studies) and 0.24 at follow-up (9 studies). Further analysis indicated that the superiority of cognitive behavior therapy to no-treatment was confined to self-report and outside-observer measures, with a nonsignificant effect size difference of 0.27 for physiological measures (7 studies). The superiority of cognitive behavior therapy to other treatments was confined to self-report measures, with an effect-size difference (over 35 studies) of 0.21. No reliable differences were found between therapies high and low on behavioral techniques. Turning to the question of differential efficacy for specific problems, the meta-analysis found no reliable evidence for this, although effect sizes for depression appeared somewhat larger than for most other problems.

A subsequent analysis (Berman, Miller, & Massman, 1984), using a larger sample of studies, showed no difference between cognitive and desensitization therapies (E.S. difference 0.06). It also revealed that the larger effect sizes for cognitive therapy occurred in studies conducted by investigators having an allegiance to that method. Finally, and perhaps most sobering for eclectic practitioners, the combination of desensitization with a cognitive method did not increase effects beyond that obtainable by either treatment alone. These results suggest that there may be important common factors in these two modes of treatment that account for the equal outcomes, and that the common-factor explanation is not limited to comparisons with verbal expressive therapies.

A similar finding was reported by Dush et al. (1983) in their review of 69 studies of a form of cognitive therapy involving self-statement modification. Each study contained at least one treatment group using self-statement modification (Meichenbaum, 1977) with adults, compared with at least one placebo or no-treatment group, and each used subjects with some clinically relevant problem, although half the subjects were recruited volunteers from college classes. Seventeen of these studies were also included by Miller and Berman (1983), as they used cognitive restructuring methods alongside self-statement modification. The "typical" treatment comprised some five sessions over four weeks and included at least three treatment features alongside self-statement modification, of which cognitive restructuring (33 studied) and modeling (32 studies) were the most widespread. Methods of coding and analysis closely resembled those of Smith et al. (1980).

The findings of this meta-analysis included a mean effect size for self-statement modification of 0.74 over 93 comparisons with untreated groups, and 0.52 over 54 comparisons with placebo groups. Other treatments obtained a mean effect size of 0.49 in comparison with untreated groups, and 0.44 in comparison with placebo groups.

Comparisons between self-statement modification and other treatments yielded no clear differences. Although systematic desensitization came off almost half a standard deviation worse than self-statement modification when contrasted with no-treatment controls, this difference vanished from comparisons with placebo controls. Studies involving relaxation training yielded weak results for both relaxation and self-statement modification. Contrasts with "other" cognitive therapies and "other" behavioral therapies (admittedly a pair of vague terms including diverse methods) yielded essentially similar effects for self-statement modification and the alternate, active treatment.

The foregoing meta-analyses reveal a mixed picture. There is a strong trend toward no differences between techniques in amount of change produced, which is counter-balanced by repeated efficacy among themselves.

Among the methodological advances that have special implications for the practice of eclectic treatments is the use of "dismantling" studies to identify the active components of a treatment procedure (Gottman & Markman, 1978). The dismantling strategy involves the controlled comparison of groups of participants undergoing the complete treatment with groups undergoing portions of the treatment. This strategy allows for the identification of elements of the treatment that are most essential in facilitating improvement. Since eclectic treatments ordinarily combine several techniques, such a strategy may ultimately illuminate those techniques that are necessary and sufficient for improvement.

To date, this design has been effectively used with behavioral and cognitive procedures and eclectic combinations of these procedures in the treatment of obesity, smoking, alcohol abuse, social skills training (nonassertiveness), sleep disorders, headache, depression, a number of anxiety-based problems, marital and sexual dysfunctions.

Evidence for specificity can be found for treatments of insomnia. Borkovec (1982), for example, suggests that relaxation and biofeedback are consistently effective, even when compared with credible placebos and counterdemand instructions. Muscle-tension release is critical for improvement. Evidence from the most rigorous studies suggests that muscle-tension release is important, although the absence of a relationship between in-treatment decline in physiological activity due to relaxation training and sleep outcomes argues against the notion that autonomic hyperactivity or its reduction are involved in the mechanism of this treatment. One possibility is that the site of effect for relaxation treatment may be cognitive. Changes in the reported frequency of intrusive thoughts at bedtime have been found to parallel improvement in reported sleep onset latency.

Research on the treatment of headache has proved more perplexing. Different types of headache have been thought to be responsive to specific treatments; for example, biofeedback (hand warming) with migraine and relaxation with tension headache. Research on the treatment of headache has been reviewed by Blanchard, Andrasik, Anler, Teders, and O'Keefe (1980). With respect to muscle-tension headache, these authors conclude from a meta-analytic comparison that relaxation and EMG biofeedback are equally effective. Experiments designed to identify the critical ingredients of EMG biofeedback have found that training procedures that increase or hold constant the level of muscle activity are just as effective as the EMG-reducing biofeedback originally conceived as a treatment for the excessive muscle activity believed to characterize tension headache. In addition, most studies have failed to obtain a correlation between EMG changes during biofeedback sessions and symptom reduction, with some participants reporting improvement in the absence of EMG changes.

A particular problem for the field has arisen from the surprising effectiveness of hand-*cooling* (i.e., thermal biofeedback in which the participant believes that the hand temperature is rising when in fact it is falling), which was originally introduced as a credible placebo control procedure! Of course, it remains possible that self-efficacy and increased awareness of the antecedents of headache, as invoked by Blanchard and Andrasik (1982) in relation to tension-headache treatment, could apply to migraine. It is clear from these authors' review that evidence for the originally presumed mechanism of thermal biofeedback, whereby biofeedback leads to decreased sympathetic activity, is patchy and unconvincing and that some common factor such as relaxation, or self-efficacy is the mechanism leading to a positive outcome.

Despite the possible important contributions of common factors, there is little evidence to support the use of treatment methods that do not directly intervene with the patient's physiological responding. Thus, treatment that may also have a specific impact include hypnosis, self-hypnosis, and autogenic training. There is little support for the use of verbal/dynamic interventions with these problems (Lambert, 1982). Along with cognitive strategies, these interventions could, however, play a role in increasing the change in lifestyle or habitual ways of coping that make the continued use of relaxation techniques most likely.

Implication 4: Eclectic therapies are most likely to capitalize on the contribu-

tions of specific techniques to effective outcome and should be recommended for practice. Since there is some evidence for the usefulness of particular techniques, eclectic therapies may be effective either because clinicians with this orientation are flexible enough to use techniques that directly address a problem or because eclectics are more open to the value of referral to clinicians who are skilled in the use of a particular technique. In either case, because of its flexibility in use of technique, eclectic therapy may be less likely to produce negative outcomes in patients.

One other implication of research on specific techniques is the serious demand it puts on eclectic practitioners. Of course the effective use of all therapies is highly demanding. But the effective use of many methods, the timing of their use, and the continued up-dating on techniques is especially demanding for the eclectic. This *Handbook* responds in part to the need to organize and systemize the overly demanding task of the eclectic therapist.

FUTURE RESEARCH ON ECLECTIC PSYCHOTHERAPY

Although most eclectic therapies are empirically based, their foundation has been borrowed from research work on separate therapy schools. Very little research has been produced by the emerging systematic eclectic approaches. For example, neither Garfield nor Beutler, who are both recognized figures in the field of psychotherapy research, has as yet reported on the effects of the eclectic system each advocates.

According to Garfield (Chapter 5), "Unfortunately, no systematic research has been conducted on the approach. . . . The only evidence that exists to support the efficacy of this approach are clinical observations and anecdotes, and this is not really adequate." Beutler, on the other hand, has initiated several studies on his matching hypothesis and has begun to study interventions according to his theory of systematic eclecticism. Despite this, Beutler has encountered significant difficulty in applying his scheme effectively and has suggested the need to develop better operational definitions of both relevant patient dimensions and matching strategies.

The work of Fuhriman, Paul, and Burlingame (Chapter 8) on Eclectic Time-Limited Therapy developed partially out of their interest in conducting outcome research. Like many of the eclectic approaches, theirs was based on a careful evaluation of empirical literature but is so recent in its development that a substantial core of empirical support has not as yet developed. To date, these authors have reported a single study on the effects of this therapy. This study contrasted the effects of experienced and inexperienced therapists who were undergoing different kinds of training in the approach. The results of this study suggested that the eclectic, brief treatment model could be effectively used by both experienced and less experienced counselors, although the clients of experienced therapists seemed to be more improved at treatment termination. The different kinds of training in the use of eclectic therapy did not result in differential effectiveness (for those who remained in treatment), although the clients of the untrained therapists had a higher rate of premature termination and dissatisfaction with treatment.

This was an interesting and well designed study that might serve as a model for the kinds of studies that need to be generated on eclectic psychotherapies. Unfortunately, the study undertaken may not be ideal as an initial study on the effectiveness of therapy. There was no expectancy, traditional treatment, or no-treatment control group with which to compare this eclectic therapy. Furthermore, the data so far published from this study do not allow one to determine the size of treatment effects or the percentage of patients that might be considered improved. Even if these data were provided, the careful selection of patients for the brief therapy offered may render the results uninformative when compared with studies of other counseling center populations who undergo traditional treatment.

Two other approaches mentioned in this *Handbook* have reported some research on their therapy. Lazarus (Chapter 3) has suggested that his approach is not intended to be added to the hundreds in existence but rather is an attempt to be at the cutting edge of clinical effectiveness by incorporating the findings of current research and practice. Despite this, he does report two uncontrolled studies of his own patients with the general conclusion that: "In terms of overall statistics, during the past seven or eight years, more than 75% of the people who have consulted me have achieved their major treatment goals."

Despite his commendable efforts at data collection and follow-up, it is disappointing to see so little systematic effort directed toward a controlled investigation of the effects of a multimodal therapy that purports to be at the "cutting-edge" of therapy. What kind of improvement rate can one expect as a result of this application of technical eclecticism? Are there patients for whom this approach is more appropriate? Would this eclectic approach offer clients anything more than the cognitive behavioral therapy to which it is most indebted? These and a host of similar questions remain unanswered at this time.

Related questions can be raised with regard to the eclectic approach advocated by Prochaska and DiClemente (Chapter 6). The transtheoretical approach, however, was directed toward the development of a "researchable" system that would result in convincing and useful outcome data. As compared with other eclec-

tic systems, it rests on a more substantial base of empirical research, derived from studies carried out on its particular effects. Unfortunately, the major portion of this research was undertaken on a limited sample of clients who were trying to give up smoking.

Even so, the outcome research initiated has favored the transtheoretical approach based on the action manual aimed at facilitating self-change. The effects of this manual, with and without a therapist present, proved more effective at helping people quit smoking than a traditional self-change approach not based on the principles and assumptions of the transtheoretical approach. The initial step toward evaluation of the transtheoretical approach must be followed by systematic research aimed at sorting out the advantages, if any, of this approach over single school or other eclectic procedures.

Despite the openness of eclectic theorists to knowledge derived from clinical practice and basic research, the eclectic approach has not yet produced a distinguishable body of research that supports its claims of superior efficacy. Therefore, in the short run, projects aimed at demonstrating the effectiveness of eclectic approaches are sorely needed. Since eclectic theorists' most persuasive argument for effectiveness lies in their claim for flexibility in dealing with a variety of patient problems, an initial study would call for the random assignment of patients to practitioners who advocate treatment within the confines of a single-school approach and to practitioners of an eclectic approach. Such a study would need to make recordings of the therapies offered in order to clarify the nature of therapeutic interventions.

The central disadvantage of this research is that it repeats the comparative, polarizing pattern that has characterized past comparative research. Unfortunately, this research may lead to the solidification of yet another therapy school rather than to agreement about the most effective intervention practices. Thus, the consequences of such research may go against the basic values of an eclectic approach. Given the large number of practitioners who are already persuaded that eclectic practice is most effective, a demonstration of this "fact" may not be needed.

Judging from the authors' comments in this *Handbook*, most would probably feel that such a comparative study is premature, that these systems are not yet well enough developed. Yet, one or two of the better developed systems could undergo evaluation at this time (e.g., multimodal therapy). The best way to test the effectiveness of eclectic therapies would be in a situation that limits selection of patients and thus taxes the adaptability of the single-school approach.

Beyond comparative studies that contrast eclectic treatment with single-school treatments or broad category approaches (e.g., dynamic or humanistic), there are a host of other studies that seem desirable. Since eclectic approaches are ordinarily based on well established treatments, experiments that focus on the use of no-treatment control or placebo-control groups cannot be recommended. Rather, it would seem most desirable to concentrate on the matching hypothesis developed by Beutler (Chapter 4) or the matching strategy of Prochaska and DiClemente (Chapter 6). Research on both of these strategies may bring us closer to prescriptive treatment, an appealing possibility.

From the point of view of past research, the developmental approach offered by Prochaska and DiClemente may be most promising for future research. For one thing, matching strategies like the one offered by Beutler have not been supported by past research (Berzins, 1977). This "matching" research, which has focused to a large degree on client personality variables and interpersonal orientation, has not resulted in a reliable

scheme that could be employed to enhance outcome. While Beutler's system may be an improvement over past systems, especially with regard to highlighting client–therapist values and the classification of treatments, it still seems less likely than Prochaska and DiClemente's developmental approach to result in a useful classification system that will enhance outcome. This conclusion is based primarily on the notion that assessing the stage or developmental position of people who are coming for help seems more likely to be directly related to treatment outcome than are diagnosis and personality traits. Developmental stage is not as far removed from the change process as personality variables and broad coping strategies.

Future research would concentrate on the matching strategies suggested by the work of Norcross, and Prochaska and DiClemente (Chapters 1 & 6) until refinement results in a more meaningful system.

Another possibility would be to combine the developmental approach advocated by Prochaska and DiClemente with the matching strategy advocated by Beutler (Chapter 4) in a research design that emphasized both current stages of change with more general coping strategies, treated with therapies that are considered optimal and minimal for both. Although such integration may prove needlessly complex, it may well be that this level of complexity is required to demonstrate superior efficacy for an eclectic approach.

Future research on eclectic therapy must come to terms with the difficulties of sorting out causal treatment factors. Although dismantling strategies may be helpful in this regard, the flexibility of eclectic treatment and integration of multiple techniques will make progress slow. However, much recent research has been directed toward the identification of effective treatments through the clearer specification of treatment procedures prescribed and directed by treatment manuals. Through the use of the manuals, therapies are being more systematically operationalized and applied.

The major advantage of treatment manuals is that they (1) standardize (to a greater degree) the treatment being offered; (2) provide a method of training therapists to offer a standard treatment; (3) allow for the development of rating scales to judge whether a therapy is being properly offered; and (4) allow researchers another method of sorting out the common factors from the unique factors associated with specific treatment approaches. The development and use of treatment manuals by the Depression Collaborative Study illustrates the possibilities of manuals and associated rating scales in psychotherapy research.

The NIMH project (Waskow, Parloff, Hadley, & Autry, 1983) involves the comparison of Cognitive Therapy (CT), Interpersonal Therapy (IPT), and Clinical Management (CM; a standardized approach to pharmacotherapy) with adult outpatient nonbipolar, nonpsychotic depression. Each of the therapies are offered in each of three different settings. The manuals have been used to guide the selection of therapists; to train therapists; to develop various rating scales to assess the effects of training; to test the degree to which the therapy offered conforms to the manual; and to measure the degree to which therapies can be discriminated. Eventually the design of the project may allow researchers to see if a particular treatment (of those considered) is more efficacious and works best with specific types of individuals, and, most relevant to our discussion, whether a specific set of therapy techniques adds anything to the factors that are common across therapies.

Although the outcome data are not yet published, there are some preliminary data dealing with the identification of therapeutic operations that are unique to a given treatment, as well as shared by treatments.

One of the therapies used in the Depression Collaborative Project is Interpersonal Psychotherapy (IPT) based on a manual developed by Klerman et al. (1979). IPT is an individual psychotherapy devised for depressed patients and aimed at the alleviation of depressive symptoms and improvement in interpersonal functioning. It is eclectic, borrowing techniques from many forms of verbal therapy. Four problem areas are identified for treatment, with specific strategies aimed at each area: pathological grief, role disputes, role transitions, and interpersonal deficits. The strategies include reassurance, a nonjudgmental attitude, social manipulation, role playing, rehearsal and teaching problem-solving skills. Therapists do not give homework but tend to be much more active than therapists offering long-term insight-oriented treatments. The manual helps therapists anticipate problems and issues in depression and focus on a resolution of these problems. Thus, the therapy moves more rapidly into focal issues with a theory of the steps necessary for improvement. For example, the manual discusses ways of handling abnormal grief through methods aimed at expression of feeling, classification of problems and reactions, mourning the loss, developing new relationships, and termination of therapy.

DeReubis et al. (1982) investigated the similarities and differences in the rated behavior of therapists using Cognitive Therapy (CT) or Interpersonal Therapy (IPT) in the treatment of depressed patients. Using a 48-item rating scale applied by 12 raters who listened to 4 sessions of therapy (two from each school), they found 34 items to discriminate between the schools. Twenty-four of the items were expected to discriminate between therapies (based on judgments of whether an item was characteristic of the CT or IPT modality); of these items 22 discriminated. However, 12 of the remaining 24 items that were thought to measure common factors were also found to differentiate the therapies. Thus, the therapies were differentiated in almost every case where it was expected and in many cases where it was not. Factor analysis of the ratings produced four factors; a CT technique, a general therapeutic skill technique, a directiveness technique, and an IPT technique. Observed scores on these factors clearly distinguished the techniques (which were perfectly classified using discriminate analysis), although no difference was expected on the therapeutic skills variable.

This finding can be viewed both positively and negatively. On the one hand it implies that therapies can be correctly classified on the basis of technique ratings. On the other hand, finding differences on the general therapeutic skills factor raises the possibility that raters were simply biased in making judgments—rating cognitive therapists high on many dimensions, and IPT therapists low—rather than rating the specific dimension identified by the scale item.

In a later study, Evans et al. (1983) reported some preliminary results on the current version of theCollaborative Study Psychotherapy Rating Scale. The purpose of this scale is to quantify differences between the therapy modalities of the depression study. The scale contains 124 items, 30 to measure each of the three treatments—Cognitive Therapy (CT), Interpersonal Psychotherapy (IPT) and Drug Management (DM)—10 to measure related therapies, 10 tapping facilitative conditions, 5 tapping directiveness, and 9 nonspecific strategies.

A sample of items to be rated, from the CT, IPT, and DM respectively, will help to make the properties of the scale clearer: "Did the therapist help the client to use currently available evidence or informa-

tion (including the client's prior experience) to test the validity of the client's beliefs?" "Did the therapist help the client explore his/her expectations and the expectations of another person regarding their relationship?" "Did the therapist discuss specific symptom relief (e.g., increased appetite, better sleep) and the temporal course of relief that the client could anticipate as a consequence of taking the medication?" Each item is rated on a seven-point scale.

The raters were 8 predoctoral students trained to rate the items but not trained in any of the therapies. Each tape (total $N = 124$) was rated by three of the eight judges, with rating teams, treatment modality, and treatment settings counterbalanced. The study design allowed for the attribution of source of ratings to rater, session, client, therapist, type of therapy, and error components. Using this procedure it was possible to conclude that 70% of the variance in the 30 cognitive therapy items could be attributed to cognitive therapy, 9% to the therapist, 10% to the session (e.g., first session, second session), 1% to the client, and the rest to raters or error.

In contrast, the 30 items used to measure how much IPT is going on in a session showed 49% could be attributed to mode, 19% to the session, 7% to the therapist, 4% to the client, and 21% to the raters or error. The Clinical Management items showed 71% attributable to modality, 24% to session, 4% to the therapist, and 10% to raters or error. The facilitative conditions were not measured as reliably, with 58% of the variance attributable to error or rater, 24% to the therapist, 6% to the patient, 5% to the session, and 6% to therapeutic modality.

These results suggest that the items so far included in the scale, especially those aimed at rating cognitive, interpersonal, and clinical management treatments, have considerable reliability and discriminate between treatments. On the other hand, items aimed at assessing facilitative conditions show less than adequate reliability and are of questionable use.

The results of the current interest in therapy manuals offer several advantages for the research and practice of psychotherapy. Most notable is the identification and distillation of the most valued techniques of specific treatment approaches. It remains to be seen if the promise of greater specificity and differential treatment will demonstrate the importance of these factors above the contribution of common factors.

The use of manuals to guide therapy crystallizes the tendency toward more rapid intervention by placing greater expectancy for time-limited treatment and for periodic, *early* assessment of the degree to which patients respond to treatment.

Thus, it moves us closer to making judgments about the effects of treatment and the necessity of altering treatment approaches and of referring patients to alternative treatments when the eclectic treatment offered does not appear to be broad enough. Finally, it provides more clear-cut guidelines for training and the evaluation of the consequences of training in very concrete ways. As a result, training for practice can move toward more competency-based criteria. And hopefully this competency in providing treatments will have the expected payoff in patient improvement and in the identification of specific effective techniques.

Although there is no reason to believe that a single course of psychotherapy should inoculate a person forever from psychological disturbance and the development of symptoms, many patients who undergo therapy achieve healthy adjustment for long periods of time. This is true despite the fact that they have had a long history of recurrent problems. At the same time, there is clear evidence that a portion of patients who are improved have a relapse and continue to seek help from a variety of mental health providers, including their former therapists. In fact, several problems such as addictions, alcohol abuse, smoking, obesity, and depression are so likely to recur that they are not considered properly studied without data collection one year after treatment.

Nicholson & Berman (1983) used meta-analytic techniques to answer the question, Is follow-up necessary in evaluating psychotherapy? In their review of research in this area they were primarily concerned with whether follow-up evaluations provided different evidence and conclusions than post-treatment evaluations. The review excluded psychotics, organic disorders, antisocial personality disorders, and addictive problems such as obesity, smoking, and alcoholism. They included studies of people with a broad range of neurotic disorders, who were self-referred rather than recruited; the studies involved both post-testing and follow-up data. The analysis was approached in several ways: (a) Does post-treatment status correlate with follow-up status?; (b) Were treatment differences apparent at the post-testing still apparent at follow-up?; (c) Are any changes at follow-up testing due to deterioration or improvements in treated groups?

The results of this meta-analytic review are complicated but, in general, all the findings suggest that treatment gains are maintained. Post-therapy status correlated with follow-up status differences between treatments apparent at the end of therapy, were virtually the same at follow-up. This finding held up whether the comparison was with no-treatment controls or another therapy. And the level of outcome was typically unchanged during the follow-up period. These findings help across a variety of treatment methods (mostly behavioral), patient populations, and sources for assessing outcome. The mean length of follow-up assessment was over 8 months but varied from 1 month to several years. Similarities between post-treatment and follow-up results were unrelated to the length of follow-up. Nicholson and Berman (1983) conclude:

Past reviews have revealed that psychotherapy produces considerable initial improvement, and our findings indicate that for a broad range of disorders this improvement stands the test of time. Thus, our evidence should be heartening both to practitioners, who are increasingly being asked to defend the efficacy of treatment, and to researchers, who have long struggled with the cost of follow-up designs. (p. 275)

It should be noted that Landman and Dawes (1982) who, with a subset of Smith, Glass, and Miller's data, examined only studies whose reported results for post-treatment and follow-up assessment were consistent with Nicholson and Berman's (1983) findings. Andrews and Harvey (1981) also found improvement to be stable over time. They concluded that improvement following treatment is stable for many months and then slowly declines at a rate of 0.2 effect-size units per year.

Little research has been done on the strategies that are most likely to result in maintenance of change. Imber, Pilkonis, Harway, Klein, and Rubinsky (1982) have suggested some possibilities for future research. The likelihood of maintenance will be increased, they suggest, if patients see change and maintenance as a result of their own efforts and if they are helped to anticipate future life crises and their reactions to them. Borrowing methods from behavioral, cognitive, and dynamic therapies such as "booster sessions" and "tapering off," they propose a four-session follow-up format spread out over a 16-week period that focuses on future stresses, attributional style, and patient strengths. As yet, no definitive research has been done on this eclectic procedure, but it appears to encompass a number of important dimensions identified through past research as important in maintenance.

In the long run, continuing progress in developing effective interventions will most likely result from the current heterogeneity in treatment modality, research strategies, and attempts at integration. Although there are numerous problems to be dealt with, such as our imprecise and poorly conceptualized attempts at measuring change, behavior change research seems to be characterized by a reasonable degree of energy and enthusiasm. We will never be finished with the task of evaluating and refining our efforts to help people deal with their psychological problems. Yet the search for more efficient, effective, and safe methods seems to be worth the effort.

REFERENCES

Andrews, G., Guitar, B., & Howie, P. (1980). Meta-analysis of the effects of stuttering treatment. *Journal of Speech and Hearing Disorders, 45,* 287–307.

Andrews, G., & Harvey, R. (1981). Does psychotherapy benefit neurotic patients? A re-analysis of the Smith, Glass, & Miller data. *Archives of General Psychiatry, 38,* 1203–1208.

Andrews, J. G., & Tennant, C. (1978). Life event stress and psychiatric illness. *Psychological Medicine, 8,* 545–549.

Asay, T. P., Lambert, M. J., Christensen, E. R., & Beutler, L. E. (1984). A meta-analysis of mental health treatment outcome. Unpublished manuscript, Department of Psychology, Brigham Young University, Provo, UT.

Bergin, A. E. (1971). Further comments on psychotherapy research and therapeutic practice. *Interpersonal Journal of Psychiatry, 3,* 317–323.

Bergin, A. E., & Lambert, M. J. (1978). The evaluation of outcomes in psychotherapy. In S. L. Garfield & A. E. Bergin (Eds.), *Handbook of psychotherapy and behavior change: An empirical analysis.* New York: Wiley.

Berman, J. S., Miller, R. C., & Massman, P. J. (1984). Cognitive therapy versus systematic desensitization: Is one treatment superior? *Psychological Bulletin, 97,* 451–461.

Berzins, J. I. (1977). Therapist–patient matching. *Effective psychotherapy: A handbook of research* (pp. 222–251). New York: Pergamon Press.

Blanchard, E. B., & Andrasik, F. (1982). Psychological assessment and treatment of headache: Recent developments and emerging issues. *Journal of Consulting and Clinical Psychology, 50,* 859–879.

Blanchard, E. B., Andrasik, F., Anler, T. A., Teders, S. J., & O'Keefe, D. O. (1980). Migraine and tension headache: A meta-analytic review. *Be-*

havior Therapy, 11, 613–631.

Bloch, S., & Lambert, M. J. (1985). What price psychotherapy?: A rejoinder. *British Journal of Psychiatry, 146*, 96–98.

Borkovec, T. D. (1982). Insomnia. *Journal of Consulting and Clinical Psychology, 50*, 880–895.

Cohen, J. (1977). *Statistical power analysis for the behavioral sciences.* New York: Academic Press.

Cooley, E. J., & Lajoy, R. (1980). Therapeutic relationship and improvement as perceived by clients and therapists. *Journal of Clinical Psychology, 36*, 562–570.

Critelli, J. W., & Neumann, K. F. (1984). The placebo: Conceptual analysis of a construct in transition. *American Psychologist, 39*, 32–39.

DeRubeis, R. J., Hollon, S. D., Evans, M. D., & Bemis, K. M. (1982). Can psychotherapies for depression be discriminated? A systematic investigation of cognitive therapy and interpersonal therapy. *Journal of Consulting and Clinical Psychology, 50*, 744–756.

Dush, D. M., Hirt, M. L., & Schroeder, H. (1983). Self-statement modification with adults: A meta-analysis. *Journal of Consulting and Clinical Psychology, 94*, 408–422.

Evans, M., Hollon, S., DeRubeis, R., Auerbach, A., Tuason, V. B., & Wismer, M. (1983, July). *Development of a system for rating psychotherapies for depression.* Paper presented at the 14th annual meeting of the Society for Psychotherapy Research, Sheffield, England.

Eysenck, H. J. (1952). The effects of psychotherapy: An evaluation. *Journal of Consulting Psychology, 16*, 319–324.

Frank, J. D. (1974). *Persuasion and healing.* New York: Shocken.

Fuchs, C. Z., & Rehm, L. P. (1977). A self-control behavior therapy program for depression. *Journal of Consulting and Clinical Psychology, 45*, 206–215.

Garfield, S. L., & Kurtz, R. (1976). Clinical psychologists in the 1970's. *American Psychologist, 1976, 31*, 1–9.

Gottman, J., & Markman, H. J. (1978). Experimental designs in psychotherapy research. In S. L. Garfield & A. E. Bergin (Eds.), *Handbook of psychotherapy and behavior change: An empirical analysis* (2nd ed.). New York: Wiley.

Gurman, A. S. (1977). The patient's perception of the therapeutic relationship. In A. S. Gurman & A. M. Razin (Eds.), *Effective psychotherapy: A handbook of research.* New York: Pergamon Press.

Herink, R. (Ed.) (1980). *The psychotherapy handbook: The A to Z guide to more than 250 different therapies in use today.* New York: Meridian.

Imber, S. D., Pilkonis, P. A., Harway, N. I., Klein, R. H., & Rubinsky, P. A. (1982). Maintenance of change in the psychotherapies. *Journal of Psychiatric Treatment and Evaluation, 4*, 1–5.

Jacobson, N. S., Follette, W. C., & Revenstorf, D. (1984). Psychotherapy outcome research: Methods for reporting variability and evaluation clinical significance. *Behavior Therapy, 15*, 336–352.

Klerman, G., Rounsaville, B., Chevron, E., Neu, C.,

& Weissman, M. (1979). Manual for short-term interpersonal psychotherapy (IPT) for depression. Unpublished manuscript, Yale University.

Kornblith, S. H., Rehm, L. P., O'Hara, M. W., & Lamparski, D. M. (1983). The contribution of self-reinforcement training and behavioral assignments to the efficacy of self control therapy for depression. *Cognitive Therapy and Research, 7*, 499–528.

Lambert, M. J. (1976). Spontaneous remission in adult neurotic disorders: A revision and summary. *Psychological Bulletin, 83*, 107–119.

Lambert, M. J. (1982). *The effects of psychotherapy* (Vol. 2). New York: Human Sciences Press.

Lambert, M. J. (1983). Introduction to assessment of psychotherapy outcome: Historical perspective and current issues. In M. J. Lambert, E. R. Christensen, & S. S. DeJulio (Eds.), *The assessment of psychotherapy outcome*, New York: Wiley & Sons.

Lambert, M. J., Bergin, A. E., Collins, J. L. (1977). Therapist-induced deterioration in psychotherapy. In A. S. Gurman & A. M. Razin (Eds.), *Effective psychotherapy: A handbook of research.* New York: Pergamon Press.

Lambert, M. J., DeJulio, S. S., & Stein, D. M. (1978). Therapist interpersonal skills: Process outcome, methodological considerations and recommendations for further research. *Psychological Bulletin, 85*, 467–489.

Lambert, M. J., Shapiro, D. A., & Bergin, A. E. (1986). The effectiveness of psychotherapy. In S. L. Garfield & A. E. Bergin (Eds.), *Handbook of psychotherapy and behavior change* (3rd ed.). New York: John Wiley & Sons.

Landman, J. T., & Dawes, R. M. (1982). Psychotherapy outcome: Smith and Glass conclusions stand up under scrutiny. *American Psychologist, 37*, 504–516.

Larson, D. (1980). Schools, styles, and schoolism: A national survey. *Journal of Humanistic Psychology, 20*, 3–20.

Lazarus, A. A. (1971). *Behavior therapy and beyond.* New York: McGraw Hill.

Levant, R. F., & Shlien, J. M. (Eds.) (1984). *Client-centered therapy and the person centered approach: New directions in theory, research and practice.* New York: Praeger.

Lorr, M. (1965). Client perceptions of therapists. *Journal of Consulting Psychology, 29*, 146–149.

Luborsky, L., Bachrach, H., Graff, H., Pulver, S., & Christoph, P. (1979). Preconditions and consequences of transference interpretations: A clinical–quantitative investigation. *Journal of Nervous & Mental Disorders, 167*, 391–401.

Luborsky, L., Singer, B., & Luborsky, L. (1975). Comparative studies of psychotherapy. *Archives of General Psychiatry, 32*, 995–1008.

Mann, A. H., Jenkins, R., & Belsey, E. (1981). The twelve-month outcome of patients with neurotic illness in general practice. *Psychological Medicine, 11*, 535–550.

Meichenbaum, D. (1977). *Cognitive behavior modification: An integrative approach.* New York: Plenum Press.

Meltzoff, J., & Kornreich, M. (1970). *Research in psychotherapy*. New York: Atherton Press.

Miller, R. C., & Berman, J. S. (1983). The efficacy of cognitive behavior therapies: A qualitative review of the research evidence. *Psychological Bulletin, 94,* 39–53.

Miller, W. R., Taylor, C. A., & West, J. C. (1980). Focused versus broad-spectrum behavior therapy for problem drinkers. *Journal of Consulting and Clinical Psychology, 48,* 590–601.

Mitchell, K. M., Bozarth, J. D., & Krauft, C. C. (1977). A re-appraisal of the therapeutic effectiveness of accurate empathy, nonpossessive warmth, and genuineness. In A. S. Gurman & A. M. Razin (Eds.), *Effective psychotherapy: A handbook of research*. New York: Pergamon Press.

Nicholson, R. A., & Berman, J. S. (1983). Is follow-up necessary in evaluating psychotherapy? *Psychological Bulletin, 93,* 261–278.

Norcross, J., & Prochaska, J. (1982). A national survey of clinical psychologists: Affiliations and orientations. *The Clinical Psychologist, 39,* 1–6.

Patterson, C. H. (1984). Empathy, warmth, and genuineness in psychotherapy: A review of reviews. *Psychotherapy, 21,* 431–438.

Pilkonis, P. A., Imber, S. D., Lewis, P., & Rubinsky, P. (1984). A comparative outcome of individual, group, and conjoint psychotherapy. *Archives of General Psychiatry, 41,* 431–437.

Prioleau, L., Murdock, M., & Brody, N. (1983). An analysis of psychotherapy versus placebo studies. *The Behavioral and Brain Sciences, 6,* 275–310.

Quality Assurance Project, (1982). A treatment outline for agoraphobia. *Australian and New Zealand Journal of Psychiatry, 16,* 25–33.

Quality Assurance Project, (1983). A treatment outline for depressive disorders. *Australian and New Zealand Journal of Psychiatry, 17,* 129–146.

Rachman, S. J., & Wilson, G. T. (1980). *The effects of psychological therapy. (Second enlarged edition)*. New York: Pergamon Press.

Rehm, L. P. (1977). A self-control model of depression. *Behavior Therapy, 8,* 787–804.

Rehm, L. P., Fuchs, C. Z., Roth, D. M., Kornblith, S. J., & Romano, J. M. (1979). A comparison of self-control and assertion skills treatment of depression. *Behavior Therapy, 10,* 429–442.

Rehm, L. P., Kornblith, S. J., O'Hara, M. W., Lamparski, D. M., Romano, J. M., & Volkin, J. (1981). An evaluation of major components in a self-control behavior therapy program for depression. *Behavior Modification, 5,* 459–489.

Rosenthal, R. (1983). Assessing the statistical and social importance of the effects of psychotherapy. *Journal of Consulting and Clinical Psychology, 51,* 4–13.

Rosenthal, D., & Frank, J. D. (1956). Psychotherapy and the placebo effects. *Psychological Bulletin, 53,* 294–302.

Schapira, K., Roth, M., Kerr, T. A., & Gurney, C. (1972). The prognosis of affective disorders: The differentiation of anxiety states from depressive illnesses. *British Journal of Psychiatry, 12,* 175–201.

Shapiro, D. A., & Shapiro, D. (1982). Meta-analysis or comparative therapy outcome studies: A replication and refinement. *Psychological Bulletin, 92,* 581–604.

Shepard, M. (1984). What price psychotherapy? *British Medical Journal, 288,* 809–810.

Sloane, R. B., Staples, F. R., Cristol, A. H., Yorkston, N. J., & Whipple, K. (1975). *Short-term analytically oriented psychotherapy vs. behavior therapy*. Cambridge, MA: Harvard University Press.

Smith, M. L., & Glass, G. V. (1977). Meta-analysis of psychotherapy outcome studies. *American Psychologist, 32,* 752–760.

Smith, M. L., Glass, G. V., & Miller, T. I. (1980). *The benefits of psychotherapy*. Baltimore: Johns Hopkins University Press.

Stein, D. M., & Lambert, M. J. (1984). On the relationship between therapist experience and psychotherapy outcome. *Clinical Psychology Review, 4,*

Steinbrueck, S. M., Maxwell, S. E., & Howard, G. S. (1983). A meta-analysis of psychotherapy and drug therapy in the treatment of unipolar depression with adults. *Journal of Consulting and Clinical Psychology, 51,* 856–863.

Strupp, H. H. (1980a). Success and failure in time-limited psychotherapy. *Archives of General Psychiatry, 37,* 595–603.

Strupp, H. H. (1980b). Success and failure in time-limited psychotherapy. *Archives of General Psychiatry, 37,* 708–716.

Strupp, H. H. (1980c). Success and failure in time-limited psychotherapy. *Archives of General Psychiatry, 37,* 831–841.

Strupp, H. H. (1980d). Success and failure in time-limited psychotherapy. *Archives of General Psychiatry, 37,* 947–954.

Wampler, K. S. (1982). Bringing the review of literature into the age of quantification: Meta-analysis as a strategy for integrating research findings in family studies. *Journal of Marriage and the Family, 11,* 1009–1023.

Waskow, I. E., Parloff, M. B., Hadley, S. W., & Autry, J. H. (1983). The NIMH treatment of depression collaborative research program: Background and research plan. Unpublished manuscript, NIMH.

Wilkins, W. (1984). Psychotherapy: The powerful placebo. *Journal of Consulting and Clinical Psychology, 52,* 570–573.

Zeiss, A. M., Lewinshohn, P. M., & Munoz, R. F. (1979). Nonspecific improvement effects in depression using interpersonal skills training, pleasant activity schedules, and cognitive training. *Journal of Consulting and Clinical Psychology, 47,* 427–439.

CHAPTER 17

Future Directions in Psychotherapy Integration

Marvin R. Goldfried and Jeremy D. Safran

The indications are very clear that the field of psychotherapy in the 1980s is highlighted by a rapidly developing movement toward integration and eclecticism. Therapists are more willing to acknowledge that existing paradigms have not stood up well under close scrutiny and have often failed to explain clinical phenomena and research evidence. An ever-increasing number of articles, chapters, books, symposia and conferences on the topic attest to the growing impact that eclecticism is making on the field.

Garfield and Kurtz's (1976) well-known survey of psychotherapy practitioners indicated that even at that time more psychotherapists designated themselves as eclectic than as belonging to any traditional psychotherapy school. More recent surveys document that between one-third to half of clinicians currently practicing classify themselves as eclectic (see Nor-

cross, Chapter 1).

A recent study by Friedling, Goldfried, and Stricker (1984) has found that therapists trained within a given orientation do not restrict themselves to methods associated with a particular approach but need to adopt a more integrated approach to intervention. Specifically, Friedling et al. surveyed the self-reported activities of graduates of a psychodynamic (Adelphi University) and a behavioral (Stony Brook) doctoral program in clinical psychology. So as to avoid the potential barriers to communication that each orientation's technical jargon might impose, the questionnaire consisted of items that were described in the vernacular (e.g., "Point out any behavior on the part of the patient/client that seems to interfere with the work of therapy."). The therapy activities themselves were generated from several texts reflecting the two orientations, translations were made into the vernacular, and faculty members from the two graduate programs confirmed that the items in question reflected the practices of their particular approach. The result-

Preparation of this chapter was supported in part by grant MH40196 from the National Institute of Mental Health. The authors would like to thank Laura Rice and Les Greenberg for their helpful comments on an earlier version of this chapter.

ing 93-item questionnaire was mailed to individuals who had obtained their doctorates in clinical psychology from each of these two programs during the previous 10-year period. A total of 110 graduates from Adelphi (67%) and 85 from Stony Brook (77%) responded to the questionnaire.

The findings indicated that 56% of the activities surveyed were used by both schools, 15% were mutually rejected by them, and 29% were used exclusively by either one school or the other. Of those activities that were derived from a psychodynamic orientation, 78% were used mutually; of the behavioral practices, 55% were used by both orientations. Clearly, neither of the two groups behaved clinically in ways that are outlined in the textbooks reflecting their orientations. This tendency to sample from therapeutic practices that fall outside one's orientation was found to be related to a number of variables. For example, graduates of Stony Brook who became practitioners were found to be more eclectic than those who were working in academic settings. Inasmuch as the graduates of Adelphi University were uniformly practitioners, this question did not pertain to them. Eclecticism was also found to be positively correlated with the percentage of adult clients seen in the practice of the behavioral group, and the percentage of patients of lower socioeconomic status that comprised the practice of the psychodynamic therapists.

It should be emphasized that this research is based on what therapists said they did, rather than on an actual sampling of their clinical practice. The potential for inconsistency between the two always exists, and indeed has been found in a recent study by Cyr and Lecomte (1983). Moreover, the fact that some degree of consensus in practice exists across orientations does not, in itself, indicate that these methods are effective. None-

theless, to the extent that commonalities do exist, they may very well reflect robust phenomena that stand a good chance of ultimately being shown to be related to successful therapeutic outcome.

Although there is an increasing acknowledgment of the need to develop a more integrative approach to psychotherapy, we are far from having any consensus as to exactly what that approach should be. This lack of agreement is no better illustrated than in the various chapters of this volume, which advocate very different eclectic models. We agree with Beutler (Chapter 4) and Murray (Chapter 14) that there exists a very real danger that the time, energy, and emotional—and at times financial—investment put into the development of a more comprehensive model of therapy may result in the generation of competing eclectic schools of thought. If this trend is carried to its extreme, we may ultimately end up with as many eclectic models as we currently have schools of psychotherapy, impeding rather than facilitating the development of a more generally agreed upon approach to therapeutic change.

Lest the reader start to wonder what an anti-integrationist chapter is doing in a book about eclectic psychotherapy, let us make it clear that we *are* in favor of integrating different approaches to psychotherapy. What we are *not* in favor of is replacing the rich and sophisticated existing systems of psychotherapy with a number of other *competing theoretical* systems—however sophisticated they may be. Clearly it is always easier to play the role of the critic than the constructive theorist. Just as the good psychotherapist attempts to help patients/clients find new alternatives before giving up old patterns, however, we recognize that the onus is on us to provide some constructive alternatives.

In addressing ourselves to the topic of "future directions" for eclecticism, we believe that it is essential first to clarify the nature of our ultimate goal. When Alice came across the Cheshire Cat sitting up in a tree and asked it which path she might take, the cat wisely replied: "That depends a good deal on where you want to get to." Similarly, we need to ask ourselves where the field of psychotherapy needs to head. Ultimately, we need to move toward the development of a unified paradigm that is both clinically meaningful and empirically grounded. It is our contention that in order to develop this paradigm we will need to begin with a serious examination of similarities and differences among different therapeutic traditions with respect to both theory and process of change. This can be accomplished only if we have some kind of overarching conceptual framework to guide us in teasing out similarities and differences among different forms of psychotherapy.

THE NEED FOR A KNOWLEDGE-ACQUISITION STRATEGY

The development of a unified psychotherapy paradigm is dependent on the prior specification of an overarching framework to guide the acquisition of knowledge in this area. In other words, we need to articulate a coherent and meaningful methodology to guide the development of theory and the execution of relevant research, so that we can begin to develop a systematic body of knowledge in a programmatic way. In particular, the scientific community must agree on conceptual tools and strategies for the acquisition of knowledge about the process of therapeutic change. A number of important questions need to be addressed, such as: What is the role of theory in the accumulation of knowledge about common principles of change? What is the role of research in the acquisition of knowledge

about common change principles? What is the relationship between theory and research?

In this chapter, we will not attempt to fully articulate such a systematic framework, as this would be an overly ambitious task. What we will attempt, however, is to raise a number of critical issues and to suggest, in a preliminary fashion, a general approach to developing a systematic body of knowledge.

It is our contention that the task of developing an integrated perspective on psychotherapy must take place both from "top down" and from "bottom up." We need to conduct scholarly examinations of similarities and differences between different psychotherapy traditions at a more conceptual level, but we also need to conduct research on the similarities and differences between psychotherapy traditions at the level of clinical practice. Moreover, we need to develop systematic ways of linking these two types of knowledge acquisition. Conceptual analyses at the theoretical level must lead to the observation of phenomena at the level of clinical process and to the empirical investigation of psychotherapy mechanisms. Observations at the level of clinical practice and associated research must feed back to the level of conceptual analysis.

From whence can this knowledge acquisition strategy be derived? Our position is that the enterprise of therapeutic rapprochement and the conceptual framework and methodology of psychotherapy process research are tied together in an integral fashion. It seems patently obvious that in searching for the common ingredients of different forms of psychotherapy, one focuses on the process or mechanisms of change in psychotherapy. And if one talks about mechanisms of change, one is already in the domain of psychotherapy process research. For this reason we believe that work done on the integration of the psychotherapies is inevitably tied to the development of the field of psychotherapy process research.

Psychotherapy process research itself, however, is very much in an early phase of development. It is worth pointing out that the development of the field of psychotherapy process research involves much more than the development of specific measurement techniques or research designs. It involves the development and articulation of a systematic perspective on how we go about looking at human change in the first place. As Rice and Greenberg (1984) have cogently noted, one of the difficulties with psychotherapy process research in the past has been the fact that too many researchers have attempted to code, categorize, and measure an infinite variety of different events and processes in psychotherapy, outside of the context of any clearly articulated rationale of how to begin approaching the question of looking at human change.

Most of the research on the process of psychotherapy that has been carried out to date has tended to be linked to a particular therapeutic orientation, typically client-centered or psychodynamic (Kiesler, 1973; Orlinsky & Howard, 1978). Possibly as a result of this idiosyncratic approach, most of the past process research has not provided us with firm conclusions on the change process. As observed by Strupp (1973),

Content analysis in psychotherapy has always impressed me as an area in which short-lived efforts abound. The pattern seems to be as follows. An investigator becomes intrigued by the possibilities of measuring one or several aspects of the communication content. He seems to say, "If we could only measure X, Y, or Z, we would really make significant inroads on the psychotherapeutic process." The answer seems to lie in the propositions of a particular theory that became the framework for a system then being developed. Almost immediately the system is applied to a substantive issue in the area, usually to the analysis of recorded interviews. Not infrequently, a system is developed

for the specific purpose of dealing with a substantive issue that the investigator wishes to explore. Soon thereafter, the investigator loses interest in the problem, and turns to other pursuits. Few colleagues find his system sufficiently congenial to put it to use in their own research, and the initial flurry of activity subsides. (p. xv)

In many respects, the diversity of codes for scoring the process of therapy can be as varied as the differing theoretical conceptions of psychotherapy itself.

In their comprehensive, critical analysis of the current status of psychotherapy process research as it relates to outcome, Orlinsky and Howard (1978) have similarly suggested that one of the major difficulties with this entire area is that we have not yet achieved an agreed-upon paradigm. They point out:

The real problem is that no one yet has persuasively shown us what the basic elements are that must be taken into account. . . . What is needed is a comprehensive list of input, process, and output factors that make sense and are subscribed to by most of the people working in the field—no matter what their theoretical predilections might be—so that their efforts may become mutually intelligible and their results comparable and cumulative. (Orlinsky & Howard, 1978, pp. 318–319)

The field, however, may be ready to begin addressing these obstacles, as reflected in the conference convened in 1983 by NIMH on psychotherapy process research, where there was considerable agreement among leading psychotherapy process researchers on a variety of key issues in the field.

In our search for an integrative psychotherapy paradigm, certain basic methodological and conceptual issues need to be addressed. This is the *what* and *how* of process research. The *what* refers to the most appropriate conceptual unit to be studied, and the *how* consists of those methdological procedures that enable us to study the critical units of the change process. Both issues will be dealt with in the remainder of this chapter.

ORGANIZING CONCEPTS

Those who are interested in developing an integrative perspective on psychotherapy are confronted with both a bewildering range of different models at the level of clinical theory and a staggering array of phenomena at the level of actual clinical practice. In this section we will discuss a number of different concepts that are useful in organizing our thinking about psychotherapy process and integration, such as, establishing a language for psychotherapy integration; dealing with an appropriate level of abstraction; establishing a comparable focus of investigation; identifying and distinguishing among psychotherapy tasks; and distinguishing between client/patient operations and therapist operations. In a later section we will make use of some of these concepts in the process of articulating an overall strategy for psychotherapy integration.

The Language of Integration

Perhaps one of the more fundamental problems that in the past has plagued attempts to effect a creative integration of different forms of psychotherapy has been the fact that theorists from different psychotherapy traditions have tended to use different languages or jargon to discuss therapeutic phenomena that may well be more similar in nature than is initially apparent. Goldfried and Padawer (1982), among others, have argued that for this reason it may be useful for therapists and researchers interested in therapeutic rapprochement to adopt a language that is relatively neutral with respect to the different psychotherapeutic traditions. The language of experimental cognitive psychology has been suggested as a candidate for this role (Arnkoff, 1980; Goldfried,

1979; Greenberg & Safran, 1980, 1981; Merluzzi, Rudy & Glass, 1981; Ryle, 1978; Sarason, 1979; Trower & Turland, 1982; Turk & Speers, 1983). The advantage of the language of cognitive psychology is not only that it is relatively neutral with respect to different psychotherapy traditions but that it is tied to the dominant paradigm in experimental psychology. The use of this language thus increases the possibility that the psychotherapy field will be open to new developments emerging from experimental psychology.

A number of different theorists from within different psychotherapy traditions are beginning to use the language of cognitive psychology. Goldfried (1979), for example, has spoken about the cognitive–behavioral treatment of anxiety disorders, using the framework of experimental cognitive psychology as a conceptual underpinning. Horowitz (1979) and Peterfreund (1980) are attempting to clarify the nature of the change process in psychodynamic therapy, using information-processing terms. Rice (1974) has discussed client-centered therapy from the perspective of cognitive information-processing theory, and Greenberg (1984) has analyzed gestalt therapy process in similar terms. Greenberg, Rice, and Safran (1984) have actually employed information-processing terminology to analyze similarities and differences between change processes involved in cognitive–behavior therapy, client-centered therapy, and gestalt therapy.

While the above-noted features of cognitive psychology qualify it as a potentially useful language for psychotherapy integration, it is important to point out that cognitive psychology is more than a language. It is a paradigm for understanding human functioning. As Safran and Greenberg (1986a; 1986b) have argued, it is thus *vital to identify the metatheoretical assumptions that underly cognitive psychology* and to evaluate how adequate they are to capture the various domains of human functioning focused on by different forms of psychotherapy. It is beyond the scope of this chapter to deal with this specific issue at greater length. The interested reader, however, is referred to Shaw and Bransford (1977) for a good articulation of the metatheoretical assumptions underlying both information-processing and ecological approaches to cognitive psychology, and to Safran and Greenberg (1986a; 1986b) for a discussion of the relevance of this issue to our understanding of psychotherapy process.

Level of Abstraction

Determining the appropriate level of abstraction to use in the comparative study of psychotherapy process is of the utmost importance (Goldfried, 1980; Goldfried & Padawer, 1982). Comparing psychotherapy process at an inappropriate level can yield similarities that are trivial or can obscure important similarities that do exist.

At the highest level of abstraction are the theoretical frameworks and philosophical stances that therapists use to explain how and why they intervene in certain ways. At the lowest level of abstraction are the observable events of psychotherapy. There is always the danger that comparative analysis at the higher levels of abstraction will obscure important similarities in psychotherapy proc-

ess, both because of differences in theoretical language and because of abstract philosophical differences that never really translate into clinical reality. On the other hand, comparative analysis at the lower levels of abstraction may obscure important similarities if therapeutic activities are topographically dissimilar but functionally the same.

Goldfried and Padawer (1982), for example, suggest that various specific therapeutic activities may have the same underlying function. They outline a number of common, general *clinical strategies or principles* that may underly topographically dissimilar clinical activities. These general strategies include inducing expectations that therapy will be helpful, providing a therapeutic relationship, offering clients/patients a more objective perspective on themselves and the world, encouraging corrective experiences, and facilitating continued reality testing. These general clinical strategies can be thought of as an intermediate level of abstraction, somewhere between higher-level theory and observable clinical procedures (see Figure 1).

It is not uncommon for theorists to postulate common change principles at this intermediate level of abstraction. This level provides one with a starting point for conceptually clustering topographically dissimilar procedures. However, it should not be thought of as an end in itself

LEVELS OF ABSTRACTION

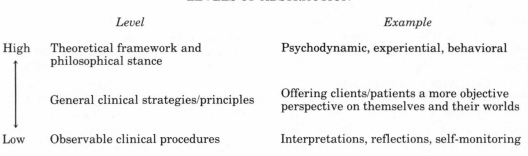

	Level	*Example*
High	Theoretical framework and philosophical stance	Psychodynamic, experiential, behavioral
	General clinical strategies/principles	Offering clients/patients a more objective perspective on themselves and their worlds
Low	Observable clinical procedures	Interpretations, reflections, self-monitoring

Figure 1. Levels of abstraction for conceptualizing therapeutic activities.

but as a beginning point in the process of teasing out similarities and differences.

It can be a useful conceptual exercise to arrange therapy activities in a hierarchical fashion, with general clinical strategies at the highest level of the hierarchy and the observable clinical procedures at the lowest level. Figure 2 illustrates how the observable clinical procedures of providing the client/patient with feedback about explicit negative thoughts or instructing the client/patient to monitor such thoughts can be seen as two specific ways of implementing the general clinical strategy of offering clients/patients a more objective perspective on themselves and their worlds.

This example illustrates that there are a number of different parameters that may be taken into account in providing clients/patients with a more objective perspective, such as who provides the objective feedback (e.g., feedback by therapist or self-observation), and the particular aspects of clients/patients or their world on which this perspective is provided. It is possible that variations across different therapeutic orientations may rest not so much on their utilization of different basic principles of change, but rather on the specific parameters associated with their implementation. In the example depicted in Figure 2, the sampling of therapy activities across orientations might reveal sim-

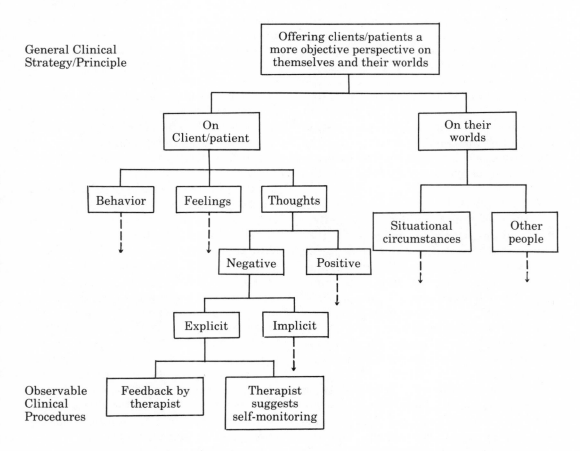

Figure 2. Illustration of therapist's activities as hierarchically arranged between general clinical strategy/principle and observable clinical procedures. The dotted arrows represent other areas for which hierarchically arranged activities may be specified.

ilarities for higher-order strategies (e.g., offering clients/patients a more objective perspective on their explicit negative thoughts), with differences emerging on more specific ways they are implemented (e.g., feedback by therapist versus the therapist's encouragement that clients/patients objectively monitor their own thoughts).

It should be emphasized that Figure 2 is both oversimplified and incomplete. Further detail could be provided on offering clients/patients a more objective perspective on their behavior, feelings, and positive thoughts, and on situational circumstances and other people in their lives. Our intention is merely to illustrate the possible existence of a hierarchical ordering of interventions between the level of general strategy and that of more specific clinical procedures. We would also like to emphasize that the differences between approaches that emerge at the lower levels of the hierarchy are as important as the similarities. An important potential focus of investigation consists of identifying the conditions that favor the use of one specific intervention over another to implement a particular general strategy.

A final point to be made is that although we advocate the investigation of similarities and differences at the level of actual clinical process rather than at a purely conceptual level, we are by no means suggesting that theorists and researchers should ignore higher level theory. Therapeutic interventions that appear functionally similar when viewed at an intermediate level of analysis may emerge as functionally dissimilar at a higher level of analysis.

Consider the following example. At an intermediate level of analysis it may appear as if the "collecting evidence" intervention in cognitive therapy and the "empty chair" intervention in gestalt therapy are functionally the same, since both achieve the objective of challenging negative self-statements. However, it is important to bear in mind that although the two interventions may look functionally similar, they are embedded within metatheoretical perspectives or visions of psychological functioning that are somewhat different. The cognitive therapy intervention exists in the context of a metatheory that views dysfunctional information processing as the ultimate problem, and the correction of cognitive distortions as a cure. In contrast, the gestalt therapy intervention is embedded within the context of a metatheory that views the disowning of one's experience as a problem, and the integration of disowned parts of the self as the cure. In the cognitive perspective, the tendency to process information in a negatively biased fashion is viewed as an undesirable tendency that must be eliminated. In the gestalt perspective, the tendency to be self-critical is viewed as part of the self in which potential strengths that are currently not being tapped reside. A therapeutic task thus becomes one of accepting and recognizing the strengths in this part of the self rather than one of eliminating it.

Our point here is that there are two different philosophical messages that are being conveyed to the client/patient. We propose that although it may look as if a similar strategy is being used at a specific point in therapy process, the ultimate impact of the strategy can be fully understood only in the context of both explicit and tacit messages about the nature of life that are being conveyed to the client/patient by the therapist. Over and above the impact of any common therapeutic strategy at a specific point in time are the values about life and human functioning that the therapist is conveying to the client/patient, which the specific intervention helps the client/patient to internalize.

We thus believe that comparative analysis in the realm of higher-level theory is as important as the comparison of psychotherapy approaches at the lower levels of analysis. Analysis at the higher levels of abstraction must nonetheless be ultimately tied to research. In the above example, if theorists hypothesize that there are important differences between the "empty-chair" procedure and the "collecting evidence" procedure, they must ultimately be able to specify how this difference will manifest itself in measurable psychotherapy change process.

It should be apparent to the reader at this point that we are speaking about subtleties that go beyond a catalogue of specific interventions on the basis of surface features, or an evaluation of whether or not two different approaches both help the client/patient to obtain an objective perspective on the self. If we are truly interested in understanding similarities and differences between psychotherapy approaches, we must develop a better understanding of the subtle psychological change processes through which different interventions achieve their impact. The remaining psychotherapy process concepts to be discussed can be thought of as tools to facilitate the development of this type of understanding.

Establishing a Comparable Focus of Investigation

In using process research to study the similarities and differences among the various approaches of psychotherapy, care must be taken to keep the focus of the investigation as comparable as possible. For example, a comparative process investigation of behavior therapy and interpersonal therapy may yield very different mechanisms of change if the cases sampled from the first orientation consist primarily of habit disorders and the cases in the second of problems in interpersonal relationships. Data reported by Prochaska and DiClemente (Chapter 6) indicate that the change processes that

are used are likely to interact with the nature of the problem, a conclusion similarly arrived at by Garfield (Chapter 5) and Murray (Chapter 14).

In attempting to narrow the focus of a comparative study of different approaches to therapy, one natural way to create that homogeneity of subject matter is to make comparisons within certain types of clinical problems, such as anxiety-related disorders, depression, addictions, marital problems, and so forth. In working with certain types of clinical problems, therapists—regardless of orientation—are more likely to share a common base of experience regarding the issues and variables related to the specific problem. Moreover, in dealing with a more homogeneous clinical population, the number of options for intervention become relatively fewer, thereby increasing the likelihood of finding some consensus. Finally, from a pragmatic point of view, there is much to be said for keeping a problem-oriented focus, as this tends to be of most concern to the practicing clinician.

Another way in which greater homogeneity of the clinical material under investigation may be obtained is based on Prochaska and DiClemente's (Chapter 6) discussion of "levels" of problems. Thus, even within given diagnostic categories, further classifications may be made on the basis of such variables as the existence of symptom/situational problems, interpersonal conflicts, intrapersonal conflicts, and so forth. We might mention in passing that we prefer to consider these "classes" rather than "levels" of problems, so as not to imply any particular model of human functioning.

Still another way to further categorize clinical material has been suggested by Beutler (Chapter 4), based on the intensity of the problem, the clients'/patients' coping style, and reactance level. This method of enhancing homogeneity is orthogonal to each of the two above suggestions.

A final conceptual tool that can be used to establish a comparable focus of investigation is referred to by Rice and Greenberg (1984) as the "client marker." According to Rice and Greenberg, the client or patient marker can be defined as a reliably identifiable aspect of client/ patient performance in therapy that signals to the therapist a readiness for a particular type of intervention. The marker concept provides another tool for establishing comparable samples in psychotherapy process research. Unlike the previously described concepts, however, the marker allows the researcher to establish homogenous samples on the basis of therapy process, rather than on the basis of stable client/patient characteristics. This approach thus affords the researcher even greater precision, because the same client/patient can display different process characteristics at different points in time.

Rice and Saperia (1984), for example, have identified the "problematic reaction" as an important marker in their version of client-centered therapy. According to Rice and Saperia, a problematic reaction takes place when clients/patients identify the reaction they have had to some stimulus, either external or internal, that they find distressing, puzzling, or difficult to understand. Their research has demonstrated that the occurrence of a problematic reaction in therapy provides a good context for the implementation of a particular type of client-centered intervention that they have termed "systematic evocative unfolding." Greenberg (1984) has identified a marker he refers to as the "split"—defined as a conflict between two partial tendencies of the self—that provides a good process context for the two-chair intervention in gestalt therapy.

A challenging and potentially fruitful conceptual and research enterprise would be to identify similarities and differences in markers for different forms of psychotherapy and different forms of interventions within different therapeutic

traditions. Do therapists from different therapy traditions intervene at the same points in the course of psychotherapy? Our guess would be that although there may be markers common to different forms of psychotherapy, different forms of psychotherapy also have their distinctive markers. For example, the expression of an automatic thought may well be an important marker for intervention in cognitive therapy, but may not have the same importance as a marker in psychoanalytic therapy. By the same token, the failure to speak about negative feelings toward the therapist may be seen as a potential marker for intervention in psychoanalytic therapy, but not in cognitive therapy. It seems reasonable to assume that therapists from different traditions who have different conceptual maps of the way therapy works would direct their attention to different aspects of client/patient performance in therapy sessions.

The value of identifying client/patient markers across different forms of therapy is that the identification of these markers may very well provide us with a clue as to therapists' implicit models of the way psychotherapy works. The empirical identification of markers may also conceivably reveal that therapists, in actuality, sometimes intervene at points in the therapeutic process that the explicit theory would not lead us to believe would be important.

Psychotherapy Tasks

The notion of "task" in psychotherapy, which has been advanced independently now by a number of theorists (e.g., Bordin, 1979; Greenberg, 1984; Rice & Greenberg, 1984), would seem to be a useful one for beginning to understand the similarities and differences among different types of psychotherapies. Here the idea is that the process of psychotherapy consists of the resolution of a number of tasks by the client. For example, the client/patient in psychoanalytic therapy may have to successfully resolve a number of tasks in order for therapy to be successful. These may include such activities as developing a transference relationship, allowing warded-off material into consciousness, and engaging in a type of parallel processing in which the transferred relationship pattern is compared with a more realistic alternative for relating to the therapist (cf. Horowitz et al., 1984).

Similarly, the client/patient in cognitive behavior therapy may have to engage in a number of specific tasks. These may include overt behavioral tasks such as completing homework assignments, as well as psychological tasks such as exploring automatic thoughts, specifying negative predictions, and examining relevant evidence. These tasks may overlap to varying extents with the tasks that are relevant to other forms of psychotherapy. Once theorists and researchers begin asking themselves the question of what the relevant tasks are in any particular form of psychotherapy, we can begin to look at the similarities and differences between the task and sequences of tasks involved in different approaches.

Psychotherapy tasks may be sequential in nature, and thereby related to a specific phase of therapy. Thus, it may be necessary for clients/patients to establish an alliance with the therapist before they can begin the task of truly looking at themselves. In Chapter 6, Prochaska and DiClemente propose that the precontemplative, contemplative, action, and maintenance stages of intervention involve very different processes, which strongly suggests that any comparative study across orientations should be carried out within the same therapeutic phase. Based on a model originally presented by Egan (1975), Fuhriman, Paul, and Burlingame (Chapter 8) propose five distinct therapy stages: role description; rapport building and specification of problem; self-understanding and anticipation

of what action is needed; "doing and reviewing"; and termination. These phases are similar to those of engagement, pattern search, change, and termination, which have also been described in the literature (e.g., Beitman, 1983; Cashdan, 1973). Thus, in conducting a comparative process analysis across different orientations, it is important to focus not only on specific types of cases but also on the particular psychotherapy tasks as they occur in each of the different phases of treatment.

Client/Patient vs. Therapist Operations

Another useful conceptual tool is the distinction between therapist operations and client/patient operations (Rice & Greenberg, 1984). A therapist operation can be defined as any intervention that the therapist implements in the course of therapy, whereas a client/patient operation refers to any activity (either overt or psychological) in which the client/patient engages during the course of therapy. An example of a *therapist* operation in cognitive behavior therapy would be directing the client's/patient's attention toward evidence that is inconsistent with his or her dysfunctional perception. An example of a *client/patient* operation in the same context would be the client's/patient's process of actively considering an alternative interpretation of events. We can hypothesize that in this particular example, the therapist operation triggers or sets in motion the client/patient operation. Although the concepts of task and client/patient operation are similar, we tend to think of the task as a more molar unit of analysis and of the operation as being more molecular. Client/patient operations can thus be thought of as subtasks that are involved in the resolution of larger tasks.

In attempting to clarify the mechanisms of change in a specific type of therapy, it is both conceptually and empirically valuable to make this distinction between therapist and client/patient operations. It is conceivable, for example, that a variety of different therapist operations can set into motion the same client/patient operation. Both interpreting the transference in psychoanalytic therapy and directing the client's/patient's attention to inconsistent evidence in cognitive behavior therapy may set in motion the client operation that Beck (1976) refers to as "decentering"; that is, a process of coming to distinguish between reality and reality as construed.

Thus, distinguishing between therapist and client/patient operations is a conceptual activity that can be useful in clarifying some of the similarities and differences in the psychotherapy process that may not be immediately apparent. Moreover, from a practical perspective, this distinction can be extremely important. If we can empirically establish catalogues of client/patient and therapist operations that are important in specific contexts, as well as therapist operations that will set into motion specific client/patient operations, then therapists can have at their disposal a variety of interventions to activate the desired client/patient operation.

An even more highly differentiated research program can potentially provide us with information about what specific therapist operations will activate what specific client/patient operations under what conditions. For example, a hypothesis worth investigating is one we suggested above, namely that both collecting evidence in cognitive behavior therapy and interpreting the transference in psychoanalytic therapy will potentially activate the client/patient operation of distinguishing between reality and reality as construed. However, under certain conditions (e.g., type of case, phase of therapy) one form of intervention might be more effective in this respect than the

other. The question for investigation, then, becomes the identification of the relevant parameters for this differential effectiveness.

From a research perspective, the process of identifying client/patient operations is much more difficult than the process of identifying therapist operations. Therapist operations are typically observable and, despite the complications involved in establishing a coding system that will yield useful information, can be coded reliably by raters. In contrast, client/patient operations are usually inferred processes that are often not directly observable. Empirically clarifying the nature of client/patient operations is thus a difficult and complex process, which we will discuss in the next section.

MODEL BUILDING: LINKING THEORY AND RESEARCH

In the preceding sections, we have outlined a number of concepts that we believe can be useful for organizing our thinking in the comparative analysis of psychotherapy process. We will now outline an overall strategy for conducting this type of analysis. Our ultimate objective—shared by others, such as Messer (Chapter 13) and Murgatroyd and Apter (Chapter 9)—is the construction of an overarching model of the psychotherapy change process that can serve as a theoretical guide to the flexible and informed selection of psychotherapy interventions that are most appropriate to the particular situation at hand.

The approach we are advocating is strongly influenced by the rational-empirical strategy (Lewin, 1951; Pascual-Leone, 1976; 1978; Pascual-Leone & Sparkman, 1978; Piaget, 1970), which Rice & Greenberg (1984) have suggested as a framework for conducting psychotherapy process research. We wish to make it clear that in endorsing the rational–empirical approach as a general paradigm for developing an integrative perspective on psychotherapy process, we are by no means excluding the use of a variety of specific process research approaches ranging from Elliot's (1984) comprehensive process analysis, to Horowitz's (1979) configurational analysis, to Luborsky's (Luborsky et al., 1984) symptom-context method. We are, however, advocating the rational–empirical approach as a superordinate perspective because it articulates explicit guidelines for integrating the activities of theory construction and empirical research.

A basic tenet of this knowledge-acquisition strategy is that it is vital that we do not engage in premature verification attempts or hypothesis testing. As Meehl (1978) has stated, one of the problems with research in psychology has been a tendency to engage in hypothesis testing before the researcher has hypotheses worth testing. This is the same concern that is central to Grounded Theory researchers in sociology (Glaser & Strauss, 1967), who maintain that one of the problems with contemporary research in sociology has been a misplaced emphasis on the verification of hypotheses to the exclusion of theory development that is *grounded* in the phenomenon of interest.

As Goldfried and Padawer (1982) point out, an important starting point for generating testable hypotheses relevant to the systematic advancement of the psychotherapy field as a scientific discipline is at the level of clinical observation. These authors refer to observations made by a variety of different scientists in different fields, that scientific development begins with direct observations and experiences, rather than with rigid experimentation or premature theoretical speculations. Birk and Brinkley-Birk (1974), for example, emphasize the importance of "saving the phenomena" that are likely to be observed by the practicing clinician. Direct observation of clinical

process thus plays an indispensable role in the ultimate development of valid theory.

At the same time, however, it must be realized that the observation of the phenomenon of interest always takes place in the context of the theory of the observer (whether explicit or implicit), and that data outside of the context of theory are meaningless (Weimer, 1979). For this reason, while the rational–empirical strategy shares the grounded theory emphasis on the intensive observation of the relevant phenomena, it begins with the process of explicating a preliminary model to guide observation. This preliminary model should include hypotheses about both therapist and client/patient operations that are presumed to take place in a specific therapeutic task.

When possible, these operations should be specified on the basis of *explicit psychotherapy theory*. For example, earlier in this chapter we hypothesized that in the cognitive behavior therapy task of collecting evidence, the therapist operation consists of directing the clients'/patients' attention to inconsistent evidence, while the client operation consists of actively considering alternative perspectives. The recent trend toward the development of psychotherapy treatment manuals (e.g., Beck, Rush, Shaw, & Emery, 1979; Klerman, et al., 1984; Luborsky, 1984; Strupp & Binder, 1984) is an important advance in the direction of specifying the relevant therapist operations within different theoretical orientations.

In most cases, existing psychotherapy models specify therapist operations more adequately than they do client/patient operations. It is the task of the psychotherapy process researcher and model builder to develop hypotheses about the nature of the relevant client/patient operations. To the extent that existing psychotherapy literature contains explicit theories about the relevant client/patient operations, this process is facilitated. For example, the hypothesis that "decentering" or "distancing" oneself from one's cognitions is an important part of the cognitive therapy change process (Beck et al., 1979) provides a useful starting point for the researcher interested in clarifying the mechanisms of change in cognitive therapy. Using this hypothesis as a starting point, the researcher then begins to ask what exactly is involved in the process of decentering and how the hypothesized processes manifest themselves in the clinical interview. Similarly, Kohut (1984) specifies a number of subtasks or operations through which a process that he refers to as "transmuting internalization" takes place in psychoanalytic therapy. While Kohut has been criticized by some (e.g., Eagle, 1984) for the apparent vagueness of this concept, there is no reason that the relevant subtasks that are either explicit or implicit in Kohut's writing cannot be operationalized and described in the language of experimental cognitive psychology.

Hypotheses about the relevant client/patient operations that are generated can serve as initial guides in the process of intensively observing samples of the relevant psychotherapy material. They constitute what Rice and Greenberg (1984) refer to as a rational, idealized model, which is subsequently modified in an ongoing, iterative fashion, in response to new information that is generated through the direct observation of therapy sessions. In this fashion, conceptual work is linked to the direct observation of the relevant phenomena. We believe that a useful approach for developing models of similarities and differences between different therapeutic traditions involves explicating at a theoretical level what some of the important client/patient tasks are in different forms of psychotherapy.

As part of the process of explicating specific psychotherapy tasks, the theorist/researcher should also attempt to specify when a particular task is appropriate. For example, clients/patients in cognitive behavior therapy who are spontaneously reappraising their automatic thoughts in a rational fashion may first have to complete the task of suspending critical judgment and fully accessing "hot cognitions" before their automatic thoughts can be successfully challenged (Safran & Greenberg, 1982). This task may not be as necessary or appropriate for clients /patients who are not spontaneously reappraising their automatic thoughts in a rational fashion. Engaging in a spontaneous rational reappraisal may thus be a client/patient marker, indicating the need for the successful resolution of the psychotherapy task of accessing relevant emotions.

The process of explicating specific psychotherapy tasks should be combined with the activity of specifying those therapist interventions that are instrumental in facilitating task resolution and those client/patient operations that are involved in the process of task resolution. We believe that the process of explicating the tasks and operations that are important in different forms of therapy is valuable in and of itself, and can lead to improved understanding of important similarities and differences. This purely conceptual aspect of the model building, however, must be combined with a research program that involves the operationalization and measurement of the hypothesized client/patient operations.

The process of specifying what procedures can be used to measure the hypothesized operations helps clinical researchers to further refine and clarify precisely what they mean by the hypothesized operations (cf. Rice & Greenberg, 1984). For example, if we hypothesize that it is important at a particular point in the process of cognitive behavior therapy for the client/patient to access a "core" rather than a "peripheral" belief (e.g., Safran, Vallis, Segal, & Shaw, in press), the process of stipulating what measurement procedures can be used to assess whether or

not a belief is indeed core requires a precise specification of what we mean by
"core." The measurement of operations
that are employed can be a combination
of both standardly used instruments, when
relevant (e.g., Elliott, 1984; Greenberg,
1984), as well as observational categories
that are developed specifically for the research (e.g., Rice & Saperia, 1984).

The generation of observational coding
categories can be considered the epitome
of the rational–empirical strategy we are
advocating. Guided by their preliminary
models of relevant client/patient and therapist operations, psychotherapy researchers inspect transcripts or recordings of
therapy sessions in an attempt to observe
theoretically relevant similarities in both
client/patient and therapist operations.
Through this rational–empirical process,
researchers begin to develop reliably code-
able observational categories that capture
similarities and differences in the change
process as reflected in different forms of
psychotherapy (L. N. Rice, personal communication, 1984). To the extent that the
observational categories that are generated specifically for psychotherapy A are
found to be theoretically relevant to psychotherapy B, the coding system provides
some indication of the degree of convergence between the two different approaches. For example, to what extent
would an observational category developed to assess core cognitive processes in
the context of cognitive behavior therapy
(Mahoney, 1982; Meichenbaum & Gilmore, 1984; Safran et al., in press) adequately capture the core conflictual
relationship theme that Luborsky (1984)
discusses in the context of psychoanalytic
psychotherapy, or the dynamic focus that
Strupp and Binder (1984) discuss in the
context of psychoanalytic therapy?

Once reliable coding categories have
been developed and preliminary models
of relevant psychotherapy process have
been refined through rigorous observation, the verification or hypothesis-testing

phase begins. Does the successful completion of a particular task hypothesized to
be important in a particular form of psychotherapy lead to good outcome? Can we
demonstrate the completion of the *same*
task, at similar phases in two different
forms of therapy? If not, how do the tasks
differ? Can we empirically demonstrate
that two different therapist operations
(from different therapy approaches) lead
to the activation of similar client/patient
operations?

As suggested above, the empirical investigation of questions of this kind should
be guided by preliminary hypotheses advanced on the basis of rational analysis
and empirical observation of therapy process. This type of rational analysis and observational activity should in turn be
guided by the type of conceptual tools we
have discussed (i.e., phases, markers, tasks,
therapist vs client/patient operations), as
it is only with the use of concepts of this
type that we can begin to organize psychotherapy process into meaningful patterns of similarities and differences.

THE PRACTICING
PSYCHOTHERAPIST

What about the practicing psychotherapist? Must clinicians wait until the the-
oretical/research strategy we are
advocating bears fruit before they have a
guide to eclectic practice? What do our
suggestions have to offer them? We believe that at least in an informal way,
practicing clinicians should always be car-
rying out the type of program we are advocating. As suggested by Wachtel (1985),
"If your theoretical perspective has remained constant throughout your career,
it's a good sign you've been looking at too
narrow a range of data" (p. 16). Therapists
should be constantly thinking about psychotherapy process and revising their
models of psychotherapy in response to
input from different theoretical systems

as well as their own observation of therapy process. If this sounds idealistic, we hasten to acknowledge that it is indeed an *ideal* we are proposing. Nevertheless, we believe that it is precisely this ideal that should be guiding us as we go about our clinical work and are involved in the training of the practicing clinician (cf. Goldfried, 1984).

One of the practical constraints associated with actually doing research in applied settings has been the need for a methodology that would allow for such work to be done. Recognizing some of these problems, several research methodologies that may be appropriate to the clinical context have recently been proposed (Barlow, Hayes, & Nelson, 1984; Kazdin, 1981; Rice & Greenberg, 1984). Even clinicians who may not have the time, desire, or skills to become heavily involved in conducting research can be active contributors to the research process. This can be done by ongoing dialogues with those who are identified primarily as clinical researchers, whereby important directions for future investigation may be delineated. As suggested by Garfield (1980), it can also take the form of clinicians collaborating with researchers who have the necessary resources and skills to undertake research in applied settings and/or objectifying the record-keeping associated with one's clinical cases. In this regard, Goldfried & Padawer (1982) suggest,

If one views the split between clinicians and researchers from outside the entire system, it becomes more evident that both groups are deluding themselves in thinking that they alone will advance in the field. Stated more positively, it is perhaps more productive to conclude that both groups very much need each other. The experience and wisdom of the practicing clinician cannot be overlooked. But because these observations are often not clearly articulated, may be unsystematic or at times idiosyncratic, and are typically kept informal,

it is less likely that these insights can add to a reliable body of knowledge. The growing methodological sophistication of the researcher, on the other hand, is in need of significant and ecologically valid subject material. Our knowledge about what works in therapy must be rooted in clinical observations, but it must also have empirical verification. (p. 33)

We thus believe that increasing the dialogue between clinicians and researchers has the potential for significantly enriching both types of activity and for contributing to the development of a more integrative perspective on the psychotherapy change process that is grounded in clinical reality. In order to promote this type of dialogue, as well as an ongoing dialogue between theorists and researchers representing different theoretical orientations, it may be useful to develop formal professional networks.

PROFESSIONAL NETWORKS AND COLLABORATIVE EFFORTS

As indicated by Goldfried and Newman (Chapter 2), the history of attempts to integrate the psychotherapies goes back to the early 1930s. There was a smattering of articles and talks in the 1930s, 1940s, and 1950s, but it was only in the 1960s that we moved from the *precontemplative* to the *contemplative* stage, to use the formulation suggested by Prochaska and DiClemente in Chapter 6 when describing the stages of change. The earlier ideas, once introduced into the literature, apparently provided a consciousness-raising function. Even so, serious contemplation was only starting, and waxed and waned for some 20 years. It has been only since the early 1980s that this enhanced consciousness has led to some *action*, the most significant of which is perhaps the formation of the Society for the Exploration of Psychotherapy Integration (SEPI). SEPI started as an informal network and, at the time of this writing, it has become an international organization of about 300 members. By means of newsletters, symposia, conferences, and informal contacts, SEPI functions not only as an important reference group for those interested in the integration of the psychotherapies; it also serves to promote educational, clinical, and research work in this area.* The question of *maintenance* of the integration movement depends on the interest and involvement of professionals. Thus far, we have observed a most enthusiastic response on the part of SEPI participants.

Professional networks such as SEPI can serve the important function of facilitating collaboration between theorists and researchers from different psychotherapy orientations, and between clinicians and researchers. The type of systematic research program we have advocated in the present chapter will require the active involvement of theorists, researchers, and clinicians who are primarily identified with different therapeutic traditions if it is to accurately capture the nature of the change process involved in different forms of psychotherapy. It goes without saying that "generalists," or those who designate themselves as eclectic psychotherapists —such as those who have contributed to this volume—have and will continue to have an important role in the development of an integrative paradigm. There is also a role, however, for those who identify themselves primarily with a specific psychotherapy tradition. It is these psychotherapy "specialists" who are in a particularly good position to guide us in the activity of constructing models of change processes. Our hope is that with the type of conceptual tools we have described in the present chapter, psychotherapy spe-

cialists will be able to engage in the type of dialogue and research activity that will ultimately result in the development of a more unified psychotherapy paradigm.

The clinical research suggestions that we have outlined in this chapter clearly involve a tremendous investment of time, energy, and financial resources. Research on the process of therapeutic change is time consuming and costly. The task of sampling therapeutic interactions—especially those that are based on competently administered interventions with certain types of clients/patients, at given phases of therapy, that additionally have frequent interim measures of change, as well as good outcome criteria—is simply too much for any given investigator to attempt. Comparative process research could be greatly accelerated if there existed a data bank available to interested and qualified researchers. Too much time and energy have been spent in the past on such mundane but nonetheless crucial tasks as developing useful tapes and transcripts to analyze. To the extent that clinical researchers need to develop these anew or have to expend considerable time in locating relevant clinical data, research progress will continue to be slow. An invaluable service that the National Institute of Mental Health can provide, perhaps in collaboration with SEPI and the Society for Psychotherapy Research (SPR), is to develop data banks and/or serve as an information source to coordinate the available clinical material.

Finally, although we would hope that the approach we have outlined in this chapter will be of some use to investigators of comparative psychotherapy process, we acknowledge that the work of articulating a coherent methodology to facilitate progress in this area has just begun. We thus believe that networks such as SEPI and SPR should be as concerned with the activity of articulating and refining a general approach to knowl-

---

*For further information about SEPI, write to Dr. Lee Birk, 398 Walnut Street, Newton, MA 02160, U.S.A.

edge acquisition in the area as they are with developing specific integrative models.

CONCLUDING COMMENTS

Our objective in this chapter has been to outline a general strategy to guide the acquisition of knowledge relevant to establishing a unified psychotherapy paradigm. We have argued that the development of such an integrative paradigm must inevitably be tied to psychotherapy process research and that various conceptual tools that are emerging from this field can be useful for purposes of organizing our thinking about similarities and differences among various forms of psychotherapy. In this context we have discussed a number of relevant issues, including: developing a common language for psychotherapy integration; dealing with an appropriate level of conceptual abstraction, establishing a comparable focus of investigation; clarifying the nature of various psychotherapy tasks; and identifying both therapist and operations and client/patient operations. We have argued that the comparative analysis of psychotherapy process must take place simultaneously at multiple levels of abstraction and that research must proceed both from the "bottom up" and the "top down." The development of theory must be guided by data. At the same time however, the observation of data must be guided by well operationalized theory, since data out of context of theory are meaningless (Weimer, 1979).

We are in no hurry to obscure the lines of demarcation between different psychotherapy traditions. Instead, our interest is one of clarifying the nature of the change processes that are active in different forms of psychotherapy. Our assumption is that we will find both differences and similarities. We believe that an understanding of both orientation-specific and more transtheoretical change processes is necessary to guide therapists who do not wish to be constrained by the politics of psychotherapy theory in their selection of interventions. Although empirical research regarding the efficacy of specific interventions is important, it is also important for us to understand the process of change. A knowledge of *what* works must be supplemented with an understanding of *why* it works.

Psychotherapists who are guided exclusively by empirical findings regarding *what* works are technicians. They may be very good technicians, but ultimately their flexibility as therapists is limited. In contrast, psychotherapists who understand *why* interventions work are able to improvise interventions in a fashion appropriate to the specific context, guided by an understanding of the relevant change processes that require activating. Understanding psychotherapy process thus permits therapists to function as true artisans rather than technicians.

We thus advocate a serious study of comparative psychotherapy process rather than the premature formulation of an eclectic system—or worse, of eclectic systems. It is understandable that clinicians would be tempted to develop formal eclectic systems at this point in time. After all, clinicians who step outside of the conceptual boundaries of one particular theoretical system need a framework to guide their clinical work, just as clients/patients in the process of changing their world views need new schemata to guide them through life.

We cannot, however, overemphasize the potential danger that the growing interest in eclecticism and psychotherapy integration may result in a renewed competition, the arena being to determine who can formulate the best eclectic or integrated system. This concern is apparently shared by others. For example, in commenting on the integration of psychodynamic and behavior therapy, Kazdin (1984) has noted:

Integrationism as a general movement represents a highly significant development in psychotherapy. However, it may be the general movement that is worth promoting rather than the specific attempt to integrate psychodynamic and behavioral views. At this point, individual positions suffer from loose concepts and weak empirical bases, problems that are not resolved and perhaps may even be exacerbated by their combination. The overall goal is establishing an empirically based and theoretically viable account of therapy. Premature integration of specific positions that are not well supported on their own may greatly impede progress. (pp. 141–142)

The motivation for continued efforts in this general area needs to be the advancement of the field, not one's own particular system. In the final analysis, we need to go beyond the politics and polemics and take a close, hard, empirical look as to what goes on during the process of change. It is only through carefully conceived and unbiased research efforts that we can ever hope to enhance our therapeutic effectiveness.

Is it idealistic to want to break through the limitations and biases imposed by our theoretical orientations? Very definitely. Is this idealism worth pursuing? We believe so. To be sure, there are numerous obstacles that need to be overcome in order to reach this goal. Nonetheless, if enough of us can accept the notion that no one orientation—be it a particular school of therapy or an idiosyncratically proposed eclectic system—has all the answers, we believe we may see some very significant breakthroughs within our professional lifetime.

REFERENCES

Arnkoff, D. B. (1980). Psychotherapy from the perspective of cognitive theory. In M. J. Mahoney (Ed.), *Psychotherapy process*. New York: Plenum.

Barlow, D. H., Hayes, S. C., & Nelson, R. O. (1984). *The scientist–professional: Research and accountability in clinical and educational settings.* Elmsford, N.Y.: Pergamon Press.

Beck, A. T. (1976). *Cognitive therapy and the emotional disorders.* New York: International Universities Press.

Beck, A. T., Rush, A. J., Shaw, B. F., & Emery, G. (1979). *Cognitive therapy of depression.* New York: Guilford.

Beitman, B. D. (1983). Comparing psychotherapies by the stages of the process. *Journal of Operational Psychiatry, 14*, 20–27.

Birk, L., & Brinkley-Birk, A. (1974). Psychoanalysis and behavior therapy. *American Journal of Psychiatry, 131*, 499–510.

Bordin, E. S. (1979). The generalizability of the concept of working alliance. *Psychotherapy: Theory, Research, and Practice, 16*, 252–260.

Cashdan, S. (1973). *Interactional psychotherapy: Stages and strategies in behavioral change.* New York: Grune and Stratton.

Cyr, M., & Lecomte, C. (1983). Practitioners: What they do versus what they think they do. Paper presented at the 91st Annual Convention of the American Psychological Association, Anaheim, CA, August.

Eagle, M. N. (1984). *Recent developments in psychoanalysis.* New York: McGraw-Hill.

Egan, G. (1975). *The skilled helper.* Monterey, CA: Brooks/Cole.

Elliot, R. (1984). A discovery-oriented approach to significant change events in psychotherapy: Interpersonal process recall and comprehensive process analysis. In L. N. Rice & L. S. Greenberg (Eds.), *Patterns of change: Intensive analysis of psychotherapy process.* New York: Guilford Press.

Friedling, C., Goldfried, M. R., & Stricker, G. (1984). Convergences in psychodynamic and behavior therapy. Paper presented at the meeting of the Eastern Psychological Association, Baltimore, MD.

Garfield, S. L. (1980). *Psychotherapy: An eclectic approach.* New York: Wiley Interscience.

Garfield, S. L., & Kurtz, R. (1976). Clinical psychologists in the 1970's. *American Psychologist, 31*, 1–9.

Glaser, B., & Strauss, A. L. (1967). *The discovery of grounded theory: Strategies for qualitative research.* New York: Aldine.

Goldfried, M. R. (1979). Anxiety reduction through cognitive-behavioral intervention. In P. C. Kendall & S. D. Hollon (Eds.), *Cognitive–behavioral intervention: Theory, research, and procedures.* New York: Academic Press.

Goldfried, M. R. (1980). Toward the delineation of therapeutic change principles. *American Psychologist, 35*, 991–999.

Goldfried, M. R. (1984). Training the clinician as scientist–professional. *Professional Psychology: Research and Practice, 15*, 477–481.

Goldfried, M. R., & Padawer, W. (1982). Current status and future directions in psychotherapy. In M. R. Goldfried (Ed.), *Converging themes in psy-*

chotherapy: Trends in psychodynamic, humanistic and behavioral practice. New York: Springer.

Greenberg, L. S. (1984). A task analysis of intrapersonal conflict resolution. In L. N. Rice & L. S. Greenberg (Eds.), Patterns of change: Intensive analysis of psychotherapy process. New York: Guilford Press.

Greenberg, L. S., Rice, L. N., & Safran, J. D. (1984). A task analysis of change events in Gestalt therapy, client-centered therapy, and cognitive therapy. Presented at the Annual Meeting of the Society for Psychotherapy Research.

Greenberg, L. S. & Safran, J. D. (1981). Encoding and cognitive therapy: Changing what clients attend to. Psychotherapy Theory, Research and Practice, 18, 163–169.

Greenberg, L. S. & Safran, J. D. (1980). Encoding, information processing and cognitive behavior therapy. Canadian Psychologist, 21, 59–66.

Horowitz, M. J. (1979). States of mind. New York: Plenum.

Horowitz, M., Marmar, C., Krupnick, A. J., Wilner, N., Kaltreider, N., & Wallerstein, R. (1984). Personality styles and brief psychotherapy. New York: Basic Books.

Kazdin, A. E. (1981). Drawing valid inferences from case studies. Journal of Consulting and Clinical Psychology, 49, 183–192.

Kazdin, A. E. (1984). Integration of psychodynamic and behavioral psychotherapies: Conceptual versus empirical syntheses. In H. Arkowitz & S. B. Messer (Eds.), Psychoanalytic therapy and behavior therapy: Is integration possible? New York: Plenum.

Kiesler, D. J. (1973). The process of psychotherapy. Chicago: Aldine.

Klerman, G., Weissman, M., Rounsaville, B., & Chevron, E. (1984). Interpersonal psychotherapy of depression. New York: Basic Books.

Kohut, H. (1984). How does analysis cure? (A. Goldberg & P. Stephansky, Eds.). Chicago: University of Chicago Press.

Lewin, D. (1951). Field theory in social science. New York: Harper & Row.

Luborsky, L. (1984). Principles of psychoanalytic psychotherapy: A manual for supportive–expressive treatment. New York: Basic Books.

Luborsky, L., Singer, B., Hartke, J., Crits-Christoph, P., & Cohen, M. (1984). Shifts in depressive state during psychotherapy: Which concepts of depression fit the context of Mr. Q's shifts? In L. N. Rice & L. S. Greenberg (Eds.), Patterns of change: Intensive analysis of psychotherapy process. New York: Guilford Press.

Mahoney, M. J. (1982). Psychotherapy and human change processes. In Psychotherapy Research and Behavior Change, 1. Washington, D.C.: A.P.A.

Meehl, P. E. (1978). Theoretical risks and tabular asterisks: Sir Karl, Sir Ronald and the slow progress of soft psychology. Journal of Consulting and Clinical Psychology, 46, 806–834.

Meichenbaum, D., & Gilmore, J. B. (1984). The nature of unconscious processes: A cognitive–behavioral perspective. In K. S. Bowers & D. Mei-

chenbaum (Eds.), The unconscious reconsidered. New York: John Wiley.

Merluzzi, T. V., Rudy, T. E., & Glass, C. R. (1981). The information processing paradigm: Implications for clinical science. In T. V. Merluzzi, C. R. Glass, & M. Genest (Eds.), Cognitive assessment. New York: Guilford Press.

Orlinsky, D. E., & Howard, K. I. (1978). The relation of process to outcome in psychotherapy. In S. L. Garfield & A. E. Bergin (Eds.), Handbook of Psychotherapy and Behavior Change. New York: Wiley.

Pascual-Leone, J. (1976). A view of cognition from a formalist's perspective. In K. S. Riegel & J. Meacham (Eds.), The developing individual in a changing world (Vol. 1). The Hague: Mouton.

Pascual-Leone, J. (1978). Compounds, and models in developmental information processing: A reply to Trabasso & Foellinger. Journal of Experimental Child Psychology, 26, 18–40.

Pascual-Leone, J., & Sparkman, E. (1978). The dialectics of empiricism and rationalism: A last methodological reply to Trabasso. Journal of Experimental Child Psychology, 26, 46–54.

Peterfreund, E. (1980). On information and systems models for psychoanalysis. International Review of Psychoanalysis, 7, 327–345.

Piaget, J. (1970). Structuralism. New York: Basic Books.

Rice, L. (1974). The evocative function of the therapist. In D. A. Wexler & L. Rice (Eds.), Innovations in client-centered therapy. New York: Wiley.

Rice, L., & Greenberg, L. S. (1984). Patterns of change: Intensive analysis of psychotherapeutic process. New York: Guilford Press.

Rice, L., & Saperia, E. P. (1984). Task analysis of the resolution of problematic reactions. In L. N. Rice & L. S. Greenberg (Eds.), Patterns of change: Intensive analysis of psychotherapy process. New York: Guilford Press.

Ryle, A. (1978). A common language for the psychotherapies? British Journal of Psychiatry, 132, 585–594.

Safran, J. D., & Greenberg, L. S. (1986a). Affect and the unconscious: A cognitive perspective. In R. Stern (Ed.), Theories of the unconscious. Hillsdale, N.J.: The Analytic Press.

Safran, J. D., & Greenberg, L. S. (1986b). Hot cognition and psychotherapy process: An information processing/ecological perspective. In P. C. Kendall (Ed.), Advances in cognitive–behavioral research and therapy. (Vol. 5). New York: Academic Press.

Safran, J. D., & Greenberg, L. S. (1982). Cognitive appraisal and reappraisal: Implications for clinical practice. Cognitive Therapy and Research, 6, 251–258.

Safran, J. D., Vallis, T. M., Segal, Z. V., & Shaw, B. F. (In press). Assessment of core cognitive processes in cognitive therapy. Cognitive Therapy and Research.

Sarason, J. G. (1979). Three lacunae of cognitive therapy. Cognitive Therapy and Research, 3, 223–235.

Shaw, R., & Bransford, J. (1977). *Perceiving, acting and knowing: Toward an ecological psychology.* Hillsdale, N.J.: Lawrence Erlbaum Associates.

Strupp, H. H. (1973). Foreword in Kiesler, D. J., *The process of psychotherapy.* Chicago: Aldine.

Strupp, H. H., & Binder, J. L. (1984). *Psychotherapy in a new key: A guide to time-limited dynamic therapy.* New York: Basic.

Trower, P., & Turland, D. (1982). Social phobia. In S. M. Turner (Ed.), *Behavioral treatment of anxiety disorders.* New York: Plenum.

Turk, D. C., & Speers, M. A. (1983). Cognitive schemata and cognitive processes in cognitive behavior modification: Going beyond the information given. In P. C. Kendall (Ed.), *Advances in cognitive–behavioral research and therapy.* (Vol. 2). New York: Academic Press.

Wachtel, P. L. (1985). Need for theory. *International Newsletter of Paradigmatic Psychology, 1,* 15–17.

Weimer, W. B. (1979). *Notes on the methodology of scientific research.* Hillsdale, N.J.: Lawrence Erlbaum Associates.

Name Index

Silverman, L.H., 34
Simek-Downing, L., 391
Simonson, N.R., 95, 331
Sims, J.H., 321
Singer, B., 14, 447, 450
Singer, M.T., 295
Siporin, M., 340
Skinner, B.F., 401, 408-410
Sloane, R.B., 14, 31, 35, 46-47, 95, 139, 164
Small, L., 233, 243
Smith, D.S., 4, 4-5, 12, 18, 379, 431
Smith, G.A., 335
Smith, K.C.P., 260, 268
Smith, M.L., 14-15, 95, 114, 136, 158, 372, 418, 420, 439-441, 443, 450-452, 460
Smith, R.C., 36
Snepp, F.P., 12
Sollod, R., 34
Sparkman, E., 474
Speers, M.A., 467
Spence, D.P., 393
Spiegel, J.P., 132
Spiegel, S., 239
Spray, S.C., 321
Staats, A.W., 39, 44, 46, 384
Stachowiak, J., 299
Staples, F.R., 14, 35, 139, 164
Steffen, J.J., 331
Stein, D.M., 440, 445
Stein, M.H., 387
Stein, N., 4, 95
Steinbrueck, S.M., 440
Steinfeld, G.J., 41, 44
Steinglass, P., 285
Steketee, G.S., 78, 335
Sterne, A.L., 116
Stevenson, J.F., 424
Stevic, R., 333
Stewart, S., 301
Stolorow, R.D., 392
Stolz, S.B., 37
Stone, A., 235, 253
Storfjell, O., 278
Strauss, A.L., 475
Stricker, G., 54, 424, 463
Strong, S.R., 95, 235, 242, 331
Strupp, H.H., 4, 12, 14-15, 33, 35, 37-39, 44-45, 51-52, 54, 94, 96-97, 102, 112, 120, 126, 138, 149, 175, 305, 333, 407, 418-422, 448-449, 466, 475, 477
Suckerman, K.R., 333
Suh, C.S., 138
Sullivan, H.S., 44, 50-51, 285, 291, 406
Sundberg, N.D., 339
Sundland, D.M., 17, 394
Svebak, S., 268, 278
Swan, G.E., 12, 13

Switzer, A., 220

Taschman, H.A., 299
Taube, C., 181
Taylor, C.A., 445
Taylor, E., 201, 204
Teders, S.J., 453
Telch, M.J., 420
Tennen, H., 115
Terdal, L., 339
Thomas, E.J., 320
Thoresen, C.E., 33
Thorne, F.C., 4, 5, 18, 20, 28, 45, 193, 205, 326
Thyer, B.A., 331
Todd, T. (Luborsky), 113
Torrey, E.F., 33
Trower, P., 467
Truax, C.B., 32, 152, 333
Tuason, V.B. (Evans), 458
Turk, D.C., 467
Turkewitz, H., 37
Turland, D., 467
Turner, S.M., 332
Turpin, G., 336
Tuttman, S., 390
Twentyman, C.T., 334

Uhlenhuth, E.H., 186
Urban, H., 324
Usher, M., 285

Vaillant, G., 216
Vallis, T.M., 476-477
van der Molen, P., 266, 268
VandenBos, G.R., 16
Velicer, W.F., 165, 191-192
Vitulano, L.A., 424
Volkin, J., 447
von Bertalanffy, L., 67

Wachtel, P.L., 3-4, 6-7, 17, 19, 35, 39-41, 42, 46-51, 54-55, 379, 383, 390, 406, 411, 433, 477
Walker, C.E., 334-335
Wallerstein, R. (Horowitz), 473, 475
Walton, D.E., 12
Wampler, K.S., 440
Wampler, L.D., 422
Wandersman, A., 35, 333
Ward, D.E., 44
Waskow, I.E., 12, 20, 255, 457
Wasserman, D., 239
Watson, G., 27
Watson, R.I., 136
Wattie, B., 331
Watzlawick, P., 68, 299
Way, J.R., 16
Weakland, J., 68, 295, 299
Weimer, W.B., 475, 480

Weiner, I.B., 6-7, 12, 289
Weissberg, J.H., 36
Weissman, M.M., 407, 457, 475
Weitzman, B., 30
Welfel, E.R., 379
Wells, R.A., 321
Welsh, G.S., 110-111
Werner, H., 8
West, J.C., 445
Wexler, D.A., 391
Whipple, K., 14, 35, 139, 164
Whitaker, J., 239
White, H., 383, 386, 389
White, L. (Tennen), 115
Whitehorn, J.C., 99
Whitehouse, F.A., 30
Wiener, D., 331, 333
Wiens, A., 242
Wilcox, N., 192
Wile, D., 89
Wilkins, W., 443
Wilner, N. (Horowitz), 473, 475
Wilson, C.C., 339
Wilson, G.T., 4, 19, 66, 87, 136-137, 153, 324, 332, 335, 336, 381, 382, 388, 438-439
Windle, C., 16
Winnicott, D.W., 390
Winokur, M., 4, 19, 42, 45-46, 48, 386, 390, 392, 409, 411-413
Wismer, M. (Evans), 458
Wodarski, J.S., 320
Wogan, M., 4, 12-13
Wolberg, L., 230, 234, 236, 326
Woldenberg, L., 210, 220-221
Wolf, E., 30, 39
Wolfe, B.E., 12, 255, 331, 333
Wolin, S., 285
Wolpe, J., 65, 126, 152-153, 326, 334, 346, 392, 401
Wood, S.M., 4, 38, 135, 379
Woodworth, R.S., 27
Woody, R.H., 31-34
Woolfolk, R.L., 391
Worthington, E.L., 331, 339
Wright, C.L., 141
Wright, L., 334-335, 423
Wynne, L.C., 295

Yalom, I.D., 151, 242, 305-306
Yates, A.J., 4, 17, 19, 41, 43, 46-48, 407-408, 411
Yogev, S., 422
Yorkston, N.J., 14, 35, 139, 164
Young, D., 245
Young, W.T., 69, 75

Zeiss, A.M., 448
Zilbergeld, B., 91
Zimering, R.T., 334
Zohn, J., 423

Subject Index

time-limited therapy
common components of, 227-
230
dynamic focus and, 407
family therapy, 300
persuasion theory and, 113-
114
psychodynamic approaches
and, 14
termination and, 147, 181
transtheoretical approach
and, 172
Shostrom Personal Orientation
Inventory (POI), 220-221
Sibling rivalry, 309-310
SIDS (sudden infant death
syndrome) family
adjustment scale, 293
Single-case design, 341
Skill acquisition, 179-180
Smoking, 172, 177, 191-192,
455, 459
Social introversion, 111
Social judgment theory, 125
Social learning theory, 285,
356-357
clinical impact and, 410
Social liberation, 165
Social psychological research,
331
Social psychology, 285
Social skills, 146, 154
training, 233, 270, 346
Social workers, 10
Socially inappropriate behavior,
266
Society for Psychotherapy
Research (SPR), 4, 479
Society for the Exploration of
Psychotherapy Integration
(SEPI),4, 6, 41, 55, 478-479
Sociology of science, 52
Somatic interventions, 75-76
Somatization, 74
Specifying, 231
Speech anxiety, 329
Spontaneous remission, 437-439
Stimulus control, 165, 167-168,
173, 191, 193
Strategic family therapy, 299
Stream of consciousness, 203,
205, 207
Stress-inoculation training,
335, 340
Structural disturbances, 266,
369
Structural family therapy, 287-
288, 293, 299
compared to psychodynamic
therapy, 399-400
Structural–phenomenological
approach, 260-261, 367-369
Structural Profiles, 73-74, 78,
87-88
Structural therapy, 193

Structuring, 330-331, 337
Subconscious, 204
Sublimation, 26
Suicide, 71, 110
Superordinate theory, 96-97,
116, 118, 354, 358, 371
language system and, 385
Supervision, 421-422, 426
Symbiotic involvement, 293
Sympathy, 262-263, 268, 270
Symptom complexity, 101-102,
119-120
Symptom-context method, 475
Symptom/situational problems,
168, 172
Symptom/situational stage, 179,
193-195
Synthetic eclecticism, 9-10, 17-
18, 67
Systematic desensitization, see
Desensitization
Systematic eclecticism, 12, 67,
400-401, see also Technical
eclecticism
critique of, 358-360
goal of, 12
superordinate theory and, 96-
98
transtheoretical approach
and, 164
versus unsystematic, 9
Systematic evocative unfolding,
472
Systems theory, 40-41, 97, 282,
295, 356-357
family systems theory, 193,
287, 299
multimodal therapy and, 67
persuasion theory and, 113,
359

Target complaint inventory,
244, 253-254
Task prescription, 307
TAT, 206
Technical eclecticism, 9-10, 17,
30, 33, 36, 65, 67, 82, see
also Systematic eclecticism
critique of, 373
effectiveness of, 455
Techniques, see Interventions
Teleological model, 216-217
Telic, 262-268, 270, 277-279,
367, 369
Telic Dominance Scale, 268,
274, 278
Tension, 73, 76, 268
reduction, 221
Termination, 42, 82, 147-148
initiated by the client, 118
as a phase of treatment, 114
structural-phenomenological
approach, 271
successful, 175-176, 180-181,

190
time-limited therapy and,
239-240
Theoretical purity, 11-12, 17
Therapeutic alliance, 231, 245,
355, 357, see also Patient-
therapist relationship
client choice and, 361
eclectic time-limited therapy
and, 366
emphasized by eclectics, 400
metamotivational states and,
369
patients' tasks and, 473
persuasion therapy and, 116
systematic eclectic therapy
and, 359
transtheoretical approach
and, 362
Therapeutic change, see
Change
Therapeutic failures, 42, 75
Therapeutic relationship, see
Patient-therapist
relationship; Therapeutic
alliance
Therapists, see also Patient-
therapist relationship
A-B typology of, 99
active role of, 147
attitudes toward brief
therapy, 258
characteristics of successful,
85
contribution to a positive
therapeutic relationship,
138
cooperation between
practitioners and
researchers, 477-479
decision-making, 20, 260,
353-356
development of eclectic
stance, 6-8
differences in response to
clients, 145
eclectics compared to
noneclectics, 12-13
empathy and, see Empathy
expectations of the client's
role, 231-232
experience level and, 252-254
experienced vs.
inexperienced, 454
as the expert on change, 176
family therapy, 288-289
flexibility, 115
focality, 244
functional, 202
group therapy and, 305
identification with the, 178,
182
match with clients, see
Matching
mental health of, 149